Making Workers Soviet

MAKING WORKERS SOVIET

Power, Class, and Identity

EDITED BY

Lewis H. Siegelbaum and

Ronald Grigor Suny

CORNELL UNIVERSITY PRESS

ITHACA AND LONDON

First published 1994 by Cornell University Press.

Printed in the United States of America

♾ The paper in this book meets the minimum requirements of the
American National Standard for Information Sciences—Permanence
of Paper for Printed Library Materials, ANSI Z39.48-1984.

Library of Congress Cataloging-in-Publication Data

Making workers Soviet : power, class, and identity / edited by Lewis
H. Siegelbaum and Ronald Grigor Suny.
p.   cm.
"Originated in a conference held at Michigan State University in
November 1990"—Pref.
Includes bibliographical references and index.
ISBN 0-8014-3022-4 (cloth : alk. paper).—ISBN 0-8014-8211-9
(pbk. : alk. paper)
1. Working class—Soviet Union—Congresses.   2. Soviet Union—
Social conditions—Congresses.   I. Siegelbaum, Lewis H.   II. Suny,
Ronald Grigor.
HD8524.M35   1994
305.5'62'0947—dc20   94-21989

To Moshe Lewin,
Ударник нашей профессии

⋆

Contents

✯

Preface

This book originated in a conference held at Michigan State University in November 1990. The impetus was Ira Katznelson and Aristide Zolberg's *Working-Class Formation: Nineteenth-Century Patterns in Western Europe and the United States*, which stimulated us to think along parallel lines with respect to Imperial Russia and the Soviet Union.[1] This theme had long figured prominently in Soviet historiography, but only in quantitative or statistical rather than analytical or interpretive terms. Typically, historians have been more concerned with registering the growth of class consciousness among the proletariat than with inquiring into how and why such a consciousness crowded out others, and more oriented toward demonstrating the preponderance of industrial workers in party and state institutions and improvements in their material and cultural well-being after 1917 than with interrogating the quality of such participation or the persistence of relations of domination and subordination within the party and state as well as on the shop floor.

In 1982, Reginald Zelnik and Victoria Bonnell convened a conference at the University of California, Berkeley, on the social history of Russian labor. For all its achievements and frustrations, that meeting was necessarily focused on Russia's workers (one might say, more accurately, Russian workers!) in the period from the 1870s through the revolution of 1917. With the single exception of Moshe Lewin, no participant at Berkeley was working actively in the post–civil war Soviet period. The October Revolution was the outside boundary of what then constituted Russian

[1] Ira Katznelson and Aristide R. Zolberg, eds., *Working-Class Formation: Nineteenth-Century Patterns in Western Europe and the United States* (Princeton, N.J.: Princeton University Press, 1986). Despite its inattention to identities of gender, race, ethnicity, and religion, this collection stimulated reconsiderations of class formation. See especially the introduction by Katznelson, pp. 3–41. This book extends the "cases and comparisons" Katznelson refers to.

labor history. Thereafter, the boundary was crossed—in no small measure because of the organizing efforts and intellectual example of Moshe Lewin, particularly in the operation of the seminar "Twentieth-Century Russian and Soviet Social History." That extraordinary collective, better known as the "Philadelphia Seminar," provided a forum for those who ventured into the uncharted territory of the 1920s and 1930s. As the turn toward Soviet and social history accelerated, developing its own dialogues—one thinks here of the pioneering work on social mobility and Soviet culture of Sheila Fitzpatrick; the "revisionist" attack on the totalitarian model; the first forays into Soviet archives that led to a cascade of monographs on Soviet society—the history of labor also benefited. Yet the more we discovered, the less adequate the old categories (borrowed from prerevolutionary labor history and the experience of an immature capitalism) became.

Many of the questions (and often the answers) in Russian labor historiography had been set in arcane debates outside scholarship, in sectarian discussions of political actors or the passionate polemics of opponents of the Soviet regime. Ironically, for a country where workers had been so central to political discourse, or perhaps because their centrality had been taken for granted, other kinds of questions—for example, about the self-conceptions of workers, the survival and development of labor's informal institutions, and the boundaries of social class—remained largely unaddressed. The Michigan State conference thus had two objectives: to encourage researchers on workers in Imperial Russia and the Soviet Union to place their specialty within a broader theoretical and conceptual realm and, at the same time, to throw into relief the peculiarities of working-class formation in a noncapitalist setting.

The participants engaged in spirited, sometimes heated discussions of the problematic of class formation and displayed a willingness to employ ideas of class, but there was no consensus about the meaning of class or its boundaries or about whether class is constituted by structures, by agents inside or outside the class, or by political and social discourses. Though analytical approaches ranged from the most "materialist" to the enthusiastically "discursive," all recognized the importance of culture and representations of class in the process of class formation.

We take this opportunity to thank all those who made this enterprise possible and who contributed to its success. They include Michael Burawoy, Kathleen Canning, William Chase, Patrick Dale, Geoffrey Eley, Laura Engelstein, John Hatch, David Hoffmann, William Husband, Robert Johnson, David Montgomery, Sonya Rose, William Rosenberg, Michael Paul Sacks, William Sewell Jr., David Shearer, and Kenneth Straus. We also gratefully acknowledge the financial support of the Russian and

East European Studies Center, the College of Arts and Letters, the Office of the Provost, and the Vice-President for Research and Graduate Studies at Michigan State University; the Committee on International Affairs, the Office of the Vice-President for Research, Horace H. Rackham School of Graduate Studies, and the Center for Russian and East European Studies at the University of Michigan; and the Center for Russian and East European Studies at the University of Toronto. Thanks go to Roger Haydon, our editor at Cornell, and Andrew Lewis, our copyeditor. Last but not least, Christine Blakeslee and Mark Orsag—the graduate student "workers" of our conference—deserve the gratitude of everyone who took part, but especially our own.

L.H.S.
R.G.S.

Archives Cited in Text

Old Acronym	New Acronym	Translation of New Title
GAChO	GAChO	State Archive of the Cheliabinsk Region
GADO	GADO	State Archive of the Donetsk Region
LGIA	TsGIA SPb	Central State Historical Archive of the City of St. Petersburg
MFGAChO	MFGAChO	Magnitogorsk Branch of the State Archive of the Cheliabinsk Region
PAIIPLO	TsGAIPD SPb	Central State Archive of Historico-Political Documents of the City of St. Petersburg
TsGALI	RGALI	Russian State Archive of Literature and Art
TsGAMO	TsGAMO	Central State Archive of the Moscow Region
TsGANKh	RGAE	Russian State Archive of the Economy
TsGAOR	GARF	State Archive of the Russian Federation
TsGIA	RGIA	Russian State Historical Archive
TsGIAgM	TsGIAgM	Central State Historical Archive of the City of Moscow
TsPA IML TsK KPSS	RTsKhIDNI	Russian Center for the Preservation and Study of Documents of Recent History

Making Workers Soviet

Lewis H. Siegelbaum and Ronald Grigor Suny

Class Backwards?
In Search of the Soviet Working Class

The experiences of Russia and the Soviet Union have long been of more than academic interest. The hopes and expectations associated with revolutionary transformation and the "building of socialism" rose and fell through this century with the achievements and suffering of the peoples of those great empires. For historians, as well as political theorists and activists, the "Russian" working class has been a central concern. As a principal actor in the great dramas of 1917 and the repository of the Marxists' imaginary historic mission, Russia's workers have been subjected to scholarly and political analysis that has obscured the particular texture of their lives as often as it has illuminated the broad outlines of a class rising to fulfill its heroic role. Narratives of growing class cohesion and radical consciousness were challenged by stories of decomposition, fragmentation, and accommodation. As older paradigms for understanding the history of Russian labor underwent their own decomposition, ubiquitous assumptions and categories were revised and replaced.

Now, in the cold light of the post-Soviet dawn, understanding the making of the Soviet working class seems less a matter of political engagement than one of archaeological excavation. But this is in itself something of an illusion. Before one can dig, one must know what one is digging for and what tools to use. Are those tools to be found among theories of working-class formation in capitalist societies? Can the characteristics of the working classes so theorized help us identify the Soviet variant?

The Locus Classicus of Class

Class is a keyword of modern times. As Raymond Williams noted, "Development of *class* in its modern social sense, with relatively fixed names

1

for particular classes (lower class, middle class, upper class, working class and so on) belongs essentially to the period between 1770 and 1840, which is also the period of the Industrial Revolution and its decisive reorganization of society.[1] Steadily displacing the more common words *rank*, *order*, and *estate*, class incorporated both the sense of social hierarchy that the older terms carried and the new sense that the emerging social system had created new kinds of social divisions.

Following Marx, Williams makes an important distinction between class as an objective social or economic category and class as a social formation that involves perceived economic distinctions and political and cultural organizations. In *The German Ideology* Marx and Engels give an example of their notion of class as a social position defined in opposition to other social groupings: "The separate individuals form a class only insofar as they have to carry on a common battle against another class; otherwise they are on hostile terms with each other as competitors. On the other hand, the class in its turn achieves an independent existence over and against the individuals, so that the latter find their conditions of existence predestined, and hence have their position in life and their personal development assigned to them by their class."[2]

In "The Eighteenth Brumaire of Louis Bonaparte," Marx shifts the definition to include consciousness of culture and interests. "Insofar as millions of families live under economic conditions of existence that separate their mode of life, their interests and their culture from those of the other classes, and put them in hostile opposition to the latter," he writes, "they form a class. Insofar as there is merely a local interconnection among these small-holding peasants, and the identity of their interests begets no community, no national bond and no political organizations among them, they do not form a class."[3] Marx's "insofar as" introduces a sense of class formation as a process of becoming or making and suggests that social conglomerates can have a more or less developed sense of class, a high or low "classness." Here one is reminded of his well-known distinction between a "class in itself" and a "class for itself," and the classic problem of movement from the former to the latter, which activists and analysts tended to overlook or simply assumed to be a natural, inevitable progression.

Much of the most fruitful theorizing about class since Marx arose from

---

[1] Raymond Williams, *Keywords, A Vocabulary of Culture and Society* (London, 1976), p. 51.

[2] Karl Marx and Frederick Engels, *The German Ideology*, ed. R. Pascal (New York, 1947), pp. 48–49.

[3] Karl Marx, "The Eighteenth Brumaire of Louis Bonaparte," in Marx and Engels, *Basic Writings on Politics and Philosophy*, ed. Louis S. Feuer (Garden City, N.Y., 1959), pp. 338–39.

attempts to understand why this movement from a class in itself to a class for itself did not happen.[4] At the end of the last century, "revisionists" such as Eduard Bernstein celebrated the lack of a revolutionary class consciousness within the European labor movement, but radical social democracts such as Lenin decried it, arguing that it had to be introduced by intellectuals from without. Whether the experience of Bolshevism vindicated Lenin's re-radicalization of Marxism divided Marxists throughout the world for decades. In the meantime, the absence of a militantly socialist proletariat in the developed and crisis-prone capitalist economies produced a rich harvest of explanations for the "opportunism" or "successful integration" of the working class. Whereas liberals have characteristically interpreted the apparent moderation of labor as a sign of maturity, Western Marxists have explored the multiplicity of class positions in advanced capitalist society. They have emphasized the mediating effect of class alliances and family relations (Eric Olin Wright), the effectiveness of capitalism to buy off workers materially and the willingness of workers to take the less risky road of playing the capitalist game (Adam Przeworski), and the power of hegemonic production regimes to coordinate the interests of workers, managers, and owners and "manufacture consent" on the factory floor (Michael Burawoy).[5]

In sum, once established in political speech, class promised social analysts a precision and certainty that it has never been able to deliver. Its purported materiality proved elusive, for class failed to perform, either as a determinant of consciousness or as a predictor of particular trajectories, and the underlying "reality" of class was far more difficult to grasp than its actuality in specific historical environments. People talked as if classes existed; they organized and even killed or were killed because of class, and yet the myriad inclusions and exclusions that made up class were always contested, not least among historians.

In the early 1960s, E. P. Thompson offered the most sustained challenge

---

[4] "In Marx's theory of history," writes Michael Burawoy, "the forces of production can advance under private property only by engendering a revolutionary working class. Marx was wrong; capitalism continues to expand, and its working class remains effectively incorporated within capitalism's limits." Burawoy, "Reflections on the Class Consciousness of Hungarian Steelworkers," *Politics and Society* 17, no. 1 (1989): 20. Burawoy goes on to argue that the theory "works much better for state socialism" because "the central appropriation of surplus engenders a shortage economy, expansion of the forces of production requires worker self-management, . . . the central appropriation of the surplus is managed directly and visibly by state organs organized at the point of production. Workers all over the country define themselves in relation to a common exploiter," and the legitimation of the extraction of surplus "only heightens the contrast between what is and what could be."

[5] See Erik Olin Wright, *Classes* (London, 1985); Adam Przeworski, *Capitalism and Social Democracy* (Cambridge, 1985); and Michael Burawoy, *Manufacturing Consent: Changes in the Labor Process under Monopoly Capitalism* (Chicago, 1979) and *The Politics of Production: Factory Regimes under Capitalism and Socialism* (London, 1985).

to the master narrative of capitalism overwhelming older social forms and giving rise to a conscious revolutionary agent. Dedicating himself to overcoming "the enormous condescension of posterity," Thompson decentered the proletariat and replaced it with craftsmen and artisans who in their struggle against proletarianization, deskilling, and political ostracism, invented the organizational forms and languages of class. In this revision, class was no longer understood as a structure or a category, but rather as a happening, as something that "eventuates as men and women *live* their productive relations, and as they *experience* their determinate situations, within 'the *ensemble* of social relations,' with their inherited culture and expectations, and as they handle these experiences in cultural ways."[6] Using and infusing old cultural forms with new meanings in their efforts to make sense of common experiences, men and women became active agents in the process of class formation.

This "culturalist" paradigm of class reinvigorated labor history, producing a vast and important body of literature on how the experience of oppression mobilized workers in nineteenth-century capitalist societies for class-based protest and higher levels of political consciousness.[7] Coincident with national liberation struggles in the Third World, the deep questioning by radical students and faculty of postwar American hegemony, ferment among industrial workers in Europe, and the powerful resurgence of feminism, this literature shared in a general optimism about the political relevance of recovering authentic experiences of earlier struggles.

To be sure, not everyone was swept away by the insurgency of the "new labor history." Despite Thompson's proviso that class happens in determinate social relations, some Marxists judged his emphasis on "agency" and the authenticity of "experience" as excessively voluntaristic, even reductionist. In Richard Johnson's view, Thompson and other "socialist-humanist historians" saw class "very much as a collective inter-subjective relationship," whereas "the economic as a set of objectively present relations only appears in an attentuated form, *through* the cultural, *through*

---

[6] Edward P. Thompson, *The Making of the English Working Class* (1963; Harmondsworth, 1968), p. 11 and "Eighteenth-Century English Society: Class Struggle without Class?" *Social History* 3, no. 2 (1978): 250.

[7] The literature is so vast that only a few representative titles can be cited here: Herbert Gutman, *Work, Culture and Society in Industrializing America* (New York, 1977); L. A. Tilly and J. W. Scott, *Women, Work, Family* (New York, 1978); Craig Calhoun, *The Question of Class Struggle: Social Foundations of Popular Radicalism during the Industrial Revolution* (Chicago, 1982); Patrick Joyce, *Work, Society and Politics: The Culture of the Factory in Later Victorian England* (London, 1982); Sean Wilentz, *Chants Democratic: New York City and the Rise of the American Working Class, 1788–1850* (New York, 1984); and Eric Hobsbawm, *Worlds of Labour: Further Studies in the History of Labour* (London, 1984). See also *History Workshop Journal*, itself a product of the "culturalist" and localist turn.

the 'inwardness of experience.' "[8] G. A. Cohen first restated Marx's own position, saying that "a person's class is established by nothing but his objective place in the network of ownership relations" and that "class position strongly conditions consciousness, culture, and politics" and then called Thompson's views "badly grounded."[9] Others, drawing on Louis Althusser's structuralist reading of Marx, unfavorably compared the mere "historicism" of Thompson's enterprise to their more "scientific" approaches, none of which required empirical substantiation![10] Indeed, debates between "culturalists" and "structuralists" rent Marxist discourse in the 1970s, culminating in Thompson's intemperate blast at Althusser in "The Poverty of Theory."[11]

By rooting class in consciousness or "feeling," Thompson and his confederates were collapsing the distinction between the class in itself and the class for itself. For some of their critics, class (in-itself) remained an important heuristic category quite apart from its articulation in language and culture. For others, even Thompson's empirical demonstration that the English working class had been made before the 1840s was flawed. As Perry Anderson noted, "It is *discontinuity, not continuity*, that is the keynote of 19th century working-class history. The sociological evolution from artisanate to proletariat . . . was accompanied by so deep a dislocation of political, ideological and cultural traditions that the new patterns which emerged in the 1880s have been dubbed by Gareth Stedman Jones . . . an effective 're-making' of the English working class."[12]

But perhaps the most telling and ultimately destabilizing critique of this new labor history stepped beyond culture into a new appreciation of language. In his brilliant reexamination of Chartism, Stedman Jones, like William H. Sewell Jr., who looked at French artisans' prerevolutionary traditions of *compagnage* and discourses of corporatism, redirected the starting point of analysis away from the material environment of an emerging industrial capitalism toward older rhetorics of radical democ-

[8] Richard Johnson, "Edward Thompson, Eugene Genovese, and Socialist-Humanist History," *History Workshop Journal* 6 (autumn, 1978): 91.

[9] G. A. Cohen, *Karl Marx's Theory of History: A Defence* (Princeton, N.J., 1978), pp. 73–77.

[10] The most egregious instance was B. Hindess and P. Hirst, *Pre-Capitalist Modes of Production* (London, 1975).

[11] E. P. Thompson, "The Poverty of Theory," in *The Poverty of Theory and Other Essays* (New York, 1978).

[12] Perry Anderson, *Arguments within English Marxism* (London, 1980), p. 45. Anderson essentially reiterates the criticism in Tom Nairn, "The English Working Class," *New Left Review* 24 (1964): 43. For Stedman Jones's essay, see "Working-Class Culture and Working-Class Politics in London, 1870–1900: Notes on the Remaking of a Working Class," *Journal of Social History* 7 (summer 1974): 460–508, reprinted in his *Languages of Class: Studies in English Working Class History, 1832–1982* (Cambridge, 1983), pp. 179–238.

racy. Stedman Jones saw Chartism not as an ideological expression of certain class interests but as a movement that used a language of class to identify and empower a particular constituency: "Language disrupts any simple notion of the determination of consciousness by social being because it is itself part of social being. We cannot therefore decode political language to reach a primal and material expression of interest since it is the discursive structure of political language which conceives and defines interest in the first place. What we must therefore do is to study the production of interest, identification, grievance and aspiration within political languages themselves."[13]

This tentative foray into (Saussurian) linguistic theory was intended as a challenge to social historians in general and labor historians in particular. It pointed up the limits of social explanation by asserting that there is no understanding of social reality outside language. Like Thompson, Stedman Jones treats class and class consciousness as one and the same; unlike Thompson, he does not posit a basic irreducible "experience," since "tacit assumptions are made about what is to count as experience, about its meaningfulness, and about its cumulative and collective character."[14] One can speak of the experience of class as its conceptual organization, as "constructed and inscribed within a complex rhetoric of metaphysical associations, causal inferences and imaginative constructions," or in other words, as discourse.[15]

Discursive theory was slow to penetrate labor history. So much had been invested in the social challenge to narrow practices of political and intellectual history that this renewed appreciation of language and discourse threatened ground gained by a whole generation of historians. Ultimately, the linguistic turn found a powerful ally in feminism and the anti-essentialist thrust of much of women's history. The incorporation of gender into discussions of class reaches back to the early 1970s when the

---

[13] Stedman Jones, *Languages of Class*, pp. 21–22. William H. Sewell Jr., *Work and Revolution in France: The Language of Labor from the Old Regime to 1848* (Cambridge, 1980). For a parallel exploration of American workers, see David R. Roediger, *The Wages of Whiteness: Race and the Making of the American Working Class* (London, 1991). Sewell has extended his critique of materialist labor history and pointed the way toward transcending it via an apprehension of "mutually constitutive complexes of meanings, scarcities, and power relations" in "Toward a Post-materialist Rhetoric for Labor History," in Lenard R. Berlanstein, ed., *Rethinking Labor History: Essays on Discourse and Class Analysis* (Urbana, Ill., 1993), pp. 15–38.

[14] Stedman Jones, *Languages of Class*, p. 20. See also Patrick Joyce, *Visions of the People: Industrial England and the Question of Class 1848–1914* (New York, 1991). Joyce argues that the culture and consciousness of working people throughout the Victorian period must be conceptualized as "populist."

[15] Stedman Jones, *Languages of Class*, p. 102. For a perceptive appreciation and critique of Stedman Jones's abandonment of the "social" in favor of the "prefigurative" power of language, see David Mayfield and Susan Thorne, "Social History and its Discontents: Gareth Stedman Jones and the Politics of Language," *Social History* 17, no. 2 (1992): 165–87.

absence or marginality of women in the narratives of labor historians was first noted. At this initial stage, much of the work of women's labor historians was "compensatory" or "contribution" history, documenting women's participation in unions and collective action. But although such inputs succeeded in diminishing the sexlessness of representations of class, they did not fundamentally question the masculine standards by which workers' activism or consciousness were being judged.

The subsequent emphasis on a distinct "women's work culture" based on cooperation and familialism—that is, the adoption of a model of separate spheres based on sexual difference—was as much a retreat as an advance. Although shattering the myth of women's passivity and dependency, it left men's labor history largely untouched and risked isolating women's labor history from the central narrative of class struggle. As Ava Baron has noted in a major review of the literature on gender and American working-class history: "The new field thus elaborated upon rather than replaced a whole series of conceptual dualisms—capitalism/patriarchy, public/private, production/reproduction, men's work/women's work—which assume that class issues are integral to the first term of each pair and gender is important only to the second."[16]

Joan Scott's deployment of poststructuralist linguistic theory represented an inventive way out of these dilemmas. Her emphasis on the multiple and contested meanings of class and on how gender has figured in those meanings radically shifted the conceptual ground on which working-class formation was understood. Defining gender as both "a constitutive element of social relationships based on perceived differences between the sexes, and . . . a primary way of signifying relationships of power," Scott found it employed in both the legitimation and contestation of those relationships. It is thus inextricably connected with class identities, whether women are present or absent.[17]

As Laura Engelstein and Geoff Eley stressed at our conference, Scott's theorization takes us beyond both the reductiveness of the distinction between the class in itself and the class for itself and the essentialism of "experience." Class instead becomes a political and cultural postulate, the assertion of a particular kind of social identity no less real than the demonstrable fact of social positions defined by relations of production. The history of a class is inseparable from the discursive claims about that class which seek to reorder the world in their own terms. Like a nation, a class is an "imagined community" with its own sense of a common past, a common present, and a common destiny. The corresponding agenda for

[16] Ava Baron, "Gender and Labor History: Learning from the Past, Looking to the Future," in Baron, ed., *Work Engendered: Toward a New History of American Labor* (Ithaca, N.Y., 1991), p. 17.

[17] Joan Wallach Scott, *Gender and the Politics of History* (New York, 1988), p. 42.

research therefore is not to try to correlate class consciousness with interest, which itself is discursively constructed, or to see languages of class
as simple reflections of underlying "realities," but to map out the landscape in which the fixing of identities (for example, the skilled male
worker) privileged certain workers and suppressed alternative possibilities,
and how such identities were reduced, expanded, challenged, and replaced
in particular historical circumstances.[18]

The shock effect of the discursive led some social historians to claim
that the privileging of language would displace attention from social determination and agency if not evaporate the social world.[19] Yet, workers
still occupy positions within the social division of labor, and productive
and reproductive relations continue to have a constraining power in people's lives. The point is not that language prefigures these relations any
more than it merely reflects them. It is that social relations, individual and
collective identities, and their representation in language work on each
other in complex ways to generate particular understandings of class and
collective behavior or action. Neither the social nor the discursive determine behavior by themselves in unmediated ways. They coexist and cannot be easily disentangled. Why workers, so complexly fragmented along
lines of gender, skill, ethnicity, and other divides enumerated by social
historians, developed at key moments senses of solidarity and shared interests can be deduced neither from the conditions in which they lived
nor from particular experiences. To the material and social must be added
the languages of class and the discourses in which the worlds of workers
are given meaning. This particular contestation over meanings and loyalties can be called politics.

Defining the Working Class of Imperial Russia

The historiography of Russia's workers in the imperial period has followed many of the patterns of Western European and American labor
history, if a few steps off the pace set in the West.[20] For many years the

[18] For a brilliant application of this agenda to German labor history, see Kathleen Canning, "Gender and the Politics of Class Formation: Rethinking German Labor History,"
American Historical Review 97 (June 1992): 736–68.

[19] See, for example, Bryan D. Palmer, *Descent into Discourse: The Reification of Language
and the Writing of Social History* (Philadelphia, 1990).

[20] And not only in the West. For two highly suggestive but very different approaches to
non-Western working-class history, see Andrew Walder, "The Remaking of the Chinese
Working Class, 1949–1981," *Modern China* 10 (1984): 3–48, and Dipesh Chakrabarty,
Rethinking Working-Class History: Bengal 1890–1940 (Princeton, N.J., 1989). For a brief
but useful summary of Latin American labor historiography, see Charles Bergquist, "Labor
History and Its Challenges: Confessions of a Latin Americanist," *American Historical Review* 98 (June 1993): 757–63.

experience of workers was collapsed into that of party and trade union organizations, and workers' attitudes were deduced from the writings of their purported social democratic leaders. The turn toward social history in Russian labor studies diminished the concern with labor politics, but, as Ziva Galili has noted, "Politics in the broader sense—the power relations of various social groups and interests—intruded in the lives of Russian workers too directly and persistently to be ignored."[21] In general, historians focused on aggregates of workers, usually in the two Russian capitals, on their migration from village to city, and the organization of study circles (*kruzhki*) and mutual-aid funds (*kassy*), unions, and relations with social democratic activists.[22]

The stories of Russia's workers under tsarism were usually told in a master narrative predetermined by the march to the October Revolution. From peasant, to peasant-worker, to hereditary proletarian, the Russian worker moved from the world of the village to that of the factory, encountering along the way more "conscious" worker-activists and social-democratic intellectuals, who enlightened the worker to *his* true interests and revolutionary political role. In his comments at the Michigan State conference, Sewell called for a "rescripting" of this grand narrative of the emergence or unfolding of an immanent sense of class as the story more of a series of social and cultural processes that led not to the "discovery" of class but to its social and cultural construction. Sewell insisted that to show how class is constituted, individual subjects must be foregrounded. As he put it, "Rather than a unified collective subject discovering the truth of its class exploitation as a consequence of unfolding experiences, this could equally and easily be a story of how the particular experiences of the Revolution of 1905 and its subsequent repression made an explanation of . . . workers' experiences in class terms offered to them by the intelligentsia, by parties and so on, seem particularly plausible." Worker

---

[21] Ziva Galili, "Workers, Strikes, and Revolution in Late Imperial Russia," *International Labor and Working-Class History*, no. 38 (1990): 69.

[22] Among others, the following works illustrate the general trends in Western writing on Imperial Russian labor history over the last few decades: Victoria E. Bonnell, *Roots of Rebellion: Workers' Politics and Organizations in St. Petersburg and Moscow, 1900–1914* (Berkeley and Los Angeles, 1983); Victoria E. Bonnell, ed., *The Russian Workers: Life and Labor under the Tsarist Regime* (Berkeley and Los Angeles, 1983); Laura Engelstein, *Moscow, 1905: Working-Class Organization and Political Conflict* (Stanford, Calif., 1982); Rose L. Glickman, *Russian Factory Women: Workplace and Society, 1880–1914* (Berkeley and Los Angeles, 1984); Leopold H. Haimson, "The Problem of Social Stability in Urban Russia, 1905–1917," *Slavic Review* 23, no. 4 (1964), and 24, no. 1 (1965); Robert Eugene Johnson, *Peasant and Proletarian: The Working Class of Moscow in the Late Nineteenth Century* (New Brunswick, N.J., 1979); Allan K. Wildman, *The Making of a Workers' Revolution: Russian Social Democracy, 1891–1903* (Chicago, 1967); Reginald E. Zelnik, *Labor and Society in Tsarist Russia: The Factory Workers of St. Petersburg, 1855–1870* (Stanford, Calif., 1971); and Reginald E. Zelnik, trans. and ed., *A Radical Worker in Tsarist Russia: The Autobiography of Semën Ivanovich Kanatchikov* (Stanford, Calif., 1986).

militance in 1917 can be scripted "as the contingent outcome of particular political struggles rather than as the kind of providential discovery of the proletariat's historical mission."

In the first chapter of this book, Reginald Zelnik rethinks the older forms of labor history. While retaining class as a concept, he follows Jacques Rancière in challenging the tyranny of representative types. His heroes, such as Vasilii Gerasimov, are individualized, and particular experiences are presented as explanatory keys to his self-identity. Gerasimov, for example, felt less identity with workers as a group, even with his fellow weavers, than he felt himself a victim, treated as an animal or a serf, whose path to humanity lay through education. Instead of locating his subjects socially in the relations of production, Zelnik insists on the centrality of the *kruzhok* in the formation of new identities, the locus where factory experience was turned "into language, discourse, *slovo*." Zelnik has moved away from "Marxist" interpretations, such as Plekhanov's, in which the transition from peasant to proletarian took place within and largely because of the new social environment in which factory workers found themselves.

Looking at Russian printers, Mark Steinberg also follows Rancière in elucidating the contribution of "advanced" workers, who through their own understanding of "universal" ideas of human dignity and rights came to see their own degraded conditions of life and work as oppressive and mutable. Rather than being catalyzed to consciousness by their social position, printers sought a social and moral community with their employers through a universal moral discourse. But after meeting resistance and condescension from their "betters," printers began to view themselves, particularly during the revolutionary confrontations of 1905, "through the prism of social class." Caught between the particularity of class and the universalism of their moral values, printers held on to both "a definition of self based on the notion of a common humanity" and a "separate identity as a class."

In her work on Petersburg metalworkers, Heather Hogan argues that the growing sense of class between 1905 and 1912, among both workers and employers, arose from a variety of experiences that made up a complex social context. In 1905 managerial authority collapsed, and workers experienced a new degree of autonomy and empowerment, but with the receding of the revolutionary wave, managers attempted to reassert their authority, particularly through the rationalization of production. Workers perceived that their labor conditions were worsening (falling wages, increased supervision from foremen) and that they were becoming socially isolated both from more impersonal supervisory personnel and from their social-democractic intellectual allies who retreated after 1907. As she puts it, "The historically specific experiences of metalworkers on the shop floor, in the city, and in the national electoral process over the 1906–12 period made the social democrats' class-based analysis of these experiences particularly compelling." Less directly focused on "the discursive," Hogan articulates the broader context of the political struggles that reinforced worker class identity after 1905 and political militance in the last years before the First World War.

In his analysis of social relations in the factories of late imperial Russia, S. A. Smith negotiates a middle position between the material and the linguistic, noting the "importance of discourse in constituting class relations, while not subscribing to the extreme view that discourse alone constitutes real objects." Specific ideological and political representations of society and social class put forth by labor activists were key, in his view, to the drawing of boundaries between workers and the "others." Here again ideas of human dignity, images of being reduced to animals or machines, worked to define a sense of exploitation, of social distance, and of the desperate need for change. Smith suggests in passing the importance of popular culture as context for reception, adaptation, and interpretation of formulations brought to the workers from outside.

Like other social identities, the definition and formation of class requires inclusions and exclusions, and much of the work on imperial labor history, with notable exceptions, has dealt almost exclusively with ethnically Russian, male workers. As Laura Engelstein reminded the conference,

> We used to say in the days of social history that Russian social history never left the politics out. Now, in the days of deconstruction, we can say . . . that the very category of worker in Russia was always, even historically, burdened by conflicting identities, by lack of conceptual wholeness, by self-contradiction, and that only in the minds of very doctrinaire revolutionaries did it enjoy the illusion of some kind of self-evident objective existence.

Pointing out "the exclusion of women both from the social world of engaged workers and from their discourse," she went on to add:

> The world of almost all these self-conscious workers is constructed in opposition to the heterosocial world of the family. The life of domestic or personal intimacy in all these stories [of Zelnik's worker-memoirists]—and we think here of Kanatchikov also—represents hierarchy, tradition, constraint. All these guys are getting out of the family. They are not getting married. The world of the noble worker activist represents male solidarity, fraternity, individualism. Gerasimov believes in a universe of brothers and sisters, not lovers and wives. He's looking for a family, but not his own family. He doesn't want to be "dad"; he doesn't even want to be "honey."

The Elusive Soviet Working Class

From the 1960s through the 1980s, an unusually cohesive cohort of Western labor historians engaged in a social-historical exploration of workers in the revolutions of 1917. Challenging an older historiography that saw the Bolshevik victory as the result of malevolent power seekers, this new generation of historians of Russia attempted to rethink 1917 as a struggle between social classes.[23] By looking below the political surface at the actions and aspirations of workers and soldiers, this "revisionist" historiography argued that a deepening vertical polarization in Russian society undermined the Provisional Government by preventing the consolidation of a political consensus—the social democrat Iraklii Tsereteli's concept of an all-national unity of the "vital forces" of the country—so desired by moderate socialists and liberals. More convincingly than any of their political opponents, the Bolsheviks pushed for a government of the lower classes institutionalized in the soviets, advocated worker control over industry, and demanded an immediate end to the war. By the early fall of 1917, a coincidence of lower-class aspirations and the Bolshevik program resulted in elected Leninist majorities in the soviets of both Petrograd and Moscow and the strategic support of soldiers on the northern and western fronts. But after a relatively easy accession to power, the Bolsheviks, never a majority in peasant Russia, were faced by dissolution of political authority, complete collapse of the economy, and fragmentation of the working-class constituency on which they based their claim to power. As Russia slid into civil war, the Bolsheviks embarked on a program of regenerating state power that involved economic centralization and the use of violence and terror against their opponents.

Western social historians of the revolution avoided an apolitical social history and quite consciously expanded the realm of the political into the factory and the regiment. Though always suspicious of the overly materialist and teleological versions of class formation familiar from Soviet works, the thrust of the new historiography was to revive class analysis rather than reject it. Their work emphasized the fractures within the working class—gender, age, level of skill, ethnicity—but aimed at explaining the extraordinary solidarity and cohesion of workers around radical political positions by the fall of 1917. Their vital synthesis of political

[23] See, for example, Diane Koenker, *Moscow Workers and the 1917 Revolution* (Princeton, N.J., 1981); Diane P. Koenker and William G. Rosenberg, *Strikes and Revolution in Russia, 1917* (Princeton, N.J., 1989); David Mandel, *The Petrograd Workers and the Fall of the Old Regime: From the February Revolution to the July Days, 1917* (New York, 1983); idem., *The Petrograd Workers and the Soviet Seizure of Power: From the July Days 1917 to July 1918* (New York, 1984); and S. A. Smith, *Red Petrograd: Revolution in the Factories, 1917–1918* (Cambridge, 1983).

and social history elaborated a social context that frustrated the efforts of moderates and promoted the fortunes of the Bolsheviks.[24]

A discourse of class was insistently present in 1917, and the achievement of the social historians was to take seriously—though not for granted—the developing sense of class interests. Rather than simply assume the inevitability of class formation, these historians demonstrated how a sense of class was conceived, perceived, and constructed. Since class formation is a matter of inclusions and exclusions, of politically eliminating some distinctions between "us" and "them" and constructing others, the social historians studied workers along with their allies and their enemies. Since classes are political coalitions of diverse elements, they illuminated divisions among workers as well as how a broad conception of a democracy of workers, soldiers, peasants, and others was constituted.

Although it is not difficult to cite instances of social reductionism or inadequate attention to the political in works by social historians, what is most striking is how in their repertoire of explanations, social historians of Russia included both "material" elements and more subjective experiences of discrimination, humiliation, and a sense of social justice. Yet social historians of 1917 tended to see the process of class formation as located squarely in the real economic and social world. For the social historian the world of deprivations and disadvantages became the primary site from which perceptions of differences arose. They saw the identity of the worker as created and reinforced by experiences of economic conflict. They paid less attention to how language and culture or representations in the socialist and bourgeois press shaped and reinforced social identities and the sense of social distance.

What might be termed the Immaculate Conceptionalization school of Soviet historiography interpreted the October Revolution as at once the teleological culmination of decades of struggle and the primal act of the working class in power. The ensuing civil war represented a baptism of fire, a sanguinary experience in which that class nearly expired. Only the dictatorship guided by the firm hand of Lenin rescued the proletariat from extinction, and after the introduction of the New Economic Policy, brought it back to (nearly) full demographic strength. What in this rendition might be thought of as the proletariat's second life begins with the onset of forced-pace industrialization in the late 1920s, proceeds to the socialization of new, predominantly peasant recruits into the new socialist work culture via shock work and socialist competition, and concludes with an increasingly mature working class reproducing itself in the context

[24] Ziva Galili, *The Menshevik Leaders in the Russian Revolution: Social Realities and Political Strategies* (Princeton, N.J., 1989); Alexander Rabinowitch, *The Bolsheviks Come to Power: The Revolution of 1917 in Petrograd* (New York, 1976).

of an ever-increasing standard of living and degree of participation in Soviet administration.

In their assessments of the impact of the civil war on the working class, Western historians have stressed its devastating, even irrevocable consequences. As Isaac Deutscher put it, "The proletarian dictatorship was triumphant, but the proletariat had nearly vanished." In so characterizing the economic and demographic catastrophes that accompanied the Reds' victory, Deutscher was doing no more than repeating the alarmed observations of several leading Bolsheviks, including Lenin. But for Deutscher, writing in the 1950s, this development constituted a great irony and was to have immense significance for the subsequent course of Soviet and indeed world history. The self-proclaimed vanguard of the proletariat, finding itself without a proletariat to lead, proceeded to rule alone, increasingly relying on its own apparatus as a substitute for the working class. "Proletarian democracy," one of the Bolsheviks' watchwords of 1917, was jettisoned in favor of the hierarchical rule of Communist Party committees, to which the factory committees, the soviets, and other authentic working-class organizations were subordinated.[25]

Other accounts speak of the "rustication" of the country and the "withering away of the proletariat" (John Keep), "leaving only its vanguard, like the smile of the Cheshire cat, behind" (Sheila Fitzpatrick). But what exactly do these historians mean by the disappearance of the proletariat? The dramatic decline in the number of industrial workers—from some three million in 1917 to just over one million by the end of 1920—is only part of the story. It was also, in Deutscher's words, that "seven years of world war, revolution, civil war, intervention, and war communism had wrought such changes in society that customary political notions, ideas, and slogans became almost meaningless. Russia's social structure had been not merely overturned; it was smashed and destroyed." Workers who had survived the associated traumas were "exhausted and prostrate"; they no longer cohered as a "vigorous and militant social class," and had "disappeared from the political stage." They were, in a word, "declassed."[26]

[25] Isaac Deutscher, *The Prophet Unarmed: Trotsky, 1921–1929* (New York, 1959), p. 7. For contemporary Bolshevik observations, see Sheila Fitzpatrick, "The Bolsheviks' Dilemma: Class, Culture, and Politics in Early Soviet Years," *Slavic Review* 47, no. 4 (1988): 606–11; Mary McAuley, *Bread and Justice: State and Society in Petrograd, 1917–1921* (Oxford, 1991), pp. 241–45, 401–16.

[26] Deutscher, *Prophet Unarmed*, pp. 5, 11; John Keep, *The Russian Revolution, A Study in Mass Mobilization* (New York, 1976), pp. 261–62; Fitzpatrick, "Bolsheviks' Dilemma," p. 601. On declassing, see also Sheila Fitzpatrick, "The Problem of Class Identity in NEP Society," in Sheila Fitzpatrick, Alexander Rabinowitch, and Richard Stites, eds., *Russia in the Era of NEP: Explorations in Soviet Society and Culture* (Bloomington, Ind., 1991), pp. 13–14, and Richard Sakwa, *Soviet Communists in Power, a Study of Moscow during the Civil War, 1918–21* (New York, 1988), pp. 40–41.

Eschewing these vitalistic metaphors, some historians have modified or rejected the notion of deproletarianization. William Chase has described the Moscow proletariat of 1920–21 as a "bifurcated class" consisting of a "small core of experienced and skilled workers, a majority of whom were males over thirty years old" and a much larger group of "inexperienced and reluctant workers," drawn from recently recruited peasants and the spouses and offspring of workers. Both groups had become estranged from the state, the former because its "revolutionary agenda" of "higher wages, better working conditions, more labor protection, improved housing and diets, greater respect," and workers' control as a means of achieving these disiderata remained unfulfilled, and the latter because of its "lack of interest in production," which was the state's paramount concern. Chase is thus able to speak of both the "distintegration" and "transformation" of the proletariat.[27]

In an article originally published in 1985, Diane Koenker departs more radically from the deproletarianization model. Drawing on demographic data from Moscow, she argues that the mobilization of young male activist workers and the flight to the countryside of unskilled recent migrants, servants, and nonworking dependents resulted in an older, more female and more urbanized working-class population. Less disposed to the "revolutionary consciousness" exhibited in 1917, those who stuck out the civil war years in Moscow resorted to strategies of survival that both reflected and enhanced their working-class consciousness. Among the indices of such a consciousness, Koenker cites "the strong sense of neighborhood and district loyalty that appears again and again in workers' memoirs" and the surge in civil marriages reflecting a more secular, urban-based culture. Class consciousness, in short, did not so much disappear as migrate from the workplace to the home, the neighborhood, and such proliferating cultural facilities as libraries, schools, and the theater. Just as the numerical decline of the urban population did not necessarily mean deurbanization, so changes in the social and gender composition and consciousness of the working class did not necessarily constitute deproletarianization.[28]

In her discussion of printers and in his of coal miners, Diane Koenker and Hiroaki Kuromiya address the effects of the revolution on labor re-

[27] William Chase, *Workers, Society and the Soviet State: Labor and Life in Moscow, 1918–1929* (Urbana, Ill., 1987), pp. 33–35. For two older Soviet studies of Petrograd workers that also distinguish between a "core" (predominantly male) element of "cadre" workers and a less proletarianized group, see O. I. Shkaratan, "O sostave fab.-zav. rabochikh g. Petrograda v gody revoliutsii i grazhdanskoi voiny, 1917–1920 gg.," *Uchenye zapiski LGPI im. Gertsena* 1957, no. 1:17–34; and V. Z. Drobizhev and A. K. Sokolov, "Rabochie Petrograda v 1918 g.," *Istoriia SSSR*, 1973, no. 1:32–54.

[28] Diane Koenker, "Urbanization and Deurbanization in the Russian Revolution and Civil War," *Journal of Modern History* 57 (1985): 424–50.

lations. In almost every respect, these two occupational groups seem to stand at opposite ends of the proletarian spectrum. Printers were quintessentially urban and oriented toward a "culture of intelligence and literacy," but coal miners were scattered in mining settlements and had a high level of illiteracy.[29] In terms of political circumstances, most printers were under Soviet power from November 1917 onward, whereas miners in the Donbas experienced frequent and often violent changes of political regime until 1920. Printers were deeply involved in the politics of representation, whereas miners were consumed by the politics of retribution and revenge.

And yet we can see evidence in both cases of an extraordinary degree of collective self-reliance and resilience. The disdain of miners for party politics and formal trade union representation and their resort to flight and *samosud* (mob law) may have been the most rational responses to the highly fluid and personally dangerous situation in which there were no universally accepted rules for industrial relations. In the case of printers, the failure of the state to fulfill its end of the "productivist" bargain— that is, to supply them with food—led to shop self-governance and a legacy of "workplace cohesion" on which printers were to draw during the years of the New Economic Policy.

Ironically, the resort to these strategies of survival placed both miners and printers beyond the limits of what the Bolsheviks defined as proletarian class interest. What was said of the Donbas miners at the Eighth Conference of the Russian Communist Party (in 1919)—that their "best elements" had disappeared and that those who remained were "psychologically smashed"—was eventually extended to other workers who failed to conform to the party's productivist, self-sacrificing vision. By 1920–21, the party leadership, faced with growing worker unrest and the meaninglessness of "customary political notions, ideas, and slogans," grew increasingly suspicious of its principal social constituency. A rhetoric of "declassing" accompanied a search for appropriate social categories— petty bourgeois, peasant, and so on—to explain the mood of workers who could not be recognized as "proletarian."[30] But the party could not

---

[29] For a recent dyspeptic view of Donbas workers before and during the 1905 revolution, see Charters Wynn, *Workers, Strikes and Pogroms: The Donbass-Dnepr Bend in Late Imperial Russia, 1870–1905* (Princeton, N.J., 1992). See also Theodore Friedgut, *Iuzovka and Revolution* (Princeton, N.J., 1989).

[30] See Koenker's arch comment, "when Bolshevik party leaders saw support slipping away, they blamed the physical disappearance of their supporters rather than changed attitudes." In Diane P. Koenker, William G. Rosenberg, and Ronald Grigor Suny, eds., *Party, State and Society in the Russian Civil War: Explorations in Social History* (Bloomington, Ind., 1989), p. 51. Ironically, Mary McAuley chides Western historians "such as Koenker, Mandel, Smith, and Rosenberg" for their "tendency . . . to enter the debate on the same terms, that is to seek the determinants of working-class political behaviour in its social background." McAuley, *Bread and Justice*, p. 401. This "tendency" is most apparent in their work on the 1917 revolution.

acknowledge for long the absence of the class in whose name it claimed to be ruling. Even while Lenin, among others, decried the lack of true proletarian qualities among workers, political artists were visually reinventing the mythological revolutionary proletarian, as Victoria Bonnell reminds us in her contribution to this book. The reversion to a broader, more inclusive definition of proletarian identity—one that stressed social origins as well as current occupation—soon followed. This is part of the "masking" of social layers Daniel Orlovsky discusses in his chapter on white-collar workers.

Class discourse functioned on many levels in the 1920s. Propagandists used it to distinguish the Soviet state from those "capitalist" states encircling the USSR, thereby rhetorically extending to an international scale the struggle that the proletariat had won in Russia. Artistic movements such as Proletkult and (from the mid-1920s) RAPP (the Russian Association of Proletarian Writers) adopted it to assert their commitment to a culture that was free of bourgeois standards. Within the professions, young Communist visionaries and self-styled "proletarians" used a language of class to challenge the hegemony of their non-Communist elders. In statuary and poster art, as Bonnell points out, "The worker was designated not just as a revolutionary but as a standard-bearer for the Bolshevik Party." Class language as a powerful tool of inclusion and exclusion played a significant role in both official and popular attitudes toward such groups as specialists, NEPmen (and NEP-women), and the non-Communist intelligentsia, each of which was tainted with bourgeois associations. It figured metaphorically in the campaign launched by the Women's Section (*Zhenotdel*) of the party to emancipate Central Asian women and in Sultan Galiev's characterization of Central Asian peoples in general. Official documents, census tabulations, studies of rural society, and admissions to higher educational institutions, the Komsomol, and the party all employed the official designations of class.[31]

The Soviet discourse of class was multivalent, even diffuse, available for appropriation by a variety of groups within the party-state. As Orlovsky claims, "The proletarian agendas were mystifying challenges and threats" for white-collar workers. Their meaning for blue-collar workers remains elusive. In his study of Moscow workers in the 1920s, William Chase treats the industrial workers, the working class, and the proletariat of Moscow as interchangeable and unproblematic categories. To be sure, Chase recognizes the existence of divisions, or in his terms, centrifugal

[31] See Gregory Massell, *The Surrogate Proletariat: Moslem Women and Revolutionary Strategies in Soviet Central Asia, 1919–1929* (Princeton, N.J., 1974); Sheila Fitzpatrick, "Cultural Revolution as Class War," in Fitzpatrick, ed., *Cultural Revolution in Russia, 1928–1931* (Bloomington, Ind., 1978), pp. 8–40; and idem, *Education and Social Mobility in the Soviet Union, 1921–34* (Cambridge, 1979).

forces, within the "working class" based on differential levels of skill, work experience, and gender. And his detailing of "life and labor in Moscow" is the first extended treatment of such "daily realities" as the scarcity of housing, crime, nightlife, and family life, each of which, he argues, functioned as countervailing centripetal forces.[32] But in his account the sociologically defined, gender-neutral working class/proletariat still retains agency. The *class,* as distinct from individuals, has attitudes, develops a revolutionary agenda, pursues certain survival strategies, and negotiates a "historic alliance." Scarce attention is paid to how official definitions of class shaped class identity.

In a recent article, "The Problem of Class Identity," Sheila Fitzpatrick has attempted to get at workers' own sense of themselves and their relationship to others by isolating certain identities or *mentalités.* She links them with three sociological types: skilled workers with ties to the land (who presumably retained an interest in village life if not the mentalité of peasants); male, middle-aged urban workers who exhibited "trade-union consciousness" and antipathies toward women, adolescents, and peasants; and young, skilled male workers who were leading candidates for upward mobility. She underscores "the fragility of individuals' class identity, on the one hand, and the social and political significance of class identity, on the other." For if the proletarian identities of at least the first two types did not coincide with the attributes found in Communist discourse—and one wonders about female workers and the "unskilled" in this respect— those whose social backgrounds were liable to cause them problems were capable of masking their "alien" class identities by "making selective use of different elements of [their] personal and family history" to adopt more advantageous ones.[33]

Fitzpatrick's historical sociology concludes with the assertion that by the end of the 1920s, "the industrial working class was a social reality . . . sufficiently coherent to be capable of collective action within the new trade union framework."[34] But was such collective action built on a recognition of *class* or something else, something not quite as universal or reductive of the differences among workers? Based on his examination of labor conflict in Moscow during the early years of NEP, John Hatch has argued that "wage and productivity pressures mobilized workers into the collective defense of their economic interests and promoted the development of working-class sensibilities." But "rural-urban migration, generational and gender differences, industrial differentiation, and sectionalism

---

[32] Chase, *Workers, Society and the Soviet State,* pp. 173–213.
[33] Fitzpatrick, "The Problem of Class Identity," pp. 28, 25.
[34] Ibid., pp. 28–29.

continued to influence and fragment workers' conceptions of class," a conclusion that coincides with Chase's assessment.[35]

Such a formulation can be tested against evidence derived from in-depth studies of particular trades. Judging from Diane Koenker's examination of printers' culture on and off the shop floor, it would appear that class sensibilities had been seriously eroded. If older workers' "alcoholic male comaraderie" pointedly excluded newly arrived younger males and women, then young printers' "partying and . . . disregard for rules and discipline" was resented by their elders and the union alike. Perhaps, she concludes provocatively, the absence of a common class enemy made class consciousness unnecessary. This may be why the metaphor of the family "was finding its way into the discourse of workers in the printing trades."[36]

In the case of the textile workers of the Central Industrial Region, Chris Ward's subject in this book, the family had a narrower and more literal meaning: "Simultaneously a unit of economic support and a unit of exploitation," the family constituted the core of the work teams or *komplekty* on the shop floor. Within the komplekty, parents exercised their authority to recruit, train, and "hard drive" their children along strictly gendered lines. Family and kinship links also spanned the "dual-axis continuum" between factory and field, thus blurring the distinction between "worker" and "peasant" and frustrating rationalizers' schemes to intensify production. This very incompleteness of proletarianization combined with a pervasive patriarchy and "the particularism of work culture" in the cotton industry to militate against an all-embracing class consciousness or even one that encompassed the entire industry.[37]

Our search for a Soviet working class has come up against a paradox. In the course of the 1920s, the industrial workforce was restored: yet the working class as a signifier of empowerment lost its salience. Small-scale entrepreneurs, NEPmen, and specialists could all arouse workers' ire—or envy. But neither the otherness of these groups, nor the party's totalizing rhetoric of the working class in power, nor even the commonality of wage labor made class imminent as a set of common understandings or a basis for collective action. Rather than assume that class was something that was fragmenting or pulling apart, we might do better to conceive of it as an emerging political construct whose employment signified loyalty to the

---

[35] John Hatch, "Labor Conflict in Moscow, 1921–1925," in Fitzpatrick, Rabinowitch, and Stites, *Russia in the Era of NEP*, pp. 67–68.

[36] Diane Koenker, "Class and Consciousness in a Socialist Society: Workers in the Printing Trades during NEP," in Fitzpatrick, Rabinowitch, and Stites, *Russia in the Era of NEP*, pp. 48–54.

[37] For an elaboration of these themes, see Chris Ward, *Russia's Cotton Workers and the New Economic Policy: Shop-Floor Culture and State Policy, 1921–1929* (Cambridge, 1990).

regime and its goals. Such an approach can illuminate a variety of previously obscure phenomena: the association of social groups or layers within the "proletarian project," which, as Dan Orlovsky argues, served to alleviate the precariousness of white-collar workers' status as well as deflect attention away from the massive increase in the size and weight of the bureaucracy; the tension, sometimes latent and sometimes overt, between loyalty to the regime (the major employer) and loyalty to one's union, enterprise, shop, or office; and the extent to which the single rhetorical framework employed in such campaigns as socialist rationalization masked but did not allow for the resolution of conflicting interests within the state system.

With the Great Turn of 1928–30, the leap into full-scale collectivization of agriculture and forced-pace industrialization, these campaigns, accompanied by a brutal assault on intellectual and religious culture, utterly transformed the social landscape of the Soviet Union. So rapid and intense were the demographic changes, so steep were the trajectories of social mobility, that there was simply no time for settling in, for a pattern of acculturation to occur. Throughout the years of the First Five-Year Plan, the USSR was, in Moshe Lewin's words, a "quicksand society," characterized by flux, uncertainty, mobility, and anomie.[38] Peasants became workers, workers became bosses, bosses frequently found themselves in prison. As the countryside disgorged its millions, the cities were "ruralized." By 1932, the number of wage earners was 22.9 million as compared to 11.9 million at the outset of the plan, and the size of the industrial workforce had reached 6.5 million, more than twice what it had been in 1928. After a brief interval during which the number of workers actually declined, expansion began anew, and by 1937, the culminating year of the Second Five-Year Plan, Soviet industry counted 8 million workers.

Having elsewhere surveyed Western historiography on Stalinist industrialization, we will confine ourselves here to how historians have conceptualized class in that context.[39] It should surprise no one that these conceptualizations have revolved around workers' relations with the state.[40] Workers have been portrayed in one of three ways: as genuine

[38] Moshe Lewin, *The Making of the Soviet System: Essays in the Social History of the Interwar Period* (New York, 1985), p. 221; see also his *Gorbachev Phenomenon: A Historical Interpretation*, expanded edition (Berkeley and Los Angeles, 1991), pp. 20–26.

[39] Lewis H. Siegelbaum and Ronald Grigor Suny, "Conceptualizing the Command Economy: Western Historians on Soviet Industrialization," in William G. Rosenberg and Lewis H. Siegelbaum, eds., *Social Dimensions of Soviet Industrialization* (Bloomington, Ind., 1993).

[40] See Sheila Fitzpatrick's comment that "we have not yet discarded the assumption that the only significant social relations in the Soviet Union are those in which society relates to government," in her "New Perspectives on Stalinism," *Russian Review* 45 (October 1986): 373. Intended as criticism, the comment itself provoked a critical response from Geoff Eley: "If the turn to social history is to be more than the spurious radicalism of social history for social history's sake, the new work needs to be explicitly linked to larger analysis of the

supporters of the system, as sullen victims, or as opportunists employing strategies to maximize their chances of survival and advancement.

As Stephen Kotkin explains in his chapter in this book, the vast bulk of Soviet historiography was dedicated to the proposition that industrialization ushered in the creation of an enthusiastic and heroic working class that under the guidance of the Communist Party, became the mainstay of socialist construction. Against this monolithically upbeat perspective, most non-Soviet commentators used to argue that enthusiasm was manufactured, that workers derived little or no benefit from industrialization but on the contrary were shackled by draconian decrees and arbitrary repression, and that their "atomized" condition precluded autonomy or organized resistance. To the extent that distinctions were made among workers—or "labor"—it was to emphasize the extreme naïveté or cultural backwardness of recent peasant migrants compared to older cadre workers and the gradual emergence of a labor aristocracy drawn from the former group.[41] Class, then, was a residual category corresponding to social location.

Staking out new ground in the late 1970s and 1980s, "revisionist" scholars interpreted the labor enthusiasm of the First Five-Year Plan as part of a "revolution from below," which complemented Stalin's "revolution from above." The shock troops of this revolution were primarily young, skilled workers who identified with the regime's assaults ("offensives") against "bourgeois" specialists, political opponents, and recalcitrant trade unionists, not to mention kulaks and "unconscious" peasants opposed to collectivization. These workers comprised a middle group between older, skilled workers, who had become disoriented by the upheavals on and off the shop floor (experiencing a "crisis of proletarian identity"), and recent migrants from the villages. Keen to demonstrate their commitment to building socialism, they volunteered for extra shifts in the factories or to serve in the brigades that were collectivizing agriculture, seemed oblivious to material privation, and, it might be added, were not always thrilled about being "promoted" into white-collar jobs.[42]

---

structured relational field *between* 'below' and 'above' in all its dimensions, ideological and political as well as socio-economic." See his "History with the Politics Left Out—Again?" *Russian Review* 45 (October 1986): 392.

[41] See Solomon Schwarz, *Labor in the Soviet Union* (New York, 1952); and for the classic account of the Soviet aristocracy of labor, Leon Trotsky, *The Revolution Betrayed* (New York, 1965), especially pp. 121–26.

[42] Donald Filtzer, *Soviet Workers and Stalinist Industrialization: The Formation of Modern Soviet Production Relations, 1928–1941* (Armonk, N.Y., 1986); Fitzpatrick, *Education and Social Mobility*; Lynne Viola, *The Best Sons of the Fatherland: Workers in the Vanguard of Soviet Collectivization* (Oxford, 1987); Hiroaki Kuromiya, *Stalin's Industrial Revolution: Politics and Workers, 1928–1932* (Cambridge, 1988).

By stressing the agency of workers and, more broadly, society, the revisionists released the stranglehold of the statist tradition. In this sense, their "history from below" was analogous to, if not directly influenced by, E. P. Thompson's breakthrough of a decade or so earlier. But the analogy goes only so far. Soviet workers did not behave as their counterparts in nineteenth-century England and North America had mainly because the political circumstances in which they lived and what they had to draw on in defining themselves in relation to those circumstances were so different. Consequently, with few exceptions, revisionist historiography does not display the identification with its subjects and their agendas that is characteristic of the work of social historians of Western European and North American labor.[43]

At the same time, the limitations of this initial reconception of the history of Soviet labor were quickly reached. It was largely confined to the late 1920s and early 1930s, a period of tremendous social upheaval when, in Alec Nove's phrase, "optimism ran riot."[44] Methodologically, the heavy reliance on official sources—and hence, categories—and the concentration on upwardly mobile and regime-supportive workers obscured the experiences and mentalités of the non- and laterally mobile as well as those subjected to various forced-labor regimes. Finally, the nominal attention to female workers and the general absence of gender from revisionists' conceptual framework significantly impaired their appreciation of the terms under which cultural revolution and class war were conducted and who was excluded from them.

Other Western scholars meanwhile were reviving and revising older perspectives. Donald Filtzer's book on the formation of modern Soviet production relations took on issues first raised in Solomon Schwarz's pioneering study published in 1952. In contrast to Schwarz, whose chief concern was to demonstrate, via an exhaustive survey of labor legislation, the state's ever-tightening grip on workers, Filtzer insisted that the state and workers fought each other to a standstill. Although the state succeeded in "atomizing" the working class, it did not—and given competition among enterprises for skilled labor and other scarce resources, could not—wrest control of the labor process. Neither coercion in the form of decrees punishing violations of "labor discipline" nor incentive systems borrowed from the capitalist West broke the stalemate. Through

---

[43] We are grateful to Geoff Eley and Keith Nield for allowing us to read and cite their draft paper "Classes as Historical Subjects? Some Reflections," which emphasizes "the closeness of the practice of social history to multiple progressive or emancipatory politics" (p. 8). For one such exception among historians of Soviet labor, see Lewis Siegelbaum, "Production Collectives and Communes and the 'Imperatives' of Soviet Industrialization, 1929–1931," *Slavic Review* 45, no. 1 (1986): 65–84.

[44] Alec Nove, *An Economic History of the USSR* (London, 1969), p. 187.

impressive empirical detail, Filtzer was able to demonstrate how workers confounded the regime's campaigns to increase productivity by engaging in both covert and overt acts of indiscipline, and how managers, desperate to hold onto scarce labor resources, colluded with them. Strictly speaking, such actions occurred on an individual basis, for the "working class" had been defeated. Its "political demoralization and organizational weakness . . . divorce[d] it once and for all from its militant traditions and destroy[ed] its ability to act collectively as a self-conscious historical force."[45]

Vladimir Andrle, an industrial sociologist, added subtle refinements to the picture drawn by Filtzer. Following Michael Burawoy's ethnographic study of workers "making out" in a Chicago engineering plant, he argued that the shop-floor culture in Soviet plants of the 1930s operated similarly "to promote stability in work relations by upholding performance standards which fell short of the expectations generated by technological investment." This was a culture of mutual interlocking dependencies based on *blat*, "the business of cultivating and using networks of personal contacts for the purpose of obtaining scarce resources which should have been distributed as state property . . . in accordance with official and impersonal rules." Cutting across official hierarchies, the reciprocities and loyalties established by workers and their immediate bosses could be, and frequently were, disrupted by both Taylorist-inspired managerial schemes and mobilization campaigns—"storming," shock work, and Stakhanovism. But the collusive responses of workers and managers undermined these efforts, returning industrial relations to the more balanced status quo ante.[46]

Andrle's analysis of "industrialization and social change in a planned economy" dispensed almost entirely with class: "The social class which interests us most, i.e. manual workers in manufacturing" was not a class at all, not even in the Marxist sense of class-in-itself, for wages in (partial) payment of labor was almost beside the point.[47] As for the more stringent criteria of a class-for-itself, Walter Connor reminds us that "becoming a class is a tall order if class is to be seen as a collectivity with a certain ability to regulate its membership; to generate a solid sense of shared identity among those members (and, perhaps, against other classes) on the basis of similar background, work situation, and relationship to au-

[45] Schwarz, *Labor in the Soviet Union*; Filtzer, *Soviet Workers and Stalinist Industrialization*, pp. 254–55.

[46] Vladimir Andrle, *Workers in Stalin's Russia: Industrialization and Social Change in a Planned Economy* (Hemel Hempstead, Eng.; New York, 1988), p. 54.

[47] For a similar argument with respect to Chinese workers after 1949, see Andrew Walder, *Communist Neo-Traditionalism: Work and Authority in Chinese Industry* (Berkeley and Los Angeles, 1986).

thority; to influence its members' behavior, and to exercise a certain amount of clout in various ways, organized and unorganized, against other classes and/or the state." Workers during the Stalin period simply did not meet these criteria. Stalin's "pervasive totalitarian rule . . . left no space for the formation or survival of classes, and, even less, organized representation of class interests: it was starkly 'uncivil.' " And again, "from the FYP [Five-Year Plan]-derived social transformations of 1928–40 through the crucible of war and on to the renewal/replacement of worker cadres through largely peasant postwar 'drafts,' the Stalin era had been inimical to processes through which class characteristics might develop spontaneously among workers or other groups."[48] Instead of working-class formation, the reverse took place during the Stalin era—not a workforce gradually becoming aware of itself as a class and expressing such an awareness in a "variety of ways, organized and unorganized," but, to cite the title and thrust of Gábor T. Rittersporn's contribution to this book, "from working class to urban laboring mass."

If as Rittersporn argues, "relations of production could not function as the main determinant of social status," the weakness or even absence of such economic determinants underscores the importance of politically discursive practices. In analyzing the "semiotics of Stalinist visual propaganda," Victoria Bonnell traces the evolution of the worker-hero as "New Soviet Man." This "visual script," which was completed during the heyday of Stakhanovism, paralleled and reinforced the highly scripted contemporary written texts and public ceremonies to demonstrate the inextricable link between the elect and Stalin, the Great Helmsman, and to encourage the nonelect to derive inspiration and guidance from them.

During this period—and for decades to come—the state jealously guarded its monopoly on the representation of class. Stephen Kotkin and Sheila Fitzpatrick address the question of how the script was read by those to whom it was directed, and how meaningful they found it. Each is concerned with the parameters of social identity. Each works within certain dichotomies—cadres and newcomers, worker-heroes and slackers, "ours" and "others," workers and managers—although assessments of whether they were overcome or outweighed by integrative mechanisms in the course of the 1930s vary.

At Magnitogorsk, the focus of Stephen Kotkin's fascinating study, all

---

[48] Walter D. Connor, *The Accidental Proletariat: Workers, Politics, and Crisis in Gorbachev's Russia* (Princeton, N.J., 1991), pp. 40–41, 70. See also Neil Harding, "Socialism, Society, and the Organic Labour State," in Harding, ed., *The State in Socialist Society* (Albany, N.Y., 1984), p. 39: "For the first time in history, . . . an industrial workforce made to the specification of the masters of the state machine . . . owed its existence, its expectations, its knowledge of the world, indeed its literacy, to that same state that controlled its avenues of movement, promotion, or even physical survival."

workers were newcomers. Here was an instance, almost laboratory-like, where the factory as community organizer and "melting pot" shaped identities. From diverse backgrounds, the labor force assembled at Magnitogorsk was reclassified according to politically charged categories of the state's devising, but it was the workers who inhabited these categories, who had to adopt "the official method of speaking about themselves" and "play the game." Did the workers of Magnitogorsk believe what they had to affirm? Kotkin is appropriately agnostic on this matter. Noting that one could " 'speak Bolshevik' one moment, 'innocent peasant' the next," he nonetheless suggests that ordinarily it was not advantageous not to believe and that "if the people of Magnitogorsk took pride in themselves for their accomplishments and rewards," we as historians would be derelict if we denied the genuineness—or legitimacy—of such feelings.

Learning to "speak Bolshevik," knowing how to behave in choreographed rituals, and maximizing the advantages of (over)fulfilling expectations was the stuff of social identification in the 1930s. As Sheila Fitzpatrick demonstrates in her chapter on worker participation in the Great Purges of 1937–38, some workers, encouraged by various "signals," denounced their bosses in terms reminiscent of the *spets*-baiting of the Cultural Revolution, if not prerevolutionary class hostilities. But others were less vindictive, and still others seem to have taken advantage of their bosses' disorientation and fear of denunciation to do pretty much what they liked on the shop floor. The contrasts she draws between the behavior of metalworkers and flaxworkers are instructive, and her entire chapter serves as a model of what can now be discovered about the purges given access to archival material from the period.

Winding up his summary, which ranges over the broad chronological and conceptual terrain of the other chapters, Moshe Lewin refers to the "historical game of 'hide and seek.' " The analogy is entirely appropriate. For many years, Soviet working-class history was hidden from Western scholars. The reasons for this had less to do with the relative inaccessibility of "appropriate" sources—though that *was* a problem—than the gravitational pull exercised by the "apotheosis of the state" on the historical imaginations and interests of investigators. Although it was known that workers were out there, they seemed either too unreachable or too unimportant to study. Later, as social historians went out in search of and found workers, a new problem arose. In what sense did Soviet workers constitute a class? Insofar as this question was addressed, the answer was certainly not in the sense that official discourse prescribed and yet also not in the sense(s) that class figured in Western capitalist societies. Did then class exist at all, or was it, as several participants at the conference suggested, merely a linguistic "echo," which, like a radioactive element, had a half-life that extended for decades beyond its real existence?

The aim of our conference was not to describe, but to find, the Soviet "working class." Its "making" was never accomplished, and the very process of class formation is not only open-ended but as much in the eye of the beholder as in the "experience" of the actors. If class is more than social stratum, more than wage level or position in the social relations of production, then its representation, the language of its composers, the discourses in which it is constituted all must be brought into a study of its constitution.

Soviet workers, coming together and working within a system called by its leaders "socialist," were quickly proletarianized, but they did not then constitute themselves as a conscious proletariat in Marx's sense of a class-for-itself. As Lewin points out, the working class had no "other" in the form of an antagonistic bourgeoisie. It operated in a noncapitalist environment without the possibility of self-organization outside of state prescription. The language of class was appropriated by party and state managers, and though autonomous discourses of workers existed within the totalizing dominance of the regime, workers had no formal modalities for wide expression and reproduction except through the state. The regime co-opted those who might have become labor's leaders and punished those who might have formed oppositions. A Soviet industrial workforce existed and grew in the first two-and-a-half decades of Soviet power; its members certainly saw themselves as members of a "working class"; but they had lost the political spaces in which they could develop independent conceptions of themselves and create their own agendas. The irony of Soviet history, that workers in an ostensibly "Marxist" state were more alienated than empowered, was also the source of its tragedy, the degeneration of the promises of social liberation and the apotheosis of a new form of tyranny over the very people in whose name the system was created.

Reginald E. Zelnik

On the Eve: Life Histories and Identities
of Some Revolutionary Workers, 1870–1905

"I want to ask you two questions; you were a first-class Petersburg worker, you made about 100 rubles." I said: "Mr. Prosecutor, we're not good enough friends to talk so freely. . . . " [His] second question was: will there be a revolution? . . . "You're a man of great experience, you've lived among all kinds of workers . . . so please give me your impression." I said . . . there'd be one, taking into account our intellectual and moral progress . . . [He] asked: when would the revolution take place? I said: in fifty years. . . . He thanked me for my honest answers.
—S. K. Volkov, "Avtobiografiia"

Douleur de l'exploitation et plaisir d'appartenir à la secte de ceux qui la connaissent.
—Jacques Rancière, *La nuit des prolétaires*

Three decades have passed since Leopold Haimson's article "The Problem of Social Stability in Urban Russia, 1905–1917," in *Slavic Review* launched an ongoing effort to pinpoint the social identities of Russia's most militant workers on the (long) eve of the Russian Revolution. If a paradigm is not just a particular theory but a configuration of notions that help us define what is or is not a worthy research project, then it is fair to say that despite some changes in conceptualization, we are still working through our analysis of Russian labor history within the framework of a social-identity paradigm.

Within the paradigm itself, however, there has been ample room for several approaches. For many, the problem of worker identity has re-

Part of this chapter was prepared while I was a fellow at the Center for Advanced Study in the Behavioral Sciences and recipient of a University of California President's Research Fellowship in the Humanities. I am grateful for financial support provided by the John D. and Catherine T. MacArthur Foundation and by an NEH Fellowship for Independent Study and Research. I thank Laura Engelstein and William H. Sewell (discussants at the MSU conference), Victoria Bonnell, Irina Paperno, Nicholas Riasanovsky, and the editors of this book for their valuable counsel.

volved around the conceptual opposition between "peasant" and "proletarian" (as in the title of Robert E. Johnson's pioneering book and in earlier studies by Theodore Von Laue).[1] Sometimes, especially but not only in Soviet works, social identity is defined as a position on a continuum of "consciousness," which is presumed to correlate closely with the peasant-proletarian dichotomy. Others have emphasized the existence of such a wide variety of subspecies of workers that any attempt to locate them neatly on a peasant-proletarian continuum would obstruct our efforts to capture particular experience. Ziva Galili underlines this multiplicity of types when she warns us that when she uses "workers" as a collective noun, she does not intend to deny "the difference of experience, attitude, and political orientation that divided workers along the lines of skill, factory size, industry, and city district, as well as sex and age."[2] (She could easily have added ethnicity and religion.)

Within Europe, a strong emphasis on "peasant" as the basic contrast with "proletarian" seems to be singularly Russian. Although the contrast may exist in other national contexts, historians of France or Germany are more likely to examine the political culture of the factory worker by comparing it with that of the traditional artisan than with that of the peasant. To test this notion one might examine the much-admired collection of essays on working-class formation in Germany, France, and the United States edited by Ira Katznelson and Aristide Zolberg.[3] The index reveals not a single entry under "peasant" or "peasantry," but indicates at least fifty pages under "artisans" and many more under specific crafts or related terms such as "journeymen."

There are, of course, good reasons for historians of those countries to focus on the factory worker–artisan relationship. In the French case, for example, the factory workforce grew slowly, and craftsmen in tiny shops dominated the labor force and labor movement for much of the nineteenth century. Anyone examining the course of popular revolutionary politics

[1] Robert E. Johnson, *Peasant and Proletarian: The Working Class of Moscow in the Late Nineteenth Century* (New Brunswick, N.J.: 1979); Theodore Von Laue, "Russian Peasants in the Factory, 1892–1904," *Journal of Economic History* 21 (March 1961), and "Russian Labor Between Field and Factory, 1892–1903," *California Slavic Studies* 3 (1964); also R. E. Zelnik, "The Peasant and the Factory," in Wayne S. Vucinich, ed., *The Peasant in Nineteenth-Century Russia* (Stanford, Calif., 1968). The peasant-proletarian contrast may be related to the binary pairs discussed in Iurii M. Lotman and Boris A. Uspenskii, "Binary Models in the Dynamics of Russian Culture to the End of the Eighteenth Century," in Alexander D. Nakhimovsky and Alice Stone Nakhimovsky, eds., *The Semiotics of Russian Cultural History* (Ithaca, N.Y., 1985).

[2] Ziva Galili, "Workers, Industrialists, and the Menshevik Mediators: Labor Conflicts in Petrograd, 1917," *Russian History/Histoire Russe* 16, nos. 2–4 (1989): 240n.

[3] Ira Katznelson and Aristide R. Zolberg, *Working-Class Formation: Nineteenth-Century Patterns in Western Europe and the United States* (Princeton, N.J., 1986).

in France would be wiser to focus on the artisan–factory worker nexus than on the peasant-proletarian nexus.

In Russia, by contrast, late but rapid industrialization, the extreme dominance of peasants as the recruitment pool for factories (even advanced machine-building plants), and the numerical and cultural weakness of the urban-artisanal sector provide plausible grounds for conceptualizing the history of labor around a peasant-proletarian nexus. The standard Soviet variant of that conceptualization has included a teleology that ends the story with the triumph of an advanced, "conscious" proletariat, dominating and leading a benighted peasantry (the Bolshevik metanarrative). An alternative to this Soviet conceptualization, one that seems very different but really only reverses its terms, replacing it with a *negative* telos, has stressed the *absence* of progress from peasant to proletarian and ends the story with the tagic victory of "backwardness" (the Menshevik metanarrative).

It is not my intent to deny the value of "peasant-proletarian" as a useful if problematic way to frame the story of Russian labor. I happily concede that there were real historical circumstances that justify this mode of constructing Russia's past. My purpose, rather, is to complicate the stories that have been composed within this framework, and in some cases to indicate its incapacity to contain the reality of the lives of politically active workers. I will proceed primarily by examining the individual stories of some of those workers, mainly but not exclusively those who have written about their own pasts. All of these were people who at some point in their lives came to identify themselves as worker-revolutionaries. Did workers of this kind imagine their own lives as a rejection of peasant culture and values? as a progressive movement over a sociocultural continuum with a peasant-proletarian axis? To what degree did they (should we) view their lives outside or prior to the factory as the moments that determined their identities? How were their contacts not only with employers and other workers, the classic actors in the Marxist family romance, but with *other* social actors, instrumental in propelling them toward new worldviews? What further readings of their life experiences would help us to make sense of the revolutions in their values that preceded revolutions in the streets?

Before we address individual cases, it is useful to take note of the work that originally constructed the typology that places Russian workers along a peasant-proletarian continuum: "The Russian Worker in the Revolutionary Movement," Georgii Plekhanov's 1892 memoir of his contacts with Petersburg workers in the 1870s.[4] Apart from the authority of the

---

[4] Georgii Plekhanov, *Russkii rabochii v revoliutsionnom dvizhenii (po lichnym vospominaniiam)*, 2d ed. (Geneva, 1902), reprinted by Politizdat (n.p., 1940) (hereafter cited as *RR*

author, the "father of Russian Marxism,"[5] that oft-cited work derives its credibility from its self-presentation as autobiography, with its social typology projected as a reflection *of* as well as a reflection *on* the author's past experience.

Without denying its utility as a source, we need to note the polemical purposes for which Plekhanov wrote this memoir, purposes he made little effort to conceal. If his first goal was to give courage to his Marxist comrades by showing that a tradition of brave Russian revolutionary workers already existed, another aim was to strengthen their hand against their populist rivals. Those rivals, though soon to turn much of their own attention to workers, still identified the peasant as the social force that would do most to help the intelligentsia bring down the old regime and replace it with a commune-based socialist order. Plekhanov, by contrast, while toying ambivalently with a quest for the ever elusive revolutionary bourgeoisie, wished to identify the urban worker as the most vital social force. It was therefore useful to depict the 1870s not only as a time when workers came to life politically (easily shown), but also as a time when they were progressing toward a "correct" understanding of their historical tasks, an understanding that populist intellectuals had failed to attain. History was preparing "new social forces" that would destroy tsarism, Plekhanov told his readers, and "the most powerful" force was the proletariat (*RR*, p. 59).

In order to tie this thesis to his polemic with populism, Plekhanov built an analytical structure, dressed in the garb of memory, that paired peasants with populists and workers with Marxists and identified the movement from the first pair to the second (that is, from peasant to worker, from populist to Marxist) as historical progress. The two lines of motion were not quite symmetrical, however, for although an individual populist could transform himself into a Marxist (as Plekhanov had) and an "unconscious" peasant could become a "conscious" worker, in the case of workers Plekhanov drew a further distinction between two types: a lower type or *fabrichnyi*, usually a weaver or spinner in a textile mill (*fabrika*), and a higher type or *zavodskoi*, usually a *slesar'* (fitter) or *tokar'* (lathe operator, turner), but never a *kuznets* (smith) or *liteishchik* (smelter), in a metalworking plant (*zavod*). Hence, the full range of this typology was from peasant to fabrichnyi to zavodskoi. Viewed as a personal trajectory the scheme entailed the actual movement of individuals from farm to fabrika *or* to zavod, but it did not suggest that individuals actually moved

---

in text and notes). *RR* was first published in *Sotsial-Demokrat* (Geneva), 1892, nos. 3 and 4. It was republished in volume 3 of Plekhanov's *Sochineniia* (Moscow, 1928).

[5] Samuel H. Baron, *Plekhanov: The Father of Russian Marxism* (Stanford, Calif., 1963).

from fabrika to zavod, that is, from the status of textile worker to that of metalworker (a rare occurrence). Rather, what was implied by the juxtaposition of fabrichnyi and zavodskoi was a pathway of disembodied consciousness, an organizational chart of intellectual and moral hierarchy, not the promotion of real individuals on a table of revolutionary ranks.[6]

Although this is not the place to probe all the questions raised by Plekhanov's schema, a few points should be considered. We may begin by recalling that until the turn of the century, fabrichnye were much more likely than zavodskie to engage in militant strike action, as is clear simply from enumerating the major strikes of those years: the 1870 Nevskii strike, the 1872 Kreenholm strike, the Petersburg textile strikes of 1878–79 (which Plekhanov knew well); see *RR*, pp. 62–63), the Morozov strike of 1885, and the citywide Petersburg strikes of 1896–97. For the most part these strikes were intense, sustained, and militant, and, for their time, displayed skilled leadership and organization; some invoked the language of collectivism and social justice, if not doctrinally articulated social*ism*; as of 1878, all involved either members of the radical intelligentsia (*intelligenty*) or workers already propagandized by them; and those of 1879 and 1896–97 entailed cooperation among workers from numerous factories. Of course there were also strikes among metalworkers in these years, but they paled in comparison.

In part because of Plekhanov's artful privileging of "advanced" metalworkers, in part because most members of St. Petersburg's first citywide workers' association (the Northern Union of Russian Workers, 1878–79) were zavodskie,[7] we are sometimes tempted to conjure up a corresponding image of the typical members of the early workers' circles (*rabochie kruzhki*).[8] But it should not be forgotten that the Northern Union's program, although breaking with populism to some degree, was replete with populist ideals, including a zealous devotion to the peasant commune, and

---

[6] Some of the material Plekhanov uses to support his typology is confirmed in other memoirs by intelligentsia, but it should also be noted that most of those memoirs were published after his, at a time when such stereotypes were well established in political discourse.

[7] On the Northern Union, see E. A. Korol'chuk, *"Severnyi soiuz russkikh rabochikh" i revoliutsionnoe rabochee dvizhenie 70-kh godov XIX v. v Peterburge* (Leningrad, 1946) and "Iz istorii propagandy sredi rabochikh Peterburga v seredine 70-kh godov," *Katorga i ssylka*, 1928, no. 1 (1928).

[8] This image was bolstered by the canonical claims of Soviet scholars, and indirectly by Western research that proves the leading role of metalworkers from 1905 to 1917, but should not be applied retroactively. For recent contributions to that literature by Heather Hogan, Diane Koenker, William Rosenberg, and Leopold Haimson, see Leopold Haimson and Charles Tilly, eds., *Strikes, Wars, and Revolutions in an International Perspective: Strike Waves in the Late Nineteenth and Early Twentieth Centuries* (Cambridge, 1989), and Robert B. McKean, *St. Petersburg between the Revolutions: Workers and Revolutionaries, June 1907–February 1917* (New Haven, Conn., 1990).

was steeped in the idiom of Christian religiosity, a far cry from Plekhanov's secular ideal.[9]

Even more to the point, many "advanced" workers of this period, active members of kruzhki, were fabrichnye. Of 141 "political" workers, almost all of them literate, who were caught in Third Section dragnets in the early 1870s, fabrichnye outnumbered zavodskie 78 to 63 (ca. 55 percent to 45 percent).[10] Nor is there any dearth of evidence about individual fabrichnye of this period, often with deep roots in the countryside, who became politically active, among them two of Russia's most famous revolutionaries, Petr Alekseev and Petr Moiseenko. It should also be noted that at Russia's first two political trials with worker defendants, every worker (two per trial) was a fabrichnyi.[11]

Finally, without denying that tsarist police were capable of wild confusion when reporting on the labor movement, I offer as evidence of the hazards of arranging workers on a tidy fabrichnyi-zavodskoi scale an 1884 report on the volatile Petersburg *uezd* (district), sent by a gendarme captain to his chief: Although most members of the local working class (*soslovie*) were "politically reliable," he warned, their reliability was not "solid." A serious source of danger was the the "fabrichnyi stratum" (*sloi*), characterized by its "permanent" presence in the labor force. Fabrichnye were both "culturally developed" and "full of vices" (qualities the captain evidently saw as going hand in hand). The typical fabrichnyi has "seen just about everything," he explained. "A poorly digested book . . . [or] occasional conversation with . . . anarchists, will lead . . . [him] down the riskiest path; he will seek . . . an excuse for his poverty not in himself . . . but in what they call social injustice. . . . The most depraved and exalted fabrichnye are . . . prepared to accept the propaganda of anarchists."

"More politically and morally reliable," the officer assured his chief, were zavodskie, mainly temporary workers, former peasants "torn away

---

[9] For the Northern Union's program, see Korol'chuk, *Severnyi soiuz*, pp. 247–51; on the use of religious idiom, see Zelnik, " 'To the Unaccustomed Eye': Religion and Irreligion in the Experience of St. Petersburg Workers in the 1870s," *Russian History/Histoire Russe* 16, no. 2–4 (1989).

[10] My data, mainly from 1872–74, are based on interrogation reports from TsGAOR, f. 112 (OPPS); Third Section documents in A. Pankratova, ed., *Rabochee dvizhenie v Rossii v XIX veke: Sbornik dokumentov*, vol. 2, parts 1 and 2 (Moscow, 1950) (hereafter cited as *RD* by volume, part, and page number in text and notes); *Deiateli revoliutsionnogo dvizheniia v Rossii: Bio-bibliograficheskii slovar'* vol. 2, parts 1–4 (Moscow, 1929–32) (hereafter cited as *Deiateli* by volume, part, and column numbers in text and notes); and various memoirs.

[11] These were the trials of V. D'iakov (1875) and of A. O. Osipov and L. I. Abramenkov (1876, the first to involve *only* workers). On the findings, see N. A. Troitskii, *Tsarskie sudy protiv revoliutsionnoi Rossii: Politicheskie protsessy 1871–1880 gg.* (Saratov, 1976), pp. 346–47. On the 1876 case, see "Chto delaetsia na rodine?" *Vpered!*, 20 July (1 August) 1876, cols. 469–73.

from the land . . . because of inadequate allotments." Not that all zavodskie were reliable: "[Even] some of them—very few, to be sure—are in-
fected by the permanent fabrichnye with drink and debauch, and with all
manner of false teaching; and with time, [they] . . . may carry their leprosy
back to the village." To prevent this contagion from spreading he proposed that the state promote such "countermeasures" as books and lectures in which "basic concepts of political economy" are explained in
popular language. The clergy too should help by exposing workers to "an
unremitting sermon of Christian morality." "Feelings of religious faith are
still alive in the Russian worker, and may yet save him from great evil."[12]

Despite its evident confusion, indeed because of it, there is much that
is instructive in this report (which might be read as prefiguring the Zu-
batov program of police-sponsored labor unions [1901–3]). Lest we attribute the captain's unexpected usage of "fabrichnyi" and "zavodskoi"
to semantic slippage, reflecting an as yet indeterminate use of industrial
terminology, note that his words are followed by a careful listing of the
number of factories of various kinds, with the accurate term always applied appropriately (metalworks are *zavody*, textile mills are *fabriki*).
Something else is going on, some kind of dim awareness that at this point
in political time a textile worker may be more menacing than a metalworker, more menacing because more literate, citified, open to dangerous
ideas, and—the two are predictably conflated—inclined to vice. Like Plekhanov, the gendarme sees a link between urban acculturation and political radicalization, but he reverses Plekhanov's two worker categories
(although he shares Plekhanov's notion that peasants, though corruptible
by urban workers, are less likely to pose a threat).

My point here is not that the gendarme was right and Plekhanov
wrong—the situation was much too murky for so bald an assertion—but
that the reality was plastic enough to generate multiple constructions of
the facts. Here we might add that "anarchist" intelligenty of the 1870s
sometimes shared the captain's view (with the signs reversed) of the radical potential of fabrichnye. Thus Kropotkin wrote in his memoir of this
period that the weavers in the cotton factories took most readily to his
agitation, whereas "our propaganda among the engineers [i.e., zavodskie]
was not notable for any particular success."[13] Although his memory was
a bit flawed (many "engineers" *were* successfully propagandized), Kropotkin had indeed singled out fabrichnye for praise in the 1870s. Of
course he differed from the captain in that he saw fabrichnye as owing

[12] "Nastroenie umov sredi rabochego naseleniia," report of Capt. Mavrin to Provincial
Chief of Gendarmes, 10 February 1884, in *RD* 2.1.635.

[13] *Peter Kropotkin's Memoirs of a Revolutionist*, ed. James A. Rogers (Garden City, N.Y.,
1962), pp. 218, 325 (see also 326).

their radicalism to close peasant ties.[14] We therefore have three views of the situation, each supporting and opposing one element in the other two. Fabrichnye are more radical and urbanized than zavodskie (gendarme), more radical but less urbanized (Kropotkin); less radical and less urbanized (Plekhanov).

We turn now to the stories of individual workers who walked a path through life from village childhoods to the exalted status of adult worker-revolutionaries. Such a trajectory necessarily entailed a major shift in their values and identities. Since I will be looking at a small number of particular cases rather than a broad population, this exercise will differ from what Annalistes would call the history of mentalités, always collective, plural, and tied to the deeply structured cultural assumptions of large entities. What follows will be more in the mode of intellectual biography, the story of smaller cohorts and especially their individual members. The subject is not the Russian worker in general, but the dedicated worker-revolutionary, an important historical character and type, but one that is often lost among more frequently studied groups such as the intelligentsia or the mass participants in strikes.

Yet it is wrong to distinguish such a worker-revolutionary, often absorbed in the process of persuing or resisting an attraction to intelligentsia identity, too sharply from an *intelligent*. By the time he was a young adult (there were no women in the first generation of revolutionary workers), he was always literate, enamored of ideas and the written word (even if engaged in painful struggle with reading and writing), and devoted to changing the world as well as understanding it. Russians have developed some awkward terms for such people—*rabochaia intelligentsiia, intelligentnyi rabochii*—terms that suggest some disorder in the identification of workers in a marginal social territory. Yet it is also wrong to distinguish too sharply between such workers and more typical participants in labor unrest, for strike activity was often a part of their story, even if what set them apart from others was that for them such activity was never enough.

Vasilii *Gerasimov* was born in or near St. Petersburg in 1852. His memoir, composed in 1881 or 1882, is the earliest example of this genre written by a Russian worker.[15] Like all members of the first generation of

---

[14] On Kropotkin's views, see Zelnik, "Populists and Workers: The First Encounter between Populist Students and Industrial Workers in St. Petersburg, 1871–74," *Soviet Studies* 24 (October 1972).

[15] *Zhizn' russkogo rabochego polveka tomu nazad. Zapiski rabochego-sotsialista Vasiliia Gerasimova* (Moscow, 1923, but printed in various editions since it first appeared in *Byloe* in 1906). I cited the 1923 edition as *Zhizn'* by page in text and notes. See also, *Deiateli*

politicized workers (born in the late 1840s to early 1850s and active in the 1870s), Gerasimov was raised in a village environment and had to *become* a worker. The process whereby a peasant youth who entered the world of factory labor sought and found a new social identity was unpredictable. *Worker* was not a necessary outcome of that search, let alone worker-revolutionary.

Shortly after his birth, Vasilii was brought by his presumably unwed mother to the Petersburg Foundling Home,[16] which placed him in the care of a peasant family in the nearby Finnish-speaking countryside. There he was raised by a series of foster families, in the last of which, that of a Lutheran village pastor, he was taught to read and write. In recalling these years, Gerasimov represents himself as an abandoned child, motherless, forlorn, in dire need of nurture, but fortunate to find that nurture among his guardians (*Zhizn'*, pp. 13–14)

If the theme of familial care and nurture, both its absence and its miraculous presence, dominates Gerasimov's memories of childhood, a new motif appears in the pages on his life as an adolescent factory worker, which began at age twelve: the contrast between the cruelty of his treatment and the humane standards set by his Finnish guardians (p. 15). At the Kreenholm factory, a giant cotton mill located on an island on the Narva (or Narova) river at the Estland border of Petersburg *guberniia* (province), Vasilii was billeted in a special barrack assigned to wards of the Foundling Home. In recalling his Kreenholm years, Gerasimov repeatedly identifies himself not as worker, spinner, or weaver, but as a *pitomets* of that home, and he regularly refers to the two hundred youngsters sent with him by the home to work at the factory as the *pitomtsy*.[17] To be sure, "pitomets" was a common term for alumni of a given school or institution, but Gerasimov, as we will see, gives the word special resonance.

As part of the cohort of pitomtsy Vasilii was assigned to Kreenholm's spinning section. The long workday was exhausting, yet in the evening the children were made to attend a factory school, a particularly onerous burden for Vasilii who, though Finnish-speaking, was taught in Russian. Beating and confinement were the normal means of disciplining young

2.1.257–59. I have treated Gerasimov at greater length in "Before Class: The Fostering of a Worker Revolutionary, The Construction of His Memoir," in *Russian History/Histoire Russe* 20, no. 1–43 (1993), and in *Law and Disorder on the Narova River* (Berkeley and Los Angeles, 1994), which includes my translation of his memoir.

[16] On the Foundling Home, see David L. Ransel, *Mothers of Misery: Child Abandonment in Russia* (Princeton, N.J., 1988).

[17] The original title of the memoir in *Byloe*, perhaps taken from the original manuscript, was simply "Pitomets vospitatel'nogo doma."

workers, and Vasilii was often subjected to these punishments, causing much of his memoir to read like a narrative of cruelty. Along with this negative theme, however, the memoir advances a positive one—group solidarity among pitomtsy.

Because Vasilii's break with his village home was final, he badly needed to find a new social identity. His fellow pitomtsy were the obvious choice, and Gerasimov recounts an early incident that illustrates his incipient sense of kinship with them. Since he was unable to pray "in the Orthodox way," expected of him as a "Russian," he was dealt the first of many rounds of moral humiliation, "several slaps in the face" by a religion teacher (*Zhizn'*, p. 16). Hoping to avoid more blows, Vasilii studied and mastered the prayers with the help of another pitomets, thereby setting the stage for the mixture of themes that would dominate his next few years: humiliation by those in authority, solidarity with his peers.

If punishment and humiliation are basic elements of his own story, Vasilii often bears witness to the similar treatment of other members of his peer group: the beating of a girl "so badly that she died," the battering of children who had "the life beat out of them" (p. 18). Reinhart Koselleck has argued that a common way to articulate or create a group identity is by "the emphatic use of the word 'we.' "[18] This is what Gerasimov does in his memoir, marking his sense of peer solidarity by repeatedly using "we," "us," or "our" when depicting the torment of pitomtsy, whether boy or girl, Russian or Finn: "*Our* food" was awful. "*Our* underwear" was filthy. "*We*" were clothed in rags. "*We* were . . . terribly afraid" (pp. 17 and 19, my emphasis).

In this way Gerasimov directs our attention not to the broader workforce but to pitomtsy in particular, especially those who arrived with him, suffered with him, and shared his punishments. Other, adult workers, by contrast, are all but absent from this part of his story, visible only as background figures. Pitomtsy are the positive pole of his identity, his primary social reference point; the world of evil adult authority figures, inversions of the kindly folk of his Finnish period, are the negative pole. It is as a pitomets that he appears to us in his first collective action, provoked by the factory's failure to provide the children with proper food (p. 19).

At age seventeen Vasilii stepped into the world of the adult workers by moving to Kreenholm's weaving section. Yet for all the importance he invests in this transition, one cannot help but remark how the young weaver continued to maintain solidarity with pitomtsy, most of whom he had left behind in the spinning section. Again this solidarity reveals itself in the context of continued acts of cruelty against his cohort. Corporal

---

[18] Reinhart Koselleck, "Begriffsgeschichte and Social History," in *Futures Past: On the Semantics of Historical Time*, trans. Keith Tribe (Cambridge, Mass., 1985), p. 83.

punishment was still applied to "us," even though "we" were now adults. One incident that haunted him was the beating to death of a worker by a foreman. Though the victim was a young adult, Gerasimov twice refers to him as a pitomets, complaining bitterly that the killer was allowed to keep his job and "torture other pitomtsy" (pp. 22–23).

Gerasimov's move to the weavers raised his status and added to his dignity. He had joined Kreenholm's "labor aristocracy,"[19] and with time even became the head of a work crew. None of this altered his solidarity with pitomtsy, but it did begin to expand the horizon of his self-identification, which now showed signs of fellowship with the entire workforce, most apparent at times of disaster such as the fatal collapse of a bridge, or an incident in which "workers" (not "pitomtsy") died when the scaffolding collapsed at a construction site (p. 22).

Yet even as his regard for a broader reference group increased, Vasilii's identification with pitomtsy remained, as may be seen in his account of the background to his temporary flight to St. Petersburg. Although the conflict that precipitated his flight was *not* connected with pitomets grievances, once he decided to flee his first move was to ask a fellow pitomets to join him. As his crew leader, Gerasimov had recently been forced to stand by helplessly while this pitomets was badly beaten by their overseers. The invitation to flee was a belated act of solidarity (pp. 24–25).

Just as suggestive of pitomets identity was Vasilii's instinctive decision to pick the Foundling Home as his destination. Not only did the two youths head straight for the Home, they identified themselves as pitomtsy and went to the director to complain against the factory owners. To their surprise their plea for sympathy was heard, causing Vasilii almost to dissolve in oceanic feeling. Taken to the area of the Home that housed "our brothers, fellow pitomtsy," he and his friend were fed and put to bed. Later, they sneaked into the Home's well-guarded girls' section, where the girls ("our sisters") showered them with compassion (pp. 25–26).

Thanks to Vasilii's pleadings, important changes favorable to pitomtsy were introduced at Kreenholm. A triumphant Vasilii returned to Kreenholm and, having scored a victory for his young comrades, began to bend his energies to the benefit of the broader factory population. The completion of this process required only one last step: his transfer to the status of "independent boarder" (p. 27), which meant that he would now provide for his own upkeep like any other worker. Henceforth his tie to Kreenholm would be contractual, unmediated by his pitomets status. An uneasy marriage between two worlds, that of pitomets and that of adult worker, could now yield to a clear commitment to the latter. Or could it?

---

[19] The term used in 1872 by a government commission; see *RD* 2.1.374.

The next part of Gerasimov's story centers around the Kreenholm strike of 1872. My focus here is not on the strike as such, but on those aspects of his account that speak to the question of identity. Gerasimov's strike narrative begins with Kreenholm's invasion by a deadly cholera epidemic. Because the first workers to suffer were stonemasons, he tells their story from the vantage point of an observer. But once the weavers are moved to action, he tells the story from within, once again using the first-person plural; but with a new point of reference: "We [weavers] gathered in a crowd and went to see the director." As the strike evolves, his identification with the weavers grows. When they elect delegates for negotiations, they are "our" (*nashi*) spokesmen (p. 29). His moral community now embraces diverse elements, united in a common cause. When managers bribe some workers, it is in order to damage "our" cause; having learned of this "betrayal," weavers seek out the "traitors" (p. 31).

Yet there is little clarity about his role in these events. Shifting temporarily to a third person "they," he seems to suggest his absence from the early confrontations. Then, once the strike is in full swing, he seems to be in the thick of things: When troops arrive to suppress it, he is among those who prepare to resist. When there are clashes with the soldiers, he seems to be among the most daring fighters. But then, despite the evident temptation of recording his brave deeds under fire, the memoir fails to enumerate his acts or give him a discernable presence (pp. 31–33).

By contrast, in relating the story of his early years at Kreenholm, Gerasimov was clear in delineating his specific feelings and experiences, and when he uses his frequent *we* constructions, his reference group is not in doubt. Yet in the pages covering the strike it is only by careful scrutiny that one begins to reconstruct his personal role; when he collapses himself into a larger "we," it is unclear whether he was physically present or is making an abstract moral identification. In light of his repeated identification with pitomtsy even after entering the world of adult workrs, his vagueness about his role may well reflect his uncertainty when acting in a broad arena of struggle, one in which pitomtsy were but a minor element. It is surely no accident that the memoir repeatedly reverts to pitomtsy themes just when it seems to have forsaken them, as when, in the middle of an account of the trial of the strikers, he pauses to relate the story of the only pitomets among the defendants (p. 33).[20]

A few months after the strike Gerasimov was again in trouble, but his offense was unconnected with the strike. Once again the problem concerned pitomtsy, and this time he describes his situation precisely. Shortly before his twenty-first birthday, he had been invited to the wedding of a

---

[20] For the findings of the trial, see *Krengol'mskaia stachka 1872 g.: Sbornik dokumentov i materialov* (Tallin, 1952), pp. 108–17.

fellow pitomets. Without permission from his overseer, he attended the festivities for several days, until he was located by guards and again placed in the dreaded punishment cell. This time, however, the confinement was "not so bad," for the neighboring cell was occupied by an interesting woman, naturally one of the pitomtsy. The two pitomtsy, maintaining a steady dialogue for a week, were "never bored." When the week was over Gerasimov abandoned Kreenholm for a new life in St. Petersburg (*Zhizn'*, p. 34).

For his first two years in the capital Gerasimov was simply a textile worker, meeting other workers, learning the ways of the city. Then, for a few months, until his arrest in 1875, he became a worker-revolutionary. Intense and exciting as this phase of his life was, in a memoir of some forty printed pages Gerasimov not only reduces this section to a couple of pages, he devotes most of it to an incident from his early days as a pitomets, presented as an account of why he became a socialist. At the age of twelve, Vasilii had been witness to the horrid fate of a girl who had come to Kreenholm in his cohort of pitomtsy. Though Olga arrived a beautiful and healthy child, after twenty days at the factory she was horribly transformed—thin, dirty, disheveled, crippled—and in two more weeks she was dead (pp. 35–36). Nearly twenty years later, this is the story Gerasimov uses to reveal how he came to grasp the injustice of the existing order. The only thing he could not yet imagine in those early years was what order could replace it. Hence the connection between Olga's story, a link with his pitomets past, and his later attraction to radical students: the students offered him a solution, "socialism," to problems he had once intuited but could not fathom. There follows just a single paragraph that actually describes his revolutionary life. It is as if we already know all we need to know about the deeper structure of his political psyche.

Gerasimov's political career was brief.[21] After working in various Petersburg cotton mills he became a weaver at the Cheshire factory, where a radical group, the *chaikovtsy*, had recently recruited about a dozen men. His first flirtation with the radical movement came in the fall of 1873 when he learned of a secret "school" for workers, but the school's or-

[21] See the indictment of D'iakov, TsGAOR, f. 112, op. 1, d. 107, ll. 2–10 (includes Gerasimov's testimony); "Materialy o propagandistskoi deiatel'nosti kruzhka V. M. D'iakova na fabrike Cheshera i drugikh fabrikakh Peterburga," in *RD* 2.2.48–60; Korol'chuk, "Iz istorii propagandy sredi rabochikh," pp. 20–26, especially the summaries of Gerasimov's interrogations); official summary of the trial, B. Bazilevskii, ed., *Gosudarstvennye prestupleniia v Rossii v XIX veke. Sbornik izvlechennykh iz offitsial'nykh izdanii pravitel'stvennykh soobshchenii* (St. Petersburg, 1906), 1:318–45; "Vospominaniia D. A. Aleksandrova," in *V nachale puti: Vospominaniia peterburgskikh rabochikh 1872–1897 gg.*, comp. E. A. Karol'chuk (Leningrad, 1975), pp. 160–62 (first pub. in *Katorga i ssylka*, 1926, no. 4) (*V nachale puti* is hereafter cited as *VNP*).

ganizer was arrested before he could enroll. It was only in the winter of 1874–75, through men with whom he shared a group apartment (*artel'*), that Gerasimov befriended his first student radical. They met through the weaver Diomid Aleksandrov—Vasilii's fellow pitomets, Finnish-speaking childhood friend, and former Kreenholm roommate—the man who had found him the job at Cheshire's. Some months earlier, through another worker, Aleksandrov had met the student Viacheslav D'iakov. Though not yet fully politicized, Aleksandrov was sufficiently impressed to invite D'iakov to meet his friends. Gerasimov liked D'iakov and his ideas (maybe they explained the fate of Olga) and the two grew close (*Zhizn'*, p. 35). D'iakov became his political guide and the artel' became a political gathering place.[22]

On D'iakov's advice, Gerasimov quit his job and adopted a new career, modeled on the lives of his new friends, that of a revolutionary propagandist. His expenses now covered by students, he devoted himself to the dissemination of written propaganda for the *narod* (people). He also engaged in oral propaganda in Russian and Finnish.[23] But his new career ground to a halt when someone alerted the police. Although he tried to flee the city, Gerasimov never made it out of town. His plan, had he escaped, was to take refuge with the last of his Finnish foster parents, the pastor who had taught him how to read and write (*RD* 2.2.49, 50). They had had no contact for years, and Gerasimov was not even sure if he was alive, yet he wished in this his hour of need to return to the scene of his childhood memories.

Arrested at the Finland station and accused of fomenting rebellion, Gerasimov denied the charge and provided only minimal information. Later, he said some things that were damaging to D'iakov, but he stuck with the story of his own innocence and protected other workers. Later still, however, he became more talkative, and may have been on the verge of testifying against Aleksandrov, a gross violation of revolutionary ethics and, perhaps more important to him, of his code of pitomets solidarity.[24] But his honor was saved when Aleksandrov cried out in their native Finnish: "Why are you afraid of these idiots?" With the support of his fellow pitomets Gerasimov resisted further interrogation and continued to do so

[22] On D'iakov's circle and its program, see Franco Venturi, *Roots of Revolution: A History of the Populist and Socialist Movements in Nineteenth Century Russia* (New York, 1960), pp. 536–38.

[23] Titles of propaganda literature confiscated from Gerasimov and others are listed in Bazilevskii, *Gosudarstvennye prestupleniia*, p. 344; *RD* 2.2.49; and TsGAOR, f. 112, op. 1, ed. khr. 107, ll. 4, 9. That he continued to be seen as a Finn is indicated by occasional references to him as "Vasilii Chukhonets" (l. 6).

[24] TsGAOR, f. 112, op. 1, ed. khr. 107, l. 5; Korol'chuk, "Iz istorii," 24–25. *RD* 2.2.49–50 omits Gerasimov's more compromising statements.

throughout the ensuing trial.[25] He and Aleksandrov were sentenced to nine years hard labor.[26]

An Italian sociologist has argued that individuals first give meaning to their social situations through the mediation of the smaller, more accessible groups to which they belong. He urges that when studying individual lives we identify the primary "regions of mediation"—families, peer groups, neighbors, chums—that serve as "pivotal hinges" between larger structures and the individual. It is in the course of "reading" their primary groups, he maintains, their "modalities and networks of affective interactions," that individuals construct a sense of self.[27] In Gerasimov's case this group was his cohort of pitomtsy, who continued to function for him as an emotional metaphor, representing and shaping his values even when he abandoned them for a larger world.

Hundreds of Russian workers joined or were otherwise touched by one or more kruzhki in the 1870s. Each of them followed a different path from a particular sociocultural background through a variety of social situations to a new, risky, often unstable self-identification as some kind of worker-revolutionary, a special incarnation of the intelligentsia's "new man" (*novyi chelovek*). In the near absence of the kind of rich memoir material provided by Gerasimov, one must strain to find whatever one can to piece together the stories of their lives and the shaping of their values. In trying to reconstruct their lives as the stories of the experiences of individual subjects, I have felt the explanatory weakness not only of neat distinctions based on soslovie or class, but also of the occupational contrasts—fabrichnyi/zavodskoi, weaver/metalworker—valued by Plekhanov. The quest for identity in the volatile world of industrializing Russia was a complex process; the elements each person was able to contribute, although historically constrained, were wonderfully varied. We continue with a sampling of fabrichnye.

Diomid *Aleksandrov*, whom we already met, was born around 1851. We know little about his early years, but what we do know from his short memoir[28] reads like a photocopy of Gerasimov's life: a pitomets childhood with Finnish guardians, a youth spent working at Kreenholm, a brief Pe-

[25] Aleksandrov, *VNP*, p. 162. There is no reference to this dramatic moment in Gerasimov's memoir. During the trial Gerasimov rebutted the testimony of government witnesses. See Bazilevskii, *Gosudarstvennye prestupleniia*, pp. 330, 332, 334, 340–41, 344.

[26] See TsGAOR, f. 112, op. 1, ed. khr. 107, ll. 114–19, and *RD* 2.2.59–60 (which summarizes the conduct of the accused).

[27] Franco Ferrarotti, "On the Autonomy of the Biographical Method," in D. Bertaux, ed., *Biography and Society: The Life History Approach in the Social Sciences* (Beverly Hills, Calif., 1981), pp. 23–24.

[28] See note 22.

tersburg career as a worker and a revolutionary, followed by arrest, trial, and exile. The opening of his memoir could have been written by Gerasimov: "At the age of eleven I left Finland and landed at the Kreenholm factory . . . , where I was turned into a machine, since I had to work every day for fourteen hours" (*VNP*, p. 160).

Like Gerasimov, Aleksandrov arrived in the capital—where he too was called a Finn—as a young adult with no previous exposure to radical ideas. In his own words, he had "many prejudices," such as a belief in God and in the tsar as "God's annointed one." When he met the student D'iakov through other workers, D'iakov, who liked to disguise himself as a worker, tried to propagandize him. But Aleksandrov saw through the disguise. Insisting that D'iakov "come clean," he assured him that he was not the low-down type who would report him—"Ia ne podlets i donosit' ne budu" (pp. 160–61). Thereafter the bond between them grew strong, and under D'iakov's guidance Aleksandrov became a revolutionary. Unlike Gerasimov, he never wavered under pressure. Absent a substantial memoir, we have no way of knowing the extent to which his *pitomets* past helped shape his self-understanding.

Willem *Preisman* was born in 1851.[29] He left no memoir and almost no direct record of his words or thoughts. What is known of his early life sheds little light on the problem at hand, but I include him here as the only other participant in the Kreenholm strike who, like Gerasimov and Aleksandrov, ended up in revolutionary circles. Apart from his age and trade (weaver), as an Estonian he was similar to the other two in religion (Lutheran) and language. Indeed, Petersburg comrades used the same ethnic label for him as for Gerasimov—"Vasilii Chukhonets." Preisman was unusual among contemporary factory workers in being classified by *soslovie* not as peasant but as *meshchanin* (petty bourgeois),[30] but the Estland town where he was registered, Alternhof, was hardly an urban center. Unlike Aleksandrov and Gerasimov, however, he had lived for a while in a real city, Reval, before moving to Kreenholm.

Unlike Gerasimov, Preisman was a leader of the strike. Put on trial in Reval, he was acquitted only because he had been in jail at the strike's peak moment. Forced to leave Kreenholm after the trial, he arrived in St. Petersburg (shortly before Gerasimov) already holding some strong views about workers' rights and employers' wrongs, but these views had not yet been translated into political language. Though literate in Estonian and

---

[29] My sources on Preisman are *Deiateli* 2.3.1261–62; *RD* 2.1.450, 459, 460; L. Shishko, *Sergei Mikhailovich Kravchinskii i kruzhok chaikovtsev* (St. Petersburg, 1906), pp. 27–28, 28n; TsGAOR, f. 112, op. 1, d. 209, ll. 64, 66, 83, 87, 190, 198, 233–44, 248, d. 210, l. 17. For his role in the Kreenholm strike, see *Krengol'mskaia stachka*.

[30] He is called a peasant in some sources, e.g., *RD* 2.1.459, 463.

able to read a little Russian, he does not seem to have been exposed to radical literature before coming to the capital.

Within a year and a half, Preisman had worked at no fewer than three Petersburg factories. Soon he became involved in kruzhki for workers, organized by intelligenty. His new life included secret meetings and discussions in taverns and apartments. One student remembered him as a militant advocate of strikes (still an unusual position among radical workers) and the use of firearms.[31] In 1874 his activities led to his second arrest, this time for political crimes. Though he insisted on his innocence, there was evidence enough against him to keep him in prison for two years. By the time of his release, the volatile weaver had parted company with radical ideas, his search for truth having led him down a path of religious mysticism.[32]

Thanks to a book-length memoir we know much more about Petr *Moiseenko* (a.k.a. Anasimov, born 1852),[33] one of Russia's most famous revolutionary workers. A native of Smolensk province, he was born a simple manorial serf, placing him on the bottom rung of the social ladder. Even after emancipation his father had little land. As was typical, Petr's upbringing was Orthodox Christian, perhaps more religious than most, and very traditional, including an arranged village marriage at age eighteen. His mother died when he was five, and though a frail and sickly child, he was, he reports, repeatedly beaten by his stepmother as well as by his master.

Clearly the unhappy village surroundings of his childhood, although conducive to bitterness, were not the soil on which new values could be cultivated. For this Petr needed experience away from home, in this case in Moscow and later in Orekhovo-Zuevo. At thirteen he was sent to Moscow to add to his family's meager income. Though he returned home intermittently, he worked in Moscow for a few years, mainly as a spinner's helper in textile mills but also in such jobs as merchant's aide and box maker. As late as his eighteenth year he was still coming home to help with the farmwork. When he returned to Moscow with his new

---

[31] Shishko, *Kravchinskii*, pp. 27–28.

[32] Ibid., p. 28n.

[33] Some sources date his birth to 1853. The edition of his memoir that I cite is *Vospominaniia starogo revoliutsionera* (Moscow, 1966). See also *Rabochee dvizhenie v Rossii v opisanii samikh rabochikh (Ot 70-kh do 90-kh godov)* (Moscow, 1933), pp. 108–75. (The excerpt in *VNP* covers only his Petersburg years.) I also use *Deiateli* 2.1.38–39 and M. Chechanovskii, *Tkach Petr Anisimovich Moiseenko. Istorikobiograficheskii ocherk s illiustratsiiami. 1852–1923* (Moscow, 1924). On his Petersburg years, see also P. Kudrina, "Eshche o P. A. Moiseenko. (Po arkhivnym dokumentam)," *Krasnaia letopis'*, 1924, no. 1: 248–59, and V. Nevskii, "Petr Anisimovich Moiseenko," *Proletarskaia revoliutsiia*, 1924, no. 1:13–16.

bride, it was to open a small business, while his wife got work as a cook. Despite his factory experience, there was still no sign of a basic identification with factory work or workers.

This may have changed after 1871, when his business venture failed and he moved to the burgeoning textile village of Zuevo (fifty five miles east of Moscow), where he and his wife took jobs as weavers. But to judge by his memoir, during his two years in Zuevo it was not his life at work that began to change his views (he tells us next to nothing about it, and nothing about what his wife was thinking), but rather his exposure to illicit propaganda literature (*nelegal'shchina*), including some of the very writings that Gerasimov would be handing out later.

Since there were as yet no kruzhki in this isolated area, Moiseenko's account of how this material first came his way is of particular interest (*Vospominaniia*, p. 15). He relates that a clerk at his factory, evidently an avid but book-starved reader, would dispatch him to the village of Orekhovo (the two settlements had not yet merged) to borrow books from the library of the Morozov factory (where Moiseenko was to help organize a famous strike in 1885). Literate since age twelve, he would use these occasions to tarry at the library. What he recalls having read there before even setting eyes on illegal works is "Fenimore Cooper and literature like that." Then, without any effort to show a connection, he explains that the illegal works were brought to Zuevo from the Nizhnii Novgorod fair by a brother of one of his factory friends. He seems to be associating American adventure novels with nelegal'shchina as a source of his moral awakening, which may explain his use of a popular adventure novel, *The Bandit Churkin*, when agitating among Morozov workers a decade later.[34]

But even the nelegal'shchina was not enough to lift the scales from Moiseenko's eyes, for, he explains, "at the time we were very religious." What did change him, he relates, was a visit, really a pilgrimage, to the Vvedenskaia monastery to behold a miraculous icon. While crossing the forest before reaching the hermitage, he and a group of friends suddenly heard the "heart-rending" scream of a woman, whom they assumed was under attack by thieves. "But to our astonishment, we saw that it wasn't bandits . . . but monks, who were taking women into the woods and raping them."

Having reached the monastery, Moiseenko's party, which apparently had not dared intervene in the rapes (he is strangely silent on this point),

---

[34] See Daniel R. Brower, *The Russian City between Tradition and Modernity, 1850–1900* (Berkeley and Los Angeles, 1990), pp. 178, 180, 213. On *Razboinik Churkin*, see Jeffrey Brooks, *When Russia Learned to Read: Literacy and Popular Literature, 1861–1917* (Princeton, N.J., 1985), pp. 123–25. In his memoir Moiseenko calls the novel "stupid" and describes how he embellished it politically when reading it aloud (*Vospominaniia*, p. 70).

attended a religious service, where they witnessed more dreadful deeds, including thievery by some monks. But most shocking of all was the sight of a deacon making sexual gestures, "displaying his entire lustful passion" (exposing himself?) before some pretty young nuns. "It seemed as if I was not in a church, but in a den of iniquity [*vertep*]" (*Vospominaniia*, pp. 15–16). Much of this, to be sure, may be exaggerated, perhaps invented, a paraphrase of ancient anticlerical tales. But it is nonetheless instructive that the only way in which a mature Moiseenko is able to reconstruct his first big break with the values of his family is not by citing some factory horror but by evoking the shock and betrayal produced when the bearers of his faith revealed their baser qualities, while a presumably almighty God, he laments, who could have stopped them with a word, allowed this to happen.

Moiseenko leaves the impression that the initial impact of this encounter was confusion, not full-blown atheism, a shaken faith, not a broken one. "We felt tormented [*muchalis'*], we looked for a way out," and decided there was only one: "to go to Petersburg [*Piter*], where we could learn about everything." Late in 1873 he and his brother (whose moral-political trajectory, though he never attained the same prominence, paralleled his own) arrived there without a kopeck, anxiously seeking old acquaintances to help them find work, any work. His brother found a job as a stablehand, while Moiseenko, thanks to *zemliaki*, found work as a weaver at the Shaw factory and lodging at the zemliaki's artel' (pp. 16–17).

In Petersburg, as we know, this was a key moment in the early history of the workers' circle, with workers like Preisman and Gerasimov just beginning their clandestine "studies." Competing with this activity, yet inadvertently promoting it, were the officially approved and more respectable (if still unconventional) schools for workers organized by the Imperial Russian Technical Society (IRTO).[35] With several weavers in his artel' already participating in one (or *both*) of these activities, it is not surprising that Moiseenko soon found himself in a kruzhok—a "holy of holies" (*sviataia-sviatykh*), he calls it—and got to know some student-teachers (including Plekhanov) (*Vospominaniia*, p. 18). Both his use of religious imagery and the alacrity with which this twenty two-year-old peasant with no political experience "threw himself on the books" (including political novels) made available to him, devouring them even while at work, suggest how much exposure to the students aided such persons in the painful process of "cultural language acquisition,"[36] and helped them to

[35] See Zelnik, " 'To the Unaccustomed Eye.' "

[36] I borrow here from the language of cultural semiotics used in a different but related context in Irina Paperno, *Chernyshevsky and the Age of Realism: A Study in the Semiotics of Behavior* (Stanford, Calif., 1988), p. 41.

impose a structure on the diffuse range of feeling they brought to the city from their pasts.

By 1875, his political ideas still not fully formed, Moiseenko had moved to a private apartment (no doubt with financial aid from students), which he used as a site for a new *kruzhok*. Though also a factory worker now, his wife had temporarily vanished from his story,[37] and apart from his brother, his zemliaki ceased to be part of his nonworking life. It is also in 1875 that he briefly crossed paths with Diomid Aleksandrov (p. 18), soon to be arrested but now just entering, despite a very different past, the same moral and political world.

Unlike the ill-fated Aleksandrov and Gerasimov, Moiseenko moved on to a celebrated career in the revolutionary labor movement. He appears as "Ivan" in Plekhanov's memoir, which treats him with a mixture of mockery and respect. (*RR*, esp. pp. 47–49, 67). Notwithstanding the Northern Union's identification with metalworkers, he was even active in that organization, as the weavers Aleksandrov and Gerasimov might well have been had they remained at large.

The weaver Petr *Alekseev*, who would surpass even Moiseenko as an icon of the revolutionary movement, was born in 1849.[38] Although he left no memoir, he did leave enough of a paper trail to repay an effort to reconstruct his moral history, especially since his famous 1877 speech at the "Trial of 50" is as concise a statement of the values of a radical worker as can be found in the literature. Alekseev was a simple peasant through and through, a *muzhik* both in origin and appearance. His father Aleksei lived in a village of Smolensk silk weavers (located in the same district as Moiseenko's home village). A poor state peasant with no last name—his "family name" was his patronymic—Aleksei had some casual work experience in a Moscow factory. His son remained in the village, leading the life of a typical peasant boy until age nine. Then, like most of the village boys, including his three brothers, Petr was sent to work in a weaving mill near Moscow, where he lived in an artel' of zemliaki. Without formal education, he had taught himself to read, though not with ease, by age sixteen. Unlike our prior cases, there is no hint of the circumstances, perhaps quite banal, that brought him to the capital. Arriving there in 1872, he followed a familiar pattern, moving from job to job, working in a zavod for part of the time, but mainly in a fabrika. Whatever

---

[37] He sometimes left her with his father's family. She too was employed at the Morozov factory on the eve of the 1885 strike (*Vospominaniia*, p. 68), making him the only first-generation revolutionary worker in our study whose activism was compatible with a lasting marriage.

[38] Sources on Alekseev include E. K. Pekarskii, "Rabochii Petr Alekseev: iz vospominanii," *Byloe*, no. 19 (1922): 80–119; *Deiateli* 2.1.25–27; *Protsess 50-ti* (Moscow, 1906). There are many references to him in the memoirs of intelligenty.

else was then on his mind, he wished to better his education, an urge that one day brought him, in the company of two coworkers from the Thornton woolens mill, to the apartment of a student who, they were told, was offering free lessons. He came to improve his reading and to study, as he put it, "eography" and "eometry."[39]

The student was a *chaikovets*, and his purpose was hardly learning for learning's sake, but the creation of worker-revolutionaries. We have no record of the words exchanged betweem him and Alekseev, but we do know that before very long Alekseev was speaking the language of the left, propagandizing other workers, moving from apartment to apartment to evade the police, and attending secret meetings that included both zavodskie and fabrichnye (an ecumenical approach he shared with Moiseenko). During the "movement to the people" he returned to the villages of his native region to propagandize other peasants. Although he picked up his new ideas from intelligenty, this did not prevent him from expressing some distrust toward them (a perspective conventionally attributed to zavodskie).[40]

Having fled to Moscow to evade the police, Alekseev was arrested there in 1875. Tried with twelve other workers at the Trial of 50,[41] he delivered (very effectively, by all accounts) a famous speech that expressed some of the most strongly held sentiments of activist workers of the period. Without attempting a close analysis, I will summarize those passages that directly address the theme of experience, values, self-awareness, and their relation to a peasant-worker's youth, recalling the images of childhood we have already seen in Gerasimov[42]:

We workers, he declares, having been thrown to the "whims of fate" (*proizvol sud'by*) by our parents, are "just beginning to stand on our own feet." Because of long hours of exhausting work and the lack of decent schools, we "get no education." Forced into factories from childhood, beaten, working under terrible conditions, he continues, we "forever dullen our mental capacities and fail to develop the moral notions first acquired in childhood." Isolated from everything civilized, we are shorn of

[39] S. S. Sinegub, "Vospominaniia chaikovtsa," *Byloe*, no. 9 (1906): 109–10.

[40] On his distrust of intelligenty, see I. S. Dzhabadari, "Protsess 50-ti," *Byloe*, no. 10 (1907): 190, in which the author, a defendant at the Trial of 50, praises Alekseev's character, but refers to his "poor intellectual quality" *(malaia intelligentnost')*. The archetypal anti-intelligentsia zavodskoi of this period is Ignatii Bachin, who appears in *RR* as "B——n." Bachin's strange marriage to an *intelligentka* ended in a murder-suicide.

[41] Though sixteen of the fifty defendants were women, all thirteen workers were men. The trial is summarized in Troitskii, *Tsarskie sudy*, pp. 168–80.

[42] The speech, first published in 1877 in *Vpered!*, has been reprinted often. I cite from *Revoliutsionnoe narodnichestvo 70-kh godov XIX veka*, ed. B. S. Itenberg, 2 vols. (Moscow, 1964–65), 1:363–67 (hereafter cited as *RN* in text and notes). On the issue of possible intelligentsia input into the wording of the speech, see Robert Otto, "A Note on the Speech of Peter Alekseev," *Slavic Review* 38, no. 4 (1979).

anything of value. Humiliated from an early age, we store up our hatred. Then as adults, we are overworked and exploited. How incredible that someone who works a seventeen-hour day for a crust of bread "almost from the cradle" now must sit on the defendants' bench! (*RN*, pp. 363–64).

Echoing a theme that had been stressed by D'iakov when he "educated" Gerasimov, Alekseev next turns to a contrast between the life of Russian workers and that of "our Western brothers" (*nashi sobrat'ia—zapadniki*). Whereas Westerners are honored if they can read, Russians are encouraged to have no education. If literate, they are still treated like animals or slaves, given nothing to read but religious works and diversions such as *Van'ka Kain*.[43] If caught reading a serious book, they are told: "Brother, you don't look like a worker—you read books" (*RN*, p. 365).

Next, Alekseev shifts from injuries done to ("us") child workers to the treatment of workers as if "we" still were serfs: There are people who imagine that we are deaf, dumb, and blind, drunkards and idlers. But we workers understand our plight; we know who gets rich while we get poor, we know that we are kept in ignorance. We won't allow this to continue. Then, working the symbolic date of February 19 into his rhetoric: "With outstretched arms, filled with feelings of joy and hope, we the Russian people thanked the tsar for our freedom"; but it was only a dream. Just as before emancipation, we (in effect, we *peasants*) are still without bread, with only useless plots of land, and we (that is, we *former* peasants, now workers) have been turned over to the capitalists, who keep us under surveillance, punish us, treat us as if we still were serfs (*krepostnye*). Then comes a series of hard-hitting statements, really an incantation, about the workers' condition, each ending with the locution "that means we're serfs!" When we ask for raises they accuse us of strikes and send us to Siberia—*znachit, my krepostnye!* When we quit our jobs because of unjust treatment they accuse us of rebellion (*bunt*), call in troops and exile instigators—*znachit, my krepostnye!* When we are prevented from complaining and are punched and kicked by any cop on the beat (*pervyi vstrechnyi kvartal'nyi*)—*znachit, my krepostnye!* (*RN*, pp. 365–66).

In the last part of his talk, the one most likely to have had nonworker input, Alekseev introduces a new motif (enraging the chief judge, who interrupts with shouts of "Shut up!" [*Molchat'!*]): degraded, bereft of intellectual sustenance, treated like serfs, workers can rely only on themselves and one other group—"intelligentsia youth" (*intelligentnaia molodezh'*). They alone have "extended us a fraternal hand," have un-

---

[43] The adventures of a semilegendary bandit, published in various genres since the late eighteenth century. See Brooks, *When Russia Learned to Read*, pp. 80, 173, 200–203. Alekseev names three other titles.

derstood and responded to the suffering of peasants. Alekseev continues in this vein with a crescendo of statements, ending with the much-quoted line that provided Plekhanov with a coda for the preface to *Russkii rabochii*) (*RR*, p. 5): "And they alone will march with us inseparably until that day when the muscular arm of millions of working people [in one variant the "sinewy working arm of the muzhik"] is raised . . . and the yoke of despotism . . . ground to dust!" (*RN*, pp. 366-67).[44]

Alekseev was sentenced to ten years hard labor, the stiffest sentence given to a defendant and, I believe, the stiffest given before 1905 to a Russian worker not involved in an assassination attempt.[45] Before long, both the man and his speech had become icons of the Russian left, both populist and, a little later, Marxist. Here, however, I am more concerned with the themes and images of the speech itself, for together with what we know of other fabrichnye, they can help us develop a composite picture of the values and identities of politicized workers.

What emerges is a self-awareness solidly grounded in, though not confined to, these workers' antecedents. For Alekseev, this had two dimensions: (1) childhood, which he depicts without nostalgia as a time of deprivation, arrested development, and lost opportunity for which the responsible parties will be brought to account, and (2) serfdom, the debased origin of the workers with whom he identifies (his "we") and his point of reference for their sufferings, though a condition that can be overcome. Both these obstacles are to be overcome through education, which in this context means not institutionally approved schooling, but a special kind of radical adult education, in a sense "compensatory," donated by young intelligenty. Still, although clasping hands with these intelligenty, Alekseev will not merge with them into a larger "we." The student youth, however revered, remains a "they."

For Moiseenko a deprived childhood is also there, as are the stigma and burden of serfdom, but there is also the added dimension of offended religious sensibility, informing his quest for education at the feet of idolized students and lending it the aura of a quasi-religious experience. There is evidence that religion (and a kind of parodoxically reverant *ir*religion), including a sense of religious awe before the book, the written word, also affected the mood of other workers' early interactions with intelligenty.[46] Curiously, among the fabrichnye it is Moiseenko who eventually adheres to a group, the Northern Union, that values worker independence, and it is the muzhik Alekseev, at first suspicious of intelligenty, who delivers the most eloquent paean to students.

[44] The "muzhik" variant is in an unpublished Third Section report, quoted in Troitskii, *Tsarskie sudy*, p. 175n.

[45] For a full list of sentences at the Trial of 50, see ibid., pp. 350–54.

[46] Zelnik, " 'To the Unaccustomed Eye'," pp. 313–23.

Never having been a serf, Gerasimov (and by extension Aleksandrov) must constitute his self-awareness, his grasp of the relation between his present and past, in different terms. The theme of childhood deprivation is present, but he is deprived *of* it, not *in* it, and there is enough joy in his early years to provide him with the material to construct a golden age, something absent in the others. His full loss will come only at age twelve, in connection with his move to the factory. But his status as a pitomets and the presence of others who share his fate allow him to cling to an identity that, though limiting, is for that very reason protective. Eventually, time and a change of venue will help him stretch his identity into another world, that of the kruzhok, though even as a seasoned political convict in Siberian exile he will write of his past in a manner that betrays the continued presence of the pitomets-child.

Though involved in strikes and intimately engaged with other workers, none of these men seems to have identified solely with a worker milieu. They identified, both positively and negatively, with their social pasts and had a strong sense, encouraged of course by a populist ideology, of the "narod" as an all-encompassing, totalizing category; at the same time, there was of course a positive but troubled place for intelligenty, *studenty*, in their social universe. "Working *people*" (*narod, liud, naselenie*), as used by Alekseev and others, though the factory hand is surely present, did not exclude anyone who labored for a living. As Alekseev's talk reveals, it was almost a synonym for "fellow victim," as "pitomets" was for Gerasimov.

How different were these fabrichnye stories from those of zavodskie of their generation? The examples that follow suggest important similarities as well as minor but instructive differences.

By conventional standards Semën *Volkov*, born in 1845, represents the quintessential "advanced" zavodskoi of the 1870s.[47] Perhaps because of his arrest in 1876, he is less well known to historians than his friends who founded the Northern Union two years later. But he shared their most obvious characteristics, the very ones used by Plekhanov to create the prototype of the (politically) conscious metalworker in *Russkii rabochii*, where, appearing as "V," he is listed among "the best, most trustworthy and influential" of Petersburg's worker-revolutionaries.[48] He

---

[47] Volkov's unfinished memoir, dictated on his deathbed in 1924, is "Avtobiografiia rabochego-revoliutsionera 60–70-kh godov xix veka," in *VNP*, pp. 141–50 (the first epigraph to this chapter is from pp. 48–49); Korol'chuk's notes are on pp. 379–81. Other sources are the memoir of Volkov's friend Dmitrii Smirnov (see note 52); Volkov's depositions while under arrest in 1874–75, TsGAOR, f. 112, op. 1. d. 215; and *Deiateli* 2.1.216–17.

[48] *RR* p. 13. Plekhanov knew Volkov well and, according to Volkov (*VNP*, p. 147), often slept at his home. Volkov claims to have been involved with others in dreaming up the plan

belonged to the *meshchanskoe soslovie* (petty bourgeois estate), was a skilled machinist, mainly at the Army's Cartridge Factory (employer of several of the first politicized metalworkers), was quite literate, at least by the time Plekhanov met him (ca. 1875), and served as librarian of one of the first workers' circles. In addition, even among metalworkers he could make the unique claim of enjoying a political *stazh* (length of service) that went back to the 1860s, when he belonged to an intelligentsia-led circle that tried to spread "collective[ist]" and "social[ist]" ideas in the Volga region (*VNP*, pp. 141–42).[49]

Despite apparent differences from our fabrichnye, Volkov's background reveals some overlapping traits. Though listed as a Gomel meshchanin, for example, he was actually born a Simbirsk serf. His parents were poor, and his father, burdened with a huge family, also worked as village carpenter. Hence his social background was similar to that of Moiseenko or Alekseev. By the same token, poverty led his family to send him away at an early age sixteen, to work at a nearby woolens mill. In other words, his first factory experience was as a fabrichnyi!

But Volkov despised this work, so he tells us, and after a few months he moved on to the provincial capital, where over a two-year period he was apprenticed as a locksmith, training that prepared him for a job in a local foundry. When a clash with his employer cost him that position, he moved from Simbirsk to the adjacent province of Kazan, where he was trained at a factory as a machinist. So now he was a zavodskoi!

At what point and under what circumstances did he begin to think politically, to identify with broader ideas and values and with people outside his own milieu? The earliest date he gives in his memoir is 1862, shortly after arriving in Simbirsk city. There, at age seventeen, he says without elaborating, he began to study the labor question (*rabochii vopros*). This seems suspect, but does suggest that he was more than minimally literate.

Volkov places his acquisition of basic literacy before his departure from his village. In an offhand remark he mentions his reading and writing teacher before he opted for self-education, a village sexton (*ponomar'*).[50] This may explain the way he formulates his only statement about why he

---

for a workers' union (p. 148), but this had to have been at least two years before the Northern Union was founded.

[49] Testifying under arrest, Volkov vigorously denied any revolutionary goals in these activities. See TsGAOR, f. 112, op. 1, d. 215, l. 99.

[50] Of the few men in my sample of 141 whose educational histories I can trace, ten (five fabrichnye, five zavodskie) began their educations in a village. Of these, only three (a fabrichnyi and two zavodskie) specified that the teacher was a cleric, but there were surely others. The second zavodskoi who learned reading from a village sexton was Mark Malinovskii, who became a militant atheist. *Deiateli* 2.3.865.

disliked his initial factory experience: The workers' lives seemed "materially and *spiritually* impoverished" (*VNP*, p. 141, my emphasis).

Volkov dates his first direct contact with people with "collective ideas" to his time in Simbirsk city. Yet the conflict that caused him to lose his job there was not political. He had burst into a rage when his boss cursed him rudely (*po-materno*), and he would have pummeled the man with a stick if other workers had not stopped him. We are still at the level of personal humiliation, the kind felt by young Gerasimov.

Despite problems with the dating, there is little doubt that sometime in the mid-1860s, in Kazan (since the 1861 "Bezdna affair" and A. P. Shchapov's ensuing speech, a hotbed of radical sentiment, with undertones of religious dissent), Volkov became involved in a cooperative store for workers, organized by intelligenty. It is possible that this "consumers' society," though authorized by the government (p. 146), later evolved into a circle devoted to the spreading of "social ideas" (p. 142). But we do not see Volkov in clear outline again until early in the new decade (1872?), in Saratov, where, employed by the new Saratov-Moscow railroad, he is again involved in a nonpolitical clash with a supervisor (this time the issue is the withholding of pay to discourage holiday drinking). Fired for insubordinate behavior (though this time it is *he* who restrains a more bellicose worker), the scrappy Volkov finally ends up in St. Petersburg in 1873 (the modal arrival year for our 141-man sample), where he begins his career with provocative talk that costs him a badly needed job (pp. 143–44).

Apart from skill and a feisty temper, just how different is Volkov the zavodskoi from our fabrichnye? To be sure, he has been exposed to socialist ideas (he claims to have engaged in propaganda in Saratov and, very briefly, Moscow), and he is ready to share his political views ("my social idea") at the drop of a hat (pp. 143–44). Evidence that prior exposure to politics has affected him is the speed with which he lands in a kruzhok, where he assumes a leadership post (treasurer-librarian). Yet the degree to which he defined his views in terms that would identify him as a zavodskoi is by no means clear, and one is hard put to find anything specific, either in his defiant conduct under arrest (see the epigraph) or in his two-year political career between his first arrest (1874) and his second, that would distinguish his views or values in any essential way from a fabrichnyi's. Although he reads Ferdinand Lassalle, the German socialist who, to be sure, brazenly privileged workers, he also tells his interrogators of his duty to go "to the people," meaning peasants. If he identifies closely with munitions workers, or more precisely with the Cartridge Factory workers in his circle, "the intellectual cream [*tsvet*] of Petersburg workers" (p. 144), this seems more an artifact of location (Vasil'evskii Island) than of ideology, just as circles of fabrichnye from the Vyborg District (mainly Cheshire workers) were bonded by a common venue. In this regard it is noteworthy that one of Petr Alekseev's closest comrades was not a fellow weaver but a machinist who worked at the same plant.[51]

Only in one respect did Volkov differ radically from other revolutionary workers, but in this he was as odd among zavodskie as among fabrichnye. In 1880, living in exile in the Far North, he took the extraordinary step of marrying an intelligentka, widow of an executed "political" who had belonged to *Zemlia i Volia*.[52] Was this a romantic relationship or yet another populist marriage of political duty? In either case it might suggest that Volkov had become a full *intelligent*, unmodified by "worker-."

Dmitrii *Smirnov*, born in 1848 and one of Volkov's closest comrades, at times his housemate, tells a story that partially duplicates Volkov's.[53] He too was one of Plekhanov's model zavodskie ("S"), a member of the meshchanskoe soslovie (but born and raised a Kostroma serf), and, by the time he entered his political phase, a skilled machinist. He too gained the rudiments of literacy in his native village, though not from a cleric, but from his peasant father, who did have a religious outlook, however, and used Church Slavonic to teach his son (Bortnik, "V 70-e," p. 222). Except briefly, a class for adults at a factory in which he worked, Smirnov never attended school.

One respect in which Smirnov differs from all the rest, zavodskie and fabrichnye, was that by age twelve or thirteen, in 1861, he was already a resident of the capital, giving him, as it were, a twelve-year head start at urban acculturation over the arrivals of 1873. Sent there by his father to apprentice with a German locksmith (p. 222), in a few years he was ready for a job in the city's burgeoning munitions industry. From 1868 to his 1874 arrest, he worked at various places, but mainly at the Cartridge factory, where he also returned after his release from prison (p. 219).[54]

Just how much of a city boy did this special history of urban work and residence make him? If one simply looks at his level of (self-)education, the answer is mixed. He was then one of only a handful of workers confident enough about his writing skills to write out a pretrial deposition in

[51] This was Ivan Smirnov, a quite well educated peasant from Tver. *Deiateli* 2.4.1534–36). See Alekseev's touching letter to him, written from prison, 7 April 1881, in *Krasnyi arkhiv* 44 (1931): 171–73.

[52] From the memoir of Dmitrii Smirnov, in M. Bortnik, "V 70-e i 80-e gody na Trubochnom zavode," *Krasnaia letopis'*, 1928, no. 2:222. The other marriage of this kind I have found in the sources is noted above, note 40.

[53] Smirnov's "memoir," a record of answers to questions submitted when he was old and infirm, was published in *Krasnaia letopis'*. It was rearranged to read more chronologically, with some omissions, in *VNP*, pp. 151–59 (Korol'chuk's notes are on pp. 381–83). My citations are from *Krasnaia letopis'*. Other sources are *Deiateli* 2.4.1530–32 (which places his birth about a year before the memoir does) and TsGAOR, f. 112, op. 1, d. 213.

[54] See also TsGAOR, f. 109 (Third Section), Secret Archive, op. 1, d. 1685, l. 2. Like Volkov, Smirnov was rearrested in 1876.

his own hand, though the grammar and spelling were replete with errors.[55] In his zeal for books he was the equal of Volkov, and he too was made custodian of his circle's library. He was also, if Plekhanov can believed, something of a dandy (*frant*), intent on sporting attractive city clothes, as was Volkov.[56]

Most germane to the question of Smirnov's "urbanization" is his attitude to his native village. In the "mad summer" of 1874, as it turns out, after thirteen years in the big city, away from home (though he surely visited his family on holidays), Smirnov, armed with his books, chose the risky path of returning to his *rodina*, Smol'nitsa village, where his father still lived, to propagandize villagers. This was *after* his first arrest and release, making him all the more conspicuous. (He made the trip with official permission, evidence that such returns were quite routine.) In his village he associated with young peasants, his "former comrades," now married, with whom he seemed to interact quite freely. He told them that a revolution was coming, that land must be seized from the gentry and given to the peasants, and "things like that." A sign of his distance from these *muzhiki*, however, was his message that they, the narod, must render aid to revolutionary workers (that is, people like him) (Bortnik, "V 70-e," p. 220). After he left, police came to search his father's home and question the muzhiki (p. 221). Apparently no one betrayed him.

Plekhanov tells us nothing of this incident. Though he mentions some exceptions, his representation of the period is of a time when truly urbanized workers of this kind became "unfit" (*neprigodnyi*) for village propaganda; they looked down on and could not get along with peasants.[57] It is interesting that the historian Korol'chuk, still looking at the workers' world through Plekhanov's long-closed eyes, made it a point to convey her doubt that Smirnov went to the peasants at all that summer.[58] Even if she is right, it is all the more striking that years later, close to death in Soviet Russia, Smirnov wished to be remembered as someone

---

[55] TsGAOR, f. 112, op. 1, d. 213, ll. 19–21.

[56] *RR*, p. 17. I know of no other reference to worker dandyism in the 1870s (in contrast to the 1890s), but there are allusions to workers who dressed so well one easily took them for *students* (TsGAOR, f. 112, op. 1, d. 215, l. 69), which is not the same thing. Of course (as Plekhanov remarks in *RR*, p. 17), students often tried to dress like workers. Curiously, it is Smirnov himself who describes his comrade Viktor Obnorskii as someone who dressed well, earned a lot of money, and hardly resembled a worker (Bortnik, "V 70-3," p. 218).

[57] *RR*, p. 18. The one "exception to this rule" on whom Plekhanov dwells at length (pp. 11–12, 18) is the metalworker Stepan Mitrofanov, a Vladimir peasant (*Deiateli* 2.3.939–40). It is only fair to note that Plekhanov granted that with long urban experience even a fabrichnyi might break psychologically with the village (*RR*, pp. 20–21). He even tells of one who developed a passionate interest in women's liberation (pp. 28–29).

[58] Questioning its accuracy, Korol'chuk omits the relevant passage from her edition of the memoir (*VNP*, p. 156n). She concedes that Smirnov went to the village two years later, but denies he propagandized among peasants.

who returned to his village to enlighten his peasant brethren. Perhaps this was *smychka*.

Unlike some other worker-memoirists, Smirnov mentions none of the mediating experiences that led to his radicalization. He is more intent— and this is not uncommon—on showing us his life as a worker-revolutionary than on telling us how he got there. Suffice it to say, then, that he was open to contact with his peasant roots, and that though a zavodskoi of first water, his political life included fellowship with fabrichnye, provided they shared his political outlook (Bortnik, "V 70-e," p. 221). Though member of a group that later expressed suspicion of students, his own attitude toward them was for a long time "reverential," as was that of his friends, who forgave students their minor vices: "We figured that that's how it was—they were gentlemen, we were workers" (pp. 222–23). As a sick old man in his last days, Smirnov still refused to believe the obvious: that Aleksandr Nizovkin, a "very sincere" and ultraradical student, had actually betrayed the workers to the police (p. 218).

Although Viktor *Obnorskii*, born in 1852, left no memoir,[59] he has held a large enough place in the pantheon of radical workers to warrant some consideration. In certain respects he represents the outer limit of the skilled, educated, urbanized zavodskoi of the 1870s (and perhaps of the 1890s as well). Much has been made of his legal classification as a Kronstadt meshchanin, but more important than soslovie, and complicating the ubiquitous question of origins, was his father's status as a retired petty officer. This means that his father may well have been raised a serf, the main recruiting ground for soldiers. Since a soldier's son was born free, unless he pursued his father's career he often ended up as a meshchanin of some town. Obnorskii was actually born in a city and may never have tasted true village life. If so, in this respect he was indeed unique among his fellows. The "city," however, was not Petersburg, not even Kronstadt, but a small backwater town in Vologda province with the Gogolesque name of Griazovets (Mudville?).

The Obnorskiis moved from there to the provincial capital (hardly a robust metropolis) in the early 1860s. Viktor's father (with financial aid from Viktor's brother Evgenii, a shadowy figure in this story),[60] was able to enroll him in the district school (*uchilishche*) instead of sending him to work. It is not clear whether Viktor graduated or had to withdraw for

---

[59] There is important information on Obnorskii in V. Levitskii, *Viktor Obnorskii: Osnovatel' "Severnogo Soiuza Russkikh Rabochikh"* (Moscow, 1929); *Deiateli* 2.3.1061–63; and *RD*, vol. 2, parts 1 and 2.

[60] Evgenii, probably the oldest of four Obnorskii brothers (I know no reference to sisters), worked for the Volga steamship company "Samolet." Viktor's other brothers joined him as workers in Petersburg, but seem to have had no serious political involvements.

financial reasons, but he was soon apprenticed to a Vologda locksmith, another step on the road to becoming a zavodskoi.[61]

Viktor arrived in Petersburg in 1869 when he was seventeen, shortly after his father's death. His precise trajectory is unclear, but one source suggests a stint at a Kronstadt zavod—not surprising given his father's military background—before settling down in the capital, (Levitskii, *Viktor Obnorskii*, p. 37), which may account for his membership in Kronstadt's *meshchanstvo* (petty bourgeoisie). Once in Petersburg he moved rather fitfully from zavod to zavod, gaining on-the-job experience as a machinist and as a lathe operator.

Political baptism came at the hands of a somewhat older worker, Stepan Mitrofanov, one of the first zavodskie to be politicized, but later chided in Plekhanov's memoir for excessive devotion to the village.[62] According to Mitrofanov, when they first met in 1869 at the Nobel factory, Obnorskii had no strong political views (Levitskii, *Viktor Obnorskii*, pp. 38–39). It was not until early 1872 that he took Obnorskii to the chaikovtsy. Both men attended Sergei Sinegub's "school" for workers, frequented mainly by fabrichnye, but when Obnorskii got work at the distant Cartridge Factory he joined its more accessible circle of zavodskie, where he became the comrade of Volkov and Smirnov.

As a member of that circle Obnorskii's life resembled theirs, with a heavy emphasis on revolutionary self-education through reading (he served a term as treasurer of the library) (*RD* 2.1.441). What did set him apart from others was an extremely strong attachment to the intelligenty, and a tendency to see them not simply as sources of values and ideas, but as social models whose image he was *almost* ready to absorb.[63] Why *almost*? Because despite his emulation of students, which included a craving to travel abroad (he made two trips to the West—to Paris, London, and Geneva) and study languages (he learned some French [*RD* 2.2.248]), and despite the vexation that his student-like departures from the capital caused his kruzhok, (*RD* 2.1.441, 445–47, 463), he always returned and was welcomed back to the worker fold. He was in fact a founder of the Northern Union, in essence an expanded union of kruzhki; one cannot help but wonder if its exclusion of nonworkers was part of a counterphobic resistance to the attraction of intelligentsia identity.

Stepan *Khalturin* was born in December 1856 (three weeks after Plekhanov). Although he left no memoir, we knew of his youth from two

---

[61] Yet such were the vicissitudes of legal designation that none of this prevented his later designation as "peasant" in the files of the criminal justice system. See TsGAOR, f. 112, op. 1, d. 213, l. 133, and d. 215, l. 157.

[62] See note 57. Though a Petersburger from age fourteen, Mitrofanov was born a serf.

[63] The best account of his special relationship with intelligenty is the testimony of A. P. Bliummer, which can be found in TsGAOR, f. 112, op. 1, d. 215, ll. 153, and 157.

unusual sources: a memoir by his nephew Ivan, who relates stories first heard from Ivan's father, Pavel (Stepan's brother) and an on-site investigation by *zemstvo* (district council) physician D. Markushevich in the village of Stepan's birth.[64] The youngest of eight children (two girls, six boys), Stepan was born in Khalevinskaia, Viatka province, to a prosperous family of state peasants. (Wrong on both counts, Plekhanov transforms them into "poor meshchane.")[65] The stone foundation and the many windows of his home proclaimed the success of his father, a trader of dry goods and agricultural products, a "kulak" by any measure,[66] whom Ivan describes as fairly well educated, "inquisitive" about the world, and very religious (confirmed by Markushevich); he even made a pilgrimage to Palestine (not confirmed by other sources). He was devoted to the education of his sons (Khalturin, "Semeinye," p. 49).

When interviewed by the doctor, Pavel and others remembered Stepan as a dextrous boy (a good juggler), good-humored and spirited. His boyhood interests were focused on technical things, including guns, and he had little use for farming or field work. (Markushevich, "Detstvo,' p. 40). Like others we have met, he had his first exposure to education, no doubt encouraged if not demanded by his father, at the hands of a parish sexton (Khalturin, p. 49). Thereafter, like Obnorskii, he continued his formal schooling at a district school, which he entered at age twelve along with Pavel, then thirteen. He managed to finish the three-year course, but except for his final exams his grades declined each year, a trend Markushevich (who had access to the school records) ascribes to a bright and hardy child's resistance to "rote learning" (*zubistrik*) ("Detstvo," pp. 41–42).[67]

In 1873, two years after graduating, Stepan, now seventeen, resumed his education by joining Pavel at a school of the democratically inclined Viatka zemstvo, a "peasant zemstvo" with a strong tax base and a commitment to educational quality.[68] A "seedbed" for the democratic intelligentsia (Khalturin, p. 50), the school was a wide-ranging four-year

[64] Ivan Khalturin, "Semeinye vospominaniia o Stepane Khalturine," *Byloe*, no. 16 (1921): 49–55; D. Markushevich, "Detstvo i otrochestvo Stepana Khalturina" *Proletarskaia revoliutsiia*, 1921, no. 3:39–43; idem, "Eshche o Stepane Khalturine," *Proletarskaia revoliutsiia*, 1922, no. 5:296–97. See also *RR*, pp. 83–90 (where an adoring Plekhanov devotes nearly 10 percent of his pages to Stepan); Iu. Polovoi, *Stepan Khalturin (1857–1882)* (Moscow, 1957), which ignores Markushevich's convincing evidence that Khalturin was born on 21 December 1856.

[65] *RR*, p. 83. Before the 1860s almost all peasants in this northern region were state peasants; gentry estates with serfs were very rare there.

[66] Such kulak-tradesmen were not uncommon in the region; see Dorothy Atkinson, "The Zemstvo and the Peasantry," in T. Emmons and W. S. Vucinich, eds., *The Zemstvo in Russia* (Cambridge, 1982), p. 120.

[67] Polevoi's hagiographic account omits any reference to Stepan's declining grades.

[68] Atkinson, "Zemstvo," pp. 119–21. I do not know where Stepan spent the two previous years; he may have returned home to try his hand at his father's business.

preparatory course for teachers, but one that also taught such useful skills as brewing, lathe operating, and the locksmith's and joiner's trades, parts of the curriculum that most attracted Stepan.[69] Although attendance was in any case subsidized, having a well-off father should have encouraged Stepan to spend the full four years at the school; but the impatient youth stayed for only a year or two, and performed rather poorly at that.

What aspirations did Stepan harbor at this point in his life? According to one of his former school chums, his interest in religion was only "slight," (Markushevich, "Detstvo," p. 43), but given the character of the school and the highly charged atmosphere of Viatka, a banishment point for political exiles, who recruited pupils into kruzhki, it is certain that he was exposed to ideas and practices conducive to "spiritual aspirations of a higher order" (Khalturin, pp. 50–51). Ivan insists that Stepan and Pavel took part in the kruzhki, read populist literature, and were drawn to then fashionable ideas such as communal kitchens. Given some of the errors in his chronology (his dating of the "Trial of 193" is off by years), Ivan's account need not be accepted in detail, but we do know that sometime after dropping out of school Stepan and some adventuresome friends were seized with the notion of going to America—hardly the typical dream of a Russian peasant or worker—to live in a utopian commune. The project may have been hastened by his father's death, for Stepan was able to finance the voyage by liquidating his share of the inheritance.

Before his plans could be realized, however, Stepan was deserted by his friends, some of whom shipped out to America with his money and travel papers. He went to St. Petersburg to catch them before they embarked, rather than to avoid the constricted life of his "godforsaken village" (*glukhoe zakholust'e*), as Polevoi would have it, and there is no basis for Polevoi's claim that he went there intending to work in a zavod and start a revolutionary life (*Stepan Khalturin*, p. 8). Once in the capital, however, it made sense for such a plucky youth to turn his sojourn into a new adventure.

Khalturin arrived early in 1875 with neither money nor a valid permit.[70] At first he took any odd job that came his way—even working as a boatman. His first opportunity to work in a more or less industrial setting came through a chance encounter with a former Viatka teacher who found him work at a railroad yard and introduced him to some intelligenty. Indeed, since his first genuine factory job came only in 1876, there is a sense in which the nineteen-year-old Khalturin was himself a kind of *raznochinets*-intelligent *before* he became a *worker*-intelligent.

[69] No other source substantiates Plekhanov's statement in *RR*, p. 83, that Stepan's father had apprenticed him to a joiner to learn that trade.

[70] The year 1875 is my own best estimate. His arrival was certainly not at the beginning of the decade, as Plekhanov states in *RR*, pp. 83–84.

In this regard the fate of one of his schoolmates, Nikolai Bashkirov (later Pavel's brother-in-law), is instructive. Just a year older than Stepan, up to age eighteen Bashkirov enjoyed a youth that was almost identical to his. They were raised together in the village, where they were very close.[71] They attended the same schools and while at the Viatka school, though in different kruzhki, were exposed to a similar intellectual climate. Unlike Stepan, however, Bashkirov completed the course. He too went to the capital in the 1870s, though unlike Stepan, who lacked the educational credentials, he came to study math and physics at the university, where he was drawn, though less deeply than Stepan, into revolutionary circles. In short, Bashkirov became a rather typical member of the student intelligentsia (a *raznochinets*, of course, since he was neither working-class nor gentry). Despite their matching social and (up to age seventeen or eighteen) educational backgrounds, we would never label him a *worker-intelligent*, as we do Khalturin.

In St. Petersburg the two zemliaki, virtually brothers, resumed their friendship. Bashkirov, though never imprisoned, was put under surveillance by police while they searched for Stepan. The line between the social identities of the two men was a thin one indeed, casting further doubt on any effort to absolutize the representational categories with which we are familiar. It is noteworthy that Plekhanov, for whom Khalturin is at one level the proletarian of proletarians, also wistfully recalls his "nearly feminine softness" and "slight resemblance to a worker," and describes his attitude toward clothes (unlike some other zavodskie) as "indifference worthy of a nihilist intelligent" (that is, a studied indifference).[72]

The rest of Khalturin's Petersburg career, closely tied to the birth of the Northern Union, is quite well known, and only a few highlights need detain us. There is no doubt that fairly soon after he began to join the workers' circles, to which he was initiated by intelligenty, Khalturin, now under the influence of Obnorskii and other zavodskie (who selected him to run their library), came more and more to see himself as a worker and, rhetorically at least, to draw invidious comparisons between workers and students. The more entangled his political imagination became in revolutionary plots (which now displaced his fantasies about America), the more skeptical he became about the strength of the intelligentsia's commitment (though he continued to interact with students as an equal, and spoke with them familiarly, *na ty*).[73] Conversely, he was known to carry on about the virtues of his fellow workers (but not zavodskie per se!) in a manner that in a later jargon would be called *ouvrièriste*, and in a still

---

[71] Bashkirov was one of Ivan Khalturin's major sources about his uncle Stepan. Ivan's memoir (note 64), in turn, is my main source on Bashkirov.

[72] *RR*, pp. 84, 88; information on Bashkirov is from Khalturin, "Semeinye," pp. 49–54.

[73] This according to Sergei Kravchinskii, as cited in Polevoi, *Stepan Khalturin*, p. 26.

later jargon, "worker-chauvinist." Sergei Kravchinskii, who knew him well, called it class "exclusiveness" (*iskliuchitel'nost'*).[74]

But did this contrasting of worker to student entail an equally hard distinction, as Plekhanov and (to a lesser extent) Kravchinskii suggest, between worker and peasant? Plekhanov's only evidence is an exchange in which Khalturin taunts him for reading books about the peasant commune ("Is this really so important?"). But even Plekhanov, while labeling Khalturin an extreme Westernizer (*zapadnik*, hinting at his proto-Marxism, later de rigueur in Soviet allusions to Khalturin and Obnorskii), admits that his "sociopolitical views" were hard to define (*RR*, p. 87). In a sense, the Northern Union and its program, which Khalturin helped compose, sums up the delicate balance of his attitude toward peasants. On the one hand, it was an exclusive association of workers (though it is the exclusion of intelligenty rather than peasants that was at stake), but on the other, it had a program that upheld the future of the commune (casting doubt on Plekhanov's reconstructed conversation). If Khalturin identified himself as a worker, he was one for whom worker and peasant shared common ground.

Moreover, Khalturin's self-identification continued to be labile, as witness his decision to withdraw his energies from the Union and, acting independently, to join the intelligenty of *Narodnaia volia* (People's Will) in their plan to murder the tsar (the notorious Winter Palace explosion of 1880). Plekhanov strains not so much to justify this action (he opposed terrorism both as a *cherno-peredelets* [member of Black Repartition] and later as a Marxist), but to show us its consistency with his image of Khalturin as a worker's worker. According to Plekhanov, Khalturin's logic was that regicide would lead to greater freedom, and freedom would allow the labor movement to expand.[75] But this kind of reasoning is not far removed from that of typical *Narodnaia volia* intelligenty. In any case, like other terrorists Khalturin was devastated when he heard the tsar had survived the blast (*RR*, pp. 92–93). Plekhanov cannot get himself to say it, but for practical purposes Khalturin had become a *narodovolets* (follower of *Narodnaia volia*), though one whose worker identity, however unstable, he refused to abandon, as we see in the following notice in *Listok Narodnoi voli* (1880): "[The man who placed the explosives] finds newspaper gossip that he is an aristocrat by origin extremely disagreeable, and he has asked the editors . . . to confirm the fact that he is of pure working-class stock."[76]

---

[74] *RR*, p. 85; Kravchinskii as cited in *Stepan Khalturin*, p. 34.

[75] Polevoi repeats this gloss on Khalturin's thinking, but with no attribution to Plekhanov or anyone else. See *Stepan Khalturin*, p. 37.

[76] Quoted in Venturi, *Roots*, p. 686 (there is a concise account of the Winter Palace incident on pp. 685–86).

On one last point we can agree with Plekhanov: Khalturin, a practical man in many respects, was also a great dreamer (*mechtatel'*), one whose dreams stretched far beyond the workers' movement (*RR*, p. 88). We have already seen this quality of imagination in his plan to travel to America. Workers could dream as well as intelligenty. Khalturin was both.

Since space does not permit as detailed a discussion of workers of the generation, born in the 1870s and 1880s, that came of age from the 1890s to the eve of 1905, I will confine myself to a summary, highlighting only a few key similarities and differences between generations.[77] In contrast to the 1870s, fabrichnye in this period, though amply represented among militant workers (including the thousands who took part in the Petersburg strikes of 1896–97), rarely appear among the memoirists. There are but a few important exceptions: Anna Boldyreva and Vera Karelina (whose short but valuable memoirs also cover some of the years between the two generations); Ivan Popov, the only fabrichnyi author of a book-length autobiography on this period (though most of it covers 1905–17).[78]

Notwithstanding the preponderance of zavodskie, many familiar themes that bear on identity and values recur in the later stories. Despite the passing of a generation, almost all the workers are village-born (not too surprising, given the industrial explosion of the 1890s, the demographics of which demanded renewed recruitment from a rural labor pool), and, up to varying ages, experience peasant childhoods, some with a strong religious foundation. The dedicated zavodskoi-revolutionary Ivan Babushkin (Lenin's favorite), a son of poor Vologda peasants, never laid eyes on a city until his fifteenth year; the equally committed zavodskoi Semën Kanatchikov—not until his sixteenth.[79] Even the exceptions are borderline cases, such as the fabrichnyi Ivan Popov, who was raised in a "village" but very near the Petersburg city limits, and who had a peasant father but one who worked in nearby urban factories. One of the "purest"

[77] For a good analysis of the "conscious worker" phenomenon of this period, see Tim McDaniel, *Autocracy, Capitalism, and Revolution in Russia* (Berkeley and Los Angeles, 1988), chap. 8. In this section I include only workers who wrote memoirs. In addition to those cited below I have used A. Fisher, *V Rossii i v Anglii. Nabliudeniia i vospominaniia peterburgskogo rabochego (1890–1921 gg.)* (Moscow, 1922); A. S. Shapovalov, *V bor'be za sotsializm* (Moscow, 1957); A. Shotman, "Zapiski starogo bol'shevika," *Proletarskaia revoliutsiia*, 1922, nos. 9 and 11; and *Ot Gruppy Blagoeva k "Soiuzu Bor'by" (1886–1894 gg.)* (Rostov-on-Don, 1921), esp. K. Norinskii and V. Shelgunov.

[78] Part of Boldyreva's memoir is in *Tekstil'shchik*, no. 1–2 (1923); a longer selection, though incomplete, is in *VNP*, pp. 249–68; Karelina's memoir of the 1890s is in *Krasnaia letopis'*, 1922, no. 4, and *VNP*, pp. 269–91 (see also Rose L. Glickman, *Russian Factory Women* [Berkeley and Los Angeles, 1984], pp. 173–80; I. V. Popov, *Vospominaniia* (Moscow, 1971), esp. chap. 1.

[79] *Vospominaniia Ivana Vasil'evicha Babushkina* (Moscow, 1955), pp. 15–16; *A Radical Worker in Tsarist Russia: The Autobiography of Semën Ivanovich Kanatchikov*, ed. and trans. R. E. Zelnik (Stanford, Calif., 1986), p. 6.

proletarian cases (there are few others) is Aleksei Buzinov, *both* of whose parents were Petersburg workers, but even in his case the father was a peasant (from Smolensk), a heavy drinker who claimed to long for village life.[80]

For what it may be worth, most of this generation still belonged to the peasant soslovie, and even those who did not were, so to speak, *meshchane* by default. Karelina, for example, like Gerasimov, was a ward of the Foundling Home (which she hated), raised by a peasant foster mother (whom she loved). Amost none had worker parents, and it is telling that the two exceptions, Popov and Boldyreva, were fabrichnye; even so, Boldyreva's parentage did not prevent her from spending her first nine years in a village. Though several lived in small cities or towns before coming to the big city (Petersburg, but in one case Moscow), they arrived without a sense of themselves as city people.

At various ages, some as early as nine, others in their teens, they all began to be exposed to the comings and goings of the city. We learn much more about the ways they experienced city life, both inside and outside the factory, than we do from workers of the 1870s, who tend to represent themselves as almost slipping into a kruzhok (after a quick contact with an engaging intermediary) and make little effort to describe their prepolitical city or (except for Gerasimov and Smirnov) factory lives. Yet even the urban experience described by the later generation had a peasant component. In part this was because much of Petersburg (not just Moscow) had remained so "peasant" in character (demographically, it had become *more* peasant). Not only had rural ways and institutions such as *arteli* and *zemliachestva* (home-region associations) been transferred there, many "city" tasks—carting, barge work on the river and canals, vending, even actual factory work (including in zavody!)—were still performed by genuine muzhiki, in peasant dress, projecting clear peasant images. Note that the "conscious" Kanatchikov, contrary to conventional wisdom (and to zavodskoi Timofeev's memoir), drew a cultural dividing line less between zavodskie and fabrichnye than between two socially distinct types of pattern-maker, one urbanized, one peasant-like, *within* a zavod population.[81]

At a more subjective level, peasant-related themes continued to figure in the workers' internal dialectic of self-identification, with even the most

[80] Aleksei Buzinov, *Za Nevskoi Zastavoi* (Moscow, 1930), p. 11.

[81] *A Radical Worker*, pp. 20–22. Timofeev, a worker who when generalizing drew a sharp line between the fabrichnyi and zavodskoi, admitted he had little personal knowledge of the former. Several pages after drawing that line he went on, now based on his *experience*, to contrast skilled zavodskie not with fabrichnye but with unskilled dayworkers in the same zavod. See P. Timofeev, *Chem zhivet zavodskii rabochii* (St. Petersburg, 1906), pp. 4 and 12–19.

skilled and cultured among them linking their "proletarianization" (a missing term in the stories of the 1870s) to the shedding of their peasant pasts, which—most markedly in the case of Kanatchikov—return from time to time to haunt them. Even Babushkin's effort to assure his readers, writing at age twenty nine after fifteen years of village life, that he has forsaken and forgotten his former life as a "peasant-ploughman," seems more a declaration of moral identity than a description of social reality (*Vospominaniia*, p. 16).

Some themes that had appeared with reference to the 1870s now reappear with greater frequency and intensity. Most striking, in a sense the opposite side of the coin of distancing oneself from the peasantry, is distancing oneself from the intelligentsia. Although we saw the germ of this development in the 1870s, the deliberate attempt by newly "conscious" workers to separate themselves from the students to whom they owed their political educations, to draw a magic circle around their own kruzhki in order to separate themselves from their "betters," is so ubiquitous in the later memoirs that it seems to constitute a requirement of the new cultural code of the radical worker. In part this may have beeen an effort to resist the temptation of upward mobility (misread by Richard Pipes, who saw the temptation but not the resistance), an analogue to Kanatchikov's effort to resist the downward pull of a peasant past. But in part, of course, it reflects the actual strain that now characterized the worker-student relationship.[82]

Another old theme now renewed with greater vigor is the role of officially sanctioned adult education in the formation of worker-intelligenty. The IRTO schools that began to spread through Petersburg's industrial neighborhoods in the 1870s with the grudging approval of the government had played a major role in awakening a thirst for knowledge among workers. In some cases, as we know, they became the catalysts that propelled their pupils, at once stimulated and frustrated by their school experience, into the arms of student radicals who took over their "educations" where the embattled IRTO schools left off. In the course of the 1890s the descendants of these schools, most notably St. Petersburg's celebrated Kornilov school, whose teaching staff was dominated by liberals and radicals of various hues, came close to exercising a cultural hegemony over an influential segment of workers, providing them with exposure to politically sensitive areas of study—especially the world of

---

[82] Richard Pipes, *Social Democracy and the St. Petersburg Labor Movement, 1885–1897* (Cambridge, Mass., 1963). For a subtle treatment of these problems, see Allan K. Wildman, *The Making of a Workers' Revolution: Russian Social Democracy, 1891–1903* (Chicago, 1967). On the workers' complex relations with intelligenty, see also my "Russian Bebels: An Introduction to the Memoirs of Semen Kanatchikov and Matvei Fisher," part 2, *Russian Review* 35 (October 1976).

literature—that touched them for the rest of their lives, even finding expression in the grateful rhetoric of their memoirs. Few among our memoirists are able to tell their tales without referring to these classes, and several affirm and vividly describe the power of their formative influence.[83] One senses that the activist workers of this era, as we have come to know them, would not have existed, or would have been very different, without these schools.

Finally, for all the importance of the schools, we must conclude by returning to the area of greatest continuity, the most durable institution in the lives of all these workers from 1872 to 1905 (when it was overtaken and partially obliterated by revolutionary events and subsequent changes in workers' institutional and cultural life): the kruzhok. The workers circle appears again and again in the stories of our second-generation memoirists, and in its basic features continues to resemble the circles of the 1870s. It remains an essential location of the workers' intellectual and moral life (the two are inseparable), the place where they take their factory experience on the one hand, the intellectual sustenance gained at "legitimate" schools on the other, and turn them both into language, discourse, *slovo* (as much verbal as written, though the verbal is poorly preserved). The kruzhok, the locus of this logos, remains a specific urban location, an apartment (individual or collective, but always collectively used), part of the city's political geography (the sites remain strikingly constant over thirty years, including the neighborhood branches of Father Gapon's Assembly of Russian Workers, 1904–5), the plebian equivalent of the aristocratic salon, a storehouse of books ("libraries"), a hectograph, occasionally a printing press, a storehouse also of memory, where so much of the typical memoir narrative is staged.

Membership in this or that kruzhok, however unstable, is a defining part of many memoirists' identity, more so, I believe, than employment in a given factory, often more unstable still. The issue of factory patriotism has been carefully debated, at least in relation to 1905 and beyond,[84] and by no means would I suggest that workers' identities were not shaped by factory experience. On the contrary, it is characteristic of all the memoirists of this period that, however intense their kruzhok activity, their work remains embedded in their narratives and memories. Unlike Jacques Rancière's Saint-Simoniens, their dreams of another life rarely entail abandonment of workplace, at least not until such time, beginning for some

---

[83] Babushkin, *Vospominaniia*, pp. 35, 45–46; Kanatchikov, *Radical Worker*, pp. 109–16; V. A. Shelgunov, "Moi vospominaniia o voskresnykh shkolakh," in *VNP*, pp. 332–40; Popov, *Vospominaniia*, pp. 49–52.

[84] Steve Smith, "Craft Consciousness, Class Consciousness: Petrograd, 1917," *History Workshop Journal* 11 (spring 1981); William G. Rosenberg, "Workers and Workers' Control in the Russian Revolution," ibid., 5 (spring 1978).

on the eve of 1905, as party loyalty and identity (Bolshevik, Menshevik, or SR) begin to assert themselves. Nevertheless, it is the kruzhok experience (mostly at night) that distinguishes them from so many of their fellows, that provides them with time and space (the time-space) to, in Rancière's words, "Resist the law of the week, the order of work and the family."[85]

As I hope is clear, it is my contention that how such workers came to new ideas, values, and identities; how having begun to adopt these identities, they experienced new growth; how they too became a kind of "new person," members of a self-identified cultural cohort with its own distinct if never quite unique set of values, cannot be adequately explained by means of a Plekhanovite progression from peasant mentality to worker mentality (through the experience of class conflict at the factory) to socialist "consciousness." That schema may still have its uses as a kind of broad-gauged ideal type, but we need to look for the other, less linear, more complex ways in which such new identities and their attendant values were sought, found, and further transformed. To be sure, this does not mean dismissing factory (or craft) solidarities as a possible, perhaps even necessary (but never sufficient) factor in the process. But we must also catch in our net how new values built on, fused with, and otherwise reshuffled themselves among the earlier notions that a worker brought to the urban factory world; and we must look for ways in which *non*-factory experience (not all of it urban), available to zavodskie and fabrichnye alike, provided workers with the wherewithal to define, redefine, and sometimes represent their lives.

---

[85] Jacques Rancière, *La nuit des prolétaires: Archives du rêve ouvrier* (Paris, 1981), p. 125 (the second epigraph to this chapter is from p. 121).

2

Mark D. Steinberg

Vanguard Workers and the Morality of Class

Moral judgment has typically been at the center of the process by which working classes are made. For individual workers to perceive that they are members of an exploited class usually requires that they do more than simply recognize that they are poor or poorly treated; they also need to believe that their personal hardships reflect unjust social relationships. And this belief requires not only the discovery that their miseries are part of a social order, but also the acceptance or construction of an ethical standard that defines this order as a violation of what is right and proper.

This moral knowledge has in different historical settings drawn on different sources: customary "moral economies" based on established craft standards and traditions of social responsibility, for example, or the experience of learning a skill, which has often encouraged workers to feel a greater measure of personal worth and a greater sensitivity to subordination and ill-treatment. Very often, however, perceptions of social injustice have reflected less common experiences and awakenings, though most of these have left only faint traces in the historical record. Most visible, for they often inspired workers to write, have been encounters with the world of culture and ideas, especially moral ideas. Like the acquisition of skill, the acquisition of cultural knowledge often made workers both painfully aware of their excluded and subordinated status in the larger society and better able to articulate nascent feelings of moral offense and to imagine emancipation.

Morally literate workers such as these, who were present in most Russian industries during the late nineteenth and early twentieth centuries, were not "typical" of their class, but they played a central role in the collective life of their class, especially in its conscious self-formation as a class. Standing at the boundary between the educated and the masses, they served as carriers and translators of ideas, words, and images that workers used to confront the larger society. But their relationship to the majority of workers, even within their own industries, as with the intellectuals with whom they shared class leadership, was complex and ambivalent.

Vanguard workers had considerable influence among workers through their active presence in mutual benefit societies, workers' clubs, trade unions, and the labor press. But they stood not only out in front of their fellow workers, but also apart from and above them, for they found repulsive the rough manners, drunkenness, traditionalism, and ignorance of the majority. Vanguard workers did not so much speak *for* other workers as preach *to* them, challenging them to think and act in unaccustomed ways. Paradoxically, though, it was precisely this feeling of moral estrangement from both their own class and the larger society—their marginality—that attracted them to the idea of a class movement that promised to erase the boundaries of class.[1]

In the Russian printing industry during the first decade of twentieth century there existed two different groups of vanguard workers—each united around its own institutions, each advocating different ideologies, and each competing against the other for influence. One group was the sort that Lenin had in mind when he spoke of a militant proletarian vanguard: workers conscious of themselves as members of a separate class, who saw the working class as collectively oppressed and exploited in the existing social and political structure and believed that this could be overcome only through class struggle and eventual revolution. But another vanguard existed, one that embraced a quite different view of the interests of workers and of the forms and goals of collective action. These workers were unashamably class-collaborationist. They viewed themselves as members not of a separate class but of a single human community and believed that the solution to workers' sufferings lay only in combining together with employers and other social elites in pursuit of a moral transformation of personal and social relationships.

The opposition between these two vanguards was reflected in their different institutional bases and different legal situations. Before the revolution of 1905, the moral-communitarian vanguard was the better organized and more influential, certainly in part because it alone was allowed to function legally. Its members joined together in mutual-assistance funds and voiced their views in the weekly journal *Naborshchik* ("The Compositor"—St. Petersburg, 1902–16), edited by the worker-turned-manager Andrei Filippov. Radical workers, by contrast, faced a government that did all it could to silence them and suppress their organizations, but also found most workers resistant to their ideas (as illustrated

---

[1] For a somewhat similar argument, see Jacques Rancière, *The Nights of Labor: The Workers' Dream in Nineteenth Century France* (1981), trans. John Drury (Philadelphia, 1989).

by the difficult history of the underground Moscow printers' union during 1904). This situation changed only starting in 1905 as the class-conscious vanguard was given a larger legal arena—trade unions and a legal labor press—and as its message began to attract a mass following (including among them worker activists who had defected from the camp of class collaboration, as they now branded it, to the camp of class struggle).

The boundary that divided these two groups, however, seems more absolute than in fact it was. When one looks closely at the ideals and the vocabulary with which they constructed their social judgments, the differences blur. This moral construction of social judgment is my subject.

During the last decades of the nineteenth century, workers in the printing industry, especially in St. Petersburg and Moscow, began organizing, with the support of paternalistic employers and managers, voluntary mutual assistance societies, joining together with employers in trade festivals and cultural activities, and voicing their views of the world in print—especially in printing industry trade journals, which first appeared in the 1860s, and, starting in 1902, in the worker-oriented weekly, *Naborshchik* ("The Compositor").

These worker activists were deeply self-conscious, and thus perceived various boundaries between themselves and the majority of workers. They saw themselves as distinguished by profession, sharing with their "colleagues," as they sometimes called other printers, even in other countries, a sense of occupational superiority both as skilled workers and, even more distinctively, as producers of a product more cultural than commercial. *Naborshchik*'s readers often encountered—and no doubt approved of—statements such as "A person who spends his entire life within the walls of a printing house cannot be compared with a carpenter, metalfitter, or other professions that have nothing in common with printing," which implies, of course, what a later issue of *Naborshchik* stated explicitly, "He is in every respect superior to the latter."[2] And since most activists set type by hand, they felt added worth since the skillfulness of their labor lay not in muscular strength or knowledge of machinery but in their ability to handle letters and words. "A compositor is not a common worker," Russian compositors often asserted, "but a working semi-intellectual [*truzhenik-poluintelligent*]."[3]

These activist workers felt superior not only to workers in other crafts and industries, but also to less developed printers. Occupation and skill encouraged feelings of pride and self-worth, but these alone were not seen to guarantee honor, which depended also on one's personal moral culture.

[2] *Naborshchik*, 25 May 1903, p. 484, and 20 July 1903, p. 590.
[3] *Naborshchik*, 29 December 1902, p. 160.

With great disdain these organized and articulate workers described the
ordinary worker, even the ordinary compositor, as ignorant, immoral,
drunken, and lacking in culture (*nekul'turnyi*). They complained con-
temptuously that the typical Russian worker—and again, even most compositors were not spared—preferred getting drunk at the local tavern to
spending his time with "books, theater, and lively and absorbing discussion in a close circle of comrades."[4] Some such worker-critics manifested
these judgments in their own lives by becoming "aristocrats": dressing in
starched shirts and neckties, refusing to speak the vulgar idiom of the
shop, and generally keeping aloof as they advanced their own moral and
cultural development. Still—echoing in a popular key the moral debt to
the people felt by many educated upper-class radicals—many believed that
it was also their duty to proselytize, to persuade their fellow workers to
live a "conscious life" aware of "thought, art, and literature," of their
own "individual dignity," and of their "obligations and rights."[5]

The accuracy of this representation of ordinary workers as lacking
"spiritual and intellectual interests or aspirations"[6] is not the issue here.
What is important are the values that such judgments reveal. Among this
active minority of workers we see an obsession with personal intellectual
and moral development—the "spiritual" and "intellectual hunger" (*du-
khovnyi golod, umstvennyi golod*) and "thirst for knowledge" (*zhazhda
znaniia*) that many contemporary observers described among Russian
workers.[7] Among printers, a significant minority attended public lectures,
concerts, literary readings, and Sunday or evening schools.[8] And many
subscribed collectively to some inexpensive newspaper, borrowed books
from public libraries, bought cheap used books, or read *Naborshchik* after
it was established in 1902.[9]

[4] *Naborshchik*, 8 December 1902, p. 113; 29 December 1902, p. 156; 26 January 1903,
p. 213; 6 April 1903, p. 382; 4 May 1903, p. 438; 11 May 1903, pp. 450–53; and 22 June
1903, pp. 533–34.
[5] *Naborshchik*, 17 November 1902, p. 63; 22 June 1903, p. 534; 4 May 1903, p. 436;
11 May 1903, pp. 450–51; and 31 August 1903, p. 657.
[6] *Naborshchik*, 22 June 1903, p. 534. Incidentally, these words were written by a compositor later killed in the march to the Winter Palace on Bloody Sunday, 9 January 1905.
[7] L. M. Kleinbort, "Ocherki rabochei demokratii," *Sovremennyi mir*, November 1913, p.
182; G. V. Plekhanov, "Russkii rabochii v revoliutsionnom dvizhenii," *Sochinenia* (Moscow
and Leningrad, 1928), 3:132. See also V. F. Shishkin, *Tak skladyvalas' revolutsionnaia
moral': Istoricheskii ocherk* (Moscow, 1967), pp. 123–24, 130–31.
[8] V. V. Sher, "Moskovskie pechatniki v revoliutsii 1905 g.," in *Moskovskie pechatniki v
1905 g.* (Moscow, 1925), p. 12; *Leninskii zakaz* (Moscow, 1969), p. 23; *Naborshchik*, 22
January 1903, p. 535; *Istoriia leningradskogo soiuza rabochikh poligraficheskogo proizvodstva* (Leningrad, 1925), pp. 91, 429; P. P. Zinov'ev, *Na rubezhe dvukh epokh* (Moscow,
1932), p. 32.
[9] *Obzor graficheskikh iskusstv*, 1 December 1880, p. 176; I. Trotskii, "Ekonomicheskie i
sanitarnye usloviia truda v peterburgskikh tipografiiakh," *Promyshlennost' i zdorov'e*, May–
August 1903, p. 97; GARF, f. 6864, op. 1, d. 216, l. 46; I. D. Galaktionov, *Besedy naborshchika* (Petrograd, 1922), p. 10. Although there are no subscription or readership data on

Of course, culture meant different things to different people. In the view of most vanguard printers during these years, there was to be found among too many workers an "uncultured" culture, expressed in a preference, for example, for "boulevard" literature, such as the adventure tales of the bandit Churkin, to "belles lettres." True culture, in their view, was more edifying. Equally important, if not more so, true culture was also drawn from an established canon. One compositor recalled being invited as an apprentice in the late 1880s to the apartment of an older compositor in which "the walls of his two small rooms [a sizable apartment for a compositor] were positively covered by shelves filled with books." Here were mainly the classics of Russian literature: Gogol, Belinsky, Turgenev, Dostoyevsky, Saltykov-Shchedrin, Tolstoy, and others. "In each one you find something new and good," commented the senior worker, "each one teaches you something."[10] Another compositor recalled that when he was an apprentice in Moscow, one "respectable elder compositor" regularly read poetry to the apprentices after work.[11] Intertwined with this ideal of being "cultured" were personal moral norms, especially temperance and a use of time that was rational and self-improving. Such workers believed that not to "drink away hard-earned wages" but to "lay some aside for a rainy day"[12] was one of the marks of a cultured worker.

Much of the effort by these vanguard printers to improve workers' morality and culture occurred around the mutual assistance funds. These funds—organized and led by an alliance of employers, managers, foremen, and workers—sought to encourage the virtues of thrift and mutual aid by offering workers insurance in case of injury, illness, or death. The funds also represented themselves as a moral alternative to the tavern as the defining center of how time after work was to be used. In St. Petersburg, for example, the Compositors' Assistance Fund began in 1877 holding annual "music and dance evenings," which were among the more popular activities of the fund. On these occasions, it was said, workers could "forget their hard daily labor," not through "the inspiration of Bacchus" but "in the whirl of a waltz or a polka." At such evenings, members and their guests were also usually offered a show—typically an eclectic mix of scenes from plays, portions of a ballet, excerpts from Russian or foreign operas, chamber music, folk songs, and vaudeville—mainly

---

Naborshchik, the response to a fund-raising campaign suggests that about one-third of all compositors in the capital were readers; letters from other cities indicate the existence of a provincial readership, but its extent cannot be measured.

[10] Galaktionov, *Besedy naborshchika*, p. 7.

[11] Po povodu tridtsatiletiia vspomogatel'noi kassy tipografov v Moskve: Vospominaniia naborshchika (Moscow, 1901), pp. 5–6.

[12] Shponik [I. D. Galaktionov], *Lebedinaia pesn'* (Moscow, 1904), pp. 5, 7. See also *Po povodu tridstatiletiia vspomogatel'noi kassy tipografov v Moskve* and *Obzor graficheskikh iskusstv*, 15 May 1878, p. 64.

performed by hired professionals but often including a few amateur performances by workers themselves.[13]

The cultural choices made by workers attracted to the activities of the funds seem to suggest subordination to a dominant culture. Indeed, these workers wished to overcome their subordination and exclusion precisely by sharing in that larger culture. It was absolutely necessary, from this point of view, that they defined culture as waltzes and polkas, orchestral music, theater, and classic literature. Likewise, because they wished to be recognized by established elites as moral individuals, they embraced the moral standards that elites demanded of them: self-help, self-development, sobriety, rational use of time. They tried to express their entry into the dominant culture even in their dress: most wore a frock coat for special occasions, and some even worked in starched shirt and necktie protected by a smock.[14]

But what did this pursuit of cultural and moral respectability actually mean? Was this evidence of simple cultural hegemony, or as historians of workers elsewhere have argued, were these efforts a challenge to workers' subordinate status, an expression, even, of an emerging class consciousness?[15] Workers themselves, in fact, often quite adroitly intertwined *both* meanings—articulating an ambiguous mixture of social and moral ideas that both accepted and challenged existing social relationships.

This ambiguous social vision is especially noticeable in the ways these workers handled the communitarian social ideal central to their outlook. As advocates of social community, these vanguard printers typically spoke of the members of an assistance fund, which included employers and managers as well as workers, as forming a single "family" united in mutual aid and "love for one's neighbor."[16] Public statements by activist compositors in these years endlessly reiterated this ideal. The journal *Naborshchik* was especially vigorous in promoting social collaboration. The editor, Andrei Filippov, was a compositor who had been promoted out of the ranks. It is perhaps unremarkable, therefore, that he should have

---

[13] *Obzor graficheskikh iskusstv*, 15 May 1878, p. 65; 15 May 1882, p. 65; 1 March 1883, p. 42; *Vestnik graficheskogo dela*, 22 December 1897, p. 249; *Graficheskie iskusstva i bumazhnaia promyshlennost'*, January 1897, p. 31, and March 1899, p. 50; *Pechatnoe iskusstvo*, December 1901, p. 85, and November 1902, p. 68; *Naborshchik*, 15 December 1902, p. 128. In Moscow, the Typographers' Assistance Fund began organizing similar evenings after 1900. See *Pechatnoe iskusstvo*, June 1902, p. 282, and *Naborshchik*, 20 July 1903, p. 586.

[14] *Obzor pervoi vserossiiskoi vystavki*, 3 April 1895, p. 4; *Naborshchik*, 15 December 1902, p. 128; and Zinov'ev, *Na rubezhe*, pp. 17, 30.

[15] Alastair Reid, "Intelligent Artisans and Aristocrats of Labour," in Jay Winter, ed., *The Working Class in Modern British History* (Cambridge, 1983), pp. 171–86; R. Q. Gray, *The Labour Aristocracy in Victorian Edinburgh* (Oxford, 1976); and G. Crossick, *An Artisan Elite in Victorian Society* (London, 1978).

[16] For example, *Vestnik graficheskogo dela*, 10 July 1897, p. 118; Shponik, *Lebedinaia pesn'*, p. 16.

insisted on the identity of the interests of employers and workers. Still, Filippov's advocacy of social community involved more than the assertion of common interests. At the heart of his arguments were always the demands of "moral virtue": "the sacred truth of love of one's neighbor," "moral responsibility," and "honor."[17] The many workers who read and wrote for *Naborshchik* shared this social ideal and frequently offered their own praise of employers who expressed "love" for their workers, showed "parental solicitude" for workers' needs, and introduced "light" into their lives.[18] Similar acclaim was spoken by workers at various workshop and trade festivals and ceremonies.[19]

This pursuit of moral community with employers was sincere, but ambivalent. Indeed, the very idea of moral community bore within itself a challenge to the status quo. Workers admired caring employers, but they also chastised the uncaring majority with the benevolence of the few. They praised the virtuous, but invariably contrasted them with employers who "trample upon the human dignity that by right belongs to their workers."[20] An illustration of this critical praise is the apotheosis of the Odessa printshop owner Vera Fesenko, who became a kind of symbol of the virtuous employer for readers of *Naborshchik*. Responding to a letter to *Naborshchik* in which Fesenko suggested that piece rates were the main cause of homelessness, drunkenness, and vagrancy among compositors,[21] the compositor Stepan Tsorn, a regular columnist in *Naborshchik*, insisted that she was being too modest. "Why do you have no drunkards?" Tsorn asked, "because you, Vera Fedoseevna, surround each of the employees of your large and, in the broadest sense, well-run printing house with humane treatment and motherly love." But sadly, Tsorn added, Fesenko was a rarity.[22] Readers apparently understood the moral of the tale, for they reiterated it in letters sent to *Naborshchik* offering their own praise of Fesenko. One typical letter described the "delight and happiness" felt by the sixty compositors with whom the author worked as they listened to one of their fellows read Tsorn's article on Fesenko. They found themselves "staring in wonderment" at the story of an employer who they concluded was "unique in Russia." The reading ended, we are told, with

[17] *Naborshchik*, 20 October 1902, p. 7; 25 February 1903, pp. 277, 288–89; 8 June 1903, p. 509; 20 July 1903, p. 581; 31 August 1903, p. 657.

[18] *Naborshchik*, 26 January 1903, p. 222; 9 February 1903, p. 251; 6 April 1903, p. 389; 25 May 1903, p. 489; 26 October 1903, pp. 782–85.

[19] *Obzor graficheskikh iskusstv*, 1 January 1884, p. 7; *Graficheskie iskusstva i bumazhnaia promyshlennost'*, March 1896, pp. 106–7; *Pechatnoe iskusstvo*, January 1902, pp. 125–28; *Naborshchik*, 14 September 1903, p. 694.

[20] *Obzor graficheskikh iskusstv*, 1 January 1884, p. 7; and almost identical words in *Naborshchik*, 9 March 1903, p. 313.

[21] *Naborshchik*, 26 January 1903, p. 224.

[22] *Naborshchik*, 9 February 1903, p. 251.

all sixty men exclaiming, "Lord, if only a third of our employers were such as she—oh, how we would live!"[23] The whole Fesenko affair was pervaded by a mixture of sincerity and irony that transformed praise of a benevolent employer into complex social criticism.

Workers not only tried to hold employers morally accountable to the ideal of moral community, they also redefined virtue to better suit their own experiences and needs. Notably, they tended to measure good on a quite tangible scale. What impressed workers about Fesenko was less her humane spirit than the practical financial assistance she gave to sick workers, her voluntary reduction in the length of the workday, and the relatively high wages she paid (and on time).[24] As here, when workers wrote about humane employers, their definition was invariably concrete: good wages and regular raises, improved hygienic conditions in the shops, financial aid during sickness, paid vacations, and pensions to widows and orphans.[25] Worker idealists of social collaboration constantly reminded employers of the hardships workers suffered: the appalling hygienic conditions in most print shops, the exhausting seven-day work week of newspaper workers, endemic poverty, abuses of apprenticeship, the harmful effects of piece rates. True "friends of the working people" were measured by how they dealt with these conditions, not by their "winged words" of "kindness and condescension."[26]

As this suggests, workers interpreted the idea of moral community in a manner not only more concrete and demanding but also more egalitarian than employers did. How workers handled the metaphor of "family," which was frequently used by both workers and employers, illustrates this. Both groups often spoke of workers as "younger brothers" within the family of printers. But whereas employers tended to emphasize the modifier—to weight the hierarchical image of social family in which workers were subordinate and even inferior, as the Russian expression *men'shie brat'ia* seems to suggest—workers focused on the substantive, the element of fraternity. This fraternal image of social family was voiced from the very first, as for example in the speech of the compositor I. Loginov at a printers' trade festival in Odessa in 1883. Praising employers who treated workers "not as workers, but as collaborators in their great endeavor," he concluded with a toast to the health of employers: "Today's fraternal holiday reveals for us the not too distant future when employers and workers, joining as one family, will advance hand in hand to their com-

---

[23] *Naborshchik*, 9 March 1903, p. 321.

[24] *Naborshchik*, 9 February 1903, p. 251.

[25] *Pechatnoe iskusstvo*, February 1902, p. 158; *Novoe vremia*, 22 March (3 April) 1895, p. 3; *Naborshchik*, 14 September 1903, p. 694.

[26] *Naborshchik*, 9 February 1903, p. 248. The phrases were quoted by Stepan Tsorn from a letter written by a worker to the newspaper *Baku*.

mon goal—service to the fatherland, pleasing our good Lord."[27] Again, praise mingled with a pointed challenge. Such statements were not uncommon, nor was the religious element. And, as here, the invocation by workers of God, Christ, or the saints often bore a critical social message: under God all are equal; the first commandment of Christ and the Saints was to "love your neighbor *as yourself*."[28] The moral vocabulary that united activist workers and employers in the years before 1905 was flexible enough to express different social experiences, interests, and needs.[29]

The egalitarian vision of social community articulated by these workers partly reflected the influence of traditional religious notions of social virtue, but no less in evidence were more secular and contemporary moral ideas. Since the early nineteenth century, public discussions of social morality in Russia, as in the West, had focused increasingly on the worth and dignity of the human person (*lichnost'*) and the natural rights that this implied. This value was to be found in the writings of popular publicists and generally in much of the daily and periodical press, in the works of popular "classic" writers such as Nekrasov, Turgenev, Saltykov-Shchedrin, Tolstoy, and Gorky, but also in much popular commercial literature, where, Jeffrey Brooks has argued, a new respect for the individual was to be found.[30] Literate workers were certainly exposed to this culture, as one compositor testified when he reminded his fellow workers of "the principle of justice and recognition of the human person [*lichnost'*] about which we read and set type every day."[31]

Whatever the sources, it is clear that the notion of the natural dignity and rights of the human person had become a part of the moral thinking of the activist workers comprising this communitarian vanguard. Their speeches and writings were filled with expressions of the worker's humanity: "Respect the human dignity in each of us." "A compositor is a man and not a machine." "The rights of the worker, as a human being, must not be trampled upon." "Employers must remember that workers are people like any other."[32] Letters, essays, and poems written by workers were filled with terms such as honor, dignity, personhood, and culture

---

[27] *Obzor graficheskikh iskusstv*, 1 January 1884, p. 7.

[28] *Naborshchik*, 6 April 1903, pp. 377–79, 389; 8 June 1903, p. 509; 15 June 1903, p. 521.

[29] For employers' contributions to the discourse and practices of moral community in the printing industry, see Mark D. Steinberg, *Moral Communities: The Culture of Class Relations in the Russian Printing Industry, 1867–1907* (Berkeley and Los Angeles, 1992), chap. 2.

[30] Jeffrey Brooks, *When Russia Learned to Read* (Princeton, N.J., 1985).

[31] *Naborshchik*, 26 October 1903, p. 796. See also *Naborshchik*, 9 March 1903, p. 313.

[32] *Naborshchik*, 1 December 1902, p. 89; 22 December 1902, p. 134; 9 March 1903, p. 313; and 14 September 1903, p. 694. For examples from other groups of workers, see Kleinbort, "Ocherki rabochei demokratii" (part 1), *Sovremennyi mir*, March 1913, pp. 27–29.

(*chest', dostoinstvo, lichnost', kul'turnost'*).[33] The defense of workers' honor was also expressed in arguments for mutual aid: one should not "suffer the humiliation" of begging from one's fellow workers in times of need, when one can preserve "self-esteem" for only a ruble a month as a member of an assistance fund.[34] And, of course, everyday behavior—sobriety, polite language, presentable dress—was viewed as a moral expression of self.

The social ambivalence contained in workers' assertion of their human worth must not be overlooked. When workers challenged employers to treat them "as men not machines," they voiced a universalistic identity as human beings, an identity shared with employers, not a class identity as workers. It was as human beings not as workers that they felt their rights had been violated. Thus, ultimately, they did not blame structures of power and control for their oppression. Although they chastised employers who "trampled on the human dignity that by right belongs to their workers," they saw here the personal sins of individual employers not the crimes of an entire social class. They sought not to overturn the hierarchy of class but to convince those in authority to recognize their moral responsibilities and join them in common cause. Similarly, they did not view the moral debasement of workers as evidence of class oppression, but rather as the personal failing of individual workers. Thus, ironically, the humanistic sense of self that enabled these workers to voice moral outrage at indignity and inequality also led them to view with moral opprobrium the workers whose humanity was most degraded.

Nonetheless, such ethics challenged a social and political order in which workers were subordinate. The assumption of an identity and worth common to all human beings, even as it drew these workers toward employers, implicitly denied the moral legitimacy of class inequality. Moreover, human dignity was not simply a universal ideal undermining the idea of class boundaries, but an antithesis to the very tangible hardships and indignities suffered by workers. Although these vanguard workers avoided an explicit vocabulary of class, they infused their writings with a very specific and concrete social anguish. When compositor-poets, for example, described workers as "dying,"[35] this was both a figurative device and a literal expression of the high illness and mortality rates among printers. And when worker-writers described the "dark kingdom of the printing

---

[33] For some typical examples, *Obzor graficheskikh iskusstv*, 1 January 1884, p. 7; letter by a compositor to *Ekho*, 2 January 1884, pp. 2–3; *Naborshchik*, 9 March 1903, p. 313, and 11 May 1903, pp. 450–51.

[34] *Naborshchik*, 30 March 1903, pp. 361–62.

[35] *Naborshchik*, 8 June 1903, p. 510; 7 September 1903, p. 682; and 5 October 1903, p. 745.

plant,"[36] this was both a metaphor for ignorance and evil and a realistic description of most print shops. The concreteness of the indignities workers experienced gave an immediacy to their ethics and sharpened its critical edge. Class made itself felt even when its name was unspoken.

By the summer of 1905, advocates of a moral community uniting workers and employers were on the defensive. Readership of *Naborshchik* plummeted (a drop in revenues forced it to become a monthly) as both readers and contributors defected to the militant and class-conscious trade union paper *Pechatnyi vestnik* (which demonstrated its preeminance by coming out weekly, as *Naborshchik* had previously done). This was a period of profound changes in social relationships in the industry. Before 1903, there had been only isolated instances of printers drawing up lists of demands or going on strike—mainly brief defensive actions against wage reductions or late payments. In the summer and fall of 1903, large numbers of printers, in southern Russia and then in Moscow, took to the streets with long lists of demands for change. But these strikes mainly foreshadowed the more lasting changes that would come only after 9 January 1905. In the wake of Bloody Sunday, strikes, trade unions, a legal labor press, and increasingly frequent encounters in these arenas between workers and socialist intellectuals all became regular facts of life in the industry.

My purpose here is not to explain how these changes in social relations came about—the influence of the wider mobilization of society is clearly central—but to examine their expression in the moral values and judgments voiced by the outspoken and activist workers who were attracted to the social ideal of class struggle.

Class was the prism through which the new vanguard viewed themselves and the world around them, a perception they shared with increasing numbers of their fellow workers. Employers testified to this shift in social attitudes. Workers in the printing industry, they complained, no longer saw themselves and their employers both as "free artists of the printed word," but wished "to be considered 'workers' [*rabochie*], since this is fashionable and up to date."[37] Even type compositors, they noted, no longer seemed to feel part of a common family with employers. As one press owner portrayed this at a meeting of employers in 1905, "There are no longer any real compositors—only hooligans."[38] Radical intellectuals and workers agreed with these observations but admired the change.

---

[36] *Naborshchik*, 20 April 1903, p. 404.
[37] *Naborshchik i pechatnyi mir*, 10 June 1905, pp. 245–46.
[38] *Naborshchik i pechatnyi mir*, 10 May 1905, p. 217.

Workers, they proclaimed, had "awakened from a long and heavy sleep."[39]

This awakening was certainly not universal. Labor leaders complained frequently about the "shameful" persistence of a "slave mentality' among workers.[40] "Despite the events of the past year," the leaders of the Petersburg printers' union commented in September 1905, "very very few among the working class truly understand their position."[41] Too many printing workers, another unionist observed, "still uphold old slavish habits, which are rooted in their flesh and blood, and want to hear nothing about the new."[42] Class-conscious activists were especially dismayed at the persistence of old-fashioned workshop ceremonies in which workers honored their employers with traditional gifts and grateful speeches; and it seemed to add insult to injury when such rituals served to thank employers for agreeing to raise wages in response to a strike.[43] Complaints about the persistence of backward mentalities continued to 1917 and beyond.[44] But even among those workers who *had* awakened to their class identity and interest, older dreams continued to shape the way they thought about "the new."

Many of the workers who comprised the new class-conscious vanguard had taken no part in earlier efforts to build a moral community with employers. The opportunities crated by the 1905 revolution and the changes in attitudes among large numbers of ordinary printers drew out new activists and gave more radical workers, marginalized before 1905, an opportunity to play a more active and visible role. Still, a number of workers who had previously been associated with the class-collaborationist *Naborshchik* did defect. For example, August Tens, once a regular correspondent to *Naborshchik*, bluntly renounced the old dream of social community in a speech in 1905 at the founding meeting for the Petersburg printers' union: "The unity of all printers, from employers to the lowest press helper, about which some dreamers fantasize, is dangerous for the workers. This would be a union of the wolf, the goat, and the cabbage. The goat would eat the cabbage and the wolf devour the goat."[45] The influence of these defectors was considerable. Tens, for example, became the head of the new union. And the new union journal for printing work-

---

[39] *Pechatnyi vestnik*, 14 August 1905, p. 3.

[40] *Pechatnyi vestnik*, 19 February 1906, p. 8.

[41] *Pechatnyi vestnik*, 18 September 1905, p. 3.

[42] *Pechatnyi vestnik*, 28 August 1905, p. 12.

[43] *Vestnik soiuza tipografskikh rabochikh*, August 1905, p. 7; *Naborshchik i pechatnyi mir*, 10 August 1905, pp. 356–57; RGIA, f. 800, op. 1, d. 427, l. 34.

[44] For evidence from diverse trades, see Kleinbort, "Ocherki rabochei demokratii" (part 1), *Sovremennyi mir*, March 1913, pp. 35–36; Shishkin, *Tak skladyvalas'*, pp. 32–33.

[45] *Pechatnyi vestnik*, 12 June 1905, p. 15.

ers, *Pechatnyi vestnik*, was staffed by a number of workers who had once written for *Naborshchik*.

Class was the defining standard of judgment in *Pechatnyi vestnik*, just as the ideal of moral community had defined and continued to define *Naborshchik*. Typical essays promoted class self-reliance, unionization, solidarity among all workers, and democratic political change. Above all, the pages of *Pechatnyi vestnik* were filled with what one manager described as "hatred, enmity, and distrust" toward social superiors.[46] Influencing the construction of this new language of class conflict, especially as socialist intellectuals became more deeply involved in the labor movement, was a Marxist analysis of social structure, productive relations, and class interest. But the influence of moral analysis was more in evidence. These workers employed a language of class protest that tended to be more emotional than analytical, more moralistic than rationalistic. When they articulated the purposes of class struggle, they were likely to represent their social opponents less as "capitalists" definable by their relations to the means of production than as "tyrants" and "bloodsuckers" definable by their moral relations to people.[47] Similarly, whereas many workers accepted the notion of irreconcilable conflict between labor and capital, they appear to have understood this less as a structural conflict of interest between classes than, in their words, a moral battle between good and evil, light and darkness, honor and insult.[48] This opposition between good and evil was not simply a convenient metaphor for class conflict. Together with other familiar values, this essentially moral view of the world helped make class sensible to workers, imbuing conceptions of the class structure with emotional resonance, but also bringing to class thinking older values and principles. The embrace of class consciousness, I would emphasize, was not, for many socially conscious workers, an intellectual rebirth or sudden awakening, as it was often portrayed, but a new emphasis—a rethinking, a recombining of older and newer ideas, and to a significant extent a realization of the subversive logic of older moral views.

The idea of the human person, of *lichnost'*, of innate human worth and hence natural rights, remained at the heart of workers' language of protest in 1905 and after. As before, outspoken workers continued to complain of offenses to workers' human dignity. They protested that for too long workers had been treated as "animals," "machines," and "slaves," "insulted," verbally abused, physically beaten, and addressed as inferiors.[49]

---

[46] *Naborshchik i pechatnyi mir*, 10 October 1905, p. 439.

[47] *Pechatnyi vestnik*, 27 November 1905, p. 6, and 24 July 1905, p. 5.

[48] For example, *Pechatnyi vestnik*, 25 September 1905, p. 1, and 30 October 1905, p. 1.

[49] *Pechatnyi vestnik*, 24 July 1905, p. 5; 31 July 1905, pp. 8–9; 11 September 1905, p. 7; 25 September 1905, p. 1; 10 October 1905, pp. 5–6; *Naborshchik i pechatnyi mir*, 19

The time had come, they said, for employers and supervisors "to respect the humanity in each human being" (*chelovek v cheloveke*), to remember that "those who work for them are people, the same if not better than themselves."[50] As was common among many other groups of workers, and other subordinate groups, injustice was defined first of all as indignity.[51]

Although there were occasional hints of moral reversal—suggestions that workers might be more human than their exploiters—the logical thrust of these criticisms was universalistic. The defining norm remained the worth of the human person. Lev Kleinbort found this value to be so widespread among Russian workers in the years after 1905 as to speak, echoing Emile Durkheim, of a "cult of the human person" (*kul't lichnosti* or *kul't cheloveka*).[52] This ideal became increasingly explicit. Printers, for example, challenged employer paternalism as "degrading" to the "free and independent human personality" of the worker,[53] condemned labor conditions at the workplace as expressions of "arbitrary authority (*proizvol*) and compulsion reigning over the *lichnost'* of man,"[54] and spoke of human rights (*chelovechnye prava*) and even of the "inalienable rights of man and of the citizen" [neot"emlemye prava cheloveka-grazhdanina].[55]

This moral challenge to the existing social order was broad in scope. With this principle in hand, workers sometimes treated even the most everyday economic demands as moral imperatives. Demands for higher wages, shorter hours, paid vacations, Sunday rest, cleaner lavatories, and hot water for tea were portrayed as "declarations of our rights—the rights of man," the right to "live as human beings ought to live." The very *act* of making economic demands was said to be a demonstration that workers "are people too."[56] Conversely, worker militants were often very

---

January 1905, p. 4, and 10 March 1905, pp. 103–5; and *Vecherniaia pochta*, 7 May 1905, p. 2.

[50] *Pechatnyi vestnik*, 7 August 1905, pp. 3–4. See also 15 May 1905, p. 3; 12 June 1905, p. 15; 23 June 1905, pp. 21–23; and 11 September 1905, p. 7.

[51] See also Kleinbort, "Ocherki rabochei demokratii" (part 1), *Sovremennyi mir*, March 1913, pp. 24–25, and (part 5) November 1913, pp. 178–82; and Shishkin, *Tak skladyvalas'*, pp. 46–47, 58–59, 69, 72, 158–61.

[52] Kleinbort, "Ocherki rabochei demokratii" (part 5), *Sovremennyi mir*, November 1913, pp. 182, 185. See also the discussion in Mark D. Steinberg, "Worker Authors and the Cult of the Person," in *Cultures in Flux: Lower-Class Values, Practices, and Resistance in Late-Imperial Russia* (Princeton, 1994).

[53] *Pechatnyi vestnik*, 28 August 1905, p. 8. See also 24 July 1905, p. 4; 14 August 1905, pp. 9–10; 18 September 1905, pp. 5–7; 2 October 1905, pp. 5–7; and 10 October 1905, p. 3.

[54] *Pechatnyi vestnik*, 24 July 1905, p. 5.

[55] *Pechatnyi vestnik*, 27 November 1905, pp. 5–6, and 11 September 1905, pp. 3–4.

[56] *Pechatnyi vestnik*, 12 June 1905, p. 15; 28 August 1905, pp. 2–4; *Pechatnik*, 14 May 1906, p. 13, and 23 July 1905, pp. 6–7; *Vestnik pechatnikov*, 11 June 1906, p. 3. Lenin,

scornful of workers who reduced the meaning of class struggle to mere material needs, to "kopeck interests" (*kopeechnye interesy*).[57]

In the trade union press, supervisors and managers were especially targeted. Here again we see the predominance of moral judgment over class analysis in how these worker activists defined exploitation. Precisely because the relationship of managers and supervisors to workers was more direct than was that of most employers, they had more opportunity to be, as workers writing to union papers often said they were, "rude," "cruel," and "despotic,"[58] and thus were treated to the most severe condemnations as "exploiters," though they did not own the means of production, and thus were less culpable than employers from a Marxist point of view. And since supervisors were usually former workers, it was felt to be doubly offensive that they should "comfortably enjoy themselves at the expense of the workers' blood, squeezing the last drops from their former comrades."[59] Militant workers sought to demonstrate in practice as well the moral bases of their accusations against supervisors, seeking to redress social wrongs in ways that suggested the moral logic that defined them as wrongs. Workers, for example, brought offending supervisors before trade union "courts of honor" (*sudy chesti*), made them apologize before assemblies of workers,[60] or, echoing peasant traditions of enforcing moral norms,[61] shamed them with "rough music"[62] or a "triumphal procession" out of the shop in a wheelbarrow or trashcan.[63]

Notions of offended dignity and violated natural rights gave great emotional and moral force to workers' protests, but also preserved an ambiguous social vision in which class anger coexisted with the ideal of an all-embracing social community. Workers' attraction to the notion that all people are by nature equal spoke not only of class-conscious protest against social subordination but also of a demand for recognition and civic inclusion that undermined class as a standard of judgment.

---

writing in 1899, concluded that this desire for a more "human" life was the central emotional element in all strikes. "O stachkakh," in *Polnoe sobranie sochinenii*, 5th ed. (Moscow, 1960), 4:292.

[57] *Pechatnyi vestnik*, 12 February 1906, pp. 10–11, and 19 February 1906, pp. 2–3. In 1917, this complaint was still heard, though inflation had increased its terms—by then workers were said to view the class struggle largely as a means of getting "big bucks" (*bol'shie rubli*). *Pechatnik*, 6 August 1917, p. 6.

[58] *Pechatnyi vestnik*, 23 June 1905, p. 25; 31 July 1905, p. 8; 14 August 1905, pp. 9–10; 21 August 1905, pp. 9–10; 28 August 1905, pp. 3–5; 18 September 1905, p. 6; and 10 October 1905, pp. 5–6.

[59] *Pechatnyi vestnik*, 31 July 1905, pp. 2–3.

[60] *Kur'er*, 21 May (3 June) 1906, p. 5.

[61] Stephen P. Frank, "Popular Justice, Community, and Culture among the Russian Peasaontry, 1870–1900," *Russian Review* 46 (July 1987): 239–66.

[62] *Golos truda*, 24 June (7 July) 1906, p. 4.

[63] *Pechatnik*, 14 May 1906, p. 16; GARF, f. 6864, op. 1, d. 207, l. 123 (1906).

The ambiguous logic of workers' claims was especially evident in the growing preoccupation among worker-activists, in the printing industry as in others, with raising the "intellectual and moral level" of workers—a phrase that appeared in virtually every trade union charter and in countless journalistic essays. The trade unions that emerged in 1905, among printers as in other industries, invariably declared their commitment to improving the "intellectual, professional, and moral development of printing workers,"[64] and in pursuit of this goal established libraries, reading rooms, and courses, and organized numerous lectures, readings, and excursions.[65] Union leaders, both workers and intellectuals, repeatedly told elected shop representatives that they were responsible as "conscious workers" not simply to collect union dues or represent workers before authority, but to bring less conscious workers "out of the mire of ignorance" by distributing among them "useful books, journals, and newspapers" and arranging lectures and excursions.[66] Although intellectuals undoubtedly encouraged workers' culture-building, worker activists not only willingly took up the banner, but they often waved it more enthusiastically, sometimes provoking intelligentsia criticism for their excessive devotion to *kul'turtregerstvo* (a disdainful term for the promulgation of culture). Too many workers, complained the Menshevik intellectual who had helped to organize the Moscow printers' union, seemed to think that "dances" were as valuable as strikes for the development of class consciousness.[67]

The criticism was accurate. These vanguard workers did indeed tend to see cultural and moral self-consciousness as inseparable from class consciousness. As such, like the communitarian worker-leaders they had supplanted, they were the harshest judges of their fellow workers, furiously condemning the drunkenness, indiscipline, crude manners, and other everyday sins that they saw among the majority. Some activist printers even argued that the *main* goal of labor organization ought to be to fight against "drunkenness and other unseemly behavior."[68] and to promote among workers "sobriety, industry [*trudoliubie*], thrift, and the thirst for knowledge."[69] To a lesser degree, all vanguard workers agreed these were necessary goals.

---

[64] *Pechatnyi vestnik*, 10 October 1905, p. 7; *Vecherniaia pochta*, 30 October 1905, pp. 3–4; *Pechatnik* (Moscow), 21 May 1906, p. 8; TsGIA SPb, f. 287, op. 1, d. 43, ll. 36–37, 147, 157 (St. Petersburg printers' union charters of 1907 and 1910).

[65] *Istoriia leningradskogo soiuza*, pp. 251, 304, 376; *Vestnik pechatnikov*, 21 April 1906, p. 7; GARF, f. 518, op. 1, d. 85a, l. 282; TsGIAgM, f. 2069, op. 1, d. 4, l. 14.

[66] *Pechatnik*, 23 July 1906, p. 14; *Protokoly pervoi vserossiiskoi konferentsii soiuzov rabochikh pechatnogo dela* (St. Petersburg, 1907), p. 11.

[67] *Protokoly*, p. 110. The speaker was V. V. Sher.

[68] *Pechatnyi vestnik*, 18 September 1905, pp. 3–4.

[69] *Pechatnyi vestnik*, 25 August 1905, p. 7.

The workers whose voices predominated in the labor press and at union assemblies launched a sustained assault on many of the everyday habits of working-class life. As part of the widespread effort after 1905 to extend workers' control at the workplace, union activists repeatedly advised shop deputies that it was their duty to make certain that their fellow workers arrived at work on time, were sober, and generally did not "disturb the proper conduct of work." Workplace rules drafted by activist workers in individual shops or proposed by the unions almost always included rules prohibiting coarse or "impolite" language, fighting, singing, playing games, or drinking during working hours, and requiring workers to arrive and leave work at the designated time and allowing absence only with "good reason." Workers guilty of drunkenness or other immoralities were punished with fines, public shaming at meetings or in the union press, or expulsion from the shop.[70]

In the labor press, vanguard workers endlessly scolded their fellow workers for all manner of personal crudeness. Swearing and obscene language, like drunkenness, was said to degrade workers' "dignity," corrupt their "morality," and encourage their "base instincts."[71] Workingmen were chastised, according to the same logic, for the insulting ways they customarily treated women. Women, it was said, "are people too," whose "honor and human dignity" must also be recognized and defended. It was not considered fitting for a conscious worker to habitually "call female workers 'prostitutes' even in the presence of the women themselves" or to treat their own wives as "slaves."[72] This crusade against what worker activists branded "moral vice" was as evident in 1917 as in 1905. In Moscow in July 1917, for example, a group of self-described "conscious workers" at one of the largest printing plants in the city announced that they found the persistent smell of alcohol among some of their fellow workers so offensive that they were organizing a "struggle" against "drunkenness, hooliganism, and debauchery."[73] This moral struggle was no less important, in their eyes, than the struggles against economic and political subordination; indeed, they were seen as inseparable.

So how different were these explicitly class-conscious worker activists from the explicitly class-collaborationist cohort? At the level of ethics,

---

[70] *Vestnik pechatnikov,* 21 April 1906, p. 8; *Pechatnik,* 14 May 1906, p. 14; 4 June 1906, p. 16; and 9 July 1906, p. 15; *Knizhnyi vestnik,* 14 October 1907, p. 1274; V. V. Sher, *Istoriia professional'nogo dvizheniia rabochikh pechatnogo dela v Moskve* (Moscow, 1911), pp. 206–7; GARF, f. 518, op. 1, d. 85a, ll. 142–43; *Istoriia leningradskogo soiuza,* p. 279.

[71] *Zhizn' pechatnika,* 20 July 1907, p. 12; *Istoriia leningradskogo soiuza,* p. 279.

[72] *Zhizn' pechatnika,* 20 July 1907, p. 12; *Vestnik pechatnikov,* 20 May 1906, p. 3; 28 May 1906, pp. 2–3; 15 July 1906, p. 3; *Pechatnik,* 9 July 1906, p. 10; TsGIAgM, f. 2069, op. 1, d. 2, l. 26 (January 1907 general meeting of compositors in Moscow); *Istoriia leningradskogo soiuza,* p. 279.

[73] *Pechatnik,* 6 August 1917, p. 15. See also *Pechatnoe delo,* 4 June 1917, p. 8.

which was central to the outlook of both, fundamental values united them. Both accepted the moral ideals of the larger culture, and both used these to attack dominant practices. Class-conscious workers were sometimes quite explicit about the need to conform to the values of ruling elites. As one worker put it in 1907, capitalists are right when they answer "our heartfelt proletarian cry, 'Allow us to live like human beings,' [with] the malicious and laconic reply: 'Then spend less time contemplating the green signboard [of the state liquor monopoly].' "[74] Conformity to established values was an essential part of the logic of the moral advocacy of both vanguards: if workers wished to be treated as equals of social elites, they must learn to act by their standards.

Moral conformity, however, did not preclude moral subversion. A critical, even class-conscious, reworking of "universal" moral values was, as we have seen, already evident in the ostensibly class-collaborationist writings of workers associated with *Naborshchik*. What was nascent there was full-blown among the workers writing in papers like *Pechatnyi vestnik* in 1905 and after. But the underlying logic was the same. Both groups viewed cultural and moral development as a means of asserting workers' humanity and dignity was human beings. Both groups viewed "drunkenness, ignorance, and darkness" as the stigmata of workers' subordination.[75]

There were significant differences, of course. Class-conscious workers were more explicit in viewing the struggle to overcome these moral evils as acts of resistance, and they were more socially self-reliant. They were also more openly utilitarian in appropriating moral norms. Drunkenness, for example, was defined as an evil especially because it hindered the class struggle by distracting workers from the movement, "obscuring class consciousness," and generally "delighting our enemies." Cultural backwardness and moral indiscipline were blamed for making workers "passive," "apathetic," "undisciplined," "lacking in hope," and unable to "stand up for their interests."[76]

There were some ways in which class-conscious workers articulated original moral values. Most important, class consciousness itself was treated as a moral principle. "Toadyism" before authority was condemned as "shameful" behavior reflecting the mentality of "slaves" and "sheep."[77] The idea that workers should act collectively to further their

---

[74] *Pechatnoe delo*, 9 February 1907, p. 7.
[75] *Pechatnoe delo*, 9 February 1907, p. 7; *Pechatnik*, 6 August 1917, pp. 5–6.
[76] *Pechatnik*, 23 April 1906, pp. 11–12; *Pechatnoe delo*, 9 February 1907, p. 7; *Protokoly*, pp. 80, 82, 109. For nearly identical examples from 1917, see *Pechatnoe delo*, 4 June 1917, p. 8, and 17 June 1917, p. 7, and *Pechatnik*, 6 August 1917, pp. 5–7, 15, and 28 October 1917, p. 8.
[77] For example, *Pechatnyi vestnik*, 19 February 1906, p. 8.

interests was treated as a moral duty. And workers who violated collective decisions, such as not joining a strike or working unauthorized overtime, were publicly threatened by union leaders with "contempt, boycott, and ostracism."[78] These were suggestive probings in the direction of moral innovation—drawing to some extent on popular traditions of communal solidarity, and especially on customary notions of "comradeship' among workers.[79] But this was still far from a separate class morality, an idea that Marxist intellectuals were already advocating. That the proletariat might be more ethical in practice than the bourgeoisie was quite plausible—but the standard of measurement had to be the same. The whole point was to expose the hypocrisy of those in power, not to relativize their behavior as right by a different morality.

In the thinking of these vanguard workers—both the explicitly class-conscious and the explicitly class-collaborationist—we see a persistently ambiguous mixing of morality and class, of universal and particularistic values, of moral deference and moral protest. The idea that workers had a natural right to "live as human beings" remained simultaneously conformist and subversive. It implied a definition of self based on the notion of a common humanity rather than on the variety of social place. At the same time, its very universalism helped workers to identify their own separate identity as a class. Recognition of the worth and rights of all people encouraged workers to become conscious of their own particular sufferings, encouraging workers to generalize in reverse, as it were, from the dignity of all persons to their own particular class humiliation.

[78] *Vecherniaia pochta*, 9 November 1905, p. 3.
[79] For a discussion of these traditions in printing workshops, see Steinberg, *Moral Communities*, chap. 3.

3

Heather Hogan

Class Formation in the St. Petersburg Metalworking Industry: From the "Days of Freedom" to the Lena Goldfields Massacre

In the years 1912–14, labor protest exploded in the metalworking industry of St. Petersburg. I argue that this extraordinary activism was shaped by a series of events in the aftermath of the October Manifesto of 1905, which created a context in which metalworkers increasingly chose to define themselves in class terms. In this process of class formation three sites of political conflict were especially important: at the point of production, as reflected in the collapse of managerial authority over the course of 1905, but most especially during the "days of freedom"; at the municipal level, as highlighted by the struggle between the Council of the Unemployed and the St. Petersburg City Duma over a program of public works, but which raised a series of community issues more generally; and in the workers' curias, as manifested in the elections for the State Duma in 1906.

However obvious it may be, I would emphasize that these conflicts occurred in a historically specific context; that is, in the highly charged atmosphere of early 1906 in St. Petersburg, which was characterized, among other things, by a fearful urban elite and the significant and growing wrath of the proletariat. It was a context, moreover, that permitted workers who experienced particular defeats (for example, on the shop floor, with the city duma) to interpret them as part of a larger defeat—a rejection by the state, their employers, and ultimately "society" of a host of demands articulated over the course of 1905. Also important in defining this context was the interaction between metalworkers and radical intellectuals and the particular language and ways of thinking that workers came to adopt. Although a small number of metalworkers had imbibed a Marxist discourse since the 1890s, and a few even earlier, it was not until the mass political activism of 1905 that significant numbers were exposed to these categories of analysis. For many metalworkers, this "new" way of thinking helped them make sense of their experiences between 1905 and 1917; and however much labor organizations were constrained by police and employers in the "years of reaction," nonetheless the labor press, the duma forum, the clubs of enlightenment, and the trade unions routinely advanced a broadly Marxist construction of contemporary reality and metalworkers routinely absorbed it.

From the Days of Freedom to the Summer Strikes of 1906

The weeks from October 17 until the bombardment of the Presnia district in Moscow on December 16 were known as the "days of freedom." It was then that Petersburg metalworkers and others sought to exercise their newly won civil rights by meeting freely, speaking openly, and reading an uncensored press. And it was then that metalworkers sought to implement these new rights directly at the point of production. Insofar as they wished to discuss their political or economic needs, they talked with their comrades or gathered by the thousands in the cafeterias and courtyards of their factories.[1] And insofar as they feared the mobilization of the right, they appropriated factory materials to forge weapons and organized "fighting detachments" for self-defense.[2] So they might have time to pursue civic freedoms, they fought to reduce the length of the workday, thus launching a struggle for the eight-hour day soon after the return to work on October 21.[3]

Employers experienced this six-week period as an unprecedented assault on their authority. In what they must have considered an all-enveloping chaos, they witnessed ceaseless meetings and violations of shop discipline, the crafting of weapons, walkouts after eight hours, and a seemingly unhindered stream of revolutionary rhetoric from social democrats and inflammatory proclamations from the St. Petersburg soviet. Top managers regularly heard remarkable reports from the shops: workers came to the factory only to talk politics, read newspapers, and in every possible way show their contempt for administrators, while the alarming incidence of physical

[1] Key documentary collections for the October–December period paint a picture of repeated meetings and spontaneous work stoppages for all sorts of reasons. See *Petersburgskie bol'sheviki v period pod"ema pervoi Russkoi revoliutsii, 1905–1907 gg. Sbornik dokumentov i materialov* (Leningrad, 1955), pp. 348–432, 500–538 and passim; and *Vysshii pod"em revoliutsii 1905–1907 gg. Vooruzhennye vosstaniia, noiabr'-dekabr' 1905 goda* (Moscow, 1955), pp. 345–525 and passim (hereafter cited as *VPR*).

[2] For one report among many on the arming of workers, see *Peterburgskie bol'sheviki*, pp. 513–14.

[3] The Semiannikovtsy were the first to act; they were followed on October 27–28 by most other factories in the Nevskii district. On October 29, the Soviet directed all workers to implement the eight-hour day beginning on October 31. *Ocherki istorii Leningrada* (Moscow-Leningrad, 1956), 3:336–37 (hereafter cited as *OIL* by volume and page).

assault on lower-level supervisory personnel reflected only too painfully the degree to which the prestige and authority of shop personnel had fallen.[4]

Industrialists were profoundly disturbed by both the political and economic implications of this crisis of labor discipline. For the continuing unrest in the factories after the October Manifesto discredited the arguments of those employers who had sought to distract workers from their economic demands by proposing instead that the labor protest was caused by dissatisfaction with the existing political order. During the days of freedom it became clear that the workers were fighting for substantive economic and social change as well as for substantive political change.

At the same time, the real cost of labor's "economic" demands came into sharper focus, since a cluster of issues surrounded the shortening of the workday. Worker efforts to "legislate" on their own the length of the workday represented a direct challenge to managerial authority. Moreover, the eight-hour day raised the problem of labor productivity and therefore entailed major questions of labor discipline, the organization of work processes, and the level of mechanization pertaining in the shops, questions made all the more vexing given the current state of the economy. In sum, precisely those economic and political issues of greatest moment to employers were challenged by the actions of labor: metalworkers spearheaded the eight-hour-day movement and constituted the backbone of the St. Petersburg soviet, which in the "days of freedom" behaved like a revolutionary government in embryo.

Meeting on November 1, representatives of seventy-two metalworking factories resolved that shortening the workday was impossible and that if workers persisted, factories would be closed. On November 7, the state took the lead by locking out workers at its Baltic, Obukhov, and other facilities; by November 16, tens of thousands of workers, the majority metalworkers, had been thrown out.[5]

The concerted actions of state and private industry soon broke the eight-hour-day strike movement. And although the soviet endeavored to regain the offensive with a dramatic proclamation, indicting the regime as provocateur and attacking the alliance between the government and the bourgeoisie, it had nonetheless sustained a major defeat.[6] Petersburg metalworkers now had to contend with mass unemployment as manufacturers utilized the unrest as a pretext to "filter" out "untrustworthy" workers. Moreover, the repressive actions of employers were facilitated

---

[4] LGIA, f. 1304, op. 1, d. 2691, l. 164 contains numerous reports on the decline of foremen's authority at the Baltic factory in the last months of 1905.

[5] OIL 3:352–53; S. Livshits, "Bor'ba za 8-chasovoi rabochii den' v Peterburge v. 1905 goda," *Krasnaia letopis'*, 1925, no. 4:131–35.

[6] For the Soviet's declaration, see *Peterburgskie bol'sheviki*, pp. 50–51.

by the cutbacks in state purchasing that attended the end of the Russo-Japanese War and the worsening economic situation.

The crisis of labor discipline that had emerged with such clarity in the "days of freedom" impelled employers and the state to scrutinize closely the assumptions that had guided their understanding of labor-management conflict. On 9–10 December 1905, the Naval Ministry closed its Baltic, Obukhov, and Izhorskii plants for what would turn out to be a seven-week period. With an almost palpable sense of exhaustion, the directors made clear that ongoing unrest made "normal work" impossible, especially since the upcoming holiday season promised still further interruptions.[7] Thus the repeated work stoppages, the seemingly endless meetings of workers, the assaults on supervisory personnel, the intense struggle surrounding the eight-hour day—had taken its toll on management.

Such was the background for discussion of a number of management studies conducted at Baltic and Obukhov. These reports stressed that wage policies were inconsistent and had failed to motivate workers; that the role and authority of foremen was ambiguous at best, confused and arbitrary at worst; that uniform regulations governing labor-management relations were largely absent; and that overall, the lines of authority were tangled. Problems in these areas were also judged to have contributed to high costs and low productivity, as had technical obsolescence and the deterioration of physical plant. In the aftermath of 1905, some of management came to see that the crisis in labor discipline was not only the result of a struggle for authority between management and an insubordinate workforce, it was also the result of the frustrations caused by fundamentally disorganized shops, outmoded equipment and production processes, woefully inadequate accounting procedures, and wage policies that failed to instill discipline.[8]

Over the course of the next several years, state plants reorganized wage policy and shop-floor practices in a number of ways. Meanwhile, a series of strikes occurring between June and August 1906 at several mid-sized machine construction plants of the capital[9] suggested that some private

---

[7] *Peterburgskie bol'sheviki*, p. 521. See also Gross's remarks to his workers on 2 December 1905. M. M. Mikhailov, "1905 god na Izhorskom zavode," *Krasnaia letopis'*, 1932, no. 1–2:247.

[8] LGIA, f. 1267, op. 1, d. 1701, ll. 76–90, 92–1030b, and f. 1304, op. 1, d. 2691. I discuss these archival materials in greater detail in my dissertation, "Labor and Management in Conflict: The St. Petersburg Metal Working Industry, 1900–1914" (Ph.D. diss., University of Michigan, 1981), esp. chap. 4.

[9] These were the Erikson Telephone Factory, the Atlas Engineering Works, the Lemmerikh Engineering Factory, Langenzipen and Company, and the Kreiton Shipyards and Engineering Works in Okhta.

employers had already moved to implement similar changes in workplace organization. In important respects, these strikes reflected a struggle to exert worker control over aspects of the work process and life on the shop floor that management had sought to alter.

The strikes at the Erikson Telephone and the Atlas Engineering plants began with clashes over issues of hiring and firing. In both cases, workers tried to cart out offensive personnel; management forthwith fired the culprits, but the workers responded by refusing to fill the jobs of their dismissed comrades. Unable to replace the needed workers, the Erikson management imposed a partial layoff; the Atlas management announced a complete shutdown.[10] What followed at Erikson and Atlas, but also at the other mid-sized machine-construction factories on strike in the summer of 1906, was the presentation of a range of demands that reflected the changing terms of struggle in the second period of the 1905–7 revolution, as well as the deployment of new tactics by both labor and management in an effort to win conflicts that were fought with exceptional tenacity.

At Erikson, workers responded to the partial layoffs by refusing all piecework and deliberately slowing output while on shop pay (*po tsekhu*); by imposing a partial strike in the assembly, warehouse and packing shops to block shipment of finished goods; and by a "go-slow" action among those workers who had been dismissed but were still on the job thanks to the two-week notification period required by the state. Eriksontsy also called upon the woodworkers' and metalworkers' unions for help. With the formation of a strike committee, workers advanced a further set of demands, which included a nine-hour workday with an hour and a half for lunch, the replacement of hourly with daily shop pay with Saturday to count as a full day, payment during working hours, the clear placement of a table of rates on piecework in each shop, pay for strike time, and amnesty for the strike.[11]

At Atlas, the announcement of a shutdown was also met by a "go-slow" action during the two-week notification period. And here, too, workers turned to the union. Frustrated by the continuing boycott on selected jobs and rejecting out of hand negotiations through the metalworkers' union, the administration closed the factory a few days prior to the end of the notification period. Workers responded by blockading the

---

[10] For accounts of the conflict at Erikson, see *Prizyv*, 21 April 1906, p. 2.; *Rabochii po metallu*, 10 October 1906, p. 6; TsGIA, f. 150, op. 1, d. 655, ll. 31–40, 121, in part reprinted in *Vtoroi period revoliutsii, 1906–1907 gody, Mai–Sentiabr 1906 goda* (Moscow, 1961), pp. 289–91 (henceforth cited as *VPRMS*). On the Atlas strike, see *Rabochii po metallu*, 30 August 1906, pp. 6–7; *Golos truda*, 4 July 1906, p. 3; TsGIA, f. 150, op. 1, d. 655, ll. 12–16a, in part reprinted in *VPRMS*, pp. 276–77.

[11] TsGIA, f. 150, op. 1, d. 655, ll. 32–34; *VPRMS*, p. 290.

entire factory; picket lines were set up that blocked not only employee access but also the shipment of finished goods. Again with the strike in progress, workers articulated further demands: a reduction of the work day to nine hours, daily rather than hourly shop pay, several specific wage demands, including one for a general increase of 30 percent in rates and base pay, recognition of a grievance committee, abolition of fines and overtime, and polite forms of address.[12]

Conflicts at Kreiton, Langenzipen, and Lemmerikh turned, variously, on issues of hiring and firing, pay cuts, attempts by workers to intervene in the determination of wage policies, and management efforts to intensify the work process.[13] Taken together, these five strikes were essentially defensive in nature and sought to protest "unfair" treatment, cuts in wages, or to reverse changes in the forms and methods of remuneration that worked to labor's disadvantage. In seeking to block the shift to hourly in place of daily shop pay and to retain full payment for the Saturday half-holiday when work ended at 2 or 3 in the afternoon (and by implication, the many pre-holidays that pertained over the course of the year), workers tried not only to maintain former levels of earning, but to forestall important changes in wage policy intended by management to recoup some of the economic losses of 1905 and to instill in workers a greater sense of time discipline. Moreover, workers tried to shape the social environment of the shop through interventions that removed personnel who had in some way wronged them and by demands for polite forms of address. At issue for workers was an insistence on dignified and humane treatment; for management, worker involvement in issues of hiring and firing, much less the carting out of supervisory personnel, encroached on the effective rights of private property and threatened or in fact entailed clearly illegal acts of violence against persons and property.

Control issues were also reflected in worker attempts to influence the pace of work by demanding the restoration of daily pay, by contesting a reduction in "extra" hands and any requirement that workers operate more than one machine tool at a time, by protesting overtime, and by

[12] *VPRMS*, pp. 276–77; TsGIA, f. 150, op. 1, d. 655, l. 16a. Although the lack of archival material prevents a detailed discussion of the underlying determinants of the Atlas strike, evidence from a later period leaves little doubt that the Atlas management was in the midst of a major reorganization of accounting procedures, and perhaps production processes, at the time of the strike. In a lecture series sponsored by the Society of Technologists in the spring of 1912, A. F. German reported on the implementation of accounting and organizational reforms at his factory. See "Organizatsiia zavodoupravleniia," special supplement to *Vestnik obshchestva tekhnologov*, no. 11 (1912): 30–49.

[13] On Kreiton, see TsGIA, f. 150, op. 1, d. 655, ll. 18–21, in part reprinted in *VPRMS*, pp. 283–84; *Rabochii po mentallu*, 22 September 1906, pp. 6–7, and 10 October 1906, p. 7. On Langenzipen see *Golos truda*, 6 July 1906, p. 3; *Rabochii po mentallu*, 30 August 1906, p. 6; and TsGIA, f. 150, op. 1, d. 655, l. 24, reprinted in *VPRMS*, pp. 266–67. And on Lemmerikh see TsGIA, f. 150, op. 1, d. 655, ll. 29–30, reprinted in *VPRMS*, p. 285.

challenging management generally over the issue of time by seeking a reduction in hours. For management, the problem turned on gaining control over labor productivity, and at least in part, employers sought to do so by manipulating forms of remuneration. Like their counterparts at the state factories, they hoped to achieve a more disciplined and productive work force through such "capitalist" incentives to hard work as monetary inducement.[14] But in so doing, management was encroaching on what labor viewed as an acceptable—humane—pace of work.

Workers, furthermore, sought to press on management new institutional forms for the regulation of industrial relations: they called for an organized representation of their interests through the trade unions; they sought the effective right to strike; and they demanded grievance committees and worker participation in wage determination. At issue here was the creation of a new institutional matrix for labor-management relations based on the presumption of equality of the sides. Also at issue was labor's newly won right to strike and form trade unions and how management now felt compelled to interpret and modify these rights.

That labor and management were confronting each other for the first time as organized social forces (in the form of the Petersburg Society of Mill and Factory Owners [henceforth PSMFO] and the Petersburg metalworkers' union) also contributed to the intensity of the struggle. Doubtless in part because of the exceptionally unstable environment pertaining in the spring and summer of 1906, each organization confused perception and reality in their respective evaluations of the strength, cohesion, and resources of the other side. Just as labor focused on the proliferation of employer organizations, their mobilization at the time of the November lockouts, and such ostensibly powerful national associations as the Congress of Industry and Trade, employers shuddered at the multiplication of worker organizations, the emergence of a Central Bureau of Trade Unions, and the unionization of some 9,500 "militant" metalworkers in the space of just three months. In fact these summer conflicts revealed significant internal weaknesses and a quite notable lack of unity; indeed, these organizations were only just in the process of formation.[15] None-

---

[14] Work paid by the hour, rather than by the day, permitted employers to calculate wages more exactly in relationship to the time actually expended. Hourly pay therefore discouraged workers from lateness in the morning and after lunch and, it was hoped, provided a disincentive to demands for a reduction in the length of the workday. For a discussion of wage reform at the state plants, see my *Forging Revolution: Metal Workers, Managers and the State in St. Petersburg, 1890–1914* (Bloomington, Ind., 1993), chap. 5.

[15] The PSMFO submitted statutes for registration with the *gradonachal'nik* (city governor) on 27 June 1906; one object of a long memorandum to P. A. Stolypin, minister of Internal Affairs, on August 19 was to protest the delay in the legalization of the PSMFO, a process that should have been completed within a month's time. The organizers for the metalworkers' union submitted statutes for registration on April 11; the founding congress of the union occurred on April 30.

theless, both sides displayed a readiness to represent the antagonist as conscious of his class interests, coherently organized in pursuit of his goals and politically aggrandizing. Thus the PSMFO's facile identification "of the so-called trade unions" with militant organizations "pursuing revolutionary goals," and its consistent refusal to accept the unions as legitimate bargaining agents for "their" workers became central points in employer argumentation and practice in this period (*VPRMS*, p. 295). Hence, too, the tendency of both labor and management to cast the conflict in absolute terms—in terms of the "principles" at stake—which encouraged each side to reject compromise out of hand.

The summer strikes therefore tended to generate new methods of struggle—work slowdowns, boycotts on jobs and work orders, picketing, and work stoppages in selected shops.[16] These tactics depended on a high degree of labor solidarity and on a willingness to utilize their knowledge of and control over the process of production. Employers saw in such tactics an intentionality heretofore absent in labor protest; and they now asserted that such tactically sophisticated methods had little in common with the spontaneous, elemental nature of labor protest they judged characteristic of the previous year.[17]

The new and threatening tactics of labor helped push employers and the PSMFO into an aggressive campaign to break the strikes and the union with blacklists and lockouts, strikebreakers and police intervention, by manipulating the judicial process, and by appealing to Stolypin. At issue from industry's point of view were the effective rights of private property,[18] the corrosive effects of the violent and revolutionary actions of "working class leaders" on the mass, and the financial viability of their enterprises, indeed the well-being of the entire industrial economy.[19] By invoking images of anarchy, the collapse of industry, and the perilous consequences of an enormous army of unemployed workers, employers pleaded with the government to recognize the challenge it confronted.

What begins to emerge at this juncture is a particular aspect of the trauma experienced by Petersburg employers over the spring and summer of 1906. For however fundamental the issues of worker control and the institutional matrix for labor-management relations may have been, these concerns were ultimately transcended by how the summer conflicts threat-

---

[16] It is also worth noting that Atlas workers resolved not to disperse to the countryside, not to take jobs elsewhere, and not to drink alcoholic beverages for the duration of the strike. *Golos truda*, 7 July 1906, p. 4.

[17] See the August 19 memorandum to Stolypin in *VPRMS*, pp. 291–95.

[18] Note the language and argumentation of an appellate brief filed by the Langenzipen Company on 22 August 1906 regarding a case first heard in the lower courts in November 1905. TsGIA, f. 150, op. 1, d. 660, l. 10.

[19] Again, the August 19 memorandum richly illustrates employer attitudes. *VPRMS*, pp. 291–95.

ened management's notion of what constituted appropriate and legitimate worker behavior. Here, in short, was an expression of the profound social fear gripping all of "society" in 1906, but played out in the specific context of the metalworking industry at a time when both workers and managers were trying to understand the changing terms of struggle. Thus it became imperative for employers to articulate how "radical" behavior on the shop floor was inimical to social order, to somehow specify the difference between "legitimate" economic grievances and what had occurred over the past two years.

The employers began by arguing that something had indeed changed. Dating the "new phase" in the workers movement from mid-April and specifically locating its expression at four machine-construction factories (Erikson, Lemmerikh, Atlas, Kreiton), they noted that the current conflicts usually began with incidents involving violence against supervisory personnel and asserted that the strikes—and most especially the development of new tactics—represented an attempt by worker leaders to regain influence over the working class that had been lost since the failure of the eight-hour-day movement in the fall. But in no way revealing that specific policy changes enacted by management had contributed to the outbreak of the strikes or that employer behavior had altered in any way, the PSMFO charged that working-class leaders "intentionally" launched strikes at carefully chosen factories, and raised "deliberately" excessive demands that the respective managements could not fulfill (*VPRMS*, pp. 291–95). At issue, it seems, was the very fact of organization, intentionality, "consciousness" if you will. Workers seemed "to know" what they were doing; and in employers' eyes, the purpose was to undermine the entire social edifice: "With iron consistency the leaders of the workers movement are pushing toward this [the collapse of industry and an enormous number of impoverished unemployed], and the whole question consists in whether or not the factories and plants can hold out until the renewal [*obnovlenie*] of state life and the cessation of anarchy" (p. 294).

In this apocalyptic vision, "rational" assessments of the costs of labor's demands were less the issue than social control, particularly so in the charged atmosphere of 1906 when accepted norms of authority seemed to be crumbling. For as the PSMFO noted with considerable alarm, what *was* to happen if workers could commit acts of terror with seeming impunity when the capital was under a state of emergency? (p. 295). In this context, therefore, the assault on supervisory personnel and the insistence on polite forms of address took on added point. Demands for respectful treatment clearly illustrated labor's "coming of age"—its rejection of relations of subordination and the infantalization that the continued use of *ty* (thou) implied. And in ways that must have seemed wholly unnerving to management, workers lashed out at former authority figures. Thus with a palpable sense of affront, a top executive at Langenzipen wrote to the PSMFO in July that his workers had been "informed that 'demands,' as well as the participation of [their] representatives, would not be recognized"; moreover, he reported that he intended to dismiss a worker who had "conduct[ed] himself especially impertinently [*derzko*]" (p. 267).

Just as surely as management would countenance no "demands" and no worker participation in wage determination, it would abide no impudence. Incensed and threatened by the "insolence and bad conduct," managers thus equated (and confused) labor's assault on their own particular notions of authority with any and all *organized* and/or collective expressions of labor's grievances.[20] Similarly, the PSMFO repeatedly equated worker tactics with acts of "terror," and then argued that the government had to provide effective protection for the factories as well as legal status for their employer organization. Only in this way might industry "hold out" until "state life" was restored and anarchy quelled (*VPRMS*, pp. 294–95).

In the end, metalworkers and their union were defeated in these bitterly contested strikes. In hard-fought conflicts lasting up to two months, workers suffered complete failure or secured extremely modest concessions.[21] Unlike the settlements of 1905 in which concessions were made by management and compromise decisions were reached, the summer strikes of 1906 were almost without exception victories for employers and thereby illustrated the greater willingness and ability of industrialists to pursue an intransigent course. Moreover, to the degree that the summer strikes turned on issues of worker control, they illustrated a widening of the sphere of conflict on the shop floor: workers were now contesting management's proprietary "right" to define the essential conditions of labor unilaterally. The summer strikes thus confronted employers with what they now interpreted as new and more threatening forms of labor protest.

---

[20] In an appellate suit brought by the Langenzipen firm in August 1906, management argued on the basis of point 4, article 105, of the *Ustav o promyshlennosti* that because of the "insolence and bad conduct of the worker" [derzost' i durnoe povedenie rabochago], the personnel and/or property of the factory had been endangered and therefore the employer had the right to dismiss the worker immediately without two weeks' notification and payment of wages. The brief asserted that the conflict involved the workers and foreman of the instrument shop alone. Workers in other shops had no cause to demand the foreman's dismissal; that they did so indicated the existence of "agitation" and "worker organization." Further, "these organizations" were directly interested in expanding an issue that concerned only a small group of workers to the workers of the entire factory and in so doing pursued "general political interests" and not the interests of the narrower group. See TsGIA, f. 150, op. 1, d. 660, ll. 8–11. The issue thus appeared to be organization per se; and the very demand to remove the foreman was judged to constitute insolence on the part of workers. Tellingly, employers relied in their argumentation on an archaic statute ("insolence and bad conduct of the worker") on a point of law that far more readily mirrored the relations of social deference than contractual relations built on social equality.

[21] On strike outcomes, see "Labor and Management in Conflict," pp. 365–67.

More motivated than in the past to scrutinize closely the patterns that structured life on the shop floor, they sought strategies that would secure managerial control over production processes all too vulnerable to interventions by labor.

Important, then, in understanding developments between late 1905 and mid 1906 were the changing terms of struggle on the shop floor. The authority of supervisory personnel had declined substantially; the confidence of management in extant structures of control had been shaken seriously. In an effort to reclaim control and the unhindered exercise of their authority, management began to experiment with changes in work practices. First at Baltic and Obukhov, then at a handful of private plants, and finally more generally through the industry over the next several years, employers undertook a process of workplace rationalization. As they did, relations between labor and management continued to shift and issues of power and control emerged more clearly.

The Unemployed Movement in 1906

The dominant reality for Petersburg metalworkers in the weeks following the arrest of the Soviet and the shelling of the Presnia district was unemployment. The massive lockout of November, the closure of the state plants in December and January, and the punitive "filtrovka" taking place throughout the private sector left thousands of metalworkers on the streets. Already in the fall of 1905, the Soviet of Workers' Deputies had established a commission on unemployment to help those locked out in the November struggles. But like the soviet itself, the activities of this group were soon halted by police repression. Some public organizations set up soup kitchens and some employed workers tried to help through voluntary deductions from their pay; nonetheless the needs of the jobless continued to mount over the winter months. During March, many of the workers who now routinely spent the day at soup kitchens began to mobilize and were joined by a few sympathetic party organizers.[22] Doubtless relying on earlier experience, they decided to elect deputies on the formula of two per soup kitchen, and on March 22, some thirty such deputies

---

[22] On the rather minimal party involvement in this movement and the nonfractional nature of it, see the comments of Vladimir S. Voitinskii, *Peterburgskii sovet bezrabotnykh, 1906–1907*, Russian Institute Occasional Papers, Columbia University (New York, 1969), pp. 4–5 (hereafter cited as *Psb*), and Petr Garvi, *Zapiski Sotsial Demokrata* (Newtonville, Mass.: Oriental Research Partners, 1982), p. 86. Malyshev's tendentious pamphlet, on the other hand, claims the primacy of the Bolsheviks throughout the movement of the unemployed. See Sergei Malyshev, *Unemployed Councils in St. Petersburg in 1906* (San Francisco: Proletarian Publishers, n.d.).

convened the first session of the St. Petersburg Council of the Unemployed.

Over the course of the next several weeks, a number of crucial decisions were made. The leaders of the council recognized the need to broaden the base of their movement and sought to establish ties to the factories and to those who still worked. Thirty more deputies were elected to the central body, and district councils were organized to link the employed with the unemployed. Equally important was sorting out a strategy that properly defined the arena of struggle. Because workers had just suffered defeat on the national level and the issues surrounding unemployment transcended the individual factory, the council resolved to focus on the municipal level. The specific needs of the unemployed also led in this direction, for as demands were articulated it became clear that fundamental community issues were at stake: the unemployed urgently needed assistance for food, rent, city pawnshop payments, and hospital fees. Most of all, the unemployed needed work. The council therefore sought a program of public works and mobilized to confront the city duma.[23]

On 12 April 1906, thirty representatives of the Council of the Unemployed converged on the city duma. The town councillors proved initially responsive, at least in part because the capital's press had been carrying frightening reports about "the forty thousand unemployed and the hundred thousand starving" and raising questions about the well-being of the urban population should hunger and social distress go unattended.[24] The city fathers quickly established a commission to develop plans for public works. Agreeing to allocate 500,000 rubles to the unemployed—175,000 rubles for immediate relief, the remainder for public works—and even acceding to the demand that an equal number of worker representatives be seated on the commission, the *dumtsy* appeared remarkably conciliatory.[25]

The apparent ease with which the duma responded to the representatives of the unemployed was doubtless conditioned by the profound and deepening social fear that had engulfed society in the wake of the fall crisis and which had grown more intense during the unsettling months surrounding the first State Duma. As the unemployed fully realized, social fear lubricated the discussions in the city duma. "Society," to quote one

[23] Malyshev, *Unemployed Councils*, pp. 15–16; *Prizyv*, 18 April 1906, p. 1; Voitinskii, *Psb*, pp. 4–5, 7–9; and *Rech'*, 25 April 1906, p. 4. See also the report of the St. Petersburg Council of Unemployed on its activities through May in *Vpered!* 31 May 1906, as reprinted in *VPRMS*, pp. 231–34.

[24] According to the subsequent recollections of the principle organizer of the Council of Unemployed, Vladimir Voitinskii, the capital's press inflated the number of jobless in the winter months of 1906. See Voitinskii, *Psb*, pp. 11–12.

[25] Malyshev, *Unemployed Councils*, pp. 21–26; Voitinskii, *Psb*, pp. 13–15. See also *VPRMS*, pp. 232–33.

of their leaflets, "was frightened by the possibility of an explosion of popular rage."[26] But it was not only apprehension about food riots, epidemic disease, or the prospect of a wave of urban crime; it was rather, an overarching anxiety over the uncertainties that still attended the political situation. Institutional flux, political instability, and what was perceived to be social chaos shaped the thinking of urban and rural elites in the spring and summer of 1906. Reflective of this pervasive unease were the thoughts that A. A. Polovtsev, an appointed member to the reformed State Council, recorded in his diary on July 5:

> The newspapers are covered with news of plunder, armed robbery, and murder; the State Duma lays claim to the role of a national convention. . . . It sends its agents in all directions to organize an armed uprising. . . . The government has failed to display energetic measures; the army has become so corrupted that even the Preobrazhenskii regiment, which stands closest to the sovereign, has gone over to the side of the revolutionaries; it is difficult to walk along the streets because of the pursuit and attack of the unemployed and the so-called hooligans; threatening clouds are gathering from all sides.[27]

Social antagonisms were expressed just as sharply in the discourse of the unemployed movement. Most dramatic was the articulation of a loose but portentous linkage between diverse segments of the urban well-to-do (census society) and the capital's industrial bourgeoisie. Wrote Sergei Petrov (Vladimir Voitinskii) about the confrontational meeting with the dumtsy on April 12:

> Workers remember that none of these gentlemen lifted a finger to mitigate the calamity of unemployment while the unemployed silently endured their situation. Or didn't the "city fathers" know that 40,000 workers in Petersburg sat with their families without a piece of bread and were starving? They could not but know this, since they themselves and those close to them sacked these workers from the very factories and mills they themselves own, evicted these families from the very houses they themselves own, threw them onto the street, deprived them of food and shelter.[28]

---

[26] *VPRMS*, p. 232. Reporting on several immediate measures recommended by the duma's commission on the unemployed, *Rech'* noted that these steps were required not only out of "philanthropic [considerations], but also out of considerations of social order." *Rech'*, 23 April 1906, p. 5.

[27] "Dnevnik A. A. Polovtseva (15 September 1905–10 August 1906; 5 March–2 May 1908)," *Krasnyi Arkhiv* 4 (1923): 116. I am grateful to Frank Wcislo for pointing out this material to me.

[28] *Prizyv*, 12 April 1906, p. 1. Or elsewhere: "But you yourselves know, comrades, how well the city takes into consideration our worker needs. Bosses [Khoziaeva]-capitalists, who control city business, will not lift a finger . . ." (p. 1).

By identifying the city fathers with the industrial bourgeoisie, the un-employed explicitly broadened the definition of the forces arrayed against the workers' movement. Conflicts that had heretofore been confined to the industrial community (albeit with the frequent intervention of the au-tocratic regime) were now expanded into a more complex and differen-tiated, but in the end deeply polarized urban community. Over the course of 1906, class and community were thus linked in new ways; and as new conflicts were joined, all involved were unavoidably forced to view power, privilege, class, and estate from a different perspective. In its reconcep-tualization of the "enemy" the Petersburg unemployed movement fore-shadowed one of the structuring realities of 1917—a conflict in which "they" (census society, but also and equally bourgeois society) were pitted against "us" (the urban *nizy* [lower strata], but also and equally the work-ing class).

Identifying "them" also contributed to a clearer definition of "us." In the struggles with the city duma over aid to the unemployed a set of attitudes was articulated that reflected the tension between workers and other segments of urban society. Thus as representatives of the unem-ployed were quick to point out, "the flower of duma liberalism" proved able to allocate funds swiftly for immediate needs, but considerably less able to implement programs of public works.[29] These hand-outs were merely charity, fully consistent with long-established relations of social dominance and subordination. But as the unemployed never tired of stressing, they wanted work not charity.[30] In their eyes, a program of public works was the central demand in their petition to the city duma on April 12; assistance with food and rent was simply an advance until work began. This insistence on jobs not charity reflected a sense of the dignity and self-worth of an autonomous individual: a job was the only appropriate way for a worker to provide for himself and his family.[31] Moreover, workers were entitled to employment from the city duma, not only by virtue of their membership in the urban community but because their current plight was the result of political reprisals. As one leaflet put it: "In view of the fact that many of us are deprived of work because we tried to gain freedom for the entire people, we demand from the city duma of Petersburg immediate work, we demand that those millions in public

---

[29] The phrase comes from Voitinskii, *Psb*, p. 18. The unemployed were to be exempted from paying certain local rates; unredeemed property in municipal pawnshops was not to be sold before June 21, fines for arrears on interest were to be canceled and payment of interest suspended for three months; monies were to be released for food, rent, and to underwrite interest payments at private pawnshops. Malyshev, *Unemployed Councils*, p. 27.

[30] "We demand not charity, but our rights, and we will not be satisfied with some sort of sop." *Prizyv*, 12 April 1906, p. 2.

[31] "Workers don't want to support [their] existence by charity or handouts. To get out of the current situation we demand work for ourselves." Ibid.

monies which are in the possession of the duma be expended on the organization of public works."[32]

Here one senses that the thinking of the unemployed was informed by a basic perception of what was fair and just. In their view, it was plainly "right" to use public monies to support the needs of the population and plainly "wrong" for employers to use starvation and homelessness to silence legitimate protest. Moreover, it now appeared that the "city fathers" were complicit in the suffering of workers. Such perceptions relentlessly expanded the dimensions of the conflict; already by late May, the alienation of the unemployed was finding rhetorical reflection in the statements of the council: " . . . at each step coming up against the sluggishness and disregard for the interests of the working class which distinguishes the Petersburg duma, the unemployed of the city of Petersburg have become convinced that they won't get much from the present census bourgeois duma of landlords and capitalists [*tsenzovaia burzhuaznaia duma domokhoziaev i kapitalistov*]. The interests of workers can only be served by a duma elected on the basis of universal, equal, direct and secret suffrage by the entire urban population" (*VPRMS*, p. 234).

These and other representations of the antagonist illustrate the ability of the council to politicize the issue of unemployment. The specificity of the unemployment of late 1905 through the spring of 1906 gave the movement these possibilities. For the political sophistication of the Council of the Unemployed derived from the militancy of the majority of its constituents, precisely those young, skilled metalworkers who were thrown out of the plants by the November lockouts and who had suffered from the "filtrovka" ever since. Although there are no reliable statistics for 1906,[33] those gathered between April and June 1906 by the Duma's Commission on Unemployment and recognized as understating the problem nonetheless illustrate the general nature of the phenomena.[34] Of the

---

[32] *Rech'*, 25 March 1906, p. 4.

[33] Estimates varied significantly and over time, with figures running from 13,000 to over 40,000. *Prizyv*, 27 January 1906, p. 3, and 5 February 1906, p. 2, reported 35,000 unemployed in January and 20,000 in early February. *Rech'*, 23 April 1906, p. 5, citing an April 20 report of the Duma's Commission on Unemployment, stated that the number of unemployed with families equaled 32,250 but that the figure was expected to rise to 43,650. It is equally difficult to define the number of unemployed metalworkers. Fedor A. Bulkin [Semenov, pseud.] variously estimated that the Petersburg metalworkers in the summer of 1906 numbered between 75,000 and 79,000. See his *Na zare profdvizheniia. Istoriia Peterburgskogo soiuza metallistov 1906–1914* (Moscow-Leningrad, 1924), pp. 130, 304. Using these numbers as a rough basis for calculation, unemployment in the metalworking industry was running somewhere between 10 and 32 percent. Bulkin, "Metallisty v revoliutsii 1905–1906 gg.," in *Proletariat v revoliutsii 1905–1906 gg.* (Moscow-Leningrad, 1930), p. 40. Bulkin himself gives the figure as 20 percent. *Na Zare*, p. 130.

[34] To my knowledge, no comprehensive analysis was ever made of this registration data. Besides the gross figures, I have only found data on the Gorodskoi, Moskovskii, and Vyborgskii districts.

12,933 registered unemployed, 7016 (54.3 percent) were skilled metal-workers; 3,149 (24.3 percent) were skilled workers in other trades; and 2,768 (21.4 percent) were unskilled laborers, primarily from the large state-owned metalworking factories.[35] Registration forms also make clear the reasons for dismissals: of the 560 registered unemployed of Gorodskoi district, 27 percent had been fired due to cuts in production, 40 percent for strikes and 23 percent for "politics." In Vyborg, 29 percent lost their jobs due to cuts in production; 34 percent for strikes, and 23 percent for "political convictions" or "conflicts" with the administration.[36]

Unemployment was plainly not the product of economic dislocation alone; it was part and parcel of the ongoing political conflict in the period after the October Manifesto.[37] And precisely because many workers believed that their suffering was the result of the deliberate decisions of state and private employers to punish politically active workers and thereby crush labor protest, they were able to hold at bay, at least temporarily, the demoralization that normally attended prolonged idleness. Moreover, because these assaults appeared focused on discrete and identifiable groups of the urban population, a sense of class was reinforced by this experience of joblessness.

The Council of the Unemployed clearly fostered a sense of class by hammering away on the theme of proletarian solidarity and on the commonality of interests linking the employed and the jobless. Unemployed comrades had fought and suffered for the cause of freedom, they argued, and hence merited full support, all the more so since employers were now manipulating the situation to undermine conditions in the factories. Only on the basis of a common front could decent wages, hours, and conditions be maintained; only with a clear sense of the need for proletarian solidarity could the jobless be held back from the temptations of strikebreaking. The council thus resolved to exclude strikebreakers from the ranks of the unemployed, as well as to register strikers and their families on the rolls, thereby making them eligible for free meals and other benefits. Moreover, the council's propagandists stressed that unemployment was

---

[35] Generalizing on the basis of the only available data (i.e., figures from the Gorodskoi, Moskovskii, and Vyborgskii districts), the clear majority of unemployed were literate, under thirty, and well paid. In Gorodskoi, 16 percent earned thirty rubles a month or less, and 64 percent earned forty rubles or more; in Vyborg, 30 percent earned thirty rubles a month or less and 20 percent earned fifty rubles a month or more.

[36] Voitinskii, *Psb*, pp. 29–31; *Vestnik zhizni*, 5 May 1906, pp. 51–52; *Volna*, 10 May 1906, p. 2.

[37] According to Voitinskii, the May 1906 registration indicated that 75 to 80 percent of the unemployed were thrown out of the factories during the November lockout and subsequent "cleansing" (p. 2). According to a report in February, the state plants were firing workers under twenty-two, especially single men, as they were considered the chief culprits in the strikes and unrest. Older men with families were allowed to remain. *Prizyv*, 5 February 1906, p. 2.

not the fault of the individual worker, but the product of capitalism. It was, therefore, the duty of every worker to support his fellow proletarians by giving aid freely and to understand that the jobless were comrades in arms, not dissolute elements down on their luck.[38] This vision of class solidarity was then actively promoted through the creation of funds in support of the unemployed. Already in late 1905, but increasingly so in 1906, workers throughout the capital practiced a voluntary 1 percent deduction from wages.[39]

The specificity of the unemployment of this period was important in another way. Young, skilled, literate, well-paid workers were tied to the city and the factory more closely than the unskilled or the day laborer; and as many observers now noted, those thrown out in late 1905–early 1906 were those least able to fall back on the resources of the village.[40] These workers were the most dependent on factory wages; they were the ones with the greatest stake in the urban community. They were, now, fundamentally dispossessed and had to turn to their comrades for help. Precisely because the throngs of unemployed illustrated that workers were in the city to stay, a clearer linkage between work and community became possible, as did stronger bonds to neighborhood and class.

As the months dragged on, however, the despair and bitterness of the unemployed inevitably grew, as did the corrosive effects of joblessness on solidarity. Angry and frustrated, the council mounted another demonstration against the city duma in mid-June to protest delays in the opening of public works projects. And although these protests secured the allocation of further monies for the immediate needs of the unemployed and although some public works projects did begin over the summer, nonetheless need continued to outstrip the available aid. With the dissolution of the State Duma on July 9 and the assault of the autocracy on labor organizations, however, the city fathers began to back away from their commitments to the jobless. By the fall they voted, by secret ballot, to terminate aid.[41] A few months later, leading industrialists pressured the city duma to put an end to the public works projects altogether.[42] In all

---

[38] Voitinskii, *Psb*, pp. 11–13, 65–66, 83–86; Malyshev, *Unemployed Councils*, pp. 28–31; and *Prizyv*, 6 April 1906, p. 1; 12 April 1906, p. 2; and 18 April 1906, p. 1.

[39] Voitinskii, *Psb*, p. 8. The labor press routinely reported contributions from the factories; for just one example, see *Prizyv*, 6 April 1906, p. 2.

[40] *Volna*, 10 May 1906, p. 2; L. M. Kleinbort, "Khronika russkoi zhizni," *Obrazovanie*, no. 4 (1906): 99–100.

[41] On the June 12 meeting, see *Rech'*, 13 June 1906, p. 6, and Malyshev, *Unemployed Councils*, pp. 42–43. On the further allocations and on the beginnings of public works over the summer, see Voitinskii, *Psb*, pp. 54–57, 65, and Malyshev, p. 48. For the bitter reaction of the Council of the Unemployed to the decision to terminate aid, see *Vtoroi period revoliutsii 1906–1907 goda, Oktiabr'-Dekabr' 1906* (Moscow, 1963), pp. 88–89 (hereafter cited as *VPROD*). See also Kleinbort, *Obrazovanie*, pp. 105–7.

[42] In mid-January, S. P. Glezmer addressed the city duma concerning his dissatisfaction

this workers perceived the power of the victorious antagonist: no longer as alarmed by the uncertainties that had surrounded the period of the first State Duma (April 27–July 9, 1906) or as threatened by a strong and coherent labor movement, the city duma and those it represented could take back the concessions they had granted out of fear.[43]

Gradually, the Council of the Unemployed began to fall apart, for however impressive the mobilization of the jobless during the first part of the year may have been, the movement could not withstand the effects of long-term idleness brought on by the withdrawal of support for the unemployed by the city duma and by the changing nature of work in Petersburg heavy industry.[44] With the waning coherence of the movement and the demoralization of extended joblessness came despair and individual acts of violence.[45] In place of the organized struggles of the spring, the outrage of the unemployed began to blend in easily with the wave of "partisan" activities developing during the fall—the notorious expropriations, but also an epidemic of assaults on factory owners and foremen, police and high city officials. But with the passage of time, this outrage was increasingly directed inward as alcoholism and suicide.[46]

The experience of unemployment and the mobilization around it proved important to the further evolution of social conflict in the city of St. Petersburg. For census society, the rising tide of social fear sharpened its perception of the costs of political opposition and thus hastened its accommodation with the autocracy. And for labor, the treatment of the

---

with this sort of program. Similarly, A. Belonozhkin, director of the Putilov Factory, worked energetically to ensure that upcoming orders for bridge reconstruction went to private contractors and not into the hands of the unemployed. See Voitinskii, *Psb*, pp. 112, 116.

[43] Wrote Voitinskii: "The pliability of the city administration in regard to the demands of the unemployed was a consequence of the lack of faith of the bourgeoisie in the final suppression of the revolution. In the beginning of 1906 [July–?] after the dispersal of the State Duma, this faith appeared. City dumas everywhere ceased their concessions to the unemployed; the Petersburg city duma from the fall of 1906 shifted from a defensive position to an offensive [one], trying to take back from the unemployed that which had been given to them earlier." *Psb*, pp. 60–61.

[44] By the second half of 1906 and more clearly during 1907, politically motivated dismissals were gradually eclipsed by layoffs due to cuts in production and the beginnings of workplace rationalization, as illustrated by the changes at the state plants, as well as by the summer strikes of 1906.

[45] This violence would include the murder of two engineers who supervised public works projects in May 1907. For a discussion of this incident, see Voitinskii, *Psb*, pp. 122–27.

[46] On the "partisan" activities taking place in the Nevskii district during the fall of 1906, see Aleksei Buzinov, *Za nevskoi zastavoi. Zapiski rabochego* (Moscow and Leningrad, 1930), pp. 115–20. For a poignant description of the devastating effects of long-term unemployment and the hopelessness that accompanied it, as well as a painful discussion of the degeneration of the organized movement of the unemployed, see Voitinskii, *Psb*, pp. 92–96, 109–11. See also *Materialy ob ekonomicheskom polozhenii i professional'noi organizatsii peterburgskikh rabochikh po metallu* (St. Petersburg, 1909), pp. 117–18.

unemployed at the hands of the city fathers was interpreted as "proof" of the linkage between census society and their employers. At the same time, the issues surrounding unemployment—food, rent, access to city hospitals—as well as public works projects for the welfare of the city as a whole (for example, stockyards, bridge repair, electric trams)—raised important questions about who "ran" the city and in whose interests and hence opened up new areas of involvement for working-class activism.

Workers and the Curial Electoral Process

I wish to note only briefly another aspect of class formation in the aftermath of 1905. Here I have in mind the elections in the workers' curia to the First and Second Dumas, as well as subsequent worker engagement with the proceedings of the national legislature. For it was not only that the electoral process and participation in the State Duma provided an important venue for social-democratic agitation and hence another vehicle for the articulation of a language of class, but that the curial system itself magnified the worker's sense of himself as a worker rather than as a citizen of St. Petersburg or the nation as a whole.

According to the complex electoral law of 11 December 1905, the right of a worker to participate in the elections was not based on his personal qualification or registration, but rather on his attachment to a particular factory or plant, specifically one at which he had worked for at least six months and one with a workforce of at least fifty males. On the day of the election, workers were to gather in their factories and select their delegate(s). These delegates would then come together in a city assembly to select fifteen electors; these electors, in turn, went on to join with the electors from the urban curia (160 in number) to elect deputies for the State Duma.[47]

Although the place of employment might well have served in the eyes of tsarist officials as "the analogue of the village community,"[48] for workers, the factory—transformed as it now was by these officials into the venue for the first stage of a national electoral process—became in yet another way a site of class formation. Little in the factory setting encouraged workers to distinguish between "national" and class concerns. Worker perceptions of the class-based nature of the national political process could only be enhanced by their employers' routine attempts to

---

[47] Terence Emmons, *The Formation of Political Parties and the First National Elections in Russia* (Cambridge, Mass., 1983), pp. 286–88.

[48] This phrase belongs to Emmons, *Formation*, p. 286.

influence electoral outcomes.[49] Politics and a particular social identity were thus neatly fused in a multitiered electoral system that began in the shop and at each subsequent stage emphasized the distinctiveness of the worker as well as minimized the opportunity for discussion and association across class lines. Meeting in segregated groups provided little chance for one group to encounter the discourse of another. Thus the worker remained a worker, not a citizen with other sources of identity beyond or in distinction to his identity at the workplace.[50]

Interesting, then, are the electoral outcomes in the workers' curia to the Second Duma and what they reveal about working-class attitudes by the winter of 1906–7. Most obvious was the complete failure of the Kadets and the other "bourgeois" parties of the center and right to attract any working-class sympathy whatsoever. Liberalism had no appeal to the working class, editorialized *Rabochii po metallu*, "Workers want not freedom for capitalist exploitation, but freedom for their struggle against it."[51] But what appears more portentous was the amorphous rage that seemed to inform worker voting behavior. For the voting demonstrated both the apparent strength of Social Revolutionaries (SRs), as well as the weakness of Menshevism, but also the relative strength of Bolshevism when representatives of the respective factions stood in direct competition with SR candidates.[52] One needs to be cautious here, because the nature of the voting process makes it problematic to generalize about worker attitudes toward party programs or party affiliation.[53] Although it is therefore dangerous to draw any bold conclusions about the strength of the Bolsheviks and SRs or to suggest the emergence of a developed consciousness of class among broad segments of the Petersburg workforce, nonetheless it seems safe to posit that the vote reflected a process of alienation that had a great deal to do with an accumulating sense of outrage directed against the state and census "society" after the October Manifesto.

[49] See the comments from the Semiannikovskii factory in *Novaia Gazeta*, 19 November 1906.

[50] My thinking on these issues has been influenced by Ira Katznelson's thoughtful essay "Working-Class Formation: Constructing Cases and Comparisons," in Ira Katznelson and Aristide R. Zolberg, eds., *Working-Class Formation: Nineteenth-Century Patterns in Western Europe and the United States* (Princeton, N.J., 1986), pp. 3–41.

[51] *Rabochii po metallu*, 28 January 1907, p. 1.

[52] For Lenin's analysis of the elections, see his *Collected Works* (Moscow, 1963), 12:62–69, 70–74, 86–92; for Martov's see his "Ianvarskie vybory po rabochei kurii v gorode Peterburge," *Otklinki* 2 (April 1907): 65–78, esp. 74–78.

[53] See the unpublished paper by Peter Holquist, "The Course of the Second Duma Elections in the Workers' *Curiias* of St. Petersburg" (Dept. of History, Columbia University, 1988), especially his discussion of why the structure of the electoral process precluded the determination of party affiliation of workers. I am indebted to Holquist for sharing his insightful essay with me.

Metalworkers in the Years of Reaction

A new era of conflict opened in urban Russia in late April 1912 when workers learned that hundreds of peacefully assembled miners from the Lena Goldfields in far-off Siberia had been shot down by tsarist troops for presenting demands to the mine's management. Yet tension had been steadily mounting even before news of the massacre ignited the explosion of labor protest in St. Petersburg. The stagnant economy of recent years and the repressive political environment of the Stolypin era provided a context in which industrialists could roll back the gains made by workers during 1905 and dismantle elements of the "constitutional" factory order they had tried to construct. Moreover, many employers now believed that the crises of the recent past required new approaches: the punishing economic loses sustained since the turn of the century focused attention on problems with factory economy, whereas the collapse of labor discipline encouraged the exploration of new methodologies of labor control. During the years of reaction, employers acted unilaterally and implemented changes in the size and form of remuneration and in time-management procedures, and selectively reorganized production processes, accounting methodologies, and staffing.[54] However necessary from a managerial point of view these changes may have been, workers experienced them as wage cuts, a more exhausting pace of work, an intensified supervision of the shop floor, and an assault on the modest civil rights granted by the government.

Correspondence from the factories printed on the back pages of the labor press well illustrates metalworker attitudes toward management's counteroffensive. Such correspondence also evidences a continuing communication between workers even as labor organizations withered in the period of reaction, as well as an ongoing sharing of experience which helped to forge a sense of the commonality of labor's concerns across the city.[55] Thus, for example, workers recorded their exhaustion with the killing pace of work and their frustration with the petty fault-finding of their foremen. Wrote one: "We work like horses. It is impossible to leave your place for a second."[56] Another felt that workers couldn't "forget for a minute that the vigilant eye of the boss, who rul[ed] with an iron hand,

---

[54] These issues are explored in depth in chapters 7 and 8 of my *Forging Revolution*.

[55] Although closed numerous times and appearing under various names, the journal of the St. Petersburg Metalworkers' Union was one of the few trade union publications able to come out with a fair degree of regularity. Although its circulation fell during the most intense period of reaction, workers nonetheless passed single copies along to comrades and read the paper collectively. The metalworkers' press was one important source for a discourse of class.

[56] *Edinstvo*, 10 August 1909, p. 13.

[was] constantly upon them."[57] At Nevskii, "The smallest delay, a minute breather [was] now seen as slacking off and frequently serv[ed] as an occasion for the foreman to send you for a dismissal slip."[58] At Baltic "orders pour out one after another and each snatches some sort of worker right."[59] And it was just as bad at St. Petersburg Metals, where workers complained that their "fattened foreman [came] up to the bench, [took] out a watch and [told] workers: set it with more traction, at a faster pace and take it with greater force [*vziat' s truzhku*]." Workers knew that nothing good could come of this, but nonetheless did everything according to orders, and "of course, working with force [broke] some part of an expensive, specialized foreign machine tool." Concluded this worker: "They go to such extremes that they themselves don't know what they want and what they are demanding."[60]

The many changes that attended management's greater concern with time discipline further contributed to the workers' sense of encroachment. The stop watch and the automatic punch clock were particularly offensive. Union sources observed that factories began to acquire automatic control clocks that "red-lined" the slightest lateness.[61] Just as disturbing was the withdrawal of "free time" before the beginning of work and after lunch; or the loss of flexibility in rules governing lateness and checking in; or the right to drink tea or smoke.[62] At issue were changes in the heretofore accepted norms of factory life, which had never been codified in the work rules but which management had tacitly accepted. In the different world of the post-1905 factory, formal regulation eliminated the small but valued "freedoms" built in by workers to modify the length and pace of the workday.

Changes in workforce composition were also disorienting. Union reports observed that women had replaced men at the Cable Factory, and adolescents had taken over adults' jobs at the Cartridge Case Plant.[63] In some places common laborers were put on machine tools, not to train them to become metalworkers *(slesari)*, but "in view of economy."[64] At Diuflon, where child labor had sharply increased in recent years, one worker bemoaned that "they look on apprentices as a cheap workforce and aren't concerned whether [they] learn something or not."[65] Wrote

[57] *Edinstvo*, 1 April 1910, p. 17.
[58] *Edinstvo*, 10 August 1909, p. 12.
[59] *Metallist*, 26 November 1911, p. 11.
[60] *Kuznets*, 20 December 1907, pp. 14–15.
[61] *Kuznets*, 20 December 1907, pp. 121–22.
[62] *Rabochii po metallu*, 9 May 1907, p. 15; *Edinstvo*, 3 March 1909, pp. 12, 13; *Materialy ob ekonomicheskom polozhenii*, p. 121.
[63] *Materialy ob ekonomicheskom polozhenii*, p. 108.
[64] *Edinstvo*, 1 December 1909, p. 14.
[65] *Zvezda*, 5 (18) March 1911, p. 20.

one Langenzipen worker: "They constantly fire and again hire, so that the workforce is extremely fluid [*tekuchii*]."[66] Combined with these sorts of changes was the expansion of supervisory staff, whose numbers seemed all the greater given that workforce size was cut or remained static in the years of reaction.[67] Perceived changes in the age, gender, and skill characteristics of the labor force experienced in conjunction with the increased presence of supervisory personnel altered the social landscape of the shop and contributed to a sense of life out of balance.

Workers also noted the different behavior of foremen once employers regained the upper hand in the aftermath of 1905. One had been "like silk" during the revolution, but had now returned to his former ways; others had "trimmed their sails to the wind." And if earlier, one could talk humanly with a foreman and bargain on rates, now he would hit the boys in the shop, scream at the workers as if they were cattle, and pass out different rates for the same work.[68]

Taken together, an acute sense of constant, oppressive supervision was linked with a perception that management was engaged in some sort of experiment that was having harmful consequences for labor's well-being.[69] Semenov workers seemed to capture an important sentiment when they wrote uneasily about the many Taylorist innovations taking place at their factory: "Although almost none of us have come to an understanding of this system [*ne razbiraetsia v etoi sisteme*], nonetheless we feel that something advances upon us [*nadvigaetsia*], and that it will be necessary to respond."[70]

Confronted with supervisors computing rates and wages in different ways, stopwatch-toting foremen ordering a faster pace, and guards monitoring the automatic punch clocks, workers variously experienced the new methods as offensive, confusing, and intimidating. But there was more. Management had sought to defuse conflict by depersonalizing relations on the shop floor. In some factories, rate setting had been taken away from the foreman (and with it the informal haggling that had been possible before) and placed in the hands of rates bureaus, time-work specialists, or engineers. Hiring practices had been codified, and in some cases

[66] *Zvezda*, 13 (26) January 1911, p. 19.

[67] *Rabochii po metallu*, 24 September 1907, p. 15; *Nadezhda*, 31 July 1908, p. 13, and 31 October 1908, p. 14; *Edinstvo*, 10 August 1909, p. 12; and *Metallist*, 26 January 1912, p. 15.

[68] *Kuznets*, 19 January 1908, p. 26; *Edinstvo*, 16 February 1910, p. 16; *Kuznets*, 20 December 1907, p. 15.

[69] *Kuznets*, 20 December 1907, p. 16; N. P. Paialin, *Zavod imeni Lenina, 1857–1918* (Moscow-Leningrad, 1933), p. 255. For an insightful discussion of the American experience with workplace rationalization, and particularly the unsettling sense of constant change felt by workers, see David Montgomery, *The Fall of the House of Labor* (Cambridge, Mass., 1987), especially chap. 5.

[70] *Metallist*, 23 February 1912, pp. 8–9.

special hiring committees had been formed to eliminate the favoritism, bribe-taking, and vodka "treats" that had often accompanied the hiring process in the past. Written documentation replaced oral communication; regulation tightened up a loose workday. As management imposed more orderly lines of command and execution, as "systems" began to replace people, work relations became increasingly structured, formalized, and impersonal.

From labor's point of view, this impersonality obscured accountability: it was no longer clear who had cut their rates, hired the adolescents to do the work of slesari, or fired the senior workers. And so when workers struck out at supervisory personnel or at the pace of work they compelled, workers were striking out more clearly than in the past at "the system"— at the reconceived managerial structures in which individual foremen had little remaining responsibility (or authority) on the shop floor. Just as important, what constituted order and regulation in the eyes of management appeared as dissimulation and evasion to workers. What for employers was a "rational" response to the crises that they faced, became for workers a bewildering set of changes that were meant to disarm them—by muddying the lines of responsibility through allegedly clear and orderly administrative systems, by making obscure the calculation of rates and wages, by pitting worker against worker in a race against time to earn at a higher rate, and by encroaching on the informal, heretofore accepted norms of the shop floor.[71]

Furthermore, these disturbing and unpredictable changes were not simply perceived in terms of bread-and-butter issues; for many, the managerial offensive seemed a punishment for the rebelliousness of the recent past as well as a vigorous attempt to restore the autocratic power heretofore held by managers over labor. By the same token, to the degree that foremen and "former" comrades "trimmed their sails" and collaborated in the imposition of the new regime, many workers doubtless felt betrayed; certainly employer efforts to take back concessions granted in 1905–6 would be experienced as such. Wrote one embittered worker in late 1906: "Bosses energetically use the situation [the economic crisis and unemployment] and under the threat of dismissal, they lower rates, make deductions, and impose severe fines. At the factories, now, such an arbitrariness reigns that would have been unthinkable a year ago."[72] Editorialized *Kuznets* in 1908:

"Attack on all fronts"—such is now the slogan of the employers. The main goal of their efforts is the destruction of all the achievements of the "days

---

[71] Conversations with Tim Mixter have contributed to my thinking about these issues.
[72] *Nevskii vestnik*, 10 December 1906, p. 10.

of freedom," a decisive return to the good old times of "unlimited" exploitation, the abolition of the last vestiges of the "factory constitution," the destruction of all types of worker organization. . . .

"We are now the bosses of the factory, not you"—openly stated the manager of the engine department to a deputation of Semiannikov workers—"If you do not want to obey, we will close the factory."

"Obey or be fired!"[73]

For Petersburg metalworkers, workplace rationalization was largely experienced as part of the defeat they suffered in 1905–6. Changes on the shop floor took place in a context in which employers felt free to act unilaterally and in which workers were mostly powerless to defend themselves. When union leaders were asked what workers had gained from the movement of 1905–6, they responded: "The answer to this question lays bare before us one of the most acute contradictions of the capitalist structure: any step of the working class on the path of liberation is utilized by capital for the establishment of new forms of oppression and exploitation. Any shortening of the workday or increase in pay is accompanied by an increase in the intensity of labor, any increase in the productivity of labor increases the cadre of unemployed."[74]

Here and elsewhere, "economics" and "politics" were conflated; the line between labor's struggle for "liberation" and capitalist exploitation within the factory was blurred. Similarly, anger about the worsening conditions on the shop floor mixed easily with despair over the difficulties of daily life. Wrote union activists in 1909: "Is it surprising that 1907–1908 gave an unheard of development of suicide among workers, of crime, prostitution, and drunkenness; that cholera rained down on the workers' neighborhoods [kvartaly] with such success, reaping an abundant harvest! Does not the responsibility for all these calamities fall on the entire contemporary social order and its representatives—the 'commercial-industrial class'?"[75]

Just as many in the unemployed movemment of 1906 had linked "the bourgeoisie" with the city's elite more broadly, so activists a few years later associated "the capitalists" with "society," holding all responsible for the terrible plight of the urban nizy. Moreover, although workers clearly identified employers as the class antagonist, their sense of class was doubtless also enhanced by the social isolation they experienced as a result of the withdrawal of the radical and liberal intelligentsia in the aftermath of 1905. Developing in the difficult years of reaction, then, was

[73] *Kuznets,* 14 February 1908, p. 3.
[74] *Materialy po ekonomicheskom polozhenii,* p. 110.
[75] Ibid., p. 118.

a generalized if still repressed rage against the "entire contemporary social order."

Also developing in the relative social isolation of the workers' kvartaly was a sense of what constituted an appropriate code of proletarian conduct. For as the labor press documented all the negative and destructive aspects of working-class life, the opposite behaviors emerged in contrast. As harsh as the condemnations of the many ways in which workers themselves participated in their own oppression often were, nonetheless the routine airing of such complaints on the back pages of the labor press acted as a most basic form of consciousness raising.

Thus workers criticized the long hours of overtime that many continued to perform or even request. Working extra hours not only took jobs away from the unemployed; it very often entailed obsequious behavior before a supervisor just to "score" a few extra hours. In such a way, workers became dependent on the whims of a foreman, allowing him to pick and choose who would get the overtime, hence sowing discord among all involved. Workers, admonished activists, needed the time to rest, to read, and to participate in social and family life.[76]

In correspondence from the factory, workers detailed the many ways in which rates were broken and offered advice on how to stop it. At Siemens-Halske, foremen tried to give out rates *after* the task was completed. But, counseled one writer, this practice could be fought since workers had the legal right to refuse any task on which an order form was not issued in advance.[77] At the Franco-Russian Factory, a foreman put two workers on one machine tool: one was to work by piece-rate, the other on shop pay and in such a way the boss was able to drive down wages.[78] With the introduction of automatic machine tools at the Pipe Factory, rates had fallen sharply for "among the workers on the automatic machine tools there [was] not one member of the union and they agree[d] to work under any condition."[79]

A Baltic worker commented that the apathy, the "deathly calm," that had come over workers had resulted in a desire either "to serve" the administration and display "trustworthiness" or an effort to earn an extra kopeck or two, without thinking about the harm this caused. Other shops at Baltic raced to complete work, thereby "giving the administration sufficient reason to lower rates," whereas "the former avant-guard of the factory"—the electro-technical shop—had become so servile that it agreed to contribute to the icon lamp funds (*lampadnye kassy*).[80] At San-Galli, a

[76] *Rabochii po metallu*, 13 June 1907, pp. 3, 4; *Zvezda*, 12 February 1912, p. 18; *Kuznets*, 25 May 1907), p. 3.

[77] *Nadezhda*, 28 August 1908, p. 19.

[78] *Kuznets*, 20 December 1907, p. 15.

[79] *Nash put'*, 3 December 1910, p. 15.

[80] *Vestnik rabochikh po obrabotke metalla*, 15 May 1908, pp. 20–21.

new foreman, "alluding to his American experience, forced us to work without interruption or rest." Argued the writer, "We must oppose the tricks of this foreman with our solidarity and not bring down one another's rates when we turn in a job."[81] At the Cable Factory, workers resolved to agitate against payment by the job (*akkord*), "in view of its baneful effect on the health [of the worker] and its demoralizing influence on labor solidarity."[82]

But workers also routinely complained about the many ways in which alcoholism undermined their cause. Rather than pay union dues or help an unemployed comrade, too many workers wasted their wages on drink.[83] And there was the problem of giving "gifts" to managerial personnel, or agreeing to do personal work for a foreman and hence becoming his "lackey."[84]

In these various injunctions against overtime and rate-breaking, drinking and pandering to foremen, workers outlined the constituent elements of a proletarian ethic, reiterating in a different voice many of the same values articulated earlier by the unemployed movement. By criticizing obsequious behaviors, workers called on one another to maintain their dignity and to behave as mature, autonomous individuals. By rejecting overtime and rate-breaking, workers called attention to issues of labor solidarity. By indicting alcoholism, workers called for self-respect; by bemoaning a passive acceptance of existing conditions, workers underscored the need for an activist, organized labor force. By protesting the crude and demeaning language of supervisors, workers sought a basic human decency. By criticizing "gifts" to administrators and contributions to the lampadnye kassy, workers called on their comrades to give to genuinely proletarian causes.

All this was easily lost in the demoralizing years of reaction; much more obvious was the absence of strike protest, the weakness of the union, and the apparent disarray of life in the conspiratorial underground. Amidst the teeming, disease-ridden slums and the dog-eat-dog atmosphere on the shop floor it was doubtless difficult to discern much proletarian comradeship. But as Iu. I. Kir'ianov has argued, both the first revolution and the years of reaction were important periods in the self-definition of Russia's classes.[85] The historically specific experiences of metalworkers on the shop floor, in the city, and in the national electoral process over the 1906–12 period made the social democrats' class-based analysis of these expe-

---

[81] *Kuznets*, 20 December 1907, p. 16.

[82] *Zvezda*, 8 (21) March 1912, p. 25.

[83] *Kuznets*, 19 January 1908, pp. 26, 27; *Edinstvo*, 12 March 1910.

[84] *Edinstvo*, 26 May 1909, pp. 13–14; 1 December 1908, p. 11; and 12 March 1910, p. 3.

[85] Kir'ianov, "Ob oblike rabochego klassa Rossii," in *Rossiiskii Proletariat: Oklik, bor'ba, gegemoniia* (Moscow, 1970), p. 121.

riences particularly compelling. In isolation and in difficult material conditions, St. Petersburg workers repressed their rage and punished themselves with destructive bouts of drinking and exhausting hours of labor; but they also began to conceive their world in stark opposition to the rest of Petersburg society. The explosive protests surrounding the Lena Goldfields massacre would suggest the degree to which the experiences of this difficult period between late 1905 and early 1912 had shaped metalworker thinking.

4

S. A. Smith

Workers against Foremen
in St. Petersburg, 1905–1917

From a theoretical point of view, the role of foremen in capitalist industry is ambiguous. First, foremen combine the socially necessary tasks of coordinating production with those of controlling labor, marrying technical competence—the extent of which varies across different labor processes—to the exercise of discipline, the extent of which also varies, according to the degree of bureaucratization and specialization of the structure of management.[1] Second, foremen are not only salaried employees who sell their labor power to and are dominated by capital but also the most junior officers in the hierarchy of capitalist command.[2] To the extent that they are the agents of control of labor, under pressure to maintain and increase productivity and to keep costs down, their relationship to the workers in their charge tends to be antagonistic. But as Michael Burawoy has argued, antagonism may be present at a structural level but not at the level at which workers understand their interests, since the interests that organize the daily life of workers are not irrevocably given by structures but are reproduced through culture.[3] Structural and cultural pressures may, therefore, combine to make for cooperation rather than conflict on the shop floor.

In St. Petersburg between the revolutions of 1905 and 1917 conflict between workers and foremen was rife.[4] Robert McKean has shown that

[1] Nicos Poulantzas, *Classes in Contemporary Capitalism* (London, 1975), part 3, chap. 3.
[2] I believe Erik Olin Wright's concept of contradictory class location is useful here. Wright abandoned this notion in his book *Classes*, but in his more recent work has partially and, to my mind, usefully rehabilitated it. Wright, *Classes* (London, 1985); E. O. Wright et al., *The Debate on Classes* (London, 1989), especially part 3.
[3] Michael Burawoy, *The Politics of Production: Factory Regimes under Capitalism and Socialism* (London, 1985), pp. 27–28.
[4] Strictly speaking, here I am concerned with the relations between workers and lower supervisory personnel in general, and not just with foremen. The latter term is used as shorthand, however, to indicate all of those who were directly involved in supervising the

the most salient feature of the economic strikes that took place on the eve of the First World War was the "dominant role played by disputes in which working people challenged in a variety of ways the all-pervasive authority of factory managers, foremen and petty workshop proprietors." He shows that in the three industries of metalworking, paper and printing, and textiles, authority issues figured in a quarter to four-tenths of economic stoppages. In particular, disputes in which workers demanded the sacking of foremen and other lower supervisory personnel comprised 19 percent of the aggregate of authority stoppages in 1913 and 21 percent in 1914. McKean comments that "these figures seriously underestimate the role of foremen and factory staff as agents of conflict, as disputes concerning fines, hiring and firing, courteous treatment and searches were almost always the direct consequence of actions taken by administrative personnel."[5] Given that the great majority of foremen were former workers, practical experience being the key to advancement, and that the social distance between them and the workforce was not great, it might seem strange that the antagonism toward them was so fierce.[6] But therein lies the paradox. For it was precisely the distance of the owners and senior management from the workforce in Petersburg's large enterprises that focused worker discontent on those immediate agents of capitalist discipline.

Yet this is to explain everything and nothing. I seek first to examine how relations between workers and lower supervisory personnel were shaped not only by the exigencies of capitalist production but also by existing cultural patterns, particularly, by the social relations of gender, age, ethnicity, and clientelism and the meanings by which they were imbricated. In Russia, as elsewhere, industrial capitalism consolidated itself by drawing on precapitalist social relations and cultural patterns—patterns that reinforced ambiguities inherent in the foreman's role under capitalist production, functioning variously to produce relations of dependence or of conflict with workers. Second, I examine how workplace conflicts became inserted into wider political struggles, by showing how the mainly Marxist labor organizers strove to disseminate a class-based view of the foreman's role. The propaganda of the Russian social demo-

---

day-to-day activities of workers on the shop floor. As we shall see, in some industries foremen were by no means the lowest representatives of the administrative hierarchy, but they were visible to and interacted with the workers on a day-to-day basis. This was not true of middle-level managers, such as shop or section directors. I shall use the masculine pronoun when referring to individual foremen, as they were overwhelmingly male. Where forewomen are included, I shall indicate that.

[5] Robert McKean, *St. Petersburg between the Revolutions: Workers and Revolutionaries, June 1907–February 1917* (New Haven, Conn., 1990), p. 253.

[6] O. V. Naumov, L. S. Petrosian, and A. K. Sokolov, "Kadry rukovoditelei, spetsialistov i obsluzhivaiushchego personala promyshlennykh predpriatii po dannym professional'noi perepisi 1918 goda," *Istoriia SSSR*, 1981, no. 6:98–99.

crats was crucial in determining how workers and foremen saw themselves and one another and how they constructed class identities. Consequently, aspects of the relationship between workers and foremen not rooted in class relations nevertheless were construed in terms of class, which over time intensified class antagonism.

There is no room here for a complete explanation of the high incidence of worker-foreman conflict. The role of lower supervisory personnel varied from industry to industry, and a comprehensive examination of worker-foreman conflict would require detailed investigation of the labor processes and the "social relations in production" of different industries. I will allude to the general causes of this conflict in passing, but I will not systematically examine the changing forms of technical and social organization of production and how they combined to form what Michael Burawoy has called the "political apparatuses of production."[7] Nevertheless I will emphasize the diversity of relationships between workers and foremen in different industries, as I investigate the cultural and historical environment in which worker-foremen relations emerged and developed over a relatively short span of time.

The Functions of the Foreman

Metal-fabrication and engineering industries dominated the industrial landscape of St. Petersburg. In 1913 42 percent of the city's factory workforce was employed in the metal and machine industries, compared with 19 percent in textiles and 11 percent in paper and printing.[8] The administrative structure of the average large metal plant appeared bureaucratic, each division or department being headed by a manager and his deputy, beneath whom were the heads of workshops and their assistants. Between them and the workforce stood the foremen (*mastera*) and assistant foremen (*podmaster'ia*), sometimes followed by crew leaders (*ukazateli*) and senior workers (*starshie*).[9] Despite this seemingly bureaucratic structure, in reality many metal plants operated more like collections of small workshops in which functional specialization was limited and in which skilled workers exercised extensive job control. In such craft settings the powers of foremen were wide-ranging, yet, as we shall see, crucially limited in

---

[7] Burawoy, *Politics of Production*, p. 13.

[8] E. E. Kruze, *Peterburgskie rabochie v 1912–14 godakh* (Moscow, 1961), p. 69.

[9] G. D. Surh, *1905 in St. Petersburg: Labor, Society and Revolution* (Stanford, Calif., 1989), p. 73; H. Hogan, "Conciliation Boards in Revolutionary Petrograd: Aspects of the Crisis of Labor-Management Relations in 1917," in *Russian History/Histoire Russe* 9, no. 1 (1982): 60.

practice.[10] After the 1905 revolution, a few companies pioneered forms
of mass production, which resulted in a growth in the number of unskilled
and semiskilled workers and increasing stratification of the workforce.
Supervisory and technical positions multiplied, entailing a reduction in
the formal powers of foremen, particularly over the quantity and quality
of output.[11] Nevertheless up to the first World War the foreman's powers
remained extensive and multifaceted: he retained responsibility for running the workshop, for rate-setting, labor discipline and the allocation of
work, and sometimes for hiring and firing.[12]

Within cotton textiles, St. Petersburg's second industry, the flow of production and the pace of the machine served as the principal means of
regulating labor. Gerald Surh has argued that in this industry foremen
were more closely identified with management than they were in metalworking, since their relationship to the workforce was neither mediated
by participation in production nor by the presence of intermediate layers
of skilled workers. The foremen and forewomen relied more on formal
authority than on personal qualities in dealing with the mill hands.[13] In
the large rubber and tobacco works of the capital relations between foremen and workers were similar.

Foremen and lower supervisory personnel were under contradictory
pressures: they were required by their superiors to ensure maximum output and expected to prevent the outbreak of conflict. It was left to the
foreman to balance these two objectives. The majority appear to have
leaned toward driving their charges, for the evidence of abuse, scolding,
beating, imposition of fines, and threats of dismissal is ubiquitous. According to the testimony of a politically moderate worker, P. Timofeev,

[10] L. H. Haimson, "Structural Processes of Change and Changing Patterns of Labor Un-
rest: The Case of the Metal-Processing Industry in Imperial Russia (1890–1914)," in L. H.
Haimson and C. Tilly, eds., *Strikes, Wars and Revolutions in an International Perspective*
(Cambridge, 1989), p. 381.

[11] H. Hogan, "Industrial Rationalization and the Roots of Labour Militance in the St.
Petersburg Metalworking Industry, 1901–14," *Russian Review* 42 (April 1983): 163–90; see
also "Novaia Industriia," in *Vestnik metallista*, 1918, no. 2:23.

[12] Unlike the subcontractor, the foreman did not employ his own labor. His salary, in
theory, was the main source of his income and he did not have the petty-capitalist interest
in costs and profits of the internal contractor. Rather arbitrarily, I have distinguished foremen from internal contractors of this type, but it should be remembered that in Russia, as
in Western Europe at an earlier date, there were large numbers of workers who were subordinated not to employers but to intermediate subcontractors. See E. J. Hobsbawm, "Customs, Wages and Workload in Nineteenth-Century Industry," in *Labouring Men* (London,
1968), p. 353. In St. Petersburg subcontracting was widespread in the docks and in construction, but it was also to be found in some metalworks. Cf. the "parties" (*partii*) of
fitters, turners, and toolmakers at the Koppel' Works; the "grasping subcontractor" (*kulak-
podriadchik*) who organized the stove-setters at Putilov, or the "brigades" (*brigady*) of the
steam-engine workshops of the Nikolaev railways. See *Pravda*, 9 January 1913, p. 4, and
30 June 1912, p. 4.

[13] Surh, *1905 in St. Petersburg*, pp. 70–71.

the "shop foreman represents the lever of factory life that presses on the worker hardest."[14] Complaints against foremen were many and bitter not least because of the myriad ways in which they could make a worker's life miserable.

In many enterprises foremen still retained some responsibility for hiring and firing. To get a job, a worker needed to know either the foreman or someone able to put in a word with him on his or her behalf. Migrants arriving in the capital would seek out kin or people from the same region—*zemliaki*—to help them find accommodations and a job. If a foreman were one's zemliak, he had some obligation to help. It could thus happen that workers in a particular section of a factory might hail from the same district as the foreman. At the Baltic Works almost all workers employed in the shipwrights' shop were natives of Staritskii *uezd* (district) in Tver' province. In the carpentry shop some seventy to eighty workers were discovered in 1917 to be either relatives or zemliaki of the foreman, Khryndikov. At the Triangle Works there were large numbers of workers from Vasilevskii *volost'* (rural district) in Tver' province.[15] One might expect these networks based on common regional origin to create vertical bonds between the foreman and his zemliaki, but they appear to have been declining in frequency as the labor market expanded and direct recruitment by the company became the norm. By the First World War they were no longer as significant in St. Petersburg as in other Russian cities.

Lacking contacts, a worker might have to bribe a foreman to get a job. Indeed, some foremen made big sums of money from selling jobs. According to the technical director at the Putilov Works, a foreman in the 1890s purchased land and a dacha for 15,000 rubles out of bribes received from jobseekers.[16] And a survey of the budgets of St. Petersburg textile workers in 1912 showed that all of those surveyed paid bribes to podmaster'ia or quality inspectors (*brakovshchiki*). The largest sums were paid by two social democrats, one a member of the inspection commission of the textile workers' union, and the other a factory union delegate, both of whom paid six rubles.[17] Corruption was so widespread that many foremen were more small businessmen than company employees.

Where piece rates were the norm, earnings often depended on the jobs or materials the foreman handed out. In the men's galoshes section of the Triangle Works, for example, according to a worker writing to *Pravda* in

[14] P. Timofeev, *Chem zhivet zavodskii rabochii* (St. Petersburg, 1906), p. 5. Some of this memoir has been translated in V. Bonnell, *The Russian Worker: Life and Labor under the Tsarist Regime* (Berkeley and Los Angeles, 1983), pp. 72–112.

[15] U. A. Shuster, *Peterburgskie rabochie v 1905–1907 gg.* (Leningrad, 1976), p. 21; LGIA, f. 416, op. 5, d. 27, ll. 7–9.

[16] A. Teplov, *Zapiski Putilovtsa* (St. Petersburg, 1908), p. 11.

[17] M. Davidovich, *Peterburgskii tekstil'nyi rabochii v ego biudzhetakh* (St. Petersburg, 1912), p. 8.

1912, foreman S frequently gave out "thin material which has an uneven backing, so that when we make galoshes, we get a lot of waste."[18] Where the execution of a particular job depended on the skill and cooperation of craftsmen, however, the foreman was obliged to bargain with them over the rate to be paid.[19] Such bargaining remained common down to 1917, even though a trend in the metal industries after 1905 was toward hourly rates of pay (the so-called "American method" of payment, which involved worksheets and the exact accounting of work time by technical staff) and complex incentive schemes. This reduced the influence over earnings of both the foreman, whose job was taken over by the central rating department, and the skilled workers, who lost the right to negotiate job rates. Some historians have suggested that this was the major cause of the high number of conflicts between workers and foremen in St. Petersburg on the eve of the war, since previous informal wage bargaining had served as safety valve for shop-floor grievances.[20] This was undoubtedly an important factor, but such conflict was not confined to industries where such rationalization was taking place.

"We Are People Too. . . . "

The 1905 revolution saw an explosion of protests by workers against inhuman treatment by lower supervisory personnel. In January 1905 workers at the Baltic Works put forward twenty demands, including ones that searches of workers—"which profane human dignity"—be abolished, and that "foremen, assistant foremen, inspectors, and the administration in general be obliged to treat workers as people and not as things."[21] This heightened sensitivity to personal dignity was not confined to skilled, relatively well educated male workers, although it was particularly strong among the self-styled "conscious" workers.[22] In 1905 the mainly female workforce at the Shtiglits Cotton-Weaving Mill issued the following statement: "There is complete arbitrariness when it comes to firing workers. The worker Petukhov worked for ten years at the mill,

---

[18] *Pravda*, 16 June 1912, p. 4.

[19] Eduard M. Dune, *Notes of a Red Guard*, trans. and ed. Diane P. Koenker and S. A. Smith (Urbana, Ill., 1993), pp. 13–14.

[20] McKean, *St. Petersburg between the Revolutions*, p. 11. See also Haimson, "Structural Processes of Change," p. 390.

[21] F. A. Bulkin, *Na zare profdvizheniia: Istoriia peterburgskogo soiuza metallistov, 1906–14 gg.* (Moscow, 1924), p. 61.

[22] Timofeev, *Chem zhivet*, pp. 96–97; A. I. Shapovalov, *Po doroge k marksismu: Vospominaniia rabochego revoliutsionera* (Moscow, 1924), p. 19. For a lucid discussion of what it meant to be one of the minority of "conscious" workers, see T. McDaniel, *Autocracy, Capitalism and Revolution in Russia* (Berkeley and Los Angeles, 1988), chap. 8.

but one day the foreman caught sight of a newspaper in his pocket and fired him, on the grounds that he was obviously involved in politics. . . . And during his time at the factory the foreman Sedov even raped several young girls. But the victims of these disgusting crimes stayed silent out of fear of losing their jobs or out of a sense of shame."[23]

During 1905 the emergence of strike committees, factory commissions, and trade unions put foremen on the defensive. A. Teplov, a technician at the Putilov Works, wrote in the aftermath of the failure of the revolution: "The nearer we got to 1905, the more importunate the craftsmen became. . . . Exhortations were ineffective and it became dangerous to oppose them. . . . Among them were many disguised students. During the strikes the staff came to the factory in fear of violence. It was quite terrifying. 'Hang the fat devils, the *burzhui*, the bureaucrats!' 'You should be given a thrashing!' the crowd shouted."[24]

Excluded from membership in Father Gapon's Assembly of Russian Mill and Factory Workers and banned from serving as electors to the Shidlovskii commission, some progressive foremen aligned themselves with the nascent labor movement by forming their own union of foremen and technicians.[25] The union deployed the language of citizenship, rather than class conflict, in a manner that was characteristic of Russia's first revolution. At a meeting on 8 October members discussed the dismissal of one of the senior foremen at the Pipe (*Trubochnyi*) Works for joining the union. The meeting expressed its "deep dissatisfaction with this grave insult to the personality of the worker [*lichnost'iu rabotnika*]," and agreed that "the police duties invested in foremen are incompatible with the dignity of the citizen and of the honorable worker [*rabotnika*]."[26] Whether because of a desire to turn over a new leaf or because of the pressure they faced from an increasingly organized working class, foremen do seem to

[23] *Revoliutsiia 1905–07 gg. v Rossii: Nachalo pervoi russkoi revoliutsii: Ianvar'–mart 1905 goda* (Moscow, 1955), p. 178.

[24] Teplov, *Zapiski Putilovtsa*, p. 32.

[25] V. Bonnell, *Roots of Rebellion: Workers' Politics and Organization in St. Petersburg and Moscow, 1900–14* (Berkeley and Los Angeles, 1983), p. 83; Suhr, *1905 in St. Petersburg*, p. 211. Father Georgii Gapon, with backing from the secret police, founded the Assembly of Russian Mill and Factory Workers in the summer of 1903. The purpose of this organization was to improve the position of workers while steering clear of politics. Gapon was popular with workers, and by January 1905, the Assembly had a membership of at least six thousand. It was Gapon who led the procession to the Winter Palace on Sunday, 9 January 1905, which was brutally dispersed, thereby setting in train the events of the revolution of 1905. In the aftermath of "Bloody Sunday" a commission was set up under Senator N. V. Shidlovskii to examine worker grievances and submit proposals to improve working conditions. A remarkable feature was that the commission included fifty delegates indirectly elected by the workers. Although the commission was a failure, the experience of the elections laid the ground for the labor unions later in the year.

[26] *Novoe vremia*, 10 (23) October 1905, p. 2. I am grateful to Gerald Surh for this reference.

have improved their treatment of workers. Beatings almost disappeared, and the incidence of physical searching of workers was reduced.[27]

Once political reaction and economic recession set in after 1907, however, the behavior of foremen appears to have deteriorated. Complaints against them multiplied during the years 1907 to 1912, but it was not until the revival of the labor movement between 1912 and 1914 that conflict once again erupted on a large scale. The new Bolshevik newspaper, *Pravda*, invited workers to write about their grievances and was inundated with reports and letters describing the abuses and insults to which they were subject. A group of workers wrote to ask for articles on themes such as *ty i vy* (the use of "you" in its familiar and polite forms) and "coarse and polite treatment."[28] In one report, "White Slaves of the Tavern," a tavern employee wrote: "The treatment of serving staff by both tavern-owners and customers is quite barbaric. 'Son of a bitch,' 'Lout,' 'Hooligan,' 'Get the Hell Out,' are all common ways of addressing fully grown adults. The treatment of young girls is worse—worse than that of prostitutes. 'Ugly-mug,' 'Old Mare,' 'Filthy Slut' are common. And young boys endure everything from verbal abuse—'Flea-ridden pup' etc.—to being punched and having their teeth knocked out."[29]

Reading these complaints, one realizes that relations between workers and foremen were influenced by more than the exigencies of capitalist production. Writing for her evening-class teacher, a woman worker wrote: "The attitude of the administration to us women is utterly obscene. They don't see us as people but as cattle. They make advances, grab us unawares, pour abuse and bad language on us and make unseemly hints. If they come across women who treat their activities with contempt, they quickly let them know they are at risk of being fired."[30] Such sexual harassment was commonplace and reminds us that relations between male supervisors and female workers were qualitatively different from those between male supervisors and male workers, for their behavior was fundamentally governed by dominant gender norms. Foremen, for example, gave preferential treatment to young women they considered attractive. In the cutting section on the sixth floor of the Skorokhod Shoe Factory, foreman I was said to "ingratiate himself with attractive women workers. . . . Seldom will one of the women escape a gentle pinch or a 'sweet' word. . . . In the sewing section foreman P addresses the women as 'ty' or hisses at them, as though he were walking along Nevskii Prospekt at night. . . . Foreman P pokes less attractive women in the ribs and roundly abuses

[27] L. Kleinbort, "Ocherki rabochei demokratii," *Sovremennyi mir*, November 1913, p. 29.
[28] *Pravda*, 23 October 1912, p. 4.
[29] *Rabochaia pravda*, 20 July 1913, p. 4.
[30] *Rabotnitsa v 1905 v Sankt-Peterburge*, ed. P. F. Kudelli (Leningrad, 1926), p. 4.

them, and ensures that any woman he dislikes, earns very little."[31] At the Art Press Printworks—where most of the women were aged fifteen to forty-five, married, and literate—"Those who are willing to go out with the foreman after work get the best jobs, whereas those who value their personal dignity regularly find themselves with not enough work to do."[32] At its most extreme, sexual harassment extended to rape. When the foreman of the rubber section at the Triangle Works tried to rape a woman worker in his office, three workers standing close by took no notice of her screams. "Apparently, they were so used to hearing this that they didn't budge from their benches."[33]

Women were far less likely to be in supervisory positions than men. Where they did serve as forewomen, it was always over other women. Though spared routine sexual harassment, women workers complain that forewomen nevertheless exercise authority in ways sanctified by patriarchal tradition.[34] At the Georges Borman Chocolate Factory, which employed some fifty women aged fifteen to twenty-two, according to a letter to *Pravda*, "The forewomen do not shrink from using words like 'scum,' and so on. Recently, on 27 August, the senior woman worker swore at one of the women after she made a mistake, and when the woman protested, she slapped her on the face. Everyone is scared of her."[35] A new recruit to the galoshes section of the Triangle Works was fined for waste: "The forewoman pounced on the unfortunate young girl and threatened to summon the foreman, who is well-known for his despotism toward women workers. The threat so terrified the girl that she fainted. . . . Yet for some reason, this and similar incidents cause merriment among the other women."[36] During the First World War Evdokiia Proskurakova, supervisor of women workers in the iron foundry of the Baltic Works, "used her power to extort coupons for meat, flour, and other items from the women. If someone failed to show up for work for any reason, she would take their rations and leave them with nothing."[37] This suggests that worker-supervisor relations were conditioned not only by the contradictory social relations of capitalist production, but also by the social relations of patriarchy.

Relations between supervisors and workers also played on age-based power relations, with some of the worst treatment being meted out to boy apprentices by owners and foremen in small workshops. The Ivanov

[31] *Pravda*, 19 August 1912, p. 3.
[32] *Pravda*, 17 February 1913, p. 4.
[33] *Pravda*, 31 August 1912, p. 3.
[34] In passing one may note that the subsequent socialist revolution failed to reverse the preponderance of men in lower supervisory positions.
[35] *Pravda*, 31 August 1912, p. 3.
[36] *Pravda*, 4 October 1912, p. 4.
[37] LGIA, f. 416, op. 5, d. 24, l. 156.

box factory on Vyborg Side employed about forty youngsters, aged twelve to sixteen. One wrote, "The foreman, Zapol'skii, is just like the owner and treats us in an intolerably crude way. They both abuse us for all they're worth, and the foreman lets fly with his fists. Generally, the factory is like a lunatic asylum, with the foreman shrieking at us the whole day as though we were cattle. . . . Isn't it about time we united and organized and showed Ivanov and his foreman that we are people, too, and not dumb animals?"[38] After 1905 there were relatively few complaints to the Factory Inspectorate about beatings. Where they occurred, the victims were invariably young boys.[39] At the Gautman bakery a boy apprentice wrote: "They beat the boys at every turn. Once a boy turned on the faucet but the sink was blocked, and at that moment Max Fedorovich came in and began to rage, using choice Russian obscenities, and then resorted to his fists. The boy fell on the floor, but the foreman continued to kick him. The workers just stood and watched as he taught the apprentice a lesson."[40] By contrast, when an adult worker at Putilov was beaten by the engineer Morgenstern in the spring of 1915, it provoked a bitter strike.[41]

The surname of this Putilov engineer reminds us of the extent to which non-Russians dominated the ranks of industrial management in St. Petersburg. Although it may not have been a typical district of the city, in Vasilevskii Ostrov in 1901 37 percent of directors of factories, 27 percent of managers, 26 percent of assistant managers, 45 percent of foremen, and 24 percent of assistant foremen were foreign.[42] Ethnicity thus also inflected transactions between foremen and workers, with foreign foremen—German and British in the main—notorious for their contempt of "uncultured" Russians.[43] At the British-owned No.2 Nevskaia Cotton Mill (formerly Koenig) it was reported to *Pravda* that "one of the Russian supervisors stands out. He is called P and both in external appearance and in his behavior he is more animal than man. Lowering his head, he rushes about shouting at any defenseless thirteen-year-old girl—of whom there are not a few—and cursing in the most obscene manner. He frequently fines the women for waste that is actually his fault, and threatens them with firing. In a word, he tries to oblige his English masters."[44] Here the woman writing emphasizes not only the male chauvinism of this foreman but the "quisling" aspect of his behavior, his desire to curry favor with his foreign employer.

[38] *Pravda*, 1 June 1912, p. 4.
[39] S. Gvozdev, *Zapiski fabrichnogo inspektora* (Moscow, 1911), p. 119.
[40] *Pravda*, 12 June 1912, p. 4.
[41] I. I. Gaza, *Putilovets na putiakh k oktiabriu* (Moscow, 1933), p. 17.
[42] S. N. Semanov, *Peterburgskie rabochie nakanune pervoi russkoi revoliutsii* (Moscow, 1966), p. 120.
[43] Haimson, "Structural Processes of Change," p. 383.
[44] *Pravda*, 15 June 1912, p. 4.

If we read the complaints of workers in the labor press about the behavior of lower supervisory personnel, we can see how industrial relations in Russia drew on and reinforced preexisting cultural patterns and power relations. If the issue of coarse and brutal treatment was a potent leaven fermenting class consciousness in Russia, it cannot be understood solely in class terms, for it was strongly inflected by social relations based on gender, age, and ethnicity.

Getting on with the Foreman

It would be wrong to infer that relations between supervisors and workers were based on nothing more than abuse and violence. Though employers expected foremen to discipline and punish, they also valued those who could command the respect of workers and induce them to work conscientiously. This was particularly true in craft settings where so much depended on the scarce skills of the craftsmen. It is harder to find out about worker-supervisor relations in such situations, since "conscious" workers wrote to the labor press to complain about tyrannical supervisors, not to praise those who behaved themselves. In the peculiar conditions of wartime, Eduard Dune paints a picture of industrial relations at the Provodnik Rubber Works in Moscow that is more cordial than that which emerges from the correspondence to *Pravda* or the trade union press: "Formally, the foremen were 'staff,' not workers, but because they had begun as workers, and learnt every detail of the production process and all the little tricks used to lessen the burden of work and increase pay, they willy-nilly pandered to the interests of the workers and were basically part of the collective."[45] Relations were similar among printers. Karavaev, foreman of the Shreder Printworks, wrote to *Pravda*, saying: "I have worked for thirty years, and I have never insulted a worker. I hope I never shall."[46] Occasionally, but only occasionally, management worried about foremen getting too friendly with the workers. In 1913, A. Kitaev, a foreman at the British-owned Nevskaia Cotton Mill, was fined five rubles after the director, Karl Ferdinandovich Kiuk, spied him shaking hands with a worker.[47] The director obviously feared that fraternization of this kind would undermine the reliability of this noncommissioned officer of capital. Only in 1917 did employer anxieties about "desertion" to the side of labor become acute.

The possibility of collaboration between craftsmen and foremen de-

---

[45] Dune, *Notes of a Red Guard*, p. 12.
[46] *Pravda*, 5 March 1913, p. 3.
[47] A. Vasenko, *Za sto let (1840–1940): K stoletiiu leningradskoi bumazhnoi fabriki im. Volodarskogo* (Leningrad, 1940), p. 99.

pended on the foremen's not putting on airs or attempting to conceal his social origins. If a foreman behaved as one of "us," that is, in a way that seemed natural and unaffected to those under him, his workers cooperated with him. Conversely, if a foreman was seen to be distancing himself, his workers tended to be hostile and uncooperative. There were two foremen and one senior worker in charge of the shop making sulfuric acid at the Okhta Gunpowder Works.

> Foreman L rose from the ranks of the workers, but has now completely forgotten this fact. He receives a good salary, but never says no when the workers treat him to cognac. . . . Foreman A is a man with secondary education who was considered "conscious" in 1905–6. Because he fawned to the management, he is now regarded as the senior foreman, almost as the assistant shop director. He is only good toward those who give shoes and clothes to him and his family. The rest he treats as idlers. The senior worker, B, has worked in the factory since the age of ten. He somehow managed to get into the clerk's office and was then promoted to senior worker. He now aspires to become a foreman and will no doubt achieve this through his denunciations and slanders, especially since there are almost no conscious workers among the workforce of eighty.[48]

Humor was one of the "weapons of the weak" used to cut the foreman down to size.[49] It was part of the culture of the workshop to invent nicknames for foremen, especially those who put on airs.[50] A supervisor in the Baltic Works, a former policeman, was known as "Pepper": "He spends the whole day clambering through the toilets and searching every nook and cranny for workers who are standing staring."[51] The director of the Phoenix Works, an Englishman, was known as "Steely": "The workers said he must have a spine of steel since he would never acknowledge a bow."[52] The foreman in the gun shop of the Putilov Works was nicknamed "Shaposhnikov" because he insisted that the workers doff their caps when they bumped into him.[53] The use of nicknames reflected the workers' ironic detachment from the official order.

Craft workers endeavored to build up "credit" with the foreman through rituals such as drinking binges or the formal presentation of gifts. These were designed to strengthen bonds of attachment within the work-

---

[48] *Pravda*, 22 September 1912, p. 4.

[49] J. C. Scott, *Weapons of the Weak: Everyday Forms of Resistance* (New Haven, Conn., 1985), p. 282.

[50] V. F. Pletnev, "Proletarskii byt: Staryi i novyi," *Gorn*, no. 9 (1923): 66.

[51] *Pravda*, 4 August 1912, p. 3.

[52] *Vyborgskaia Storona: Iz istorii bor'by rabochego klassa za pobedu velikoi oktiabr'skoi revoliutsii: Sbornik statei i vospominanii* (Leningrad, 1957), p. 16. "Steely" met a tragic end, axed to death by one of his employees. Such incidents were very rare.

[53] *Pravda*, 24 June 1912, p. 3. The root of this surname is *shapka*, the word for "cap."

shop and create a fund of goodwill on which both sides could draw.[54] One of the ways in which skilled men could secure good relations with a new foreman was to give him a rousing welcome and invite him to participate in an initiation ceremony. In return, the foreman was expected to treat the workers to drinks. In a foundry, for example, a new foreman would be given an "address" (*adreso*), which entailed his being invited to fix the first hole in a mould waiting to receive molten pig iron with a rod decorated with colored paper. After the ceremony he would buy the workers a round of drinks, though Timofeev tells of one who flatly refused to do so. The same source claims that such practices were already in decline by 1905. Yet in the machine shop at New Lessner in 1912 a new foreman "introduced himself to the eight or ten fitters, who shouted 'Hurrah.' Even more shamefully, they raised him aloft. Of course, they did so only so that he would give them vodka, and he did not stint them, treating them to five roubles worth, which, naturally, they drank at once. . . . Now they are expecting great and wonderful kindnesses from this foreman."[55] Such bibulous customs may have been on the wane, but they were not defunct even in the 1920s.[56]

In a situation where the absence of rights was generalized, workers of all types relied on informal strategies to defend themselves against their immediate bosses. Such strategies can be usefully analyzed through the lens of clientelism.[57] Seeing no escape from their situation, some workers ingratiated themselves with the foreman by telling tales on their fellows or by giving gifts. Spying and informing were endemic in the years after 1907, for employers were eager to expel workers who had been active during the revolution. P. Vasil'ev, one of a group of fitters transferred from the Sestroretsk Armaments Works to the Aivaz Works, was nicknamed the "Sugary One." In return for a soft job as a sorter, which earned him seventy-five rubles a month, he provided the foreman with written and oral reports on his fellow workers, telling him who were "extreme elements," who were "yardmen" (that is, untrained in their jobs), and who were plain lazy.[58] Tale-telling was common among women workers. At the James Beck Cotton Mill it was said: "The women all tell tales on

[54] H. Medick, "Plebeian Culture in the Transition to Capitalism," in R. Samuel and G. Stedman Jones, eds., *Culture, Ideology and Politics: Essays for Eric Hobsbawm* (London, 1982), p. 92.

[55] Timofeev, *Chem zhivet*, p. 94; *Pravda*, 15 June 1912, p. 4.

[56] C. Ward, *Russia's Cotton Workers and the New Economic Policy: Shop-floor Culture and State Policy, 1921–29* (Cambridge, 1990), pp. 93–94.

[57] Carl Lande, "The Dyadic Basis of Clientelism," and J. C. Scott, "Patron-Client Politics and Political Change in Southeast Asia." Both articles are in *Friends, Followers and Factions: A Reader in Political Clientelism*, eds. S. W. Schmidt, L. Guasti, C. Lande, and J. C. Scott (Berkeley and Los Angeles, 1977).

[58] *Pravda*, 28 February 1913, p. 4.

one another and try to hurt one another in every way. Gossip and toadying have built a firm nest for themselves. There are some who have become experts, but they generally act carefully, according to the proverb, 'The sow told the hog and the hog went to Ivan Egorov.' People are fined or dismissed because of this."[59] At the St. Petersburg Company for the Manufacture of Canvas Products there were said to be fifty women in a workforce of ninety-two: "They treat one another badly and engage for the most part in telling tales on their comrades, hoping in this way to distinguish themselves in the eyes of the administration."[60]

The "conscious" minority waged war against these divisive and collusive strategies. "For conscious workers, aware of their class interest, all giving of gifts is unacceptable," wrote a correspondent to *Pravda*.[61] On 10 July 1913 at the Shtiuder Timber Works 28 rubles and 50 kopecks were collected for the foreman, Gaevskii. One worker wrote:

> Perhaps Gaevskii is a very good man, but the issue we must face is whether we should be increasing his pleasure or improving our own lives which are oppressed by capital. Gaevskii enjoys a good reputation with the management, who have increased his salary to 125 rubles a month, and this ensures him satisfaction enough. . . . Nice presents for nice people is fine, but the moral price can be high. Consider who, in our eyes, is really a good man: is it the one who climbs the job ladder or the one who cares about the collective welfare of the workers?

The writer suggested that if the workers were determined to make a collection for the foreman, they should donate it in his honor to some collective cause such as a workers' library or to strikers' families.[62] Another worker wrote to protest that one of his colleagues, on being promoted to assistant foreman, had splashed out ten rubles for drinks, arguing that the money would have been better spent on orphans, on the "Knowledge Is Light" educational society, on the newspaper *Rabochaia pravda*, or on a factory library or canteen. "I am not some opera Mephistopheles and was neither scornful nor mocking. But it is necessary to arouse some shame among this drunken lot."[63]

Although it might express sincere respect for a decent foreman, gift-giving was generally self-interested in motive: gifts were protection money, the price one paid to ensure that the foreman would not be the bane of one's life. Even the correspondents to *Pravda*, deeply hostile to such be-

---

[59] *Pravda*, 4 January 1913, p. 4.
[60] *Pravda*, 17 February 1913, p. 4.
[61] *Pravda*, 27 September 1912, p. 4.
[62] *Pravda*, 28 July 1913, p. 4.
[63] *Rabochaia pravda*, 31 July 1913, p. 4.

havior, perceived it as largely cynical in intent, a ploy to get in with the foreman. That such patterns of behavior disappeared quickly once collective organization was permitted—though there are still occasional complaints in *Pravda* in 1917 about the buying of leaving presents for foremen and employers—suggests that there was no widespread normative adherence to such strategies. We know that within the culture of the craft worker, sneaking on one's fellows was considered dishonorable, but there is evidence that it met with general censure on the part of the mass of workers, despite being fairly widespread.[64] We hear of informers being beaten up, of "being given a race" (*gonka*) or a "cleaning behind the gates" (*chistka za vorotami*) or a "smack on the chops" (*skulovorot*). And the words for bootlicking and toadying—*podkhalimstvo, podlipaly*—themselves powerfully pejorative, were in wide circulation.[65]

Compared with other agrarian societies undergoing industrialization, patron-client relations in the full-blown sense appear to have been relatively weak in St. Petersburg. There are, for example, almost no instances of foremen supporting strikers, whereas in Shanghai, where clientelism was far more deeply rooted, such solidarity was common.[66] Of a strike in November 1912 at the Old Sampsionievskaia Mill it was said: "The supervisors [*podmaster'ia*] in the weaving and sizing sections went on strike, but only out of decency, and when the strike ended, they went back to the factory, crying to the foremen—'We tried to stop them.' "[67] The paucity even of such instances of ambivalent support may be taken as an index of the relative weakness of clientelism proper. Certainly, such relations were not sufficiently strong to stultify efforts by labor movement activists to represent the foreman ideologically as the enemy rather than ally of the worker.

The Foreman as the Agent of Capital

In the years following the 1905 revolution the trade union and social-democratic press tried to combat older notions, widespread among the "backward masses," of the foreman as a "benefactor" (*blagodeiatel'*) or

---

[64] Compare the Gujerati engineering works studied by N. R. Sheth, where the skilled workers said they disliked flattering the bosses but claimed that the unskilled workers did it all the time: N. R. Sheth, *Social Framework of an Indian Factory*, 2d ed (Delhi, 1981), p. 119.

[65] Pletnev, "Proletarskii byt," p. 66; this was still true in the 1920s, see H. Kuromiya, "The Crisis of Proletarian Identity in the Soviet Factory, 1928–29," *Slavic Review* 44, no. 2 (1985): 291.

[66] S. A. Smith, "Workers and Supervisors in St. Petersburg 1905 to 1917, and Shanghai, 1895 to 1927," *Past and Present*, May 1993, pp. 131–77.

[67] *Pravda*, 14 December 1912, p. 4.

patron. Instead it endeavored to represent the foreman as the agent of capital. All processes of representation are selective, and it is interesting to note how the image of the foremen retailed by the trade union and socialist press omitted reference to his function in coordinating production or to the fact that he sold his labor-power to capital,[68] but constantly iterated his function as the last link in the capitalist chain of command. The image was popularized in a more accessible idiom by the "conscious" worker, who likened the foreman to a "little whip" (*knutik*), whose sole aim in life was to intensify the exploitation of workers. He was, they averred, a traitor to his class, who had made his personal escape from the ranks of the oppressed at the expense of his fellows.[69]

In propagating class politics, socialist intellectuals and "conscious" workers deemed it vital to police the boundary between the world of the worker and the world of management, the better to define and strengthen workers' esprit de corps. Struggling trade unionists insisted on keeping foremen out of the labor unions. Figures emanating from a survey of the metalworkers' union in St. Petersburg in 1908 show that the only members exercising any kind of supervisory function were a handful of gang leaders (*desiatskie*) and quality inspectors (*brakovshchiki*).[70] As industrial recovery slowly got under way after 1910, opportunities for promotion to supervisory positions multiplied, and isolated voices were heard within the union urging admittance to assistant foremen (*podmaster'ia*), though not to foremen proper. The assistant foremen, it was argued, had not lost contact with the workers and their presence within the union would help bridge the gap between workers and technical personnel. The union board, however, decisively rejected this proposal.[71] In their eyes, the liminal figure of the foreman blurred class boundaries and confused the definition of what it meant to be a worker. It is worth noting that such an exclusive policy was at variance with that pursued by certain British trade unions in the nineteenth century, which made efforts to get foremen into the trade unions, the better to keep them under control.[72]

Worker antagonism to the foreman was not, of course, created by so-

---

[68] Roger Chartier, *Cultural History: Between Practices and Representations*, trans. Lydia G. Cochrane (Ithaca, N.Y., 1988), p. 6.

[69] Bulkin, *Na zare*, p. 212.

[70] *Materialy ob ekonomicheskom polozhenii i professional'noi organizatsii peterburgskikh rabochikh po metallu* (St. Petersburg, 1909), p. 94.

[71] Bulkin, *Na zare*, p. 297.

[72] Foremen were members of the Boilermakers' Society and of the construction workers' unions. See J. Melling, "Non-Commissioned Officers: British Employers and Supervisory Workers, 1880–1920," *Social History* 5, no. 2 (1980): 207; R. Price, *Masters, Unions and Men: Work Control in Building and the Rise of Labour 1830–1914* (Cambridge, 1980), p. 39.

cialist propaganda. As the most visible and seemingly powerful representative of industrial management on the shop floor, his daily activities in and of themselves were enough to provoke worker disaffection.[73] As Barrington Moore argues, the social relations of the workplace engender resentment and moral outrage more directly than do the wider relations of society: "In the workplace there are visible and concrete human beings who appear responsible for injustice. . . . This aspect distinguishes such situations from the more general distress of hunger and bad housing."[74] The contribution of socialist propaganda was to work up this discontent ideologically so that the foreman became linked metonymically to a system of exploitation and injustice that stretched well beyond the confines of the workplace. Not only could he symbolize a wider system of capitalist exploitation, he could also symbolize the wider system of tsarist autocracy. As the bosses' "little whip," the foreman stood for "capitalism," and as the "little tsar" of the workplace, he stood for the general condition of *bespravie*—the denial of civil and political rights—endemic to the tsarist political system. The figure of the foreman was thus peculiarly potent in discursive terms, for it focused grievances rooted in capitalism and autocracy alike, thereby facilitating the articulation of manifold economic and political discontents in the language of class.

From the perspective of the social-democratic project, however, much shop-floor resistance to lower supervisory personnel remained prepolitical. Favored tactics included physical attacks on foremen under cover of darkness, the sending of anonymous threatening letters or round-robin petitions with inscriptions such as "We are all against you, blood-sucker. Just wait, we'll get our revenge."[75] The most dramatic form of resistance was the ritual of carting out an administrator from the workplace in a wheelbarrow. A group of workers would steal up behind an errant supervisor, throw a sack, suitably lined with oil or soot, over his head and then, to catcalls and whistles, trundle him out of the factory.[76] The cart was known colloquially as "local transport" or the "landau."[77] Dune writes:

> I know from my father's stories that there were rare occasions at the Provodnik plant when a whole workshop of 300 to 500 workers would rise

[73] D. P. Koenker and W. G. Rosenberg, *Strikes and Revolution in Russia, 1917* (Princeton, N.J., 1989), p. 139.
[74] Barrington Moore, *Injustice: The Social Bases of Obedience and Revolt* (London, 1979), p. 203.
[75] A. M. Buiko, *Put' rabochego: Zapiski starogo bol'shevika* (Moscow, 1934), p. 18; N. P. Paialin, *Zavod imeni Lenina, 1857–1918* (Moscow, 1933), p. 150.
[76] Timofeev, *Chem zhivet*, pp. 98–99.
[77] *Istoriia Putilovskogo zavoda, 1908–17 gg.*, eds. M. Mitel'man, V. Glebov, and A. Ul'ianskii, 3d ed. (1961), p. 527; Gaza, *Putilovets*, p. 27.

against the foreman. On coming to work, the foreman would discover a sack nailed to the door of his office as a warning. If the warning did not suffice, he would be thrust into the sack, carried into the yard and dumped into a wheelbarrow and, amid general laughter, mirth and joking, carried through puddles or to the dung-heap in the stable yard. A foreman who had floundered in a sack amid the hoots and jeers of the crowd, or wallowed in a puddle while trying to crawl out of the sack would not easily forget it, and would bear the stigma for a long time. In order that the instigators should remain undetected, this would all happen without warning or in some other department, as the foreman was passing through a crowd of workers.[78]

The targets of this form of symbolic retribution, used by men and women alike, were usually male supervisors, though sometimes factory directors or strikebreakers might also be the victims.

It was the strike, however, which was the most important means of resisting tyrannical supervisors. Of the many strikes against administrative personnel on the eve of the First World War, the most dramatic was that against a foreman at the New Lessner Works in 1913. It began after foreman Laul accused a young Jewish worker, Iakov Stronin, of theft—an accusation which caused Stronin to hang himself. The strike received remarkable support from workers throughout the country, who donated over 11,000 rubles. It ended in failure, after a remarkable 102 days, with management firing the strikers and importing skilled labor from Sweden.[79] A contemporaneous strike at the Robert Krug Works against foreman Ianson also ended in failure after twenty-seven days.[80] During the war the proportion of economic strikes attributable to issues of authority remained approximately comparable with prewar levels, that is, in the range of a quarter to a third of all disputes, but these strikes became concentrated in the metal industries.[81]

Foremen on the Run

The February Revolution unleashed a ferocious onslaught on the old factory order, which included the mass expulsion of unpopular administrative personnel by workers. Workers drew a direct parallel between the overthrow of the tsarist autocracy and that of the autocratic order in the workplace, insisting that the establishment of the "constitutional factory"

[78] Dune, *Notes of a Red Guard*, p. 14.
[79] *Severnaia pravda*, 11 August 1913, p. 3. A. Y. Badaev, Bolshevik deputy in the Fourth Duma, says that about 18,000 rubles was collected, "the largest sum ever collected during a strike." A. Y. Badaev, *Bolsheviks in the Tsarist Duma* (London, 1987), p. 96.
[80] *Pravda*, 25 July 1913, p. 4.
[81] McKean, *St. Petersburg between the Revolutions*, pp. 421–22.

required the purging of the staff officers of the ancien régime.[82] The extent of expulsions in the largest plants is astonishing, though no global data for Petrograd exist. At the Triangle Works in the first heady days of the revolution more than one hundred administrative and technical staff were ejected.[83] In the first three "days of freedom" more than forty members of the administration at the Putilov Works were expelled.[84] At the Sestroretsk Armaments Works fifty-six members of the administration were removed during the month of March.[85] At the Petrograd Cartridge Works about 80 percent of the administration were rejected by the workforce, and at the Admiralty, New Admiralty, and Galernyi Island Shipyards forty-nine staff were removed from their posts by decision of a general meeting of workers.[86]

The Provisional Government tried to ensure that these removals were ratified by the newly established conciliation boards, which consisted of an equal number of representatives of management and workers. But these bodies proved powerless to obstruct the general will of labor. The three conciliation boards at the Baltic Works, a large shipyard run by the Admiralty, heard no fewer than 113 appeals by supervisory personnel against their expulsions.[87] Conciliation Board No. 1 examined fifty-nine cases, of which six involved foremen, twelve assistant foremen, thirty-four crew leaders, and seven workers. Of a total of 126 charges presented in these fifty-nine cases, the largest number—40—concerned rudeness and contempt for workers' needs, underlining just how sensitive workers were to issues affecting their dignity. Thirty charges involved the setting of unduly low wages or piece rates; 14 concerned incompetence in the job; and 11 involved persecution of workers for their political beliefs or for wage militancy.[88]

Some of the cases at the Baltic Works are worth looking at in closer detail. In the paint shop on March 9 a general meeting decided to expel V. Miliaev, shop foreman for seven years. He appealed to the conciliation board: "The workers concede that they can recall no rudenesses or injustices on my part. But now that we have a new system, they desire a foreman elected from their ranks, because they think that such a person will be easier to get on with and will defend their interests." The concil-

---

[82] S. A. Smith, *Red Petrograd: Revolution in the Factories, 1917–18* (Cambridge, 1983), chap. 2.

[83] I. A. Baklanova, *Rabochie Petrograda v period mirnogo razvitiia revoliutsii (mart–iun' 1917 g.)* (Leningrad, 1978), p. 79.

[84] B. M. Freidlin, *Ocherki istorii rabochego dvizheniia v Rossii v 1917 g.* (Moscow, 1967), p. 248.

[85] Baklanova, *Rabochie Petrograda*, pp. 80–81.

[86] Smith, *Red Petrograd*, p. 55.

[87] Baklanova, *Rabochie Petrograda*, p. 77.

[88] H. Hogan, "Conciliation Boards," p. 59.

iation board upheld his appeal against expulsion, but in April a meeting of the paint shop resolved "under no circumstances to allow the return of the old foreman, Miliaev, since he does not know his job and is completely ignorant of the painters' craft. In addition, he showed no desire to develop the factory since he farmed out work to subcontractors."[89] In the foundry the senior foreman was accused of "organizing espionage on the workforce and of imposing such vigilance via his agents that it was impossible to form any organization other than a monarchist one."[90] The memory of injustice rankled, going back in one instance as far as 1901. In the accumulator shop white-collar employees voted by fifty-four to thirty-four to get rid of the assistant director, N. G. Gaidukhin, "for rudeness to employees and for depravity toward A. Tikhomirova, an office worker, who was arbitrarily sacked by him, and who attempted suicide in the works grounds."[91]

In thirteen out of the eighteen cases involving foremen or their assistants that came before the first conciliation board at the Baltic Works, the board felt it had no choice but to uphold the expulsions, since it was powerless to revoke them. In conflicts involving the very lowest ranking supervisors, such as crew leaders and senior workers, however, the board did succeed in exerting some influence over the workers. Out of forty-one such cases, twenty-six were resolved peacefully, or by downgrading the crew leader to the status of a rank-and-file worker. This suggests that workers considered these people not to have deserted the ranks of labor in the same way as foremen.[92]

Although the purges were largely complete by the end of March, conflict between workers and foremen persisted over the next several months, albeit on a smaller scale. At the Nevskaia Footwear Factory the foremen sent a letter to the factory committee on 21 June 1917, "protesting categorically the attitude of workers toward us. If we make a justified reprimand we are greeted with unprintable abuse."[93] At the same factory the foreman, P. Konovalov, complained that when he asked the worker Dudin why he had entered another section of the factory without a pass, he answered, "What business is it of yours?" and proceeded to be very rude. When told he risked dismissal, he threatened the foreman with violence.[94] The most abrasive conflict between foremen and workers took place at the Triangle Works. In early June the women of the galoshes section decided to demote twenty forewomen on the grounds that they were no

---

[89] LGIA, f. 416, op. 5, d. 24, ll. 52–58.
[90] Ibid., l. 155.
[91] Ibid., l. 7.
[92] Hogan, "Conciliation Boards," p. 61.
[93] LGIA, f. 1182, op. 1, d. 96, l. 32.
[94] Ibid., l. 40.

longer needed. The union of foremen appealed to the council of elders (that is, the factory committee) to intervene, and the council called for their reinstatement. This infuriated the workers, who said that they would accept nothing less than the outright dismissal of the forewomen, and even threatened to cart them out of the factory. The council of elders referred the matter to the works conciliation board, which deferred making a decision for want of evidence. The union of foremen then insisted that the matter be resolved by the Central Conciliation Board and also demanded that the board examine the cases of all foremen and forewomen expelled at the time of the February Revolution. Receiving no satisfaction, the union of foremen on 21 June announced that it was going on strike. The strike appears to have been partly successful, for the workers agreed to the reinstatement of the twenty (though it is not clear whether as ordinary workers or as forewomen), and in return the foremen dropped the demand for the reinstatement of those expelled in March.[95] Similar conflicts took place at the Metal and Nobel works.[96]

The February Revolution encouraged workers to claim the right to elect foremen. On 7 March 1917 the factory committee of the Nevskaia Footwear Factory announced that "only the workers will elect the foremen and those in charge."[97] In the state-owned sector, in particular, the election of administrative personnel at every level was widespread: in early March workers at the Baltic and Izhora works elected the entire administration, after most of the previous state appointees had fled, believing that only full election was compatible with the industrial democracy and collegial management.[98] On April 15 a conference of representatives of factories under the Artillery Administration and the Naval Ministry tried to curb enthusiasm for electing administrations. The constitution ratified by the conference spoke of directors, shop directors, and engineers being "accepted with the agreement of the factory committee" and of the workers' right to "object" (*dat' otvod*) to those who could not guarantee normal relations with them.[99] It was this right to object to members of the administration, rather than to elect them directly, which was most typical of practice in the capital. But foremen, as the lowest level of the administrative hierarchy, continued to be directly elected by the workers in both the state and private sectors. The industrial census carried out in the autumn of 1918 revealed that in Petrograd no fewer than 56 percent of

[95] *Delo naroda*, 24 June 1917, p. 4; *Birzhevye vedomosti*, 24 June 1917, p. 5. I am grateful to Diane Koenker for the latter reference.

[96] *Oktiabr'skaia revoliutsiia i fabzavkomy* (1927), parts 1 and 2, ed. with introduction by S. A. Smith (Millwood, N.Y., 1983), p. 156.

[97] Z. V. Stepanov, *Fabzavkomy Petrograda v 1917 godu* (Leningrad, 1985), p. 83.

[98] *Trudy pervogo vserossiiskogo s"ezda delegatov rabochikh zavodov, portov i uchrezhdenii Morskogo Vedomstva* (Petrograd, 1917), protocol 1, p. 3.

[99] *Oktiabr'skaia revoliutsiia i fabzavkomy*, part 1, p. 34.

foremen's positions had been captured by workers in the period since the February Revolution of 1917.[100]

The upheavals of 1917 forced administrative personnel to reexamine their professional identity and class allegiance. Even though worker hostility toward them remained strong, both foremen and white-collar workers sought to align themselves with the labor movement. One woman recalled that at the cotton mill where she worked "in the February Days the supervisors came to us to beg forgiveness. Fedot was the first to speak, bowing to us, he said: 'Girls [*baby*], forgive me.' Then each supervisor came up in turn. Finally, even Filipp, the guard, approached us: 'As I served the old order, so shall I serve you.' "[101] For their part, labor unions softened their former antipathy. On 24 April 1917 the council of delegates of the woodturners' union decided, after a lot of argument, and by only thirty-eight votes to twenty-nine, to admit foremen to union membership, on condition that they had been elected by the workers.[102]

A significant index of the change in orientation of foremen was the revival of their trade union. By October the union of factory foremen and technicians had up to six thousand members in the capital.[103] At the V. I. Rykatkin Works the foremen on May 1 demanded that "no owner has the right to take on any foreman without the consent of the union of foremen."[104] Though suspicious of the Bolsheviks, the Petrograd branch of the foremen's union declared after the seizure of power: "We have always regarded ourselves as an integral part of the proletariat, and have always been interested in strengthening the gains of labor over capital. . . . We call on our members to join with the workers and support them in their creative work by every means—without yielding to their political views—and to be respectful toward those organizations in the factory which receive the sanction of the proletariat. In cases of insult, abuse, or infringement of your rights, the union will powerfully defend you, but our best defense will be tact and sincere love for the proletariat."[105]

Conclusion

The collapse of industry, combined with escalating civil war, quickly undermined workers' power on the shop floor. In a bid to reverse the

[100] O. V. Naumov, L. S. Petrosian, and A. K. Sokolov, "Kadry rukovoditelei, spetsialistov i obsluzhivaiushchego personala," pp. 99–110.

[101] *Leningradskie tekstilia*, no. 6–7 (1927): 7.

[102] *Ekho derevoobdelochnika*, 19 October 1917, p. 11.

[103] *Professional'noe dvizhenie v Petrograde v 1917 g.*, ed. A. Anskii (Leningrad, 1929), p. 347.

[104] *Oktiabr'skaia revoliutsiia i fabzavkomy*, part 1, p. 146.

[105] A. Lozovskii, *Rabochii kontrol'* (Petrograd, 1918), pp. 93–94.

catastrophic decline in industrial productivity, the Bolsheviks soon came to advocate one-man management of industrial enterprises and the restoration of the authority of "bourgeois specialists." By the 1920s little remained of the worker democracy that had briefly flourished in 1917–18. Yet resistance to one-man management did not vanish completely. There were periodic attempts, especially by the more skilled workers, to reassert the principle of election of supervisors, such as during the movements for shock work and socialist competition after 1929 and in the Stakhanov movement of 1935–38.[106]

With the inauguration of the New Economic Policy, foremen recovered much of the authority they had lost in 1917. Once again they enjoyed wide discretion in the day-to-day running of the shop, being responsible for job training, setting output norms, recording output, assigning skill levels *(razriady)*, and enforcing general labor discipline. Conflict between workers and foremen was rekindled, especially over the determination of output norms and labor discipline. The old complaints of rudeness, favoritism, bribery, and sexual harassment by foremen were heard once more.[107] Yet conflict never reached the intensity of prerevolutionary times, in part, no doubt, because the powers of the foreman were no longer what they once had been. The absence of stringent market disciplines— even at the height of NEP—forced the party-state to intervene in the workplace to promote productivity in a way that was quite new.[108] The party cell and trade union committee, though by no means agencies of the state in any unilateral sense, encroached on the prerogatives of the foreman.[109] And organs such as the enterprise rates-and-conflict commissions and the arbitration boards, which investigated alleged violations of collective agreements, further limited his competence.[110] Between 1926 and 1933, especially, when the vogue for "scientific organization of labor" *(nauchnaia organizatsiia truda)* was at its peak, the technical norm bureaus, the bureaus of allocation and scheduling, the departments of labor, and the rationalization bureaus also significantly constrained the foreman's exercise of authority, in theory if not always in practice.[111] Fi-

---

[106] Hiroaki Kuromiya, *Stalin's Industrial Revolution: Politics and Workers, 1928–31* (Cambridge, 1988), p. 187.

[107] Lewis H. Siegelbaum, *Stakhanovism and the Politics of Productivity in the USSR, 1935–41* (Cambridge, 1988), pp. 131, 135, 139, 166; Lewis H. Siegelbaum, "Masters of the Shop Floor: Foremen and Soviet Industrialization," in Nick Lampert and Gábor T. Rittersporn, eds., *Stalinism: Its Nature and Aftermath: Essays in Honour of Moshe Lewin* (London, 1992), p. 127.

[108] Siegelbaum, *Stakhanovism*, p. 8.

[109] Kuromiya, *Stalin's Industrial Revolution*, p. 188.

[110] Siegelbaum, "Masters of the Shop Floor," p. 131.

[111] Vladimir Andrle, *Workers in Stalin's Russia: Industrialization and Social Change in a Planned Economy* (London, 1988), p. 158; Siegelbaum, "Masters of the Shop Floor," pp. 139–40.

nally, after 1929 the peculiar structural pressures generated by the command economy and "taut" planning propelled foremen not infrequently to side with workers against the enterprise directors, norm setters, or Stakhanovites.[112]

The diminution in the power of the foreman on the shop floor was thus a key factor in the attenuation of worker-foremen conflict in the 1920s and 1930s. But the latter was also a function of the profound change in political climate. Before 1917 the foreman had been transformed by socialist propaganda into a symbol of the economic and political tyranny to which workers were subject. After the Bolshevik seizure of power the conditions that had sustained this discursive construction changed radically. The language of class ceased to be an oppositional discourse and was no longer able to articulate and legitimate worker grievances in the old way. This is not to say that it could not still authorize workers to make claims—including ones against the Bolshevik state—but since it mimicked the official discourse of the state, its effectiveness as a language was much reduced.

By the 1920s the language of class, which had assumed such extraordinary salience in St. Petersburg in the period between the two revolutions, both within the labor movement and within the public sphere, was in decline. We have seen that it was the achievement of Marxist intellectuals and the "conscious" minority of workers to subsume the manifold discontents of the abused and exploited into a strident language of class, even though class relations were heavily inflected by non-class-based social relations and precapitalist cultural patterns. Women workers' anger, for example, at sexual harassment became interpreted as an aspect of class exploitation, even though it was hardly functional to capitalist production. Similarly, the ubiquitous demands for humane treatment were also construed as instances of class oppression. Though there is no doubt that the claim that "we are people too" was powerfully pertinent to exploitation in the workplace, it related fundamentally to issues of justice, dignity, and human rights that were in no way peculiar to the capitalist mode of production.

This raises a final point of a more general nature. The pertinence of dignity issues to the development of class consciousness in prerevolutionary St. Petersburg may cause us to question the limits of a theoretical approach that seeks to grasp labor-capital relations entirely through the lens of "exploitation." Russian workers certainly complained of "exploitation," but it was invariably in the context of bewailing their inhuman treatment. They used the term in a moral rather than a Marxist sense.[113]

---

[112] Andrle, *Workers in Stalin's Russia*, pp. 166–69; Siegelbaum, *Stakhanovism*, p. 166.
[113] This counterposition is something of a conceit. Norman Geras has shown that Marx's

It was the reality of domination, the lack of rights, more than of exploitation in the economic sense, that most rankled with them. It was their treatment as "things" and not as "people," which spoke most powerfully to their sense of being an oppressed class. It seems important, then, to pay attention to the dimension of domination which characterizes labor-capital relations in all societies when thinking about the meaning of class. It may rightly be objected that there would be a loss of analytical power if the concept of class were evacuated of its exploitation-based core, yet the reluctance to incorporate relations of command and obedience into it, makes it of limited use to historians trying to understand how class structure constrained and motivated workers to act.

---

discourse, notwithstanding his explicit denial that the wage relation was unjust and his repudiation of any transhistorical notion of justice, is replete with moral judgments (cf. his regular references to exploitation as "robbery"), and concludes that Marx thought of capitalism as unjust *malgré lui*. Norman Geras, "The Controversy about Marx and Justice," *New Left Review* 150 (March/April 1985).

5

Hiroaki Kuromiya

Donbas Miners in War, Revolution, and Civil War

The Donbas, or Donets Basin, Russia's Ruhr, is located in eastern Ukraine and southwestern Russia. Numerous coal mines are scattered throughout an area about the size of the state of Vermont. These mines accounted for 87.1 percent of the country's coal production in 1913 and 79.3 percent in 1917. The southern industrial region, of which the Donbas was the center, also produced 73.7 and 71.3 percent of Russia's pig iron in those years.[1] The coal miners were the largest workforce in the Donbas. Their numbers rose rapidly and steadily from 84,857 in 1900 to 168,440 in 1913 and to 283,773 (including some 70,000 prisoners of war) in February 1917, accounting for nearly 90 percent of the country's colliers. From a comparative perspective, it is surprising that Western historians have neglected the revolution in such an important industrial center.[2]

Commenting on Donbas politics, Lev Trotsky was reported to have

---

[1] See G. D. Bakulev, *Razvitie ugol'noi promyshlennosti Donetskogo basseina* (Moscow, 1965), pp. 128, 203, 662, 664.

[2] For a typical pre-glasnost Soviet work, see *Istoriia rabochikh Donbassa*, vol. 1 (Kiev, 1981). Western historians have recently begun to explore this area. See Susan Purves McCaffrey, "The New Work and the Old Regime: Workers, Managers and the State in the Coal and Steel Industry of Ekaterinoslav Province, 1905–1914" (Ph.D. diss., Duke University, 1983); idem, "Origins of Labor Policy in the Russian Coal and Steel Industry, 1874–1900," *Journal of Economic History* 47 (December 1987); idem, "The Association of Southern Coal and Steel Producers and the Problems of Industrial Progress in Tsarist Russia," *Slavic Review* 47, no. 2 (1988); Charters Stephen Wynn, "Russian Labor in Revolution and Reaction: The Donbas Working Class, 1870–1905" (Ph.D. diss., Stanford University, 1987); Theodore H. Friedgut, *Iuzovka and Revolution*, vol. 1, *Life and Work in Russia's Donbas, 1869–1924* (Princeton, N.J., 1989); idem, "Professional Revolutionaries in the Donbass: The Characteristics and Limitations of the *Apparat*," *Canadian Slavonic Papers*, 27 (September 1985); and idem, "Labor Violence and Regime Brutality in Tsarist Russia: The Iuzovka Cholera Riots of 1892," *Slavic Review* 46, no. 2 (1987). Yet all these works stop at World War I. Despite its title, Friedgut's first volume does not cover the post–1914 years.

remarked: "One can't go to the Donbas without a gas mask."[3] Indeed, the Bolsheviks were baffled by the long periods of political doldrum occasionally interrupted by violent riots by coal miners which comprised the political atmosphere of the Donbas.[4] Their militancy, however, was independent of party politics. The tumultuous years of war, revolution, and civil war generated a far more difficult political situation in the Donbas than in Moscow or Petrograd. Even after the civil war ended, the Donbas coal-mining industry remained a significant trouble spot. (One might also recall the strikes in the summer of 1989.) Anyone who worked there would have needed a political gas mask.

It is possible that baffling political development of Donbas colliers during war, revolution, and civil war will seem less baffling if we focus on three issues. The first issue is the alternation of rebellion and conformism characteristic of the colliers' labor protest.

The second is the political dimension of labor-management relations. In 1917 in the Donbas collieries the labor-management conflict was particularly violent, reflecting the sharp polarization of Donbas society. Miners tended not to bother to strike but resorted to direct action against management. I will examine how this action related to party politics.

The third is the political dimension of the civil war experience in the Donbas, for there, unlike in the capital cities, "the victory of labor over capital" was not "achieved remarkably, and perhaps deceptively, easily."[5] Like Bulgakov's Kiev, the Donbas repeatedly changed hands among the Reds, Whites, Blacks (anarchists), and Greens (peasant armies). With the Whites, former bosses returned and restored the old regime to the mines. Many colliers did flee the Donbas and avoided the conflict, but unlike Moscow, where "this confrontation was removed from the direct daily experience of most workers,"[6] in the Donbas, the war was the "direct daily experience" of those who chose to stay. The experience could not help but have had a lasting influence on the subsequent politics of the region.

---

[3] Quoted in *XI z'izd Komunistychnoi partii (bil'shovykiv) Ukrainy, 5–15 chervnia 1930 r. Sten. zvit* (Kharkiv, 1930), p. 373.

[4] The coexistence of industrial militancy and political conservatism was also seen among the Ruhr coal miners. See S.H.F. Hickey, *Workers in Imperial Germany: The Miners of the Ruhr* (Oxford, 1985).

[5] Sheila Fitzpatrick, "New Perspectives on the Civil War," in Diane P. Koenker, William G. Rosenberg, and Ronald Grigor Suny, eds., *Party, State, and Society in the Russian Civil War: Explorations in Social History* (Bloomington, Ind., 1989), p. 15. See also idem, "The Bolsheviks' Dilemma: Class, Culture, and Politics in the Early Soviet Years," *Slavic Review* 47, no. 4 (1988): 600.

[6] Diane P. Koenker, "Urbanization and Deurbanization in the Russian Revolution and Civil War," in Koenker, Rosenberg, and Suny, *Party, State, and Society in the Russian Civil War*, p. 99.

Buntarstvo and Conformism

Some say the mining environment itself creates rebelliousness: the social and geographical isolation of the miners, "their habits and intensely felt need of cooperation," and "the psychological burden imposed upon them by the danger and arduousness of their job."[7] There is in fact no shortage of examples. Yet, as has been pointed out by many observers, the isolation that miners endured and the intense solidarity they enjoy may also produce the opposite—conformism or submissiveness. In June 1990, for example, Romanian miners were mobilized by the government to terrorize its critics. Historically speaking, these two tendencies, rebelliousness and conformism, have often been observed in the same miners. The conduct of French miners in the nineteenth century, for example, was characterized by a "series of brutal explosions interrupting long periods of calm."[8]

This generalization seems to apply to the Donbas as well. The Donbas miners were widely known for their *buntarstvo* (rebelliousness). For example, 1892 witnessed the so-called cholera riots in the Donbas, which involved anti-Semitic pogroms.[9] In the 1905 revolution the Donbas colliers again rebelled against the regime. They acted like militant revolutionaries, but at the same time they actively participated in looting and violence—especially against Jews.[10] Between riots, however, they were quiet. The onset of war in 1914 aroused their patriotic feeling.[11] They formed no union until 1917. Economic strikes, some very large, did occur during the war, but they were not particularly significant.[12] Whatever influence the Bolsheviks might have had among them before the war[13] was largely lost during it, whereas the Mensheviks, with their support for the war and emphasis on economic as opposed to political struggle, rose in popularity.[14] The "wine riot" in Luhans'k (Lugansk) in July 1914 embodied these two characteristics of Donbas workers: rebelliousness and conformism. Young Donbas patriots, mobilized for the war and assem-

[7] See Gaston V. Rimlinger, "International Differences in the Strike Propensity of Coal Miners: Experience in Four Countries," *Industrial and Labor Relations Review* 12 (April 1959): 394: "The underground dispersion and isolation of the workers make good labor-management communication, which is an asset to industrial peace, considerably more difficult in mines than in factories."

[8] Ibid., p. 399.

[9] For this, see Friedgut, "Labor Violence and Regime Brutality in Tsarist Russia."

[10] See Wynn, "Russian Labor in Revolution," chaps. 7 and 8. For the pogroms, see also *Khrushchev Remembers* (Boston, 1970), pp. 266–69.

[11] See, for example, A. A. Shliapnikov, *Nakanune 1917 goda. Vospominaniia i dokumenty o rabochem dvizhenii i revoliutsionnom podpol'e za 1914–1917* (Moscow, 1920), p. 276.

[12] *Oktiabr' i gorniaki* (Moscow, 1927), p. 13.

[13] See Ralph Carter Elwood, *Russian Social Democracy in the Underground: A Study of RSDRP in the Ukraine, 1907–1914* (Assen, Netherlands, 1974), p. 254.

[14] Iu. I. Kir'ianov, *Rabochie Iuga Rossii, 1914–fevral' 1917 g.* (Moscow, 1971), pp. 186–87.

bled in the city, sought a drink before departing to the front. The result was rioting, looting, and pogroms.[15]

Undoubtedly, the "respectable" society of Russia looked down on the miners as "dark masses" (*temnye liudi, temnye massy*) just as they looked down on the peasantry. From their perspective, the miners scarcely differentiated themselves from the countryside, from which the majority of them in fact had sprung. Even in the years immediately before the revolution, every summer 30 to 35 percent of Donbas miners left for agricultural work.[16] Primitive and squalid working and living conditions, described by Theodore H. Friedgut, encouraged mobility among the colliers.[17] Furthermore, by any definition the literacy of Donbas colliers was very low. In 1897 only 31 percent (as against the industrial average of 50 percent) could read simple sentences, and in 1921 barely 40 percent.[18] In 1922 more than two thirds of miners never read newspapers or books.[19] The *byt* (everyday life) of miners also appeared to respectable society to be very brutal. Gambling, wild drinking, and crime were rampant. One of their favorite pastimes was collective fist-fighting among various groups of *zemliaki* or ethnic groups, which often resulted in deaths.[20] The Donbas

[15] Aleksandr Gambarov, "Ocherk po istorii revoliutsionnogo dvizheniia v Luganske, 1901–1921 gg.," *Letopis' revoliutsii*, 1923, no. 4:80; *Rabochee dvizhenie na Ukraine v period pervoi mirovoi imperialisticheskoi voiny, iiun' 1914 g.-fevral' 1917 g. Sbornik dokumentov i materialov* (Kiev, 1966), pp. 12–17; and A. Rashkov's review in *Litopys revoliutsii*, 1929, nos. 5–6:352.

[16] Iu. I Kir'ianov, "Vliianie pervoi mirovoi voiny na izmenenie chislennosti i sostava rabochikh Rossii," *Voprosy istorii*, 1960, no. 10:99, and idem, "Krest'ianstvo stepnoi Ukrainy v gody pervoi mirovoi voiny (1914–1916 gg.)," in *Osobennosti agrarnogo stroia Rossii v period imperializma* (Moscow, 1962), p. 24.

[17] See Friedgut, *Iuzovka and Revolution*. The labor turnover of Donbas miners (annual rate of discharges to the average number of employed) usually exceeded 100 percent. This was much higher than that of coal miners in other countries that suffered from the same problem. The turnover of coal miners in the Ruhr, for example, fluctuated between 37 percent and 69 percent, with the exception of 1914, which recorded 102 percent, an impact of war. See Gerhard Adelmann, ed., *Quellensammlung zur Geschichte der sozialen Betriebsverfassung Ruhrindustrie unter besonderer Beruecksichtung des Industrie- und Handelskammerbezirks* (Bonn, 1960), 1:145–46. See also Elaine Glovka Spencer, *Management and Labor in Imperial Germany. Ruhr Industrialists as Employers 1896–1914* (New Brunswick, N.J., 1984), pp. 46–47.

[18] S. I. Potolov, *Rabochie Donbassa v XIX veke* (Moscow-Leningrad, 1963), p. 133, and *Promyshlennost' i rabochii klass Ukrainskoi SSR v period vosstanovleniia narodnogo khoziaistva (1921–1925 gg.): Sbornik dokumentov i materialov* (Kiev, 1964), p. 293.

[19] Kir'ianov, *Rabochie Iuga Rossii*, p. 105.

[20] See, for example, F. Zaitsev, "Bolsheviki Iuzovki do 1918 goda," *Literaturnyi Donbass*, 1933, nos. 10–12:155–56; also see *5-letnii obzor deiatel'nosti Soiuza gornorabochikh v Donetskom basseine (1920–1925 gg.) i kratkii ocherk rabochego i professional'nogo dvizheniia gorniakov Donetskogo basseina do 1920 goda* (Artemovsk, 1925), p. 13. (*Zemliaki* refer to those migrant workers from the same village or regions.) Fist-fighting was not peculiar to miners but often marked traditional holidays in traditional Russian society. (See B. V. Gorbunov, "Narodnye vidy sportivnoi bor'by kak element traditsionnoi kul'tury russkikh [XIX–nachalo XX v.]," *Sovetskaia etnografiia*, 1989, no. 4, and Helmut Altrichter, *Die Bauern von Tver. Von Leben auf dem russischen Dorfe zwischen Revolution und Kollektivierung*

industrialists feared the periodic buntarstvo of miners as irrationality inherent in their primitive nature. According to one prominent Donbas manager, "Masses will always be masses" [*Tolpa vsegda ostaetsia tolpoi*].[21]

It has been suggested that the southern industrialists were disposed to "welfare liberalism."[22] Yet every dealing with the colliers tended to undermine these liberal inclinations and reinforce prejudice and fear. To their astonishment and despair, rationality did not appear to apply to the Donbas miners. "With very rare exceptions," for example, higher wages did not to lead to higher productivity. The higher the colliers' wages, the fewer days they worked and the less strenuous their work became. Consequently, their earnings remained more or less constant, usually at subsistence levels, and independent of the rates.[23] Whatever their moral economy, to the industrialists they seemed irrational and ill-equipped for "modern," "rational" economic life.

The sick-funds law of 1912 is another case in point. In Moscow, Petrograd, and elsewhere, the sick funds were accepted by both labor and management, and contributed quickly to the creation of surrogate trade unions and cultural organizations of labor.[24] Yet in the Donbas they were rejected by both parties: labor was angered by the requirement to contribute to the funds; and the employers, also disappointed by the financial burden imposed on them feared as well that withholding sick-fund contributions from miners' wages would cause labor unrest.[25] Thus few sick funds existed in an industrial area with notably high accident and illness rates.

If management considered labor "dark masses," the latter viewed the former as savage exploiters. It is true that as the mining industry developed in the twentieth century, a growing number of colliers came to settle and enjoy the benefits of modern urban life in the making in the Donbas,[26]

[Munich, 1984], pp. 105, 107.) Fist-fighting was not always just a pastime; given an ethnic component, such as the friction that existed between Russians and Tartars, it was actual conflict.

[21] A. I. Fenin, *Vospominaniia inzhenera. K istorii obshchestvennago i khoziaistvennago razvitiia Rossii (1883–1906 gg.)* (Prague, 1938), p. 52.

[22] See the works by McCaffrey cited in note 2. See also Alfred J. Rieber, *Merchants and Entrepreneurs in Imperial Russia* (Chapel Hill, N.C., 1982), p. 235: "The southern entrepreneurs displayed toward their workers a concern which was hierarchical rather than paternalistic."

[23] E. Taskin, *K voprosu o privlechenii i uderzhanii rabochikh na kamennougol'nykh kopiakh Donetskago Basseina* (Kharkov, [1899?]), p. 15.

[24] For the case of Moscow, see Diane Koenker, *Moscow Workers and the 1917 Revolution* (Princeton, N.J., 1981), pp. 73–74.

[25] See Kir'ianov, *Rabochie Iuga Rossii*, pp. 197–203. The industrialists demanded that the government provide national sick funds.

[26] See Friedgut, *Iuzovka and Revolution*, chap. 7. See also John P. McKay, *Pioneers for Profit. Foreign Entrepreneurship and Russian Industrialization, 1885–1913* (Chicago, 1970), pp. 265–67.

which in turn increasingly differentiated the mining population. Yet the workday of the average miner was characterized by brutal exploitation and affront. An elaborate system of fines affecting every aspect of a worker's conduct on the job often deprived the Donbas miners of 10 to 25 percent of their wages.[27] Bribes were a way of life in the mines. Refusal of requests could result in all kinds of inconveniences, including loss of job. The wives of the bosses in turn exploited the wives of workers by demanding gifts. The police openly solicited money from the miners, and deductions were made from their wages for the church, school, and *soldatki* (wives of soldiers). All this was compounded by the exploitation by cooperatives run by management, and by the elders of *artel*s, or work gangs, which subcontracted underground work with management.[28] During World War I, the constant threat of dispatch to the front made the exploitation of labor easier, and wartime inflation decreased miners' real wages by 30 to 50 percent.[29]

Exploitation was accompanied by rudeness to colliers from all ranks of administrators from director down to gang boss. Miners periodically struck with demands, among others, for respectable treatment. Ironically, when strikers were arrested, they were often subjected to the most humiliating corporal punishment—flogging in public.[30] This "medieval" practice, which virtually treated workers as serfs and continued until after 1917, symbolized Russia's remarkable failure to "modernize" labor-management relations,[31] an important cause of the eventual downfall of the autocracy.

In the Donbas, the polarization of society into the respectable (*verkhi*) and the downtrodden (*nizy*),[32] thus, took an extreme form, symbolized by the "enlightened" aboveground and the dark underground. The exploitation of labor, too, took an extreme form in this industry. The mobility, illiteracy, and ties to the countryside were not peculiar to the mining workforce, but they were much more pronounced here than, for example, in the metalworking and metallurgical industries. So it was far more difficult for the colliers than for others to create organizational bases from

[27] Kir'ianov, *Rabochie Iuga Rossii*, p. 64.

[28] See M. Ostrogorskii, "Rabochee dvizhenie v Gorlovsko-Shcherbinoskom raione Donbassa (v gody imperialisticheskoi voiny)," *Litopys revoliutsii*, 1928, no. 3:87–88, 93.

[29] Kir'ianov, *Rabochie Iuga Rossii*, p. 77.

[30] Ostrogorskii, "Rabochee dvizhenie," pp. 98–99 (which refers to 1916), and Zaitsev, "Bolsheviki Iuzovki," p. 157 (which refers to 1892).

[31] For ideological barriers to modernization in Russia, see Reinhard Bendix, *Work and Authority in Industry: Ideologies of Management in the Course of Industrialization* (Berkeley and Los Angeles, 1974). For a German experience, which is characterized by "mutual learning process," see Lawrence Schofer, *The Formation of a Modern Labor Force, Upper Silesia, 1865–1914* (Berkeley and Los Angeles, 1975).

[32] For this, see Leopold H. Haimson, "The Problem of Social Stability in Urban Russia, 1905–1914," *Slavic Review* 23, no. 4 (1964), and 24, no. 1 (1965).

which to fight for improved living and working conditions.[33] The divisions within the colliers made the task all the more difficult. Buntarstvo was a counsel of despair. Certainly what James C. Scott has called "everyday forms of resistance" regarding peasants[34] applied to the miners as well. Underground work, difficult for management to supervise, left the miners some room for deception and pilfering. Yet to use another concept of Scott's, their "hidden transcripts"[35] were that the miners, like the peasants, assumed that "authority could not be challenged, and that rebellion was possible only when constraining authority has been eliminated." Their behavior was similar to that of Russian peasants and soldiers.[36]

Confrontation in 1917

In 1917 the deep social division in the Donbas manifested itself in violent explosions of conflict between labor and management. It appeared as if, unlike the more "sophisticated" workers of Moscow or Petrograd, the Donbas colliers struck back with vengeance in the immediate aftermath of the February Revolution. They showed only mild interest in such institutions as collective agreements and conciliation boards and took direct action against managers in the form of search (obysk), removal from the mines, and arrest.[37] What happened in the Donbas in 1917 was thus characterized as "an unbroken, continuous conflict."[38]

The February Revolution was followed immediately by what mine administrators termed "excesses" on the part of colliers: the introduction of a de-facto eight-hour workday, the willful removal and "forcible arrest" of contractors, senior officials, engineers, and technicians.[39] Throughout

[33] Ziva Galili, *The Menshevik Leaders in Russia's Revolution: Social Relations and Political Strategies* (Princeton, N.J., 1989), p. 98, speaks of "the highly organized workers of the Donbas mining regions," but it did not seem to have been the case. The unionization of miners proved difficult even after the February Revolution. See *Rabochee dvizhenie v 1917 godu*, ed. V. L. Meller and A. M. Pankratova (Moscow, 1926), p. 246.

[34] James C. Scott, *Weapons of the Weak: Everyday Forms of Peasant Resistance* (New Haven, Conn., 1985).

[35] James C. Scott, *Domination and the Arts of Resistance: Hidden Transcripts* (New Haven, Conn., 1990).

[36] See John Bushnell, *Mutiny amid Repression: Russian Soldiers in the Revolution of 1905–1906* (Bloomington, Ind., 1985).

[37] See V. Ia. Boshcherskii, "Stachechnoe rabochee dvizhenie v Donbasse v period podgotovki Oktiabria," *Rabochii klass i rabochee dvizhenie v Rossii v 1917 g.* (Moscow, 1964), and A. M. Lisetskii, *Bol'sheviki vo glave massovykh stachek (mart–oktiabr' 1917 g.)* (Kishnev, 1974), pp. 267–68.

[38] M. Balabanov, "Konflikty v Donbasse v 1917 godu," *Materialy po izucheniiu istorii professional'nogo dvizheniia na Ukraine*, vol. 1, *Professional'noe dvizhenie v 1917 godu* ([Kharkov], [1928?]). pp. 65–66.

[39] See the complaints of managers cited in *Rabochee dvizhenie v 1917 godu*, p. 123. See also *Gornozavodskoe delo*, 15 April 1917, p. 15605, and *Robitnychyi kontrol' i natsional-*

1917 the Donbas industrialists bombarded the Provisional Government with requests for assistance and intervention. According to one such proclamation of 27 May 1917, "the dictatorship of the working class has been established in its most primitive form. The working class, carried away by tempting perspectives depicted to it by irresponsible leaders [*vozhaki*], awaits the advent of a golden age. Terrible will be its disappointment, which it is impossible not to foresee."[40] By August 1917, it was reported that in the Donbas no state authority, inviolability of domicile, or personal safety existed at all.[41]

Between March 1917 and January 1918, there occurred 149 conflicts in the Donbas collieries, of which 127 occurred in the summer and autumn (from 1 July to 20 September). The main causes for conflict were "interference with internal order" (72 cases), disputes over wages (38 cases), the length of the workday (15 cases), and the closure of mines and firing of workers (15 cases).[42] These data suggest that power in the workplace was the major bone of contention and that the miners were more given to settling old scores with management than to demanding sharp increases in wages and reductions in work hours.

What happened in the Chistiakovo (in Ukrainian, Chystiakove) pit of the South Russian Coal Company at the end of March was typical. One day workers' delegates came to the main office of the company and demanded, among other things, the removal of a mechanic, against whom three accusations were lodged: (1) before the revolution he imposed excessive fines; (2) he prevented workers from earning proper wages by assigning only two workers to tasks that required three or four; and (3) he did not place the order for a spare gear for a steam winch, even though its cogs had long been broken and threatened to disrupt work. The mechanic responded: (1) the fines were necessary because of the miners' "poor work," but they were assessed in accordance with the company rules and after February he had not fined them; (2) he had a long experience in the mining business, and therefore he knew better how many hands were adequate and where; and (3) the gear, ordered fourteen months before, had not been delivered yet. The main office found the accusations unfounded, and the mechanic went on a "holiday." When he came back, he was dumped in a wheelbarrow and carted around "all the mines" by workers. Simultaneously, his telephone line was cut and his

---

izatsiia promyslovosti na Ukraini. Zbirnyk dokumentiv i materialiv, berezen' 1917–berezen' 1921 rr. (Kiev, 1957), pp. 140–41.

[40] *Rabochee dvizhenie v 1917 godu*, p. 126.

[41] See *Bor'ba za vlast' Sovetov na Donu, 1917–1920 gg. Sbornik dokumentov* (Rostov-on-Don, 1957), pp. 78–79.

[42] Balabanov, "Konflikty," pp. 52–54. These are far from complete data on "more or less big conflicts" that were eventually solved.

horses were taken away to prevent him from working. The conciliation board, recommended by the management, refused to elaborate on this affair on the grounds that the case was not one of a conflict of interests but one of a "mutual misunderstanding." The workers refused to guarantee the mechanic's safety.

Eventually the case was handed over to the "comrades' court" of miners. Held in early June, the court declared: (1) that before the revolution the mechanic dealt despotically with his subordinates; (2) that of late he still maintained the same attitude toward workers and acted disrespectfully toward their organizations; and (3) that holding a responsible position, he left the mines without reporting to the miners' committee, which had to take the responsibility on itself for the order of work. The court decided to force him to quit his position. The management, however, preempted the inevitable outcome by dismissing him first, yet allowing him to live in his flat until a new mechanic took over. Thereupon, the workers forced him out of both his flat and the coalfields.[43]

Similar events were legion. The workers either occupied or wrecked those flats taken away from engineers and white-collar employees.[44] Neither the newly created workers' soviets nor the Prosecutor's Office was able to do much to calm the situation.[45] When a fire broke out at the Iakovenko Brothers Coalfield in June, for example, a crowd of agitated workers arrested the director, Engineer Kogan. Taken to the executive committee of the soviet, he was threatened by the crowd with *samosud* (a kind of kangaroo court).[46] Many other directors, engineers, and foremen were subjected to house arrest and beatings, and under duress agreed to increase workers' wages.[47]

Miners often organized large meetings to conduct *samosud* of engineers and foremen, just as peasants did of criminals and violators of community rules and customs. It was intended as the ultimate humiliation. For instance, in August 1917, the foreman at the Union Coal Company, Maikut, was condemned for having demanded order in work. (Such demands were taken by the workers as encroachments on their hard-won freedom.) After much altercation, Maikut was told by the crowd of workers that the only way out was for him to take off his service cap (*furazhka*), kowtow in all directions, and beg the workers for mercy.[48] At the Iasinovka coalfield, there was an extreme case in which the workers

---

[43] Ibid., pp. 60–61.

[44] GADO, f. 306, op. 1, d. 32, l. 2.

[45] See *Robitnychyi kontrol' i natsionalizatsiia promyslovosti na Ukraini*, pp. 135–36.

[46] *Gornozavodskoe delo*, 24 June 1917, p. 15938. The attack on the mine itself may have been motivated by anti-Semitism.

[47] See a vivid example in GADO, f. 305, op. 1, d. 6, ll. 29–29 [verso].

[48] *Gornozavodskoe delo*, 25 November 1917, pp. 16342–43.

murdered an assistant mine director.[49] Coal managers bitterly complained that such anarchy sharply decreased labor productivity.

Many humiliated and threatened managers refused to return to work unless apologies and a guarantee of safety were offered. When such offers were not forthcoming, they did not come back to the mines.[50] To counter the workers, the industrialists resorted to lockouts and closings. By the beginning of September, 200 coalfields had been closed, and some 100,000 workers thrown into the streets.[51]

If in the summer of 1917, "illegal" acts, strikes, and workers' control in the capital cities of Moscow and Petrograd were largely motivated by their desire to maintain production,[52] the concern of Donbas colliers seem to have been elsewhere. They maintained, for example, that horses taken from management were to be used to evacuate workers' families in case of imminent civil war.[53]

Despite their consistent and determined actions, the political identification of Donbas colliers in 1917 was a complex process. The autocracy was discredited, so was liberalism, long regarded as the bosses' politics, which was, in any case, utterly incompatible with workers' action. It was left to the Mensheviks, the Socialist Revolutionaries, the Bolsheviks, and to a lesser extent the anarchists to fight for political hegemony. In the November elections to the Constituent Assembly the Bolsheviks won a minority victory, but even then the Mensheviks and SRs dominated many soviets, miners' committees, and trade unions.

In this place where illiteracy prevailed (the majority of miners read nothing, in any case) and few elements of modern politics and civil society had ever existed, rumor and demagoguery were said to have found fertile ground. By all accounts, the anti-Bolshevik agitation proved very effective. The Bolsheviks' antiwar campaign was so unpopular with miners that some Bolsheviks were lynched by crowds in Iuzovka (Iuzivka, subsequently Stalino, and currently Donets'k).[54] The Bolsheviks were branded as German spies who wanted Russia to be defeated and the tsar reinstated. Lenin's "sealed train" was evoked all the time. Such demagoguery "confused workers, who bent both right and left. In those days [March 1917]

[49] GADO, f. 305, op. 1, d. 6, l. 38. In June, when the question arose of what to do with former policemen and gendarmes, the Donbas industrialists jumped on the suggestion that they be sent to the mines. See E. Osipov, "Gornorabochie i gornopromyshlenniki v 1917 godu," *Materialy po istorii professional'nogo dvizheniia v Rossii* (Moscow, 1925), 4:402.

[50] See, for example, GADO, f. 306, op. 1, d. 41, ll. 4–11.

[51] *Rabochee dvizhenie v 1917 godu*, p. 228.

[52] See William G. Rosenberg and Diane P. Koenker, "The Limits of Formal Protest: Worker Activism and Social Polarization in Petrograd and Moscow, March to October, 1917," *American Historical Review* 92 (1987), p. 319.

[53] *Robitnychyi kontrol' i natsionalizatsiia promyslovosti na Ukraini*, p. 156.

[54] Ed. Medne, "Oktiabr'skaia revoliutsiia v Donbasse," *Letopis' revoliutsii*, 1922, no. 1: 49.

whoever told them whatever, they applauded everyone all the same."[55]
The notorious but disastrous Kerensky offensive of June 18 only added
to the anti-Bolshevik rhetoric. In meetings, the workers were inflamed to
"pogrom-like moods" to "Beat the Bolsheviks." When in the aftermath
of the July uprisings in the capital, Trotsky and Lunacharsky were arrested and Lenin and Zinoviev went into hiding, the Donbas miners became even more hostile to the Bolsheviks.[56] Workers were fed propaganda
to the effect that Lenin, Trotsky, and Steklov were all Jews who were
guilty of the ruin of Russia.[57] Rumors about German gold, allegedly received by the Bolsheviks, died hard in the Donbas.[58]

This was a nightmarish development for the Bolsheviks, yet hardly a
comfort to the Mensheviks and SRs, who were calling in vain for moderation. The contrast between the militancy and the vulnerability to rumor
and demagoguery among the miners led Trotsky to the following description of Donbas miners in 1917:

An excellent example of this *quid pro quo* between the Compromisers and
the masses, is to be seen in an oath taken at the beginning of July by 2,000
Donetz miners, kneeling with uncovered heads in the presence of a crowd of
5,000 people and with its participation. "We swear by our children, by God,
by the heaven and earth, and by all things that we hold sacred in the world,
that we will never relinquish the freedom bought with blood on the 28th of
February, 1917; believing in the Social Revolutionaries and the Mensheviks,
we swear we will never listen to the Leninists, for they, the Bolshevik-
Leninists, are leading Russia to ruin with their agitation, whereas the Social
Revolutionaries and Mensheviks united in a single union, say: The land to
the people, land without indemnities; the capitalist structure must fall after
the war and in place of capitalism there must be a socialist structure. . . . We
give our oath to march forward under the lead of these parties, not stopping
even at death." This oath of the miners directed against the Bolsheviks in

[55] P. Kazimirchuk, "Revoliutsionnoe dvizhenie v Gorlovo-Shcherbinovskom raione Donbassa (Vospominaniia)," *Letopis' revoliutsii*, 1923, no. 3:45, 47.

[56] Ibid., pp. 51, 53, 55. In Iuzovka, after the July events miners chased around their
Bolshevik fellow workers with picks, forcing many activists to deny that they were Bolsheviks. See F. Zaitsev, "Kak my tvorili Oktiabr' (1917–1918 gg. v Iuzovke)," *Letopis' revoliutsii*, 1925, no. 4:136–37, and idem, "Oktiabr' v Iuzovke," in *Oktiabr'skaia revoliutsiia.
Pervoe piatiletie* (Khar'kov, 1922), p. 622. For a more favorable view of Donbas miners,
see I. Vishniakov, "V bor'be za diktaturu proletariata v Donbasse (1916–1918 gg.)," *Litopys
revoliutsii*, 1928, no. 2:225.

[57] Kazimirchuk, "Revoliutsionnoe dvizhenie (Vospominaniia)," pp. 63–64, and *Donetskii
proletarii* (Luhans'k), 3 (16) August 1917, p. 2. The prevalence of anti-Semitism among the
colliers was hardly surprising when one recalls that in November 1917, in the midst of the
revolution, the Bolshevik party organization in Iuzovka had to discuss, and condemn, persistent anti-Semitism among its own members. See *Bolshevistskie organizatsii Ukrainy v
period ustanovleniia i ukrepleniia Sovetskoi vlasti (noiabr' 1917–aprel' 1918 gg.)* (Kiev,
1962), pp. 325–26.

[58] See, for example, *Donetskii proletarii* (Kharkov), 9 (22) December 1917, p. 3.

reality led straight to the Bolshevik revolution. The February shell and the October kernel appear in this naive and fervent picture so clearly as in a way to exhaust the whole problem of the Permanent Revolution.

By September the Donetz miners, without betraying either themselves or their oath, had already turned their back on the Compromisers.[59]

The influence of the Mensheviks and SRs may be explained sociologically. Those workers who came to be settled in the Donbas had much to lose and may have been more receptive to Menshevik moderation, whereas peasant workers were attracted to the agrarian policies of the SRs. Yet Trotsky's description also suggests that the Donbas miners followed the direction of no single political party: they rejected the Bolsheviks on the issues of land and peace and the Mensheviks and SRs on the issue of direct action. If this was true, one indeed needed a gas mask to work in the Donbas.

Certainly, in the Donbas, as elsewhere, Bolshevik influence surged in the summer and autumn. For example, in the August elections to the Lugansk (Luhans'k) City Duma, the Bolsheviks turned out to be the most popular party.[60] In the September elections to the Lugansk soviet, the Bolsheviks won 82 seats out of 120.[61] Moreover, in the November elections to the Constituent Assembly, the Bolsheviks did win a minority victory: "In the most important districts and cities in the Donets-Krivoi Rog Basin," of the total 577,010 votes, 186,543 (32.3 percent) were cast for the Bosheviks, 132,604 (23 percent) for the Ukrainian SRs, the Peasant Union, and other Ukrainian groups; 107,917 (18.7 percent) for the Russian SRs; 30,899 (5.4 percent) for the Mensheviks, and 42,606 (7.4 percent) for the Kadets. In some cities the Bolsheviks fared far better: 48 percent in Lugansk and 47 in Iuzovka.[62] In the coal mines in particular, the Bolsheviks defeated the Mensheviks, the SRs, and the Ukrainian nationalists by a wide margin (16,775 votes against 362, 2043, and 889).[63] How complete the available data on the Donbas mines are is far from clear, however, because only 20,279 votes were cast.[64]

[59] Leon Trotsky, *The History of the Russian Revolution*, trans. Max Eastman (London, 1977), pp. 792–93.

[60] *Donetskii proletarii* (Luhans'k), 9 (22) August 1917. Lugansk was a traditional Bolshevik stronghold. See George Denike in *The Making of Three Russian Revolutionaries: Voices from the Menshevik Past*, ed. Leopold H. Haimson in collaboration with Ziva Galli y Garcia and Richard Wortman (Cambridge, 1988), pp. 342 and 355.

[61] N. Goncharenko, *Oktiabr' v Donbasse* (Luhans'k, 1961), pp. 165–66. The majority of the Bolshevik delegates were representatives of metalworkers.

[62] I. K. Rybalka, "Rabochii klass Ukrainy na vyborakh vo Vserossiiskoe i Vseukrainskoe uchreditel'nye sobraniia," *Istoriia SSSR*, 1965, no. 1:119–20.

[63] *Donetskii proletarii* (Kharkov), 18 November (1 December) 1917. See also TsGAOR, f. 7952, op. 6, d. 13, l. 3, and Steven L. Guthier, "The Popular Base of Ukrainian Nationalism in 1917," *Slavic Review* 38, no. 1 (1979), 44.

[64] An SR newspaper bitterly complained that Donbas miners, carried away by bootleg

Whatever the case, in the Donbas the SRs retained considerable political power, as evidenced in the election results. The SRs and the Mensheviks combined to surpass the Bolsheviks politically. For example, when the unionization of the miners finally took place in October 1917, much more belatedly than other trades, the Bolsheviks sent the largest contingent (47) to the first union conference, but they were outnumbered by the Mensheviks (41) and the SRs (37) combined. The leadership of miners' unions remained in the latter's hands until 1919.[65] On 31 October 1917 the Iuzovka Soviet adopted a resolution proposed by the Menshevik Internationalists, which condemned the Bolshevik seizure of power in Petrograd and appealed for a "homogeneous democratic government." The Bolsheviks' counterproposal was rejected by the majority. Eventually the Bolsheviks had to force out their opponents to capture the Iuzovka soviet.[66] In some other soviets in the Donbas, the Bolsheviks gained leadership with great difficulty.[67] Because no one party could manage the soviets in the name of workers, recalls and reelections were frequent.[68] When the Bolsheviks disbanded the Constituent Assembly in January 1918, "some coalfields, which have always followed us [Bolsheviks]" became troublesome. At meetings, many workers asked why the Bolsheviks dissolved the assembly: "You yourselves held the elections, didn't you? But now you've dispersed it." (This was attributed to Menshevik-SR agitation.) Thus "indifference and distrust toward the Bolsheviks" were created among the miners.[69]

The new government appeared to the Donbas miners to have deprived them of "the freedom bought with the blood of the twenty-eighth of February, 1917," which they had sworn never to relinquish "by our children, by God, by the heaven and earth, and by all things that we hold sacred in the world." From late 1917 onward, the worsening economic situation further complicated the matter. The new Bolshevik masters soon became

---

vodka and gambling, forgot their "civil duty—voting in elections." See *Klich naroda* (Iuzivka), 5 November 1917, p. 4. According to another account, only five to eight percent of miners participated in various organizations *(Gornozavodskoe delo,* 15 November 1917, p. 16279).

[65] *Rabochee dvizhenie v 1917 godu,* p. 248, and *5-letnii obzor,* pp. 35–95.

[66] See *Donetskii proletarii* (Kharkov), 9 (22) December 1917, and *Pobeda Velikoi Oktiabr'skoi sotsialisticheskoi revoliutsii i ustanovlenie Sovetskoi vlasti na Ukraine, okt.–dek. 1917 g.* (Kiev, 1957), 2:285. For the strength of the Mensheviks in the Donbas, see also Leopold H. Haimson, ed., *The Mensheviks: From the Revolution of 1917 to the Second World War* (Chicago, 1974), p. 139 (George Denicke).

[67] See N. G. Goncharenko, *V bitvakh za Oktiabr' (mart 1917–mart 1918 gg.)* (Donetsk, 1974), pp. 144–50, 155–57.

[68] *Rabochee dvizhenie v 1917 godu,* pp. 242–43. The state of affairs in Iuzovka, for example, was described as "multiple power" *(mnogonachalie). Litopys revoliutsii,* 1928, no. 3:371.

[69] P. Kazimirchuk, "Revoliutsionnoe dvizhenie v Gorlovo-Shcherbinovskom raione Donbassa. Ianvar'–aprel' 1918 goda," *Letopis' revoliutsii,* 1923, no. 4:125.

as harsh as old masters and, when things became difficult, threw workers into the streets just as readily as the old masters had.[70] Some party members came to behave like dictators, and those who had entered the party on the spur of the moment turned against it.[71] It was also reported that the soviets, miners' committees, and other worker organizations, which had "bolshevized" themselves, soon "discredited themselves so thoroughly that they lost all influence among the workers." Instead of an organized force, there operated "an unrestrained elemental force" (*bez-uderzhnaia stikhiia*);[72] anarchism had spread among the workers. To save the Bolsheviks it would take a civil war.[73]

Civil War

The experience of civil war and foreign intervention in the periphery of the former Russian empire, which brought about the restoration of old regimes, differed sharply from the experience of the heartland. In the south, the Reds, Whites, Blacks, and Greens fought against each other.[74] In the Donbas, the battle was so fierce that some twenty political regimes were set up one after another.[75] In the particularly chaotic months of February–May 1919 Konstantinovka (Kostiantynivka) in the center of the Donbas changed hands twenty-seven times.[76] In the process, 30 percent or more of the Donbas colliers perished.[77]

Labor's violent attack on management, as some workers were well aware, led inevitably to management's retaliation. From August 1917 onward, the Donbas industrialists importuned the Provisional Government to dispatch Cossack regiments and declare martial law in the Donbas; by early October A. K. Kaledin's squadrons had occupied almost the entire region.[78] As the seizure of power by the Soviets spread through the Don-

[70] See *Protokoly I-go delegatskago oblastnogo s"ezda professional'nago soiuza gornora-bochikh Donetskago, Krivorozhskago i Solianogo Basseinov*, 25 March–1 April 1918 (Kharkov, 1918), p. 22.

[71] *Bor'ba za vlast' Sovetov Donbassa. Sbornik dokumentov i materialov* (Stalino, 1957), p. 313 (Gorlovka-Shcherbinovka party conference in February 1918). For an analogous process of labor opposition to the Bolsheviks elsewhere, see William G. Rosenberg, "Russian Labor and Bolshevik Power after October," *Slavic Review* 44, no. 2 (1985), and Alexander Rabinowitch, "The Petrograd First City District Soviet During the Civil War," in Koenker, Rosenberg, and Suny, *Party, State and Society in the Russian Civil War*.

[72] *Protokoly I-go delegatskago oblastnogo s'ezda*, p. 60.

[73] See Kazimirchuk, "Revoliutsionnoe dvizhenie. Ianvar'–aprel' 1918 goda," pp. 125–27.

[74] See Peter Kenez, *Civil War in South Russia, 1918: The First Year of the Volunteer Army* (Berkeley and Los Angeles, 1971), and idem, *Civil War in South Russia: The Defeat of the Whites* (Berkeley and Los Angeles, 1977).

[75] *5-letnii obzor*, pp. 8–9.

[76] *Istoriia rabochikh Donbassa*, p. 182.

[77] TsGAOR, f. 5459, op. 1, d. 1, l. 62.

[78] *Rabochee dvizhenie v 1917 godu*, pp. 229–35. See also *Bor'ba za vlast' Sovetov Don-*

bas, the confrontation developed into armed fighting. Already in December, White terror was in full swing in the Donbas. In Iasinovka (Iasynivka), for example, the Kaledin bands dissolved the workers' soviet, tore Red banners, broke the furniture, murdered twenty workers, and dumped their bodies into cesspools and dung piles. In Makeevka (Makiivka), in revenge for armed resistance, Cossacks plucked out the eyes of arrested workers and cut their throats. Workers who came up from the underground were chopped up and shot; others were thrown alive down mine shafts. Altogether, 118 miners (including 44 Austrian POWs) were shot in Iasinovka and Makeevka.[79] Elsewhere, the Cossacks rounded up the workers at the mines themselves, and exiled them to unknown places; managers evicted the families of arrested workers from their flats.[80]

Red terror was likewise brutal. Officers, cadets, and Cossacks would be arrested and shot, and their bodies left on public display.[81] On 7 January 1918 the Red Guards arrested the director of the Berestovo-Bogodukhovska (Berestovo-Bohodukhivka) coalfield, Engineer Porakov, and a cadet (the son of an employee) for alleged cooperation with the Cossacks. They were sentenced to be shot and executed the same day.[82] Managers, engineers, foremen, and other specialists were suspected of sabotage and subjected to harsh treatment.[83] On 7 January 1918, for example, a riot by hungry colliers in the Nikolai (Mykola) coalfield resulted in the murder of a foreman, the only remaining member of the administration.[84]

The occupation of the Donbas by German and Austrian troops and the Skoropads'kyi coup d'etat in April 1918 restored the old regime to the mines and factories. Those managers who had fled returned to recover their mines, and those who had stayed reasserted their authority. The triumphant former masters sent their regards and devotion to the Hetman (*Iasnovel'mozhnyi Pan Hetman*)[85] and called for a thorough review of all labor legislations enacted under the Provisional and the Soviet govern-

---

bassa, p. 143, and P. V. Volobuev, *Proletariat i burzhuaziia Rossii v 1917 godu* (Moscow, 1964), pp. 248, 256–61.

[79] Vishniakov, "V bor'be," pp. 228, 230–31, and *5-letnii obzor*, pp. 38–39. See also T. Kharechko, "Bor'ba za Oktiabr' v Donbasse. Organizatsiia biuro revkomov i Tsentroshtaba v Donbasse," *Letopis' revoliutsii*, 1927, nos. 5–6:141–42.

[80] *Donetskii proletarii* (Kharkov), 13 (26) December 1917.

[81] See P. V. Kovalev, *Sostoianie Donetskogo Basseina v oktiabre–ianvare mesiatsakh 1917/18 g.* ([Moscow?], [1918]), p. 3.

[82] GADO, f. 306, op. 1, d. 32, l. 3 [verso]. See also R. Ia. Terekhov, *Tak nachalas' bor'ba. Iz vospominanii* (Stalino, 1957), p. 84.

[83] Kovalev, *Sostoianie Donetskogo Basseina*, p. 3, and Kazimirchuk, "Revoliutsionnoe dvizhenie Vospominaniia)," p. 65, and "Revoliutsionnoe dvizhenie. Ianvar'–aprel' 1918 goda," p. 126.

[84] Kovalev, *Sostoianie Donetskogo Basseina*, p. 4.

[85] *Gornozavodskoe delo*, 31 June 1918, pp. 16554–55 (18 May speech by N. F. von Ditmar, a leading Donbas industrialist).

ments.[86] Thus, the working hours were increased, wages cut, the unions ignored or closed, and strikes virtually outlawed.[87] It was symbolic of the restoration that savage corporal punishment was widely reintroduced. In Iuzovka, for example, forty politically suspect workers were subjected by Skoropadskii's men to twenty-five or more blows by a ramrod; one of them died from this punishment.[88] The violence and brutality of the political revenge frightened even the managers who feared that the workers would flee the mines en masse.[89]

Their fear was justified. The exodus of POWs, begun already in 1917, was accelerated by the occupation, and many colliers deserted the mines to avoid the fighting and to search for food.[90] Donbas miners "now were enrolled in the Red Army, now left the coalfields retreating with the Soviet Government, now went to the Kuban or other grain-producing areas to escape famine, now returned to their native village, now went back to the coalfields." The population movement was such that it was described as a "great migration of peoples."[91] According to one source, the number of Donbas miners thus declined progressively from 215,000 in March 1918 to 78,239 in October 1918, a sixty-four percent drop in seven months.[92] Coal production accordingly plummeted from 24,836 to 8,910 thousand tons from 1917 to 1918.[93]

The dire shortages in the labor force led desperate managers to round up the recalcitrant workers from their flats and barracks by armed force.[94] Yet wages often remained unpaid. Strikes erupted everywhere. In the Sofievka (Sofiivka) coalfield, for example, on 24 September 1918 a spontaneous strike took place for the payment of the August wages. On that day, the trade union under the Menshevik leadership managed to convince the strikers to end their action, but the following day the strike resumed. The administration promised to pay by 28 September, and the union's appeal ended the strike. The promise was not kept, however, and the colliers struck anew.[95]

In spite of the strike waves, the restored capitalist regime managed to

[86] Ibid., pp. 16574–75.
[87] See B. Kolesnikov, *Professional'noe dvizhenie i kontr-revoliutsiia. Ocherki iz istorii professional'nogo dvizheniia na Ukraine* (Kharkov, 1923), pp. 46–50. See also the case of Adam Svitsyn, director of the New Russian Company, in *Gornotrud*, 1919, no. 2:9.
[88] *5-letnii obzor*, p. 48. For other cases, see Pavlo Khrystiuk, *Zamitky i materialy do istorii ukrains'koi revoliutsii 1917–1920 rr.* (Vienna, 1921), 3:46, and *Vestnik profdvizheniia Ukrainy*, 15 September 1924, p. 9.
[89] *Gornozavodskoe delo*, 15 May 1918, p. 16524.
[90] See, for example, *Donetskii proletarii* (Kharkov), 23 March 1918, and *Protokoly I-go delegatskago oblastnogo s"ezda*, p. 47.
[91] *5-letnii obzor*, pp. 9–10.
[92] E. M. Skliarenko, *Robitnychyi klas Ukrainy v roki hromadians'koi viiny (1918–1920 rr.). Narysy* (Kiev, 1960), p. 24.
[93] Bakulev, *Razvitie*, p. 662.
[94] *5-letnii obzor*, p. 47.
[95] GADO, f. 306, op. 1, d. 25. l. 9.

increase the productivity of labor. The remaining workforce, which was said to be composed largely of "old" (that is, skilled) workers with families, sought to earn as much as possible to feed their families. The capitalists exploited them intensely.[96] The same pattern was repeated in 1919 under the Denikin regime.[97]

From late 1918 (when Skoropads'kyi was overthrown by the Directory) to mid-1919 (when almost the entire Donbas fell to Denikin), the Donbas again became a theater of savage warfare and class revenge. Workers were terrorized by the Whites simply because they were workers.[98] In December 1918 in Iuzovka, for example, at General S. V. Denisov's order, one out of every ten arrested workers was to be hanged. Hundreds of corpses were kept hanging for days in major streets.[99] In January 1919, in Enakievo (Ienakiieve), Gorlovka (Horlivka), and Shcherbinovka (Shcherbynivka), more than 500 workers were shot.[100]

With Denikin, former managers returned again. The pre-February regime was restored to the mines and factories. This time they were said to be concerned not so much with increasing their profits as with getting revenge.[101] Yet the workers were ruthlessly exploited, in any case, and deaths from starvation and epidemics were reported to be "not rare in Enakievo, Kadievka [Kadiivka], and other districts."[102] Here and there wildcat strikes occurred.[103] Yet, as in 1914–17, strikers were threatened with, and punished by mobilization to the front, with the result that the strike movement was more limited under Denikin than under Skoropadskii.[104] In the Donbas White rule continued until the end of 1919.

If the workers were terrorized by the Whites, the engineers and technicians were battered by the workers. When the Whites retreated, workers would beat up engineers and technicians, even those sympathetic with the Soviet government, considering that the time for revenge had come.[105] Nor did the Soviet government trust the specialists as a group, since many of them had—willingly or not—cast their lot with the Whites.[106] Whatever

---

[96] *Narodnoe khoziaistvo*, 1919, no. 3:28.

[97] See *Oktiabr' i gorniaki*, pp. 49–50.

[98] See *Robitnychyi kontrol' i natsionalizatsiia promyslovosti na Ukraini*, p. 495.

[99] *Pravda*, 4 December 1918.

[100] *Gornotrud*, 10 April 1919, p. 20.

[101] Kolesnikov, *Professional'noe dvizhenie i kontrrevoliutsiia*, p. 172. More generally, see M. Mal't, "Denikinshchina i rabochie," *Proletarskaia revoliutsiia*, 1924, no. 5.

[102] *Gornotrud*, 25 September 1919, p. 7.

[103] Note, for example, the Makeevka case in *Professional'noe dvizhenie*, 5 December 1919, p. 3.

[104] Kolesnikov, *Professional'noe dvizhenie i kontrrevoliutsiia*, p. 308.

[105] *Protokoly III-go oblasnogo delegatskogo s"ezda professional'nogo soiuza "Gornotrud" Donetskogo Basseina, Krivorozhskogo i Solianogo raionov, 26 aprelia–6 maia 1919 g.* (Kharkov, 1919), p. 67.

[106] See *Narodnoe khoziaistvo*, 1919, no. 5:29.

their political views, during the civil war many specialists were shot by the Reds on grounds of rumor about their political disloyalty.[107] White terror was met by Red terror with equal severity. In December 1919, half of the mining specialists fled the Donbas with the defeated Whites.[108]

The Donbas colliers underwent terrible sacrifices during the civil war. In December 1919 the Donbas, "this economic center of the Soviet Republic," was described as "having become a cemetery of Donbas miners and metalworkers."[109] A journal of the miners' union congratulated their members on their brave fight:

> Among the miners there were not such deep degradation and depravity as seen in the ranks of other industrial workers, not excluding even the vanguard metalworkers. In the Donbas [we] even didn't know what the Kirstov movement was.
>
> The dark, ignorant miners have come out honorably from the ordeal of those gloomy days. . . . With the exception of some rare instances in which individual workers or groups of workers showed a friendly attitude towards the [White] authorities, the miners as a whole, after a brief depression, were opposed to the Voluntary Army.[110]

Surprisingly, then, once the Whites were gone and the Reds came back, some 80,000 remaining Donbas colliers, among others, found themselves decried by the Bolshevik Party:

> All the best [elements] of the [Ukrainian] proletariat have gone to Russia and to the Red Army, and few have returned. The remainder are those who have families and private property: not a few have a house by the coalfields and factories and have stayed there. They are psychologically smashed. They have no work, but engage in petty speculation. This is understandable, because they want to eat, but their proletarian consciousness, which isn't very high to begin with, is now completely crushed.[111]

They were even told that in the Donbas the working class had disintegrated into *Makhnovshchina* (members of the Makhno anarchist move-

---

[107] See, for example, V. A. Menzhosov, "Oktiabr' 1917 goda i tekhnicheskaia intelligentsiia Donbassa," in *Novye stranitsy v istorii Donbassa, Stat'i* (Donetsk, 1992), 1:110.

[108] See *Ekonomicheskaia zhizn'*, 25 February 1920.

[109] *Vos'maia konferentsiia RKP(b): Dekabr' 1919 goda. Protokoly* (Moscow, 1961), p. 86 (Ia. A. Iakovlev).

[110] *Gornotrud*, 22 March 1920, p. 16. The Kirstov movement was a kind of *zubatovshchina* under the Denikin rule, strong in Kiev and Odessa. For a view favorable more of miners than of metalworkers, see also Kolesnikov, *Professional'noe dvizhenie i kontrrevoliutsiia*, p. 113.

[111] *Vos'maia konferentsiia RKP(b)*, p. 104 (V. P. Zatonskii). For a similar criticism of Donbas colliers, see *Gornorabochii*, 1920, no. 3:44.

ment) and that the proletariat did not exist.[112] Some workers did join the Makhno insurrections.[113] Yet this disparagement by the Bolshevik Party was symptomatic of the troubles lying ahead, which it attributed to the "declassed proletariat."[114] The civil war brought the Bolsheviks and the miners closer in their fight against common enemies. With the end of the war came not peace but turbulence. In the years of economic crisis that followed the civil war, the Donbas miners resorted repeatedly to strikes, and the "great migration of peoples" could not be halted.[115]

Implicit in the reproach by the Bolsheviks, however, seemed to be the party's suspicion of the political loyalty of those who stayed on under the Whites. To be sure, this was not explicitly stated, but it would have been absurd for the party to assume their loyalty without reservation. It feared that the frequent change of powers, that is, the availability of political alternatives, had made the population less firm in their support of the Soviet government.[116] In any case, that many workers chose to remain and even recorded a high productivity of labor under the Whites was not palatable to the Bolsheviks.

Conclusion

An extreme case is often extremely revealing. The Donbas is such a case. If on the eve of World War I there existed a sharp polarization of Russian society into *verkhi* and *nizy*, in the Donbas the depth of mutual alienation appeared unfathomable. On the one hand, the miners as a group still constituted a semi-peasant, migrant, and "dark" force, which led an extremely wretched life. On the other hand, the Donbas industrialists, many of whom represented foreign capital, embraced more "enlightened" and liberal inclinations than their colleagues elsewhere. Their "welfare liberalism," however, did not mean that economic exploitation was less harsh. In real-life industrial relations they did not adhere to their modern notions. In times of crisis, brutal repression and medieval methods of punishment prevailed. The alternation of miners' violent rebellion and submissive conformism was conditioned not merely by the peculiarity of a mining environment but also by labor and management's mutual contempt and fear.

[112] *Vos'maia konferentsiia RKP(b)*, p. 107 (D. Z. Manuil'skii).

[113] See, for example, D. Kin, *Denikinshchina* (Leningrad, 1927), p. 116.

[114] For this problem in general, see Fitzpatrick, "Bolsheviks' Dilemma."

[115] I discuss this in a book on the Donbas coal-mining industry from 1917 to 1941 I am currently writing.

[116] This fear is clearly seen in *Sbornik otchetov Narodnykh komissariatov USSR, Upolnomochennykh Narodnykh komissariatov RSFSR pri Sovnarkome USSR i tsentral'nykh uchrezhdenii Ukrainy* (Kharkov, 1921), p. 23.

There were clear signs of disunity within the Donbas colliers. Even in 1917, for example, when unionization became possible and even fashionable, they, unlike many other groups of workers, hardly bothered to form trade unions. There were also indications that they had a clear sense of who their enemies were (representatives of the old regime) and what they wanted (freedom and, for some, land). When the autocracy fell, the Donbas colliers appeared to have little illusion about any form of politics.[117] What Leopold H. Haimson has called the "absence of a minimal consensus—not merely about an institutional framework and a political and social order but also about a moral order"[118]—was manifested in extreme form in the Donbas. In 1917 the militancy of miners assumed the form of revenge and developed largely independently of party politics. Certainly, the Bolshevik influence increased in the course of 1917, yet it was not overwhelming. This was somewhat ironic, for the Bolsheviks were the most uncompromising toward the old regime and capitalists. The miners could not be easily organized or accommodated to party politics. Their apparent vulnerability to political manipulation was a reflection of their lack of belief in any form of politics.

These political developments were extreme but not necessarily peculiar to the Donbas colliers. The restoration of the old regime during the civil war, however, distinguishes the Donbas from other industrial centers in the Russian heartland. The civil war gave the Donbas workers political choices that Moscow or Petrograd workers did not have. Even though the war united the Bolsheviks and the Donbas workers against their common enemies, the former suspected that those miners who remained and worked in the Donbas had sympathized if not collaborated with the Whites and the Greens. This civil war experience posed a very serious conceptual and practical challenge to the Bolsheviks. If the Bolshevik Party regarded as true proletarians those Moscow or Petrograd workers who held out through the civil war years and as "semi-proletarians" those who fled to the countryside, then can the same criteria be applied to the Donbas colliers? Were those workers who settled in the Donbas and stayed on under the Whites, Blacks, and the Greens "true proletarians"? Should those migrant peasant workers who fled from the Donbas, presumably with the retreating Bolsheviks, be viewed as "semi-proletarians"?

[117] They may be compared with the Russian and Armenian workers of Baku who through 1917–1918 "were concerned about safeguarding the freedoms won in February and consolidating their economic position through the labor contract." See Ronald Gregory Suny, *The Baku Commune, 1917–1918: Class and Nationality in the Russian Revolution* (Princeton, N.J., 1972), p. 346.

[118] Leopold H. Haimson, "The Problem of Social Identities in Early Twentieth Century Russia: Observations on the Commentaries by Alfred Rieber and William Rosenberg," *Slavic Review* 47, no. 2 (1988): 516.

To work in the Donbas, the Bolsheviks certainly needed a political gas mask.

From the party's point of view, this lingering suspicion was compensated for by the profound enmity of workers toward the representatives of the old regime. Those who stayed on under the Whites and the Greens may have worked desperately to survive. Yet their enmity was tempered with their bitter civil war experiences. Thus, "specialist-baiting" was kept extraordinarily alive among the Donbas colliers. It does not appear to be a coincidence that the Shakhty affair, the 1928 trial of Donbas coalmining engineers and managers and an event that marked Stalin's revolution from above, took place in the Donbas. Perhaps Stalin knew exactly what kind of political gas mask was needed.

6

Diane P. Koenker

Labor Relations in Socialist Russia:
Class Values and Production Values
in the Printers' Union, 1917–1921

The Bolshevik Party came to power in October 1917 on the promise of a socialism that would more justly allocate society's economic resources. This socialist promise was widely supported by Russia's urban workers; the Bolsheviks received 46 percent of the vote in Petrograd and Moscow in the elections to the Constituent Assembly that followed the October Revolution, and all socialist parties together received two-thirds of the vote. Nor was socialist sentiment confined to the cities. Parties representing the various strands of Russian socialism also collected two-thirds of the national total in November 1917.[1] But few of these voters knew precisely what they could expect from "socialism" beyond the popular goals of land, bread, and peace. The fact was, the implementation of socialism on a national scale had never been attempted before. Russian Marxists possessed a great deal of theory about capitalism but very little about what a socialist society should or could be.

The nature of the socialist workplace was uncharted territory especially for workers. The aspirations they expressed in their political and economic protests in 1917 give some idea of what they expected from a socialist revolution, but offer little indication of how their aspirations would be implemented within a socialist economic structure. They had demanded food, jobs, workshop democracy, improved health and work conditions, shorter hours, and paid vacations. Many expected that all this

Support for the research and writing of this essay was gratefully received from the University of Illinois, the National Endowment for the Humanities, the National Council for Soviet and East European Research, the International Research and Exchanges Board (IREX), the Fulbright-Hays Faculty Research Program of the U.S. Department of Education, the Australian National University, and the Midwest Universities Consortium on International Affairs (MUCIA).

[1] Calculated from figures in Oliver H. Radkey, *Russia Goes to the Polls: The Election to the All-Russian Constituent Assembly, 1917* (Ithaca, N.Y., 1989), pp. 34, 80.

could be provided once the capitalists had been deprived of the surplus they had so long expropriated.

But *how* these things would be provided, how workers would interact with management, the state, and each other under socialism—these questions had no ready answers. Lenin, in *The State and Revolution*, begged the question of labor relations; he argued the state would eventually wither away, as Engels had predicted, but whether and how factory authority would also go the way of the state remained outside Lenin's field of vision. Leading theorists from both Marxist political parties, the Bolsheviks and the Mensheviks, also argued among themselves.[2] And so the dictatorship of the proletariat (itself a disputed construct) was established without benefit of a theoretical consensus on the role of management and authority in the workplace, the issues of labor discipline and remuneration, or the rights of workers in a workers' state.

The ensuing civil war scarcely provided Russia with controlled laboratory conditions for the socialist experiment. Military and economic emergencies fueled bitter political struggles and sharply limited resources available for the task. It is impossible, in fact, to separate the building of socialism from the specific political and economic context of the civil war. The system that emerged by 1921, with the Bolsheviks in power, reflected this bitter experience, interpreted through the interaction of theory and practice. No wonder that socialists failed to agree on the conclusions they drew from this complex interaction.

The experience of the printing industry during the civil war years offers a vivid illustration of the struggle to accommodate theory and practice, a struggle that manifested itself in a search for alternative solutions to the problem of building socialism. The printers' union between 1917 and 1921 was the focus of a bitter struggle between Mensheviks and Bolsheviks, and even among Bolsheviks, a struggle fought precisely over the nature of socialism and the role of workers and trade unions in a socialist state. I will concentrate on the evolution of labor relations in the printing industry, primarily in Moscow and Petrograd, both from the perspective of union leadership and state policymakers, and from the perspective of workers on the shop floor. The evolution of labor relations under socialism was inextricably linked with the "re-formation" of the working class, as workers sought to adapt their old consciousness to the new realities of state ownership of the means of production and to define a role for themselves in the new order.

Both perspectives, that of the union office and that of the shop floor, were mediated through the struggle for control between Mensheviks and

[2] See Carmen Sirianni, *Workers' Control and Socialist Democracy: The Soviet Experience* (London, 1982), chap. 7.

Bolsheviks from 1917 to 1920, when the Bolsheviks shut down the last independent branch of the printers' union in Moscow. This is an important story, and one that will be a major element of the larger study of which this is a part. At the risk of seeming to "depoliticize" the development of socialist labor relations, I will concentrate here on the elements of labor relations in order to focus on how new socialist values and definitions were shaped by the shop-floor and everyday experience of workers in revolutionary Russia.

Models of Labor Relations

No labor-relations "system" emerged from policymaking circles in the immediate aftermath of the October Revolution. But as the fragile Soviet regime sought to establish its authority in the face of economic chaos and political and military challenge, pieces of a system were fashioned through an avalanche of central decrees. Throughout the civil war, issues concerning labor relations provoked heated political debate, pitting communists against each other as well as against rival socialists. The debate and the decrees focused on five major areas—in printing and in industry as a whole.

Most immediate were the nature and rights of workplace authority, of management. Should ownership be private or public? If private ownership remained, how much state regulation was appropriate, and what would be the mechanism of regulation? Or, if public ownership prevailed, would this take the form of national, local (city or region), or workplace ownership? And what was the appropriate amount of superordinate regulation of such public properties? Although the impulse to central planning and state regulation arose in Russia during the war, as it did elsewhere in Europe, the virtues of central planning were not universally accepted in 1918. Initially, the Soviet regime permitted continued private ownership, with the public interest represented by state regulation. Such a relationship proved unworkable, and most Russian industrial enterprises were nationalized by decree on 28 June 1918. The printing industry, however, was not included in this compulsory nationalization scheme.[3]

For socialized industry, the question of administrative structure remained open: should industry be centrally or locally administered? How much autonomy should individual plants possess? What should be the mechanism for allocating resources or gaining access to raw materials, orders, and customers? The demands of the civil war economy inexo-

---

[3] *Sbornik dekretov i postanovlenii po narodnomu khoziaistvu (25 oktiabria 1917 g.–25 oktiabria 1918 g.)* (Moscow, 1918), pp. 226–29.

rably pressed policymakers to advocate greater and greater central authority and control, but this outcome was by no means the only one possible under social ownership of industry.[4] Within individual plants, a critical question was whether authority would be vested in a committee, or whether social justice could properly be supervised by a single individual. "One-man management" was more efficient and worked better with the developing centralized apparatus; Lenin argued forcefully and successfully for its universal implementation,[5] but workers and trade unions frequently resisted. In many places they retained collective systems in which plant administration consisted of representatives from workers, the union, and central economic organs.

For workers whose claims for workplace democracy in 1917 had fueled the conflicts that resulted in the socialists coming to power, the issue of workplace authority in socialized enterprises was critical. How much power would workers have in enterprise decision making? Would factory committees administer plants and participate in their administration or merely exercise oversight and hold veto power over decisions made by specialist managers? How would workers assert their claims to better work conditions, their determination to be bossed by sympathetic and not tyrannical supervisors? Many socialists in higher positions felt workers' interests would be sufficiently defended by the state acting in the name of the proletariat, and by the exercise of authority by individuals who *had once been* workers.[6] (This argument may have been especially irrelevant to printers: as Mark Steinberg has indicated, many bosses even in the prerevolutionary printing industry were former workers who had risen through the ranks.) The extent of workers' power on the shop floor remained a gray and contested area. It was not settled by the revolution, by the 14 November 1917 decree on workers' control, or by the 1918 decree on nationalization. As it is a critical element in any system of labor relations, it will be important to return to this issue in the specific context of the printing industry in the years 1917–21.

The question of productivity and how to promote it constituted a second crucial area of labor relations. What were appropriate socialist incentives to production? Among positive incentives, would wages disappear in favor of a psychology of production, "from each according to his ability, to each according to his need"? In the breakdown of the economy after 1917, the Russian Republic came near to effecting a system, labeled by

---

[4] See E. H. Carr, *The Bolshevik Revolution, 1917–1923* (Harmondsworth, 1966), 2:62–105, 176–200.

[5] Ibid., pp. 191–94.

[6] This is a theme of the work of Sheila Fitzpatrick, particularly in *Education and Social Mobility in the Soviet Union, 1921–1934* (Cambridge, 1979) and "The Bolsheviks' Dilemma: Class, Culture, and Politics in Early Soviet Years," *Slavic Review* 47, no. 4 (1988), 599–613; see also the discussion following "Bolsheviks' Dilemma" with Ronald Grigor Suny and Daniel Orlovsky (pp. 614–26).

historians "social maintenance," in which the state provided a bare minimum of subsistence to all workers regardless of output.[7] Some saw this as the wave of the future, others as a stopgap measure to cope with crippling scarcities of food and other resources. The question remained open whether positive pecuniary incentives were necessary and desirable under socialist production. Also undetermined were the forms such incentives could take: were skill-based differentials compatible with socialism? Was the "family wage," in which a wage was based on family size and one's position in the family as much as on work, an appropriate element of socialism or would it discourage individual productivity? Were specific schemes tied to productivity—piece rates, bonuses, norms—compatible with and appropriate to socialist labor relations, or were they necessary only in capitalist systems?[8] Nonpecuniary incentives—appeals to patriotism or enthusiasm, such as designating heroes of labor and volunteer work Saturdays—might also play an important role in socialist productivity.

The reverse side of these positive incentives was labor discipline: would there be a need to enforce discipline in a socialist enterprise, and how should it be done? Capitalist industry had employed close supervision, fines, and threats of dismissal to ensure discipline. The wartime state added to this the threat of military mobilization. Some socialists expected that under socialism, only "unconscious" workers would have to be compelled to work, but here too the nature and extent of compulsion remained to be defined.

A third area of contention was the problem of conflicts. Would disputes arise under socialism between workers and management, and if they did, how should they be resolved? The classic form of conflict, the strike, was widely considered to be inappropriate under socialism. Workers, by withholding their labor, harmed the collective interest of all workers now, not the private interest of capital. Arbitration, conciliation, and judicial procedure—labor tribunals—were hailed as socialist alternatives to labor stoppages. Political pressure in a democratic system could also replace labor stoppages as a means to settle conflicts. But if all else failed, should workers be permitted to strike or to engage in other forms of direct action (sit-ins or slow-downs) against their own society? The question perplexed Soviet policymakers for as long as the Soviet Union existed.[9]

Linking these three areas of labor relations was the crucial fourth one,

[7] See Paul Ashin, "Wage Policy in the Transition to NEP," *Russian Review* 47 (July 1988): 295; and William J. Chase, *Workers, Society, and the Soviet State: Labor and Life in Moscow, 1918–1929* (Urbana, Ill., 1987).

[8] See Ashin, "Wage Policy in the Transition to NEP," pp. 293–313.

[9] "Zabastovki v SSSR: Novaia sotsial'naia real'nost'," *Sotsiologicheskie issledovaniia* 1 (1989): 21–36; Sergei Stankevich, "Legal Strikes," *Moscow News*, 29 October 1989, pp. 8–9.

the role of trade unions, their relationship to the state and its economic organs, their relationship to workers on the shop floor. Would trade unions exist outside the state's economic apparatus or within it? Was it possible for unions to disagree among themselves, and if so, could individual unions follow their own policy or were they bound by the union movement as a whole? What was appropriate union practice: would "trade union rules" be centralized and authoritarian, or federal and democratic? Were workers' interests identical to those of the state and its organs—higher productivity—or somehow different? It was precisely on the question of union independence that Bolsheviks and Mensheviks were most sharply divided, but the Bolsheviks themselves were split over this issue. The "trade union debate" dominated communist political discussion in 1920.[10]

Equally central to the problem of labor relations under socialism was the nature of the state. Would the socialist state subsume all sectors of society, or would the state function as superarbiter, balancing conflicting demands on its resources, resolving inevitable conflicts among different elements of society? In the economy, would the state function as regulator or manager? How centralized would state power and authority be? Where would control over its coercive forces lie? And who would regulate state policy—was a dictatorship of the proletariat incompatible with socialist democracy? To raise these questions opens a vast realm of political theory and socialist practice, and to consider them fully would take this essay far from its main task. Although the specific issue of the state received much less contemporary discussion than, for example, the role of trade unions, the emergence of a centralized state with control over all institutionalized activity and with a monopoly of coercive power played a critical role in the development of labor relations in the printing industry, as elsewhere.

No consensus on a system of labor relations emerged from these discussions and conflicts, but alternative approaches polarized into two basic variants. One was productivist and statist, the other "workerist" and independent. One subsumed all social life into state institutions, the other permitted trade unions to play an autonomous role in civil society.

The First All-Russian Trade Union Congress in January 1918 and the Second, one year later, were dominated by Bolsheviks, who fully endorsed the primacy of production. Bolshevik printers carried this message to their supporters: "Trade unions, as the class organization of the proletariat, should undertake the primary task of organizing production and renewing

---

[10] Carr, *Bolshevik Revolution*, 2:220–22; see also William G. Rosenberg, "The Social Background to Tsektran," in Diane P. Koenker, William G. Rosenberg, and Ronald Grigor Suny, eds., *Party, State and Society in the Russian Civil War: Explorations in Social History* (Bloomington, Ind., 1989).

the shattered productive forces of the country."[11] Productivist interests could only be served by state regulation of all printing enterprises and by centralized economic administration, with orders and policies transmitted from state economic organs through trade unions to the trade unions' local agents, the factory committees. The latter, although their appointments were ratified by workers, remained responsible for promoting production. In any conflict between workers' welfare and production, production came first: only higher productivity could produce a higher standard of living. Factory committees and unions likewise served as the industry's disciplinary body, with the power to fire workers for absenteeism or for challenging administrative decisions. They also implemented the centrally contracted wage and bonus systems. Conflicts in this productivist system, where the unions and managers represented workers' collective best interests, could only be individual, not collective.[12]

Trade union independence was the keystone of the alternative model of labor relations, which was embraced by the Menshevik Party. Regardless of the economic system under which workers were employed, the interests of workers as sellers of labor conflicted with the interests of those who purchased their labor. Only trade unions independent of their employers could properly represent the workers' interests. For proponents of this model, the nature of plant ownership was irrelevant for the tactics of trade unions. Whether workers confronted socialist or capitalist managers, they needed to defend their immediate interests first. Unions could do this through organized collective bargaining: gathering information, preparing proposals, and negotiating on behalf of the sellers of labor as equals with the buyers of labor. The rules of their interaction would be defined through the democratic process, not by arbitrary use of state force. In the independent model of labor relations, as in the statist model, production was in workers' best interests. Within this system of bargaining, workers were prepared to accept output norms and negotiated wage scales.[13] Menshevik union leaders therefore agreed to participate in the economic agencies that directed their industry, the better to be able to represent the interests of workers.[14] Strikes that halted production were also to be discouraged, but the right to strike had to be retained as the final weapon of workers in defense of their interests.[15]

[11] *Pervyi s"ezd vserossiiskikh professional'nykh soiuzov, 1918* (Moscow, 1918), p. 119.

[12] In the printing industry, discussion of this model can be found in *Vserossiiskii pechatnik*, 15 February 1921, pp. 2–9 and 15 March 1921, p. 7, and in *Moskovskii pechatnik*, 15 February 1921, pp. 3–4.

[13] *Pechatnik*, 27 November (10 December) 1918.

[14] *Pechatnik*, 30 May 1919 (decision of the board meeting of May 8). The Menshevik Nikolai Chistov joined the collegium of the Moscow polygraphic division in February 1920. TsGAMO, f. 699, op. 1, d. 60, l. 17.

[15] *Pechatnik*, 17 (30) April 1918, pp. 8–9.

Two additional models of labor relations can be constructed from the practical experience of the civil war economy. Both Communists and Mensheviks warned against the implementation of an anarchist model, whose key feature was ownership and management of an enterprise by the workers themselves. Such a model was incompatible with a centrally administered socialist economy. Independent factories, operating as "federated republics," would never subordinate their immediate interests to the collective good.[16] Without markets (which were capitalist) and without central authority, there would be no way to allocate resources to these plants or to distribute their output. Furthermore, neither party's leaders had much confidence in the ability of Russia's "backward" labor force to master the complicated science of factory management. Worker self-management, in the conditions of Russia's economic collapse, would lead to workers selling off the capital stock of their plant and going to the countryside on the proceeds. It was therefore a recipe for the rapid collapse of Russia's remaining industrial capacity. Such a model received little theoretical support from printing workers, but practical experience pushed workers toward such a system, as we will see.

Mensheviks and communists also denounced what they labeled the "narrow-minded" (*obyvatel'skii*) worker's model of labor relations. As Trotsky had argued, too many workers, left to their own devices, would choose a system that guaranteed a maximum of compensation for a minimum of work. Capitalism or socialism, dictatorship or democracy, dependent or independent trade unions, the "broad interests" of class or society—were equally irrelevant to the narrow-minded worker, who chose whichever alternative provided for his immediate material interests.[17] Printers "live their own lives, live only for what today's need prompts them to do."[18] If one system did not deliver, he would choose another. Printers were indifferent to which party promised bread, clothing, and freedom to travel in search for food, argued the communist union journal. "He wants to have all this—and that's enough."[19] For socialists, this attitude was dangerously shortsighted. Trotsky proposed to combat it by force, the Communist unionists by education, and the Mensheviks by organization. On the shop floor, however, workers practiced a tenacious resistance to the politics of sacrifice advocated by their leaders, using whatever means practicable to defend their self-interests. The real differ-

---

[16] *Vtoraia vserossiiskaia konferentsiia soiuzov rabochikh pechatnogo dela* (14–21 dekabria 1917 g.) (Moscow, 1918), p. 63.

[17] A recent study of workers under socialist governments in France and Spain argues that workers were just as resistant to work under these regimes, much to the displeasure of the socialist governments. See Michael Seidman, *Workers against Work: Labor in Paris and Barcelona during the Popular Fronts* (Berkeley and Los Angeles, 1991).

[18] GARF, f. 5525, op. 1, d. 10, l. 14 (discussion at 1919 congress).

[19] *Vserossiiskii pechatnik*, 10 June 1920, p. 3.

ence between the so-called narrow-minded workers and far-seeing socialists was where they drew the limit to "self": at themselves, their family,
their workshop, their industry, their class, their country, or the world.

The role played by "class" in these debates about labor relations lost
clarity as Russian society moved rapidly away from the classic social
structure of capitalism (before, indeed, it had even arrived at such a structure). The Menshevik supporters of union independence seemed most
wedded to a structural definition of class and most comfortable leading a
union that struggled with employers using the familiar labels of a capitalist terrain. As these capitalist employers succumbed to state regulation
and expropriation, the meaning of "class" became increasingly blurred.
The Communists, as we shall see, were much more willing to use the old
language of class to signify new conceptions of friends and enemies that
had little in common with classic Marxist categories.

Printers and Their Industry

Does the experience of printers in the Russian Revolution provide a fair
representation of the "proletarian" experience? Not if we take as the idealized proletarian some stereotypic machine-builder, muscular coal miner,
or kerchiefed cotton-spinner. Printers possessed certain unique characteristics that separated them, quite self-consciously, from others in the proletarian family. Their place of work was generally in the urban center
rather than the industrial suburb, and their daily work brought many of
them into close contact with journalists and writers, with the printed
world of ideas. The nature of their work required them to be not only
highly skilled but literate as well, and a culture of intelligence and literacy
evolved among printers. Mark Steinberg expertly analyzes the culture and
worldview of the activist stratum of this group elsewhere in this book.
Printers contributed to society not raw or finished goods like coal or steel,
but the transmission of ideas and values; many printers considered themselves, therefore, to be especially valuable to society in general and to the
working class in particular.[20]

But like other industrial workers, printers worked in production with
their hands and with skills learned through years of apprenticeship and
on-the-job practice. As Steinberg has shown, printing activists in the years
before 1917 had forged a self-identity as proletarian repositories of a
moral humanism. With other proletarians, they shared the status of ex-

---

[20] *Istoriia Leningradskogo soiuza poligraficheskogo proizvodstva (1904–1907 gg.)* (Leningrad, 1925); Mark Steinberg, "Culture and Class in a Russian Industry: The Printers of
St. Petersburg, 1860–1905," *Journal of Social History* 23 (spring 1990): 513–33.

ploited sellers of labor, and they rejected a narrow craft unionism that separated typesetters from press operators (characteristic among printers in most other industrial societies) in favor of an all-encompassing industrial unionism. Whether Menshevik or Bolshevik, they prided themselves on their bona fide revolutionary history, which began in Russia with industry-wide strikes in 1903 and extended to activism in the 1905 and 1917 revolutions.[21]

With the fall of the old regime in February 1917, printers joined with other Russian workers to organize trade unions, to bargain collectively with their employers, and to engage in political action on a local and national scale. The end of tsarist censorship opened the way for a flourishing printing trade, and employment opportunities expanded. Printers mounted a series of citywide strikes across Russia, and improved their material position in many other places without strikes, through collective bargaining backed by strong union organization. But internally, printers were beset by divisions similar to those found among other groups of workers: between skilled and unskilled (in printing, the newspaper compositor emerged as the highest paid in the profession), and among adherents of various socialist parties. Unions were officially outside partisan divisions, but the printers' union became a bastion of Menshevism in 1917.[22] To counter this influence, smaller groups of Bolshevik supporters in Petrograd and Moscow formed caucuses and "subdistricts" and agitated among their fellows for the adoption of their line. This partisan struggle became increasingly vocal and bitter in the second half of 1917, at the same time as the general collapse of the Russian economy began to affect the well-being and future prospects of printers everywhere in Russia. The collapse of production became catastrophic in the months after the Soviet seizure of power in October 1917.

The printers' trade, their skills, their position in the economy, and their self-image made many of them perceptive observers of society and the working class. Their access to the technologies of the printed word allowed them to describe their position and to comment on society in a remarkable range of periodicals before and after the 1917 revolution. And their politics placed them in the very center of the struggle to define the

[21] *Pechatnik*, 28 October (10 November) 1918, p. 4; *Vtoraia moskovskaia gubernskaia konferentsiia rabochikh poligraficheskogo proizvodstva (Stenograficheskii otchet) 12 maia 1921 g.* (Moscow, 1922), p. 31; *Tretii vserossiiskii s"ezd soiuzov rabochikh poligraficheskogo proizvodstva i poligrafotdelov (2–6 iiunia 1921 g.) Protokoly i postanovleniia s"ezda* (Moscow, 1921), p. 13; *Istoriia Leningradskogo soiuza*, pp. 99–120, 133–406.

[22] The reasons for this political position are complex and deserve more discussion than is possible here. The Mensheviks' opponents argued that printers, as "labor aristocrats," were inherently reformist. Later in their struggle to conquer the union, the same opponents argued this was not necessarily so. *Pravda*, 5 January 1919.

goals of the revolution. In short, printers offer a unique and valuable window on the struggle for socialism in Russia.

Models in Conflict: The Printers' Union, 1917–1918

Printing workers had a long history of organization, one dogged by penetration by police spies and periodic prohibition. With the fall of the tsarist regime in February 1917, printers in scores of cities across the Russian empire again formed unions, elected officers, worked to strengthen their organizations, and engaged in collective bargaining. But despite their relatively long experience in union affairs, it was not until the end of 1917 that representatives of forty-eight local unions met in Petrograd to form an all-Russian trade union of workers in the printing trade.[23] The structure of the union reflected standard Russian practice. The December 1917 conference elected a central council; local unions continued to be governed by boards of directors (*pravleniia*) elected by a general vote of members; boards were assisted by councils of representatives (*sovety upolnomochennikh*) elected by workers at their place of work.[24] Workers in individual print shops also elected factory committees, whose relationship to the union structure would constitute a focus of dispute in the coming years.

The majority of trade unions had pledged their allegiance to the Bolsheviks by October 1917, but not printers. In Moscow and elsewhere, printers elected Menshevik majorities to their boards and Mensheviks as their union representatives. The Moscow branch of the union was nearly alone among the city's unions in opposing the "premature" seizure of power in October.[25] Petrograd printers were more radical, and replaced their Menshevik board with a Bolshevik one in November. Nationwide, the printers' union continued to support Menshevism: Mensheviks outnumbered Bolsheviks at the December national conference by fifty delegates to seventeen.[26]

The function of the union was to defend workers' interests. With socialists in power, however, the "workers' interest" was no longer a simple calculation, and these interests were challenged on two fronts in the weeks after the October revolution. On one hand, printers were engaged in pro-

---

[23] *Vtoraia vserossiiskaia konferentsiia*, 1917, pp. 10–11.

[24] The term for this body was unique in the union movement; other unions called their analogous institutions "assemblies of delegates" *(sobraniia delegatov)*.

[25] The degree of support among printers for the Socialist Revolutionaries is hard to determine. The Menshevik Party had the more dynamic leaders and dominated the political discourse. An indeterminate number of printers claimed membership in the SRs, but their voices are indistinct in the historical record.

[26] *Vtoraia vserossiiskaia konferentsiia*, 1917, p. 10.

tracted economic struggles with their employers, who resisted implementation of citywide collective agreements.[27] Conflicts over interpretation of the contract—on layoffs, work rules, nonpayment, and short pay—absorbed the Moscow union's energies in 1917 and 1918.[28] Continuing inflation provoked rank-and-file demands for raises outside the collective agreement. One print shop demanded a 150-ruble bonus in September 1918, another claimed 200 rubles.[29] The union had to resolve these claims to preserve equity, ultimately convincing the Moscow Trade Union Council to adopt an across-the-board increase of 200 rubles for all workers in the industry.[30] This was familiar territory for the adherents of the independent model of labor relations.

On the other hand, workers also faced conflict with the new proletarian dictatorship. One of the first moves of the regime was to close down newspapers that openly opposed Soviet power. This violated the right of press freedom, which the Mensheviks as well as many Bolsheviks supported, and it also put many printers out of work. (Whether or not printers opposed Communism because they felt they would not be able to make a living under a proletarian dictatorship must remain an open question for now, but it is an important one.) In any case, the Petrograd union's council of upolnomochennye demanded on November 6 that press freedom be restored or they would call a general strike.[31] Many printers recoiled from using a political strike against their own government, and it was at this point that new Petrograd union elections turned out the Menshevik board and put a Bolshevik majority in their place.[32] The shop upolnomochennye, though, were not reelected, and the council of upolnomochennye retained its Menshevik majority. The balance of political power in Petrograd was so even that the council could force the directors to send two Mensheviks

[27] Documents about collective agreements can be found in TsGAMO, f. 699, op. 1, d. 4. Other individual cases are reported in TsGAMO, f. 699, op. 1, d. 5, l. 7; *Pechatnik* 5 (1918): 13.

[28] TsGAMO, f. 699, op. 1, d. 34; *Pechatnik*, 31 January (13 February) 1918, p. 19; 18 (31) March 1918, p. 17; 27 September (10 October) 1918, pp. 7–8; 28 October (10 November) 1918, p. 12.

[29] TsGAMO, f. 699, op. 1, d. 4, ll. 164, 160.

[30] *Pechatnik*, 27 September (10 October) 1918, p. 5; 27 November (10 December) 1918, p. 2.

[31] Accounts differ on this meeting. The communist union history recorded the vote as 120–78, with 32 abstentions. *Materialy po istorii professional'nogo dvizheniia rabochikh poligraficheskogo proizvodstva (pechatnogo dela) v Rossii*, ed. F. Smirnov, N. Gordon, and A. Borshchevskii (Moscow, 1925), 1:91 (hereafter *Materialy*). This unremarkable book lay in the Lenin Library *spetskhran* until early 1989. A Menshevik newspaper reported that Bolshevik speakers avoided the meeting, and that the vote was 173–60. *Rabochaia gazeta*, 7 November 1917. The union journal, under Menshevik editors, reported only that the resolution received a majority. *Pechatnoe delo*, 8 December 1917, p. 5.

[32] *Materialy*, p. 91.

and two Bolsheviks to the first national congress of trade unions in January. The Bolshevik board had initially voted to send only Bolsheviks.[33]

Workers' interests as masters of the proletarian state also came into conflict with their interests as wage earners in Moscow, when local Bolshevik authorities shut down the liberal newspaper *Russkoe Slovo*. This case raised all the contradictions of socialist labor policy and presaged conflicts to come. In response to *Russkoe Slovo*'s inflammatory opposition to Soviet power, the Moscow soviet sequestered its print shop, owned by the printing magnate I. D. Sytin, and closed the newspaper on 28 November 1917. An armed guard occupied the shop and ordered its workers home. The next day, on the eve of the meeting of the Constituent Assembly (subsequently postponed by the Bolshevik regime until 4 January 1918), workers met to protest the use of force; they declared a strike against the government. The union's Menshevik leaders intervened and persuaded the Moscow soviet to retain the workers to print the soviet's paper, *Izvestiia*, on the same terms as before. Workers became soviet employees, and they signed a collective agreement. Two weeks later, when the soviet failed to pay these workers, they struck again, charging a breach of the agreement. The soviet and its local labor commissar immediately labeled this a political strike and refused to negotiate. Red Guards occupied the print shop, and its 1,500 workers were dismissed with sixteen days' severance pay. The unemployed printers refused to accept their dismissals and continued to strike.[34]

Was this a political strike now, or an economic one? The union and the *Russkoe Slovo* workers claimed they wished only to be paid their rightful wages. They were branded "saboteurs" simply because they had dared to defend their economic interests, they complained, because they had the audacity to consider the Moscow soviet an ordinary employer.[35] The union asked for the usual neutral party to arbitrate the dispute between workers and their "new owners."[36] But the soviet replied it did not recognize neutral arbitration, that the labor commissar was now the supreme authority.[37]

When word leaked that the print shop's expropriated owner, Sytin, had given the workers money to tide them over the Christmas holidays, the *Russkoe Slovo* strikers now genuinely seemed to be colluding with the class enemy. They ended their strike on January 18 and appealed for unemployment benefits, only to find that even their peers had turned

[33] *Pechatnik*, 31 January (13 February) 1918, p. 15.
[34] *Materialy*, pp. 142–56, provides some of the correspondence in the affair.
[35] *Pechatnik*, 31 January (13 February) 1918, p. 19.
[36] *Materialy*, pp. 150–55.
[37] Ibid., p. 156.

against them. On January 27, the Moscow union's council of representatives declared that the strike had been political from the start, that there was no difference now between economic and political actions. With growing unemployment, printers should not devote the scarce resources of the union unemployment fund to those who chose to quit work for political reasons. The strikers responded with what would become a familiar theme in the months ahead: the workers' government was treating workers worse than any capitalist employer had.[38] Such sentiment was quickly labeled counterrevolutionary.

A precedent had now been set. According to the Moscow soviet, the socialist employer was not simply another boss but the embodiment of the revolution. To challenge one's economic superior was now to challenge the revolution: such an equation immediately placed the independent union movement at an ideological disadvantage, creating a precarious moral status from which the independent trade union movement never recovered.[39]

The language in this conflict reveals the ambiguities that socialist power had brought to the discourse of class. The union charged that the Moscow soviet was acting as a "strikebreaker," "locking out" workers. Their actions were those of a tsarist governor, not of a "class-proletarian" government.[40] In the debate about this conflict, "class" and "proletarian" lost their meanings and were replaced by other identities. The *Russkoe Slovo* workers claimed the "workers' government" had chased them out of the factory "that we created through our own sweat and blood."[41] Their identity, in other words, came not from their relationship to the society at large, but from their role at the point of production. Yet other workers hostile to the *Russkoe Slovo* printers accused them of betraying the revolution, of having been blinded and duped by the "enemies of the working class."[42] For them, a worker was a member of the class only if he or she acted according to the interests of the class as a whole.

The *Russkoe Slovo* strike polarized the Moscow printers' union. Bolshevik printers strengthened their party organization and began to publish their own journal, *Revoliutsionnyi Golos Pechatnika*.[43] A month later, the Moscow upolnomochennye again supported (by a narrow margin) the Bolshevik position.[44] Printers' radicalism at this moment seemed genuine:

---

[38] *Pechatnik*, 31 January (13 February) 1918, p. 21.

[39] The significance of this episode in establishing the nature of labor relations in Moscow is suggested by the extent of the discussion in the history of the Moscow union in *Materialy*.

[40] *Pechatnik*, 31 January (13 February) 1918, pp. 19–20.

[41] *Materialy*, pp. 154–55.

[42] Ibid., p. 159.

[43] I was unable to find a copy of this journal in Moscow libraries; it is attacked in *Pechatnik*, 31 January (13 February) 1918, p. 4.

[44] *Pechatnik*, 18 (31) March 1918, p. 14.

the events of October, the resistance of the old ruling classes to the decrees implementing socialism, the promise of a socialist order, had legitimately pushed the sentiment among printers—some of the most moderate workers in Russia—toward the identification of their private interests with those of the Soviet state. But the Bolsheviks could not capitalize on this victory in Moscow or in the national union.[45] Instead, rank-and-file sentiment among printers and other workers began to shift away from the Bolsheviks, toward the Mensheviks, the party of the socialist alternative.

As economic conditions continued to deteriorate, printers lost confidence in the statist solution. Once the Communists had gained control of the union in Petrograd, argued Menshevik unionists, their adoption of "state socialism" had led to the immediate closure of many print shops. According to an editorial in *Pechatnik*, "Every type of 'control,' 'requisition,' 'nationalization,' and blind systemless evacuation [with the government to Moscow] conclusively weakened the union and harmed its authority among the masses."[46] From local shops in Petrograd came the call for a general meeting, the ultimate source of authority in the union movement. The meeting on March 24 attracted some five thousand printers, who turned the Communist board's report into a trial of Communist economic management. Workers condemned the communist monopoly on advertisements and the publication of classic literature. They charged the government had requisitioned print shops but could not provide them with any work. Private shops refused orders for fear they would be shut down and confiscated for printing the wrong thing. All this contributed to growing unemployment, the opposite of what workers expected from socialism.[47] In a tumultuous conclusion, the meeting adopted a resolution denouncing the union's failure to defend workers' interests in the four months it had been led by Communists. The board had not called a single general meeting, there was no plan or direction to the union's work, no consideration of the pressing problems of evacuation from Petrograd, or of unemployment. The meeting called for new leadership elections within two weeks.[48]

The elections in Petrograd returned the Mensheviks to power with 6,300 of 9,300 votes.[49] In Moscow, new leadership elections were preceded by a lively campaign of shop-floor meetings. Communists sought to pass a series of resolutions against the current board, promising "rivers of milk with banks of jelly" if elected to run the union, branding the Menshevik leaders as scoundrels and counterrevolutionaries for their un-

---

[45] *Vestnik vsrpd*, 20 March 1918, p. 6, and 20 April 1918, p. 4.
[46] *Pechatnik*, 18 (31) March 1918, p. 11.
[47] Ibid.
[48] *Pechatnik*, 18 (31) March 1918, p. 11; *Vestnik vsrpd*, 20 April 1918, p. 14.
[49] *Gazeta pechatnika*, 16 December 1918, p. 4.

willingness to embrace the October Revolution. But the Mensheviks countered with their own resolution campaign. In a secret ballot with 10,000 members voting (half the union membership, but a big increase over the 2,500 who had last voted in 1917), the "independents"—supporters of the Menshevik position—won fifteen seats on the board to the Communists' ten.[50]

Armed with this mandate, the Moscow union leaders attempted to prove that it was a union that defended its members' interests. The collective agreement (*tarif*) won the previous October expired in April 1918, and the union struggled to negotiate a new one, a task complicated by growing unemployment and rapid inflation. Private owners already felt constrained by a series of government decrees requiring them to contribute to unemployment and insurance funds,[51] but agreed in late April to a stipulated wage increase, with promised productivity gains and plans for an orderly reduction of the labor force to be negotiated by a commission of representatives from both sides.[52] The agreement was backdated to April 1, but to be valid it had to be approved by the Moscow Council of Trade Unions and by the commissar of labor. Both of these, unlike the union, subscribed to the productivist model of labor relations. Their concern, in principle, would be to ensure that gains in these particular workers' welfare be balanced by a corresponding contribution to the national economy. The commissar approved the new contract "in principle," but the trade union council rejected the agreement after a month's deliberation, claiming the pay scale was too high. In individual disputes, however, the labor commissar upheld the tarif anyway and even authorized a flat rate increase in July, although it was higher than the citywide pay scale decreed by the Moscow Council of Trade Unions.[53] In 1918 Communist labor policy was not yet unanimous.

Persistent conflicts over the tarif and its modifications continued to tax union resources. Workers at the Vazhenkov print shop sent the union a long letter complaining of union inaction in a series of disputes over pay, vacation time, and work rules. Some eight or ten trips to the union had resulted in nothing; their elected delegate refused to make these fruitless journeys any longer, and the factory committee had to make three additional trips without ever finding the responsible union official at his desk. Their owner knew the union was powerless, so he acted with increasing impunity.[54] Significantly, the workers of Vazhenkov did not publicly voice

---

[50] *Pechatnik*, 17 (30) April 1918, pp. 6–8.
[51] These are discussed in the journal of their society, *Biulleten' moskovskogo obshchestva tipo-litografov*, 1918.
[52] *Pechatnik*, 17 (30) April 1918, pp. 15–16.
[53] *Pechatnik*, 27 November (10 December) 1918, pp. 1–2.
[54] TsGAMO, f. 699, op. 1, d. 34, ll. 178–79.

their complaint at such a "difficult time" for the union: their dissatisfaction with union performance did not extend to disapproval of its overall independent political line. The union's Menshevik activists were already under great pressure for their political activism; the party had been expelled from the Moscow soviet in June.[55] But the union's ability to serve its members in the realm of "ordinary" class struggle was also constrained by the application of the state's productivist vision of labor relations, by the refusal of Communist board members to fulfill any union functions, and by increasing divisions within the printing industry labor force. All these pressures sapped the collective force the union needed to counter the resistance of private employers.

Private enterprise still existed in the printing industry in mid and late 1918, particularly in Moscow. By the end of 1918, 325 Russian typographical enterprises had been socialized, some 18 percent of the total in the republic. At the same time, only thirteen enterprises in Moscow had been nationalized, but many others had passed from private ownership to some form of collective, or "socialized" control.[56] The term "socialization" covered a wide range of authority; the *Russkoe Slovo* printshop in Moscow had been sequestered by order of the Moscow soviet, and that body's presidium assumed managerial authority. Sequester here was prompted by the need to suppress a voice of the opposition but also by the soviet's desire to print its own organ, *Izvestiia*, in a suitable shop. The convenience of an in-house print shop prompted other agencies to appropriate other shops, resulting in a chaotic grab of printing resources. The biggest institutions, such as the military and transport commissariats, seized the largest and best shops, locking up their resources and operating them outside the regular channels of the economy.[57] In Petrograd, socialization proceeded from the bottom up. During the short Communist tenure at the head of the union, pressure came from workers in scores of shops, demanding, "If power is now in the hands of the working class, then there cannot be any talk of print shops, as the weapon of Soviet power in its struggle with the bourgeoisie, remaining the property of the bourgeoisie."[58]

To manage this chaotic march toward socialization, the Supreme Economic Council (VSNKh) created a special division early in 1918 to co-

---

[55] Vladimir N. Brovkin, *The Mensheviks after October: Socialist Opposition and the Rise of the Bolshevik Dictatorship* (Ithaca, N.Y., 1987), p. 224.

[56] *Vserossiiskii pechatnik*, 20 March 1920, supplement, p. 1.

[57] Vysshei sovet narodnogo khoziaistva, poligraficheskii otdel, *Obzor deiatel'nosti 1918–1920 gg.* (Moscow, 1921), pp. 1–2; *Plenum Tsentral'nogo komiteta vserossiiskogo soiuza rabochikh poligraficheskogo proizvodstva (7–11 dekabria 1920 g.). Doklady i rezoliutsii* (Moscow, 1921), p. 15.

[58] *Materialy*, pp. 94–95.

ordinate administration of all public print shops.[59] This polygraphic division would appoint commissars to supervise enterprises, and it would rationalize the supply of materials, set wage policy, and distribute orders, labor, and output. The polygraphic division and its local branches (fifteen provincial affiliates were created by the end of 1918)[60] became the refuge for Communist printers ousted or alienated from printers' union activities; these activists, such as Nikolai Gordon in Petrograd and Aleksandr Borshchevskii in Moscow, used their new managerial positions on behalf of the productivist model of labor relations.

Experience soon revealed that self-socialization was no panacea. Discharged soldiers in a military print shop in Petrograd decided to form their own collective rather than face unemployment. But on their own, they could not generate enough business to keep operating, and they turned to the Petrograd soviet for help.[61] Some workers blamed the bourgeoisie for refusing to channel their orders through the state printing network.[62]

Within individual print shops, workers' control had been legislated in November 1917 to operate in private enterprise. The tarif concluded between the Moscow union and the employers' association in April 1918 further codified the rights of factory committees to enforce the agreement, to approve hiring and firing of workers.[63] But the practical meaning of such agreements became rapidly obscured by rampant socialization and ad hoc interpretation.[64]

In private shops, factory committees negotiated with their employers and exercised the right to approve hiring and firing decisions, but seemed no more powerful at this level than they had in 1917, when factory committees arose spontaneously as workers' representatives.[65] In the growing circle of public enterprises, workers' control had more scope. The Menshevik union organ, *Pechatnik*, pointed out a peculiar case to illustrate their distaste for unrestrained workers' control, the anarchist model of labor relations. Workers at the print shop of the Soviet of Soldiers' Dep-

---

[59] The predecessor of the polygraphic division, a "technical council," was created on 9 January 1918, with representatives from the commissariats of enlightenment, labor, and finance, from the Soviet Executive Committee, the union, and from workers in nationalized enterprises. *Sbornik dekretov*, p. 320.

[60] A polygraphic division under the Moscow Council of the Economy was created in January 1919. *Vserossiiskii pechatnik*, 20 March 1920, supplement, p. 1. It would come to rival the national polygraphic division in importance. Conflict also reigned between the Petrograd and central polygraphic divisions. GARF, f. 5525, op. 1, d. 38, ll. 19, 22.

[61] *Pechatnoe delo*, 1 April 1918, p. 13.

[62] *Pechatnoe delo*, 10 June 1918, p. 12.

[63] TsGAMO, f. 699, op. 1, d. 4, ll. 37–44.

[64] See S. A. Smith, *Red Petrograd: Revolution in the Factories, 1917–1918* (Cambridge, 1983), chap. 9.

[65] TsGAMO, f. 699, op. 1, d. 34, ll. 1–3, 12, 178–79.

uties voted to accept their factory committee's offer of a complete distribution of current assets "as a reward for the labor they had endured."
Two who objected to the economic irrationality of the move were fired,
and workers refused all attempts by the union to reinstate them. You see
how workers' control operates in practice, said the journal. The paying
out of dividends and the firing of dissidents was no different from capitalism.[66]

The new owners of these shops, state institutions, also disapproved of
such practices, and the more normal form of factory management in the
public sector was collegial administration, elected or at least approved by
the workers themselves. Perhaps most such collegia worked as well as
they could under conditions of a deteriorating economy, but many cases
of abuse reached the pages of the union journal. These cases suggested
that worker participation in management bodies did not necessarily
change traditional manager-worker relations, that worker managers could
be as authoritarian as their bourgeois predecessors.

The Petrograd branch of VSNKh's polygraphic division, dominated by
Communist printers, considered itself all-powerful, and ignored work
rules, tarifs, and norms established in agreement with the union.[67] At
Moscow's Seventh State Print Shop, a Communist stronghold, the workers' elected collegium soon refused to consult with the factory committee
and even threatened to fire them if they protested.[68] At the First State
Print Shop, when the factory committee threatened to resign unless the
collegium paid it more heed, the collegium said the committee's departure
would make its own work that much easier.[69] At Girshfeld's bookbindery
in Moscow, the factory committee chairman and control commission behaved as "Tsar and God" toward workers, promising Christmas bonuses
only to workers who refrained from criticism.[70]

In shops where one-man management (Lenin's own preference) replaced
collegial administration, workers faced the same kinds of authoritarian
management they thought existed only under capitalism.[71] Workers at a
military print shop complained that when a former printer named Lekh-
man arrived to direct their work, the shop became hard labor (*katorga*)
instead of a livelihood.[72] At the shop of the Soldiers' soviet, where workers
early in 1918 had shared out dividends, the new commissar, Gurevich,
attempted to fire the factory committee chairman over a disagreement.

[66] *Pechatnik*, 18 (31) March 1918, p. 18.
[67] *Pechatnik*, 27 September (10 October) 1918, p. 16.
[68] Ibid., p 21.
[69] *Pechatnik*, 25 January 1919.
[70] Ibid., p. 15.
[71] *Pechatnik*, 27 November (10 December) 1918, p. 13, for an example at the print shop
belonging to the Moscow district military commissariat.
[72] *Pechatnik*, 28 October (10 November) 1918, p. 14.

Eventually he summoned the militia, who refused to carry out his order. Gurevich next called a general meeting to appeal to the workers, but they too denounced his autocratic behavior and added that his ignorance of the printing trade was leading the shop to utter ruin.[73]

Increasingly, such embattled commissars and committees called on the forces of state power to discipline their unruly workers. Workers at the nationalized print shop of Ostrogozhsk (Voronezh province) complained in 1919 of excessive layoffs and loss of back pay. The chairman of the town's Revolutionary Committee gave the order (in the manner of Trotsky, the Red Army commander-in-chief): "Shoot every tenth man—and the rest will be silent."[74] Printers at another nationalized printshop were told they would be branded as "saboteurs" if they failed to complete an order for the military commissariat, despite workers' claims that the order was technically impossible to complete on time.[75] Factory committee members in suburban Bogorodsk were arrested when they protested the nationalization of their shop.[76] Workers at the shop of the newspaper *Voice of the Toiling Peasant* faced firing if they did not sign a statement of loyalty to the regime.[77] And when workers at the Sixth State Print Shop in Moscow refused to work on December 4, a religious holiday sanctioned by the union, the next day an armed detachment of Red Army soldiers along with members of the Cheka occupied the shop. They served papers on three dissidents and promised a permanent armed occupation if protests continued.[78]

From the point of view of trade union productivism, the purpose of centralized state pressure on recalcitrant printers was to raise production in the industry. The Menshevik union publicized these instances to show that the interests of employers, whether socialist or capitalist, were inevitably in conflict with those of workers. They argued also that such arbitrary and thoughtless administration had further plunged the industry into ruin. Communists claimed on the contrary that industry would only recover if they were able to devote all activist resources to organizing production, not to defending workers' rights. Whoever was right, the printing industry continued to collapse. In Petrograd, unemployment had already affected 15 percent of the printing labor force in early 1918. Newspapers had closed, orders from industry were down, Russian print shops now faced competition from German firms hiring Russian prison-

---

[73] *Pechatnik*, 27 September (10 October), 1918, p. 20.
[74] GARF, f. 5525, op. 1, d. 22, l. 19.
[75] *Pechatnik*, 27 November (10 December) 1918, p. 12.
[76] Ibid.
[77] *Pechatnik*, 27 September (10 October) 1918, p. 20.
[78] *Pechatnik*, 25 January 1919, p. 15.

ers-of-war to set type and print books.[79] The departure of the government to Moscow further reduced the demand for printed work in Petrograd. Unemployment rose to four thousand printers by autumn 1918, and many more printers now left the city for refuge in the countryside.[80]

The Mensheviks' trade union dream of a united working class standing up to its employer disintegrated. "Unity," such as there was, became an artificial construct, enforced by state and Communist institutions. Latent divisions within the workforce now became more acute. Demobilized soldier-printers challenged noncombatants for scarce jobs, and others took on overtime assignments, which only exacerbated growing unemployment.[81] Women bore the brunt of industrial demobilization policies that allowed only one member per family to be employed in a given print shop: "They want to take from us the right to a share of bread, a right of every citizen," they protested in one instance.[82] Despite the tarif in force in Moscow, newspaper typesetters in state enterprises received 50 percent more than those employed under the collective contract.[83] New tarif proposals pitted skilled workers against unskilled, fanning a perpetual source of discord. The printers' union actually proposed a smaller differential between the highest and lowest pay categories than the government's economic organs.[84] Urban workers chastised their colleagues with rural ties, who now walked away from the city with two months' severance pay instead of staying on to help restore industrial production.[85] Workers were also divided by disputes over which branches of printing were hazardous enough to warrant extra summer leave or special ration entitlements.[86]

The centrality of class as a way to explain and integrate the revolutionary experience continued to erode. Of course, "class" was always a fluid and multivalent concept, as others in this book have argued. Class can be defined in structural terms, based on the relations of production. Class can be constituted in action, in the struggle over the control of production. In both these senses, the socialization of the printing industry confused the meaning of working class. Class can also be defined through the language used to explain and give meaning to social relations and lived experience, and neither the Communists nor their independent opponents wished to yield control over that language. After the national

[79] *Vestnik vsrpd*, 20 April 1918, p. 4.
[80] *Vestnik vsrpd*, 20 October 1918, p. 5; *Pechatnik*, 27 September (10 October) 1918, pp. 15, 16.
[81] *Pechatnik*, 10 (23) June 1918, p. 16; 15 (28) July 1918, p. 17.
[82] *Pechatnik*, 17 (30) April 1918, p. 11; 31 January (13 February) 1918, p. 19.
[83] *Pechatnik*, 28 October (10 November) 1918, p. 9.
[84] *Pechatnik*, 27 September (10 October) 1918, pp. 3–4.
[85] *Pechatnik*, 31 January (13 February) 1918, p. 19.
[86] *Pechatnik*, 27 September (10 October) 1918, pp. 9, 10.

printers' union rejected the productivist model in early 1918, a Communist typesetter published a letter questioning the class position of these workers: do they belong to the working class, or to some other? Do they have interests in common with ours or separate ones? Concluding that printers had joined the ranks of the saboteurs of production, he claimed they had brought a new stain and shame to the "leaden army," once considered to be the avant-garde of the working class. Then the writer switched metaphors. "We have seceded from the great worker family, and every individual member of this family will look at us with contempt and indignation."[87] The metaphor of "family" as a way of constructing worker solidarity had already been a common feature of the linguistic landscape, and it would continue to help form workers' views of their identity.[88]

Similar fissures split apart the entire Russian working class in these months, shattering the class-based sense of purpose that had contributed to the Bolshevik victory in October 1917. Among printers, political party divisions now assumed an even more prominant role, as Communists and Mensheviks tried to rally support for their respective visions of labor relations and the socialist revolution.

Workers' dissatisfaction with Communist policies reached a peak in May and June of 1918. A growing opposition movement in Petrograd called for new elections for the soviet and the convocation of an independent workers' congress.[89] Responding to the Petrograd initiative and to the expulson of Mensheviks and SRs from the All-Russian Soviet's Central Executive Committee, Moscow's printers held a mass rally at the Zimin circus on June 16, denouncing the curbs on the freedoms of speech and press and demanding an end to the persecution of all those who disagreed with the regime. This is not workers' power, they claimed, but power by a group of fanatics. The meeting concluded by warning that if the representatives who carried this message to the Soviet were arrested, the printers were prepared to launch a political strike whenever the union board called them.[90] Communist influence among workers seemed weaker in mid-1918 than ever. And at the same time, the simmering civil war now threatened the regime's survival with the revolt of Czechoslovak troops in Siberia. The task of building socialism in a wrecked economy was compounded by a renewed military emergency, and the Communist

[87] *Pechatnoe delo*, 31 January (13 February) 1918, p. 9.

[88] See Diane P. Koenker, "Class and Consciousness in a Socialist Society: Workers in the Printing Trades during NEP," in Alexander Rabinowitch, Sheila Fitzpatrick, and Richard Stites, eds., *Russia in the Era of NEP: Explorations in Soviet Culture and Society* (Bloomington, Ind., 1991).

[89] M. S. Bernshtam, ed., *Nezavisimoe rabochee dvizhenie v 1918 godu: Dokumenty i materialy* (Paris, 1981).

[90] *Pechatnik*, 10 (23) June 1918, pp. 9–10.

regime responded with emergency measures against all who would oppose their policies. In Petrograd, Communist printers found their minority position intolerable, and they began an intensive campaign to win control of their union by fair means or foul.

The details of this process offer important insights into the methods the Communists used to maintain control over society and the working class. Essentially, Communist printers created a rival "red" printers' union, and although dual unionism was officially anathema, the Communists used their party connections with the All-Russian Central Council of Trade Unions (VTsSPS) as well as the party apparatus to win rulings favorable to their splinter group. The independent union survived longest in Moscow, but it too was squeezed out of existence by a combination of political maneuvers and flagrant repression, the methods of "Cheka, prison, and bullets," as one independent unionist labeled it.[91] The communists captured control of the Petrograd union branch in November 1918 by physically storming the union office and throwing out the Menshevik leaders there. The all-Russian union became a communist union after VTsSPS recognized its congress as legitimate in August 1919, despite rival claims from a Menshevik-led congress. The Moscow union kept electing Menshevik leaders until June 1920, when the Moscow Trade Union Council dissolved the board of directors as "counterrevolutionary" and instructed the union to reorganize itself without Menshevik participation.[92] The union apparatus was henceforth permanently in the hands of the Communists.

The application by the communists of the term "yellow" neatly illustrates how the term "working-class" came to be synonymous with "proletarian state." In July 1918, the growing movement of worker dissatisfaction with the regime erupted in political strikes. Although the printers' union had not explicitly called its members to participate, the Menshevik and SR parties had clearly endorsed such an action. Communist printers, led by Gordon, denounced the union leaders for their complicity in this antiproletarian protest: a strike against the Communist regime was tantamount to calling for the restoration of the bourgeoisie and stabbing the "class revolution" in the back.[93] These Communists proclaimed their full disassociation from the printers' union, whose "yellow banner" read "back to capitalism!" In other words, because the union

[91] *Pervyi vserossiiskii s"ezd soiuza rabochikh poligraficheskogo proizvodstva*, p. 59; *Pechatnik*, 25 January 1919, p. 2.

[92] *Vestnik vsrpd*, 16 November 1918, p. 3, and 1 December 1918, p. 19; *Pechatnik*, 27 September (10 October) 1918, p. 16; 28 October (10 November) 1918, p. 2; 27 November (10 December) 1918, p. 10; *Materialy*, pp. 104–15 (recollection by the Communist leader Gordon); GARF, f. 5525, op. 1, d. 10, l. 198; and *Professional'noe dvizhenie*, 22 August 1919, p. 4, and 26 June 1920, p. 3.

[93] *Petrogradskaia pravda*, 13 June 1918.

opposed the regime, it must therefore be a capitalist union, a yellow union.

In vain, the Menshevik union leaders tried to explain the true meaning of "yellow union." Yellows were not workers who stayed out of trade unions and worked for less than the union wage. Yellows were strike-breakers recruited by capitalists to defeat organized unions. Unions that struggled with capital were red unions, and the printers' union was such an organization, a "union that leads the struggle with employers for better conditions of labor, a union that is not yellow, but a revolutionary, red, militant union, striving to achieve those goals which the proletariat as a class has set for itself."[94] European and American socialists would not dare label our union yellow, they sniffed. (To take the final step and argue that if any union was yellow, it was the state-sponsored Communist union, was not something these socialists were prepared to do.) The Communists retained the term yellow in their vocabulary of insults, and henceforth their most inflammatory attacks on the independent union invariably smeared them with the yellow hue.

The Productivist Union in Power and the Shop-Floor Response, 1920–1921

Although the Communists used repression and brute force to defeat their Menshevik opponents, they also won rank-and-file support through the positive appeal of their model of labor relations. A productivist union, one in step with the regime, would take better care of its members through its coordinated effort to raise production. Produce more, and you will eat better, was their message. But the years of party struggle had taken their toll. The rank-and-file seemed thoroughly disaffected from the union and its policies. A few large shops struck in defense of the disbanded Moscow board of directors; they saw their factory committee representatives arrested and replaced with more compliant ones.[95] The union and regime were now free to implement their model of labor relations, to demonstrate how centralized and coordinated economic leadership would raise production and improve the welfare of the working class.

Symbolizing the new productivist line, the union's permanent secretary, Aleksandr Tikhanov, also assumed the leadership of the economic organ administering the industry, the polygraphic division of the Supreme Economic Council. But he faced competition in Moscow, now the center of

---

[94] *Pechatnik*, 28 October (10 November) 1918, pp. 2–3.
[95] E.g., at the First Model State Print Shop: TsGAMO, f. 699, op. 1, d. 74, ll. 39, 40; GARF, f. 5525, op. 2, d. 5, l. 29.

the Russian printing industry, from the Moscow polygraphic division, led by another Communist, Aleksandr Borshchevskii. Only late in 1920 was the situation resolved by subordinating the central polygraphic division to the Moscow division.[96] Worse was the status of production in the industry: there were insufficient supplies of ink, grease, kerosene, spare parts and type, reported a workers' inspection team in May 1920. Because of fuel shortages, 80 percent of enterprises were unable to work a full day. Skilled workers had disappeared, there was no transport to haul paper or fuel. Presses and buildings had not been repaired since 1914. Management conducted its work unsystematically, it failed to account for materials. Poor food supply forced workers to leave their jobs to search for bread for themselves and their families.[97]

The polygraphic divisions had no power or authority to solve many of these problems. Their first priority was to optimize the remaining scarce resources: this meant a drastic concentration of enterprises. Presses, type-cases, and workers from small establishments were transferred to enterprises with the best sanitary and fuel conditions.[98] But most pressing was the need to stimulate individual and collective productivity with material rewards. Workers on the shop floor remained resistant to working for nothing, and together the union and economic administration attempted to implement one wage system after another in the effort to lure workers back to work. Collective tarifs measured in money had become worthless along with the money supply. Bonuses payable in kind were officially adopted, but the system of measuring output was so complicated that the system could not actually be implemented.[99] Further, promised supplies of food were insufficient to reward individuals for higher productivity; what supplies reached the union ended up being divided equally among all workers, and even then, workers complained the amount was too little to live on.[100] Union officials blamed the situation on the undervaluing of printers by the higher economic and trade union organizations. But V. V. Shmidt, the People's Commissar of Labor, replied this was nonsense: printing was recognized to be an important industry, but no union had defended its members as poorly as this one. If the union would only properly gather the facts and defend its requests, he promised to listen.[101] To keep up what levels of production they could, union officials sought to appease workers in piecemeal fashion, here managing to put a shop on

[96] GARF, f. 5525, op. 2, d. 49, l. 51.

[97] Ibid., l. 30.

[98] *Plenum Tsentral'nogo komiteta VSRPP, 1920*, p. 19; *Vserossiiskii pechatnik*, 20 March 1920, supplement, p. 4; *Moskovskii pechatnik*, 15 April 1921, pp. 4–5.

[99] *Moskovskii pechatnik*, 15 April 1921, p. 10.

[100] *Vserossiiskii pechatnik*, 15 March 1921, p. 8.

[101] *Plenum Tsentral'nogo komiteta VSRPP, 1920*, pp. 40–41.

the higher Red Army ration, there responding to individual requests for boots, underwear, gloves, fabric, or overcoats.[102] This helped to keep individual shops in competition with one another and to strengthen the primacy of the workplace as a unit. Internal divisions, by skill, gender, or age, mattered less now than the survival of the workshop unit.

The struggle for resources was similarly chaotic. The Moscow polygraphic division calculated that it employed three hundred individuals full-time in the effort to obtain supplies for the industry.[103] Their system of allocating these supplies was in turn laden with bureaucracy and red tape. The director of one print shop described the process of securing oil, grease, and kerosene: first, he had to apply to the polygraphic division's subdivision on supply, which after two days would issue a voucher on the appropriate center. The center would then issue a voucher authorizing its warehouse to dispense the material, and by then there was usually little left of what had initially been requested.[104] Other complaints came about the polygraphic division's inability to administer the industry. Presses taken for repair disappeared for months at a time.[105] The polygraphic division was too ignorant of local conditions to allocate labor and materials rationally.[106]

Workers on the shop floor expected more from their union and from socialism. Gathering to express their anger at conditions in March 1920, Moscow printers denounced the regime's failure to deliver its promised bonuses for December, its refusal to authorize the union to send a special train to acquire food for its members. "Our impoverished conditions, our starving families, have forced us to gather here," cried one worker.[107] We are branded as saboteurs by the workers' and peasants' regime only because we ask for bread for our children. The faces of starving children give birth to that mood which the regime labels 'sabotage,' " said another.[108] The regime responded that the solution was to abandon support of the Menshevik union, whose leaders cared more about political opposition than about the welfare of their members.[109] Three months later, Menshevik union leaders were forcibly ousted by authorities in the central trade union council.

But a year later, in May 1921, after ten months under the new pro-

---

[102] GARF, f. 5525, op. 2, d. 5, l. 9; op. 2, d. 33 (these protocols of the Moscow union board are full of such requests); op. 3, d. 64 (Petrograd union), ll. 11, 32; TsGAMO, f. 699, op. 1, 63, l. 21.

[103] *Vserossiiskii pechatnik*, 20 March 1920, supplement, p. 7.

[104] *Moskovskii pechatnik*, 15 February 1921, p. 8.

[105] GARF, f. 5525, op. 3, d. 103.

[106] *Vtoraia moskovskaia gubernskaia konferentsiia*, 1921, p. 69.

[107] TsGAMO, f. 699, op. 1, d. 12, l. 4.

[108] Ibid., l. 5.

[109] *Vserossiiskii pechatnik*, 29 June 1920, pp. 1–2.

ductivist Moscow union, a conference of the province's printers remained angry. "We were urged to elect a new board to replace the yellow one, and this would place us in the forefront of the red army," said one delegate. "But there have been no improvements, we do not even receive the bare minimum standard of living. How can we work calmly?"[110] Another agreed: "A year of the existence of the red board, from which we dreamed we would receive relief, and what do we have? A statement that they have organized 610 meetings."[111]

Printers at the Sixteenth State Print Shop were especially enraged. A month before this conference, they met to complain about the irregular distribution of pay-in-kind, demanding that all printers in Moscow receive the same high level of rations as certain shops designated as "exemplary," demanding cash payments, soap, shoes, clothing, and the right to move freely.[112] Their demands remained unsatisfied and they refrained from striking in May only in the hope that the provincial conference would force the union to ameliorate their conditions.[113] Two months later, food supplies were again promised with no result. Once again, the workers here stopped work, "because they have many times deceived us. For example, they promised to issue in-kind payments for January, February, and March within two weeks, but we received only part of this after two months. Therefore we will not trust comrade Kolpakov [from the union] and we will not appear at work until we see food delivered to the door of our factory."[114]

These workers and others resisted as they could. Trade union archival evidence and statements in conference protocols suggest that strikes were endemic throughout the period, although the extent of these stoppages cannot be measured because such actions were not reported in the press. (The relevant trade union documents further suggest that strikes were commonly dealt with by the party bureau within the union rather than by the union board or its secretariat.)[115] Absenteeism was a worse problem; workers left work for days at a time, even in the face of strict union sanctions against such "indiscipline."[116] The absenteeism problem was only solved with an improvement in the regularity and amount of pay.[117]

[110] *Vtoraia moskovskaia gubernskaia konferentsiia*, 1921, p. 15.

[111] Ibid., p. 17.

[112] TsGAMO, f. 699, op. 1, d. 134, l. 1.

[113] Ibid., l. 3.

[114] Ibid., l. 20.

[115] TsGAMO, f. 699, op. 1, d. 136, l. 19: a report on the situation at the twentieth State Print Shop to the party bureau.

[116] Measures to combat absenteeism *(progul)* included moral pressure, fines, dismissals, and "repressive measures," namely, disciplinary courts, and where necessary, concentration camps. GARF, f. 5525, op. 3, d. 103, ll. 3–8.

[117] *Moskovskii pechatnik*, 15 February 1921, p. 8; 1 March 1921, p. 11; 1 May 1921, p. 15.

Theft of factory property also increased, as workers took paper, light bulbs, anything they could steal that could be exchanged for food on the black market.[118]

Such behavior indicated to both Communists and Mensheviks the "immaturity" of Russia's working class, its "narrow-mindedness," its lack of a proper "socialist consciousness." For Mensheviks, the low cultural level of the "masses," even in the highly skilled printing industry, was one reason that Russia was not ready for socialism and why the Communist experiments in socialist labor relations were doomed to fail.[119] Communists preferred to blame short-term factors for the behavior of this mass: the "best workers" had volunteered for the Red Army or were posted to Soviet commissariats. What remained even in the printing industry were women, youths, and semi-peasants whose exposure to a proletarian ethos was too brief to generate the proper consciousness.[120]

But were both parties correct in characterizing even the printers, with their traditions of intellectualism and independence, as a "mass" driven only by their stomachs, not their heads? I would argue that these activists were blinded by old dichotomies between "economic" and "political" consciousness, and that both failed to appreciate the fundamental connection between welfare and politics. The issue of food had been an important political catalyst in revolutionary Russia: the demand for better distribution of bread and flour had frequently been the only issue in widespread strikes across Russia before February, and the demonstrations that toppled the tsar in February 1917 were sparked by shortages in the bread supply in Petrograd. It was the failure of the Provisional Government to improve the supply of bread and foodstuffs that contributed to its loss of popular support in October 1917. Subsistence was seen to be a basic human right. The Communists in power blamed their failure to improve the food supply on many obstacles beyond their control—loss of territory, blockade, and war, but workers' protests over the regime's continuing failure to supply food meant not only that workers were starving but also that the socialist government had broken the social contract. It was illegal and dangerous to couch these protests in terms of rights and of the social contract in 1920. In 1920, as in 1916, the cry, "We are starving" was politically neutral and therefore safer than the claim, "You do not protect our welfare."

But of course, workers *were* starving. Early in 1918 the regime enacted

---

[118] TsGAMO, f. 699, op. 1, d. 136, ll. 5, 36; d. 145, ll. 20, 23, 24; GARF, f. 5525, op. 3, d. 106, ll. 175–209.

[119] *Vestnik vsrpd*, 20 March 1918, p. 12; 20 April 1918, p. 7; *Pechatnik* 5 (1918): pp. 7–8.

[120] *Vserossiiskii pechatnik*, July 1919, p. 11; 10 June 1920, p. 1; 15 February 1921, p. 9; *Materialy*, 93.

measures intended to make urban food supply totally dependent on the state: a ban on free trade in grain, curbs on workers' rights to travel beyond the city limits to purchase grain, severe punishment for "speculation." Even collective food purchases by unions required government permission.[121] But the state struggled in vain to satisfy the subsistence needs of its dependents. By January 1919, for example, only five or six days' reserve of flour remained in the capital.[122] Moscow printers were entitled to one pound of bread a day in 1920, but there, as elsewhere, delivery was not guaranteed.[123] Production plummeted as workers devoted all their time and resources to foraging for food, and many died. At the large First Model State Print Shop in Moscow, a representative reported that they were burying a colleague a week in 1920. In fact, 174 died here in eleven months from mid-1919 to May 1920, 9.5 percent of the plant's workforce. The average death rate for all government print shops in this period was the same.[124]

Even at this margin of subsistence, however, supposedly "narrow-minded" printers remained conscious of more than their stomachs. They were especially incensed that workers in the tobacco, leather, chemical, and metal industries, whose products had immediate value in exchange for food, lived better than the printers whose printed word had been as valuable for the revolution as bayonets and bullets.[125] We do not want privileges, argued the delegate Kazatskii in 1921, "We speak only of equalization. . . . It is not a misfortune when everyone suffers, but if I suffer and my neighbor finds a way not to suffer, then this creates unrest."[126]

The failure of the regime to feed its citizens was a political failure, and printers recognized this. It was not Lloyd George who blocked Russia's food supply but the regime's policy of seizing grain by force, they had argued in December 1919.[127] "The workers' power does not support workers' interests!"[128] In March 1920, they said the Communists took power over the economy, but did not know how to use it, throwing the

---

[121] TsGAMO, f. 699, op. 1, d. 60, ll. 25, 38.

[122] *Gazeta pechatnika*, 19 January 1919, p. 3.

[123] TsGAMO, f. 699, op. 1, d. 12, l. 2; d. 74, ll. 8, 32; GARF, f. 5525, op. 1, d. 34, l. 6.

[124] TsGAMO, f. 699, op. 1, d. 12, l. 5; Vysshei sovet narodnogo khoziaistva, poligrafi-cheskii otdel, *Obzor deiatel'nosti*, p. 34.

[125] TsGAMO, f. 699, op. 1, d. 74, l. 32. Such comparisons surfaced in angry meetings in December 1919, March 1920, and at the Moscow province conference in May 1921. GARF, f. 5525, op. 1, d. 34; TsGAMO, f. 699, op. 1, d. 12; *Vtoraia moskovskaia gubernskaia konferentsiia, 1921*.

[126] *Vtoraia moskovskaia gubernskaia konferentsiia, 1921*, p. 18.

[127] GARF, f. 5525, op. 1, d. 34, l. 10 (speech of Rostov, a union board member, at a general meeting of Moscow printers).

[128] Ibid., l. 17 (interruption of a speech by a union official at the December 1919 general meeting of printers).

workers a "bare bone," a promise of an extra ration of three-eighths of a pound of bread.[129]

Both Communists and Mensheviks accused each other of exploiting the workers' subsistence demands, of engaging in "demagoguery."[130] One unionist argued that 80 percent of printing union members, who belonged to no party, cared only about food.[131] But in the town of Penza, when local Communists promised cheese and butter to workers who joined the red union, just like those who had earlier left the independent union, printers said no. "We are workers, not sandwich makers."[132]

How were workers and union leaders to translate this anger into programmatic terms, which both sides claimed to represent "class" interests? Opponents could be labeled with foul names. Communists charged that the "leaden army" under the Mensheviks "smelled like decay and mold, as from the swamp," the independent union was a "yellow sore," a "yellow depravity." The Mensheviks countered by attacking the Communists' bureaucratization of the union: you have taken away the soul of workers, and instilled in the union the soul of pencil-pushers and typists, one of them claimed at their national congress in 1921.[133]

What did it mean now, in 1919 and 1920, to be a "worker"? Printers observed the desperate struggle among workers for extra hazard pay, for special rations, and for access to vacation rest homes, and mourned, "Look at this atmosphere, which now prevails in the working class."[134] Printers were treated like "stepsons" rather than printers.[135] They all knew that "not one class has starved like the printers." "Class" here meant the class of tobacco workers, the class of textile workers, what other critics had labeled "closed corporations."[136] And yet, at the fiercely pro-independent First Model Print Shop (formerly Sytin), the plant whose strike against its Soviet employers polarized the union in 1918, workers still clung to their class labels. Rejecting the official slogan for May Day in 1920, "On the First of May We Will Harmoniously Go Forth for the All-Russian Subbotnik" (a clearly productivist slogan), they adopted instead, "Freedom and Independence of Class Organization," and "Unite the Proletarian Front."[137]

---

[129] TsGAMO, f. 699, op. 1, d. 12, l. 5 (speech by Kondrashev, a worker from the Second State Print Shop).

[130] GARF, f. 5525, op. 1, d. 34, ll. 7, 18; *Tretii vserossiiskii s"ezd, 1921*, p. 9.

[131] *Vtoraia moskovskaia gubernskaia konferentsiia, 1921*, p. 15.

[132] *Vestnik vsrpd*, 15 August 1919, p. 7.

[133] *Revoliutsionnyi pechatnik* (Petrograd), 1 January 1919, p. 9; *Tretii vserossiiskii s"ezd, 1921*, pp. 15, 14.

[134] *Vtoraia moskovskaia gubernskaia konferentsiia, 1921*, p. 17.

[135] TsGAMO, f. 699, op. 1, d. 74, l. 32.

[136] *Vtoraia moskovskaia gubernskaia konferentsiia, 1921*, p. 31.

[137] TsGAMO, f. 699, op. 1, d. 74, l. 26.

This core of pride in their status as workers, their proletarian collectivism and egalitarianism found greatest scope for expression at the level of individual print shops. The failure of the centralized economic apparatus to support workers and their families reinforced the centrality of the workshop, which assumed more and more welfare functions. To some extent, the factories did become the "federated republics" denounced by activists. Factory meetings and factory committees allocated wages, dispensed food, distributed clothing, secured empty buildings for workers' housing, and assigned their workers to apartments there.[138] Factory-level tribunals ruled on violations of law and workplace rules.[139] Factory committees arbitrated personal conflicts and pronounced on proletarian morality: workers who swore at others, who drank on the job, or who demonstrated "indifference" to their work were reprimanded or fired. One typesetter Filippov always used obscene language toward his co-workers; his factory committee ordered him transferred to another enterprise. A printer named Lebedev was fired by his factory committee for coming to work drunk (not so heinous a crime) and raising a row (more serious).[140] Cultural life also devolved on the factories, which sponsored libraries, clubs, and even their children's schools.[141] All these tasks were intended to be fulfilled by central unions, but they were inadequate to the job. Their records reveal a litany of despair over their inability to administer wage policy and production; other union goals of cultural transformation, promotion of occupational health and safety, and the protection of women and youth remained distant dreams in this period. Whatever was done in these realms during the civil war was done at the level of the individual shop.

Such workplace cohesion contributed to the political mobilization of printers even after their independent union had been decapitated, and workplace protests over the food situation in shops like these eventually forced the regime to change its policies. The New Economic Policy would reintroduce free trade, end requisitioning, and permit private enterprise and a market economy: all of these were elements of the Menshevik critique from the start of communist rule. This new policy required new thinking from the printers' union, and it could potentially have altered the relations among workers, unions, and management.

---

[138] Such functions were routinely performed by the three Moscow print shops whose records I studied: the First Model State Print Shop, the Sixteenth State Print Shop, and the Twentieth State Print Shop. TsGAMO, f. 699, op. 1, d. 74, ll. 2, 13, 17; d. 145, l. 4; TsGAMO, f. 699, op. 1, d. 134, ll. 1, 13; TsGAMO, f. 699, op. 1, d. 136, ll. 8, 42.

[139] TsGAMO, f. 699, op. 1, d. 74, ll. 72–73; d. 145, ll. 20, 23.

[140] TsGAMO, f. 699, op. 1, d. 74, l. 11; d. 134, l. 28 (swearing); d. 145, l. 61 (drink).

[141] TsGAMO, f. 699, op. 1, d. 134, l. 68; d. 145, l. 72.

Conclusion

The struggle for the printers' union during the civil war ultimately yielded two distinct alternative systems of labor relations. The Communist system, based on the belief in the absolute harmony of interests between proletarian state and worker, placed production above consumption, state interests above local interests, central authority above democracy. It also made class identity unnecessary and superfluous. In a Communist utopia, with a perfectly planned economy, such a system might promise efficiency and yield a material surplus that could raise the welfare of all. In the real world of war and revolutionary conflict, the system's implementation came quickly to rely on imperfect and arbitrary authority, which met challenges unsystematically and increasingly through use of force and repression.

The Menshevik system was less perfect in the abstract. It recognized that even under socialism workers and employers had interests in conflict, and they sought to regulate those conflicts through compromise, through institutionalized bargaining, through preserving for trade unions an autonomous civil status apart from the state. It recognized that such a system could only function in a democratic state, that democratically established rules and procedures could most peaceably protect the interests of workers and employers. In such a socialist system, the state should be an ally, but it should never be permitted unlimited power.

The system that emerged by the spring of 1921 was the communist system modified to the extent that workers themselves had been able to resist its most repellant aspects. The overall management of industry in 1921 was no more democratic than it had been in 1914; indeed, it was much more highly centralized, hierarchical, and bureaucratic. In a political democracy, workers might influence central economic policy through the political process, but the communist system of management left them with little formal leverage. Nevertheless, the workplace in 1921 reflected important changes from before the revolution: local democracy and self-organization were possible, and workers continued throughout the civil war to exercise the important right won in 1917 to reject supervisors they could not work under.[142] A variety of forms of participation—factory committees and commissions, as well as Communist Party organizations in each enterprise—organized the rank-and-file to deal with their immediate problems. The enterprise emerged from the civil war a more central unit of public life than was probably imagined in either Communist or Menshevik visions of socialist revolution. And even though the class label

[142] Examples at the First Model State Print Shop: TsGAMO, f. 699, op. 1, d. 145, ll. 29, 50.

was used to describe the workers of these enterprises, class solidarity was not necessarily the outcome of their activities.

Workers also succeeded in imposing their preferred incentive system on communist visionaries. The adoption of the New Economic Policy was an implicit admission that coercion and other negative incentives had failed. So too had ration schemes that did not use money and the direct supply of clothing and fuel, if only because supplies had been so irregular. Wage differentials based on skill proved to be the only way to lure skilled workers back into production; wages dependent on fulfilling output norms—including piece rates and bonus systems—also proved to be more successful in raising production than standard compensation for all regardless of work.[143]

But unlike the adversarial capitalist system, the victorious new system of labor relations also relied on proletarian enthusiasm. Appeals to patriotism during the civil war had certainly helped to raise productivity and squelch conflicts.[144] Voluntary labor Saturdays (*subbotniki*) generated productive enthusiasm from the stratum of Communist supporters.[145] Participation in management, in many forms, also emerged as a way to involve workers in the drive for production. As factory committees became bogged down in the routine of administering material and daily life, workers were called on to elect their "most reliable" comrades to the workers' and peasants' inspectorate, a body charged with monitoring production performance.[146] Later in the NEP, factories would employ production conferences and factory newspapers as nonpecuniary methods of raising workers' interest in production.

Collective resolution of conflicts remained a casualty of civil war labor relations, as adversarial collective bargaining virtually disappeared. Since classes had disappeared from production relations, so should conflict. Overarching agreements on wages and work conditions became a function of state policy; decrees by the Council of People's Commissars, the Supreme Economic Council, or the Commissar of Labor replaced negotiation and arbitration. Such central policies could be debated at party, soviet, and trade union congresses, but their adoption came through the highly centralized administrative process, not through democratic or local initiative. Within the terms of these agreements, individuals could appeal to their unions about violations or for special treatment; disputes about

[143] Ashin, "Wage Policy in the Transition to NEP," pp. 293–313, offers an illuminating analysis of policy in this period.

[144] See Thomas Remington, *Building Socialism in Bolshevik Russia: Ideology and Industrial Organization, 1917–1921* (Pittsburgh, Pa., 1984), p. 81.

[145] A recent study is William Chase, "Volunteerism, Mobilisation, and Coercion: Subbotniki, 1919–1921," *Soviet Studies* 41 (January 1989): 111–28.

[146] TsGAMO, f. 699, op. 1, d. 134, l. 42.

improper job assignments, personnel conflicts, poor work habits, labor indiscipline, and inappropriate behavior were dealt first within factory committees and then in union-level comrades-discipline courts.[147] The strike was never formally outlawed, but its implications were so threatening that the word disappeared from common usage. Workers might engage in "stoppages," but a "strike" by 1921 was a serious political act and punished accordingly.

The trade union that emerged from the civil war was a subordinate participant in the formulation of industrial policy, and the mechanism through which centrally determined policy was implemented. Unions need not compete for resources for their workers, because wise central authorities would determine in advance the optimal allocation of resources. The trade union that led the printers in the NEP pledged to organize production and raise the cultural level of its members, but it was disinclined to fight for any interests that were not identical with those of the Russian workforce and economy as a whole. Trade unions also emerged as highly centralized institutions: trade union locals received instructions from union central committees, whose policies in turn depended on directives from the VTsSPS as well as the central economic organs. Within each trade union unit, decisions were made in advance by the party cell directing the unit.[148] If workers had gained some authority at the shopfloor level since the days of tsarism, their exercise of authority at higher levels of power and decisionmaking was sharply circumscribed in favor of the party vanguard.

The centralization of power and authority also strengthened the role played by the state in labor relations. No socialist would deny that the state had a role to play: even the independents were happy to invoke state power to enforce favorable settlements in disputes with private entrepreneurs or to legislate the participation of capitalists in unemployment and social welfare funds. The socialism that emerged from the civil war was a centralized state socialism, which relied on the power of the state's coercive agencies—the Cheka and the concentration camp—to ensure adherence to its centrally defined goals and policies. The goodness of the goal—maximal social welfare—justified concentrating all power in the hands of the central apparatus, subordinating trade unions, and punishing

---

[147] *Otchet Moskovskogo gubernskogo otdela VSRPP s sentiabria 1920 g. po mart 1921 g.* (Moscow, 1921), pp. 84–99, gives a summary of cases in Moscow, and GARF, f. 5525, op. 3, d. 106, in Petrograd.

[148] TsGAMO, f. 699, op. 1, d. 136, l. 19. The primacy of the party is confirmed by newly opened documents from the trade union party organizations, as for example, in TsGAIPD SPG (the former Leningrad party archive), f. 435, op. 1, d. 14 (minutes of the meetings of the party fraction of the Petrograd union of printers for 1919).

political dissent. In the end, printers had to throw in their lot with this state, because they were allowed to choose no other.

By 1921, the Communist system of labor relations had triumphed in the printing industry more by virtue of the Communist monopoly on state power than by the system's inherent workability or intellectual appeal among printers. But in practice, the system was forced to compromise by pressure from below, because printers refused to give up all their rights and independence to their union or to the state. In their resistance to communist policy in the winter and spring of 1920–21, these and other workers insisted on their right to choose the system that best protected their welfare. The communist government was able to restrict the choices open to workers by outlawing opposition socialist parties and by ruthlessly limiting the right to discuss alternatives beyond factory walls. The regime also once and for all seized control of the language of class. Oppositionist printers were a "yellow blemish," "yellow bastards," "scoundrels," "diseased" swamp dwellers, "enemies of soviet power," "traitors," and "lackeys of capital."[149] The official history of the printers' union in the civil war was now told as a simplistic tale of valiant communists overcoming the treacherous Menshevik manipulation of the hearts and minds of virtuous proletarians in the printing trade.[150] The consideration of alternatives, socialist or otherwise, was henceforth beyond the limits of permissible discourse.

[149] *Revoliutsionnyi pechatnik*, 27 July 1919, p. 17; GARF, f. 5525, op. 2, d. 11, l. 7; *Vserossiiskii pechatnik*, 10 June 1920, p. 4, and 29 June 1920, pp. 4–5.
[150] For example, in *Vserossiiskii pechatnik*, 1 December 1921, p. 2; *Moskovskii pechatnik*, 15 January 1921, pp. 4–11.

7

Chris Ward

Languages of Trade or a Language of Class? Work Culture in Russian Cotton Mills in the 1920s

I

Like Gaul, the historiography of the Russian working class is divided into three parts; if the first two are fairly well mapped the third is still largely *terra incognita*. In part 1, the prerevolutionary period, historians are concerned with "becoming." Even where they are trying to uncover the structures and culture of the working class in situations bounded by time and place, they are still "remembering forwards." Because it is hard to escape the giant shadows cast by the events of 1917 there is always a subtext, more or less manifest in the literature. In one way or another what we tend to read are stories of how the Russian working class, however defined or imagined, became—or failed to become—revolutionary.

In part 2 the profession changes tack. It opens up new pathways, traverses new landscapes. Now historians experience workers as revolutionary actors either in their own right or as interlocutors with revolutionary parties or heroes, or, conversely, they focus on this or that group of workers, or workers in this or that region, which declined to act in a revolutionary manner. Later on they co-opt these workers, as willing or unwilling participants, in texts describing and analyzing the processes of state formation. In all events "becoming" gives way to "being" within the high drama of revolution and civil war.

But what happens in part 3, once the Rubicon of 1917–20 has been crossed? In the historiography of the prerevolutionary and revolutionary period there is a fruitful tension between the idea of class, workers' activities and identities, and the disintegration of one state form and its replacement by another. Thereafter it seems to me that until comparatively recently, historians have been unsure of the direction and focus of their research. Is the category of class still useful and does it properly describe aspects of the postrevolutionary landscape? Are workers a legitimate or interesting area of study once they have played out their historical role, and if so, how should they be characterized? As enthusiastic partners in socialist construction, as sullen victims of a revolution gone wrong, or as upwardly mobile actors keen to exploit the new opportunities offered by the revolution's partial liberations? Class can be mobilized as an organizing concept in parts 1 and 2 without too much trouble because "becoming" and "being" impart meaning, coherence and direction to historians' efforts. They give historians confidence that they "know" what they are studying. But how should we approach the discourse of class after the revolution, and what is the Russian worker "for" in descriptions of the postrevolutionary landscape?

If there is a particular set of problems located around direction and focus, my own solution to this (self-imposed) conundrum is to turn these problems on their head. Precisely because the extraordinarily powerful referent of 1917 is absent, or at least "behind" us, we can try to look at workers *in situ*, in their own time and place, without being mesmerized by a "big event," which tends to pull and twist the notion of class around a particular historical problem.[1] If we ask whether or not we can use the term "working class" in relation to the Soviet industrial labor force of the 1920s, our landscape of inquiry is less bounded. We are more likely to be able to beat new pathways that are divorced from the proximity of a big event. Although the interconnections of past and future remain as traditional concerns of the historian, the pull of the future is weaker, and so the direction and focus of our research is less likely to be overdetermined by shadows cast by the future.[2] To put it another way, we may have more space to "decongest" the notion of class, locating workers in their own time and place without reference to some wider event.[3]

My own work has paid scant attention to these matters. *Russia's Cotton*

---

[1] I do not mean to suggest that 1917 necessarily marks a sharp break between all aspects of the two parts of the same land. Rather, I am trying to indicate how knowing about the revolution fundamentally affects the drift of our research. It is possible, for instance, that the variety and vitality of class-based studies of nineteenth-century Britain is due, to some extent at least, to the fact that there was no big event of social and political revolution. Had one occurred research would doubtless have been wrenched in a particular direction for much of the twentieth century.

[2] There are, of course, other referents that may overdetermine postrevolutionary historiography. Much effort is now directed towards exploring workers' participation in—or aversion to—the construction and maintenance of other big events, such as Stalinism, for example. But it still seems to me that once the revolution is over, historians have more freedom of movement, because the significance of events like these are still not packaged in the historical profession's mind in quite the same way as those of the revolution and civil war.

[3] I am thinking here of Katznelson's formulation: " 'Class' as a term is too frequently used in a congested way, encompassing meanings and questions that need to be separated from each other." I. Katznelson and R. Zolberg, eds., *Working-Class Formation: Nineteenth-Century Patterns in Western Europe and the United States* (Princeton, N.J., 1986), p. vii.

Workers and the New Economic Policy might be described as an exercise in traditional empirical British historiography, an account in which theoretical implications are ignored or taken for granted.[4] Nevertheless, on reflection, it seems to me that my research on the cotton workforce could be construed as a test case for ways of looking at the problem of class after 1917, since I was less concerned with remembering forwards, with searching out the imminence of big events (the cotton workforce's contribution to the rise of Stalinism, for instance), and more interested in looking at aspects of workers' lives within the context of the NEP.

In what senses can we use the term "working class" in relation to the Soviet cotton workforce of the 1920s (and, by implication, in relation to workers in other industries)? I shall try to open up a discussion focused around the four parameters of class suggested by Katznelson and Zolberg.[5] These are class as *structure*, class as *ways of life*, class as *dispositions*, and class as *collective action*. I shall also try to relate my account to Michael Burawoy's analysis of the cotton industry in Europe, Russia and the United States.[6] To this end the next section will look at the work culture of the mill, at aspects of life and labor in the Soviet cotton industry during the 1920s. This in turn will form the basis for a further discussion of class.

II

Since class as an organizing concept is intimately, though not exclusively, bound up with relations of production, any definition of a working class must engage the allocation of roles in production. In NEP Russia the microworlds of production—technology and the labor process—shaped cotton workers' lives in two important ways: on the one hand providing a stage for the construction of identities, on the other, a field of action conditioning responses to central policy prescriptions.

Technological Setting

The equipment and chain of production of a typical Russian cotton mill in the 1920s was as follows. As they entered the factory, tightly packed

[4] See my *Russia's Cotton Workers and the New Economic Policy: Shop-Floor Culture and State Policy 1921–1929* (Cambridge, 1990) and the doctoral dissertation on which it is based; "Russian Cotton Workers and the New Economic Policy" (University of Essex, 1986).

[5] Katznelson and Zolberg, *Working Class Formation*, chap. 1.

[6] M. Burawoy, *The Politics of Production: Factory Regimes under Capitalism and Socialism* (London, 1985), especially chap. 2.

Table 7.1. Age of fine-spinning and weaving machinery in Soviet cotton mills, 1927

Year of installation	Percent of self-actors	Percent of ring-frames	Percent of power looms
Before 1890	25.2	9.5	18.8
1890–1899	38.4	35.0	27.3
1900–1909	19.0	28.0	23.6
After 1909	15.3	23.5	17.8
Not known	2.1	4.0	12.5

Sources: Tekstil'nye novosti 10–11 (October-November 1927): 365; L. Ia. Shukhgal'ter, ed., *Vnutrizavodskoi kontrol' kachestva. Sbornik statei i instruktsii* (Moscow-Leningrad, 1927), p. 5.

bales of raw cotton were stripped down on openers and then passed to scutching-frames, which beat, crushed, and wound the raw material onto large drums. From here cotton was sent to carding-frame rooms where fibers were combed into roughly parallel lines prior to primary spinning. Collectively, opener, scutching, and carding rooms were described as the mill's initial processing department. When cotton moved into the preparatory department, it went first to drawing-frame rooms, which ran out thick slivers of cotton, and from there to flyer-frame rooms, which produced rovings—thick-spun cotton suitable for final spinning. Three types of flyers were in common use; slubbing-, intermediate-, and jack-frames, each progressively thinning down the rovings. Finally, roving spools were transported to fine-spinning halls where self-acting "mules" or ring-frames spun fine threads of diverse thicknesses (counts) appropriate for various types of weaving or sewing. In weaving sheds most looms were simple single-shuttle Lancashire power looms. Jacquard looms, for pattern weaving, were rare, and multishuttle auto-looms rarer still. In almost all mills motive power was provided by steam engines running machinery via extended belt-drive systems.

Technological Idiosyncrasy

The first thing to note about all this equipment is its advanced age (table 7.1). By 1927 just over half of all looms and fine-spinning frames had been purchased in the nineteenth century, and it was not uncommon for operatives to be working equipment installed before 1850. Moreover, in comparison with Western Europe and the United States, technicians were always scarce, and became scarcer still as emigration thinned out their ranks after the revolution. Consequently, though a glance through the sources suggests that what we are faced with are serried rows of standard frames that could be operated by any worker (or set of workers) trained

Table 7.2. Cloth types in cotton weaving sheds, 1926

Cotton trust	Number of cloth types		Average number of looms per type
	standardized	unstandardized	
Ivanovo-Voznesensk	20	42	532
Vladimir-Aleksandrov	22	12	459
Moscow	16	4	367
Ozery	20	—	260
Presenesk	25	21	250
Iaroslavl'	7	3	191
Orekhovo-Zuevo	30	34	167
Tver'	36	37	156
Egor'evsk-Ramenskoe	17	34	156
Serpukhov	21	24	117
Bogorodsk-Shchelkovo	34	46	93
Leningrad	30	55	65

Sources: Izvestiia tekstil'noi promyshlennosti i torgovli 21 (June 1926): 4; *Trudy pervogo vsesoiuznogo s"ezda po ratsionalizatsii v tekstil'noi promyshlennosti, 19–24 maia 1926 goda* (Moscow-Leningrad, 1926), p. 100.

Note: Finished cloth was categorized as either "standardized" (conforming to an all-Union specification) or "unstandardized" (the traditional product of a given mill or region). The giant Ivanovo-Voznesensk Trust wove 20 standardized and 42 unstandardized types with an average of 532 looms per type, for example. The much smaller Leningrad Trust, on the other hand, with 55 unstandardized and 30 conforming to all-Union standards—a total of 85 cloth types—averaged only 65 looms per type. Leningrad's weavers were therefore more "idiosyncratic" than those in Ivanovo-Voznesensk.

up in a given trade, this was not the case. As machinery aged it deviated from the standardizing and deskilling intentions of the machine maker and became "idiosyncratic." There was a tendency, inherent in the industry, for workers to trim, set, and repair their own frames, and so operatives could not easily be moved from one machine (or machine group) to others of the same type without reducing productivity and output and perhaps disrupting the culture of a given shop. In short, workers (or work groups) tended to specialize in operating a given frame (or set of frames), having been trained up on those frames.

All this had important implications for the shop floor and beyond—for relationships within the workforce and between workers, foremen, managers, trust officials, the trade union, and state agencies; for the construction and maintenance of patterns of identity within a given shop; and for the degree of control that operatives could exercise over their lives at work.

I shall return to some of these matters in a moment, but it should also be noted that idiosyncrasy was part and parcel of the production process, regardless of any historical factors impinging on technology. Though standard products might be obtained from any shop—measured as count in spinning halls or cloth type in weaving sheds—they could not be obtained via standardized work routines, even if workers could have been moved around at will on machinery that supposedly behaved in standardized manner. Because the raw material handled by workers and machinery was a natural product, no one bale was ever quite the same as the next. The vagaries of soil and climate conspired to alter the quality of each particular cotton strain as it entered the mill—chiefly from Central Asia, to a lesser extent from Egypt, Persia, India, or the southern United States. Skilled sorters in initial processing departments judged the quality and raw material type and classified sorts by number (VII for the poorest quality, I for the best). But since these could only be averages, the behavior of the raw material could still vary unpredictably as it passed through the production chain.

This necessarily affected the labor process. Workers in initial processing departments might have to spend more or less time stripping and cleaning their frames, for example, and fine spinners might find themselves "doffing off" (replacing exhausted roving spools) or "piecing up" (rejoining broken threads) more or less frequently. An additional source of idiosyncrasy resulted from the wide range of counts spun throughout the 1920s and the multiplicity of cloth types in weaving sheds. This fragmented the labor process in fine-spinning halls, and many weavers tended to be grouped around, or to specialize in, a relatively narrow product range (table 7.2). Additionally, weavers might have to modify their work practices in response to variations in the quality of semifinished goods received from other rooms or factories.

Work Teams

As cotton moved down the production chain its unit size decreased. Consequently, the number of spindles and workers in each room of the mill increased. Typically, in the initial processing, preparatory, and spinning departments, there might be one bale opener, four scutching-frames, ninety carding-frames, fifty drawing-frames, ten thousand spindles on flyer-frames, and eighty thousand spindles on ring-frames and self-acting mules. But this does not mean that there was a simple aggregate increase in the number of atomized individual workers in each room. Most operatives worked in teams, or *komplekty*, but the number of operatives in komplekty varied, not only between different rooms and production processes, as would be expected, but also within rooms engaged in one and the same production process. In part this had to do with the eclectic nature of capital substitution: variations in the kinds of machines purchased before the revolution for a particular process in particular mills gave rise to variations in manning levels. On scutching-frames, for in-

Table 7.3. Machinery in the Glukhovskaia mill's flyer-frame room, 1926–27

Machine maker	Year of installation	Number of operatives
Platt Brothers (U.K.)	1881	1
"	1882	1
Bülow (Germany)	1897	3
Hetheringtons (U.K.)	1898	1
Hetheringtons	1899	2
Platt Brothers	1904	2
"	1905	1
"	1908	4

Source: Predpriiatie 7 (July 1928): 19.

stance, levels diverged markedly between regions and mills throughout the 1920s—usually one female operator to one, two, or three frames— and although formally machine speeds and loadings were determined by cotton sort and weight, the adjudged competence of a particular operative was also taken into account. On slubbing-frames one or two women operated one machine, or two women shared two frames, or one woman worked on two frames alone. Adolescent girl helpers were added to intermediate- and jack-frames because doffing occurred more frequently, but numbers still varied: the range of sources for this section of the mill indicates one helper for every one or two frames, or for four frames one spinner and one assistant or one spinner and two girls. The situation in flyer-frame rooms was no less haphazard (table 7.3). It was in such circumstances that Taylorist propagandists anxious to recast production complained about the difficulties they faced when investigating the labor process, difficulties caused by differences in work practices, terminology, and procedures from one mill to the next.

Britain, the Labor Process, and the NEP

But historical factors shaped the labor process in other ways. Power looms, self-acting mules and ring-frames, flyer- and drawing-frames, bale openers, and scutching- and carding-frames all came, for the most part, from Britain. Not only was the *technology* British, the *labor process* was also British. Expatriate managers, foremen, and supervisors, arriving from Lancashire, Yorkshire, or the Scottish Lowlands in the nineteenth century, imposed their particular taken-for-granted world of production on Russia's newly recruited factory labor force. Their influence persisted long after the industry's foundation. "Englishmen played a big part in establishing many of our spinning and weaving factories," noted one Soviet engineer in 1926. "Not only was the machinery from Britain, the organ-

Table 7.4. Komplekt sizes of self-actor pairs, 1922

	Warp spinning			Weft spinning		
	Number of spindles per frame (× 2)			Number of spindles per frame (× 2)		
Counts	500–675	676–875	876–1000	500–775	776–1026	over 1026
61–120	–	3	3	–	3	3–4
45–60	–	3	3–4	–	4	4–5
29–44	3	4	5	4	5	6
21–28	4	5	6	5	6	7
13–20	5	6	7	6	7	8
9–12	6	7	8	7	8	9
5–8	7	8	9	8	9	10

Source: TsK VPST, *Tarif tekstil'shchikov* (Moscow, 1922), p. 47.
Note: As count fell (the lower the number the coarser the thread spun) and thus rovings were exhausted more quickly, so the komplekt expanded. The same obtained if frame sizes increased. So, for example, two 1050-spindle frames spinning count 7 weft would have a komplekt of 10 (9 + spinner), whereas two 700-spindle frames spinning count 100 warp would have only 3 (2 + spinner).

izational form was also British." He went on to say that the labor process still followed the British model.[7]

The point is most apparent if we look at self-actor halls. Here the komplekt comprised spinner, piecers, and doffer-creelers. Piecers repaired yarn-sheet breakages as the carriages moved back and forth, doffer-creelers doffed off full spools of finished thread and "creeled up" (set up) new rovings as the spools were exhausted. As in Britain, spinners exercised a wide degree of control over the labor process. Following early nineteenth-century British practice one spinner always looked after a pair of "wheels,"[8] but the number of piecers and doffer-creelers varied considerably. Traditional prerevolutionary variations in *komplekt* sizes were institutionalized in the textile workers' union handbook of 1922 (table 7.4), and by 1928 the state had formally recognized the spinner's control over komplekt sizes (table 7.5).

But the contemporary situation conspired to magnify the spinner's role on the shop floor in other ways. In comparison with the prerevolutionary period komplekt numbers tended to increase following the introduction of the NEP. This occurred because self-actors were best for spinning high counts on good-quality fiber. Good-quality cotton reduced the piecing workload, whereas high counts resulted in a slow rate of "draw"—move-

[7] *Tekstil'nye novosti* 8–9 (August–September 1926).
[8] The physical layout of Russian self-actor rooms was based on the Lancashire pattern established in the 1790s, one frame facing the other so that the komplekt could attend easily to the yarn sheet of each.

Table 7.5. Komplekt sizes and self-actor spinner's wage scale, 1928

Sort/count	Spindles per frame pair	Spinner's pay scale (points 13–16) & komplekt sizes			
		13	14	15	16
I sort	Up to 1350	–	–	–	3
cotton	1352–1750	–	—	—	3
(counts	1752–2160	–	–	–	3
100 +)	Over 2162	–	–	–	4
I sort	Up to 1350	–	–	3	–
cotton	1352–1750	–	–	3	–
(counts	1752–2160	–	–	3	–
70–88)	Over 2162	–	–	4	–
I–II sort	Up to 1350	4	3	–	–
cotton	1352–1750	4	3	–	–
(counts	1752–2160	4	3	–	–
45–68)	Over 2162	5	4	–	–
II–IV sort	Up to 1350	4	3	–	–
cotton	1352–1750	4	3	–	–
(counts	1752–2160	5	4	–	–
30–44)	Over 2162	6	5	–	–
IV–V sort	Up to 1350	5	4	3	–
cotton	1352–1750	5	4	3	–
(counts	1752–2160	6	5	5	–
22–28)	Over 2162	7	6	5	–
V–VI sort	Up to 1350	6	5	4	–
cotton	1352–1750	6	5	4	–
(counts	1752–2160	7	6	5	–
16–20)	Over 2162	8	7	6	–
VI sort	Up to 1350	6	5	4	–
cotton	1352–1750	7	6	5	–
(counts	1752–2160	8	7	6	–
10–14)	Over 2162	9	8	7	–
VII sort	Up to 1350	7	6	5	–
cotton	1352–1750	8	7	6	–
(counts	1752–2160	9	8	7	–
up to 8)	Over 2162	–	–	–	–

In all but the top two cotton sort/count categories spinners could choose between higher wages and fewer komplekt members or lower wages and more komplekt members.

Source: TsK VPST, *Tarifno-spravochnik rabochikh khlopchato-bumazhnogo proizvodstva* (Moscow, 1928), pp. 34–35.

ment back and forth of the carriages—and in these conditions komplekt sizes tended to be small. But as the demand for high counts weakened as a result of changes in social structure occasioned by the revolution—the departure and decimation of the middling and upper ranks of society— the call for low counts, for weaving coarse calicos, rose as a result of the imperatives of the *smychka* (the economic "Link" between the town and countryside—the Leitmotiv of the NEP). Low counts accelerated the draw rate and led to an increased number of thread breakages. What is more, in general these low counts had to be spun from poor-quality Central Asian cotton—substituting for the lost imports of the prerevolutionary years— thus further increasing the piecing workload. The net result of political and social revolution was the larger komplekt sizes illustrated in tables 7.4 and 7.5. Additionally, because repair skills were in such short supply, spinners were expected to set, trim, and maintain their own pair of wheels without reference to technical personnel.[9] Finally, self-actor spinners also directed the activities of the following "auxiliary workers" when they passed through the "jenny-gate" (the long narrow corridor separating the two yarn sheets of a pair of wheels): one tube sorter, three to four roving carriers, four ropers (supplying ropes and belts), and four thread carriers. Some spinners, therefore, exercised primary authority over more than twenty operatives (komplekt members plus auxiliaries) on the shop floor at various moments throughout the working day. In January 1928 *Izvestiia tekstil'noi promyshlennosti i torgovli* measured variations in the workload that could result from the combination of the divergent work practices of particular komplekty, machine idiosyncrasy, and fluctuating cotton quality. The journal discovered that over a four-hour period the piecing workload varied markedly, not only between two komplekty running a pair of wheels, but also between frames operated by a single komplekt.

The komplekt, however, was more than just a work team. Spinners trained up members of their own komplekty. Doffer-creelers served their time before becoming piecers, and "senior" piecers awaited the spinner's retirement before taking over the pair. Evidence from worker biographies makes the point: in the mid-1920s A. I. Shevarev, a fifty-three-year-old spinner, had spent forty years in the Tverskaia mill; two years as a doffer-creeler, twelve as a piecer, twenty-six as a spinner. In 1917 twelve-year-old boys were recruited as "little" piecers for what were to become Leningrad's Sovetskaia Zvezda and Krasnaia Nit' mills; if they survived the civil war, these youngsters would become the senior piecers, and in due course the cadre spinners of the NEP years. None of this was welcome to rationalizers, but the shortage of technicians and the steady acceleration

---

[9] "The spinner," asserted a 1926 monograph, "is responsible for his own pair." Other sources held that spinners "must fully understand the complex workings of their machines." They were to carry out auxiliary servicing and were "in command" of machine repair. They decided when the pair would be halted for cleaning and adjustment, and they were responsible for ensuring correct count and quality. See D. D. Budanov, *Obshchie poniatiia o NOT'e v chasnosti v tekstil'noi promyshlennosti* (Ivanovo-Voznesensk, 1926), p. 73; N. T. Pavlov, *Sel'faktor* (Moscow, 1926), pp. 117–18; A. F. Shvarabovich, *Kak uberech' sebia ot neschastnykh sluchaev v khlopchatobumazhnom proizvodstve* (Moscow, 1926), p. 43.

of machine idiosyncrasy before and after 1917 made the continuation of the British model of the labor process particularly appropriate, wedding komplekt members to a particular pair of wheels for their working lives.[10]

Though self-actors provide the most extreme case of the varieties of idiosyncrasy and their import, it is also apparent that to a lesser extent heuristic work practices prevailed on *vater-mashini* (ring-frames), the direct descendants of eighteenth-century British throstle spinning frames. Even though on average ring-frames were newer than self-actors (table 7.1), idiosyncrasy proceeded apace because of the advanced age of the machine stock, and subordinate komplekt members looked to the spinner to teach them the skills of the trade on a particular set of frames in the hope of promotion sometime in the future.[11] Similarly, in weaving sheds it was accepted practice for weavers to set the "loom stroke"—the number of shuttle strikes per minute—and to undertake minor repairs on their own initiative. It was also common for women nearing retirement to take on their daughters as assistants and train them up so that they could "inherit" their looms.

As in self-actor halls all these "production operatives" were surrounded by a welter of comparatively poorly paid auxiliaries presently shut out from komplekty, workers who might get the chance of promotion to a frame when the state embarked on *uplotnenie* drives (Taylorist experiments, speed-ups, or rationalization schemes). These auxiliaries comprised waste processors, bin stackers, carriers, labelers and greasers in opener rooms; needle solderers, needle setters, comb strippers, can boys, and greasers in carding rooms (plus a card-grinding komplekt made up of first, second, and third grinders ranging from experienced workers to adolescent trainees); bobbin sorters, bobbin strippers, loaders, and machine repairers and their assistants in flyer-frame rooms (plus roving sampler and cleaner komplekty, each with experienced and ranking members); and numerous fetchers and carriers in ring-frame rooms and for Jacquard, power, and auto-looms in weaving sheds. The textile workers' union held up a mirror to this complex and extraordinarily localized world of production, listing 588 trades in the cotton industry in its 1922 and 1925 handbooks and, following the partial success of the mid-1920s rationalization drive, 544 trades in the 1928 handbook.

---

[10] M. Shaginian, a popular writer of the 1920s, noted that Leningrad's self-actor spinners "grew and aged with" and became "partisans" of their own wheels. *Nevskaia nitka* (Moscow, 1925), p. 16.

[11] "The doffers who work under the direction of the ring-frame spinner," recorded one specialist, "these immediate candidates for the post of spinner, are interested in the acquisition of corresponding practical skills at work." Ia. Kvasha and F. Shofman, *Semichasovoi rabochii den' v tekstil'noi promyshlennosti* (Moscow, 1930), pp. 54–55.

Tsekhovshchina

What we are beginning to see is that the primary point of reference for the operative was not the abstraction of the mill (still less "the cotton industry"), but the reality of the shop. Each shop was a world unto itself, sharply differentiated from other shops. Indeed, very large mills like the Nikol'skaia, situated in Orekhovo-Zuevo and employing some 20,000 operatives, were really production sites rather than factories. Much like Leningrad's giant Kirov engineering works the Nikol'skaia's rooms and sheds were in fact separate buildings sprawling over many acres. Elsewhere, in Iaroslavl's Krasnyi Perekop mill, for example, some rooms had been built as far back as the eighteenth century. We must also bear in mind that not all production sites contained the entire range of the production process: some were weaving mills with varying combinations of power, Jacquard, and auto-looms, and some were spinning mills with no weaving sheds, but not all spinning mills had self-actors, ring-frames, or the full complement of flyer-frames.

The interstices that allowed *tsekhovshchina* (shop loyalty, or shop feeling) to flourish were, therefore, the product not only of eclectic capital substitution or machine and raw material idiosyncrasy, they arose also from regional specialization (as table 7.2 indicates). No less important were the physical parameters of the mill. The architecture of large industrial enterprises created room for the elaboration of subcultures within the arena of production; for closure, exclusivity, for the denial of space to management or this or that subgroup of workers. Particularly in spinning departments the mill's internal architecture played its part in sustaining komplekt working. The layout and size of frames was determined, not by some neutral assessment of the most efficient physical distribution of labor power, but by mediations between preexisting forms of the distribution of labor in the early British Industrial Revolution, the deskilling intentions of British machine makers, and the market imperatives of nineteenth-century Britain, which obliged masters to "stretch-out" their frames. A radical restructuring of the labor process in NEP Russia was scarcely conceivable without breaking up the long spindle banks in self-actor and ring-frame halls and tearing down and rebuilding the entire mill corpus.[12] Even "production communes," Komsomol work teams

---

[12] The self-actor started life in Lancashire as "Crompton's Mule"—a domestic frame no larger than a motorcycle with only half a dozen or so spindles. By the early nineteenth century factory-based semiautomatic mules in Lancashire were commonly over one hundred feet long. Similarly, by the 1850s spindle banks on ring-frames were so large that no more than a dozen could be fitted into an average mill corpus. Photographs of British, Russian, or Soviet mills reveal that physical parameters were identical.

Table 7.6. Production communes on self-actors in Leningrad's Ravenstvo mill, 1930

Number of frames per commune	Number of spindles per frame	Count	Number of commune members	Average number of commune members to two self-actors
6	900	12 weft	42	12
1	732	10 weft		
6	732	20 warp	32	9.1
1	732	20 warp		
7	900	38 weft	22	6.3
10	894	20 weft	30	6
30	894 to 900	38 weft	90	6
1	732	10 weft		
7	732	20 warp	36	4.5
8	732	20 warp		

Source: S. Zhukovskii et al., *Pervaia udarnaia* (Moscow-Leningrad, 1931), p. 74.

that emerged in the late 1920s and purported to break with traditional forms of the division of labor, were constrained by physical realities: averaged out, the number of workers per pair of wheels in self-actor halls (table 7.6) bears an uncanny resemblance to the komplekt sizes shown in tables 7.4 and 7.5.[13]

Gender and Kinship

Inflecting into these subgroups which crystallized around machinery was the factor of gender. All supervisors and foremen were male. This gender demarcation was also apparent in production and auxiliary tasks. In opener rooms men directed the work of three or four female loaders. In scutching rooms operatives were always female. In carding rooms women attended the machinery but men decided when the frames would be shut down for cleaning and repair. Drawing-frame operatives were female, as were slubbing-, intermediate- and jack-frame operatives.[14] Ring-frame operatives were always women but self-actor spinners were always men, and though self-actor piecers and doffer-creelers might be of either sex, women could rise no higher than senior piecer on the trade ladder. Only in weaving sheds were gender divisions blurred somewhat,

---

[13] Burawoy's remarks on the search for socialism in production are pertinent here: "We can no longer avoid the distinct problem of destroying and reconstructing the apparatuses of production . . . Does collective self-management require *a new technology*, a new labour process?" Burawoy, *Politics of Production*, p. 112 (my emphasis).

[14] In July 1929 twenty adolescent males refused to work on flyer-frames in the Soviet Union's first new cotton mill—the Krasnaia Talka in Ivanovo-Voznesensk—complaining of "women's work." *Rabochii krai*, 20 July 1929.

perhaps because operatives were traditionally recruited from the pool of peasant handloom weavers.

Gender demarcation came to the mills with British machinery and British expatriates—Lancashire imposed itself on Russia—but the main point I want to make here is as follows: if the *division of labor within komplekty* was to a greater or lesser extent under the control of komplekt leaders, the *allocation of functions within* komplekty was strictly delineated. Here one might speak of the *primacy* of gender throughout virtually all rooms and departments. With the partial exception of self-actor halls (where spinners were in effect operative-managers),[15] and the clear exception of weaving sheds, women worked the frames while men supervised.

We can extend our investigation of the role of gender in production to encompass the role of the family. Komplekty were not haphazard constructs conjured into being by management. Typically whole families (often extended families) worked in the mill—especially in the Central Industrial Region (CIR), somewhat less so in Leningrad where the range of industrial work opportunities outside the cotton industry was greater—and consequently kinship networks pervaded komplekty. The family was simultaneously a unit of economic support and a unit of exploitation. Kinship networks inside komplekty allowed workers to time-share jobs should the family have other commitments or some off-mill economic interests—a point to be explored below—and tended to render machinery the de facto property of a family, thus ensuring economic security across generations.[16] On the other hand, komplekt leaders could "hard drive" their kin (increase the workload of their assistants) as a way of sidestepping the burdens of uplotnenie.[17]

Tie with the Land

The significance of off-mill economic interests—the land—impinged on the shop floor and interacted with the factor of kinship. Unfortunately, I

---

[15] A 1928 time-and-motion study found that self-actor spinners spent about 20 percent of their working day in tasks "subsidiary to production" (managing the komplekt) compared to 9 percent for ring-frame spinners and 2 percent for power-loom weavers. *Izvestiia tekstil'noi promyshlennosti i torgovli* 1 (January 1928): 44–45.

[16] "Wherever possible," observed an American visitor to Russia's mills in 1912, "two members of the same family operate a set of looms or the same spinning frames, etc. The arrangement is particularly satisfactory in the case of a family with small children; the husband takes one shift and his wife the other, and the children in the home are never left alone." R. M. Odell, *Cotton Goods in Russia* (Washington, D.C., 1912), p. 37.

[17] In 1928 self-actor spinners in Leningrad's Ravenstvo mill were making their komplekty turn up for an extra unpaid hour before the start of the morning shift to set up the frames with rovings. They also shut down the frames for an unofficial unpaid Easter holiday, thus financially penalizing their less well paid komplekt members. Piecers and doffers acquiesced in such treatment since their chances of advancement depended on the spinner. *Golos tekstilei*, 11 November 1928.

have not been able to discover any sources that link the degree of "tie with the land" to particular trades or rooms. We have to be content with statistical and other information that merely generalizes between regions, or at best mentions the degree of landholding in particular mills in passing.[18] What is clear is that the level of interpenetration between the rural economy and the shop floor was lowest in Leningrad and highest in the CIR, and that within the CIR tie with the land was most evident in mills located in the countryside, least evident in metropolitan regions (Moscow, Ivanovo-Voznesensk, Vladimir) with small provincial centers (Shuia, Rodniki, Iur'ev-Pol'skii) coming somewhere between the two.

I have postulated a dual-axis continuum of relationships to land as a way of going beyond the common-sense conclusions evident in the sources (that is, that the levels of interpenetration were lowest in urban areas and highest in rural districts).[19] One axis of the continuum points to the degree of wage-dependence on the mill (the level of separation from the means of subsistence); the other to the degree of time-dependence (patterns of residence that in terms of time spent traveling to and from the shop, would make the mill or the land more or less attractive economic propositions). The main conclusions I have come to are as follows:

1. Industrial *stazh* (length of service in industry) was related in no clear way to the level of proletarianization—long-stazh operatives could have a considerable economic investment in the rural economy; conversely, short-stazh workers might have no connections at all with the land.
2. Because they were not fully separated from the means of subsistence operatives with a high level of off-mill economic interest were more able to resist uplotnenie drives than those with no source of income aside from wage labor.
3. More generally, the range of interconnections with the rural economy in the CIR functioned as an economic safety-net should the mills close, temporarily or permanently.
4. In the CIR managers had difficulty keeping labor on the shop floor at peak periods in the agricultural calendar.
5. Uplotnenie drives predicated on strict time-keeping or split shifts discriminated against workers living farthest away from their shops, regardless of the level of landholding.
6. The recruitment of new labor into the mills caused by normal secular

[18] The three best sources are V. V. Il'inskii, *Ivanovskii tekstil'shchik. Sostav i sotsial'naia kharakteristika rabochikh-tekstil'shchikov ivanovskoi promyshlennoi oblasti* (Ivanovo-Voznesensk, 1930); A. G. Rashin, *Sostav fabrichno-zavodskogo proletariata SSSR* (Moscow, 1930); and N. Semenov, *Litso fabrichnykh rabochikh, prozhivaiushchikh v derevniakh, i politrosvetrabota sredi nikh. Po materialam obsledovaniia rabochikh tekstil'noi promyshlennosti tsentral'no-promyshlennoi oblasti* (Moscow, 1929). Incidental evidence can be found in trust and trade union publications.
[19] See my *Russia's Cotton Workers*, chap. 5.

changes in workforce composition and, after 1927, by the introduction of the seven-hour/three-shift system, probably served to increase the level of tie with the land among the CIR cotton workforce.

7. And finally, such recruitment served also to intensify the degree of family working in all shops and trades.

Recruitment and Training

It should be evident that—given the degree of tie with the land (in the CIR at least)—the lineaments of recruitment served to maintain and reinforce a long-standing symbiosis between the world of the village and the world of the mill.

The village impinged on the shop in two ways worth exploring here. First, the workers with ties to the land were in some measure indifferent to time. This can be seen in how work discipline was consistently being strengthened and reconstituted and was reflected in the endless official criticisms of "half-peasant" or "backward" operatives, operatives who were more interested in the land than in the mill.[20] Second, the continuous flow of a rural-based *sostav* (staff, workforce) into the mill tended to forestall attempts to reconstruct the labor process: many operatives could refuse to acquiesce in uplotnenie drives, for example, since withdrawing labor—temporarily or permanently—did not necessarily ruin the family. Even if we imagine state agencies sacking the entire workforce of a given shop in a struggle over the labor process, the rationalization dilemma would still remain: in the CIR, the biggest cotton district, new operatives would have to be recruited from the countryside.

But we should not think of recruitment as necessarily threatening to unravel the culture of a given shop, or even as necessarily introducing strains and tensions between workers, managers, and state agencies. Symbiosis worked the other way round as well. The peculiarities of the labor process inherited from Britain coincided with the imperatives of Russia's social structure. As in Russia, British cotton mills of the late eighteenth- and early nineteenth-centuries also recruited farm laborers, small-holders, or domestic workers with other economic interests. As in Britain, Russian komplekty with clearly defined hierarchies were designed to train up raw recruits. Due to the acute shortages of factory schools in the 1920s, they remained, along with individual apprenticeship, the main method of training in the mill. And if youngsters without blood ties to a particular master or komplekt wanted to secure places on the frame they tried to insinuate

---

[20] Remarks like these can be found almost daily in *Golos tekstilei*, the textile workers' union newspaper.

Table 7.7. Distribution of registered unemployed cotton workers, October 1927

	Leningrad	Moscow	CIR ex Moscow
Preparatory departments			
Drawing-frame operatives	9	74	147
Flyer-frame operatives	77	48	325
Fine spinning rooms			
Ring-frame operatives	112	60	794
Self-actor komplekt			
Spinners	0	27	115
Piecers	0	99	567
Weavers	495	185	1496
Unskilled operatives (auxiliaries)	565	799	4050

Source: L. E. Mints and I. F. Engel', eds., *Statisticheskie materialy po trudu i sotsial'nomu strakhovaniiu za 1926–27 goda*, 4th ed. (Moscow, 1927–28), vol. 4, table 4, pp. 14–15.

themselves into kinship networks, not by relying on a bureau of labor or a trade union, but via *magarych*—a system of patronage whereby the adolescent, or his or her parents, "petitioned" and created "friends" in the shop through gifts of money or vodka.[21]

Finally, if komplekt working, machine, raw material, and product idiosyncrasy led to the appropriation of control over training by komplekt leaders (making what was virtually a carbon copy of the system elaborated in early nineteenth-century Britain functional in the context of NEP Russia), it is also the case that these factors led to the restriction of entry into various trades.[22] Though unemployment was high in NEP Russia, and though the entire cotton workforce was usually characterized by official agencies as unskilled, raw recruits could not be put to the frame. The formal designations of operatives as "skilled," "semi-skilled," or "unskilled" are best understood as attempts to objectify the parameters of skill, but they were unreal measures of workforce competence. Rather, we should think in terms of experience at the frame, a subjective measure of competence directly related to time served in komplekty. There were doubtless many thousands of peasants and town-dwellers anxious to get places in the cotton industry during the NEP, but precious few were experienced operatives able to take on work when confronted with the realities of production (table 7.7).[23]

[21] *Magarych* was not geographically specific, nor was it only a postrevolutionary phenomenon. It was commonplace before the revolution and pervaded all cotton districts and rooms in the 1920s.

[22] "Mule [self-actor] spinners take time off and do as they like," complained *Golos tekstilei* in 1927, "because they know they are in short supply." *Golos tekstilei*, 21 June 1927.

[23] There were catastrophic falls in productivity when thousands of new workers were hurriedly recruited to the mills with the introduction of the seven-hour/three-shift system.

Recruitment should perhaps be characterized as the beginning of a process of socialization into a particular mill. In combination with all the other factors mentioned above it served as the starting point of a mechanism for the replication and transmission of a long-standing culture of work across generations, regardless of the political form of the state. The various daily destinations of workers (different destinations for different members of the family) taught youngsters what was women's work, what was men's work, what was adolescent work, and what was adult work. Within the context of the mill's architecture tsekhovshchina imprinted and sustained that sense of otherness peculiar to various trades: appendix 1 surely indicates that there was little in common between self-actor and ring-frame spinners, still less between A. I. Shevarev, a power-loom tenter, and some young girl fresh from the countryside stacking bins in opener rooms. Indeed, unless they were related the three would probably never meet at all. Finally, komplekty delineated the boundaries of the possible in terms of life chances while simultaneously elaborating and strengthening group bonding via machine idiosyncrasy. In sum, recruits inherited a complex and variegated world of production focused around particular shops, trades, and spaces.

III

What are we to make of all this in terms of our search for a working class in NEP Russia and its relationship to work culture? We can now return to Katznelson's four typologies of class mentioned at the beginning of this chapter.

Class as Structure

If class is taken as a structure produced by capitalist economic development—"privately owned autonomous forms that seek to make profit-maximizing decisions" in Katznelson's formulation[24]—then the notion that the cotton operatives of the 1920s formed part of a working class has some substance. Though state intervention in industrial production was the sine qua non of the Bolshevik regime, the imperatives of the NEP refracted through the cotton industry (and not only the cotton industry) produced competition between mills and a simulacrum of bourgeois economic imperatives. Khozraschet (commercial accounting) looks like profit maximization. The preoccupation with the smychka suggests a

---

[24] Katznelson and Zolberg, *Working-Class Formation*, p. 14.

market-driven economy. Trustification pointed toward the autonomiza-
tion of decision making. Speed-ups—uplotnenie drives—brought in their
wake piece rates and changes to the working day.

All this would have been familiar to workers and managers in capitalist
countries. Even if the Revolution overthrew one state form and gave birth
to another, once the heroic period of the civil war had been replaced by
the NEP it is apparent that there had been no fundamental transformation
of production relations or of the labor process. To put it another way, if,
following Burawoy, the level of state intervention in production and the
degree of competition among mills are two of the determinants of factory
regimes everywhere,[25] it seems that the differences between socialist Russia
and capitalist Europe or the United States were ones of quantity, not of
quality.

But the benefits of elaborating this point are, for my purposes, limited.
They lead us inexorably in the direction of systems comparison—toward
discussions of whether or not the NEP represented state capitalism, state
socialism, or some other form—and away from a concern with the history
of the workforce, which, in such analyses, is handled chiefly by reference
to how it locks into a given system. Thus characterized there is a temptation to treat the phenomena of class as surface phenomena: and since
a system or state form becomes the focus of interest, there is a tendency
to conflate, exaggerate, or ignore differences in lived experience between
workers—between, say, cotton workers in Lancashire and cotton workers
in Ivanovo-Voznesensk—without actually examining the evidence on the
physiology of the workforce. We cannot explore other meanings of class
without leaving to one side the discourse of macroeconomic structure.
Instead, we must look inside and around the industry itself.

Class as Ways of Life and Dispositions

Regardless of any political or cultural transformations that may have
occurred in the context of revolution and civil war, it is doubtful whether
during the NEP Soviet cotton workers can be described *simply* as part of
a working class.[26] Except insofar as they happened to work "in the cotton
industry"[27] it was by no means the case that all operatives were proletarianized "in the full sense of lacking ownership or control over the means

[25] Burawoy, *Politics of Production*, fig. 1, p. 91.
[26] I am ignoring the official rhetoric of "class" produced by Marxist-Leninist ideology.
[27] That is, in more or less large-scale factories where capital substitutes for labor. According to the 1926 census about 480,000 operatives worked in large-scale cotton mills.
There were about 300 functioning mills in 1927, giving a rough average of 1,600 workers
per mill in the late NEP years.

of production and over the labour power of other workers"[28]—or, one might add, in the full sense of having been separated from the means of subsistence.

This brings us back to the cluster of elements surrounding recruitment, production, and the labor process. Returning to the discussion in section II allows us to extend the 'ideal-type' determinants of factory regimes suggested by Burawoy.[29] Thus elaborated these are as follows:

1. *State intervention in relation to production* is "internal" in a fully-developed command economy (penetrating the factory), but "external" in a laissez-faire economy (remaining outside the factory).

2. *Inter-mill competition* is "limited" in a command system, but "anarchic" under classical capitalism.

3. *Separation from the means of subsistence* is "complete" for workers thoroughly proletarianized, but "incomplete" for those with access to land (for instance).

4. *Labor supply* can be characterized as "short" or "surplus," depending on factors like skill profile and geographical match between industry and population.

5. *Subsumption of labor* or the degree of power exercised by managers is "formal" where workers have considerable control over the labor process and "real" where workers are powerless in the face of shop-floor managers or foremen.

6. *Entry to trade* is "restricted" where some workers control apprenticeship, but "open" where managers can assign workers to production tasks at will.

7. *Gender demarcation* is "complete" where trades or tasks are gender specific, "incomplete" where they are not.

8. *Spatial separation of trades* is "complete" where different production tasks take place in different rooms, "incomplete" where they do not.

9. *Raw material* is "standardized" or "idiosyncratic" (natural raw materials tending to be idiosyncratic, semifinished or man-made materials tending toward standardization).

10. *Machinery* is "standardized" or "idiosyncratic" (mass-produced machinery starts out as standardized but tends toward idiosyncrasy with age).

11. *Product* is "standardized" or "idiosyncratic," according to determinants 1, 2, 4–6, and 9–10.

I do not wish to assign any particular hierarchical significance to the different elements of this schema, but it is useful to think of them as vectors—not fixed points determining class consciousness or every aspect of workers' identities—with different groups of workers located at different moments on each vector over time. Nevertheless, by representing each

---

[28] Katznelson and Zolberg, *Working-Class Formation*, p. 4.
[29] Burawoy, *Politics of Production*, fig. 1, p. 91.

vector diagrammatically for NEP cotton operatives (appendix 2) we can catch a glimpse of just how variegated was the world of work.[30] Two of the remaining three of Katznelson's typologies of class—class as ways of life and class as dispositions—can be explored by reference to these vectors. The "near experience" of class was, it seems to me, bounded by work and the workplace, giving rise to a "language of trade."[31] Equally "dispositions" (formed groups, maps of lived experience, cultural formations and institutional expressions of these—komplekty, for instance), were trade bounded, with the extra factor of the long-standing symbiosis between mill and village added in.

Class as Collective Action

I submit that the language of class is not particularly useful for describing the cotton workforce of the 1920s, and that we should instead be thinking of a language of trade, one that interacts with the degree of separation from the means of subsistence. The language of class may have been immanent in the cotton industry but was obfuscated by the divisiveness of the labor process and the symbiosis between mill and village. This is apparent if we turn to the last of Katznelson's four typologies of class—class as collective action—by glancing at cotton workers' responses to pressures emanating from the state during the NEP.

The first of these, the strike movement of 1925, was a response to uplotnenie drives predicated upon multi-machine working (assigning more

[30] If I have paid a great deal of attention to self-actor spinners in this essay it is because they were located at one extreme of most vectors. Auxiliary workers were at the other extreme, the placing of other groups of workers was more variable. In this context it might be worth mentioning that I am not entirely convinced of Burawoy's taxonomy of the relative standing of occupations in the Russian cotton industry. Though factory-based weaving came to Russia before mechanized spinning, reversing the British pattern, the dynamics of the nineteenth-century cotton industry eventually reversed the early Russian pattern: by the late nineteenth century mechanized spinning had virtually wiped out domestic spinning and the consequent increase in thread production served to preserve, and perhaps stimulate, the putting-out system in weaving. Peasant handloom weavers were commonly recruited to the weaving sheds in the 1920s, but I have found nothing that suggests that they enjoyed a particularly high status in the eyes of other operatives. Reginald Zelnik's illuminating study of the Kranhölm mill in the prerevolutionary years, which suggests that weavers rather than spinners were regarded as skilled and were the focus of organized labor unrest, is something of a puzzle here: could the Kranhölm experience be related, not only to the mill's location (Estonia), but also to how much earlier Emancipation came to the Baltic regions than to Russia proper? Conversely, there seems little doubt that as in Britain, *Russian* (as opposed to Baltic) self-actor spinners formed a kind of "aristocracy" in the mill. A possible solution to this apparent contradiction is, as Burawoy has suggested, that the labor process in Estonia's Kranhölm mill was based on the German model, whereas that obtaining in Russian mills was predicated on British practices.

[31] Katznelson and Zolberg, *Working-Class Formation*, p. 4.

frames to a worker or komplekt than was customary), speed-ups, and the imposition of piece rates. But the strikes were not generalized throughout the cotton regions. Leningrad remained quiescent, in part because very few workers had sources of off-mill income to fall back on, but also because of the particular configuration of the labor process: the old capital was first in line for good-quality imported fiber which at once reduced the piecing workload in spinning rooms and checked the spread of "bad spinning"—threads spun "off the count"—which made life more difficult for weavers. This made the burdens of uplotnenie less onerous and the financial benefits of piece rates more attractive for all workers.

In the CIR, on the other hand, multi-machine working and piece rates were generally disadvantageous, given the poorer quality of the native raw material. Strikes flickered across all districts in the CIR, but not all shops stopped work. Piece rates may have been attractive to operative-farmers living close to the mill. Moreover, machine idiosyncrasy deflected the drive toward multiframe working, and spinners could hard drive their komplekty, and thus the full force of uplotnenie was most likely to fall on weavers and auxiliaries. In addition, although access to off-mill income was more commonly available than in Leningrad, it was distributed unevenly throughout the workforce. Not all operatives could necessarily afford to initiate or sustain a stoppage.[32]

A second attempt at uplotnenie, the introduction of the seven-hour/three-shift system early in 1928, did not give rise to any marked level of collective industrial action. Though many established komplekt leaders were disadvantaged by the new system because they lost exclusive control of their frames, and though segments of the established culture of work were therefore disrupted,[33] any movement toward the expression of collective discontents was fragmented by the interpellation of a host of new factors: disagreements over shift placings; the sudden chance of advancement for many komplekt members; the promotion of auxiliaries to the frame, and increased employment prospects for family members and the subsequent strengthening of kinship networks throughout the mill. For the most part, therefore, conflict was contained within the parameters of the shop. Generally speaking, workers quarreled with each other. They did not confront the state and its agencies.

In both instances—in 1925 and again in 1928—the Bolshevik regime's acceptance of the continuation of those factors which simultaneously differentiated various groups of workers from one another and blocked the

---

[32] "We fight one against the other," observed one CIR operative in 1925, "though each feels that it's necessary to organize."

[33] According to *Zhenotdel* (the women's section of the Communist Party), women were "afraid of losing their own machines, their workmates on their shift, or they consider that it would be more convenient to work nights." *Kommunistka* 3 (March 1928): 29.

full implementation of uplotnenie did not happen by default. Rather, it was the product of a particular juncture of historical and contemporary social and political imperatives. If maintaining the smychka via khozraschet and uplotnenie put pressure on the cotton workforce, the state's projects were at once assisted and hindered by the divisiveness of village ties and the labor process.

IV

Historians like to cross unexplored territory. To map the geography of class, to decongest it, we must pace out the shop floor, try to understand its imperatives, and attempt to illuminate the interstices and fixities of the landscape of labor. The shop floor of course, was by no means the only landscape in which identities were formed, but it did serve as one significant field of action for workers, and it did help to structure their responses to many of the problems they faced. We also must bear in mind that the fixities and interstices of particular industries were produced by the interactions of workers, managers, machine makers, and machinery. They were not "given" by technology.[34] Social and labor historians should take a hard look at the labor process in the various industries populated by the class they want to describe, not least because the shop floor is an important arena in which the wider aspects of working-class culture and national politics are concentrated and acted out.

In this context I would like to conclude with a short observation on the role of cotton workers in the big event of the revolution. Despite the divisiveness of the cotton industry, operatives in Ivanovo-Voznesensk managed to construct the first soviet in 1905 and in 1917 the CIR was a stronghold of radical Bolshevism. In both instances the cotton workforce could be characterized as acting as a "class-for-itself." Nevertheless, it is probable that the primordial cause of workers' actions cannot be located just by reference to the mill. My research suggests that although in cotton at least, the point of production may have been the "decisive arena for the formation of the working class,"[35] this is apparent only in structural terms, not in terms of the three other typologies of class listed by Katznelson. Here "class-in-itself" can be broken down into the more appropriate typologies of the language of trade. Furthermore, it seems to me that Burawoy's formulation that the "historical anomaly of English working-class reformism and the revolutionary spirit of Russian workers" can

[34] Burawoy's contention that "base *and* superstructure are both arenas of objectivity *and* subjectivity" is particularly suggestive in this context. Burawoy, *Politics of Production*, p. 111.
[35] Ibid.

be explained chiefly by reference to the physiology of the shop floor requires modification.[36] It may well be that the particularism of work culture in the Russian cotton industry described in this essay was strengthened by the peculiarities of the NEP, but even if this was the case it was not generated by it. Operatives were only building on the experience of the tsarist period, on foundations laid by British machinery, British expatriates, and the British model of the labor process established in nineteenth-century Russia. And the labor process in British and Russian cotton mills was not so different. Patriarchy pervaded all shops. The subsumption of labor was, in some instances, formal. Not all operatives were separated from the means of subsistence. An important place must therefore be allowed for other ways in which working-class identities were structured and sustained; for the penetration of socialist ideology from without, and for that slow accretion of generalized perceptions of the injustices of the ancien régime throughout the middling and lower ranks of Russian society.[37]

Appendix 7:1

"Don't ask me about this infernal machine!"

"Why not?"

"Because, I'm telling you, it's high time it was sent to the devil!"

With these words the Ukrainian manager clapped his hand on the back of a large clumsy frame. The machine took up a lot of space and had a long, awkward body, something like a grand piano.

This, several years ago, was the occasion of my first meeting with the mule. Since then I've gotten to know a lot of people in the industry, and each has had their own attitude to it. . . . I began to appreciate that there are really only two views about the mule. One is sharply against it. The other belongs to people who know something of the world and who—as we say—like to measure their cloth seven times before they cut it. These are solid, quiet and reserved men; we could say that they are "mule patriots." They know how to tame this lion, and it is a point of honor for them to say that he is the best and most submissive of beasts—if only he is treated properly. The other view comes from young people; impatient, hot-headed, and always ready to put their trust in all things American. . . .

"Send it to the devil," repeated my temperamental manager. "What use

---

[36] Ibid.

[37] It is remarkable that although Russian workers could select from many varieties of socialism inherited from the West, they constructed, in association with the radical intelligentsia, a form of socialism predicated in the final analysis on the transformation of the *state*, not on the transformation of the labor process.

is it? It's already been scrapped in America, and they make threads more neatly there on the ring-frame. We're also learning how much better the ring-frame is, and then we'll throw this junk on the scrap heap. Look— the mule takes up almost twice as much room as the ring-frame. We install a mule with a thousand spindles, but put a ring-frame in its place and we'll get 1750—almost twice as many. Working the mule's a thankless task. It's complicated and it requires training. You have to put the spinner on a high wage-scale, and besides that he's got to have assistants, because one person alone can't cope with it. The thread they produce isn't cheap, and in our hard times the buyer won't dip into his pocket for it. But now take a look at the ring-frame—profit and simplicity! The ring-frame uses female labor, and wages are lower because the work's simpler. Ring-frame thread isn't expensive, and it gives an immediate return to the mill. I ask you, why do we still bother with these monsters!"

"But things aren't as simple as that," replies the mule patriot, slowly weighing his words. "Look at the root of the matter. To you it's just an expensive and unnecessary machine, and there's no profit in it because it's uneconomic. You should think of economy like a woman—a woman doesn't measure economy in centimetres. And even if the mule comes off worse in terms of price, profit and convenience, all the same, some are still for carrying on with it. . . ."

"But how is mule thread better than ring-frame thread?"

How? Here the mule patriot smiles to himself and hands you two spools of thread. One from a ring-frame, the other from a mule. You take them and hold them, and for a moment they seem the same. But if you have a good eye, and that sixth sense which is a combination of touch, vision, instinct, and understanding, you will gradually become aware of the difference. What is this difference? Mule thread is more alive than ring-frame thread; ring-frame thread is dry and inert. This is strange, but without a doubt it's exactly the impression you get, and it lies in some peculiar quality of mule thread. It is as if it were finer, more even, more supple to the touch. It is closer to that genius of a man's hands that creates thread. And so you yourself come to your own decision while the mule patriot patiently waits for the thread to offer up its own explanation. . . .

"Check the quality of the finished product," continues the mule patriot. "Cloth made from mule thread will fit you properly. It'll give with every movement, it'll be flexible, like something living. Now cloth from a ring frame—that's another matter. It puckers and creases and it's uncomfortable under a coat. So if you're buying in the market you've only got to use your hands to tell the difference. . . ."

Source: M. Shaginian, *Nevskaia nitka* (Moscow-Leningrad, 1925), pp. 33–36.

Appendix 7:2

State intervention in production	INTERNAL	<——————— New Economic Policy ———————>	EXTERNAL
Intermill competition	LIMITED	<——————— New Economic Policy ———————>	ANARCHIC
Separation from the means of subsistence	COMPLETE	<--- Leningrad ——— Metropolitan CIR ——— Provincial CIR ——— Rural CIR --->	INCOMPLETE
Labor supply	SHORTAGE	<----- Self-actor spinners -- Other komplekt heads --- Jacquard looms --- All komplekt members --- Power looms --- Auto-looms --- Auxiliaries --->	SURPLUS
Subsumption of labor	FORMAL	<----- Self-actor spinners ——— Other komplekt heads ——— Weavers ——— Komplekt members ——— Auxiliaries --->	REAL
Entry to trade	RESTRICTED	<----- Self-actor halls ——— Initial processing & preparatory departments, ring-frame halls ——— Weavers ——— Auxiliaries --->	OPEN
Gender demarcation	COMPLETE	<----- Initial processing & preparatory departments, all fine-spinning halls ——— Auxiliaries, Weaving sheds --->	INCOMPLETE
Spatial separation of trades	COMPLETE	<----- All rooms --->	INCOMPLETE
Raw material	STANDARDIZED	<----- All rooms ----->	IDIOSYNCRATIC
Machinery	STANDARDIZED	<----- All rooms ----->	IDIOSYNCRATIC
Product	STANDARDIZED	<----- All rooms ----->	IDIOSYNCRATIC

8

Daniel Orlovsky

The Hidden Class: White-Collar
Workers in the Soviet 1920s

On 22 June 1929, M. I. Kalinin gave one of the major speeches at the Eighth All-Union Congress of the Union of Soviet and Commercial Employees. Kalinin, later president of the Soviet Republic, was then the chairman of the Central Executive Committee of the USSR (a largely ceremonial post overshadowed by positions in the Sovnarkom or ministerial bureaucracy and by the Politburo and Secretariat of the Communist Party itself). One of Kalinin's major themes was the ongoing purge of state employees that had again turned upside down the world of white-collar employees. In June of 1929, Stalin's reheated class war was already in full swing. The five-year plan was under way, as was collectivization. The so-called Right Opposition (Bukharin, Tomsky, Rykov, and their allies among the technical intelligentsia and party cadres who supported a softer line toward the peasantry and so on) had already been routed from their not very deep trenches. For the union membership, purges were already the order of the day—the state against itself—another of a long series of antibureaucratic campaigns that dominated the discourse and political landscape of the 1920s (and indeed, in an even more virulent form, the 1930s as well).[1]

Kalinin, much to his credit, decried this "campaign" mode of reforming or transforming the bureaucracy. It was too destructive, he claimed, and usually got rid of the wrong people. Purging, he argued, should never be carried out on the basis of social origin (he understood well the masked quality of Soviet society and the utter lack of correspondence between social origin and political consciousness). Purges, understood in this case

---

[1] The campaign mode of the 1930s was legitimized and became a permanent feature of the political and social landscape during the 1920s. For a discussion of the power and varied meanings of what I term the discourse of antibureaucracy, see my "Anti-Bureaucratic Campaigns of the 1920's," to appear in a volume of Kennan Institute Conference papers on reform in tsarist and Soviet Russia, edited by Theodore Taranovski (Cambridge: Cambridge University Press, forthcoming).

as a campaign mode of bureaucratic reform, should be carried out strictly on the basis of individual performance and competence. Kalinin appealed to the provincial union functionaries to purge only the "responsible" types. (Here he cited Stalin's dictum to go after the "big bureaucrat.") In Riazan, for example, he noted that 1500 employees had been dismissed, but not the real troublemakers. "It was wrong, as many now did, to think of purging as an honor. We need quality purges, purges that are permanent so that 75 percent of banished functionaries do not reappear in other Soviet positions." Purges require foresight and planning, he argued. In Tomsk, according to Kalinin, one thousand purged employees were replaced by blue-collar workers who had no qualifications to become office workers, bookkeepers, typists, or higher specialists.[2] This he said was a bad tendency, "mechanical affirmative action," and there were far too many reports of miserable workers in new white-collar posts. "In the Central Executive Committee, we only take in five workers, and then only if we can give them full support and a trial period to see how they like the new occupations." It was dangerous, he argued, to remove valuable production workers from the factories to give them less meaningful white-collar jobs. He called on his audience to think of the factory and its leadership and only remove blue collar workers very very carefully. "A valued person makes good money in the factory, so don't promote a metalworker into a typist, don't make them into bureaucratic paper pushers." He insisted that a policy promoting hundreds of thousands of blue-collar workers is not in touch with the issues, that a campaign mode of promotion will destroy thousands of lives.

For Kalinin, the preferred solution to the call for affirmative action was to promote white-collar workers themselves within the soviet and commercial apparatus. Why, he wondered, was there no commentary in the media about this kind of promotion to more responsible positions? (To answer his question: at that time to speak of white-collar workers instead of pure proletarians was not politically correct and the silence in the media was a reflection of the hidden nature of the white-collar "class.") Why, he wondered, is the press so negative toward the Soviet apparatus? He observed that in twelve years the white-collar workers had fulfilled enormous state tasks and created a huge cadre of selfless functionaries and called on these functionaries to defend themselves as a corporate body and a profession. He pointed out that the factory system had more former tsarist officials than the apparatus did and called for an end to the tyranny of the managers. He called on the members of the employees' union to raise their self-consciousness and professionalism and closed with a plea to the white-collar workers to acquire more of a corporate sense of them-

[2] All of the above taken from *Nasha gazeta*, 22 June 1929, p. 2.

selves, in short to stand up for their rights and status even as they helped to lead the way forward in the construction of the new socialist economy and state. He called the Soviet and commercial employees a proletarian army, proletarian in the material and popular sense (though not in terms of social origin), and urged them to give this proletarian army ideological content and working-class political and economic sense. The white-collar workers are not, as some would have it, an intelligentsia proletariat. They were raised on petty bourgeois values. Our job—the job of the union and the party—is to instruct them in proletarian interests, ethics, and way of life. This is possible, and this immersion of white-collar workers in proletarian society will strengthen the Soviet apparatus and insure the link of workers and peasants and the building of socialism.[3]

In the Soviet Union during the 1920s the white-collar workers, a group largely, but not exclusively peopled by employees, were a hidden class (although the term "class" is problematic), precisely because they were so closely identified with and identified themselves with the proletarian project, the idea of the proletariat or of a proletarian state that had come to dominate the discourse and politics of state building during the revolution. To call them a hidden class suggests that in some ways they were as important as the working "class," and reflects how they appeared under the rubric of employees (*sluzhashchie*) only to disappear from time to time back into the larger proletarian category . One would have to sift through the official rhetoric and documents quite carefully to unravel the white-collar thread from the whole proletarian cloth. They have also been "hidden" from our view by a conspiracy of silence. Largely ignored by historians of the Soviet period (Western and Soviet), by historians of the revolution in 1917, and by historians of late Imperial Russia alike, white-collar workers have generally been folded uncritically into the working class, or worse yet confused with the so-called bourgeois specialists, who had their own problematic history during the civil war and the 1920s.[4]

---

[3] Ibid.

[4] It is instructive that even the most recent attempts to map the social terrain of the 1920s pay scant attention to white-collar workers or to the key questions of occupations and layering. See, for example, Maureen Perrie and R. W. Davies, "The Social Context," in Davies, ed., *From Tsarism to the New Economic Policy: Continuity and Change in the Economy of the USSR* (Ithaca, N.Y., 1991), pp. 29–46. See also Catherine Merridale, *Moscow Politics and the Rise of Stalin: The Communist Party in the Capital, 1925–32* (New York, 1990). Merridale notes the large numbers of white-collar workers in the party, but focuses her analysis almost exclusively on "workers," thus lending credence to the regime's public front and the stale categories of decades of Soviet scholarship. Sheila Fitzpatrick offers some insight into the "objective" vs. subjective nature of class identity in the 1920s in her recent "The Problem of Class Identity in NEP Society," in Sheila Fitzpatrick, Alexander Rabinowitch and Richard Stites, eds., *Russia in the Era of NEP: Explorations in Soviet Society and Culture* (Bloomington, Ind., 1991), pp. 12–33. Fitzpatrick speaks of masked identities, but only from the point of view of *vlast'*, that is, she argues that state power (and by implication society as well), was interested in unmasking class aliens hiding behind acceptable occupations or false class identities. I argue here that the state was itself doing the masking with

This research on white-collar workers grows out of earlier work on the role of the lower middle strata, a concept meant to include both white-collar workers and certain middle-level status groups and occupations, professionals, and intellectuals in the Russian revolution.[5]

The story of Soviet white-collar workers should not be viewed in isolation as a feature of the peculiar experience of a massive agrarian society (with a long history of bureaucracy) undergoing revolutionary transformation. Comparing the white-collar workers of the Soviet Union of the 1920s with their interwar counterparts in Europe is particularly useful for understanding the role of this sizeable and politically significant social group in the development of corporativist nondemocratic political systems—to include fascism.

Here the Italian case may be particularly instructive. The Italian historian Liugi Salvatorelli and the social theorist and Marxist activist Antonio Gramsci both observed and commented on the role of Italy's lower middle class in the articulation of corporativism during the 1920s.[6] Salvatorelli labeled the Italian middle classes "literate illiterates."[7] Members of this group could be found especially in bureaucratic offices, scholastic halls, and petty professional activities. Salvatorelli spoke to the culture of this group and noted that they possessed a "smattering" of grammatical and formulaic culture, but that they lacked the critical and synthetic abilities to use their knowledge to evaluate the contemporary political scene. Grasmci colorfully described them as "monkey people," and fascism as their latest "performance" in the theater of national political life. The monkey people, according to Gramsci, "supply daily news, they do not create history, they leave traces in the newspapers, they do not offer material to write books."[8] The Italian regime attempted to manage the problems of lower-middle-class social marginality by building a new mythology of corporativism that provided for membership in the new national society through participation in the "free" unions (*syndicati*). Such corporations provided metaphors for "framing and reinterpreting experience" and for channeling private initiative into the public sphere through the overarching presence of the fascist state. In the Italian model, one had to be a part of a collective (and subject to collective labor contracts for example) in order to be part of the nation. As in the Soviet case (as will be shown), white-collar workers and intelligentsia in general were

---

the assistance of social groups who found it expedient to adopt or adapt to acceptable social categories.

[5] On the intelligentsia (including some professionals) in 1917, see O. N. Znamenskii, *Intelligentsiia nakanune velikogo Oktiabria (fevrial'–oktiabr' 1917 g.)* (Leningrad, 1988).

[6] The material that follows is drawn largely from Mabel Berezin, "Created Constituencies: The Italian Middle Classes and Fascism," in Rudy Koshar, ed., *Splintered Classes: Politics and the Lower Middle Classes in Interwar Europe* (New York, 1990), pp. 142–63.

[7] Ibid., p. 142.

[8] Ibid., p. 143.

to play the role of mediators in a new society that was to transcend the class struggle and indeed, the entire problem of class in industrializing societies. The goal was the manipulated expressions of solidarity among the various participants in production (an example would be collective labor contracts). The state would be the great unifier and "encourager" of private initiative, and the professionals and intellectuals were to assist production and be the guardians of the new collective morality.[9] Under this system, the fiction of class collaboration would replace the much-feared class conflict. Early Soviet society and Marxist ideology offered parallel possibilities.

Two aspects of Russian society need to be mentioned at the outset—layering and masking. The first refers to the tremendously rich variety of social and occupational groups that emerged in late tsarist Russia (at the turn of the century) and their enormous impact on the revolution of 1905 and especially on the two revolutions in 1917. The second refers to the conscious and unconscious efforts of the actors, theoreticians, and commentators of the time and of subsequent politicians and historians to mask this social reality by developing the sociologically crude and reductive, but politically effective discourse of a class struggle among workers, peasants, and the "bourgeoisie." In fact the conclusion one is tempted to draw after four months of archival work on the 1920s is that the more fragmented and layered that Soviet society became (a process that only increased in intensity with the October Revolution, the early attempt to abolish the market in War Communism, the onset of civil war, and so on), the more stridently it claimed an essentially proletarian nature. In short, the more important and larger the social and political role of non-blue-collar factory workers (and agrarian laborers), the greater the pressure for state power to act out its proletarian fantasies. The state sought social integration by articulating an affirmative proletarian universalism. One might say that the revolution had placed on the table both strict and broad interpretations of the composition of the proletariat. During the early and mid-1920s, the broad view prevailed, but economic failures (accompanied by parallel failures in social integration) later in the decade led to a reassertion of the narrow conception of class (and class war) and even more obsequious attempts of non-factory workers to fit into the proletarian model.

This is not to say that during the 1920s there was no body of workers that comprised a conscious, socially coherent, politically unified class in the Marxist sense, or that components of such a group did not identify with the regime or even defend its economic interests against authority.

---

[9] In a word strikingly resonant with the experience of tsarist Russia, this group was even termed the "Third Element" (ibid.).

Rather it is to note that the formation of such a coherent and conscious group was neither straightforward nor predictable, that its forms did not necessarily conform to either Marxist or non-Marxist theories of class. The process of class formation was full of contradictions that involved other "proletarians" who were not factory workers. It also involved a series of substitutions that derived from the elimination of the bourgeoisie and the market and their replacement by state power (itself a form of social power) in its varied and sometimes masked forms.[10] For the white-collar workers the proletarian agendas were mystifying challenges and threats. How after all could Taylorism be applied to office work, much less storming? Is one's loyalty to *vedomstvo* (home institution), union, class, or occupational group? Did the language of class and class conflict mask the ongoing struggles of all of these formations over the substance of power in the 1920s?

The Russian Revolution had a profound impact on social roles and identities.[11] This is hardly surprising since any revolution at least for a time throws open the realm of possibility to an entire spectrum of social groups previously limited by the structures of the old regime. The Russian Revolution offers another dimension to this problem, namely that of ideological masks. The Bolsheviks declared the revolution to have been made in the name of the proletariat. They even proclaimed a partnership between this proletariat and the peasantry, a holy union that was to persist as a cornerstone of party dogma, if not political reality, until the end of the 1920s.[12] The trouble is that neither social nor even political reality corresponded to the requirements of ideology. This should not be surprising. Russian society had been rapidly evolving since the mid-nineteenth century. In the two decades immediately prior to the February Revolution of 1917, new social groups and new occupations had emerged that did not correspond to the legal categories of the estate (*soslovie*) system. Factory workers, professionals, white-collar workers, and others had to be worked into the official estate categories.

We know that the working class was shattered during the civil war,

[10] The argument is similar to one made by Diane Koenker in her essay "Class Consciousness in a Socialist Society: Workers in the Printing Trades during NEP," in Fitzpatrick, Rabinowitch and Stites, *Russia in the Era of NEP*, pp. 34–57, which was first delivered at the National Seminar on the History of Twentieth-Century Russian and Soviet Society, Bloomington, Ind., 1986.

[11] See Leopold Haimson, "Civil War and the Problem of Social Identities in Early Twentieth Century Russia," in Diane Koenker, William G. Rosenberg, and Ronald G. Suny, eds., *Party, State and Society in the Russian Civil War: Explorations in Social History* (Bloomington, Ind., 1989), pp. 24–47. Also the articles by Sheila Fitzpatrick, "New Perspectives on the Civil War," and "The Legacy of the Civil War," pp. 3–24 and 385–98 in the same collection.

[12] See M. A. Molodtsygin, *Raboche-krest'ianskii soiuz 1918–1920* (Moscow, 1987).

though only recently have we seen that too much has been made of the deurbanization and declassing phenomena.[13] Workers in the industrial center managed to turn to other traditional sources and locations of class identity once the bourgeoisie was eliminated. How else, after all, was one to define a social identity when a major source of that identity was gone? The cities, as Brower shows, were full of survivors (*obyvateli*), a rather amorphous urban mass that in a time of unbelievable hardship dealt in the essential goods and services of day-to-day life.[14] During the 1920s the weighty presence of white-collar workers in the urban mass and indeed in the provincial towns and countryside as well is documented in the 1923 census of cities and towns and the All Union Census of 1926. These were the last relatively accurate and professional censuses carried out prior to the purges of the Central Statistical Administration (TsSU) in the late twenties. (The TsSU was itself a bastion of lower-middle-strata prerevolutionary professionals, zemstvo statisticians, and the like.)

In the countryside the white-collar worker emerged with new force as functionaries in the soviets and in the party and other state institutions, building on the structure of occupations already in place as a result of institution building in the decades leading to 1917 and the revolution itself. In the post-October civil war countryside a new, vast, and ever increasing group of peasants-turned-functionaries quickly took hold. In the words of Orlando Figes, the "rural official elite of the emergent party-state apparatus was formed as the village democracy of the peasant revolution disintegrated under the social pressures of the civil war."[15] Figes writes,

> The problem of governing the countryside after 1921 was in many ways more fundamental than it had been prior to 1917. The social autonomy and the economic power of the village communes had been greatly increased as a result of the revolution. The new state administrators in the VIKs and the village soviets were, unlike their predecessors under the Tsar, mainly drawn from the peasantry; they were for the most part, barely literate, inexperienced in government, poorly disciplined, and strongly inclined towards localism.[16]

The new functionaries were drawn from the marginal and landless elements of rural society and included, according to Figes, ex-servicemen,

[13] See the excellent articles on this by Daniel Brower and Diane Koenker in Koenker, Suny, and Rosenberg, *Party, State and Society*.

[14] See I. Got'e, *Time of Troubles* (Princeton, N.J., 1988), for an account of the hardships as experienced by a member of the intelligentsia.

[15] Orlando Figes, *Peasant Russia, Civil War: The Volga Countryside in Revolution (1917–1921)* (Oxford, 1989), p. 355.

[16] Ibid., p. 245.

general laborers, craftsmen, migrants, rural youth, and women. White-collar work in the village and canton (*volost'*) centers helped to define a social and political division between the agrarian world of the communes and the rapidly growing party-state, which would come to represent the outside world and its projects of industrialization, education, and the like.[17]

Even the party opposition known as Democratic Centralists called attention to the nature of rural cadres in the soviets. T. V. Sapronov and V. V. Osinski, leaders of this movement, were wholly in favor of *ispolkom* power in provincial and rural soviets, but believed that the elected membership of these soviets consisted largely of antiproletarian, petty-bourgeois obyvateli. In a debate at the Seventh All-Russian Congress of Soviets in 1919, this Democratic Centralist charge was answered by the great defender of the white-collar workers, M. Kalinin. Kalinin argued for wide enlistment of the ordinary citizen as follows: "Some say, 'But you are enrolling the obyvateli?' What is the obyvatel'?—a person, standing on the petty bourgeois point of view, accustomed to living according to routine. We should tear these people out of their routines, we should shove them into soviet work. Can those who are alienated from the soviets really be enlisted in the larger goal of soviet construction? We must push the obyvatel' [philistine] mass forward."[18]

Even a cursory examination of the census materials shows the existence of a large white-collar social formation—a group that in numerical strength fully equalled or exceeded those who were categorized as workers.[19] Statistics reveal the urban population of the Russian empire to have been reduced by eight million (from 28.4 million to 20.1 million) or 30% during the years of war, revolution and civil war from 1913-1920.[20] Despite ongoing famine and pestilence, economic recovery was far enough

[17] See ibid. for figures on the social composition of *volosti*, district soviets, and executive committees (*ispolkomy*).

[18] Quoted in the stenographic *otchet* of the Seventh All-Russian Congress of Soviets (Moscow, 1920), p. 221. I am grateful to Lars Lih for the reference. Interestingly, both Sapronov (the Democratic Centralist) and the food supply official P. K. Kaganovich accused Kalinin of putting the soviets in the hands of obyvateli (vulgar urbanites) and *meshchane* (bourgeois), and of petty-bourgeois *raskliabannost'* (literally, lack of discipline, disorganization brought on by a sort of weak sloppiness). See pp. 225–27 and 244.

[19] One of the few Western scholars to underscore the existence of large numbers of white-collar workers in the 1920s was William Chase in his pioneering study of the Moscow working class, *Workers, Society and the Soviet State: Labor and Life in Moscow, 1918–1929* (Urbana, Ill., 1987), pp. 121–29.

[20] V. B. Zhiromskaia, *Sovetskii gorod v 1921–1925gg.: Problemy sotsial'noi struktury* (Moscow, 1988), p. 44. All figures that follow are taken from Zhiromskaia's reproductions of 1923 and 1926 census materials.

along by 1923 to spur a population increase of 8.7%. The urban population had reached 22 million at the time of the 1923 census. In European Russia (exclusive of Siberia and Ukraine) the urban population numbered 11,194, 100 or 51.2% of the empire's total. The figures on social composition of the cities and towns of this region for 1923 and 1926 reveal almost an equal number of blue- and white-collar workers and a large number of other census categories that hid significant additional numbers of employees.[21]

	Blue collar	White collar
USSR, urban population	2,332,713 (25.3%)	2,231,116 (24.2%)
RSFSR	(26.0%)	(26.2%)
European Russia	(26.2%)	(26.9%)

Other urban social groups—USSR as a whole

Free professions	78,976 (0.8%)
Enterprise owners (with hired labor)	39,435 (0.4%)
Enterprise owners (family labor, to include NEP women and men often from employee or shop background)	475,019 (5.1%)
Individuals engaged in economic activity (undefined)	942,717 (10.2%)
Family helpers of above	(8.5%)
Dependents of state and social institutions	746,307 (8.1%)
Unemployed	905,424 (9.8%)
Retired	110,682 (1.2%)
Declassed population (gentry, priests, bourgeoisie, and those indicating no source of income)	550,495 (6.0%)

Factory workers constituted a very small percentage of the urban population. Much more numerous were the white-collar workers in all their variants, many of whom were hidden in the other categories of the census. Not only were white-collar workers hidden in the census categories and in most official communications and analyses of "society," their presence was also downplayed in trade union membership statistics, which makes it easy to miss how they could be found in all sorts of enterprises and institutions in the Soviet state. One must look beyond the union in which they were segregated (the Union of Soviet and Commercial Employees) to all other unions (blue-collar and intelligentsia alike), because all these unions had significant white-collar memberships.

[21] The following is taken from V. B. Zhiromskaia's reproduction of 1923 and 1926 census materials in *Sovetskii gorod v 1921–1925 gg.: Problemy sotsial'noi struktury* (Moscow, 1988), p. 44.

In European Russia between 1923 and 1926, the period of Lenin's death and the great political struggles between Stalin and the Left and Joint Oppositions, the period of the Lenin Levy in the party (an early wave of affirmative action, intended to increase the numbers of workers from the bench in the proletarian's party), the absolute numbers of both factory workers and white-collar employees increased dramatically. In the central industrial region, for example, workers increased by 298,511 and employees by 190,527. In 1926, the workforce there included 43.8 percent factory workers and 30.4 percent employees. This represented a growth rate from 1923 to 1926 of 51 percent for the workers and 32.7 percent for employees. Similar figures exist for Leningrad and Karelia. In the central agricultural (black-earth) and middle Volga regions, employees were more numerous than factory workers. The black-earth factory workers numbered 69,687 in 1923 (15.9 percent) and 75,099 in 1926 (16.8 percent), whereas employees numbered 96,351 in 1923 (21.9 percent) and 102,633 (22.8 percent) in 1926. For the middle Volga region in 1923 there were 79,827 workers (19.4 percent) and in 1926, 89,064 (20.1 percent). White-collar employees numbered 102,607 in 1923 (24.9 percent) and 112,158 in 1926 (25.3 percent). Unemployment among blue- and white-collar workers ran at 8.4 and 6.4 percent, 11.3 and 7.2 percent for the central agricultural and middle Volga regions. Data for individual cities confirm the presence of large numbers of employees and others with no connection to factory life. In 1923, the Moscow region contained 31.1 percent workers and 26.5 percent employees, and in the city of Moscow, 26.6 percent of the population counted as workers and 27.4 percent as employees. In European Russia both the working class and the white-collar workers and employees grew dramatically. Industrial recovery and growth meant not just more workers, but more white-collar employees as well. This was a structural and ideological fact that stemmed from the state control of industry and the statization of the economy under War Communism and even under NEP. This may also be said of many categories of the urban intelligentsia, that is, the middle- and lower-middle-strata managers, engineers, and other professional groups (including education personnel), who in most instances were more highly educated and received comparatively large salaries. Using the census category of intelligentsia, we see in the USSR and European Russia the following urban totals: for the USSR as a whole, 424,861 (1923) and 544,184 (1926); for European Russia, 254,448 (1923) and 297,286 (1926). The census included (1) senior administrative and juridical; (2) senior technical, (3) senior medical, and (4) cultural and educational personnel (with categories 1 and 4 by far the largest with 75 percent of the total).

The Union of Soviet and Commercial Employees

Writing in 1929, the former Menshevik turned union activist M. Gegechkori, in a pamphlet designed to acquaint union rank and file with the benefits bestowed by membership, argued that the union card was the member's passport into the proletariat.[22] Gegechkori (who was soon to be purged) showed ironic foresight in his companion claim that all those outside the union were by definition the class enemy. The union was a mechanism by which a new ideology could be anchored firmly in society (as part of *obshchestvennost'*). By the mid-1920s, the Union of Soviet and Commercial Employees was the largest single trade union in the Soviet Union. It was a union with a history in the sense that it was comprised of occupational groups with histories of union activity going back to the turn of the century and both the 1905 and 1917 revolutions. The Bolshevik post-October drive to create large artificially unified "production" unions resulted in the merging of literally dozens of regional and occupational unions (shopkeepers, clerks, bookkeepers and commercial employees, zemstvo employees, government officials and the like) that had roots in either the prerevolutionary years or in 1917–18. The Bolsheviks had ridden white-collar support to important victories in a variety of grassroots institutions during the revolution, but there remained many non-Bolsheviks including neutrals, Mensheviks, and SRs in the vast white-collar army. The union on the eve of NEP was a mediator, an important institution that served to shape and control a large social force in ways that could never be accomplished by party, Komsomol, or vedomstvo (The first two were too elitist and the latter too limited in membership and hierarchical). The union brought together both commercial and bureaucratic employees (in the soviets and commissariats). At the end of the civil war and during the early NEP years, the union was the primary source of food, clothing, housing, and education as well as a wide range of cultural and recreational opportunities.

There were several important turning points for the union during the 1920s: the implementation of the New Economic Policy, the death of Lenin, the power struggles of the mid- and late 1920s, collectivization and industrialization and the beginnings of the new class war at the end of the twenties. It is instructive, for example, that in 1921 as NEP was declared, union leaders spoke of the need to shape a proletarian union out of the disparate social and occupational groups inherited from the lower-middle-strata revolutionary movement. They admitted in their executive sessions what rhetoric tried to hide, namely that not all by any means of

---

[22] M. Gegechkori, *Chto dolzhni znat' sovetskie i torgovye sluzhashchie o svoem soiuze* (Moscow, 1929).

their members were reconciled to the Revolution—and that NEP itself could work against adaptation to the revolution and construction of socialism. Union leaders noted a "psychological reaction" among white-collar workers to the advent of NEP, what they called an unhealthy and possibly quite dangerous tendency to "retreat," to "demobilize," to back away from production.[23] The union hastened to warn its members that NEP did not mean a change in mission, just in method. NEP remained a *proletarian* mission, with a proletarian goal, the economic reconstruction of the nation, and white-collar workers must strive to bring it into being even though the reappearance of private trade might result in the reappearance of exploitation. NEP, again according to Kalinin, was not just for production workers, but for office and shop personnel as well. It was clear to all that better wages and improvements in living standards depended on identification with the proletarian tasks (NEP). Union officials also commented on the swelling of the *apparat* during the civil war years, a situation that would be hard to rectify given the hidden social identities and agendas of so many individuals in the maelstrom of revolution. They also emphasized the potential freedoms of NEP—less regulation and less social leveling.

In September 1921, union leaders proclaimed the need to build the new socialist society by making NEP work, by helping the administration adjust to the new economic conditions. Radical *perestroika* was placed on the agenda, and this at first meant either deep staff cuts (staffs had indeed become bloated during the civil war) based on simple reductions to achieve economies or outright purges based on social and/or political criteria. In the early 1920s the union supported staff cuts. By 1924, the union began to advocate the fixing of tables of organization as a means of securing job permanence for its members. Fixed tables of organization would at least afford some protection against cost-cutting campaigns such as the Regime of Economy. This campaign mode of solving the "bureaucratic problem" would be extended to include rationalization (NOT),[24] the Regime of Economy, and transformation or revitalization of the (rural) soviets.[25]

The New Economic Policy brought special challenges, both in the workplace and in the larger society. The renaissance of a private sector called for a reassertion of the traditional union function of defending worker interests against employers. It was not just that capitalists, however petty, were once again doing business and therefore inevitably had to appear as

---

[23] *Golos rabotnika*, 1 September 1922.

[24] Nauchnaia Organizatsiia Truda.

[25] On these campaigns, see Davies, *From Tsarism to the New Economic Policy*; Orlovsky, "Anti-Bureaucratic Campaigns of the 1920's;" and Daniel Thorniley, *The Rise and Fall of the Soviet Rural Communist Party, 1927–39* (New York, 1988).

exploiters of wage labor. Union leaders considered managers in the state sector potential exploiters as well. The union again had to take up the fight for wages and benefits, better workplace conditions, workplace safety, and public health. It had to battle against administrative abuse as well as private-sector exploitation. In social terms, the Union had a massive cultural and educational mission. A wide array of skills were needed for the growing industrial economy, horizons had to be broadened, and thousands of people acculturated to life in the administrative archipelago of socialism. Even greater skills were needed to promote proletarianism, that is, to make sure that the white-collar constituency fit in to the emerging society, that its own already distinctive culture could blend in with that of blue-collar factory workers.

The Union of Soviet and Commercial Employees had approximately 570,000 members by 1921. By 1926 it would have about 1.2 million, but even then it would be a paper tiger. Commitment to the Bolshevik agenda was hardly a criterion for membership. The union had little money and a weak apparatus in the provinces and borderlands. Much of its energy in the first half of the 1920s went into building its organization and assuring its apparatus of operating funds. Its task was to become a union of "workers," of proletarians, which would be more difficult than for true blue-collar unions since it had members who did not necessarily produce anything, and "who only with difficulty had adjusted to or accepted the socialist revolution and who still fully did not understand its goals." Throughout the decade, the union was faced with the challenge of "drawing closer to the masses." In essence this meant the establishment of an effective factory- and office-level presence supported by local professional union activists. The union had to be capable of mobilizing its members (and indeed all employees) not only to insure support for union objectives, but also to head off embarrassing or politically damaging words or deeds that could be construed as unproletarian. This meant that it would have to seem open to the opinions and needs of its rank and file and at least promote an atmosphere or mythology of democracy in order to legitimize not only the union but the entire society-building enterprise of the proletarian state to its membership.

Union members came from all layers and occupations of the prerevolutionary white-collar and professional movements. A great number joined the movement in 1917. They helped build the unions, soviets, cooperatives, and an array of other "proletarian" institutions that helped bring the Bolsheviks to power.[26] Many others joined during the first two years of the civil war, when it was already clear that membership in the sanctioned organizations of the proletarian state was a safer and more

[26] See my forthcoming *Russia's Democratic Revolution*.

promising bet than indifference or opposition. Despite the influx of large numbers of new members during the revolution and civil war, the mid-1920s witnessed an even larger and more politically significant period of membership growth that involved younger postrevolutionary cadres new to the challenges of office work.

Maintenance of one large union was not just a product of post-October Bolshevik *gleichschaltung*. There was a degree of self-interest at work here among white-collar activists who had joined the party only recently, if at all. They knew that working within the framework of a single large "production" union, on a par with the other large production unions (metalworkers, printers, transport workers, textile workers) could best serve their career interests as well as the social and economic agendas of their diverse occupational groups. They had learned during the revolution and the civil war what it meant to scramble for scarce resources when divided into hundreds of weak occupational and regional unions. By nature, white-collar workers tended to a separatism that had to be controlled in the interests of all. Bank and financial employees for example, had always regarded themselves as a cut above the ordinary clerks and bookkeepers. To solidify its position in the new proletarian state, the union also had to grow, to absorb new categories of members, and new occupations. Union capital was its own growing labor force well dispersed in key institutions. Organized into a union this labor power could stand as a counterweight to the much distrusted economic managers (*khoziastvenniki*) and ministerial administrators. This, it was hoped, would mean a place at the table with the dominant production unions and the economic administration. It would remain to be seen, of course, whether the union could translate its influence into political clout with the party leadership. Thus the union was delighted to welcome into its ranks the so-called paramilitary personnel (OGPU, militia, prison staff, and the like). Other union concerns in the early NEP years were finances, the collection of dues, and cooperation with RKI and TsKK on rationalization schemes.[27] The message to the rank and file and to those outside the union alike was that white-collar workers were vital to the tasks at hand, economic reconstruction and rationalization, and that the union was the unifier of the "grandiose mass" in the ranks of the apparatus of the Soviet republic.

Another ubiquitous theme during the mid-1920s was democratization, which usually translated into the need to build an effective presence in the workplace through factory committees and other lower-level union organizations. For example, the union promoted the use of wall newspapers (*stengazety*) to raise the cultural level of members and to heighten

---

[27] Rabochaia-Krest'ianskaia Inspeksiia, or Rabkrin. Tsentral'naia Kontrol'naia Komissiia ([Party] Central Control Commission).

their participation and social consciousness (*aktivnost' i obshchestven-nost'*).[28] The union recognized that in the local committees shop (*tsekh*) interests might prevail over the general interest of the mass. *Stengazety* would help the union identify activists to counter "shopism" and to further union policies. With the onset of a faster-paced economic reconstruction in 1924, the union no longer saw itself as a passive bystander in the formulation of economic policy. It claimed to be a player, a force to be reckoned with by the enterprise managers and higher-level (trust) officials.

The union would work hard to retain its constituent groups—since numbers meant power, both political and economic. There were moves during the mid-twenties to separate the commercial employees, but the union held fast. It was only in 1931 that the party, having already swept away the union leadership, dismantled the union itself by breaking it into three smaller unions representing its major constituent occupational categories (government, commercial, and financial employees).

The union performed the ritual of lamentations at Lenin's death, and it is easy to see how union activists might have sincerely considered him a true friend of the white-collar worker. Lenin, after all, had treated this group as a potential ally in 1917. He had understood that there could be no Soviet state without them. Lenin might have attacked bureaucracy and bureaucrats, but he was careful not to implicate employees as a class. They in turn would refer frequently throughout the 1920s to a letter he sent in November 1922 to the All-Union Congress of Trade Unions praising white-collar workers. Lenin asked them to join the crusade against bureaucracy and to work for simplification of the apparat. These became standard union campaign slogans throughout the 1920s.[29]

For union activists and rank and file alike, declining real wages seemed to be a more pressing issue than Lenin's untimely end (the union wanted stabilization of the *chervonets* ruble—the monetary unit adopted in 1922 as equivalent of ten gold rubbles—and monthly pay adjustments). In 1924, the union went on a campaign against overtime. There were many abuses by administration and economic managers—and these were emblazoned across the pages of the union press. Abuses of overtime, for example, allowed crafty economic managers to blackmail or otherwise harass employees to put in longer hours. The often unstated threat was that refusing overtime could mean dismissal. Furthermore, some higher-level white-collar workers saw overtime as an entitlement, a salary supplement equivalent to the piece rates earned by factory workers.[30] Labor turnover or instability (*tekuchest'*) was also was a problem, especially in

---

[28] *Golos rabotnika*, 15 January 1924.
[29] This was part of the sanctification of the discourse of antibureaucracy.
[30] *Golos rabotnika*, 15 January 1924.

the more skilled occupations. The notion of a free labor market went against state policy and union interests. High unemployment rates throughout the mid-1920s resulted in a variety of schemes to offer some financial aid and retraining to those out of work, and to shore up the labor exchanges.[31] Union leaders were concerned that managers were filling vacancies outside the labor-exchange framework, that is, by hiring new migrants from the provinces rather than from the ranks of local unemployed white-collar workers. For white-collar workers, NEP in practice sometimes meant the reappearance of the long-hated and festering workplace conditions of the decades leading up to 1917.[32] Long hours, lack of vacation or rest time, horrendous workplace and living conditions, low wages, patriarchal and authoritarian managers—all these reappeared during the "halcyon" days of NEP. There was a danger that employees would lose what they had won in the revolutions of 1917 and afterward—their sense of empowerment, their organizational strength, their sense of participation in the proletarian movement and its state, of being among the "ins" of the new society rather than the "outs." The union lustily joined the anti- NEP crusade of 1924–25, publishing articles and editorials with such titles as "Dirty Dealers of the NEP World" and "NEP Gangrene." The union and employees were in the forefront of the battle to defeat the market. The union urged the state and the state-sponsored cooperatives (and their employees) to take wholesale trade away from the private sector. They were also to assist in the rationalization and simplification of the commercial apparatus and in the various campaigns for quality in production and service alike.[33] The commercial sector was particularly nettlesome for the union because it was particularly prone to breakdown, corruption, inefficiency, and worker abuse.

There was also a need to differentiate the white-collar workers from the more highly educated specialists, who were usually in positions of authority over white-collar workers. Here the state and the union were in a bind. White-collar workers resented the higher wages paid to specialists. Yet the wage differentials had been sanctioned by Lenin himself. The economic organs (acting as an interest group) wished to maintain higher wages for specialists, some of whom were members of the Union of Soviet and Commercial Employees. Here the union argued that the state must gain a better handle on its human (i.e., specialist) resources via more accurate censuses and verifications of educational qualifications, skill levels, and actual work performed. The union also opposed *sovmestitel'stvo* or

---

[31] Unemployment among union members peaked in April 1927 at 278,000, up from 180,000 the previous October.

[32] These are well described in A. M. Gudvan, *Ocherki po istorii dvizheniia sluzhashchikh v Rossii*, part 1, *Do revoliutsii 1905 goda* (Moscow, 1925).

[33] *Golos rabotnika*, 15 January 1924.

the holding of more than one position.[34] Evidently, specialists received unfair advantages from management from the white-collar point of view.[35]

The union never lost an opportunity to attack market or "spontaneous" (*stikhiinyi*) forces. These were the enemy of not only white-collar workers but also of the *smychka* or the necessary union of town and countryside, worker and peasant. These forces had spilled over into the apparatus and were a primary cause of bureaucratic dysfunction. As early as 1924, for example, the union press attacked the "petty bourgeois NEP spontaneity that has exploited the weaknesses in our apparatus."

Wages were always important. A review of wages in 1922–23 showed that the average wage for the entire union was up (by the end of 1923) 196.1 percent of the Gosplan index. There were, however, rather large differentials by sector. State Bank employees' wages were up 343.3 percent, for example, whereas militia wages had increased by only 71.2 percent.[36] The union was active in pushing for collective wage agreements, in part to promote white-collar interests, but also as a means of combating the ever present tendency to fragmentation. Such agreements furthermore, provided something of a raison d'etre for union officialdom, another means of asserting their legitimacy among the economic managers and state bureaucrats.

By 1927, the union was fully supporting the Stalin line in high politics without fully realizing what this might mean if the new militancy should trickle down to confront their own operations. Indeed, it had publicly attacked the Left and United Oppositions and Trotsky in particular in its press and in its congresses during the crucial years of the mid-1920s. And the party had responded with kind words at the Fourteenth and Fifteenth Party Congresses. Employees had come a long way, the party admitted, in their journey into the proletariat. But by 1927 there were ominous signs on the horizon. Once again the economic situation was deteriorating as was the well-being of white-collar workers. With some 213,000 unemployed and NEP legislation that permitted factory and office managers to hire outside the labor exchanges, the rank and file had a new set of grievances. Union leaders noted the rise in peasant migrants to the cities and peasants in the countryside who were taking up posts in the village soviets and militia. This satis-

---

[34] Ibid.

[35] The need for accurate counts of qualified personnel was a constant theme of the 1920s. And indeed many state and party institutions conducted censuses of engineers and other specialists. These included the Commissariat of Labor, Rabkrin, the various unions, and other institutions.

[36] *Golos rabotnika*, 31 January 1924. Wages for administrative employees in the soviets were up 148.2 percent, economic sector employees 209.1 percent, and cooperatives 217.7 percent.

fied the leadership's desire to bring in fresh cadres, new recruits to the white-collar social formation. Yet it also raised a new round of cultural questions, including the most important question of how to turn these new cadres into proletarians.

Cultural Transformation

A wide range of issues fell under the rubric of culture. Union leaders were always concerned with the literacy and skill levels of old and new white-collar workers. The union's cultural work was carried on largely in employees' clubs. These were organized to provide something of the feeling of extended family as well as support in the form of child care, intellectual edification (lectures, courses, and the like), transmission of high culture (plays, music, literature), organization of group vacations, and sports. The union was very concerned with raising the cultural level of employees so that they might become *obshchestvenniki*, or politically conscious and active *participants* in the production process and union work and accepted members of the proletarian commonweal.[37] Sometimes the solutions proposed were naive. In the late 1920s, for example, the cultural department of the union organization for the province of Moscow issued a slender volume on the occasion of "book day." The goal was to help the member plan her or his winter reading, since "our 'mass' reader (ordinary clerks, typists, shop personnel, militia, and so on) still has not learned to read according to plan" (the appendix listed more serious books for more advanced readers in higher white-collar occupations).[38] For the masses, cultural officials placed a premium on what was striking and colorful as well as capable of capturing the interest of resistant readers. Similarly, in the mid-1920s the union exhorted its activist cadres to bring employees home to dinner to impress them with the culture of more advanced and conscious households. Education was a prime concern. Although it is true that the employees themselves had rather low levels of education, most often no more than several years of primary school, they had rather high aspirations for their children.[39] The trade union of white-collar workers was the main conduit of youth into institutions of higher education during the Soviet 1920s. The Soviet state turned primarily to the offspring of white and not blue-collar workers for this privilege, and

---

[37] At one point in 1929 a union leader equated the terms "bureaucrat" and *neobshchestvennik* (antisocial element).

[38] *Chto chitat' sovtorgsluzhashchemy* (Moscow, 1928).

[39] See the union congress registration cards (*ankety*) for delegates to the various Union of Soviet and Commercial Employees All-Union congresses for the 1920s in TsGAOR, f. 5468, op. 10.

the union had considerable influence in these admissions decisions.[40] During the 1923–24 academic year for example, 34.9 percent of the 53,400 students in higher technical institutes came from employee backgrounds as opposed to only 17.5 percent from worker backgrounds and 16 percent from peasant. Fully 30.8 percent of these students were drawn from the nebulous "other" category.[41] It is odd that despite all calls for "affirmative action" during the 1920s, the pattern of educational recruitment that gave preference to white-collar children was barely disturbed until the great turn at the end of the twenties. Still, access to higher education may be viewed as a good indicator of just how far the party-state was willing to go in joining the white- and blue-collar workers into a single proletariat. As in the case of wages and other benefits, education was a source of friction between the two social groups.

At issue at the Seventh All-Union Trade Union Congress was the destruction of the traditional commercial culture of the sales clerk. According to union activists, the marketplace role of the sales clerk as the essential helpmates of the consumer had been destroyed when they were transformed into bureaucrats (*chinovniki*) by the statization and elimination of the market on the one hand and the economics of extreme scarcity on the other. "Instead of being mediators between consumer and goods, and entering into the process of consumer choice, they are reduced

---

[40] In Moscow 1926 figures show that grades 7, 8, and 9 had 56.81, 68.54, and 68.02 percent of white-collar offspring among the student body with only 27.15, 17.50, and 18.61 percent coming from the "working class." In the entire Russian Republic (1926–27) the white-collar figures for the same grades were 40.5, 46.2, and 45.9 percent, for workers 21.5, 16.0, and 15.0 percent, for peasants 21.5, 18.3, and 19.6 percent (signifying the high degree of peasant mobility into the employee category), and "other" a very large 16.5, 19.5, and 19.5 percent, which indicates a great deal of masking. See TsGIA (RSFSR), f. 1575, op. 6, d. 244, l.1, and *Narodnoe prosveshenie*, May 1929, pp. 71, 73, both quoted by Larry Holmes in his paper, "With Just Cause? Komsomol's Critique of Narkompros and School Policy, 1919–1928," presented at the annual AHA meeting, Chicago, 1991. The entire subject of education in the 1920s is treated masterfully in Larry E. Holmes, *The Kremlin and the Schoolhouse: Reforming Education in Soviet Russia, 1917–1931* (Bloomington, Ind., 1991). Important information on the social backgrounds of prerevolutionary students and their corporate characteristics is contained in Samuel D. Kassow, *Students, Professors and the State in Tsarist Russia* (Berkeley and Los Angeles, 1989). See also S. Zhaba, *Petrogradskoe studenchestvo v bor'be za svobodnuiu vysshuiu shkolu* (Paris, 1922), and T. I. Til', "Sotsial-demokratisheskoe dvizhenie molodozhi 1920-kh godov," in *Pamiat': Istoricheskii sbornik*, 3d ed. (Paris, 1980), pp. 165–283.

[41] Nicholas Lampert, *The Soviet Technical Intelligentsia and the Soviet State* (New York, 1979), p. 70. Lampert claims that most ITR personnel had employee backgrounds as did most chief engineers during the 1920s and on into the 1930s. On technical education in general and the question of social mobility, see Sheila Fitzpatrick, *Education and Social Mobility in the USSR 1921–1934* (Cambridge, 1979). In support of my view, Catherine Merridale has documented in her study of the Moscow Party organization the fact that *vydvizhenie* (she translates this as "promotion") was not working as planned during the early and mid 1920s. The numbers were small, the blue-collar workers resisted promotion, and the host institutions were inhospitable. Merridale, *Moscow Politics*, pp. 192–98.

to authorities in a bureaucratized distribution system. They can only say, yes we have it, no we don't. Either take it or get out—the customers stand in line and we have become bureaucrats." Many an old veteran of the long union movement bemoaned this reduction in status from *prikaz-shchik* (shop assistant) to *chinovnik* and the harsh working conditions of the state commercial enterprises and even of the co-ops of the 1920s.[42]

Another example would be the NOT movement and its utopian drive to rationalize Soviet institutions and bureaucratic practice.[43] Here the ideal was the assembly line, the mechanization and routinization of office work. But this was the assembly line in the Soviet context, with goals and means somewhat different from Henry Ford's automobile factories. One of NOT's chief theoreticians and propagandists, E. Rozmirovich, put it this way: "The goal of the party is to bring the masses into the state administration. This means workers and peasants. The peasants, especially, are culturally unfit and unsuited for office work. We will not try to alter their culture, rather we will eliminate by means of mechanization and routinization, the agency of human will in administrative work. At that point peasant culture will not stand in the way."[44] It won't matter any more.

Social Composition and the Power of Youth: A New Look at *Vydvizhenie*

The union's experience with the promotion of workers from the bench into white-collar jobs calls for another look at patterns of social development and social mobility in the 1920s, especially at what may be called "affirmative action" or what is sometimes termed "pushing up" or "promoting" (*vydvizhenie*). Western scholars first learned of this phenomenon through the pioneering work of Sheila Fitzpatrick. The white-collar experience requires some modifications in the argument that the Russian Revolution at least from 1917 to 1929 was in large part the story of the social mobility of workers (by implication largely blue-collar) from the workbench into administration. First, forced affirmative action (as opposed to recommended affirmative action, as opposed to the Lenin Levy and the lip service paid to Lenin's own idealized version of bringing the

---

[42] *Sed'moi s"ezd professional'nykh soiuzov SSSR (6–18 dekabria 1926 g.): Plenum i sektsii: Polnyi stenograficheskii otchet* (Moscow, 1927), p. 464.

[43] See Marc R. Beissinger, *Scientific Management, Socialist Discipline, and Soviet Power* (Cambridge, Mass., 1988), and E. A. Rees, *State Control in Soviet Russia: The Rise and Fall of the Workers' and Peasants' Inspectorate, 1920–34* (London, 1987).

[44] Taken from Rozmirovich's lead article in the first issue of *Tekhnika upravleniia* (Moscow, 1925).

masses into administration) was not the party's goal until the very end of
the 1920s and even then the mission was poorly understood and even
more poorly carried out. I take issue with the blue-collar to managerial
class interpretation of the Russian Revolution, at least as applied to the
1920s. It misses the social dynamics because such a view adopts wholesale
the categories of Soviet propaganda and historiography (the division of
society into workers and peasants and employees). The revolutions of
1917 were plebeian revolutions, but the historiography has not been careful to define those plebeians. My material drawn from the union congress
registration cards (*ankety*) of 1919–1930 and the other materials pertaining to the union central committee and congresses show a white-collar to
white-collar mobility and a peasant to white-collar mobility that reproduced the structure of the earlier revolution of the lower middle strata
from 1905 to 1917 (including white-collar domination of access to education) during the 1920s and the impermeability of the social borders
between white- and blue-collar workers.[45] Factory workers did not want
to become clerks and vice versa. There seems to have been little mobility
for the rank and file white-collar employees upward into managerial
ranks, though this certainly must have been possible for the relatively
small numbers who took up the majority of spaces in the Soviet institutions of higher and technical education during the 1920s. The 1927 union
congress is full of material (repeated again in 1929) about the failures of
affirmative action through indifference, the hostility of managers and
workers alike, sabotage on the office floor, lack of care in selecting prospects, and absolute lack of follow-up counseling and other forms of aid.
There was however, a concerted effort by union activists to implement
affirmative action for white-collar workers themselves. There were strong
feelings that looking to workers from the bench was a big mistake when
competent potential administrators could be found among the white-
collar rank and file. As late as October 1931, the Commissariat of Labor
(NKTrud) asked Sovnarkom to improve the economic and working conditions of the promoted. At issue were laws that took away certain worker
entitlements from individuals who had been promoted and away from the
bench for one year or more. NKTrud asked that such workers be guaranteed the supply rights of workers of the category from which they had
been promoted. These workers were also to be allowed access to certain
supply institutions reserved to the working class for as long as they remained in service in the apparatus.[46]

The union and the state had to fight the apolitical nature of the employ-

---

[45] Material taken from union congress records, TsGAOR, f. 5468, op. 10, d. 17, and
especially, the *ankety* for 1921, 1927, and 1929.

[46] TsGAOR, f. 5515, op. 1, d. 278, l. 37.

ees at all times. They didn't want to engage in cultural work or campaigns. Their excellent journal, *Golos rabotnika* (Voice of the Functionary) until 1926, and from 1926 on their daily newspaper, Nasha gazeta (Our newspaper) were miserably undersubscribed. *Nasha gazeta* had 120,000 subscribers; *Gudok*, the paper of the transportation union, had 480,000. Union leaders always feared being outflanked or overtaken by other institutions such as the Komsomol, with its own newspaper and capacity for high-profile, ideologically correct interventions in the murky waters of public opinion.

By the mid twenties the ankety reveal a wholesale turnover in leading trade union personnel at all levels, but particularly in the provinces. The typical social profile of congress delegates, who were almost always union officeholders and activists, reveals that they were the offspring of white-collar families and had no more than an elementary education. Delegates to the Fifth All-Union Congress of the Union of Soviet and Commercial Employees in 1922, a group that might still be regarded as transitional, reflected the mixed prerevolutionary and revolutionary composition of union membership. Of the 219 delegates, 10 percent had been in the union (its antecedents) in 1905 with another 22.8 percent having joined in 1906–16 and 34.3 percent in 1917. The remaining 32.5 percent had come in between 1917 and 1921. A whopping 43 percent were active in union work before 1918. Sixty-three percent of the delegates claimed "individuals of mental labor" as their category of social origin with another 12.3 percent claiming the provenance of shop personnel. Only 18.3 percent claimed any hereditary connection to the world of physical labor.[47] The parents of the majority of these individuals were low-level clerks and functionaries. The majority of delegates themselves had no more than a primary education, and though almost 80 percent belonged to the Bolshevik Party, the vast majority of these had joined only after the October Revolution.

Only four years later, however, the pre-October cohort had all but disappeared. By 1926–27 these activists were almost exclusively the children of the October Revolution. That is, they were too young to have been in the events of 1917 and usually joined the union or the party in the early 1920s. Their ankety show educational and social profiles roughly similar to those of the 1922 cohort, though there are more instances of workers or worker offspring entering the white-collar work force. Yet the delegates comprise an entirely new group that reflected the regime's desire to integrate women and the nationalities. There was also an increase in the number of delegates with party or Komsomol membership. This mid-

[47] *Golos rabotnika*, 15 January 1923.

to late 1920s collection of union activists represented nothing less than a turn to youth and a turnover in union officialdom from the early twenties when there were still many white-collar activists and union members who had experienced the struggles of 1905 and 1917. In this sense the cultural revolution of 1928–31 had already taken place during the middle years of the decade, during the apogee of NEP, amid the obscure yet massive social group of white-collar workers. This youth culture in the union prevailed during the 1920s and apparently provided a large cohort of employees and union officials who would actively support Stalin's agenda. Still, the nature of their occupations, concerns, and workplace culture seems to have carried over from the earlier period. A summary of statistics for delegates to the union's 1927 congress revealed that only 29 percent of the delegates were party members (though another 9 percent were candidates and 8 percent belonged to the Komsomol). Thirty-seven percent of the delegates were between twenty and thirty (which means of course that at the time of the October Revolution they were between ten and twenty). Fifty-six percent of the delegates claimed an "employee" social origin (as compared to 18 percent who declared themselves to be workers) and, tellingly, only 34 percent were Russian. Jews and Tatars numbered 21 percent and 11 percent of the delegates respectively. A full 45 percent of the delegates had completed primary educations. Only 1 percent of these individuals had entered the union or its predecessors between 1905 and 1917. The figure for 1917 was 18 percent. Another 22 percent entered during the years 1918–20. The largest group of experienced union activists, 35 percent, had joined the union during the years of the New Economic Policy.[48] At the 1927 congress Figatner claimed that total union membership had reached 1,217,315, including 226,780 unemployed.[49] Figatner applauded the influx of new people and proclaimed the need to reach out to youth and "renew" the union even further through generational change. Figatner also made a point of answering the charge that the union harbored a public menace in the form of old chinovniki who had been hiding out in the state administration. He cited figures to show that by 1927 this was far from the case and that the union again had worked to channel youth into the Soviet bureaucracy.

The idea of the state against itself popularized by G. Rittersporn was already visible during the civil war, but certainly blossomed during NEP. One could see this in the competition among commissariats and the unique role of Rabkrin. But these were the kinds of conflicts that white-collar workers as a social group were able to transcend by playing on all sides of such conflicts. They were also present in all other trade unions

[48] TsGAOR, f. 5468, op. 10, d. 17.
[49] TsGAOR, f. 5468, op. 10, d. 17.

(including industrial ones and in such large organizations as the transport and education workers' unions). The 1920s spawned a fetishism of *uchet* or counting human resources, a need to identify and fix in place scarce human resources and a need to unmask illegitimate social categories. But this unmasking could not go too far, because all institutions as political players were implicated in the protection of their human capital. The Union of Soviet and Commercial Employees, for example, had its own section of specialists and economists as did all the other production unions. This dispersal of the professionals and specialists was to be sure part of a deliberate strategy on the part of the regime to divide this potentially nettlesome group and prevent the re-creation and growth of traditional professional unions and organizations. Numerous official institutions (TsSU, the party, the Commissariat of Labor, the VMBIT, and the like)[50] frequently attempted to count these specialists in the 1920s and early 1930s.

As further evidence of the state against itself, the party leadership launched a massive antibureaucratic campaign after 1926 linked to the Fifteenth Party Congress's resolution to rationalize economic planning.

White-Collar Workers and the Soviet Experience

The roots of both the highly stratified classical Soviet society organized by occupational niches and today's emerging civil society go back to the layered social order of the 1905–17 period that witnessed the creation of new occupational groups, including the free and proto-professions and the rising lower middle strata.[51] Occupation was unusually important in this layered social order between the revolutions.[52] Also unusual was the weakness in this society relative to Western societies of the connection of occupational groups and professionals to the means of production or the market as opposed to bureaucratic organizations as a source of status and power. In the West, capitalism created the office and the need for masses of white-collar workers (and rather rapidly the feminization of that kind

---

[50] VMBIT is the Russian acronym for All-Union Interagency Bureau of Engineers and Technical Personnel.

[51] See Moshe Lewin's brilliant analysis of the recent Soviet social pattern and its antecedents in *The Gorbachev Phenomenon* (Berkeley and Los Angeles, 1988).

[52] For a suggestive discussion of the importance of occupation in the context of Weimar Germany, see Thomas Childers, "The Social Language of Politics in Germany: The Sociology of Political Discourse in the Weimar Republic," *American Historical Review* 95 (April 1990): 331–58. See also Harold Perkin, *The Rise of Professional Society: England since 1880* (London, 1989). On the issue of gender and the feminization of clerical work in the United States, see Lisa M. Fine, *The Souls of the Skyscraper: Female Clerical Workers in Chicago, 1870–1930* (Philadelphia, 1990).

of work). In Russia, there was a deeply rooted white-collar presence in the traditional economic and political power structures. In Russia and especially in the Soviet Union, the bureaucracy and office created large-scale industrial and agricultural enterprises. The Russian culture of the "free professions" was also unusual. For the white-collar workers the revolutionary era 1905–30 began in ambiguity (in social identity) and ended with it in the so-called Stalin revolution of 1928–29. Along the way they were active participants (or determinants) in revolutionary state building. Their participation in the revolutionary process contained a paradox. On the one hand, as a social group they were fragmented and disunited, a variety of unions and groupings organized on occupational and regional lines. In many instances and from many perspectives they were even hidden from view by the language (discourse) of the revolution—as proletarians or as peasants. They could be bureaucrats even while speaking the language of antibureaucracy. They could be proletarians even while maintaining a distinct culture and competing with the factory proletariat for scarce resources, wages, and the like. And they could be peasants even if they had long since left the fields for service in the Red Army, cooperatives, or village offices. On the other hand their combined skills and activism gave them a collective weight, a capacity for social pressure. This can only be understood by disregarding traditional Soviet categories and studying their relations with the state, mediating institutions, and other social groups. White-collar workers claimed, "we come into contact with people, we are mediators, we don't work with objects or produce them, we have a higher cultural level, higher literacy rates. Yet we need to transform our mental laborers into members of the commonweal or social activists [*obshchestvenniki*]." The Union of Soviet and Commercial Employees thus brought together many of these individuals who came into direct contact with the population at the grassroots level. The members were among the chief mediators between the new proletarian state and its social constituencies and not producers in the sense of factory workers or peasants. To the extent that the marketplace was to be replaced by socialism, white-collar workers of all varieties could only experience growth in their mediating role and pressures toward institutionalizing those roles in bureaucratic frameworks. Commercial employees in the cooperatives and the growing state sector had every reason to wish to wrest commerce from the hands of the new NEP "bourgeoisie." NEP provided these employees with a new kind of exploiter in private enterprise—a new kind of social being to define themselves against—employers who reenacted the role of the hated shop owners of the 1905–17 period. It was much harder to focus on the state as exploiter as its bureaucratic anonymity presented the typical shop employee with a less clearly defined target (and after all, the state was ostensibly a "proletarian" state).

The history of organized white-collar labor in 1917 and as far back as the 1905 Revolution weighed heavily on the early Soviet experience of the white-collar workers. At those key historical conjunctures organized white-collar workers, including shop personnel, post and telegraph employees, railroad and pharmacy employees, and so on, were instrumental in the development of the larger working-class movement and in its political victories. Throughout the revolutionary era of 1905 to 1930, then, the alliance (troubled and ambiguous as it was) between blue- and white-collar workers (and other members of the lower middle strata) formed something of a second *smychka*, a little noticed, but potent union parallel to the more celebrated and troubled union of workers and peasants. Looked at another way, in its attempt to assimilate other social formations and become "universal," the proletarian state found it no easier to assimilate the white-collar workers so necessary to its existence than to absorb the numerous non-Russian nationalities into a new Soviet national identity.

Still, by the end of the 1920s white-collar workers had still not overcome even their own internal differences. Gegechkori's agitational pamphlet mentioned earlier reaffirms this point. He admitted that many had disputed the unification of commercial and soviet administrative employees in one union. Commercial employees had argued that they alone were the true proletarians, not the administrative types, no matter how low their position in the hierarchy. Gegechkori answered by invoking the production principle. For him, commerce was now part of the state structure and thus there was no contradiction. Gegechkori also pointed out that white-collar workers needed membership in a strong and large union if they were to enter the proletariat. This kind of ongoing white-collar fragmentation could only make more difficult the absorption of the entire white-collar group into a reconstituted proletariat. The union, he warned, was in danger of taking in "petty bourgeois" urban intellectuals, professionals, artisans, Nepmen, and the like, who understood that membership conferred proletarian status. He also pointed out that 500,000 union members of "peasant mentality" were fresh from the villages. Gegechkori warned that now above all was not the time for white-collar workers to adopt an apolitical stance (*apolitichnost'*).[53]

The experience of white-collar workers in the 1920s raises serious questions about our interpretations of NEP. For those who would otherwise idealize this period, the white-collar experience provides some bedrock of social reality (the life experiences of a significant number of people engaged in crucial occupations) against which we may measure the claims to viability for the NEP system. White-collar workers saw NEP was tem-

---

[53] All taken from Gegechkori's pamphlet published in Moscow, 1929.

porary, deeply threatening, and incapable of providing either the material security promised by the revolution or the status commensurate with the importance of occupational roles. The October Revolution did not end class conflict, and the proclamation of a proletarian society should not blind us to the fragmented and conflict-ridden social reality of the NEP period. For the white-collar rank and file, NEP brought unemployment, increasing marginality, uncertainty, and out of this uncertainty a constant pressure to prove one's loyalty to the proletariat and its agendas. NEP represented "spontaneity," the hated and feared forces of *stikhiia* as symbolized by the market. Consciousness and control were dominant themes of white-collar politics during the 1920s. All the antibureaucratic campaigning of the 1920s was a mask. There was a tremendous social pressure to increase bureaucracy since more bureaucracy really meant more security, status, and power for the employees, and for middle- and lower-level officials already in the state apparatus.[54] No wonder then about the appeal of the Stalin version of full employment with its great crusades and campaigns to industrialize and collectivize agriculture—all of them to be administered in "command-bureaucratic fashion," all requiring massive increases in clerical and commercial functionaries. The union materials of 1930 and 1931 reveal not just slavish devotion to the Stalin project, but also genuine faith in it, the sort of faith that Germany and the West had in those who promised them full employment in the wake of the Depression. Indeed, Stalin's recovery project preceded recovery in the West, which enabled the party-state apparatus to say, "Look what we provided for our employees when Western economies were still in shambles." During the 1920s public identification of white-collar workers and their organizations with the proletarian project (*zadachi*) diverted attention from many smaller class and occupational conflicts between white-collar and blue-collar workers over scarce resources, and between both groups and the specialists (technical intelligentsia and engineers) and the even more threatening economic managers (*khoziaistvenniki*). This latter conflict spilled over into an opposition between wage labor and ministerial bureaucrats in their role as employers.

The 1920s brought new challenges and new meanings to trade unionism. The trade union controversy in 1919–20 had resulted in a victory for Lenin's middle-ground approach both that avoided the democracy of the Workers' Opposition and Trotsky's vision of militarized labor. Lenin's thinking appears to have been similar to his naive ruminations on the

---

[54] This is the argument, from a somewhat different angle, in Don K. Rowney, *Transition to Technocracy: The Structural Origins of the Soviet Administrative State* (Ithaca, N.Y., 1989). Rowney sees a continuity in the takeover of the new Soviet apparatus by the technical intelligentsia and specialists and other lower-order types during the course of the early twentieth century.

nature of bureaucracy and the efficacy of popular control as a mechanism for overcoming bureaucratic dysfunctions. Lenin somehow believed that the large bureaucratic production unions could perform the functions of defending and educating workers within a noncapitalist framework. He believed that they could be both soviet and democratic, that they could be subject to party-state discipline and still avoid the dead hand of bureaucratization, that the stifling of spontaneity would still produce consciousness. When the dust settled, the unions were to act as educators and as protectors of labor against NEP private enterprise and even against the ministerial bureaucracy and industrial and commercial establishments. The unions provided access to education, to scarce goods, including food and clothing, to apartments to spots in vacation resorts and sanatoria, and to culture in the form of books, theater, music, and the rich life of the union clubs. In this the unions were taking over some of the traditional functions of the market, but more telling for the Russian context, the ministerial bureaucracy itself. This would be a major source of friction between the "state" and its constituent parts (once again, the state against itself) throughout the 1920s.

The unions were faced in the 1920s with the unprecedented challenge of maintaining and forging new links with their mass base. The fixation on mammoth production unions (even where such a concept was awkward at best as among white-collar, education, and medical workers, and so on) was related precisely to the fear of layering and disunity (the weakness of class) and social fragmentation in the emerging revolutionary society. The unions were to educate, to help conduct the Leninist cultural revolution in the mechanical anti-Bogdanov sense and to train the masses for low-level, low-status jobs in the new Soviet apparatus. How to promote the new way of life (*byt'*) was a problem, and the union mobilized grassroots field correspondents (*rabkory*) and used stengazety with the aim of "instilling social consciousness" and building a union apparatus that was intertwined with the lives of ordinary functionaries. Union leaders realized that paper pushing and formal contacts were not enough, though it was not clear just how the visits to activist households might move the agenda of cultural transformation forward. As shown earlier, the union was preoccupied with wage policy, antibureaucracy, and how to curb excesses and abuses rampant in the far-flung state and commercial institutions of Soviet Russia. In the case of white-collar workers this meant union responsiveness to large numbers of new white-collar youth, some of whom were drawn from peasant ranks, as had always been the case in the earlier decades of the twentieth century. How to fit the old white-collar culture into a new emerging proletarian culture when the former was being swamped with obyvateli and peasants and the latter was largely a myth was a great problem for the union. Resourcefulness (*gibkost'*) was the order of the day, in 1921 as in 1929. Union leaders constantly spoke of the need for shrewdness and flexibility in linking white-collar interests to those of the proletarian state and the working class as a whole.[55]

The white-collar experience raises the issue of contamination of the working-class state and the possibility that such contamination resulted in a form of socialist corporativism. Since such a large and important percentage of the new Soviet state was white-collar and since the factory proletariat was small and in the process of reconstitution during the 1920s, social contamination of the proletarian state meant that a set of vital occupations were locked into place and their disparate social occupants organized as a substitute for class. White-collar positions were filled by increasing numbers of youth, women, the offspring of the previous generation of white-collar workers and peasants. These varied social groups could not overcome gender, status, ethnic, and national differences to live up to the pure proletarian ideal. Apart from the shop personnel, it seems that the Soviet case did not produce a feminization of clerical work, despite the influx of women into the apparatus. Office positions were too important a source of livelihood for males, and they would never recede from the office as happened in the United States, for example. As in the case of fascism, the state attempted to impose a universal set of social and cultural norms on diverse social groups and interests. The field of conflict was defined by cultural norms and enforced by the wielders of political power. The lower middle classes and intellectuals and professionals along with their associational monopolies (trade union syndicates, professional organizations, and the like) became the vital mediators and social cement of these universalizing utopias. White-collar workers were vital to this project in a double sense. They were the necessary nonproductive but facilitating mediators of industrial society and the modern bureaucratic state. They were also a large and potentially organizable political force that had to be moved in from the margins and made to coalesce with the dominant mythologies and cultural norms of the regime. This could take the form of attachment to class or to state as universal or to both. Society in this case was able to penetrate and take over the state and impose its own value system. This was a bureaucratic value system more than it was proletarian in any Marxist or even Leninist sense. From the beginning the vedomstvo or bureaucratic institution was paramount in the mobilization of social power. As was often the case in earlier Russian and Muscovite history, the dynamism of this kind of social formation inevitably shaped emerging blue-collar consciousness. Factory workers had to define themselves against bureaucrats rather than against

[55] TsGAOR, f. 5468, op 12, d. 2, l. 196.

the bourgeoisie. White-collar social power fought on several fronts during the 1920s—both for and against the bureaucracy of which they were a part. For example, antibureaucratic campaigns were a fixture of the 1920s. These attempts to mobilize public opinion (usually defined as mass opinion, or obshchestvennost') were meant to signal solidarity as much as fix the perennial bureaucratic problem. White-collar workers were arrayed on both sides of the issue as the problem and the cure. On the one hand, they had to defend themselves through the union against workplace abuses such as overtime (which undercut the eight hour day, which was regarded as one of the major triumphs of the February Revolution). On the other hand, they had to promote the regime of economy, which always meant cuts in permanent staff (the *shtat*). Ironically, the emergence of a full-blown *nomenklatura* system in 1925 was a form of protection for white-collar functionaries. It meant a fixing in place of social currency that had become debased during campaigns and an end to arbitrary reductions in staff. It was a means of controlling if not eliminating the bureaucratic wars of the 1920s which always produced white-collar casualties. By the same token, the union chose to fight constantly against what it regarded as a major problem during the twenties, that of labor mobility or turnover. Though one might argue that for all the uncertainties of the 1920s the white-collar workers did very well (in relation to other social groups), the campaign mode, the filling of the air with charges and countercharges, the rising public consciousness of at least the possibility if not reality of white-collar corruption, bureaucratic incompetence, blockage of desired political and economic initiatives, the attempt to mobilize a public opinion against the bureaucrat, whoever he or she may be—all of this left an indelible imprint on the emerging Soviet political consciousness, and all of it formed a convenient starting point for the antibureaucratic, quasi-populist campaigns of the 1930s (such as the purges). There was an irony here too in that the irrationality and pressure of the antibureaucratic campaigns only made employees less secure and more prone to accept the security offered by the Stalin program. In fact, it is not too far-fetched to see them as willing partners in the formulation of such a program.

Soviet history and the history of the Soviet working class run against the grain of historical language in that class formation and the proletariat were conceived of as the inevitable products of industrial or capitalist societies and market economies. The formation of a proletarian class was to have taken place in the crucible of capitalism. The social reality and ideal of a proletariat was meant to be defined in relation to market institutions. The Soviet case is different. As a result of the October Revolution and the antimarket ideologies and practices of War Communism, the proletariat indeed came to power (in the form of the Bolshevik Party and the supporting institutions of plebeian democracy), but by the onset of NEP in 1921, no longer had a "bourgeoisie" or a "market" against which to define themselves. To be sure both existed in limited forms, but they were on the outside and never powerful enough to attain hegemony. So, the shattered working class of the civil war era had to reconstitute itself in a radically new historical context, surrounded and nurtured by a set of state economic and political institutions that acted as the primary employer of skilled white- and blue-collar labor. Enter the white-collar workers. Because of the revolutionary ideology of proletarianism and because of their own proletarian-oriented prerevolutionary history, and most of all because of their skills and their obvious importance to any industrial institutions, they had to become proletarian or part of a newly reconstituted proletariat. Yet what is equally important here (for the notion of class formation) is the structural component of the new state sector. The state sector under War Communism strove for its own brand of universalism, for the abolition of the market. This tendency did not disappear under NEP. It was not even muted. The trusts and Vesenkha (Supreme Council of the National Economy) could hardly be said to have represented private enterprise, and the same is more obviously true of the ministries. Thus from the beginning of the 1920s social and occupational groups could only be formed within this enlarged and growing state sector. Ambiguity resulted. The proletariat was forced to consider as a part of itself the white-collar workers and vice versa. Patterns of social development and consciousness were placed on rails. In other words a structure was set up during the revolution and civil war in which the working class, by virtue of its symbiotic relationship with employees, could only grow in tandem with a large social formation that fulfilled functions in commerce, industry, and administration that were at best mediative and at worst located in the camp of the new exploiters (bureaucrats, economic managers, and administrators). Social mobility came to be channeled along these rails, both during the 1920s and during the industrialization and collectivization drives. The result was a vast increase in blue-collar as opposed to white-collar workers (though they too increased exponentially). But raw numbers was not the whole story. The state-dominated "administrative command" economy was organized to provide for white-collar and administrative hegemony. The reformed proletariat was in the position of subordination to itself, or at least to competition from within, in the form of the white-collar component. Upwardly mobile peasants, migrants to the cities, and even blue-collar workers who were "pushed up" into managerial or lower white-collar ranks all filled out these social categories, which were essentially already in place at the end of the civil war.

State building and society went forward together during the early 1920s. But neither class formation nor state formation was a clean-cut affair. White-collar occupational groups showed a marked tendency to gravitate away from the union toward the more powerful and richer commissariats, economic units, and the like. The difficulties of organizing a single powerful white-collar union symbolized the difficulties this numerous and powerful group had in terms of coalescing as a class. Commercial and Soviet employees have very different agendas and profiles. Again, the excessive emphasis on class in Soviet history and in the history of the revolution may indicate the strength of layering, fragmentation, even an inability to unite and form classes-for-themselves except to defend themselves against *vlast'* (state power).

We return to June 1929 and the Eighth All-Union Congress of the Union of Soviet and Commercial Employees. Figatner delivered the keynote report for the union central committee. By this time Figatner was fighting for his job, a fight he was, of course, destined to lose. The party leadership had already found allies in the union who had identified Figatner with Tomsky and the Right Opposition. Still Figatner played out his role in the face of a hostile union audience. He opened his speech with the idea that the congress was meeting at an extraordinary time. "Before the working class," he argued, " stands great tasks—the *perestroika* of the entire economy, town and village, socialist competition, and the possibility of overtaking capitalism." According to Figatner, the sharpening class struggle required the union organization's most acute attention. Nepmen and kulaks were trying to use the state apparatus to subvert the proletarian tasks. Here Figatner had in mind the well-publicized examples of bureaucratic and clan corruption in Astrakhan and Smolensk. "Our union is responsible before the working class," he loudly proclaimed. But even at this stage as Stalin's revolution was already underway, we may still ask if the union and its members belonged to the working class. Figatner proclaimed the need for self-criticism as a part of the daily white-collar consciousness. The fabric of daily life was the proper place for consciousness raising and not the more and more frequent campaigns of the mid and late 1920s. After twelve years of class formation and reformation, of white-collar workers fitting in and helping to define both the proletarian state and society, it is strange to imagine the voice of Figatner in 1929 as he fearfully warned his audience of the danger of losing the proletarian connection and of turning into something "monstrous."[56] In defense of his own work (and that of his union central committee) Figatner argued that "we have issued the directives and tried to shepherd this work" to prepare employees for what amounted to an examination of their politics and consciousness. Catcalls and hostile speeches from the floor greeted this speech. Figatner was ousted, but the rank and file re-

---

[56] All quotations are from *Nasha gazeta*, June 1929.

mained—as did the new wave of union activists ready to step into the positions of the organizers of the 1920s. The union faced collectivization and industrialization with new energy—its representatives and members knowing that there might be the usual uncertainties of white-collar life, but potential benefits as well. This social formation was truly a bedrock of socialist construction.

The fate of the Union of Soviet and Commercial Employees at the end of the 1920s sheds some light on the triumph of the Stalin bloc. Part of its success derived from reformulating well-worn themes of the 1920s and by mobilizing social forces, including the white-collar workers, to stand with the proletariat against the class enemy—Nepmen, specialists, managers, bureaucrats, old intelligentsia, and the disenfranchised. In this sense there is something profoundly nonrevolutionary about the Great Turn at the end of the 1920s. State building was also the building of a society.

9

Gábor T. Rittersporn

From Working Class to Urban Laboring Mass: On Politics and Social Categories in the Formative Years of the Soviet System

Inquiring about the formation of a working class may easily expose the researcher to the charge of trying to construct a social category that, under the pressure of objective conditions, is supposed to become a self-conscious agent of a radical turn in the history of humanity.[1] After all, why else be curious precisely about the working class instead of studying nuns, philatelists, or smokers? On the other hand, if the material available at the moment of this writing permits at least some very general conclusions about the impact of objective conditions on workers in the formative years of the Soviet system, it is still insufficient to draw far-reaching conclusions about the implications of their self-understanding. These dilemmas and circumstances explain why, even though it always seems useful to insist that our research reports put forward but a few interim results of a work in progress, this precaution is far more than a stylistic convention in our case.

I hope to find a place for workers in the social hierarchy of the prewar USSR. Rather than take for granted that an understanding of the determinants of social stratification or class formation can be located in the division of labor, occupational categories, and the authority patterns they may imply, I will try to evaluate the impact of the period's historical circumstances and political factors on the structure of Soviet society. Because this approach leads me to the tentative conclusion that it is far-fetched to speak about a working class in the period under review, I will explore this question in terms of whether the behavioral patterns of workers that reveal a pattern of social tension and conflict bespeak a tendency of their development into a well-defined group with a degree of autonomy from the political system and with features clearly distinguishing them

---

[1] For an influential account of such an understanding of the proletarian condition, see Georg Lukács, *Geschichte und Klassenbewußtsein* (Berlin, 1923), pp. 164–228.

from other social categories. I will also assess some characteristics of their perception of their relations with the rest of society as well as certain peculiarities of the influence of age, reactions to political campaigns, and geographic and social mobility to determine the extent to which these advanced or hindered the formation of a distinct group identity among workers.

The question whether or not we can speak about a Soviet working class in the 1930s stands a good chance of appearing as hopeless academic pettifogging. It seems well established that after the social and economic cataclysm of the revolutionary period and the civil war, an industrial pro-letariat was by and large reconstituted in the course of the 1920s, and its assertiveness vis-à-vis the authorities, including those who purportedly represented the interests of the toilers, leaves little doubt that this was a distinct social class.[2] However, the influx of newcomers, especially in the wake of the industrialization drive, the increasing uncertainty of prole-tarian identity, and the success of the political leadership in manipulating manifestations of the workers' discontent[3] seem to militate against apply-ing the notion of a working class after the upheaval of 1928–32. Never-theless, the strong presence in the 1930s of a specific work and shop-floor culture, the emergence of lifestyles typical of the worker milieu, and the difficulties the regime experienced bringing about the political socializa-tion of labor appear on the whole comparable to phenomena that had characterized the making of a proletarian class elsewhere.[4]

For all that, it is by no means simple to define the Soviet working class in the years—and indeed decades—that followed the industrialization campaign. It is certainly tempting to reserve the label for those and all those performing manual work in industry. But even if a definition of this kind can motivate a perfectly legitimate curiosity to study a more or less precisely circumscribed group, it involves the risk of making it impossible to identify features that such a group may have shared with other social categories. Moreover, the definition of workers above all as an occupa-

[2] Walter Süß, *Die Arbeiterklasse als Maschine: Ein industrie-soziologischer Beitrag zur Sozialgeschichte des aufkommenden Stalinismus* (Berlin, 1985), pp. 50–76; William J. Chase, *Workers, Society, and the Soviet State* (Urbana, Ill., 1987), pp. 103–21, 228–39, 243–47, 258–61: Hans-Henning Schröder, *Industrialisierung und Parteibürokratie in der Sowjetunion* (Berlin, 1988), pp. 70–83.

[3] Hiroaki Kuromiya, *Stalin's Industrial Revolution: Politics and Workers, 1928–1932* (Cambridge, 1988), pp. 87–99, 110, 171–72, 213–17, 227–28, 310–18.

[4] Lewis H. Siegelbaum, *Stakhanovism and the Politics of Productivity in the USSR, 1935–1941* (Cambridge, 1988), pp. 41–45; Vladimir Andrle, *Workers in Stalin's Russia* (London, 1988), pp. 51– 66, 165–68; Patrick Dale, "The Instability of the Infant Vanguard: Worker Party Members 1928–1932," *Soviet Studies* 35 (October 1983). For Western patterns of the emergence of a working class see Jürgen Kocka, *Lohnarbeit und Klassenbildung* (Berlin, 1983), pp. 117–23, 137–54.

tional category implies that social stratification in the formative period of the Soviet system can be grasped in terms of the hierarchies that material production had established among white- and blue-collar labor as well as among major economic sectors. Understanding the working class specifically and social categories generally as functions of the positions they occupy in the relations and process of production[5] may be justified in societies where authority patterns are founded mainly on the profitability of business interactions among management, producers, consumers, and the state; however, it is doubtful that anything like the profit-oriented interplay of economic and governmental mechanisms determined the structure and functioning of the productive sphere in the USSR and even more doubtful that it had a decisive impact on social relations, especially in the 1930s.

A prolonged period of peasant refusal to market food products, urban unrest, growing uncertainty about the political loyalty of technical specialists, and increasing hesitation within the leadership about how to reassert the regime's authority were the major factors that precipitated collectivization and industrialization. In spite of the regime's claims that it was laying the foundations of a planned economy, the construction of a modern industry was launched in a way that amounted to the "disappearance of planning in the plan," proceeded through ad hoc drives to often arbitrarily selected targets and to punish everyone who could be made a scapegoat when the drives failed, and resulted in a crisis that became indistinguishable from the everyday functioning of economic mechanisms.[6] The overriding importance the regime assigned political rather than economic gain explains the weight of costly administrative procedures in the shaping of developmental strategies at the beginning of the 1930s, while the failure of subsequent attempts to impose economic priorities suggests that even these attempts were dictated by the same political considerations that had established the primacy of administrative fiat. The Stakhanovite campaign, the most ambitious attempt to rationalize the economy in the 1930s, disorganized production, increased social tensions, and contributed to the aggravation of the period's political con-

[5] Karl Marx and Friedrich Engels, *Werke* (Berlin, 1957–), 6:397–423 and 593–99 and 23: 181–91.

[6] Moshe Lewin, *La paysannerie et le pouvoir soviétique* (Paris, 1966), pp. 193–222; idem., "The Disappearance of Planning in the Plan," *Slavic Review* 32, no. 2 (1973); Alec Nove, *An Economic History of the USSR* (Harmondsworth, 1972), pp. 187–209; R. W. Davies, *The Socialist Offensive—The Collectivization of Soviet Agriculture, 1929–1930* (London, 1980), pp. 39–41, 56–60; Kendall Bailes, *Technology and Society under Lenin and Stalin* (Princeton, N.J., 1978), pp. 69–121, 280; Michal Reiman, *Die Geburt des Stalinismus—Die UdSSR am Vorabend der "zweiten Revolution"* (Frankfurt, 1979), pp. 71–144; Tatiana Kirstein, *Die Bedeutung von Durchführungsentscheidungen in dem zentralistisch verfaßten Entscheidungssystem der Sowjetunion* (Berlin, 1984), pp. 176–203; Kuromiya, *Stalin's Industrial Revolution*, pp. 22–30, 81–86, 139–72, 288–96; Schröder, *Industrialisierung*, pp. 216–30, 317–23.

flicts, instead of realizing its initial goal of subjecting both management and labor to control through economic leverages and organizational constraints.[7] Though the intention behind the drive was an optimal use of production factors, the course it took led to the depletion of resources, to a fall in quality, to the disorganization of technological processes, plants, and cooperation among enterprises, to the overspending of the wage fund, to a dangerous deterioration in the servicing of equipment, and to the marginalization of efforts to develop Soviet models of the "scientific organization of labor" or to import foreign accomplishments in this field.[8]

In view of these circumstances and because—whatever their attitude toward or reactions in the wake of campaigns such as industrialization or Stakhanovism—workers were not really the ones who launched these drives on a national scale, it is perhaps no less appropriate when trying to define social categories in the USSR of the 1930s to concentrate on their access to political decision making and their influence over the implementation of decisions than on their place in the production process. Even if an approach of this kind may play down the importance of the work and life environment of occupational groups, it is likely to bring out common features in the behavioral patterns of different groups that would otherwise probably remain obscure. Such an approach may be justified in any case by the frequency in this period of changes in occupational status that could not be followed immediately by a change in attitude, behavior, or worldview.

This seems particularly true in the case of workers, many—if not most—of whom were yesterday's peasants: about 68 percent of all workers and employees came from the villages in 1928–32 and 54 percent in the years between 1933 and 1937.[9] At the same time, some 100,000 former benchworkers who were promoted during the First Five-Year Plan to become administrators in industry, made up about 22 percent of this corps of cadres in 1933, when more than 80 percent of party members in white-collar positions had started their career as workers or peasants.[10]

---

[7] Robert Maier, *Die Stachanov–Bewegung 1935–1938* (Stuttgart, 1990), pp. 86–114, 217–65, 292–306; Gábor T. Rittersporn, *Stalinist Simplifications and Soviet Complications: Social Tensions and Political Conflicts in the USSR, 1933–1953* (Reading, Mass., 1991), pp. 34–36; idem., "Héros du travail et commandants de la production," *Recherches*, no. 32–33 (1978); Siegelbaum, *Stakhanovism*, pp. 99–169.

[8] Maier, *Die Stachanov Bewegung*, pp. 253–91, 307–29; Siegelbaum, *Stakhanovism*, pp. 89–90, 103–4.

[9] R. P. Dadykin, "O chislennosti i istochnikakh popolneniia rabochego klassa SSSR (1928–1937 gg.)," *Istoricheskie zapiski*, no. 87 (Moscow, 1971): 46, 48; A. I. Vdovin and V. Z. Drobizhev, *Rost rabochego klassa SSSR 1917–1940 gg.* (Moscow, 1976), pp. 115–16. Unfortunately, the available data do not allow a separation of workers and employees of peasant origin from other workers and employees, though it is probable that among the former the proportion of villagers was somewhat higher.

[10] *Sostav rukovodiashchikh rabotnikov i spetsialistov Soiuza SSR* (Moscow, 1936), pp. 18–19; I. N. Iudin, *Sotsial'naia baza rosta KPSS* (Moscow, 1973), p. 186.

Everything points to the assumption that the higher the position a former worker was to occupy in the administrative—and consequently social—hierarchy, the more he was bound to be implicated in a complex set of relations, interactions, and mechanisms established by the interplay and mutual dependence of institutions, agencies, groups, and sociopolitical processes.[11]

This is understandable, as this hierarchy became the only agency authorized to make decisions and enforce their implementation, and because this monopoly and the determination to defend it against encroachment by the rest of society tended to transform all of its moves into political actions. Moreover, every relation it maintained with society at large was a political relationship, which seems to explain why the peacefulness of these relations or the economic soundness of these actions were secondary to the defense of the decision-making monopoly. The status of people invested with the prerogatives of this monopoly was inevitably distinct from the status of those who were merely supposed to suffer its consequences. From this point of view, all those excluded from the privilege of formal decision making belonged to other social categories whose main distinguishing feature was the lack of an institutional framework to defend their interests and to influence political processes.

This applied even to specialists and cadres on whose expertise depended the management and development of agencies and techniques of administration, material production and distribution and scientific and cultural action. Specialists and executives were able to manifest their interests through how they exercised their professional activities, the corporatist implications of which were likely to oppose them to their superiors and especially to the masses. But the administrative hierarchy they belonged to institutionalized the prerogatives of decision makers. Specialists and other groups with simple managerial or supervisory functions therefore formed a middle stratum—and in many respects a buffer zone—between those holding leading posts in the party and state apparatus, whose dominant role and unity of organization and action were guaranteed by their decision-making monopoly, and those whose professional activities were not deployed within or on behalf of the apparatus and who were, therefore, incapable of organizing. Seen from this angle, workers comprised part of a category situated at the antipode of the elite of decision makers, the only political class of the system.[12] Despite the notable differences

---

[11] For an understanding of this implication and of the pressure it exerts on individuals as part of a "civilizing process," see Norbert Elias, *Über den Prozeß der Zivilisation* (Frankfurt, 1976), 2:312–434.

[12] This political understanding of class owes a good deal to theories on elites, middle classes and social conflict of Gaetano Mosca, *The Ruling Class* (New York, 1939), pp. 50–69, 103–19, Vilfredo Pareto, *Traité de sociologie générale* (Geneva, 1968), pp. 610–13, 1293–1305, 1501–2; Emil Lederer and Jakob Marschak, "Der neue Mittelstand," in G. Albrecht et al., eds., *Grundriß der Sozialökonomik* (Tübingen, 1926); Emil Grünberg, *Der*

between the occupational status and self-image of industrial labor and that of the farm population, this category included the peasantry that was also excluded from direct access to the sphere of action of the administrative hierarchy.

My attempt to define the essential activities of social categories in political terms seems justified not only by the problematic connection between relations of production and social stratification but also by the impact of these activities on the system. The "essential activity" of the elite was the defense of its decision-making monopoly. Because the elite defended this monopoly even concerning simple technical aspects of production or cultural practices and lifestyles, its actions tended to transform a bewildering range of issues into questions of submission or opposition to authority and to introduce political relationships into most of walks of life. At the same time, however, actions and even behavioral patterns of other social categories also had a good chance of becoming politically significant, susceptible as the elite was to construing them as challenges to its initiatives. To be sure, there was an enormous difference between the impact of the activities of officials vested with firmly institutionalized prerogatives and the influence exerted by individuals deprived of any possibility to organize. Nevertheless, the political nature of this influence not only evinced a certain kinship between elite and popular reactions in the 1930s but influenced the character of these reactions.

That relations of production could not function as the main determinant of social status implied that economic and motivational means of control were unable to guarantee regular and reliable operation of the administration. In the absence of a more or less coherent system of incentives and success indicators related to the interactions among producers, consumers, and the state, the execution of orders, conformity to regulations, and political stability were the only yardsticks to measure the performance of the elite and the middle stratum, and their positions in the administrative hierarchy constituted the main source of prestige and privilege. It was the marginal status of such incentives and indicators that ensured the dominant position of the elite, though it was far from certain, under these conditions, if plans, orders, and regulations were consistent with available material, technical, administrative, and human resources.

Mittelstand in der kapitalistischen Gesellschaft (Leipzig, 1932), pp. 176–85; C. Wright Mills, *White Collar* (New York, 1953), pp. 290–94, 340–50; idem, *The Power Elite* (New York, 1959), pp. 269–324; and Ralf Dahrendorf, *Klassen und Klassenkonflikt in der industriellen Gesellschaft* (Stuttgart, 1957), pp. 49–54, 70–77, 159–80, 190–202. It implies that the administrative hierarchy and its leading posts define the elite and the middle stratum whose personnel may undergo even radical turnover without substantial change in the behavioral patterns and modes of action supposed by the defense of the hierarchy's prerogatives. Cf. Rittersporn, *Stalinist Simplifications and Soviet Complications*, pp. 51–55, 321.

Failure to execute orders or comply with regulations was likely to entail reprimands, demotion, or penal sanctions, but limited resources and the cadres' understandable intention to stay in office motivated frequent deviation from rules, deviation that the uncertainty of success indicators made extremely difficult to control.

The efforts of individual officeholders to retain their positions in the administrative hierarchy tended to conflict with the supreme interests of the regime, to subvert relations of authority between leading and subordinate agencies and cadres, to disorganize the functioning of the administration, and to aggravate tensions between the apparatus and the rest of society. Still these efforts were by no means evidence of any intent to oppose the regime and as a rule, they consisted in the skillful use of prerogatives officeholders had at their disposal by virtue of their positions.[13] A sign of the adaptation of cadres to the realities they confronted, this behavior represented genuine entrepreneurship, that is, the innovative combining of elements of their sphere of activity within the constraints of the regime.[14] It did not differ fundamentally from how workers most frequently interfered with the regime's policies. Slack discipline or absenteeism amounted to a similar accommodation to the constraints of their conditions and to the administration's difficulties in enforcing regulations such as the 1932 measures intended to curb truancy and high turnover rates.[15]

It is tempting to explain this close resemblance of behavioral patterns by invoking the relative homogeneity of the recruiting pool of both workers and officialdom; after all, the majority of the latter were promoted from factories and the villages.[16] In all probability, however, the phenomenon also expressed the paradoxical situation of individuals who, as subjects of political action, were not entitled to manifest their preferences concerning the exercise of state power outside officially sanctioned—and severely circumscribed—channels and forms, whatever their social status happened to be. Admittedly, cadres were able to make use of levers of institutionalized authority that were likely to make even isolated actions very efficient—hence the suspicion of "hostile maneuvers" and "wrecking," as well as the categorical criminalization of their supposedly deviant behavior after the mid-1930s. As for workers, it was above all the fre-

[13] For these phenomena within the apparatus, see G. T. Rittersporn, "Soviet Officialdom and Political Evolution," *Theory and Society* 13, no. 2 (1984), and "Soviet Politics in the 1930s," *Studies in Comparative Communism* 19, no. 2 (1986).

[14] See Joseph Schumpeter, *The Theory of Economic Development* (New York, 1961), p. 75.

[15] Donald Filtzer, *Soviet Workers and Stalinist Industrialization: The Formation of Modern Soviet Production Relations, 1928–1941* (London, 1986), pp. 108–15, 135–36.

[16] Sheila Fitzpatrick, *Education and Social Mobility in the Soviet Union 1921–1934* (Cambridge, 1979), pp. 239–42.

quency and extremely widespread character of manifestations of their insubordination that tended to become a cause for concern for the elite. The latter's countermeasures rarely made explicit a conflict between the regime and its alleged ruling class, notwithstanding the remarkably repressive clauses of certain legal acts destined to curb the unruliness of labor.

Nevertheless, at times, worker reactions were also countered as political crime, for the most part in cases when they amounted to a more or less open and consciously assumed sabotage of the relations between labor and the apparatus. Thus assaults on the person and property of activists, shock workers, and Stakhanovites and premeditated breakage of equipment or even failure to denounce theft of public property stood good chances of being taken as opposition to the regime.[17] It also occurred that the courts were exhorted to clamp down on "hooligan misbehavior of a counterrevolutionary character,"[18] a phenomenon whose treatment by the authorities exemplifies the problems posed by popular reactions and by workers as a social category.

Collectivization and industrialization triggered a mass migration to the cities, which became "ruralized" in a matter of years.[19] The migrants imported into the urban environment their habits, including easy recourse to violence that had been increasingly plaguing village life in the 1920s.[20] One-fifth of convicted "hooligans" were workers in 1928; their share rose to one-third by the first half of 1933.[21] It is in these circumstances that exemplary penalties were urged by the regime's spokesmen, who emphasized that these had to be "ruthlessly" applied also against workers and that "hooliganism" amounted to "sabotage" and political crime.[22] As this rise in petty violent offenses occurred in the wake of the veritable civil war that accompanied collectivization,[23] the authorities were perhaps not entirely mistaken to surmise that the aggressiveness of the masses expressed something more than simple interpersonal conflicts. On the other hand, nothing indicates that this kind of delinquency diminished after the early 1930s. On the contrary: the abolition of suspended and noncustodiary sentences and an attempt to implement a harsher schedule of pun-

---

[17] *Ugolovnyi kodeks RSFSR* (Moscow, 1937), pp. 135–37, 139, 155 (hereafter cited as *UK*); *Sovetskaia iustitsiia*, 1935, no. 11:11, 36:2 (hereafter cited as *SIu*); *Sotsialisticheskaia zakonnost'*, 1937, no. 1:83 (hereafter cited as *SZak*).

[18] *SIu*, 1935, no. 18:10.

[19] Moshe Lewin, *The Making of the Soviet System* (New York, 1985), pp. 220, 303.

[20] Helmut Altrichter, *Die Bauern von Tver* (Munich, 1984), pp. 109, 125, 129–30, 258–59.

[21] *SIu*, 1934, no. 2:16.

[22] Editorial, *Pravda*, 3 May 1934, p. 1; *SZak*, 1935, no. 5:10; *SIu*, 1935, no. 10:3–4; no. 11:11–12.

[23] See Davies, *Socialist Offensive*, pp. 182–85, 228–49, 256–60.

ishment for "hooligans" in 1940 suggest the persistence of the problem, the more so since it also proved necessary to establish "special judicial sections" in large cities to deal with these types of offenses.[24]

For all that, official discourse ceased to equate hooliganism with "counterrevolutionary" offenses. Despite their manifestly great numbers and the need to "strengthen repressive measures" against them, "hooligans" ended up being downgraded to simple "disorganizers of socialist communal life."[25] This was not inconsistent with current legislative practice. To be sure, the vague formulation of previous legislation made it perfectly applicable to any new forms of opposition that might appear. It is also true that if the elite wanted to maintain the fictions of the workers' state and social harmony, it was well advised to avoid referring to the political aspects of popular behavior that endangered relations between the apparatus and labor. Nevertheless, after the mid-1930s the authorities did not seem particularly concerned with political offenses that arose from work relations; indeed, even legal acts concerning agriculture ceased to refer to them after early 1936,[26] despite the tensions inherent in food production and procurement in the collectivized rural economy. Authoritative warnings that opposition by rank and file workers to the Stakhanovite campaign that did not involve violence or wrecking was by no means to be mistaken for a "counterrevolutionary" offense and should not entail prosecution[27] suggest that there was an increasing tendency to treat these occurrences as simple acts of revolt by individuals who did not necessarily represent a political danger, even though covert resistance against the drive was by no means infrequent.

Everything points to the assumption that in spite of the gravity of social tensions this revolt demonstrated, the regime was able not only to co-opt many of its manifestations, but also to constitute a framework for the ensuing conflicts and, in a sense, their limit. The regional official who believed that he detected the "enemy's method to discredit the leadership" in a letter signed by twenty-one workers claiming that Kirov's assassination had been possible because of cadres such as those in their factory,[28] was not entirely in tune with a powerful political trend in the weeks

[24] UK (1947), p. 154; Ugolovno-protsessual'nyi kodeks RSFSR (Moscow, 1947), pp. 196–97 (hereafter cited as UPK).

[25] UK (1947), p. 154.

[26] The last available act making an infraction in agriculture punishable as a "counterrevolutionary" offense dates from February 1936 and relates to the Stakhanovite campaign, as does the last such act concerning industry promulgated at the end of 1935. UPK (1937), p. 147; SIu, 1935, no. 36:2.

[27] SZak, 1936, no. 1:4, no. 7:70; SIu, 1936, no. 5:2; no. 4:3.

[28] See the handwritten remark on the margin of a copy of this letter made, in all probability, by the addressee, I. P. Rumiantsev, old Bolshevik and member of the Central Committee. Smolensk Archive WKP 355, p. 114 (hereafter cited as WKP). A less vehement letter on the subject by another group of workers is in WKP 355, p. 187.

following the "Great Moscow Trial" of August 1936. The clearly spontaneous multiplication during these weeks of letters complaining of acts of "sabotage" allegedly committed by local officials or administrative and technical cadres in industry[29] did not bode well for a great number of people in positions of authority. But the conflicts they indicated were not necessarily of a character to turn workers against the system as such. After all, the imagery of the "wrecking cadre" and mobilization of workers for "anti-saboteur" campaigns had proved their worth for the regime as expedients to manipulate a "class war" against intractable specialists and unreliable officeholders at the outset of industrialization, and the crisis of the Stakhanovite drive was accompanied by a quick offensive against "saboteurs" that ended shortly before the "underground work" of "enemies" was "rediscovered" in the summer of 1936.[30]

What is more, the logic of the system found its expression in the fiction of "sabotage," inseparable as this fiction was from the increasingly unmanageable working of governmental and economic mechanisms, and from the fact that nothing could be more alien to the administrative hierarchy—which was responsible for the chaos as well as for the inevitable failure of all attempts to install some order—than the idea that its very existence as the only legitimate institution of decision making and action happened to be at the origin of the regime's disorganization.[31] However sincerely indignant over the arbitrary reduction of their wages the workers may have been and however grave the potential of genuine social conflict behind their sentiment of being humiliated by the high-handed manners of their chiefs, their anger at these bosses benefiting from undeserved advantages, and their suspicion that all the hardships of their living and working conditions were the result of deliberate wrecking by their superiors,[32] they still expressed their grievances in a way that reproduced a central element of the regime's official self-understanding.

From this point of view, the extent to which the imagery of "sabotage" was cynically manipulated by certain politicians is not very important. Nor is the extent to which those who were trying to use this fiction against all sorts of real and imaginary "enemies" believed it, even though all the indications are that it constituted a dominant explanatory paradigm for the period's confused realities in both official and popular milieus.[33] What

---

[29] *WKP* 195, p. 182; *WKP* 196, pp. 77, 89, 230; *WKP* 355, p. 220.

[30] Sheila Fitzpatrick, "Cultural Revolution as Class War," in Fitzpatrick, ed., *Cultural Revolution in Russia 1928–1931* (Bloomington, 1978), pp. 8–27; Bailes, *Technology and Society*, pp. 69–121, 280; Kuromiya, *Stalin's Industrial Revolution*, pp. 14–17, 31–35, 105–6, 292–94, 310–18; Schröder, *Industrialisierung*, 216–30, 317–23; Siegelbaum, *Stakhanovism*, pp. 117–20; Maier, *Die Stachanov Bewegung*, pp. 380–81.

[31] Cf. Rittersporn, *Stalinist Simplifications and Soviet Complications*, pp. 43, 47–48, 53–54, 74–76, 117, 170–71, 265.

[32] A typical case of the outburst of this conflict can be found in *WKP* 195, pp. 20–23.

[33] For an exploration of this problem, see G. T. Rittersporn, "The Omnipresent Conspir-

counts is how the official discourse limits the exposure of social conflict and its manifestations within the institutional framework of the regime to which rebellious workers appealed when asking that their hated higher-ups be punished.[34] It is hardly surprising, in these circumstances, that their revolt was as easy to instrumentalize by officeholders to settle personal scores among themselves[35] as it was by the regime to put pressure on officialdom as a whole.

To be sure, this mobilization entailed the risk of proving excessively successful, because at times the subversion of system-inherent hierarchical relations endangered the positions of people or groups whom high-placed sponsors of the drive had not targeted, and occasionally it even encouraged open attacks on the regime as such.[36] But even these excesses were likely to be accommodated within the confines of the system. Campaigns could be and were called off or suspended in case of necessity, despite the tactical disadvantages to their sponsors.[37] On the other hand, excesses such as those involved in the chaotic struggle of each against all that these mobilization drives were liable to provoke made integral part of the regime's modus operandi, and it was doubtful if this could be altered without destroying the system.[38] Although it contributed to the intensification of social tensions and political conflicts, the refusal of workers to obey the orders of their superiors under the pretext that they were potential "wreckers"[39] was also an element of this system-inherent chaos. Similarly, the regime's hopelessly unavailing attempts to rectify its functioning through periodically encouraging a struggle against "sabotage" contributed to the chronic and on the whole inevitable disorder of the system.

Workers did not fail to profit from the administration's disarray in the wake of such attempts and slackened discipline, as in 1937 when their insubordination and absenteeism grew proportionally with the confusion provoked by the fight against the "enemies."[40] As this fight and an obvious fear to apply management methods that had been denounced as

---

acy: On Soviet Imagery of Politics and Social Relations in the 1930s," in Nick Lampert and G. T. Rittersporn, eds., *Stalinism: Its Nature and Aftermath* (London, 1992).

[34] *WKP* 195, pp. 19, 24.

[35] For the ins and outs of a case in which local officials succeeded in exploiting workers' hostility against management in their personal rivalry see ibid., pp. 25, 33, 37–38.

[36] See, e.g., T. Karpenko, "Vnutripartiinaia demokratiia," *Pravda*, 12 August 1936, p. 3; editorial, *Pravda*, 22 April 1937; B. Levin, "Uroki odnogo bol'shogo partsobraniia," *Pravda*, 22 April 1937, p. 2; D. Vadimov, "Bezotvetstvennost'," *Pravda*, 19 May 1937, p. 2; idem, "Plokho poniataia demokratiia," *Pravda*, 19 May 1937, p. 2; "Bol'she poriadka," *Pravda*, 11 May 1937, p. 3; *Partiinoe stroitel'stvo*, 1936, no. 18:33; *Bol'shevik*, 1937, no. 9:84.

[37] Rittersporn, *Stalinist Simplifications and Soviet Complications*, pp. 131–34.

[38] Ibid., pp. 54–55, 170–71, 219–20, 287–88, 325, 328–29.

[39] Editorials, *Pravda*, 29 April 1937, 24 June 1937, and 25 March 1938.

[40] Editorials, *Pravda*, 11 May 1937, 14 and 25 August 1937, 24 January 1938, 27 March 1938; D. Vadimov, "V Donbasse bez peremen," *Pravda*, 14 May 1937, p. 6; idem, "V Donbasse sabotiruiut bor'bu s progulami," *Pravda*, 23 May 1937, p. 6; A. Vinnikov, "Proizvoditel'nost' truda," *Pravda*, 5 October 1937, p. 2; *Bol'shevik*, 1937, no. 16:19, no. 19:7.

"wrecking" deterred cadres from taking unpopular measures,[41] the un-ruliness of labor understandably became an important stimulus to efforts to close the ranks of the administrative hierarchy, even at the price of tacitly rehabilitating a good deal of "saboteur" practices. Characteristi-cally, these efforts were accompanied by calls for mobilizing the judiciary to combat slack discipline and by allusions stopping short of designating the workers themselves as "wreckers."[42] And it is perhaps even more char-acteristic that if the proclivity of ordinary people to denounce "wrecking" officeholders and cadres had played a prominent role in the image-building of the "enemy of the people" in the autumn of 1936, two years later *leniency* in the enforcement of disciplinary measures was censured as "acting against the people."[43]

For all that, 6.9 percent of the personnel of the most important indus-trial branches had to be punished in the space of a single month for hav-ing infringed the first measures to reestablish order and curb migration among enterprises, about a year after their enactment.[44] This came at a time when some 54 percent of workers of these branches had been em-ployed in the same plant for less than two years.[45] Only a relatively small proportion of these people were new recruits to the shop floor. Most of them belonged to a labor force whose turnover rate was so high that in 1932–35 and again in 1937 the number of workers leaving jobs ex-ceeded total industrial manpower.[46] The promulgation of a series of harsh regulations and laws penalizing even "idleness" at the workplace and imposing custodial sentences for the unauthorized change of one's job[47] leaves no doubt of the determination of the regime to crack down on troublemakers. Nor does the injunction of a Central Committee res-olution to "implant discipline even through repression."[48] The labor laws of the last prewar years hit a great number of people: more than 2 mil-lion persons were sentenced under their terms in 1940, that is, some 6

[41] Editorials, *Pravda*, 24 January 1938, 8 February 1938, and 9 February 1938.

[42] "Po-bol'shevistski borot'sia," *Pravda*, 10 December 1938, p. 3; G. Ivanovskii, "Lishit' lodyrei," *Pravda*, 14 December 1938, p. 3; I Zal'tsman, "Komandiry proizvodstva i tru-dovaia distsiplina," *Pravda*, 25 December 1938, p. 2; *SIu*, 1938, no. 17:10, 12; *Bol'shevik*, 1938, no. 7:32, no. 23–24:10.

[43] Maier, *Die Stachanov Bewegung*, pp. 382–85; Rittersporn, *Stalinist Simplifications and Soviet Complications*, pp. 83, 93–94, 100–101; Siegelbaum, *Stakhanovism*, pp. 136–37; *Bol'shevik*, 1936, no. 23–24:16.

[44] A. V. Mitrofanova, "Istochniki i popolneniia sostava rabochego klassa v gody tretei piatiletki," in A. G. Rashin, ed., *Izmeneniia v chislennosti i sostave sovetskogo rabochego klassa* (Moscow, 1961), p. 216.

[45] *Industrializatsiia SSSR, 1938–1941 gg.* (Moscow, 1973), p. 213.

[46] *Industrializatsiia SSSR, 1933–1937 gg.* (Moscow, 1971), pp. 421, 511–12.

[47] *KPSS v rezoliutsiiakh i resheniiakh s"ezdov, konferentsii i plenumov TsK* (Moscow, 1971), 5:324–32; *Partiinoe stroitel'stvo*, 1939, no. 2:51, no. 3:64; *UK* (1947), pp. 110–11, 113–14, 116–18, 121; *UPK* (1947), p. 191.

[48] *Izvestiia TsK KPSS*, 1990, no. 2:188.

percent of the entire blue- and white-collar staff of the national economy.[49]

Nevertheless, it is doubtful that the elite tended to equate the restiveness of labor with political opposition. Despite the severity of the legislation, the available documentation does not allow us to conclude that articles of the criminal code on "counterrevolutionary" offenses were applied against undisciplined workers. As the realization of the regime's economic programs represented a crucial aspect of the exercise of that state power which had to be asserted at all costs in the main sphere where the administration was supposed to defend the system's authority in direct contact with the masses—the sphere of production—the unruliness of the workforce had a clear political dimension. In all probability, however, the representatives of the regime did not fully appreciate themselves the political implications of disciplinary problems at the workplace. The noisy campaigns against "enemies" throughout the 1930s and the underlying imagery of political engagement as merely taking sides with or against the party's "general line" were hardly conducive to a vision of politics in terms of labor relations. On the other hand, even when these relations were understood as an important part of the regime's political problems, the reluctance to cooperate with the administration beyond what was strictly necessary was bound to be seen in elite milieus as a mark of success in alleviating the political charge of labor-management relations and in marginalizing genuine political protest by workers.

Scarce as they are, the available data suggest that such an appreciation might have been somewhat—although by no means excessively—optimistic. Opinion polls among wartime refugees show that workers were much less inclined to see the "intelligentsia" and "employees" as unfairly treated by the regime than were these potential members of the administrative hierarchy themselves, who were far more ready to find (or imagine) that they had common ground with the workers.[50] The workers and the "intelligentsia"—as groups—considered each other harmful. Workers thought that considerably less harm was done to them by "employees" than by "intellectuals." For their part, "employees" feared workers as a source of potential danger more than the latter feared "employees."[51]

Researchers in this area have made no effort to define social categories in terms of subordinate or superior positions and have relied on Soviet

---

[49] V. Zemskov, "Sorokovye, 'trudovye'," *Soiuz*, no. 18 (1990): 9; *Narodnoe khoziaistvo SSSR, 1922–1982* (Moscow, 1982), p. 399.

[50] Alex Inkeles and Raymond Bauer, *The Soviet Citizen* (Cambridge, Mass., 1959), pp. 301, 305; Alex Inkeles, *Social Change in Soviet Russia* (Cambridge, Mass., 1968), pp. 89, 93.

[51] Inkeles and Bauer, *Soviet Citizen*, pp. 308–9.

definitions as well as on the categories according to which the respondents identified themselves. Their "employees" in all probability included most of managerial and many technical cadres of the sample, though apparently not engineers.[52] Thus—and especially given the understanding of the term by the Soviets themselves—the relatively weak tensions perceived by workers between their group and "employees" and the relative intensity of these tensions felt by the latter seem to indicate that conflict between labor and management was less problematic for workers than it was for "employees." By contrast, the relatively strong perception of strained relations with the "intelligentsia" suggests the successful functioning of the buffer zone between the elite and the masses whose direct contacts with "intellectuals" were restricted mainly to those with engineering personnel, but who were nevertheless rather disposed to resent professionals in general.

These data hardly permit conclusions about the readiness of workers to manifest political preferences openly; however, two findings of the survey seem to reflect actual attitudes toward traditional forms of expressing political opinions. When asked, workers as a group were more likely to say that people should be forbidden to say things detrimental to the state than the "intelligentsia" were (though, rather characteristically, less than "employees"); but workers under thirty were more inclined to favor freedom of speech than their peers who had good chances to belong to the administrative hierarchy.[53] For all that, the same young workers were considerably less disposed than their comrades in their thirties and forties to concede to people the right to assemble "if the purpose of the meeting [was] to attack the government," though it must be added that workers over fifty were even more hostile to the idea of granting this freedom, which was in general opposed by the majority of workers. Moreover, young "intellectuals" and "employees" were also much more reluctant in this respect than their older colleagues.[54]

Between 1930 and 1933, the proportion of workers under twenty-two rose from 24.7 percent to 41.3 percent in the main industrial branches where 34.3 percent of the workforce was younger than twenty-five even

---

[52] Ibid., pp. 72–75.

[53] Alice Rossi, *Generational Differences in the Soviet Union* (New York, 1980), p. 305; Inkeles and Bauer, *Soviet Citizen*, p. 248.

[54] Rossi, *Generational Differences*, p. 303. According to Inkeles and Bauer the wording of the question was responsible for the preference of the majority of respondents for restrictions on this right (*Soviet Citizen*, p. 504), but Rossi is probably correct to emphasize that the problem must have been their understanding of an assembly as an organized group (*Generational Differences*, pp. 305–6). This argument seems all the more convincing, since the respondents proved rather reserved toward the idea of granting the freedom to set up political organizations (Inkeles and Bauer, *Soviet Citizen*, p. 36).

in 1939.[55] The proportion of young workers was particularly high in rapidly developing sectors (37–39 percent of the personnel in machine-building were under twenty-three in 1935) and in new industrial regions.[56] In one way or another, the majority of these workers had been involved with or affected by the mass migration between town and countryside and among the cities between 1928 and 1935.[57] Unstable living and work environments, frequently disrupted familial and personal relationships and the failure of the cities to provide a cultural model as reference for positive identification, must have combined to create and reinforce a feeling of disorientation and uprootedness among the masses, and especially young workers.[58]

It was not for nothing that by the end of the 1920s the evolution of press photography evinced a shift in the regime's vision of workers whose representation in their individual, occupational, and proletarian reality became marginalized to give place to the allegory of an idealized "new man" at the same time as the images of politicians occupied more and more space and as that of the Supreme Leader acquired the iconographic features of the celebration of a ruler.[59] The suggestion in official discourse of the protecting omnipresence and omniscience of a strong leadership was by no means a mistaken response to the chaotic realities of the regime and to the insecurity of the masses, and it is highly characteristic that portraying the *Vozhd'* as a veritable *Vaterfigur* and the workers as his sons began in connection with the first Stakhanovite stars.[60]

At the beginning of the campaign the majority of Stakhanovites were young and of peasant origin[61] Very probably, their freshly won status functioned as a substitute for a traditional community that many if not

[55] *Sotsialisticheskoe stroitel'stvo SSSR* (Moscow, 1934), pp. 344–45; *Industrializatsiia SSSR, 1938–1941*, p. 214.

[56] Vdovin and Drobizhev, *Rost rabochego klassa SSSR*, p. 135.

[57] On the whole, some 77 million arrivals to and 60 million departures from cities were recorded in these years. *Trud v SSSR* (Moscow, 1936), p. 7. Although many of these people were seasonal workers or persons periodically leaving villages and later returning there, the figures convey an idea of the phenomenon's magnitude in a country whose population was about 152 million in 1928, perhaps 163 million in 1932, and some 158 million in 1935. E. M. Andreev, L. E. Darskii, T. L. Khar'kova, *Istoriia Naseleniia SSSR, 1920–1959 gg.*, no. 3–5, part 1, of *Ekspress-informatsiia, seriia: Istoriia statistiki* (Moscow, 1990), p. 141. Seasonal workers made up some 10 million of the migrants between 1928 and 1932 and perhaps 9 million in 1933–35. Vdovin and Drobizhev, *Rost rabochego klassa SSR*, pp. 120, 122.

[58] Lewin, *The Making of the Soviet System*, pp. 313, 256.

[59] Rosalinde Sartorti, *Pressefotografie und Industrialisierung in der Sowjetunion* (Berlin, 1981), pp. 97, 236–45, 256–60, 275–81.

[60] Siegelbaum, *Stakhanovism*, p. 150; Maier, *Die Stachanov Bewegung*, pp. 179–80. See also Katerina Clark, *The Soviet Novel* (Chicago, 1981), pp. 114–25.

[61] V. A. Kozlov and O. V. Khlevniuk, *Nachinaetsia s cheloveka* (Moscow, 1988), pp. 153–54; Maier, *Die Stachanov Bewegung*, pp. 115–17, 123–24, 151–52; Siegelbaum, *Stakhanovism*, pp. 170–73.

most Soviet people came to feel as much deprived of as parentless and formerly vagabond youth who were remarkably visible among participants of the drive.[62] More than the popular tradition of proving one's worth through achievement, more than a desire for recognition and status lay behind their thirst for setting or surpassing records, for competing with record holders, and for improving their conditions as individuals, even to the obvious detriment of their comrades; in all likelihood Stakhanovites were looking for a sort of compensation for the hardship, deprivation, and humiliation they probably suffered in the wake of collectivization.[63] The apparently spontaneous pressure by workers on management to create favorable circumstances for records channeled a good deal of discontent toward forms of protest consistent with the regime's needs and, as the well-publicized presence among Stakhanovites of former convicts suggests, expressed something of the revolt that fueled "hooliganism."[64] It was not too difficult, therefore, for the political leadership to instrumentalize the campaign in an attempt to modify the operation of economic mechanisms, and it is understandable that—encouraged as they were as a counterforce to "conservative" management and "reactionary" specialists as well as dependent on the central authorities—Stakhanovites came to spearhead the struggle against "wrecking" cadres.[65]

Not all Stakhanovites were young people or of peasant background, and, after all, only a relatively small proportion of young workers or former villagers were Stakhanovites. Nevertheless, the behavior of the heroes of the drive seems indicative of the urge most newcomers may have felt to make the best of a situation in which their per capita living space did not allow more than 70 percent of them to come together with friends except in courtyards and streets, but in which as shock workers they would have some chance of winning better living conditions as well as access to better food supply.[66] To be sure, industrial production needs a stable rhythm and standard procedures more than it needs heroic exploits, so that Stakhanovism and most of its essential ingredients were condemned to give way to rather ordinary patterns of everyday factory routine.[67] This state of affairs must have contributed to a worker skepticism comparable to the skepticism of peasants about the desirability of making

---

[62] Maier, *Die Stachanov Bewegung*, pp. 126, 170.

[63] Siegelbaum, *Stakhanovism*, pp. 76–78, 90–91, 94, 187–90; Maier, *Die Stachanov Bewegung*, pp. 77, 91, 101, 123, 151–54.

[64] Maier, *Die Stachanov Bewegung*, pp. 78, 81–82, 125–26.

[65] Ibid., pp. 93–95, 391–94, 398–403; Siegelbaum, *Stakhanovism*, pp. 77, 79, 81–84, 95–96, 205–6, 252–54.

[66] L. N. Kogan and B. S. Pavlov, *Molodoi rabochii vchera, segodnia* (Sverdlovsk, 1976), pp. 55, 63–65, 162.

[67] Andrle, *Workers in Stalin's Russia*, pp. 190–99.

a career. It is also probable that the aftermath of the Stakhanovite campaign contributed to the frustrated feeling of the youngest among them about the possibility of climbing the social ladder, a frustration that was shared even by skilled workers.[68]

Nevertheless, workers did experience social mobility in the 1930s. Even if the careers of those who succeeded in reaching white-collar status are the most likely to attract attention, the overwhelming majority of workers who improved their conditions did not leave the shop floor. Many of them started in construction—a sector where in Leningrad the proportion of former peasants increased from 13.3 percent to 82.9 percent in the course of 1931.[69] More than two million people left this branch for others, with better work conditions, as the construction fever abated during the subsequent five years.[70] Over all, the majority of workers improved their skills and qualifications in this decade, and this was especially the case among young people.[71] Admittedly, the massive effort of vocational education and betterment went hand in hand with the evolution of a technological policy founded on the extreme fragmentation of the work process, so that in many respects this effort resulted in a de facto deskilling of an increasingly better schooled labor force.[72] Nevertheless, it certainly helped many workers to attain higher wage categories.

This prospect and that of advancing in the shop-floor hierarchy must have been all the more attractive, since avenues of upward mobility between social categories grew ever more narrower in the course of the 1930s. There was a more than 10 percent fall in the recruitment of people of worker background into institutions of higher education in the five years following 1933, and by 1938 42.2 percent of students were "employees" or their children against 39.9 percent who came from worker families.[73] Data for the subsequent years hardly exist, but the trend seems to have continued because even at the university of an industrial city such as Gor'kii, students of worker origin constituted only 20 percent of freshmen by 1952.[74] "Sociocultural capital" played an increasing rôle in advancing mobility already in the 1930s: 59.3 percent of the party members

---

[68] Inkeles and Bauer, *Soviet Citizen*, pp. 93–97.

[69] Ia. M. Drakhiia et al., *Leningradskie rabochie v bor'be za sotsializm, 1926–1937* (Leningrad, 1965), p. 152.

[70] Dadykin, "O chislennosti i istochnikakh," pp. 49–50.

[71] Vdovin and Drobizhev, *Rost rabochego klassa SSR*, pp. 197–99, 204–10; Kogan and Pavlov, *Molodoi rabochii*, p. 39.

[72] Süß, *Arbeiterklasse als Maschine*, pp. 156–68, 218–26; Lewin, *The Making of the Soviet System*, p. 250.

[73] M. P. Kim, ed., *Sovetskaia intelligentsiia* (Moscow, 1968), p. 190.

[74] A. A. Terent'ev et al., *Sotsiologiia i vysshaia shkola* (Gor'kii, 1975), p. 58. Seventy-two percent of their classmates were from families of "employees."

who did white-collar jobs in 1933 had started as workers and 21.9 percent as peasants against some 41.5 percent and 4.7 percent by 1941.[75]

Though the educational level of party activists already figured among the qualities that seemed to justify their worth in the eyes of the authorities in 1934, the first criterion of the militants' probity was still their proletarian origin.[76] Nevertheless, things changed in the ensuing five years, to the extent that by 1939 the diplomas of recently promoted officials were praised and little mention was made of their social background.[77] To be sure, the purging from the party of people on the grounds of being "class-alien elements," or having concealed this state of affairs,[78] suggested that belonging to the purported ruling class of the system was still a highly valued asset in the mid-1930s. In the same way, charges that managers were "cut off the workers" and did not treat them with due respect and the official praise of Stakhanovite initiatives as an antidote to the inertness of administrative and technical cadres,[79] were bound to create the impression of a regime honoring labor. It is probable that these circumstances were likely to convince many workers of their privileged status within the system and to make them accept the paternalism of the party-state as well as its claim to represent the interests of the laboring masses. It is equally likely that far from all workers noticed that not the spread of proletarian virtues but the "raising of the cultural level" of labor and the eventual disappearance of class differences through its projected integration in the category of technical cadres was inscribed in the Stakhanovite campaign, whose stars were publicized as people striving to assimilate middle-class manners and values.[80]

Nevertheless, the behavioral patterns of hundreds of thousands of workers who received penalties within the first weeks that followed the hardening of the measures against slack discipline in 1940[81] were somewhat at variance with their potential identification with the regime. To be sure, unauthorized absence from or change of one's workplace did not denote anything that would even remotely resemble opposition to the system. In fact, the wayward conduct of large masses of workers can be

[75] Iudin, *Sotsial'naia baza*, p. 186; the 1941 figures are calculated on the basis of data in *Izvestiia TsK KPSS*, 1990, no. 5:200.

[76] *XVII s"ezd VKP(b)* (Moscow, 1934), p. 530.

[77] *XVIII s"ezd VKP(b)* (Moscow, 1939), pp. 106, 239, 529, 556, 581, 596, 610.

[78] J. Arch Getty, *Origins of the Great Purges: the Soviet Communist Party Reconsidered, 1933–1938* (Cambridge, 1985), pp. 54, 83.

[79] B. Tsakov–V. Solov'ev, "Troekratnoe golosovanie" *Pravda*, 9 April 1937, p. 2; N. Bezrukov, "Deliagi," and B. Andreev, "Sila samokritiki," *Pravda*, 12 April 1937, p. 2; Siegelbaum, *Stakhanovism*, pp. 81–84, Maier, *Die Stachanov Bewegung*, pp. 93–94.

[80] Bailes, *Technology and Society*, pp. 316–18; Siegelbaum, *Stakhanovism*, pp. 222–42.

[81] Oleg V. Khlevniuk, "26 iunia 1940 goda: illiuziia i real'nosti administrirovaniia," *Kommunist*, no. 9 (1990): 92.

understood as following the line of the least resistance when seeking to ameliorate their conditions. Still, it evinced a strong inclination to put considerations of individual well-being ahead of the purported public good and a notable distance from the collectivist values in whose name the regime was imposing its policies.

On the other hand, the remarkable lack of eagerness of workers to join the supposed vanguard of the proletariat, which resulted in a steady decline of their share among new recruits in the party in the immediate prewar years,[82] might indicate that they were distancing from the regime consciously. The purges of the first half of the 1930s did a good deal to bring about a sharp decrease of benchworkers among the membership.[83] But their reluctance to enroll must have contributed to the fall of their representation to 18.2 percent by early 1941 against 40.9 percent in 1933. Put another way, if 8 percent of workers were party members in 1933, party saturation of this social category was only 2.9 percent by the beginning of 1941.[84] In terms of social position as opposed to background, 62.4 percent of the members were white collar on the eve of the war, whereas 33.6 percent of the membership came from their milieu as compared to only about 7.8 percent in 1933.[85] These data do not seem to suggest that workers invested too much hope in the possibility to make themselves heard through the only political organization that carried weight in the system. They must have noticed that the importance of one's "sociocultural capital" had increased even in the alleged vanguard of the working class and that their chances to rise in the social hierarchy did not improve substantially when they joined the party.[86]

But whatever their possibilities of upward mobility, workers fared much better in this respect than peasants, whose most likely promotion was to

[82] *Izvestiia TsK KPSS*, 1990, no. 5:199, 201.

[83] *Istoriia KPSS* (Moscow, 1971), vol. 4, book 2, p. 283; *Partiinoe stroitel'stvo*, 1939, no. 5:36.

[84] *Izvestiia TsK KPSS*, 1990, no. 5:200–201; Iudin, *Sotsial'naia baza*, p. 128. The 1933 data do not include the army but are comparable to the 1941 figure, which refers only to "territorial organizations" of the party. In 1933 16.7 percent of "employees" were party members; in 1941 19.2 percent were.

[85] *Izvestiia TsK KPSS*, 1990, no. 5:199–200. The 1933 figure is calculated on the basis of data in Iudin, *Sotsial'naia baza*, pp. 128, 164. One can estimate that about one-third of the 1933 membership was in white–collar positions.

[86] Between 1933 and 1941 the number of benchworkers among the membership declined from 1,311,967 to 584,791, whereas that of "employees" rose from 1,002,421 to 2,012,543. Though—besides the purges—promotion had a certain part in the sharp fall of worker representation, the majority of 1941 "employee" party members came from white-collar families whose descendants accounted for some 18.8 percent of Bolshevik "employees" in 1933 (188,455 persons) against 53.8 percent (about 1,082,748 people) in 1941 (calculated on the basis of data in *Izvestiia TsK KPSS* 1990, no. 5:200, and Iudin, *Sotsial'naia baza*, p. 186).

farm brigade leader or chairman, jobs that wartime refugees found less attractive than that of a rank and file worker.[87] Though hundreds of thousands of peasants had been trained to become tractor and combine drivers, a considerable proportion of them left for the cities almost as soon as their training ended,[88] which does not seem to indicate that better-paid mechanized jobs in villages were more popular than virtually any urban occupation. Many refugees of the older generation stated that they had wanted to be peasants but could not do so, prevented as they were by collectivization, whereas the younger a peasant happened to be, the more likely he was to be dissatisfied with his occupational status.[89] Even though the professional attainment of young workers clearly did not match their aspirations, it is highly improbable that they (or workers in general) had the feeling of being situated at the bottom of the social hierarchy.

The possibility of still having a relatively enviable status occluded the fact that, despite their advantages—which did not prove sufficient in the last prewar years to prevent a remarkable slowdown of migration toward cities[90]—workers had no more direct access to policymaking bodies than peasants and that, from this point of view, they belonged to the same social category. On the other hand, notwithstanding the serious headache persistently slack work discipline gave the regime, manpower shortages tended to prevent even (or especially) the harshest labor laws from being consistently enforced. Management, after all, was well advised to prefer social peace on the shop floor and the prospect of plan fulfillment to strained industrial relations and the loss of badly needed labor.[91] This circumstance both contributed to the blurring of the lines of social stratification and the masking of its implications.

To be sure, these lines did not go unnoticed by workers who did develop certain elements of a group identity. Nevertheless, some components of this identity, such as its distinctiveness from peasant self-understanding, were hardly conducive to realizing basic similarities in behavioral patterns with villagers and their commonly shared experienced of having been dispossessed of institutions of interest representation. Others, such as the

---

[87] Inkeles, *Social Change*, p. 196.

[88] Stephan Merl, *Sozialer Aufstieg im sowjetischen Kolchossystem der 30er Jahre?* (Berlin, 1990), pp. 164–65, 170–71, 173–74, 179–81, 256–57. Although this kind of migration decreased after 1932 when almost half of tractor drivers left the MTS, the proportion of runaways fluctuated every year between one-third and a quarter of the entire contingent of tractor and combine drivers.

[89] Rossi, *Generational Differences*, pp. 209–10, 212.

[90] Mitrofanova, "Istochniki i popolneniia," pp. 208–9; Dadykin, "O chislennosti i istochnikakh," pp. 48–49.

[91] Filtzer, *Soviet Workers and Stalinist Industrialization*, pp. 236–43.

focus on conflict with the "intelligentsia," prevented workers from identifying daily manifestations of social tensions in their immediate environment as antagonism between themselves and the elite. Even though these tensions could lead to open political conflict with higher-ups, this was liable to take place in the buffer zone between the elite and the masses. Moreover, such conflict made integral part of the former's attempts to regulate the operation of the administrative hierarchy and easily lent itself to manipulation by those who belonged to the apparatus.

These circumstances explain the outbursts of tension whenever an occasion presented itself, though not why on some occasions of this kind workers in all seriousness demanded the authorization of opposition political parties—as did, by the way, peasants.[92] At the same time, however, these circumstances also indicate that insofar as the constitution of workers into a genuine political class was concerned, it occurred above all in the sphere of *mentalités* and in negative terms in the formative period of the Soviet system. That is, it was limited to a certain consciousness of the need to achieve autonomous institutionalization of the defense of their interests and of the obstacle the regime represented to attempts to grasp, let alone realize, this requirement. If there are some indications that despite powerful countervailing influences, Soviet workers were by no means unaware of the advantages of independent interest representation, their ways of acting out their conflict with the regime are rather far from bespeaking an understanding of the nature and consequences of system-inherent constraints. Their adaptation to such constraints, when all is said and done, was characteristic of an urban toiling mass rather than a political class of labor.

[92] *WKP* 109, p. 30, *WKP* 357, p. 11, *WKP* 499, pp. 125–27, 183–85.

10

Stephen Kotkin

Coercion and Identity: Workers'
Lives in Stalin's Showcase City

"Magnitka taught us how to work. Magnitka taught us how to live."
—Elena Dzhaparidze, *Slovo o Magnitke*

Weary of the anonymity of barracks life, the residents of barracks no. 8 in Magnitogorsk tacked a sign near the entrance with a list of all those living inside. It gave their name, year of birth, place of origin, class origin, trade, Komsomol and party membership (or lack thereof), and location of employment. As Cherneev the initiator of the action explained, "When someone saw the list—for example, that Stepanov, a fitter, a Komsomol, a shock worker, fulfills his plan such-and-such percent, works on the construction of the blast furnaces—one immediately understood what kind of people lived here."[1] Such acts of self-identification became routine, and enveloped the entire society.

When studying the workers of tsarist Russia, historians have found their chief task to be explaining how it came to pass that, as Reginald Zelnik puts it, "within a period of less than sixty years, the workers of the most politically 'backward' European country were transformed from a small segment of a caste of peasant-serfs into Europe's most class-conscious and revolutionary proletariat."[2] Precisely the opposite question

The author gratefully acknowledges helpful comments and suggestions by Sonya Rose, Michael Burawoy, Lewis Siegelbaum, the other participants of the conference, and an anonymous reader for Cornell University Press. Funding for the research and writing of this essay was provided by the International Research and Exchanges Board, the Social Science Research Council, the Harriman Institute, and Princeton University.

[1] Cherneev added that they also put up a copy of Stalin's "six conditions," as enunciated in his 1931 speech, plus some slogans, and issued a wall newspaper. GARF, f. 7952 (istoriia fabrik i zavodov), op. 5, d. 319, ll. 28–29.

[2] Reginald Zelnik, "Essay Review: Russian Workers and the Revolutionary Movement," *Journal of Social History* 6 (winter 1972–73): 214–37. For an excellent review of the literature and a sophisticated attempt at synthesis, see Tim McDaniel, *Autocracy, Capitalism, and Revolution in Russia* (Berkeley and Los Angeles, 1988). Additional comments can be found in Stephen Kotkin, "One-Hand Clapping: Russian Workers and 1917," *Labor History* 32, no. 4 (1991), pp. 604–20.

might be posed about Soviet workers: how did it come about that within a period of less than twenty years, the revolutionary proletariat of Europe's first self-proclaimed state of workers and peasants were turned into Europe's quietest working class? A substantial part of the answer to that question, and to the question of the character and potency of Stalinism, is contained on that simple scrap of paper tacked onto a Magnitogorsk barracks.[3]

Ordinarily, the study of a working-class town would be expected to devote considerable attention to worker self-expression, even if only in extreme situations (such as during strikes and demonstrations), and to explore the causes of worker unrest. But in Magnitogorsk there were neither strikes nor riots, and the only demonstrations were state-organized glorifications of the regime and its leadership. In this sprawling steeltown, organized worker protest was conspicuous by its absence.

For the Soviet regime and its defenders, this was no paradox. The absence of strikes followed logically from the proposition that workers themselves held power and thus by definition welcomed the policy of industrialization, "their" policy, with enthusiasm. That there *was* mass enthusiasm lends an ostensible plausibility to this Soviet view. Indeed, although there is scattered evidence of worker discontent in the contemporary Soviet press, manifestations of worker consciousness in official sources were overwhelmingly supportive of the status quo.[4]

Rejecting state-censored expressions of worker consciousness, non-Soviet commentators at first adopted two sets of explanations for the apparent "quietism" of the Soviet working class under Stalin. One view held that the regime's structure and repressiveness precluded any possibility of worker autonomy and collective action, an argument bolstered by the testimony of many former Soviet citizens.[5] Another view, not in-

---

[3] What follows is adapted from chapter 5 of my book *Magnetic Mountain: Stalinism as a Civilization* (Berkeley and Los Angeles, 1994).

[4] Donald Filtzer, *Soviet Workers and Stalinist Industrialization: The Formation of Modern Soviet Production Relations, 1928–1941* (Armonk, N.Y., 1986), pp. 76–87, provides an overview of press reports that contain "negative" information. The Jay K. Zawodny Collection at the Hoover Institution Archives contains some of the best interviews with former Soviet workers. Merle Fainsod, who studied the party archives from Smolensk, a predominantly agricultural region, noted that "the documents provide unimpeachable evidence of widespread mass discontent with Soviet rule." Fainsod, *Smolensk under Soviet Rule* (Cambridge, Mass., 1958), p. 449. It seems highly likely that such evidence could be found in the Cheliabinsk oblast security police files, which as of 1991 remained inaccessible.

[5] This view has been expressed by Solomon Schwarz, who wrote a number of well-informed pieces on workers under Stalin for the contemporary Menshevik émigré newspaper *Sotsialisticheskii vestnik*, and later developed his articles into the first major English-language study of the subject, *Labor in the Soviet Union* (New York, 1951). Schwarz's book, written during the early years of World War II and meant to cover the period 1928–41, was envisioned as an antidote to Soviet propaganda about the achievements of workers under so-

compatible with the first, saw the lack of worker political activism in the disintegration of the working class as a result of the civil war and the so-called peasantization of the workforce that began in the early 1930s, when the surviving working class was "diluted" by "raw recruits." The new proletarians were characterized by a cultural backwardness characterized by a desire to be ruled by a strong tsar-father and no inclination to pursue their "proper" working-class interests.[6] Against the Soviet assertion of harmony between worker and regime, these scholars assumed the existence of an objective antagonism, even when an overwhelming preponderance of the available sources indicated support.

In reaction to the assumption that the regime and the people had no common interests, a wave of "revisionist" scholarship arose. Agreeing with certain of their predecessors on the existence of widespread support for Stalin and his programs, revisionists regarded such support not as the "false consciousness" of a "backward" proletariat, but as an expression of genuine self-interest linked to worker advancement or social mobility. Such a view tended not only to accept at face value the absence of visible social discontent but even to suggest the presence of genuine social cohesion.[7] It would be hard to imagine an interpretive controversy with the opposing sides farther apart: either disgruntled workers who despised the regime, or contented workers who applauded it (whether "falsely" or "correctly"). Perhaps the time has come to redefine the questions.

There can be no doubt that the regime was repressive, that the influx

---

cialism. The author thus gave detailed exposition to the Draconian labor laws and their obviously repressive intent. At the same time, however, he documented the violations and circumventions of those same laws—without making it clear what such findings meant for his principal argument about the Soviet regime's "control" over labor. Not until Donald Filtzer's 1986 book did anyone attempt a synoptic reevaluation of labor under Stalin. Filtzer sought to resolve the seeming paradox that had emerged in Schwarz's work whereby continued and severe repression by the regime was shown to have coexisted with effective circumvention of regime dictates by workers.

[6] This is the position of Trotsky, who sought to pinpoint the "social base" of the usurping bureaucracy. Such a view was also espoused by the Mensheviks in their journal, *Sotsialis-ticheskii vestnik*. (Solomon Schwarz, one of the main contributors to the Menshevik publication, implicitly adopts this view in his book on Soviet labor, cited in note 5.) John Barber, in his many unpublished but nonetheless influential essays for the Birmingham Centre for Russian and East European Studies, adopts a variant of it. Soviet historians have also promoted the notion that "backward" peasant workers adversely affected the "consciousness" of the working class. See A. I. Vdovin and V. Z. Drobizhev, *Rost rabochego klassa SSSR 1917–1940 gg.* (Moscow, 1976). In yet another variation, Vladimir Andrle ascribes the willingness of workers to denounce innocent people in exchange for rewards to the flux characteristic of an "unsettled and uprooted society." See his *Workers in Stalin's Russia: Industrialization and Social Change in a Planned Economy* (New York, 1988). It seems that no one likes to characterize admiration for dictatorship as a rational choice exercised by conscious individuals.

[7] Sheila Fitzpatrick, *Education and Social Mobility in the Soviet Union, 1921–34* (Cambridge, 1979).

of millions of peasants changed the composition of the labor force, and that many thousands of workers "moved up" to become administrators and party officials. But the usefulness of all these conceptions for understanding workers' lives and behavior is limited for at least two reasons. First, these categories are trapped within the terms of the phenomena they are trying to analyze. Moving from the primary to the secondary sources, one is struck by the extent to which the categories and debates of contemporaries pervade subsequent "analyses." Historians are able to study the "peasantization" of the workforce in the 1930s, to take one example, precisely because the authorities thought in such terms and collected data accordingly. For us it should be important that large numbers of peasants entered the working classes not because they were "backward" or even peasants but because the regime defined them this way and treated them as such.

Second, these conceptions are limited by their polarization along a single axis of repression and enthusiasm with the evidence such that one can "demonstrate" worker support by referring to official sources and worker opposition by citing émigré ones. But how, in fact, do we recognize social support? What constitutes evidence of it? Is the absence of organized political protest a sign of atomization or of social cohesion, or of neither? Does it make sense to analyze social support in terms of groups, and if so, by what criteria should such groups be differentiated? By income and social status? Level of education? Membership in the party? Class? Finally, what is the relative usefulness of official sources versus émigré ones which often tell a diametrically opposed story?

Amid such an incongruity of views in the understanding of workers under Stalin, an important advance was made by Donald Filtzer. Taking up where Solomon Schwarz left off (although without saying as much), Filtzer combined a diligent and sophisticated reading of the contemporary Soviet press with an equally exhaustive review of émigré testimony, and displayed a fine appreciation of paradox and contradiction. Characterizing Stalinist industrialization as inherently exploitative in a Marxist sense, he assumed that workers ought to have recognized their "class interests" and resisted the expropriation of their "surplus value" by the emerging elite, or bureaucracy. But workers did not do so.

By way of explanation Filtzer revived the argument that the old working class was crushed by industrialization: depoliticized, it could manage only individualized responses, such as changing jobs and getting drunk. He also argued that although a new "working class" had formed, its members were not up to collective action, preoccupied as they were with personal survival in the difficult circumstances of widespread shortages, speed-ups, physical intimidation, and public ridicule. At the same time, Filtzer did show that workers often "resisted" the new terms of work, just not on a collective basis. He recognized the importance of worker self-expression as demonstrated in a variety of behaviors (turnover, soldiering) otherwise dismissed as evidence of disorientation and *anomie*. Yet he did not treat the remarkable proliferation of statements about workers' identities made by workers and others, including the authorities, with the same seriousness.[8] As a result, his analysis of the terms on which workers became part of the Stalinist enterprise, though the best to date, is unnecessarily incomplete.

I adopt a different approach. I will attempt to trace the various ways of seeing and conceptualizing work, the work process, and the worker that were then prevalent. My points of departure will be the identification of certain problems: productivity, worker discipline and aptitudes, social origin, and political loyalty. My aim will be to show how these conceptualizations affected the workers' lives and self-understanding. Such formulations are not reducible to "ideology." They are better thought of as dynamic relations of power. For this reason, the task is to approach them not from the point of view of meaning, or symbolic constructs, but as a question of maneuver and countermaneuvers—in short, as part of what Michel Foucault called the little tactics of the habitat.

The far-reaching effects that resulted from understanding work and workers in particular ways were made possible by the links of these formulations with the practices and techniques that the regime introduced to address the problems identified. Those techniques ranged from questionnaires, to the numerical assignment of skill levels, output quotas, and piece rates to labor books, to autobiographical confessions. It is to the techniques themselves and the context into which they were introduced that I turn to analyze how what was said about work and the workplace determined how workers were understood by others and how they understood themselves.

Work, Worker, and Workplace under Socialism

On hearing in February 1932 that the first Magnitogorsk blast furnace was blown in, a telegram was dispatched in the name of the party and the state and signed by Stalin. "I congratulate the workers and the ad-

---

[8] Filtzer, *Soviet Workers*, pp. 254–55. Expecting a proper "Marxist" response by exploited workers, Filtzer had trouble with actual manifestations of worker consciousness, reluctantly admitting that "expressions of discontent did not necessarily reflect a sophisticated political awareness of events or alternatives. Frequently they were couched in the most reactionary nationalist, anti-Semitic, and male-chauvinist terms." Unfortunately, he did not explore this point. Nonetheless, Filtzer's discussion of workers under Stalin has much to commend it, and we will draw on it at points in the discussion.

ministrative and technical personnel of the Magnitogorsk metallurgical complex on their successful fulfillment of the first order of the construction program," Stalin said, adding: "I have no doubt that the Magnitogorsk workers will likewise successfully fulfill the main part of the 1932 program, will build three more blast furnaces, open-hearth furnaces, and rolling mills, and will thus fulfill with honor their duty to their country."[9]

As Stalin's telegram, among many other documents, shows, in the Soviet context work was not simply a material necessity but also a civic obligation. Everyone had the right to work; no one had the right not to work.[10] Failure to work (in a "socially useful" manner) was a punishable offense, and the chief punishment was forced labor (*prinuditel'naia rabota*). Convicts were required to work not merely to make good their "debt" to society but above all to be able to rejoin that society as transformed individuals. Work served as both the instrument and measure of normality.[11]

On top of this, anyone who belonged to the social group "workers" shouldered the historical responsibilities that, according to the regime's ideology, fell to this special class. As is well known, Marxism-Leninism conceptualized social structure in class terms.[12] Class analysis, which provided a coherent and simplified worldview and thus a ready-made interpretation of any event or situation, explained and justified numerous state policies, including the liquidation of the "kulaks" as a class and their deportation to places such as Magnitogorsk. Class analysis also helped make possible numerous campaigns and mobilizations for increased vigilance or greater industrial output that were predicated on emotional appeals against class enemies, both inside and outside the country. And it allowed mere individuals to become a part of the movement of history.

Whereas under "capitalism" work was thought to consist of the appropriation of "surplus value" by a small number of individuals for their own benefit, under socialism such exploitation by definition did not exist: there were no "capitalists." Instead, people worked for themselves, and by doing so were building a better world. Not all work sites were equally "strategic,"

[9] *Pravda*, 30 March 1932, reprinted in Stalin, *Sochineniia* (Moscow, 1953), 13:133. A copy of the original can be found in RTsKhIDNI, f. 558, op. 1.

[10] These strictures were set down in the 1936 constitution. Under article 12, work became compulsory. Under article 118, it was listed as a right.

[11] Sentences of up to six months' forced labor were to be served at the convicted person's usual place of employment with a reduction in pay (not more than 25 percent). Sentences of more than six months were also served at one's regular place of employment, unless the sentence specified "deprivation of freedom," which meant relocation to a labor colony. A new RSFSR Corrective Labor Code was introduced in 1933, replacing the one from 1924. It is excerpted in *Sbornik dokumentov po istorii ugolovnogo zakonodatel'stva SSSR i RSFSR, 1917–1952 gg.* (Moscow, 1953), pp. 367–78.

[12] Leszek Kolakowski, *Main Currents of Marxism*, 3 vols. (Oxford, 1978–81), especially vol. 3, chaps. 1–3.

but through class analysis the output of an individual miner or steel smelter acquired international significance as a blow against capitalism and a contribution to the furthering of socialism. In other words, the exertions of every worker at the bench were inscribed in an international struggle.

Class analysis served as a sophisticated technique of rule, and armed with this class-based view of the world, the Soviet leadership pursued as one of its chief goals the creation of a specifically Soviet working class. Although the country had supposedly experienced a proletarian revolution in 1917, twelve years later the leadership still worried about what it considered to be an embarrassingly small proletariat. With the crash industrialization program the ranks of the proletariat expanded greatly, indeed even more than the planners had originally foreseen.

About the only target of the first Five-Year Plan that was not merely reached but surpassed was the one for total employment, and the bulge in the country's workforce was even greater during the Second Five-Year Plan.[13] Magnitgorsk was a case in point. By 1938, less than ten years after the arrival of the first group of settlers, the Magnitogorsk metallurgical complex employed almost twenty thousand people in its various shops, from the blast furnaces to the state farms.[14] Several thousand more people were employed by the construction trust Magnitostroi, the coke plant, and the railroad.[15] As of 1940, the city's total workforce numbered approximately 51,100 people.[16]

[13] The plan foresaw an increase from 11.9 million employed in 1928–29 to 15.8 million by 1932–33, but in 1932 the actual number of people employed was 22.9 million. In heavy industry proper, there were 6.5 million people employed in 1932, as against 3.1 million in 1928. In other words, in less than five years, both the number of employed in general and the number of people employed in industry doubled. *Sotsialisticheskoe stroitel'stvo SSSR* (Moscow, 1936), p. 508. After a brief period when the number employed decreased slightly, from 1934 on employment climbed again. By 1937, the end of the Second Five-Year Plan, total employment reached 27 million. *Results of Fulfilling the Second Five-Year Plan* (Moscow, 1939), p. 104. Even though the latter figure fell short of the plan target of 28.9 million, it capped an increase in the workforce in one decade of over 15 million. When one recalls that by 1921–22, following years of war, revolution, and civil war, employment had shrunk to approximately 6.5 million, including only 1.24 million in industry, it becomes clear how far the country had come in providing a proletariat for the "proletarian revolution."

[14] *Magnitogorskii rabochii*, 16 May 1938. This was down from the summer of 1936, when there were 25,882 people at the steel plant, of whom 20,749 were categorized as workers *(rabochie)*, 1,273 as employees *(sluzhashchie)*, 1,894 as engineers and technicians *(ITR)*, 1,244 as young service personnel *(MOP)*, and 723 as apprentices *(ucheniki)*. The previous year, August 1935, the factory had employed 24,114 people. *Tekhniko-ekonomicheskie pokazateli raboty zavoda* (Magnitogorsk, 1936).

[15] According to John Scott, "the entire coke and chemical plant employed about 2,000 workers. Of these, some ten percent were so-called engineers and technical personnel, including foremen, superintendents, planners, and so on." Scott, *Behind the Urals: An American Worker in Russia's City of Steel* (Bloomington, Ind., 1989), p. 156; see also *Magnitogorskii rabochii*, 9 June 1937.

[16] This figure included 21,500 in industry, of whom 10,589 worked in ferrous metallurgy

This new workforce created virtually *ex nihilo*, had to be trained, and that training was conceived in specific terms.[17] For new workers, learning how to work became more than a question of exchanging agricultural time and the agricultural calendar for the eight-hour shift, the five-day work week, and the Five-Year Plan. Anxious to create a Soviet working class, the leadership was no less concerned about workers' political attitudes and allegiance. New workers had to be taught how to work, and all workers had to be taught how properly to understand the political significance of their work. Soviet-style proletarianization meant acquiring industrial *and* political literacy, understood as the complete acceptance of the party's rule and willing participation in the grand crusade of "building socialism."[18]

To attain such goals much faith was placed in the transformative powers of the factory system. With the socialist revolution, the factory, far from being a place of exploitation and of shame—as it was reputed to have been under capitalism—was to become a palace of labor manned by politically conscious, literate, and skilled workers filled with pride in their work.[19] In the event, most new workers, even those who eventually staffed the factories, began as construction workers, and it was in construction

---

proper. GAChO, f. 804, op. 11, d. 105, l. 37. In December 1931, there had been 54,600 workers on the site, virtually all of whom were employed in construction. RGAE, f. 4086, op. 2, d. 42, l. 28. The number of construction workers declined precipitously toward the end of the 1930s when little new construction was undertaken. By 1940, there were 4,200 workers in construction, whereas at the end of 1936, there had been 8,800. (The comparison is not exact, since the data for 1936 include engineers and technicians.) *Magnitogorskii rabochii,* 18 December 1936.

[17] That many workers began as unskilled and illiterates, as "peasants," certainly affected how this training was conceived and implemented. But all workers regardless of social origin had to go through a "training" in life and work. Among the resolutions adopted at the 1932 first Magnitogorsk party conference on what was called "cultural construction" was one concerning the need for "the re-education [perevospitanie] of the new strata of workers." *Rezoliutsiia pervoi Magnitogorskoi partkonferentsii po kultstroitel'stvu na 1932 g.* (Magnitogorsk, 1932), p. 4. Statistics on the social composition of the Soviet workforce are given in Adolf Rashin, "Dinamika promyshlennykh kadrov SSSR za 1917–1958 gg.," in *Izmenneniia v chislennosti i sostave sovetskogo rabochego klassa: Sbornik statei* (Moscow, 1961), pp. 7–73. A discussion of published contemporary statistical sources can be found in John D. Barber, "The Composition of the Soviet Working Class, 1928–1941," CREES Discussion Papers, Soviet Industrialization Project, no. 16 (Birmingham, England, 1978).

[18] Such fears were expressed in a typical instructional pamphlet from 1929 on party membership purges: "These new workers ... have never seen and known what class struggle means, and why and how discipline is needed in the ranks of the proletariat. ... For them the factory is neither the property of the working class that was taken by the working class from the capitalists, nor the child of the proletariat that has been erected by Soviet power, but rather a place in which they can earn a little extra to strengthen their own farms." I. I. Korotkov, "K proverke i chistke proizvodstvennykh iacheek," in E. M. Iaroslavskii, ed., *Kak provodit chistku partii* (Moscow, 1929), p. 83.

[19] An excellent example of this thinking can be found in the children's book by N. P. Mislavskii, *Magnitogorsk* (Moscow, 1931).

that they confronted the problem of what were called "socialist attitudes [*otnosheniia*] to labor."[20]

Construction work during the five-year plans was performed in rushes, or "storms," a style that, although likened to "the very old, rural, rhythm-setting work cry [*vziali*],"[21] was christened with a new term, shock work (*udarnyi trud*).[22] Predicated on the belief that vastly higher productivity could be achieved through a combination of labor exploits and better work organization, shock work was facilitated by the generally low level of mechanization and carried out in gangs or brigades. To be sure, the obsession with dramatically raising productivity was sometimes associated with the introduction of new technology. But in construction, where shock work was most widely developed, given the level of technology, most often extra effort became the main method of "rationalization."[23]

The authorities sought to extend the shock brigades into a mass move-ment (*udarnichestvo*) through a series of campaigns and mobilizations, the most important of which began in 1929 and was called socialist com-petition. Socialist competition took the form of a challenge, often in writ-ing, of one factory, shop, brigade, or individual by another. Challenges were also made of the plan in the form of a counterplan (*vstrechnyi*), or a proposal to accomplish more in less time. In practice, what this meant was that singular feats of daring and overexertion compelled almost eve-ryone else to do likewise or risk ridicule, suspicion, and, in some cases, arrest.

Theoretically, socialist competition differed from competition under capitalism in that the aim was not supposed to be the triumph of a victor but the raising of everyone up to the level of the most advanced (*pere-dovik*). Such terms as tugboating (*buksirovat'*) and sponsorship (*shefstvo*) were used to express the goal of lifting up the less advanced. Yet although intended as a socially cohesive device to raise productivity, socialist com-petition more often served as a means of dividing enthusiastic militants

[20] "The construction of the Magnitogorsk factory," the Central Committee decreed in 1931, "should become a practical school for the creation of new methods and forms of socialist labor." See "O stroitel'stve Magnitogorskogo metallurgicheskogo zavoda," *Pravda*, 26 January 1931; reprinted in *Partiinoe stroitel'stvo*, February 1931, pp. 94–96.

[21] Moshe Lewin, *The Making of the Soviet System: Essays in the Social History of Interwar Russia* (New York, 1985), p. 37.

[22] According to Lewis Siegelbaum, " 'Shock work' is a term that originated during the Civil War period to denote the performance of particularly arduous or urgent tasks. It acquired new meaning in 1927–1928 when isolated groups of workers, primarily members of the Komsomol, organized brigades to fulfill obligations over and above their work as-signments. These ranged from cutting down on absences and abstaining from alcohol to overfulfilling output norms and reducing the per unit cost of production." *Stakhanovism and the Politics of Productivity in the USSR, 1935–1941* (Cambridge, 1988), p. 40.

[23] Lewis Siegelbaum, "Shock Workers," in *The Modern Encyclopedia of Russian and So-viet History* (Gulf Breeze, Fla., 1983), 35:23–27.

willing to attempt extraordinary feats of labor exertion (shock work) from more established workers and workers who generally tried to avoid political effusions.

The effects of the productivity campaigns involving shock work were reinforced by the new wage policy introduced in 1931, when "equalization" was condemned and replaced by differentiation. Wages were individualized and, through the device of piece rates, geared to each unit of output. Each worker was assigned an output quota, or norm, and outstanding work performance, defined as production above the norm, was to be rewarded.[24] In theory, as more and more of the workforce moved over to piece rates, wages could become a powerful lever for raising productivity. In practice, managers and especially foremen, desperate to hold onto "scarce" labor power, readily credited workers for fictitious work and, in any case, could award supplementary payments and bonuses to workers to make up for deductions that resulted from the failure to fulfill norms.[25]

Not surprisingly, there were fierce struggles over the calculation and assignment of norms and considerable invention in the measurement and recording of output—so much invention that although a large majority of workers in Magnitogorsk theoretically worked above their norms, production at the plant continually fell below plan targets.[26] (Meanwhile, the number of norm-setters and piece-rate calculators proliferated.)[27] Yet although the impact of the differentiated wage policy on productivity may have been questionable, its effect on the understanding of workers was plain. Workers were individualized and their performance measured on a percentage basis, which permitted ready comparisons.[28]

[24] Rewards were individualized, but others could be carried along in the recipient's wake. Trade union lists of "workers" awarded special vacation trips because of outstanding performance, for example, almost always included the shift boss and shop chief where the worker was employed. MFGAChO, f. 118, op. 1, d. 80, ll. 96–101.

[25] Scott, *Behind the Urals*, p. 72. The proliferation of bonuses followed a compelling logic. The regime could rail against overpayment of wages, but those individuals charged with enforcing output quotas and piece rates were under more pressure to meet production targets, and the only way to meet production targets was by enlisting the cooperation of the workforce. The ability to regulate wages strictly, like much else, became hostage to the measurement of production in terms of quotas and the overriding concern to achieve those quotas, even if only on paper. See Filtzer, *Soviet Workers*, p. 232.

[26] The wage schedule based on norms was undermined by the uneven pace of production, which fluctuated with interruptions in the supply of raw materials and the end-of-the-quarter storms to fulfill the plan. For a discussion of how the unpredictability of production was institutionalized, and thereby became predictable, see *Voprosy profdvizheniia*, 1933, no. 11: 65–71 (a study of the Kulakov factory), as cited in Filtzer, *Soviet Workers*, p. 211.

[27] Scott, *Behind the Urals*, p. 75.

[28] For data on wage differentials in 1933, see Scott, *Behind the Urals*, p. 49; for data as of 1 January 1937, see *Obzor raboty zavoda za ianvar 1937g.* (Magnitogorsk, 1937), p. 17. Over time, average nominal wages generally rose, although they could be reduced, as dem-

Shock work, combined with socialist competition, became a means of differentiating individuals as well as a technique of political recruitment within the working class. As such, its effectiveness was augmented by the calculated use of publicity. Mobile displays of honor and shame, colored red and black, carried lists of workers' names. Airplanes were used to stand for those racing forward, crocodiles for those lagging behind. "Lightning sheets" were issued in which the best workers and worst "slackers" were named, and banners were awarded to the victors of competitions. With the banners circulating as the fortunes of brigades rose and fell, sometimes from shift to shift, work could become a sort of sport.[29] Before long permanent honor rolls for recognizing a shop's "best workers" were posted, adding to the pressure on workers.[30]

This extensive politicization of work was facilitated by the presence in and around the work place of agencies other than management. Each construction area and factory shop, for example, had its own primary party organization, which maintained a strong party presence through membership and meetings. The party also sought to reach out to the non-party mass in the factory, a task for which each shop employed "agitators," that is, people whose job it was to discuss political issues and present interpretations of domestic and international events.[31]

One agitator in Magnitogorsk's mill 300, Z. S. Grishchenko, delivered twelve reports on the domestic and international situations and conducted six readings of newspapers during the course of a single month in 1936. To be able to lead discussions and steer them in the desired direction, Grishchenko prepared by scrutinizing as many Soviet newspaper as possible, paying particular attention to the speeches and directives of Stalin and the party leadership. He could also rely on agitation manuals pub-

---

onstrated by data from the mine. *Stakhanovskii opyt magnitogorskogo rudnika: Sbornik statei* (Moscow, 1939), p. 187.

[29] See, for example, the incidents related in GARF, f. 7952, op. 5, d. 306, ll. 23–24.

[30] Foremen and brigade leaders also felt pressured to designate workers under their charge as shock workers, to demonstrate their leadership skills to the higher bosses and to keep their workers happy. In a satire that appeared in the factory newspaper, a brigade leader said to have no time for socialist competitions or verifying norm fulfillment percentages nonetheless recognized the need to designate his charges as shock workers. In the satire, he assembles the brigade and begins reading off their names: " 'Burnin!' he shouts. 'Enter into the ranks of shock workers?' 'Enter him,' someone yells out. Next to the name Burnin appears a mark and he becomes a shock worker." In such fashion Burnin goes through the entire list, and each time someones calls out "Enter him." Those he accidently passes over are named at the end and added. But he forgets about himself, as someone points out. By this time the rest of the brigade has left. No one remains to shout "enter him," so the brigade leader is left out, foiling his plans to make his whole brigade into shock workers. *Magnitogorskii metall*, 28 August 1935.

[31] In late February 1936, the party organization organized a special meeting of agitators at which secretary Rafael Khitarov delivered a report outlining the nature of their work. *Magnitogorskii rabochii*, 14 March 1936.

lished by the party's agitprop department. Grishchenko was said to take extra time to tutor those workers who appeared unable to grasp the issues, or who had somehow fallen behind.[32]

Not all of the two hundred and fourteen agitators at the steel plant as of 1936 were as motivated or thorough as Grishchenko appears to have been, and the effects of such agitation varied. When asked why he failed to conduct agitation, one organizer in the coke shop remarked, "What will I babble [to them]?" He added ominously, "And what happens if I confuse something, make a mistake, then I will be charged!"[33] Such hesitancy could draw backing from reports in the central press, which ridiculed how agitators visited a shop and interrupted production to harangue workers about the problems of lost work time.[34]

But shops continued to be visited by agitators, whose work was considered integral to promoting production even though their agitation sometimes subverted it. A speech by Stalin at an All-Union Gathering of Stakhanovites in November 1935, for example, was printed, distributed, and discussed throughout the Magnitogorsk steel plant in a massive effort to induce entire shops into accepting "obligations" for increased output. Typically, such exhortations for increased output—indeed, all discussion of domestic events—were placed against the international background, which was made to seem anything but remote, yet could be extremely complex. Only one month into his new job as agitator for mill 500, the activist Sazhko reported that workers asked a great many questions about foreign news, especially after his presentations on the Italian-Abyssinian War and the 1936 Soviet-French Diplomatic Agreement.[35]

If the presence of the party in the factory was the most visible, that of the security police, or NKVD, was no less consequential. In the Magnitogorsk complex, just as in every Soviet industrial undertaking, government bureau, or higher educational institution, there was a so-called "special department" connected with the NKVD. The special departments, whose work was secret and separate from the factory administration, employed networks of informants, operated without limits, either from law or custom, and generally made sure that everyone, manager or worker, assisted them in their undertakings.[36] For NKVD officials, the

---

[32] *Magnitogorskii rabochii*, 15 December 1936.

[33] *Magnitogorskii metall*, 3 November 1935 and 30 June 1936.

[34] See the example given in Andrle, "How Backward Workers," p. 155, cited from *Voprosy profdvizheniia*, 1934, no. 7:50.

[35] He complained that the lack of a decent map hindered the sessions. *Magnitogorskii rabochii*, 4 March 1936.

[36] See Scott, *Behind the Urals*, pp. 84–85. Scott's claim that "until 1935 . . . there were few arrests. But material was accumulating in dossiers" was echoed by, among others, the manager of a Soviet factory in the Ukraine who fled the country. See Viktor Kravchenko, *I Chose Freedom* (New York, 1946), p. 75.

discovery of security problems was a surefire means to advance their careers.

Trade unions, too, were prominent in the workplace, even though in a workers' state, trade unions could not perform their traditional roles, as under capitalism, of defending worker interests against owners, since the workers were, technically, the owners. Instead, unions in the USSR were enlisted in the regime's efforts to achieve higher productivity, with the unsurprising result that they commanded little respect from the workers. This situation, known to the Soviet leadership, soon changed.[37] According to John Scott, workers' assessments of trade unions were altered in 1934 and 1935, when the unions reorganized their work and assumed responsibility for the wide range of social welfare activities sponsored by the regime.[38]

In 1937 alone, the Magnitogorsk branch of the metal workers' union had a budget of 2.7 million rubles, plus a social insurance fund of 8.8 million rubles (financed by pay deductions). That year, more than 3 million rubles of social insurance funds were distributed for pregnancy leave and temporary or permanent incapacity. Trade union funds were also used to buy cows, pigs, sewing machines, and motorcycles for workers, send workers' children to summer camp, and pay for sport clubs. Trade unions had become central to Soviet workers' lives.[39]

Soviet production space was a focal point for the intersection of a variety of agencies: the party, the NKVD, and trade unions, as well as safety inspectors and health experts. Their many concerns ranged from increased steel production and proper ventilation of the shops to political education, police intrigue, and to injured workers or their families. That there were contradictions between some of these aims and that some organizations worked at cross-purposes only underscored the singular importance of the workplace. Although management, the party, the NKVD, the trade unions, and technical experts were all present in the factory, they wielded varying degrees of influence. Some concerns obviously enjoyed a higher priority, none more so than the broadly defined notion of state security (*gosudarstvennaia bezopasnost'*), a reflection in part of the international "class struggle."

In the Soviet workplace the terms at issue were neither workers' ownership nor control; both already existed by virtue of the regime's self-definition as a worker's state. The matters of contention were the performance of the workers and all actions and attitudes that were related to their work performance, including actual or suspected political loyal-

[37] G. K. Ordzhonikidze, *Stati i rechi* (Moscow, 1957), 2:458.
[38] Scott, *Behind the Urals*, p. 36.
[39] *Magnitgorskii rabochii*, 6 February 1938.

ties. Within such parameters, the relentless campaigns to boost productivity and political awareness through enhanced individual performance were logically promoted as expressions of advanced worker consciousness, and as the distinctive character of labor in a socialist society. No doubt the quintessential campaign in this regard was Stakhanovism, a movement sponsored by the regime following the coal-hewing feats of a Donbas miner, Aleksei Stakhanov, achieved one day in August 1935.[40]

After Stakhanov's "record" shift, attempts were organized to achieve analogous breakthroughs in other industries, and then to convert these record-setting shifts into longer mobilizations. Across the country, 11 January 1936 was declared a Stakhanovite Twenty-Four-Hours (*sutki*), which was followed by a Stakhanovite Five-Day (*piatidnevka*) between 21 and 25 January, a Stakhanovite Ten-Day (*dekada*), then a Stakhanovite Month, and so on, until 1936 was christened the Stakhanovite Year.[41] Some Stakhanovites seem to have become obsessed with making records, coming to the shop early, checking over the work space, keeping it clean, and inspecting the machinery.[42] Other workers, however, were said to have "incorrectly" understood the Stakhanovite Ten-Day: when the rush period ended, they drew the conclusion that "we worked for ten days, now we can relax."[43]

But relaxation was not part of the official program. In early 1936, newspaper headlines proclaimed the advent of "new norms for the new times."[44] Nikolai Zaitsev, chief of Magnitogorsk open-hearth shop no. 2, admitted in unpublished remarks that although Stakhanovism in his shop began only in January 1936, already by February the norms were raised, from 297 to 350 tons of steel per shift. Zaitsev added that no one was meeting the new norms.[45] In this vein, one worker in the coke shop was

[40] See particularly Siegelbaum, whose analysis of Stakhanovism as "both a state policy and a social phenomenon" takes full account of the many associations the word evoked: certain workers, certain methods of work, vocational schooling, as well as periods of intense work activity. *Stakhanovism and the Politics of Productivity*, pp. xii, 145.

[41] The central space of the city, Factory Administration Square, where holidays were publicly celebrated and political demonstrations were held, was (temporarily) renamed Stakhanovite Square. *Magnitogorskii rabochii*, 12 January and 4 May 1936.

[42] GARF, f. 7952, op. 5, d. 313, l. 88.

[43] *Magnitogorskii rabochii*, 1 March 1936. One Soviet historian of Magnitogorsk, writing soon after Stalin's death, disclosed that in just twelve days in January 1936, the number of Stakhanovites almost doubled, from 2,496 to 4,471. To this fact, however, he added that because there were not enough supplies, materials, or instruments, the efforts were not sustained but exhausted in "storms," during which workers did not take sufficient care of their machines. Valentin Serzhantov, "Metallurgi Magnitki v bor'be za osvoenie novoi tekhniki v gody vtoroi piatiletki," *Iz istorii revoliutsionnogo dvizheniia i sotsialisticheskogo stroitel'stva na iuzhnom Urale* (Cheliabinsk, 1959), pp. 236–37. An identical assessment for the Soviet automobile industry is given in V. Sakharov, *Zarozhdenie i razvitie stakhanovskogo dvizheniia v avtotraktornoi promyshlennosti* (Moscow, 1979), pp. 144–45.

[44] *Magnitogorskii rabochii*, 5 March 1936.

[45] GARF, f. 7952, op. 5, d. 397, ll. 45–46, 50. By contrast, Boris Bogoliubov, a "prisoner

reported to have told the factory newspaper, "With the norms now in existence I can't work as a Stakhanovite. If the norms are lowered, then I can call myself a Stakhanovite." Another reportedly said to the same source that "in winter I can work as a Stakhanovite, but in summer it is so hot by the ovens, I can't stand it."[46]

The center of the Stakhanovite movement in Magnitogorsk was the blooming mill, where behind the celebrated records lay much sweat and blood. "Nowadays work in the blooming mill has become very difficult physically," the Stakhanovite operator V. P. Ogorodnikov remarked, also in an unpublished discussion. "Earlier it was easy, because we handled 100 to 120 ingots, and for two to three hours of each shift we rested. Now we work practically the full eight hours, and it is very difficult."[47] The increased burden on the blooming's management, moreover, was no less great.

Fedor Golubitskii, who took over as chief of the blooming mill in 1936, evinced what must have been a prevalent view of labor relations, whereby it was the manager's task to "study people." He suggested that a manager had to get to know subordinates, how to interact with them, what their needs and moods were. Above all, he said, it was necessary not to lose contact with the masses. But Golubitskii conceded that during the periods of heightened activity associated with Stakhanovism, the shops were "working as if at war," and his job had become "a serious strain."[48]

Notwithstanding the pressures, Stakhanovism involved what appears to have been a genuine record-mania that transformed the task of rolling or smelting steel into sport. Under the heading "A Remarkable Year," an article commemorating the first anniversary of Stakhanov's record shift appeared under the name of Dmitrii Bogatyrenko, a worker in the blooming mill. In looking back over the year, Bogatyrenko divided it up by the number of ingots cut in "record-breaking" shifts:

12 September 1935	Ogorodnikov	211
22 September	Tishchenko	214
25 September	Bogatyrenko	219
9 October	Ogorodnikov	230
[?] October	Bogatyrenko	239

specialist" who was deputy chief of the mine, claimed in unpublished remarks recorded on 28 November 1936 that "at the mine, all norms were mastered. This didn't happen very easily, but all norms were mastered." Ibid., d. 304, l. 113.

[46] *Magnitogorskii metall*, 3 November 1935.

[47] GARF, f. 7952, op. 5, d. 312, l. 11.

[48] GARF, f. 7952, op. 5, d. 306, ll. 84–87, 101. For further discussion of the pressures brought to bear on management by Stakhanovism, see *Za industrializatsiiu*, 18 January 1936; *Sotsialisticheskii vestnik*, 28 December 1935; and Kravchenko, *I Chose Freedom*, p. 188.

He concluded succinctly: "This is what enthusiasm could accomplish."[49]

Such gamesmanship, which was lavishly reported in the newspaper (often with accompanying photographs), seems to have captured the imagination of an emergent Soviet working class. In unpublished remarks, Ogorodnikov explained that "My wife asks, 'Why don't you go anywhere, or do anything?' Why? Because I have to leave for work early, prepare everything, check things over, make sure everything's right. Work in the blooming mill is a contagious disease, [and] once you catch it, it sticks."[50] After their back-to-back records on 11 January 1936, both he and Chernysh received brand-new motorcycles.[51] For helping to organize record shifts, shop bosses were also given various awards, including large money bonuses, sometimes as high as 10,000 rubles. In March 1936, just before taking over as chief of the blooming mill, Golubitskii became one of four people in Magnitogorsk to be awarded automobiles.[52]

The Stakhanovite movement was noteworthy for opening broad new vistas for Soviet workers, whose meteoric rise was something to behold. Aleksei Tishchenko, who by the age of seventeen was a stevedore at a Donbas mine, came to Magnitogorsk in the fall of 1933 and was immediately made an apprentice bridge-crane operator in the blooming mill. By May 1935, the twenty-five-year-old Tishchenko was a full-fledged scissors operator, and over the next few months competed with other young Turks for the record of most ingots cut in a single shift.[53]

The advance on the job of such young Turks as Tishchenko was usually guided by one of the few established workers on hand. One *obermaster*, or head foreman, in mill 300, Mikhail Zuev, a veteran worker with fifty years' experience, asserted that whereas in the past, master artisans concealed the secrets of their skills, in the socialist society of 1936, he willingly imparted his skills to the new generation. The sixty-one-year-old Zuev, who had been "mobilized" to Magnitogorsk from Mariupol in March 1935, was frequently called on to make speeches, usually with the title "All Roads Are Open to Us," in which he would relate to the younger

---

[49] Bogatyrenko also pointed out that in the shop at the time of his article (August 1936) there was considerable idle time, that equipment often gave out, and that 215 ingots was still not a normal occurrence. Moreover, he revealed that "a few times I challenged the [other operators] to competitions," but there was "no support from the party or trade union, and no feeling of public support." *Magnitogorskii rabochii*, 14 August 1936.

[50] GARF, f. 7952, op. 5, d. 312, l. 11.

[51] *Magnitogorskii rabochii*, 14 August 1936.

[52] *Magnitogorskii rabochii*, 28 January and 1 March 1936.

[53] *Liudi Stalinskoi Magnitki* (Cheliabinsk, 1952), pp. 104–5.

generation how for more than thirty years he worked for "exploiters," but since the October Revolution he worked "only for the people."[54]

Pay increases for some Stakhanovites, predicated on the bonus system, were purposefully dramatic. The Zuev family—father Mikhail and three sons (Fedor, Vasilii, and Arsenii) whom he had trained—earned almost 54,000 rubles combined in 1936, when Mikhail Zuev topped all workers in Magnitogorsk with an annual salary of 18,524 rubles.[55] In December 1935, Zuev had become one of the first Magnitogorsk workers to receive the second highest state medal, the Order of the Red Banner.[56] The following summer, he received a trip (*putevka*) for his entire family to Sochi.[57]

Second to Zuev in earnings was Ogorodnikov. The blooming operator earned 17,774 rubles in 1936, part of which he spent on the construction of an individual house. "My house cost 17,000 rubles," Ogorodnikov related in an unpublished interview. "I paid 2,000 rubles [down] of my own money, and will pay another 7,800 in installments over twenty years. The rest the factory is paying." Before the revolution, perhaps only a factory's owner and top technical staff could put together that much money and buy a private home.[58]

Probably no Magnitogorsk Stakhanovite did better than Vladimir Shevchuk. A foreman (*master*) in the medium sorting mill (mill 500), Shevchuk was said to have averaged 935 rubles a month in the second half of 1935, and 1,169 in the first half of 1936. When asked what he did with all his money, he explained that he spent much of it on clothes. "My wife has three overcoats, a good fur coat, and I have two suits," Shevchuk reported. "Plus, I deposit money in the savings bank." He also had a rare three-room apartment and that summer had taken his family to the Crimea on vacation. Along with a bicycle, gramophone, and hunting gun, he was awarded the Order of the Red Banner. Shevchuk upheld his part of the bargain when, according to the *Magnitogorskii rabochii*, he "greeted" the death sentence handed out to the Trotskyites in 1936 "with a feeling of deep satisfaction."[59]

Shevchuk, Zuev, Ogorodnikov, Tishchenko, Bogatyrenko, Chernysh,

---

[54] *Magnitogorskii rabochii*, 21 November 1936; GARF, f. 7952, op. 5, d. 300, ll. 61–81.
[55] MFGAChO, f. 10, op. 1, d. 243, l. 3.
[56] At the same time, four bosses and one other worker received the Order of Lenin. *Magnitogorskii rabochii*, 11 December 1935.
[57] MFGAChO, f. 99, op. 1, d. 1091, l. 81.
[58] GARF, f. 7952, op. 5, d. 312, l. 14.
[59] *Magnitogorskii rabochii*, 27 August 1936; GARF, f. 7952, op. 5, d. 313, l. 140. The newspaper also reported that books (and also groceries) were being delivered to the homes of Stakhanovites. Workers complained, however, that they had no time to read, and that in place of the groceries they had ordered substitutes were delivered, and even these were of dubious quality. *Magnitogorskii rabochii*, 8 April and 17 June 1936.

and several others became household names. An August 1936 photo-
graphic display in the newspaper commemorating the first anniversary of
Aleksei Stakhanov's record included a list of twenty Magnitogorsk Stakhanovites: four from the rolling mill, one from the blast-furnace shop,
one from the open-hearth shop, and the rest from around the factory.
They were identified as the workers who had been placed on the plant's
honor roll (*pochetnaia doska*) and "earned the right to make a report to
Stalin and Ordzhonikidze."[60] One scholar has suggested distinguishing
between "ordinary" and "outstanding" Stakhanovites, limiting the latter
designation to perhaps a hundred or so for the entire country. Rather
than outstanding, it makes sense to call them "high-profile," for that is
how we know of them.[61]

Such publicity surrounding "high-profile" workers was of course part
of a calculated strategy. "To bathe individuals [*liudi*] from the people
[*narod*] in glory is of enormous significance," Ordzhonikidze had said in
Pravda. "In capitalist countries, nothing can compare with the popularity
of gangsters like Al Capone. In our country, under socialism, heroes of
labor must become the most famous."[62] Not long after Ordzhonikidze's
remarks were published, Rafael Khitarov, Magnitogorsk party secretary
during the heyday of the Stakhanovite movement, declared that Stakhanovites were "revolutionaries" in production.[63]

Khitarov compared the Stakhanovite campaign with party activism,
blending Stakhanovism into the political discourse on raised vigilance and
equating the "discoveries" in the workplace supposedly made possible by
Stakhanovism with those in the party organization, supposedly made possible by the exchange and verification of party cards. Not all Stakhanovites were party members, however. Ogorodnikov, who was apparently
prevented from joining the party owing to his class background, wrote
that "when I'm rolling steel and I overtake [Dmitrii] Bogatyrenko [a party
member], no one notices. But when Bogatyrenko overtakes me, then that's
good. I was like a partisan."[64]

Whether such intense competition between Ogorodnikov and Bogatyrenko was all that healthy became one of the principal themes of an unpublished manuscript about Stakhanovism in Magnitogorsk, written
during the course of events. The author remarked on the pressures felt in
each shop by each shift and shop boss to produce records, pointing out

---

[60] *Magnitogorskii rabochii*, 30 August 1936.

[61] Siegelbaum, *Stakhanovism and the Politics of Productivity*, p. 179.

[62] As quoted in S. R. Gershberg, *Rabota u nas takaia: Zapiski zhurnalista-pravdista trid-
tsatykh godov* (Moscow, 1971), p. 321.

[63] *Magnitogorskii rabochii*, 10 March 1936. The article originally appeared in *Pravda*, 4
March 1936.

[64] GARF, f. 7952, op. 5, d. 312, l. 49.

that one by one the machines broke down and that one worker in the record-breaking blooming mill lost his leg. And he wrote of the "unhealthy atmosphere" that had arisen in the shops where annointed workers went around "thinking they were Gods."[65]

Tensions caused by Stakhanovism were high. Ogorodnikov, who claimed that he was discriminated against in the shop and called "a self-seeker and a man only after money, an un-Soviet element with a kulak heritage," bolted from the mill on 30 March 1936, relocating to Makeevka and in the process causing a national scandal. It required the intervention of the People's Commissariat of Heavy Industry (NKTP) to return him to Magnitogorsk.[66] A related case involved the forced return of Andrei Diundikov, a distinguished worker with four years' experience in the blast-furnace shop, who had departed in a huff because "he couldn't understand why some people were awarded automobiles and he wasn't."[67]

Resentment arose not only among high-profile Stakhanovites but between them and the rest of the workers, as well as management. One Magnitogorsk shop chief, Leonid Veisberg, after pointing out that "we frequently create conditions, let's say, a bit better than usual, for the establishment of a record," privately expressed dismay that individual workers "failed to recognize that without such assistance they would not be heroes."[68] Without stating his own view, Zaitsev of the open-hearth shop commented that engineers resented Stakhanovites, who were made into heroes at the expense of equipment.[69]

Zaitsev added that some workers held the view that Stakhanovite methods were dangerous for the equipment—not surprising, since during the first attempts to introduce "Stakhanovite methods" in the open-hearth shop, the furnaces were burnt out. Meanwhile, the *Magnitogorskii rabochii* reported that one of the scholars at the Mining and Metallurgical Institute lectured that Stakhanovite practices of speeding up the steelmaking process had adverse effects on machinery. "Overloading ovens," the professor warned, "was technologically absurd." The newspaper countered that the factory's shops were proving the opposite.[70]

As the newspaper emphasized, Stakhanovism made possible "assaults" on the technical "capacity" of machines and equipment, much of which had been imported from capitalist countries. Questioning capacities was said to be a way of discovering and unleashing supposed "hidden reserves,"

[65] GARF, f. 7952, op. 5, d. 364, ll. 58–61, 66.
[66] *Za industrializatsiiu*, 12 April 1936; *Magnitogorskii metall*, 24 April 1936; *Magnitogorskii rabochii*, 12 May 1936; and TsGAOR, f. 7952, op. 5, d. 312, ll. 5–11.
[67] *Magnitogorskii rabochii*, 16 March 1936.
[68] GARF, f. 7952, op. 5, d. 305, l. 59.
[69] GARF, f. 7952, op. 5, d. 307, ll. 45–46, and d. 397, ll. 45–46, 50.
[70] *Magnitogorskii rabochii*, 14 October 1936.

thereby proving the superiority of Soviet workers and work methods, asserting Soviet independence from foreigners and foreign technology, and impugning the motives of foreign suppliers—all of which served to heighten the political awareness of the populace. After each new record, Soviet managers would announce that projected capacities set by foreign engineers were being "reexamined" and "revised" by "Soviet specialists."[71] These supposed leaps in productivity acquired further political significance in the context of the international "class struggle." "The Stakhanovite movement," the Magnitogorsk newspaper instructed, was "a blow to fascism."[72]

"Revising" capacities upward could backfire, however, as managers, engineers, and workers came to learn when serious, sometimes fatal accidents resulted; production had to be halted or curtailed, and arrests made. In August 1936, the newspaper reported that the chief of the pressing (*obzhimnyi*) shop of the blooming mill, Vasilev, was fired (and replaced by Golubitskii) when the shop had to operate at half-capacity for three days. Vasilev was then turned over to the courts, for "exceeding what was permissible" and allowing the machinery to be "injured." In norm-busting, who decided what was permissible, and how a decision was to be arrived at, remained unclear.[73] What was clear was that both excessive zeal in promoting Stakhanovism and the failure to do so could be dangerous.[74] One nonparty engineer who apparently did oppose Stakhanovism was criminally charged amid a shower of adverse publicity.[75]

Workers, for their part, could scarcely fail to see that Stakhanovism resembled a sweating campaign, and one that placed inordinate strain on managers and created much friction between managers and workers, as well as between foremen and workers—with often questionable results in

[71] Avraamii Zaveniagin, "O peresmotre moshchnostei oborudovaniia i norm," *Magnitogorskii rabochii*, 9 March 1936.

[72] *Magnitogorskii rabochii*, 5 April 1936.

[73] Mysteriously, the newspaper made no mention of the Stakhanovite campaign, which at that time was in full swing, and must have had something to do with the fact that Vasilev "exceeded what was permissible." *Magnitogorskii rabochii*, 27 August 1936.

[74] GARF, f. 7952, op, 5, d. 309, l. 74.

[75] "In mill 300 No. 1 during the Stakhanovite Ten-Day in February [1936]," the city newspaper wrote, "engineer Kudriavtsev (head of a shift), instead of mobilizing the workers' collective for the overfulfillment of the record of the shift of Makaev . . . adopted the stance of discrediting the shop chief and the shift of Makaev, announcing that the shop chief credited extra tons to Makaev's shift." The report further stated that "Kudriavtsev refused to conduct and lead countershift meetings, announcing that this was a matter of concern to the trade union and the party and not to the engineering personnel." Removed as shift boss, called a saboteur, expelled from the Engineer's and Technicians' Council (he was not a party member), Kudriavtsev was soon arrested. Makaev became the new shift boss. *Magnitogorskii rabochii*, 22 and 30 January, 9 February 1936; MFGAChO, f. 118, op. 1, d. 106, l. 23. According to the recollections of Fedor Golubitskii, Kudriavtsev was released by the NKVD and managed to leave town. GARF, f. 7952, op. 5, d. 306, ll. 55–56.

production.[76] But the costs of open opposition for workers were also high. One steel smelter's helper, said to have remarked that Stakhanovism was an attempt to enslave the working class, was arrested in November 1935 and sentenced to forced labor.[77] No less significant, however, were the benefits of acceptance. Stakhanovism meant that the most difficult jobs in the "hot shops" were invested with the greatest prestige, affording anyone who would take them up high status and pay.[78]

Stakhanovism reinforced tendencies already present in the ongoing articulation of industrial activity as a problem of labor productivity, which in turn was understood as a question of "rationalization," that is, inordinate individual exertion, reflecting the attainment of advanced consciousness. The "Stakhanovite" was soon hailed as a new type of worker, and Stakhanovism came to eclipse (without entirely replacing) shock work as the archetypal form of "socialist labor." Throughout 1936, the number of Stakhanovites in Magnitogorsk grew daily, until by December more than half the steel plant had earned either the classification *Stakhanovets* or *udarnik* (shock worker). That so many workers were so designated is eloquent testimony to how workers and management embraced such classifications, and the new relations that arose out of them.[79]

With material incentives reinforced by moral ones, workers of all ages, not just younger ones, struggled to overfulfill their norms and earn credentials as 150- or 200-percenters—identifications that were duly recorded in a worker's personnel profile and pay schedule, and with luck, reported in the city newspaper for all to read. A certain amount of stratification among workers obviously took place, yet its significance has per-

[76] One Soviet eyewitness spoke the opinion of many people in Magnitogorsk when he testified that with Stakhanovism, one shift would produce above plan, the next shift nothing. GARF, f. 7952, op. 5, d. 306, ll. 77–78.

[77] MFGAChO, f. 118, op. 1, d. 106, l. 23. Another worker, Anton Vasilchenko of the medium sorting mill, who appears to have been dekulakized in 1931, was accused of refusing to help set up conditions for a record by the Stakhanovite Shevchuk. Vasilchenko was arrested, charged with counterrevolution under article 58, and dispatched to the Cheliabinsk oblast court. The published details of his supposed crimes were not very convincing. He was apparently made a scapegoat in a case that was publicized in the newspaper under the title, "The Class Enemy in the Shop." *Magnitogorskii rabochii*, 30 January 1936.

[78] This was in sharp contrast with American steel plants at this time, where minority groups such as blacks and Hispanics usually received the roughest and most dangerous jobs in the hot shops, indicating the low status of both the jobs and the workers. Edward Greer, *Big Steel: Black Politics and Corporate Power in Gary, Indiana* (New York, 1979), pp. 72–89.

[79] The Commissariat of Heavy Industry issued several instructions on classifying superior workers, most of which involved a system of quantitative norm fulfillment. By contrast, in one directive issued in August 1936, Gurevich, the chief of the Main Administration for Metallurgy (GUMP), wrote that Stakhanovites were differentiated from shock workers by the quality of their work and the conditions of their place of work and machinery. This was obviously an attempt to counter the tendencies of seeking quantity at the expense of quality and machinery. *Magnitogorskii metall*, 30 June and 4 August 1936.

haps been somewhat exaggerated (bosses remained bosses, after all). The more important development was that in the general hubbub, all workers, not just Stakhanovites, were enveloped in extensive publicity about their importance and membership in a distinct social group.[80]

The constant references to workers as members of a new Soviet working class retained a large audience. Vasilii Radziukevich, who came to Magnitogorsk in 1931 from Minsk (via Leningrad), recalled five years later that when he first arrived the blooming mill was still in crates. He helped build it. When in 1936 the mill celebrated its third anniversary, Radziukevich was a skilled worker in one of the even newer sorting mills.[81] The Rubicon for such people was the acquisition of a trade. P. E. Velizhanin, after arriving in Magnitogorsk on 29 December 1930, was randomly included in a brigade of assembly workers to work on boilers, which he had never before seen. "At that time," he recalled four years later, "I had no conception of what a boiler assembly worker [*nagrevalshik*] was or what he did." But by 1934 he had mastered his new profession.[82]

Radziukevich's and Velizhanin's fate was that of tens of thousands.[83] They obtained a set of work clothes (*spetsovka*) and real boots (*sapogi*) in place of bast sandals (*lapti*), a change that marked their arrival as skilled workers. Moreover, their ascent in the work world was often paralleled by their movement from tents to dormitory barracks to individual-room barracks to perhaps their own room in a brick building. True, the work was often backbreaking. And it remains questionable whether in private workers felt that they had traversed a notable trajectory from victims of exploition to masters of production, from forlorn, illiterate,

---

[80] Siegelbaum has argued that the principal goals of the state's promotion of Stakhanovism, in addition to raising productivity, were to undermine the autonomy of managers and to create a new proletarian culture supportive of the state. In the process, the working class was supposedly divided between a privileged stratum and a nonprivileged majority, with the former's weight and influence ensuring general adherence to regime values and the resulting intraclass tensions inhibiting the development of class solidarity. But Siegelbaum neglected the persistence of a "class outlook," or sense of common fate, among workers. Notwithstanding the extreme individualization and ostensibly successful stratification, workers knew that they were not bosses. According to Moshe Lewin, who was evacuated to the USSR from Poland during the war, "You couldn't come to a worker and tell him in private that he was a member of a ruling class. When I worked in the Urals, workers knew who they were and that it was the *nachal'stvo* that had all the power and privileges." Siegelbaum, *Stakhanovism and the Politics of Productivity*, chap. 6; "Moshe Lewin, Interview with Paul Bushkovitch," in *Visions of History*, ed. MARHO (New York, 1983), pp. 295–96. One former Soviet citizen testified that workers felt great fear, "but you know, we did like each other, I mean the workers. Everybody was in the same boat." Jay K. Zawodny, "Twenty-Six Interviews," I/2, Jay K. Zawodny Collection, Hoover Institution Archives.

[81] GARF, f. 7952, op. 5, d. 300, ll. 149–54.

[82] GARF, f. 7952, op. 5, d. 315, l. 14; d. 300, l. 47.

[83] V. N. Eliseeva, "Bor'ba za kadry na stroitel'stve Magnitogorskogo metallurgicheskogo kombinata v gody pervoi piatiletki," *Uchenye zapiski Cheliabinskogo pedagogicheskogo instituta* (Cheliabinsk, 1956), vol. 1, part 1, p. 221.

uncouth slaves to builders of a new world and a new culture. Even if, the rhetoric of the regime notwithstanding, workers knew they were not bosses, however, they also knew that they were part of a Soviet working class, and that whatever its shortcomings, such a status was different from being a worker under capitalism—axioms that appeared to be confirmed by their own life courses.

Behind the exhortations to self-improvement lay a concrete process of continuous education centered on the labor process. Filatov, who came to Magnitogorsk in January 1931, gave the following response to a question about his work history: "I began as an unskilled laborer, then I went into a brigade and strove to raise my pay category [*razriad*] and to improve my skills. Had I been literate, I would have attended courses, but as an illiterate I only went to the literacy circle [*likbez*]." But Filatov was soon "graduated" from his literacy course, and then moved on to production-related matters. "Now I read, write, and solve problems," he added. "And I'm learning the ins-and-outs of blueprints."[84] It was from such people that several of the high-profile Stakhanovites had sprung.[85]

And if the workplace was like a school, schools became an extension of the workplace, as workers struggled to acquire literacy, master a trade, and continually raise their skills. In the early years, there were many informal courses and study circles, including open-air discussions on the job and "technical hours," introduced in 1931.[86] Later, the authorities encouraged workers' participation in so-called supplemental training (*dopolnitel'noe rabochee obrazovanie*, or DRO) in a variety of ways, the most important of which was the examination for the technical minimum (*gostekhekzamen*), analogous to basic literacy.[87]

In and out of the workplace virtually everyone in Magnitogorsk, even those who worked full time, attended some form of schooling, which reinforced the socialization and politicization processes visible at work.[88]

---

[84] GARF, f. 7952, op. 5, d. 100, l. 110.

[85] Aleksei Shatilin, for example, a miner from the Donbas who came to Magnitogorsk in 1931, became one of Magnitogorsk's celebrated Stakhanovites after having been selected in 1934 to train for the position of blast-furnace operator. Shatilin, *Na domnakh Magnitki* (Moscow, 1953), pp. 4–5. Many Magnitogorsk Stakhanovites, such as Shatilin, were drawn from experienced workers, although their experience was in far less skilled occupations. According to 1936 trade union data on 2,335 Magnitogorsk Stakhanovites, 1,028 had ten or more years' work experience. Of 3,665 shock workers analyzed, 999 had three or less years' experience and 1,203 had ten years' or more. MFGAChO, f. 118, op. 1, d. 106, l. 4.

[86] V. F. Romanov, "Magnitogorskii metallurgicheskii kombinat," *Voprosy istorii*, 1975, no. 9:108.

[87] By the end of 1935, according to the city newspaper, 3,500 people had passed the state examination for the technical minimum in basic professions. *Magnitogorskii rabochii*, 2 February 1936. See also Scott, *Behind the Urals*, p. 218 and GARF, f. 7952, op. 5, d. 200, passim.

[88] Improving one's work capacities went beyond simply acquiring a trade and honing one's skills. Workers were given instruction materials, such as small booklets that included

John Scott attributed the workers' hunger for education to wage differentials, and to the assurance of being able to obtain a job in any profession one has learned or supplemented.[89] To these reasons must be added a sense of adventure and, above all, self-accomplishment.[90] Those singled out by the authorities as "precisely the new type of worker" were said to "understand that the success of their work consists in the uninterrupted raising of their skill levels."[91]

Of course, workers could scarcely afford to be complacent. Not merely their potential advancement on the job but their access to food, clothes, and shelter was preferentially distributed through the centrally managed supply system. Strong moral pressure was also exerted on individuals to demonstrate a desire for self-improvement. But many people were only too glad to take up the party's threat-backed summons and continuously struggle to better themselves.

It is within this cursorily sketched context of the special importance attached to labor and to being a worker, the tying of each individual's labor to the international class struggle, the use of output norms and piece rates to individualize and make quantifiable a worker's performance, the obsession with productivity and the organization of the work process as a series of campaigns, the understanding of worker training as political education, the prominence of political agencies in the workplace, and the strong imperative for self-improvement that we can begin to evaluate the significance of the emerging social identity evident in the list posted on the entrance to barracks no. 8.

The Identification Game

For a Soviet worker, reporting on one's work history became an important ritual in defining oneself before others, and one of the most im-

---

metric tables, multiplication tables, and advice on behavior. As the French historian Michelle Perrot has written, "Industrial discipline represents only one form of discipline among others, and the factory belongs, with the school, military, penitentiary, and other systems, to a constellation of institutions which, each in its own way, contribute to the rule-making process." Michelle Perrot, "The Three Ages of Industrial Discipline in Nineteenth-Century France," in John Merriman, ed., *Consciousness and Class Experience in Nineteenth-Century Europe* (New York, 1979), p. 149.

[89] Scott marveled at the "student body in Magnitogorsk night schools, [which was] willing to work 8, 10, even 12 hours on the job under the severest conditions, and then come to school at night, sometimes on an empty stomach and, sitting on a backless wooden bench, in a room so cold that you could see your breath a yard ahead of you, study mathematics for four hours straight." Scott, *Behind the Urals*, p. 49.

[90] "For me it was truly interesting to master the ever newer equipment," Petukhov, an assembly worker in blast-furnace construction, noted in an unpublished interview. GARF, f. 7952, op. 5, d. 318, l. 21.

[91] GARF, f. 7952, op. 5, d. 305, l. 35.

portant details of one's work history was the time and place of one's original work experience. It was not uncommon for workers to trade boasts about who started work at the youngest age: fifteen, twelve, and so on.[92] Extra value was attached to that initial experience if it had been gained in industry, especially in one of the older and better-known industrial enterprises, such as Putilov (renamed Kirov) in Leningrad or Gujon (renamed Serp i molot) in Moscow. The ultimate boast was when one could trace one's lineage back to a family of workers: father, grandfather, great grandfather. Such was the proud background of Pavel Korobov, a blast-furnace apprentice who was descended from a "dynasty of blast-furnace operators" and who catapulted to the Magnitogorsk factory directorship during the days of dizzying social mobility in 1937.[93]

Elements of a worker's identity stressed achievements, but identification could also be "negative." For example, if a worker was "breakdown" prone, he or she would be labeled as such (*avariishchik*), which was cause for dismissal. In 1936 the newspaper carried a list of breakdown-prone individuals and a table of their breakdown frequencies.[94] With the passage of time, the negative components of a worker's record received greater and greater emphasis. What remained constant, however, was that everyone had to have a work history, and one conceived in politically charged categories.

Materially speaking, a worker's record was made up of various documents, such as the questionnaire (*anketa*), periodic professional evaluations (*kharakteristiki*), and the short-form personnel file (*lichnaia kartochka*), which all workers filled out on being hired and which were subsequently updated. Later, workers were required to have a "labor book" (*trudovaia knizhka*), without which they were not to be hired.[95] But the technique of defining workers by their work histories was in operation well before labor books were introduced.[96]

Because the practice of identifying individuals through their work history was so widespread, it could be seen in almost any official document. The reverse side of one archival file consisting of worker memoirs was found to contain a list from either 1933 or 1934 of individuals granted "shock rations." The list specified name, profession, party status, record on absenteeism, appearances at production conferences, study or course

---

[92] GARF, f. 7952, op. 5, d. 300, l. 52.

[93] *Magnitogorskii rabochii*, 28 October 1936. Also see on this theme *Rabochie dinastii* (Moscow, 1975): "From generation to generation the elevated designation 'worker' is passed on" (p. 4).

[94] *Magnitogorskii rabochii*, 21 April 1936.

[95] *Izvestiia*, 21 December 1938.

[96] One can find the rationale behind the labor book of 1938 already in the central press of 1931. See *Izvestiia*, 14 January 1931, as cited in Schwarz, *Labor in the Soviet Union*, pp. 96–97.

attendance, rationalization suggestions, norm fulfillment percentages, and socialist competitions entered. What made such records particularly significant was that they were not simply collected and filed away but used as a basis to distribute material benefits.[97] Work histories were also reported in public, thereby becoming an important ritual for gaining admission to peer and other groups.

Oral presentations were promoted through evenings of remembrances, which in turn formed part of an ambitious project to write the history of the construction of the Magnitogorsk factory. For the history project, which was never published, hundreds of workers were either interviewed or given questionnaires to fill out. Not surprisingly, the questions were formulated so as to elicit discussion of certain topics (and discourage discussion of others). Much of the discussion was directed at the Stakhanovite movement, which is mentioned in a great many of the memoirs (the majority of which were recorded in 1935 and 1936).[98] Moreover, as is clear since some memoirs are handwritten and contain grammatical mistakes, whereas others are neatly typed without errors, the workers' accounts were at least in part rewritten.[99] It would be erroneous, however, to conclude that the workers' memoirs were "biased" and thus of little or no value. That workers were encouraged to write about certain matters and avoid others is precisely the point. Indeed, that sometimes workers "erred" and had to be corrected, both for grammar and content, shows how they were implicated in a process of adopting the official method of speaking about themselves.[100]

It is, of course, highly significant that workers' memoirs would be sought and celebrated at all. In fact, whether or not he or she was being interviewed for the factory history project, a Magnitogorsk worker was frequently called on to discuss his or her biography. On the day they arrived, dekulakized peasants were interviewed extensively for their biography, which was thought to be an indication of the degree of danger

[97] GARF, f. 7952, op. 5, d. 301, l. 83 [verso].

[98] One form contained sixteen questions, almost all of which related to work experiences, although some sought to establish the social and geographical origins of the respondent, as well as the length of time spent in Magnitogorsk. Bosses were also interviewed. GARF, f. 7952, op. 5, d. 301, l. 79.

[99] GARF, f. 7952, op. 5, d. 301. Very few of the reminiscences left behind were by women. An exception was the case of Raisa Troinina. Ibid., d. 319, l. 1ff.

[100] GARF, f. 7952, op. 5, d. 318, l. 20. There is internal evidence that the memoirs were at least partly written by workers themselves. Within the repetitive tropes, one can see considerable differences in style and emphasis. Moreover, many "delicate" or otherwise proscribed matters are openly discussed. And unlike most of the "worker letters" published in the newspaper, in the memoirs there was only one instance (out of more than one hundred) when the author concluded with the exclamation: "Long Live the Party of the Bolsheviks, Long Live the Genius Leader Stalin, Long Live the World Giant [Magnitka]." Ibid., d. 318, l. 20.

they posed.[101] But noncriminal workers were also prompted into relating their social origin, political past, and work history for security reasons. More often, they were encouraged to "confess" simply as a matter of course, as something one did.

Even when these self-confessions extended to nonwork activities, moreover, they tended to revolve around work. On the seventh anniversary of socialist competition in 1936, some Magnitogorsk workers were "surveyed" on their activities after work. Of the ten answers published in the city newspaper, virtually all began with a discussion of the relation between plan fulfillment and personal satisfaction (given that both wages and esteem were tied to plan fulfillment, such an equation was not as ridiculous as it might sound). Virtually every worker claimed to read in their spare time, not surprisingly, since reading and the desire for self-improvment were considered necessary. Most revealing of all, almost all spent their "time off" from work visiting the shop, in the words of one, "to see how things were going."[102]

Identification with one's shop was apparently strong. An apprentice, Aleksei Griaznov, who recalled in November 1936 that when he arrived three years earlier there had been only one open-hearth oven (now there were twelve), kept a diary of his becoming a bona fide steel smelter (*stalevar*). Excerpts were published in the factory newspaper telling of his developing relationship with his furnace.[103] The city newspaper, meanwhile, quoted Ogorodnikov to the effect that Magnitogorsk was his "native factory" (*rodnoi zavod*).[104] The expression *rodnoi*, normally applied to one's birthplace, captured the relation these workers had with their factory: it had given birth to them. For these people there was no dichotomy between home and work; no division of their lives into separate spheres, the public and the private: all was "public," and public meant the factory.

Not only workers, but also their wives were encouraged to make the shop the basis of their lives. "Here at Magnitka, more than anywhere else," asserted Leonid Veisberg, "the whole family takes part in and lives the life of our production." He claimed that there were even cases when wives would not allow their husbands to spend the night at home because they had performed poorly in the shop. And such disapproval was not motivated by considerations of money alone. Wives took pride in their husband's work performance, and many got directly involved. Wives' tri-

[101] As related to me by Louis Ernst, an eyewitness, in an interview in Doniphan, Missouri, on 30 April 1986 and confirmed by surviving dispossessed peasants interviewed in Magnitogorsk in 1987 and 1989.

[102] *Magnitogorskii rabochii*, 29 April 1936.

[103] *Magnitogorskii metall*, 4 January 1936; GARF, f. 7952, op. 5, d. 306, ll. 204–22.

[104] *Magnitogorskii rabochii*, 12 May 1936.

bunals were organized to shame men to stop drinking and to work harder, and some wives regularly visited the shop on their own, to inspect, offer encouragement, or scold.[105]

Just how the new terms of social identity were articulated and made effectual, sometimes with wives' participation, can be seen in a long letter preserved in the history project archives from the wife of the best loco-motive driver in internal factory transport, Anna Kovaleva, to the wife of the worst, Marfa Gudzia. I quote it in full:

Dear Marfa!
We are both wives of locomotive drivers of the rail transport of Magnitka. You probably know that the rail transport workers of the MMK Magnito-gorsk metallurgical kombinat are not fulfilling the plan, that they are dis-rupting the supply of the blast furnaces, open hearths, and rolling shops. . . . All the workers of Magnitka accuse our husbands, saying that the rail work-ers hinder the fulfillment of the [overall] industrial plan. It is offensive, pain-ful, and annoying to hear this. And moreover, it is doubly painful, because all of it is the plain truth. Every day there were stoppages and breakdowns in rail transport. Yet our internal factory transport has everything it needs in order to fulfill the plan. For that, it is necessary to work like the best workers of our country work. Among such shock workers is my husband, Aleksandr Panteleevich Kovalev. He always works like a shock worker, over-fulfilling his norms, while economizing on fuel and lubricating oil. His engine is on profit and loss accounting. . . . My husband trains locomotive drivers' helpers out of unskilled laborers. He takes other locomotive drivers under his wing. . . . My husband receives prizes virtually every month. . . . And I too have won awards. . . .

My husband's locmotive is always clean and well taken care of. You, Marfa, are always complaining that it is difficult for your family to live. And why is that so? Because your husband, Iakov Stepanovich, does not fulfill the plan. He has frequent breakdowns on his locomotive, his locomotive is dirty, and he always overconsumes fuel. Indeed, all the locomotive drivers laugh at him. *All the rail workers of Magnitka know him—for the wrong reasons, as the worst driver. By contrast, my husband is known as a shock worker* [my italics]. He is written up and praised in the newspapers. . . . He and I are honored everywhere as shock workers. At the store we get every-thing without having to wait in queues. We moved to the building for shock workers [*dom udarnika*]. We will get an apartment with rugs, a gramophone, a radio, and other comforts. Now we are being assigned to a new store for shock workers and will receive double rations. . . . Soon the Seventeenth Party Congress of our Bolshevik Party will take place. All rail workers are obligated to work so that Magnitka greets the Congress of Victors at full production capacity.

Therefore, I ask you, Marfa, to talk to your husband heart to heart, read

[105] GARF, f. 7952, op. 5, d. 305, ll. 40–41.

him my letter. You, Marfa, explain to Iakov Stepanovich that he just can't go on working the way he has. Persuade him that he must work honorably, conscientiously, like a shock worker. Teach him to understand the words of comrade Stalin, that work is a matter of honor, glory, valor, and heroism.

You tell him that if he does not correct himself and continues to work poorly, he will be fired and lose his supplies. I will ask my Aleksandr Panteleevich to take your husband in tow, help him improve himself and become a shock worker, earn more. I want you, Marfa, and Iakov Stepanovich to be honored and respected, so you live as well as we do.

I know that many women, yourself included, will say: "What business is it of a wife to interfere in her husband's work. You live well, so hold your tongue." But it is not like that. . . . We all must help our husbands to fight for the uninterrupted work of transport in the winter. Ok, enough. You catch my drift. This letter is already long. In conclusion, I'd like to say one thing. It's pretty good to be a wife of a shock worker. It's within our power. Let's get down to the task, amicably. I await your answer. Anna Kovaleva.[106]

In Anna Kovaleva's words, Marfa's husband, Iakov Gudzia, was known to all as the worst locomotive driver, whereas her husband, Aleksandr Kovalev, was known as the best. Whether Iakov Gudzia wanted to see himself in such terms was in a sense irrelevant; that was how he would be seen. For his own benefit, it was best to play the game according to the rules. Gudzia's locomotive was dirty and overconsumed fuel. What kind of person could he be? What could his family be like? Indeed, after sending off the letter, Kovaleva discovered that Marfa Gudzia was illiterate. But Marfa was more than simply functionally "illiterate": she did not know, nor apparently did her husband, how to live and "speak Bolshevik," the obligatory language for self-identification and as such, the barometer of one's political allegiance to the cause.[107]

Publicly expressing loyalty by knowing how to "speak Bolshevik" became an overriding concern, but we must be careful in interpreting these acts. Strictly speaking, it was not necessary for Anna Kovaleva to write

---

[106] GARF, f. 7952, op. 5, d. 303, ll. 3–5.

[107] The dramatic and far-reaching Bolshevization of the Russian language—to say nothing of the many others that were spoken in the Soviet Union—was noted by contemporaries. Indeed, the four-volume interpretive dictionary, *Tolkovyi slovar' russkogo iazyka*, issued between 1934 and 1940 self-consciously set out to lay "the basis for a new phase in the life of the Russian language and at the same time to indicate the new norms that are being established for the use of words." A. M. Sleishchev, *Iazyk revoliutsionnoi epokhi: Iz nabliudenii nad russkim iazykom poslednykh let (1917–1926)*, 2d ed. (Moscow, 1928). See also Michael Waller, "The -Isms of Stalinism," *Soviet Studies* 20 (October 1968): 229–34. An interesting comparison is furnished by Victor Klemperer, *LTI, Lingua Tertii Imperii: Die Sprache des Dritten Reiches* (1957; Leipzig, 1991). Part memoir, part detached analysis, Klemperer's book offers an amusing analysis of the Nazi penchant for acronyms, and links "speaking Nazi" *(nazistisch sprechen)* with the goal of securing popular belief in an ersatz religion.

this letter herself, although she may well have. What was necessary was that she recognize, even if only by allowing her name to be attached to the letter, how to think and behave as the wife of a Soviet locomotive driver should. We should not interpret her letter to mean she believed in what she likely wrote and signed. It was not necessary to believe. It was necessary, however, to participate as if one believed—a stricture that appears to have been well understood, since what could be construed as openly disloyal behavior became rare.

Although the process of social identification that demanded mastery of a certain vocabulary, or official language, was formidable, it was not irreversible. For one thing, swearing—*blatnoi iazyk*—could usually serve as a kind of "safety valve." And we know from oral and literary accounts that a person could "speak Bolshevik" one moment, "innocent peasant" the next, begging indulgence for a professed inability to master fully the demanding new language and behavior.[108] Such a dynamic was also evident in the interchange between Marfa and Anna.

With wives writing to other wives, husbands were in a way permitted to continue their faulty behavior. Intended to put pressure on another woman's husband, such wives' letters actually may instead have taken much of the pressure off the transgressor: the wife could constantly reiterate the formula and the husband could constantly deviate from it. It might even be said that a kind of unacknowledged "private sphere" reemerged, a pocket of structural resistance based on the couple, playing the game according to the rules and yet constantly violating them.[109]

If indirect or less than fully intentional contestations were built into the operation of the identification game, more direct challenges of the new terms of life and labor could be dangerous. Yet even these were not impossible—as long as they were couched within the new language itself, and preferably with references to the teachings of Lenin or Stalin. In at least one case encountered in the city newspaper, people were allowed to use certain of the officially promoted ideals to challenge regime policy through the very public-speaking rituals normally intended as exercises of affirmation.

Women, when they were quoted in the newspaper, rarely spoke as anything other than loyal wives. One exception was March 8, International Women's Day, when women were spotlighted as workers.[110] Another ex-

---

[108] Cleverness and dissimulation, time-honored "peasant" attributes, perennially induced a sense of wonder in the authorities. See, for example, Daniel Field, *Rebels in the Name of the Tsar* (Boston, 1976).

[109] This analysis of a variant on the Russian wife's traditional role as moralist with the husband as misbehaving drunk was suggested to me by Laura Engelstein.

[110] One such spotlight fell on Nina Zaitseva, a brigade leader in the ore-crushing plant. *Magnitogorskii rabochii*, 8 March 1936.

ception was the short-lived but startling debate in the pages of the newspaper following the introduction of "pro-family" laws in 1936, when women were heard protesting against the new policy. One woman assailed the proposed fee of up to 1,000 rubles to register a divorce as far too high. Another pointed out that the prohibitive cost for divorces would have the effect of discouraging the registration of marriages, which she implied would be bad for women. Still a third condemned the restrictions on abortion even more forcefully, writing that "women want to study and to work" and that "having children . . . removes women from public life."[111]

Even as this example shows, however, the state-sponsored game of social identity as the one permissible and necessary mode of participation in the public realm remained all-encompassing. There were sources of identity other than the Bolshevik crusade, some from the past, such as those of peasant life, folklore, and religion, the fact of one's native village or place of origin (*rodina*), and some from the present, such as age, marital status, and parenthood. And people continued to confront understandings of themselves in terms of gender and nationality. But all of these ways of speaking about oneself came to be refracted through the inescapable political lens of Bolshevism.

Take the case of nationality. Gubaiduli, an electrician in the blast-furnace shop, purportedly wrote a letter that appeared in the city newspaper.

> I am a Tatar. Before October, in old tsarist Russia, we weren't even considered people. We couldn't even dream about education, or getting a job in a state enterprise. And now I'm a citizen of the USSR. Like all citizens, I have the right to a job, to education, to leisure. I can elect and be elected to the soviet. Is this not an indication of the supreme achievements of our country? . . .
>
> Two years ago I worked as the chairman of a village soviet in the Tatar republic. I was the first person there to enter the kolkhoz and then I led the collectivization campaign. Collective farming is flourishing with each year in the Tatar republic.
>
> In 1931 I came to Magnitogorsk. From a common laborer I have turned into a skilled worker. I was elected a member of the city soviet. As a deputy, every day I receive workers who have questions or need help. I listen to each

[111] *Magnitogorskii rabochii*, 11, 16, and 1 June 1936. These voices—published by the male editor—are unique not simply because they are female. Together they constitute the single instance of an unequivocal rebuke of official policies in the newspaper during the Stalin era, and would seem to indicate the deep dissatisfaction of certain women with the policy shift. For similarly critical letters published in *Pravda* and *Komsomol'skaia Pravda*, see Janet Evans, "The Communist Party of the Soviet Union and the Women's Question: The Case of the 1936 Decree 'In Defense of Mother and Child,' " *Journal of Contemporary History* 16 (1981): pp. 757–75.

one like to my own brother, and try to do what is necessary to make each one satisfied.

I live in a country where one feels like living and learning. And if the enemy should attack this country, I will sacrifice my life in order to destroy the enemy and save my country.[112]

Even if such a clear and unequivocal expression of the official viewpoint was not written entirely by Gubaiduli himself, whose Russian language skills may in fact have been adequate to the task (as was the case with many Tatars),[113] what is important is that Gubaiduli "played the game," whether out of self-interest, or fear, or both. Perhaps he was still learning how to speak Russian; he was certainly learning how to "speak Bolshevik."

As every worker soon learned, just as it was necessary for party members to show vigilance and "activism" in party affairs, it was necessary for workers, whether party members or not, to show activism in politics and production. The range of proliferating activities thought to demonstrate activism included making "voluntary" contributions to the state loan programs (for which shop agitators and trade union organizers conducted harangues); taking part in periodic *subbotniki* (literally—Saturdays, actually any time workers worked without compensation); putting forth "worker suggestions" (*predlozheniia*) for improvements (which were quantified to demonstrate compliance and then usually ignored); and holding production conferences (*proizvodstvennye soveshchaniia*).

Regarding the latter, the newspaper inveighed against their tendency to degenerate into "a meeting fetish" (*mitingovshchina*), and one may suppose that tangible results were not always those intended.[114] Much the same could be said about so-called suggestions.[115] But God help the shop that tried to do without these practices, for workers often took them seriously. According to John Scott, at production meetings "workers could and did speak up with the utmost freedom, criticize the director,

---

[112] *Magnitogorskii rabochii*, 28 July 1936. His remarks were published as part of the celebration of the new 1936 constitution.

[113] In 1938 the city had around 15,000 *natsmen*, or members of national minorities, a designation reserved primarily for non-Slavs, especially Kazakhs and Tatars. *Magnitogorskii rabochii*, 12 April 1938.

[114] *Magnitogorskii rabochii*, 17 March 1936.

[115] During the first eight months of 1935, twenty-two suggestions were advanced in the coke-chemical plant, six of which were acted on (although only five were realized). The other sixteen were declined. "In such a way," wrote the factory newspaper, "really only five rationalization suggestions, which benefit the shop, were advanced." Moreover, the paper pointed out that these were made by engineers and foremen, not rank-and-file workers. The spotlight provided by the newspaper sent a clear and unavoidable message to the plant's party and trade union organizers: in upcoming months results better be more substantial. *Magnitogorskii metall*, 23 August 1935.

complain about the wages, bad living conditions, lack of things to buy in the store—in short, swear about anything, except the general line of the party and a half-dozen of its sacrosanct leaders."[116]

Scott was writing of 1936, a time when the regime encouraged criticism of higher-ups "from below," and such freewheeling populist activism was common. Just as often, however, official gatherings could be characterized by strict formalism, making activism "from below" a charade.[117] And we know from émigré testimony that workers were held back from expressing their grievances by the fear of informants.[118] But when the signals came from above that it was time to open up, workers always seemed to be ready to do so. And woe to the foreman or shop party organizer who failed to canvass and take account of worker moods before introducing a resolution, or a new rule.[119]

Certain workers no doubt looked for every opportunity to ingratiate themselves, while others perhaps tried to steer clear of the highly charged rituals. But there was really nowhere to hide. If before the industrialization drive virtually two-thirds of the population was self-employed, a decade later such a category scarcely existed: virtually everyone was technically an employee of the state. Simply put, almost no legal alternatives to the state existed for earning a livelihood.[120] Here the contrast between Bolshevization and the "Americanization" of immigrants in the United States is instructive.

Americanization—a variety of campaigns for acculturation—could also be extremely coercive.[121] But not every American town was a company town, and moreover immigrants living in such places could often leave in

[116] Scott, *Behind the Urals*, p. 164.

[117] An excellent case in point is the process of upward norm revision as described by Kravchenko, in *I Chose Freedom*, p. 189.

[118] Unequivocal evidence on the fear of informants comes from the testimony of former Soviet citizens (not from Magnitogorsk) in J. K. Zawodny, "Twenty-Six Interviews," Hoover Institution Archives, Stanford, Calif., and from the Harvard Interview Project. During the same period, informants were widely used by American corporations, in violation of the law, which provoked Senate investigations and indignant denials by industrial executives. Frank Palmer, *Spies in Steel: An Expose of Industrial War* (n.p., 1928).

[119] It was not that speaking out freely at any time was completely prohibited; one had to learn how and when to speak out. Scott described a workers' meeting in a large Moscow factory in 1940. "I saw workers get up and criticize the plant director, make suggestions as to how to increase production, improve quality, and lower costs," he wrote. "Then the question of the new Soviet-German trade pact came up. The workers unanimously passed a previously prepared resolution approving the Soviet foreign policy. There was no discussion. The Soviet workers had learned what was their business and what was not." *Behind the Urals*, p. 264.

[120] According to the 1926 population census, *Vsesoiuznaia perepis' naseleniia 1926 goda* (Moscow, 1929).

[121] See the analysis of the great American steel center, Pittsburgh, by Nora Faires, "Immigrants and Industry: Peopling the 'Iron City,'" in Samuel Hays, ed., *City at the Point: Essays on the Social History of Pittsburgh* (Pittsburgh, 1989), pp. 3–31.

search of greener pastures elsewhere. Even if they stayed, some had the option of becoming shopkeepers, merchants, or small-holders and achieving a degree of independence (I am the product of such a family). As an arena of negotiation, Americanization, however oppressive, afforded more possibilities and thus even in its most oppressive moments contained within it far more latitude than Bolshevization did.

Even so, it should not be thought that Soviet workers were passive objects of the state's heavy-handed designs. For one thing, many people gladly embraced the opportunity to become a "Soviet worker," with all that such a designation entailed, from unabashed demonstrations of complete loyalty to feats of extraordinary self-sacrifice. The acquisition of the new social identity conveyed benefits, ranging from the dignity of possessing a trade to paid vacations, retirement pensions, and social insurance funds (*posobie*) for pregnancy, temporary incapacity, and death of the family's principal wage earner.[122] The new identity was empowering, if demanding.

Moreover, notwithstanding the existence of an imposing repressive apparatus, there were still many strategems available with which to retain some say over one's life, in and out of the workplace. Workers reacted to the oppressive terms of work, for example, with absenteeism, turnover, slowdowns (*volynka*), and removing tools and materials from the job in order to work at home for private gain.[123] To be sure, the regime fought back. There was, for example, the law of 15 November 1932, which provided for dismissal, denial of ration cards, and eviction from housing for absenteeism of as little as one hour.[124] Yet the very circumstances that had in a sense called forth this desperate law rendered it extremely difficult to enforce.

The rapid industrial expansion, combined with the inefficiency and uncertainty characteristic of a command economy, resulted in a perpetual labor shortage. "Throughout the city," wrote the Magnitogorsk newspaper, "hang announcements of the department of cadres of the metallurgical complex explaining to the population that the complex needs

---

[122] The rules governing these social welfare benefits were laid out in *Kodeks zakonov o trude, s izmeneniiami do 1 iiulia 1934 g.* (Moscow, 1934), pp. 36–37, 85–92.

[123] This is one of the chief arguments of Filtzer, *Soviet Workers.* See also Lewin, *The Making of the Soviet State*, p. 255. Whereas Filtzer treated all dysfunctional behavior by workers as resistance, John Barber has argued that absenteeism or drunkenness did not constitute conscious or deliberate opposition. Yet although Filtzer may have indeed gone too far in attributing motives to Soviet workers, surely the main point is that the regime's treatment of the kind of behavior Filtzer points to as a political problem, even when such behavior was more or less "innocent," had to make workers aware that being late or absent from work willy-nilly constituted a political statement and would be dealt with accordingly. Barber, "Working-class Culture and Political Culture in the 1930s," in Hans Guenther, ed., *The Culture of the Stalin Period* (New York, 1990), pp. 10–13.

[124] *Sobranie zakonov i rasporiazhenii* (1932), no. 78, item 475; see also no. 45, item 244.

workers in unlimited numbers and of various qualifications."[125] Desperate to hold on to and even acquire more laborers, managers would often not heed instructions ordering them to fire workers for violating the stringent rules, or forbidding them to hire workers who had been fired elsewhere. In the battle against absentees, workers "booted out of one place, were taken in at another," as the Magnitogorsk newspaper continually complained.[126]

The state policy of full employment further reinforced workers' leverage.[127] Workers discovered that in the absence of unemployment or a "reserve army," managers and especially foremen under severe pressure to meet obligations could become accommodating. What resulted could be called a kind of unequal but nonetheless real codependency. Workers became dependent on the authorities who, wielding the weapon placed in their hands by a state supply system that created perpetual scarcity, were able to determine the size and location of a worker's apartment, the freshness and variety of his or her food, the length and location of his or her vacation, and the quality of the medical care available to him or her and to additional family members. But the authorities in turn depended on the workers to achieve production targets.

None of this is meant to diminish the importance of overt coercion. The workers' state did not shrink from the use of repression against individual workers, especially when the general "class interests" of all workers was alleged to be at stake. We know from émigré sources that the authorities searched for any signs of independent worker initiative and were extremely sensitive to informal gatherings among workers, lest some type of solidarity outside the state develop.[128] But a far more subtle and

[125] *Magnitogorskii rabochii*, 26 July 1939. In the first eleven months of 1936, four thousand workers were said to have left their jobs at the steel plant and construction trust. *Cheliabinskii rabochii*, 30 December 1936. During the first four months of 1937, around 1,500 workers were said to have quit. Recruiters were said to be spending state money but recruiting no one, and little was being done to retain those workers already present. *Magnitogorskii rabochii*, 25 January 1938.

[126] *Magnitogorskii rabochii*, 9 April 1934. For the repercussions of the labor shortage, see Filtzer, *Soviet Workers*, pp. 62, 261.

[127] See David Granick, *Job Rights in the Soviet Union: Their Consequences* (Cambridge, 1987). I am indebted to Kenneth Straus for directing me to this source and for fruitful discussions of Filtzer's work.

[128] One former Soviet worker not from Magnitogorsk offered the following testimony: "In the early 1930s I and several of my friends used to drink a little bit of beer or wine together, and we used to gather in the same place on Saturdays. Sometimes, we drank vodka, sometimes we went to a movie. After a while, the party and the members of the Komsomol put pressure on us to break up our gatherings. They were afraid of *gruppovshchina* [group formation]. Let's say you write an application, and that you put in a request for something and several men sign it. That's *gruppovshchina*. Immediately, the local Communist Party and trade union people will call one guy after another and reprimand him. But they will not call the whole group; they will deal with each individual, separately." Zawodny, "Twenty-Six Interviews," II/14.

in the end no less effective method of coercion was at hand: the ability to define who people were.

The argument is not that the new social identity grounded in a kind of official language of public expression was erroneous, or that it was accurate, but that it was unavoidable and, furthermore, that it gave meaning to people's lives. Even if we find the notions absurd, we must take seriously whether a person was a shock worker or a shirker, an award-winner or breakdown-prone, because Magnitogorsk workers had to. What is more, if the people of Magnitogorsk took pride in themselves for their accomplishments and rewards, or felt disappointment at their failures, we must accept the reality of these feelings, however disagreeable we may find the social and political values that lent these social assessments significance.

Unavoidable as the new terms of social identity were, however, they must not be thought of as some kind of hegemonic device, which explains everything and therefore nothing.[129] Rather, they should be seen as a "field of play" in which people engaged the "rules of the game" of urban life. The rules were promulgated by the state with the express intention of achieving unquestioned control, but in the process of implementation they were sometimes challenged and circumvented. Workers did not set the terms of their relation to the regime, but they did, to an extent, negotiate these terms, as they quietly understood.[130] That negotiation, however unequal, arose out of the restrictions, as well as the enabling provisions, of the game of social identification. It was largely through this game that people became members of the public realm, or, if you will, of the "official" society.

Life in Magnitogorsk taught cynicism as well as labor enthusiasm, fear as well as pride. Most of all, life in Magnitogorsk taught one how to

---

[129] Gareth Stedman Jones has written that "there is no political or ideological institution that could not in some way be interpreted as an agency of social control. . . . Since capitalism is still with us, we can with impunity suppose, if we wish to, that at any time in the last three hundred years the mechanisms of social control were operating effectively." Similarly, he urged caution in the use of Gramsci's notion of hegemony, which "can only give a tautological answer to a false question if it is used to explain the absence of a revolutionary proletarian class consciousness in the sense envisaged by Lukacs." When Stedman Jones attempted to put forth an alternative explanation for workers' apparent "quiescence" under capitalism, however, he violated his own strictures regarding the place of culture and language, invoking—as he himself admitted in a critical reflection on his own essay—"the determinant place of relations of production . . . far too unproblematically." Stedman Jones, "Class Expression Versus Social Control? A Critique of Recent Trends in the Social History of 'Leisure'," in Stedman Jones, *Languages of Class: Studies in English Working Class History, 1832–1982* (Cambridge, 1983), pp. 76–89.

[130] "You simply had to be smart with them," explained one former worker, not from Magnitogorsk. "Very often you even felt good that you could outsmart all those restrictions." Zawodny, "Twenty-Six Interviews," I/5. See also "Moshe Lewin, Interview with Paul Bushkovitch," pp. 294–96.

speak and identify oneself in the acceptable terms. If ever there was a case where the political significance of things said, or discourse, stood out, it was in the articulation of social identity under Stalin. This subtle mechanism of power, within the circumstances of the revolutionary crusade, accounted for the strength of Stalinism. Fifty years later, surviving workers in Magnitogorsk still spoke the way they and their contemporaries did in the memoirs from the 1930s.

11

Sheila Fitzpatrick

Workers against Bosses:
The Impact of the Great Purges
on Labor-Management Relations

In the Great Purges, industrial managers were arrested in very large numbers as "enemies of the people," accused over an almost two-year period in 1937–38 of a variety of real and imaginary offenses from endangering workers' health by violating safety regulations to committing acts of intentional sabotage and entering into conspiracies with foreign intelligence agents and Trotskyists. At the top level of the management hierarchy (the factory manager and his deputies, as well as the chief engineer in big plants), an individual's likelihood of falling victim was very high, and the period beginning with the Piatakov trial was one of nightmarish uncertainty and apprehension. Lower in the hierarchy, the risk diminished. All the same, anyone holding a position of authority in the plant, even a relatively humble one like trade union secretary or foreman, was to some degree at risk, since he might be caught up in one of the elaborate scenarios of counterrevolutionary conspiracy concocted by the NKVD when a major "enemy of the people" was exposed.

Workers, by contrast, were much less likely to fall victim to the Purges. Naturally some workers were swept up by accident, chance associations, or as a result of malicious denunciation. But it was officeholders who were primarily at risk, and the proportion of workers-at-the-bench who fell into this category (e.g., those who served as local trade union organizers without being released to full-time, paid, trade union employment) was small. If workers had any direct involvement in the dramas of unmasking "counterrevolutionary conspiracies" in industry, it was usually as witnesses for the prosecution. But generally they were just part of the popular audience for the terror that Stalin unleashed against the elites in 1937–38.

It would be extraordinary if this situation had not had some impact on labor discipline and labor-management relations at the enterprise level, not to mention broader issues of Soviet working-class organization, iden-

311

tity, *mentalité*, and so on. Yet so far there has been very little discussion of this in the scholarly literature. The Great Purges are scarcely mentioned in Solomon Schwarz's classic work on Soviet labor in the 1930s,[1] and Donald Filtzer also virtually ignores them in his recent book, apart from noting that an increase in worker insubordination was an "unintended by-product" of the managerial purges in industry.[2] Lewis Siegelbaum makes the interesting comment that "the Great Purge in industry . . . was both 'the state against itself' and workers against their bosses, higher state authorities not only failing to mediate and moderate the latter struggle, but actually aiding and abetting it,"[3] but this is only a side issue in his study of Stakhanovism.

Since the subject is therefore relatively unfamiliar, it is worth considering the possible variety of ways in which the large-scale purging of Soviet industrial managers as "wreckers" and "enemies of the people" might have affected Soviet workers' attitudes and behavior toward management and relations between labor and management within the factory. In the first place, discipline was likely to suffer, since the arrests and the atmosphere of suspicion surrounding managers must have undermined their authority. In the second place, as Siegelbaum suggests, there is the intriguing possibility that the collective cloud of suspicion hanging over the Soviet managers may have encouraged a revival of militant class consciousness on the part of workers—that is, a reversion to the old "workers-against-bosses" mentality that had supposedly become obsolete once the bosses became representatives of the workers' state. But this issue has to be handled very carefully, since there are indications that the regime was actually trying to produce and manipulate such an effect.

Workers are unlikely to have reacted uniformly to the wave of terror against industrial managers. The emotional responses to the accusations against the managers run from indignation (where the accusations were believed) to skepticism or concealed sympathy with the victims, and the responses to their disgrace and removal run from indifference ("Nothing to do with me") through perceptions of opportunity (such as for individual revenge or advancement) to satisfaction ("Serves them right") based on envy, malice, or a sense of class grievance. Of particular interest in this situation are responses that recall the "*spets*-baiting" and anti-authoritarian strains of the Cultural Revolution; responses that suggest a revival of the capacity for labor organization and collective action that was beaten down by the regime at the beginning of the 1930s; and the

---

[1] Solomon M. Schwarz, *Labor in the Soviet Union* (New York, 1952).

[2] Donald Filtzer, *Soviet Workers and Stalinist Industrialization: The Formation of Modern Soviet Production Relations, 1928–1941* (Armonk, NY, 1986), p. 130.

[3] Lewis H. Siegelbaum, *Stakhanovism and the Politics of Productivity in the USSR, 1935–1941* (Cambridge, 1988), p. 258.

responses of Stakhanovite workers—or, more exactly, those workers' responses that can be related to the Stakhanovites' assigned role as goad, watchdog, and scourge of management.

Signals

The signal that Soviet industrial managers were at risk as a group came from the show trial of Piatakov and other leading Communist industrialists at the beginning of 1937. Despite earlier warning signs, notably the rash of accusations in the spring of 1936 that Donbas industrialists were deliberately sabotaging the Stakhanovite movement,[4] and the more recent Novosibirsk show trial of industrialists accused of deliberate "wrecking" in connection with a series of accidents in Siberian coal mines,[5] the thrust of the new Moscow trial came as a shock. The Communist leaders of Soviet industry had enjoyed unusual honor, praise, and privilege during Sergo Ordzhonikidze's tenure as People's Commissar of Heavy Industry since 1930. They were associated with the Soviet Union's central preoccupation of those years, the first five-year plans, and with what were perceived as the regime's greatest successes.

Even former oppositionists were swept up in the general enthusiasm for industrialization, and industrial administration and management was one of the areas in which they felt they could serve with a clear conscience. Georgii Piatakov, an economist by profession and former member of the Left Opposition, was Ordzhonikidze's first deputy at the Commissariat of Heavy Industry from the early 1930s until his arrest in mid-1936. His arrest was a great blow to Ordzhonikidze, who understood it as a sign that his cherished cohort of industrial managers was in danger, fought with all his might to prevent the show trial, and killed himself in January 1937, reportedly after an altercation with Stalin.

At their trial in January 1937, of which long verbatim reports appeared in all national newspapers, Piatakov and the other defendants were accused of treasonous, counterrevolutionary conspiracy with the exiled Trotsky and Western intelligence agencies, expressed most notably in the intentional sabotage of Soviet industry by causing industrial breakdowns and disastrous accidents like the explosion at the Tsentral'naia mine in Kemerovo in September 1936, which had already featured prominently in the Novosibirsk trial.

[4] On the rash of accusations of sabotage of the Stakhanovite movement in the spring of 1936, see ibid., pp. 117–20.
[5] See Robert Conquest, *The Great Terror* (London, 1971), pp. 222–24. See also report of the plenum of the Kemerovo gorkom that discussed the Kemerovo disaster in *Sovetskaia Sibir'*, 9 October 1936, p. 3.

At the Central Committee plenum of February-March, Stalin and Molotov spelled out the political message of the trial.[6] Industry was full of wreckers and saboteurs who escaped discovery because, in contrast to past cohorts of enemies, they were usually Communists. The leaders must be exposed to scrutiny from below (*proverka snizu*) as well as scrutiny from above.[7] The "little people"—workers and low-level cadres—could often see more clearly than the big people, and their word should be heard. In this connection, Stalin recalled the case of Nikolaenko, a rank-and-file party member who had been "waved away like an annoying fly" when she tried to point out that something was rotten in the leadership of the Kiev party organization.[8] As must have been clear to Soviet listeners, Nikolaenko was one of those numerous citizens who had become habitual writers of letters of complaint and denunciation.[9] She had even reportedly been expelled from the Ukrainian party as a "slanderer" in 1936.[10]

How these signals were translated into specific instructions is still obscure because the instructions themselves were never published. A partial reconstruction is possible, however. On 29 November 1936, a week after the Novosibirsk trial, the state prosecutor of the USSR ordered that all major industrial accidents should be investigated for signs of intentional counterrevolutionary sabotage.[11] Lazar Kaganovich, the Politburo member in charge of the trade unions, instructed the union leaders that their members should be encouraged to write letters exposing abuses in industry and that the letters should be taken seriously.[12]

The February-March plenum of the party's Central Committee led to

---

[6] Stalin's speech to the plenum on March 3, "O nedostatkakh partiinoi raboty i merakh likvidatsii trotskistskikh i inykh dvurushnikov," is in I. V. Stalin, *Sochineniia*, ed. Robert H. McNeal (Stanford, Calif., 1967), 1:189–224, and his concluding statement to the plenum on 5 March ("Zakliuchitel'noe slovo") is in ibid., pp. 225–47. Molotov's speech to the plenum was published as "Uroki vreditel'stva, diversii i shpionazha iapono-nemetsko-trotskistskikh agentov," *Bol'shevik*, 1937, no. 8:12–45. The previously unpublished minutes of the February-March plenum have been appearing in *Voprosy istorii*, starting with no. 2–3 of 1992.

[7] Stalin, "O nedostatkakh," p. 232.

[8] Stalin, "Zakliuchitel'noe slovo," pp. 239–40.

[9] The sending of *zhaloby* and *donosy* to newspapers, local party and Soviet officials, prosecutors, and the NKVD, as well as to Stalin and other top party leaders was an amateur activity—distinct from that of the paid or suborned NKVD informer—whose scope in the Stalin period is only now becoming evident to researchers. The great majority of these letters contained allegations of criminal behavior or abuse of power by the writers' bosses or people in their immediate environment whose perks and privileges they envied. On the complaints and denunciations sent to *Krest'ianskaia gazeta*, the national peasant newspaper, see Sheila Fitzpatrick, *Stalin's Peasants: Resistance and Survival in the Russian Village after Collectivization* (New York, 1994).

[10] Conquest, *Great Terror*, p. 227.

[11] Conquest, *Great Terror*, p. 223, citing *Sovetskoe gosudarstvo i pravo*, 1965 no. 3.

[12] From the statement of a speaker at the plenary meeting of a trade union central committee in May 1937: TsGAOR, f. 7679, op. 3, d. 86, l. 16.

at least two specific sets of secret instructions. The first was that there should be monthly meetings of management with Stakhanovite workers ("soveshchaniia administrativno-khoziaistvennogo aktiva so stakhanovtsami") in the factories, as well as regular gatherings of Stakhanovite workers at the oblast level. The stated purpose in both cases was to promote worker participation and industrial democracy. The means by which this noble purpose was to be achieved was the eliciting of public ad hominem criticism of industrial bosses from workers and the encouragement of public denunciation of bosses as wreckers and saboteurs.[13]

The second instruction of the plenum concerned work safety in industrial enterprises.[14] The factory committees of the trade unions were told that it was time for a stringent review of safety violations and poor working conditions, with plant directors being held liable for deficiencies. Criminal prosecution might often be called for. In some case, the question of intentional sabotage might have to be raised.

The general message directed to workers, particularly Stakhanovites, at these first months of 1937 may be summarized as follows.[15]

Your bosses, especially the top-level managers of the factory, may be enemies of the people. You should watch for the signs that enemies are at work, and denounce them fearlessly, no matter how powerful and respected they may be, both in public and private communications.

Have there been accidents in which workers lost their lives, caused allegedly by "negligence"? This is probably intentional sabotage. If so, a prime candidate for suspicion is the factory director or one of his close associates. Regardless of whether accidents have actually occurred at your plant, are safety precautions regularly violated? That may be a more subtle form of sabotage—an attempt to provoke worker discontent by raising the level of work-related injuries and illnesses.

Are you a Stakhanovite or would-be Stakhanovite who thinks the bosses in your factory have not given you the necessary support and cooperation? Or, for that matter, are you a Stakhanovite who did receive support from the bosses but was not adequately protected against the hostility of other workers who regarded you as a norm-buster? In either case, consider the

---

[13] A reference to this unpublished directive is in *Ural'skii rabochii* (Sverdlovsk), 4 January 1938, p. 2. Minutes of one such meeting in 1938 (from the archives of the flaxworker's union) are cited later in this chapter. For elaboration of the purpose of the Stakhanovite meetings, see Zhdanov's comments in *Trud*, 21 March 1937, p. 2.

[14] See the discussion in a trade union central committee meeting of 17 April 1937 on "realization of the decisions of the February plenum of the TsK VKP(b) on reviewing the situation with regard to work safety." TsGAOR, f. 7679, op. 3, d. 90, l. 138.

[15] This is taken primarily from Stalin and Molotov's speeches to the Central Committee plenum, together with major commentaries on the plenum, such as Zhdanov's report on plenum to Leningrad party meeting, published in *Trud*, 21 March 1937, p. 2; *Pravda*'s editorial on the show trial, 2 February 1937, p. 2; V. Sobolev's article "Likvidatsiia posledstviia vreditel'stva," *Trud*, 16 February 1937, p. 2; and so on.

possibility that the bosses in your factory are trying openly or covertly to sabotage the Stakhanovite movement.

Are your bosses authoritarian, making you afraid to criticize them? Is it hard for workers with complaints to get access to the top management? Do they expect workers to treat them deferentially? Is there a local cult of personality of the factory director (portraits, placards on May Day etc.)? These may all be signs that the bosses are hidden counterrevolutionaries.

Finally, have you a personal grievance against anyone? Is there one particular boss who has treated you badly? Did you ever offer a criticism or suggestion at work that was ignored? Do you know of any minor wrongdoing that might indicate the presence of graver crimes? Have you ever been insulted, abused, passed over for a bonus, unfairly punished? If so, this is your moment. The person who offended [you] was probably an enemy of the people, and it is your duty to unmask him.

In their speeches at the February-March plenum, both Stalin and Molotov compared the present threat with that of the Shakhty and Prompartiia "wreckers" of the period of the First Five-Year Plan.[16] The difference, of course, was that the Shakhty wreckers had been non-Communist "bourgeois specialists," whose technical expertise had allegedly enabled them to pull the wool over the eyes of the Communist industrialists with whom they worked, whereas this time it was the Communist industrialists themselves who turned out to be guilty. No doubt this analogy was intended to serve several purposes, but one purpose was probably to test workers' reactions. In the 1920s, workers had regarded "bourgeois specialists" with suspicion and class antagonism even before the trials and often responded with enthusiasm to the signal that they were fair game for "specialist-baiting" (*spetseedstvo*).[17] When Stalin and Molotov drew an analogy between the Piatakov and Shakhty trials, this seemed to suggest that "boss-baiting" was as appropriate now as "*spets*-baiting" had been then—and even, taking the implication further, that workers had a temporary license to treat Communist industrial managers as something like class enemies.

Stalin toyed again with this rather perverse and mischievous notion when he toasted the "little people" instead of the big industrial bosses at a reception for industrial leaders and Stakhanovites in October 1937.[18] In his speech, a scarcely veiled threat to Soviet industrial bosses was artfully

[16] Stalin, "O nedostatkakh," pp. 202–4; Molotov, "Uroki," pp. 24–25.

[17] On *spetseedstvo*, see Sheila Fitzpatrick, "Cultural Revolution as Class War," in Fitzpatrick, ed., *Cultural Revolution in Russia, 1928–1931* (Bloomington, Ind., 1978).

[18] "Rech' na primete rukovodiashchikh rabotnikov i stakhanovtsev metallurgicheskoi i ugol'noi promyshlennosti, rukovoditeliami partii i pravitel'stva, 29 oktiabria 1937 g.," in Stalin, *Sochineniia*, 1:253–55. In honoring the "small and middling" cadres, Stalin stated explicitly that he was not making the usual toast "za zdorov'e rukovoditelei, shefov, za vozhdei, za narkomov."

intertwined with a teasing comparison—no sooner raised than repudi-
ated—of contemporary Soviet industrial managers with the old exploiting
class of prerevolutionary capitalist managers.

> In general, one must say about leaders that they, unfortunately, do not al-
> ways understand to what a height history has raised them under the Soviet
> system. They do not always understand that to be a leader of the economy
> in these circumstances means . . . being awarded the high trust of the work-
> ing class, of the people. In the old days, in the time of capitalism, industrial
> leaders—all kinds of directors, administrators, shop heads, foremen—were
> considered chained guard-dogs for the capitalist owners. The people hated
> them as enemies, believing that they directed the economy in the interests of
> the owners, for the sake of the capitalists' profits. Under our Soviet system,
> by contrast, there is every reason why industrial leaders enjoy the trust and
> love of the people. . . . With regard to the industrialists, comrades, the peo-
> ple's trust is a big thing. Leaders come and go, but the people remains. Only
> the people [narod] is eternal. Everything else is transient.[19]

Undoubtedly there were echoes here of the class-war sentiments that
had been so powerful in the working class and the Bolshevik Party in
1917 and again during the Cultural Revolution at the end of the 1920s;
however, there were also significant differences. It was "the people," (narod), not the working class, to whose resentments and grievances against
their bosses Stalin was appealing. Moreover, in 1937 Stalin's praise of
"little" and "humble" people had a sinister ring, for these terms immediately recalled the "little people" like Nikolaenko who secretly wrote in
and denounced their bosses.

Responses

Large-scale arrests by the NKVD of leading industrial managers as
"wreckers" and "enemies of the people" began early in 1937.[20] The actual
arrests were not publicized except in rare instances, but the associated
process of publicly criticizing and discrediting industrial managers was
clearly visible in the national and provincial press. Throughout the spring
of 1937, the newspapers reported a seemingly endless series of meetings

[19] Ibid., pp. 253–54.
[20] For data on the impact of the Great Purges on Soviet industrialists, see Roy A. Med-
vedev, *Let History Judge: The Origins and Consequences of Stalinism*, 2d ed. (New York,
1989), pp. 444–45; Hiroaki Kuromiya, "Stalinist Terror in the Donbas: A Note," in J. Arch
Getty and Roberta T. Manning, eds., *Stalinist Terror: New Perspectives* (Cambridge, 1993),
pp. 215–22; and Sheila Fitzpatrick, "The Impact of the Great Purges on Different Elite
Strata: A Case Study from Moscow Telephone Directories for 1937 and 1939," in Getty
and Manning, *Stalinist Terror*, pp. 247–60.

at big industrial enterprises at which the directors and other senior personnel gave speeches of increasingly harsh "self-criticism," and the workers and other employees offered their own criticisms, suspicions, and denunciations of management.

According to the conventions of these meetings, a plant director who tried to avoid stirring up ad hominem attacks and denunciations of "wrecking" was failing in his duty,[21] probably because he was trying to cover up his own misdeeds. A director who treated an industrial accident at the plant as an accident was at best naive. A factory meeting that uncovered no wrongdoing and unmasked no enemies of the people or accusations of sabotage was obviously a cover-up. A meeting that identified only enemies that were already known (that is, already under arrest) was a sham. Accusations once launched were almost impossible for the victim to refute at the time without inflaming general hysteria (though it was sometimes possible to quash them successfully later if management kept its nerve).

Although all workers and other "little people" had been called on to criticize their bosses, the invitation was directed particularly at Stakhanovites. At this point, we need to pause to consider what was meant by the term "Stakhanovite." Strictly speaking, Stakhanovites were workers who had not only overfulfilled their production quotas but had done so by finding ways to rationalize production and maximize output. But there were other overtones to the term. From the standpoint of fellow workers, Stakhanovites were often seen as norm-busters, betrayers of shop-floor solidarity. From the standpoint of management, Stakhanovites often had equally undesirable attributes: they were workers who demonstrated the real production capacity of the plant, thus breaking the unspoken compact between labor and management in a planned economy to mislead the central planners and keep the plant's production targets low. In this sense, the Stakhanovite role was a peculiar Soviet version of whistle-blowing. Like the worker and peasant correspondents (*rabkory* and *sel'kory*) who took it on themselves to write regular reports to newspapers on wrongdoing in their factories and villages in the 1920s, though to a lesser degree, Stakhanovites were in some sense conceived of as "the eyes of the party" in their local milieu.

Thus, by appealing to "Stakhanovite" workers to take the lead in crit-

---

[21] See, for example, the critical and disapproving reports of factory meetings where the director set the wrong tone by avoiding "painful questions," with the result that speakers "talked in generalities" and criticized the plant management only "sotto voce." *Zvezda* (Dnepropetrovsk), 28 May 1937, p. 2. Or of a factory director who habitually urged plant employees not to "ruin a man's reputation for nothing" when they accused someone of intentional sabotage. *Severnyi rabochii* (Iaroslavl), 6 April 1937, p. 3. Or of a director who tried to confine discussion at factory meetings to "a narrow circle of immediate economic questions." *Molot* (Rostov), 10 April 1937, p. 3.

icizing management and unmasking saboteurs, the party leadership was not so much literally appealing to workers who were recognized production Stakhanovites as appealing to the potential Stakhanovite (in the sense of whistle-blower or informant against bosses) in all workers. It must be said that the response—at least initially, and in public—was disappointing.[22] Most workers were hesitant about criticizing their bosses to their faces. No doubt some also remained silent out of skepticism, disgust, or boredom with the whole ritual of unmasking wreckers.[23]

In the mining town of Shakhty (home of the Shakhty "wreckers" of 1928 whose show trial had launched the Cultural Revolution), workers carried the ritual of unmasking to the point of absurdity, though whether they did this in innocence, indifference, or malice is impossible to determine. Instead of gravely debating the signs of possible industrial sabotage and then diligently searching for possible culprits, they cut through to the heart of the matter and held an *election* to determine which managers and engineers should be labeled wreckers. A similar travesty was reported at another plant, where the list of elected wreckers was posted on bulletin boards.[24]

An additional forum for criticism of industrial managers was provided by the reelection of party committees that began in April 1937 under the slogan of strengthening party democracy. The hallmark of these elections was rank-and-file Communist participation and the stimulation of that "initiative from below" of which Stalin had spoken at the Central Committee plenum. A radical turnover of party officers was expected and required. Contrary to normal practice, and to the confusion and dismay of the participants, no lists of nominees for office (*spiski*) were provided by higher party bodies.[25]

In the past, it had always been routine procedure to elect the director of an industrial enterprise—who was invariably a Communist—to the factory's party committee. In the new climate of suspicion and criticism,

[22] See, for example, the report of the first meeting of the managerial aktiv of a Donbas coal-mining trust with Stakhanovites: "For the first time, voices of criticism and self-criticism were heard here. But one must say they are timid voices, not completely bold." *Sotsialisticheskii Donbass* (Stalino), 24 March 1937, p. 3. Even when Stakhanovites voiced their criticisms, the plant directors did not always pay much attention: see, for example, the example from Vladimir Ilich plant in Moscow in *Rabochaia Moskva*, 4 September 1936, p. 3.

[23] This is the dominant attitude seen by Kravchenko, an engineer who in 1936–37 was head of a subplant at the Nikopol Metallurgical Combine. See Victor Kravchenko, *I Chose Freedom* (London, 1949), p. 235 and passim.

[24] *Za industrializatsiiu*, 21 August 1937, p. 1. This story was told by V. I. Mezhlauk, then (but not for much longer) a deputy commissar of heavy industry, at a congress of workers in the machine-building industry. Clearly Mezhlauk was expressing opposition to the current waves of managerial witch-hunting in industry.

[25] *Pravda* and other newspapers provided extensive coverage of these elections in the period March to May 1937.

however, many factory directors in Moscow failed to win reelection to their plants' party committee.[26] Furthermore, Communist workers seem to have been considerably more responsive than other workers to suggestions that they should boldly criticize their factory bosses. During the party elections at the huge Stalin Auto Plant in Moscow, where three thousand Communists worked, there was "passionate" and even "irresponsible" criticism of managers by workers from the floor, according to *Pravda*. One particularly eloquent worker used the terms "Goebbels," "barbarian-bureaucrat," and "donkey's ears" to describe various plant managers.[27]

A vivid impression of the climate of suspicion and desperation that prevailed in industry—or rather, in the upper echelons of factory administrations—is conveyed in an account written by a woman, probably young and inexperienced, who was the newly appointed party secretary at Kaganovich Brake Factory in Moscow. The author was clearly torn between sympathy with the besieged managers of the plant and suspicion that they really were saboteurs. On the one hand, she reported without rebuttal the anguished complaints of the director that "the atmosphere at the plant was unbearable, managerial authority [*edinonachalie*] had been shattered, the party committee is giving the orders, people are terrorized, the commercial director has handed in his resignation, the chief accountant has fled, the Plan has not been fulfilled, . . ."

On the other hand, she got the feeling that the old cadres were hiding something from her. There had been a serious accident at the plant—but was it *really* an accident? Was it pure coincidence that the commercial director had been fired from a previous job? That two sons of the plant's accountant had been exiled? As for the factory director, the new party secretary tried to give him the benefit of the doubt, but there were so many worrying signs. He had given bonuses to Trotskyists and hired persons of dubious background. He was known to have accompanied the notorious enemy of the people, Piatakov, on an overseas buying trip, even though he now denied it. Why would an innocent man have seemed so "utterly dejected" as he had reportedly been at the time of the Piatakov trial? The more one thought about it, the more sinister and suspicious everything seemed.[28]

Such suspicions were presumably being fed by a growing stream of denunciations coming in to party committees, the NKVD, and other organizations. The writing and reading of denunciations was a furtive activity, even after Stalin and Molotov's encouragement, and they were

---

[26] *Pravda*, 25 April 1937, p. 2.
[27] *Pravda*, 22 April 1937, p. 2.
[28] *Pravda*, 16 August 1937, p. 2.

rarely referred to or explicitly cited in public. Sometimes people publicly boasted of having written a *donos* on someone who had since been arrested as an enemy of the people, but the reaction of fellow workers was usually at least passively hostile.[29] It is difficult, therefore, to gauge the exact volume and intensity of the phenomenon at any given time. A useful indicator is the number of complaints received by industrial trade unions.[30] In the first four months of 1937 alone, the central committee of the union of workers in the precious-metal industry received 991 complaints from workers, compared with 372 complaints in the whole of 1935 and 561 complaints in 1936.[31]

Some more information on denunciations came out in 1938–39 when the party leadership was trying to put on the brakes and discourage the letter writers. Cases of victimization of persons falsely denounced earlier were publicized.[32] There were reports such as the one from the big Sverdlovsk plant, Uralmash, that "a group of slanderers terrorized and disrupted party, soviet, and industrial work for a long time. The slanderers, speaking out at meetings, cried out loudest of all about vigilance and flooded party committees and investigative organs with an uncountable number of statements and *donosy*."[33] The damage done by "slanderers" (that is, the writers of complaints and *donosy*) was criticized by Andrei Zhdanov in his report to the Eighteenth Party Congress in 1939 repudiating mass purging.[34]

One consequence of the purging of industrial managers was deterioration of labor discipline at many enterprises.[35] It was observed that worker

[29] See, for example, the exchange at a meeting of the city party organization in Khabarovsk when one of the "little people" from the railroad depot criticized the top management of the railroad for failing to respond to "workers' signals"—evidently meaning his own *donosy*—about Trotskyite infiltration. *Tikhookeanskaia zvezda* (Khabarovsk), 1 April 1937, p. 3.

[30] On the basis of the *Krest'ianskaia gazeta* correspondence files of 1938, my impression is that little significant distinction can be made between complaints *(zhaloby)* and denunciations at this period. The category of letters filed by *Krest'ianskaia gazeta* under the heading "Zloupotreblenie i vreditel'stvo" (TsGANKh, f. 396, op. 10 and 11) does not contain complaints in any normal sense; it is full of letters accusing local officeholders of a multitude of specific abuses of power, criminal acts, ties with enemies of the people, and personal offences against the writer. The authors of these letters often said they had sent copies to the NKVD and the procuracy.

[31] TsGAOR, f. 7679, op. 3, d. 86, l. 16.

[32] See, for example, the case of a Communist woman weaver, active in the trade union movement since 1917, who was denounced for having been acquainted with a Trotskyist in 1923. *Profsoiuzy SSSR*, 1938, no. 2:5.

[33] *Ural'skii rabochii* (Sverdlovsk), 2 February 1938, p. 2.

[34] See A. Zhdanov, "Izmeneniia v ustave VKP(b). . . . Ob otmene massovykh chistok," in *XVIII s"ezd Vsesoiuznoi Kommunisticheskoi Partii (b), 10–21 marta 1939 g. Stenograficheskii otchet* ([Moscow], 1939).

[35] Donald Filtzer expresses skepticism about the alleged deterioration of discipline of mid-1937, writing that "it is impossible to determine whether matters had really grown worse from the regime's point of view or whether it had merely decided to try and reassert control

absenteeism was growing,[36] and that the arrest of management wreckers, which should have improved the situation, inexplicably seemed to have had the opposite effect.[37] It was said that workers and even foremen were regularly taking off early from work and refusing to obey instructions from managers.[38] Later reports spoke of unspecified "antistate tendencies" and "disorders" (*besporiadki*) at plants and warned that these could only serve the interests of enemies of the people.[39]

The nature of the connection between the purges of industrial managers and the breakdown of labor discipline was explained most clearly by Iulii Kaganovich, brother of Lazar and first secretary of the Gor'kii obkom (regional party committee) in mid-1937. Alarmed by the rapid rise in violations of labor discipline in the industrial enterprises of the oblast, he cross-examined representatives of the "Red Sormovo" plant—whose director had recently been arrested as an enemy of the people—about why foremen were condoning truancy of workers and shop heads were not penalizing the foremen for slackness. They told him that the reason was that "the commanding cadres have not recovered from their shock [*rasteriannost'*]," presumably a reaction to the arrests, and that managers at lower levels "have let discipline lapse" because "they are afraid they will be accused of suppressing self-criticism [*samokritika*]."[40]

Rasteriannost'—shock, confusion, disarray—is a word that crops up quite often in 1937 to describe the mental state of people who had not yet been arrested but feared they might be.[41] Their fear of being accused of "suppressing *samokritika*" if they tried to discipline workers[42] was a current code for something very like blackmail: if a worker was punished

---

over a situation that in reality differed little from 1935 or 1936, when it had provoked no reaction." Filtzer, *Soviet Workers*, p. 140. Although such skepticism is always prudent in dealing with Soviet published sources, I think it is unwarranted in this instance. Apart from the frequency and inherent plausibility of the reports, there is a recurring note of evasiveness and euphemism that suggests to me that the phenomenon was being downplayed rather than exaggerated in the press.

[36] See, for example, director Birman's statement on the Petrovskii Metallurgical Plant, made to the Dnepropetrovsk oblast party conference after several months of extreme tension at the plant and repeated sessions of criticism and self-criticism in *Zvezda* (Dnepropetrovsk), 19 May 1937, p. 2.

[37] Editorial, *Severnyi rabochii* (Iaroslavl), 3 September 1937, p. 1.

[38] *Rabochii put'* (Smolensk), 18 July 1937, p. 1. See also "Bolshevik *samokritika* and labor discipline," *Pravda*, 24 June 1937, p. 1.

[39] *Rabochii put'* (Smolensk), 16 October 1937, pp. 3–4.

[40] See reports in *Gor'kovskaia kommuna* (Gor'kii), 23 July 1937, p. 2, and *Za industrializatsiiu*, 4 August 1937, p. 2.

[41] The Rostov newspaper even referred to industrial cadres whose *rasteriannost'* was so great that it led to "self-release from leadership"—that is, they quit their jobs and ran away. *Molot*, 29 April 1937, p. 1.

[42] See also "Bolshevik *samokritika* and labor discipline," *Pravda*, 24 June 1937, p. 1.

by his boss, he might take revenge by denouncing the boss as an enemy of the people.

There are also reports of a revival of "*spets*-baiting" in some ways reiminiscent of that which had flourished during the Cultural Revolution. Then the victims had been nonparty engineers, generally trained before the revolution and regarded by many workers as part of the old exploiting, privileged classes. Most of that cohort of engineers was gone by 1937, a new cohort of young Communist engineers had entered and was entering the factories, and the former sharp distinction between "Reds" and "experts" no longer applied. Managers and engineers were jointly referred to as "ITR,"[43] and they seem to have suffered almost equally in the Great Purges.

The interesting aspect of the "*spets*-baiting" of 1937-8, however, is that the major target seems to have been *young* engineers, newly arrived at the plants (often as replacements for old cadres that had been purged) and suffering both because of their own inexperience and because of the purge-related breakdown of discipline in the factories. It was reported in the fall of 1937, for example, that young engineers sent to work at a ship-repairing plant in Saratov found their position impossible because of the hostility they encountered from the workers, as well as from the plant director and the party committee. There was no disagreement or rebuke from management when the leader of a fitter's brigade stated at a factory meeting that "all young specialists are wreckers. We need to promote 'our own' people and not take people from somewhere outside."[44]

A year later, an inspector sent out from Moscow to check up on and advise a new director of the Novomoskovskii Tin-Rolling Plant in Dnepropetrovsk filed a vivid and alarming report of the situation. The new, inexperienced men in the top jobs had no authority and were respected neither by the old cadres that remained nor by the workers. A running feud had developed between the new director, the party secretary, and the head of the trade union committee. When anything went wrong, everybody automatically shifted the blame onto the director: "It's the director's fault" had become an all-purpose, standard excuse. The chief engineer (evidently also new and inexperienced) was regarded as incompetent, and it had become "established practice" not to carry out his instructions. At one meeting, for example, "the head of the rolling shop, comrade Savvateev, informed the chief engineer that he would not carry out his instructions [because] he thought they were wrong, and moreover

---

[43] *Inzhenerno-tekhnicheskie rabotniki* (as against blue-collar workers and white-collar employees in the industrial workforce).

[44] *Kommunist* (Saratov), 3 September 1937, p. 3.

stated that 'I will do the same in the future.' " In this atmosphere of managerial confusion and demoralization, accidents and work stoppages had become routine. "Labor discipline is in very bad shape (people have got out of hand [*razboltalis'*], and everyone is looking out for himself)."[45]

Case Studies

The two sets of case studies of the impact of the purges on labor-management relations that I will examine in the rest of this article come from Soviet trade union archives.[46] These archives are incomplete and fragmentary for the late 1930s, and the two trade unions whose files I use are among the few blue-collar unions with a good run of local material for 1937 or 1938.[47] The first set consists of files from three metalworking plants in the Urals[48] and one in Moscow.[49] The second set comes from the flaxworkers' trade union and includes the minutes of two regional conferences of Stakhanovites as well as materials from individual plants in Smolensk and Ivanovo oblasts. The first set covers the period January–August 1937—that is, the first stage of the Great Purges—and deals with enterprises in which almost all the workers were men. The second set covers the period from July 1938 to February 1939—the end of the Great Purges—and deals with enterprises in which most of the workers were women.

Metalworkers, 1937

In the three Urals plants, the Great Purges had already made an impact in the first months of 1937. There had been arrests of managers and/or accusations of "wrecking" in connection with industrial accidents or health dangers at the plants.[50] The impact seemed to be greatest at the

[45] TsGANKh, f. 4086, op. 2, d. 4896, l. 139.

[46] TsGAOR, f. 7679, op. 3 (fond TsK soiuza rabochikh dobycha tsvetnykh metallov SSSR), and f. 5457, op. 26 (fond TsK soiuza l'ianoi promyshlennosti).

[47] Unfortunately, there seems to be no single trade union archive that provides good material on both 1937 and 1938. The metalworkers' union, whose 1937 material I use, had nothing useful from 1938. Similarly, the flaxworkers' union, whose 1938–39 material I use, had nothing useful from 1937.

[48] The New Kyshtym Electrolytic Copper Plant, the Kyshtym Foundry, and the Krasnouralsk Copper-Smelting Works.

[49] The Moscow Electrodes Plant.

[50] At the Kyshtym Foundry, the head of the trade union committee said that "wreckers' hand had not passed by our enterprise" but gave no details. TsGAOR, f. 7679, op. 3, d. 111, l. 23. At the Krasnouralsk Copper-Smelting Works, the chief engineer was serving as acting director (which could mean that the director had been arrested), and the heads of the plant's party and trade union organizations had recently been removed for "facilitating wrecking." TsGAOR, f. 7679, op. 3, d. 123, ll. 9 and 15.

New Kyshtym plant, where some wreckers had already been unmasked and more disclosures were expected. Evidently the director, although still in office, had been damaged by the disclosures and was expected to become the next victim. Noting that "we must carry the struggle with wreckers to its conclusion," one speaker at a plant trade union meeting said: "It's obvious that the director will be removed, since this can't go on much longer." A previous head of the trade union committee, who had been accused of misappropriating funds, had possibly already been expelled from the party[51] and seemed to be on the brink of being declared an enemy of the people.[52]

Although the exact substance of the accusations of wrecking in the Urals plants are not known, it is clear that they involved toleration by management of hazardous conditions, contamination of the working environment, and the workers' accidents and illnesses related to them. At two out of the three of the Urals plants, there were formal investigations and discussions of work safety in the first months of 1937, evidently stimulated by the revelations of the Novosibirsk and Piatakov trials and the instructions from the center that followed (see above, pp. 313–15).

At the Kyshtym Foundry, the plant's physician presented a report on traumatism and illness at the factory which was discussed in March.[53] Speakers attributed the high incidence of TB, malaria, and flu to the draughts in the shops, which all had broken windows. "Management could have used money from the profits that were made to cope with all this," said one speaker. The chairman of the factory committee put the discussion squarely in a Purges context:

> At the present time, both VTsSPS and the central committee of our union attach great importance to the issue of work safety measures in the Urals. The wreckers' diversionary hand has not passed by our enterprise. Evidence disclosed at the Kemerovo trial, amounting to intentional poisoning of workers [by enemies of the people], testify to the fact that the class enemy is using the [issue of] protection of labor for its own infamous purposes. The union's central committee warned us to be vigilant and not to tolerate the outrageous conditions that exist here. Let us take some examples from the steel-rolling shop: the windows are broken, the door is broken, there are draughts through the shop. This clearly points to an attitude of negligence and indifference, if not to wrecking.[54]

[51] Contradictory statements on the man's current party status were made by two speakers (Babushkin and Glazkov). TsGAOR, f. 7679, op. 3, d. 111, ll. 43 and 44.

[52] TsGAOR, f. 7679, op. 3, d. 111, ll. 43–45.

[53] Meeting of the social-insurance soviet together with members of the [Party and?] trade union aktiv and heads of shops at Kyshtym Mechanical Factory, 21 March 1937. See the report by physician Veller on traumatism and illness at the factory in TsGAOR, f. 7679, op. 3, d. 111, ll. 21–24.

[54] Ibid., l. 23.

Given this threatening preamble, the conclusion that the problems were the result of "negligence and indifference" was relatively tame, as was the meeting's decision "to ask the directorate of the plant to order the shop heads to correct deficiencies in work safety procedures."[55] This was, in effect, to reject the options of calling for criminal prosecution of managers who allowed violation of safety regulations or accusing them of intentional sabotage. It should be noted also that the question was discussed by the *aktiv*—in effect, by politically active middle- and lower-level cadres—rather than by a general meeting of workers or a meeting of management and Stakhanovites of the type recommended by the February-March plenum.

The Krasnouralsk Copper-Smelting Plant was polluted by gas, with adverse consequences to the health of the workers, and had had a number of gas-related accidents in the previous year (1936). In February, the plant held a general meeting of workers on the issue of working conditions and safety precautions that was attended by a representative from the Central Council of Trade Unions and the secretary of the local raikom (district [party] committee). It was generally agreed by all speakers that the plant was unhealthy because of the gas, and that the reason measures had not been taken to correct the situation was lack of funds. According to the acting director, in order to remove the gas from the shops it would be necessary to install a ventilation system costing 3 million rubles. "Piatakovs" (that is, wreckers) were to blame for the center's failure to allocate this sum earlier, he said, making no effort to make this assertion of intentional wrongdoing credible. He added that installation was now scheduled for August, but seemed skeptical that it would in fact occur, since "we don't have the money."[56]

No formal meeting on work safety is recorded in the files of the New Kyshtym Electrolytic Copper Factory, though working conditions there were also poor, and there had been allegations of wrecking and probably arrests of managers early in 1937. In June, a speaker at a trade union meeting drew a causal connection between the two, which, as reported, mocked rather than endorsed the current party line on intentional counterrevolutionary wrecking. He said, "Safety measures are poor, there is a lot of overtime, people are working without free days, the water is unboiled, and from this it follows that management is trying to make the workers ill."[57] No other speaker took up the theme.

The Moscow Electrodes Plant differed from the three Urals plants in that there is no indication in its files for the first half of 1937 of arrests

---

[55] Ibid., l. 24.
[56] TsGAOR, f. 7679, op. 3, d. 123, l. 15 (statement of acting director).
[57] Ibid., l. 44.

of managers, accusations of wrecking, or any other direct symptom of the
Great Purges. Nevertheless, here too work safety was a big issue. At the
end of January, the factory director, Linde, gave a report on the subject
to the factory committee.[58] In the ensuing discussion, a number of workers
complained strongly about working conditions and health risks. One
speaker, chairman of a shop committee, said:

> The turners work in the cold, the door is open, and there is a draught. The
> turners have to walk around to keep warm. They are not issued special work
> clothes. The dust which is present in the furnace shop has an effect on the
> health of the workers. They don't get much soap. The showers are crowded
> and colossal lines form.

Others pointed to an increasing rate of sickness at the plant, and complained that management had been promising to fix all the problems for
three years now, but nothing had been done.

But the spokesmen for management were equally assertive.

> GUSEV. Our plant is still new, it went into operation when the building was
> not completely finished, and therefore we cannot get rid of defects so quickly.
> A large amount of blame lies on the workers themselves. They never shut
> [sic] the ventilators. Last year we gave workers special work clothes, but the
> workers didn't give them back [illegible words]. You repair the doors and
> tomorrow they will again have resumed their former appearance, because
> the workers treat them carelessly and nobody shuts them.

> LINDE [plant director]. Comrade Gusev is right, you can't work on electrodes
> without dust, you can put in ventilators but still they will not create the kind
> of air you'd get at a resort. Our plant grew, the number of people increased,
> and therefore the showers became crowded. It isn't right to say that all the
> blame lies on the management.

All the same, that was what the meeting decided to do. On the motion
of Savelev, probably the party secretary at the plant, it was resolved

> to ask the prosecutor of Stalin district to bring charges against the directorate
> of the factory for callous indifference to questions of protection of labor and
> work safety.[59]

Despite this resolution, however, no charges were filed because "the factory committee failed to send the materials through to the procuracy."

[58] TsGAOR, f. 7679, op. 3, d. 129, l. 12.
[59] Ibid., l. 14.

Apparently no repairs were made either, since it was reported in June that "the ventilation still does not work."[60]

Stakhanovite initiatives were not much in evidence at any of the four plants. At the Kyshtym Foundry, it is true, a general meeting of Stakhanovite workers was held at the factory early in August, and the plant's party secretary did his best to stimulate sharp criticism and denunciation of managers by quoting Stalin's warnings about enemies and the need for vigilance, but to no avail.[61] A few weeks later, an oblast-level meeting of Stakhanovites was held in Sverdlovsk. Its message that a factory director who did not actively support the Stakhanovite movement was objectively aiding enemies of the people was duly relayed back to the workers at Kyshtym—not by a Stakhanovite worker, however, but by their own director, who had attended as the foundry's representative![62]

It was said at one of the factory committee meetings at New Kyshtym—the plant where the purges seem to have made the greatest impact in the first half of 1937—that "the workers were under pressure [before] and are only now beginning to say a little of what was on their minds."[63] The speaker, P. N. Oreshkov, was a member of a family of skilled workers that was obviously highly respected at the plant. What was on his mind, however, was not wrecking and enemies of the people—which never appear in these files as subjects of real discussion—but inflation and its impact on real wages ("If I, a worker, earn 'a hundred' rubles, then what will I be able to get for those 'hundred' rubles?")[64]

When the New Kyshtym plant held trade union elections in June, the spirit comes across as generally thoughtful and serious as the different candidacies were considered and objections raised. Despite the fact that the factory committee's former chairman had been disgraced and possibly expelled from the party, witch-hunting was not the order of the day. This particular factory had a solid cohort of worker-activists like the Oreshkovs who evidently inhibited such a development (at least up to mid-1937). They were often, though not invariably or permanently, charged with various official responsibilities, such as chairmanship of the factory committee. In their comments during the lengthy election discussions, they displayed a sense of working-class identity and pride, but no hostility toward managers and engineers as such. Rather, they seemed inclined to distinguish between ITR who were themselves former workers "pro-

[60] Ibid., l. 78.
[61] TsGAOR, f. 7679, op. 3, d. 111, ll. 93–94.
[62] Ibid., l. 102.
[63] Ibid., l. 43.
[64] Ibid.

moted" into management or higher education, with whom (on this small body of evidence, at least) they felt comradeship, and those of other social background, with whom they felt less comfortable.

The "vigilance" these workers exercised in the trade union elections was not the Great Purges variety but an older kind of class vigilance. They argued, for example, about whether it was proper to nominate a shop head, a newly graduated engineer, to the factory committee: one speaker held that people with higher education were useful additions, whereas another objected ("Comrades, we need to elect candidates from the workers"), and the candidacy was defeated by a wide margin.[65] They also gave close attention to the question of whether various worker candidates (who, like most of these workers, came from peasant families) did or did not have kulak backgrounds.[66] This was not a "signaled" topic of investigation in 1937, and from the tone of the comments of the New Kyshtym activists, it seems that they raised such questions simply because they themselves considered them important.

This is not to say that the vindictive spirit necessary for real worker participation in the Great Purges was wholly absent from New Kyshtym. One speaker, a stoneworker from the construction shop who was clearly not part of the established circle of worker-activists, came out with a string of denunciations and grievances that were very much in the "Stakhanovite" spirit Stalin and Molotov were encouraging:

> Sukpasova [not further identified] was a Trotskyist. In 1936, they gave her a prize and sent her for a vacation at a resort. Who is to blame here, the director or the party committee[?]
>
> ...In 1936, they gave a prize to the director and the chief engineer, and in addition 13,000 [rubles] was given for prizes for the best employees. However, that money has still not been distributed. I would like to know why they give prizes to ITR and do not give prizes to workers.[67]

Another speaker, a woman who was likewise not a member of the established aktiv, complained that proper attention was not being paid to "the unmasking of the class enemy," and named two employees in the factory's supply department as "class enemies," (*liudi . . . ne nashi*).[68]

[65] Ibid., l. 52.
[66] Ibid., ll. 51–52.
[67] Ibid., l. 44.
[68] Ibid., l. 45. From the semiliterate phrasing of this comment, it seems unlikely that the speaker was trying to draw any distinction between unmasking "class enemies" and unmasking "enemies of the people." It is more likely that she had confused the two categories.

Flaxworkers, 1938–1939

The files from the flaxworkers' union archive that will be discussed in this section differ sharply in many respects from those of the metalworkers that were examined in the previous section.[69] The most remarkable characteristic of the flaxworkers' files is the truculent, insistent, and disrespectful manner in which individual workers and foremen challenged and criticized senior managers at meetings, and the defensive, intimidated, ill-assured manner in which the managers responded. The boldness with which workers spoke of and to top managers in these public sessions of 1938 and 1939 has no counterpart in the recorded behavior of metalworkers in 1937 (though John Scott describes something similar in Magnitogorsk after the arrest of a plant manager in 1936).[70] In their criticism, the flaxworkers often seemed to be treating management as a tainted class, collectively under suspicion of political disloyalty as "bourgeois specialists" had been during the Cultural Revolution. At other times, to be sure, the workers' dismissive tone toward managers suggested a more down-to-earth emotion—for example, the impatience that a tired, ill-housed woman worker with a chip on her shoulder might feel toward a callow young engineer just out of college or a thirty-five-year-old director on his first senior management job.

What are the factors distinguishing the two sets of data that might explain the difference in content? The most obvious difference is time: the metalworkers' files used in the last section come from the first half of 1937, whereas the flaxworkers' files used in this section cover the period from the second half of 1938 through the first months of 1939. This means, of course, that the time separating the two sets of files coincides fairly exactly with the period in which one would expect the Great Purges to have had maximum impact in industry. It seems plausible that labor-management relations at the enterprise level should have changed significantly over that period (though Scott's report would then be anomalous), and that much of the difference we see can be explained by the fact that the managerial purge, which was just beginning in the first set of files, had essentially run its course in the second, leaving turbulence and an untested cohort of young, nervous directors in its wake.

But there are also other differences that may be relevant. We are dealing

[69] The four files used here—from TsGAOR, f. 5457, op. 26, dd. 435, 427, 584, and 585—are all from the archive of the central committee of the trade union of workers of the flax industry (wages department). They are dated from late July 1938 to February 1939.

[70] "During the first few days, chaos reigned in the plant. A foreman would come to work in the morning and say to his men, 'Now today we must do this and that.' The workers would sneer at him and say: 'Go on. You're a wrecker yourself. Tomorrow they'll come and arrest you. All you engineers and technicians are wreckers.'" John Scott, *Behind the Urals* (Bloomington, Ind., 1973), p. 195.

with different sectors of industry (metallurgical and metalworking, on the one hand; flaxworking, on the other), different geographical locations (Moscow and the Urals in the first case, Smolensk and Ivanovo oblasts in the second), and, perhaps most important, a different kind of workforce. Whereas the metalworkers were almost entirely male, the flaxworkers were predominantly female. In addition, it is probable that there was a more significant and numerous cohort of older, experienced workers and workers who were party members among the metalworkers than among the flaxworkers.

There is ample evidence in the flaxworkers' files that the Purges had had a substantial impact on the life of the plants. There were many references to the recent extraordinary turnover of managerial personnel and wrecking by "Trotskyist-Bukharinite bandits,"[71] and this was said to be a cause of the breakdown of labor discipline that was the top item on the agenda of most meetings at this period. At a gathering of young Stakhanovites of the flax industry in Ivanovo oblast in July 1938, the Komsomol organizers fell into a panic and started desperately trying to shift the blame when it was found that a newly arrested "enemy of the people" (Vlas Chubar) had inadvertently been included in the meeting's honorary presidium.[72] At another meeting, the problem of denunciation was raised in connection with a deputy head of department who was in the habit of writing false denunciations about his boss and making slanderous accusations against co-workers.[73]

Until the very last of the meetings in these 1938–39 files, the underlying premise of discussion seemed to be that if something had gone wrong, management was to blame. This point was hammered home by workers, and sometimes also by foremen.[74] For example, the minutes of a meeting of plant managers with Stakhanovites[75] at an unidentified flax combine (probably either Smolensk or Ivanovo) on 13 August 1938 show the combine's director and chief engineer silently enduring a barrage of criticism about management's poor performance and its responsibility for the breakdown of discipline in the plants, high labor turnover, and the combine's failure to meet production quotas. Most of those who spoke at the meeting put the blame for all the problems squarely on top management, claiming that the director and his deputies were too often absent on business trips and spent too little time in the shops.[76] The resolution, however,

---

[71] TsGAOR, f. 5457, op. 26, d. 430, l. 22; d. 585, l. 57; d. 584, l. 117; and so on.

[72] TsGAOR, f. 5457, op. 26, d. 427, ll. 62, 66–68.

[73] TsGAOR, f. 5457, op. 26, d. 435, l. 17.

[74] See, for example, foremen's criticism at a meeting at an unidentified flax plant on 3 August 1938, ibid., l. 7.

[75] The file, TsGAOR f. 5457, op. 26, d. 435, is headed "Protokoly soveshchanii administrativno-khoziaistvennogo aktiva i stakhanovtsev fabrik . . . 1938–39."

[76] TsGAOR, f. 5457, op. 26, d. 435, ll. 7–10.

broadened the criticism to apply to *all* ITR, stating flatly that "the exceptionally poor work of the plant in July and the first ten days of August
was because the administrative-technical personnel, starting with the director and ending with the sub-foremen, did not head the struggle for
raising labor discipline, and sometimes violated labor discipline themselves."[77]

It is hard to read the 1938 minutes without sensing that the workers
knew it was "open season" on managers and were getting some satisfaction out of criticizing them publicly with little fear of retaliation. At the
same time, there clearly were good reasons to criticize the managers, given
their low morale and inexperience. At a meeting held in Iamshchino (Smolensk oblast) on 20 October 1938, at which the "management is to
blame" theme held its usual prominent place, factory directors pleaded
with workers for greater tolerance of young managers and engineers in
view of their inexperience and the enormous problems they had inherited
as a result of past "wrecking."

> SOBOLEV [director of Zvorykino Combine] . . . Until very recently, we had a
> group of wreckers here . . . For the past half year, the situation at the com-
> bine has been as follows: the whole leadership of the combine consists of
> new men, Soviet people, mainly young, fresh from the schoolroom, [that is]
> from higher technical schools . . . The chief engineer is a young man pro-
> moted up from the ranks, comrade A. V. Goriachkin. The shop heads are
> also young: Chikalova, a Komsomol girl, Kuznetsova, and a whole list of
> other fine young specialists.[78]

> SMOKIN [director of the Smolensk Flax Combine, Iamshchino] . . . If the en-
> gineers and technicians at the Zvorykino Combine are young, it's the same
> with us. Our chief engineer is a Komsomol, the head of the weaving plant
> is a Komsomol, the head of the combing plant, comrade Muranova, is
> twenty-two years old. The trouble was that the basic cohort coming in 1938
> only graduated from college in 1936. Our young ITRs had to learn on the
> job and at the same time teach the workers.[79]

Other than the directors, however, nobody expressed much sympathy
for the new young ITRs, and the tone of workers' comments often veered
close to class hostility. Take the Iamshchino meeting, whose agenda included adjudication by jury of a competition for the best flax factory. One
jury member, evidently a worker, indignantly criticized ITR from the Smolensk combine for keeping aloof from the working class: "Comrades, the

[77] Ibid., l. 11.
[78] TsGAOR, f. 5457, op. 26, d. 584, ll. 117–18.
[79] Ibid., l. 140.

ITR have got swelled heads. Katz said to me today: 'You [*ty*] went to the wrong place to find out about the defects of our Combine.' (And where did I go? I went to the workers—and I consider that correct.) 'You should have asked the engineers and technicians.' No, comrades. If you are going to be a Soviet specialist, you need to learn from the workers, and you aren't doing it."[80]

One of the most interesting aspects of the flaxworkers' criticism of management is the highly visible part played by Stakhanovites. The Stakhanovites' criticisms of management were strident and at times threatening, recalling the Stakhanovite whistle-blowing function that was so much emphasized by the party leadership at the beginning of 1937. For example:

Our plant works badly, but earlier it always fulfilled the plan and was the first in the district. . . . Have our workers really forgotten how to work[?] It is the leaders [*rukovoditeli*] that have forgotten how to work, not the workers. We have no director. The party organization works badly, the same goes for the trade union organization, and that is why the plan is not being fulfilled. . . . *I ask all organizations to intervene . . . and look at what is happening at our plant* [my emphasis].[81]

When the wrong skein was put on [the machine], I told the [section] chief that if this matter was not corrected, I would go to the shop head, and if he did nothing I would go further, to the chief engineer, to the director of the Flax Combine, and yet further, to the Glavk itself—nothing would stop me, I would go through the whole lot of them.[82]

In one case, harsh criticism of plant leaders by a Stakhanovite worker—one of the few males in our sample—was accompanied by an apparent reference to purging (note the use of the verb *pochistit'*) and an intimidatory paraphrase of Stalin:

At our combine we have three directors, and not one had the decency to come here [for the conference]. Our director was at the All-Union Meeting of Flax Workers at the trade union central committee, and they straightened out his thinking properly there [ego tam pochistili kak sleduet]. . . .

As comrade Stalin said, "We have no bad people; there are [only] bad leaders."[83]

[80] Ibid., ll. 175–76.

[81] Trusova, a Stakhanovite worker at the Marx plant, speaking at a meeting of young Stakhanovites in Ivanovo oblast, 29 July 1938. TsGAOR, f. 5457, op. 26, d. 427, ll. 31–34.

[82] Brainina, a Stakhanovite worker at the Smolensk Combine, speaking at a conference of Stakhanovites in the flax industry in February 1939. TsGAOR, f. 5457, op. 26, d. 585, ll. 75–78.

[83] Vorontsov, a Stakhanovite worker at the Melenkovskii Combine, speaking at the July 1938 meeting in Ivanovo. TsGAOR, f. 5457, op. 26, d. 427, ll. 33–34.

At times, these worker critics of management seemed to be speaking specifically as Stakhanovites, asserting the special status of that group of workers and the obligation of management to give it special treatment. At a conference at the Zvorykino Combine early in 1939, for example, Stakhanovite Smirnova commented thus on the director's report: "She asks who is to blame for the poor work of the flax combine? Is it not the administration which is to blame, not paying any attention to Stakhanovites and Stakhanovite brigades?"[84]

More frequently, however, the Stakhanovite critics seemed to see themselves as representatives of the whole collective of workers at the plant, playing the role of militant labor spokesmen rather than the accepted Stakhanovite role. This throwback to the old (pre-1930, perhaps in some respects even pre-1920) patterns and rhetoric of labor-management confrontation is one of the most striking and unexpected aspects of the 1938–39 discussions in the flax industry. For example, Trusova, the Stakhanovite from the Marx plant in Ivanovo, sounded more like a belligerent trade unionist or shop steward than a norm-buster: "With respect to protection of labor, I told Zakharov, the head of the plant, that they are forcing people to work two or even three shifts, they are forcing them to work on their day off. I said I will not allow them to do that, but Zakharov stated that he would fire me. But that doesn't scare me, I will do what is necessary."[85]

The same was true of Brainina, the Stakhanovite worker from the Smolensk Combine, whose altercation with Ivanov, a senior official from the Glavk in Moscow,[86] was the most dramatic and extended confrontation between representatives of labor and management recorded in these files. The exchange took place at a conference of Stakhanovites in the flax industry. Not only did Brainina represent herself as a spokeswoman for her fellow workers, she was also so represented by Ivanov—who accused her of playing up to her constituency of "backward" workers and forgetting her special obligations as a Stakhanovite.

According to Brainina, the fall in output at the spinning plant was all the fault of the bosses and the Glavk that kept changing them, and the workers were fed up.

> The bosses [nachal'niki] of the spinning plant have been changed five times . . . and now comrade Smirenin is the sixth. . . . [In one section] they replaced eight bosses and now comrade Plaks is already the ninth, and you can see

[84] Protocol of conference held in the premises of the Stakhanov school at the [Zvorykino?] flax combine, 2 February 1939. TsGAOR, f. 5457, op. 26, d. 435, l. 20.

[85] TsGAOR, f. 5457, op. 26, d. 427, ll. 31–34.

[86] Ivanov was deputy head of the Chief Administration (Glavk) of the Flax Industry of the People's Commissariat of Light Industry.

the sort of work that comes out of that. Can the bosses really know their people when they are changed like gloves on a fine lady, and people are essentially left to fend for themselves[?]

. . .Comrade Shcherbakov was at our aktiv and talked a lot about all the problems that are hindering the work, and even the boss of the Glavk himself knows about those problems, but what help have they given? Nothing, except for promises. We have the right to demand help and support. If you look at production, we produce a lot of spoiled items [*brak*], and we will go on doing it, not because we want to but because the machines are not set right. They keep promising things, but the workers do not believe the promises and therefore do not go to the meetings, or if they go it is to be convinced yet again that they will promise and not deliver.

Brainina complained bitterly about the bad working conditions at the plant, stressing particularly the problems of women workers.

Of course, all that has an influence on the mood of the women workers. Where is the concern for the individual person who must give the state high-quality production? If someone talks about production problems or bad living conditions at our plant, they brush him away like an irritating fly instead of listening sensitively to our signals, scolding us if we deserve it and helping us when that is necessary.[87]

Brainina's speech infuriated Ivanov, who knew her from when he had been director of the Smolensk Flax Combine before his promotion to the Glavk.

You know, . . . a speech like that, where you badmouth the whole collective of engineers and technicians, newly appointed administrators, leaders, and the whole Glavk without saying a word about how i.e., in what way you were badly treated—that's slander. You didn't leave anything at Smolensk Flax Combine untouched, you just threw mud at everything from top to bottom.

I worked at Smolensk Flax Combine myself, and that was when conditions were worse. Here are the workers now who are the best Stakhanovites, here are the ITR, who are now setting an example to everyone—they didn't whine then as you are doing. We had no toilet, we had to go out to the courtyard of the Combine in the cold, we had no wash basins, there was no such spinning plant as you have now—yet all the same there was none of this whining. I don't believe you [when you say] that everything at the Combine is no good.

In Ivanov's book, Brainina was a troublemaker pure and simple.

---

[87] TsGAOR, f. 5457, op. 26, d. 585, ll. 75–78.

This isn't the first time I've listened to you. I listened to you when I worked as boss of the factory, I am listening to you [now] when I work as boss of the Glavk—and your speeches were just the same then as now. People are pledging themselves to compete for the Red Banner, and look how you spoiled this meeting. You talked as if it was impossible to carry out the pledges.

If she had any sense of responsibility as a Stakhanovite, Brainina would be naming names of *workers* who were slacking on the job or performing below standard. But, Ivanov complained, she stubbornly refused to do this.

Why have you not told us anything about workers who treat equipment badly—do you really not know even one woman worker who feeds the roller badly? You are a Stakhanovite—how are you passing on your experience to the young technical personnel who have only just graduated from technical schools? You are giving them no help. In my opinion, the applause that greeted your speech here came only from backward people.

Ivanov's sympathy with the beleaguered managers at the Combine was obvious:.

Comrade Smirenin has set an example of how to work and done a great job, [but] do you think that Smirenin can keep an eye on everything? . . .

All the problems that you spoke of must be solved. All that has to be done. But I would like to hear what method you suggest. They threw out Nikolskii and sacked Nosov. A third [manager] turned out incompetent and they fired him, and now we have Pavlov, who they say has received a prize. Comrade Smirenin, who puts his heart into his work at the plant, was promoted; such a bad sector, but he is already improving it—the factory is approaching 100 percent fulfillment [of plan. But] you are not helping him—he can't work twenty-four hours a day—and you haven't identified even a single delinquent [worker].[88]

The date of the meeting at which Ivanov crossed swords with Brainina was February 1939, and the main item on the agenda was labor discipline, with special reference to the recent introduction of workbooks and the law of 28 December 1938 "On measures for the regulation of labor dis-

[88] Ibid., ll. 79–90.

cipline. . . ."[89] The new law introduced harsher measures against absenteeism (a single infraction could now in theory bring automatic dismissal and loss of company housing) and frequent job-changing (which could result in loss of part of the worker's pension). From what was reported at the meeting by plant managers,[90] it was clear that discipline at the flax plants had indeed sunk to a low level, and moreover, as Ivanov commented, that the new legislation was not yet being taken seriously by workers ("I have heard rumors that now that a few people have been punished, the wave has passed and everything will calm down[.] That interpretation is quite wrong and you musn't believe it").[91]

Ivanov's toughness with Brainina was clearly related to the new law, which he evidently understood as a basic shift of policy away from tolerance or even encouragement of "boss-baiting" by workers toward a reestablishment of more traditional patterns of respect and obedience in the factories. Ivanov firmly rejected the idea that management was to blame for everything that went wrong with production in the flax industry. On the contrary, he seemed to be suggesting, the workers' indiscipline and poor work habits were largely to blame; and it was the task of Stakhanovites to help management identify and punish less conscientious workers, not to side with lazy workers against management. "The purpose of our meeting here is to uncover idlers and self-seekers [among the workers]," Ivanov announced firmly.[92] His message, in short, was that "open season" on managers was over. It was time for workers to knuckle down and Stakhanovites to stop acting like demagogic labor agitators and get back to their proper job as pacesetters and norm-busters.

The 1939 labor laws have usually been seen by scholars as a response to the war threat or a pure totalitarian reflex, but Ivanov's exposition seems to imply a different interpretation. He presents them as measures designed to *restore* order, discipline, and respect for authority at the workplace after their collapse during the Great Purges. This explanation is

[89] Resolution of Sovnarkom USSR of 20 December 1938, "O vvedenii trudovykh knizhek," in *Resheniia partii i pravitel'stva po khoziaistvennym voprosam* (Moscow, 1967), 2:662–64, and Resolution of Sovnarkom USSR, the Central Committee of the Communist Party and VTsSPS, "O meropriiatiiakh po uporiadocheniiu trudovoi distsipliny, uluchsheniiu praktiki gosudarstvennogo sotsial'nogo strakhovaniia i bor'be s zloupotrebleniiami v etom dele," 28 December 1938, *Resheniia*, 2:665–72.

[90] Earlier in the meeting, the director of Medkesskii Flax Combine had provided a detailed account of labor discipline violations and "flitting" in his plants, emphasizing particularly that the majority of those who quit in 1938 were hired again in other capacities, and were in fact successfully manipulating Soviet labor laws to get extra benefits and time off. He said that if the Combine refused to hire such people, they went straight to the local prosecutor and filed charges. TsGAOR, f. 5457, op. 26, d. 585, l. 34.

[91] TsGAOR, f. 5457, op. 26, d. 585, l. 90.

[92] Ibid., l. 79.

quite plausible, and historians of Soviet labor policy should surely take note of it. As a shop head commented at the same meeting in February 1939: "It is no accident that the party and the government have directed attention to labor discipline, . . . because the period of 1938 and part of 1937 at Smolensk Flax Combine was a period . . . when labor discipline was absent, people did whatever they felt like, and the work went very badly."[93]

Conclusion

Although any general conclusions about labor-management relations must be tentative, I suggest the following.

First, the Great Purges undermined the authority of managers and engineers in the plants and encouraged workers to break rules, ignore orders, and treat their bosses disrespectfully. On the one hand, this was a consequence of the mass arrests of old managerial and specialist cadres as "enemies of the people" in 1937–38 and the cloud of collective suspicion that hung over the ITR. On the other hand, it was evidently also related to the lack of respect that workers felt for the new and inexperienced ITR cohort that replaced the old cadres because of the youth and (for the time being) incompetence of many of its members.

Second, there were elements of "boss-baiting" by workers that recalled the "*spets*-baiting" of the Cultural Revolution. Nevertheless, it is noteworthy that the metalworkers were initially slow to respond to the regime's signals that industrial bosses were collectively under suspicion: to all appearances, these workers felt a certain kinship with at least some of their bosses, notably those of working-class background who were in lower- or middle-level management positions. The flaxworkers of 1938–39 were much more belligerent in their attitudes to managers, treating them with something approaching or at least reminiscent of class hostility. Even they, however, showed nothing like the degree of malicious pleasure in "boss-baiting" that was displayed by peasant witnesses in the show trials of rural officials held in the fall of 1937.[94]

Third, the belligerent flaxworkers were predominantly women, whereas the bosses criticized by them were virtually all men. This is a dimension of conflict that may have been very important, and might explain some (though not all) of the difference in reaction between flaxworkers in 1938–39 and metalworkers in 1937. In general, we know

---

[93] Ibid., ll. 66–67.

[94] These trials, which were held in many *raionnye* (district) centers throughout the Soviet Union, are described in my article, "How the Mice Buried the Cat: Scenes from the Great Purges of 1937 in the Russian Provinces," *Russian Review* 52 (July 1993): 299–320.

remarkably little of the specifics of labor-management relations in predominantly female industries in the Soviet period. It is possible that some of the striking unfamiliarity of the tone of the flax-industry discussions can be attributed to the strong gender component of its power relations. By the same token, the sense of residual kinship between workers and working-class managers that is evident in the metalworkers' files but not in those of the flaxworkers may have had an element of male as well as class solidarity.

Fourth, Stakhanovite workers in the metallurgical industry failed almost completely to respond to the regime's urging to unmask wreckers and saboteurs among industrial managers in the first half of 1937. On the other hand, it was Stakhanovite workers who took the lead in attacking managers in the flax industry in 1938–39, and to some degree their behavior fitted the "approved" Stakhanovite pattern of keeping managers up to the mark by an implicit threat to go to outside authorities with complaints.

Fifth, at the same time, the flax-industry Stakhanovites of 1938–39 seemed to diverge from the "approved" Stakhanovite model by acting as spokeswomen to management for the grievances and interests of *all* workers—as if they had taken on the labor-representation role that before 1930 had been filled by the trade unions. This, if confirmed by further detailed research on labor in the late 1930s,[95] would change the accepted picture of labor-management relations quite substantially. It would also suggest that the status of Stakhanovites as "leading" (*peredovye*) workers may have contained within it a wider range of leadership possibilities than we have hitherto suspected.

Sixth, despite the evident breakdown of discipline and the assertive behavior of Stakhanovite flaxworkers as spokespersons (presumably self-appointed) for the workers' viewpoint in confrontation with management, there were some types of labor protest that remained conspicuous by their absence, at least according to the evidence of these files. The Stakhanovite flaxworkers spoke about workers' grievances, but they still spoke as individuals, never hinting at the possibility of collective industrial action. Their implicit threat was to denounce rather than to go on strike: they said, "I will inform the proper authorities" or "I will take my complaint right up to the top," not "We will go out on strike."

Last, the 1939 legislation tightening labor discipline may have been related much more to its deterioration during the Great Purges than to

[95] In this connection, it would be worth looking to see if the election of large numbers of Stakhanovites to membership and chairmanship of factory committees in the 1937 elections (see figures in *Profsoiuzy SSSR*, 1938, no. 1:77) had any discernible impact in producing more assertive behavior and a more belligerent stance vis-à-vis management.

the regime's preparations for war. It should be noted that the much tougher labor discipline law that followed in 1940 can be linked much more plausibly to the imminence of war, and that the two pieces of legislation need not and probably should not be explained by the same set of circumstances.

12

Victoria E. Bonnell

The Iconography of the Worker
in Soviet Political Art

Every revolution needs its heroes. In social revolutions of the modern era, the new heroes have not only been individuals but collectivities—social groups such as the sansculottes in France of the 1790s or the proletariat of twentieth-century Russia. A revolution is a carnivalesque reversal that turns the world upside down. Those who were despised under the old regime are adulated under the new. Revolutionaries have used verbal and visual means to create a new iconography that exalts the heroic collectivity. We can see this pattern at work in the French Revolution of 1789. During the Jacobin dictatorship, the people, or to be more precise, the sansculottes, were elevated to the status of heroes in political rhetoric and political practice. The figure of Hercules, who was depicted as slaying the hydra of the ancien regime, came to symbolize the sansculottes.[1] Hercules and Marianne—the symbol of liberty—dominated the political iconography of the French Revolution.[2]

When the Bolsheviks came to power in October 1917, they set about identifying and promoting their own heroes. In the spring of 1918, Lenin unveiled a "monumental plan of propaganda" aimed at creating public statuary of revolutionary heroes to replace those of the tsarist era. Some fifty or sixty monuments subsequently appeared, representing a wide range of Russian and European political, artistic and cultural figures.[3]

---

[1] Lynn Hunt, *Politics, Culture, and Class in the French Revolution* (Berkeley and Los Angeles, 1984), pp. 104, 106, and more generally, chap. 3; François Furet, *Interpreting the Revolution* (London, 1981).

[2] On Marianne, see Maurice Agulhon, *Marianne into Battle: Republican Imagery and Symbolism in France, 1789–1880* (Cambridge, 1981); Hunt, *Politics, Culture, and Class.*

[3] The original list contained twenty-one Russians and nineteen Europeans. For a complete list, see Richard Stites, *Revolutionary Dreams: Utopian Vision and Experimental Life in the Russian Revolution* (New York, 1989), pp. 88–89. Additional material on this topic can be found in *V. I. Lenin i izobrazitel'noe iskusstvo. Dokumenty. Pis'ma. Vospominaniia* (Moscow, 1977), pp. 253–85; Nina Tumarkin, *Lenin Lives! The Lenin Cult in Soviet Russia*

Lenin's enthusiasm for monuments to deceased heroes was intended, above all, to make credible and comprehensible the inexorable march of history projected by Marxism-Leninism. The historical actors monumentalized by Lenin's plan—a motley group of assassins, authors, rebels, and martyrs—acquired special heroic significance once they were located in the action that culminated in October 1917.[4] In the Bolshevik master narrative, these heroes anticipated and prepared the way for the collective hero of world history: the proletariat. Party rhetoric and propaganda of the early years, with its relentless emphasis on the Proletarian Revolution and Dictatorship of the Proletariat, left no doubt concerning the centrality of the worker in the new pantheon.

Soon after seizing power, party leaders turned to the problem of disseminating their message to the population at large. With encouragement and leadership from Lenin and his commissar of education Anatoly Lunacharsky, party members came to understand that the creation of compelling visual symbols—"invented traditions" as E. J. Hobsbawm has called them—was a key aspect of the campaign to capture public enthusiasm, inculcate novel ideas, and implant loyalty in a semiliterate population accustomed to the elaborate pageants and visual imagery of the old regime and the Russian Orthodox Church. Political posters, monumental sculpture, and displays at holiday celebrations (especially May Day and November 7) provided the major vehicles for Bolshevik visual propaganda.

At the time of the October Revolution, the Bolsheviks had little experience with political art. Under the repressive conditions of the tsarist regime, no public displays were permitted except those authorized by the government or the Church. Publication opportunities were circumscribed, and the satirical journals produced by left-wing groups during the 1905 revolution had all but disappeared after 1907. When the Bolsheviks took power, therefore, they had not yet developed a visual image to represent the working class, comparable, say, to Hercules in the French Revolution.

The creation of a compelling visual language proved to be particularly critical in the campaign to establish the "working class" as the heroic collectivity of the Bolshevik revolution and of world history more generally. In a country where at least 85 percent of the population still lived in villages in 1918, the identity and characteristics of the "working class" remained murky and mysterious. The Bolsheviks faced the task not only

---

(Cambridge, Mass., 1983), pp. 66–67; J. E. Bowlt, "Russian Sculpture and Lenin's Plan for Monumental Propaganda," in Henry A. Millon and Linda Nochlin, eds., *Art and Architecture in the Service of Politics* (Cambridge, Mass., 1978).

[4] The list included Ryleev, Pestel, Karakozov, Khalturin, Zhelyabov, Perovskaya, Kalyaev, Radishchev, Chernyshevsky, Plekhanov, Bakunin, Fourier, Owen, St. Simon, Marx, Engels, Lassale, Jaures, Voltaire, Marat, Luxemburg, and Liebknecht.

of establishing the heroic position and role of the worker but also bringing an image of the new worker-heroes to the population at large. Verbal propaganda, however ubiquitous, could not achieve this objective.[5]

During the early years of Soviet power, political artists groped for a visual language that viewers could comprehend. Given the diverse cultural background of the population, they drew on a variety of sources: religious and folk art, classical mythology, and the imagery of Western European labor and revolutionary movements. Before long, a new iconography had arisen in Soviet Russia, an iconography with its own distinctive lexicon and syntax. As in religious art of the Orthodox tradition, a set of standardized images was created, depicting worker-heroes (saints) and class enemies (the devil and his accomplices) in accordance with a fixed pattern (the so-called *podlinnik* in church art).

Although the party had no single visual image of the worker when it took power, a year later the representation of "the worker" had acquired a very definite form. He was almost invariably depicted as a *kuznets*, or blacksmith (see figure 1).[6] His distinctive markers are the blacksmith's hammer *(molot)*, a leather apron, and sometimes an anvil. Typically, he has a mustache (a beard was associated with the male peasant), a Russian shirt, and boots (peasants wore bast shoes). Sometimes, he is presented as bare to the waist, but more often he wears a shirt. He is neither very youthful nor particularly old; generally, he has the appearance of a mature and experienced worker, perhaps in his twenties or even thirties. The imagery of the worker in late nineteenth-century and early twentieth-century socialist iconography is overwhelmingly male, and Soviet visual propaganda conformed to this pattern.[7] A female version of the blacksmith does not emerge until early 1920 (see figure 2).[8] She is a replica of the male worker and is presented as his assistant. Since women virtually

[5] See Peter Kenez, *The Birth of the Propaganda State: Soviet Methods of Mass Mobilization, 1917–1929* (Cambridge, 1985), for an excellent account of these efforts.

[6] Alexander Apsit's November 1918 poster, "God proletarskoi diktatury, Oktiabr' 1917–oktiabr' 1918" (Year of the proletarian dictatorship, October 1917–October 1918), exemplifies the new image. This poster is item no. 1760 in the Russian-Soviet poster collection at the Hoover Archive (hereafter cited as RU/SU and item number). In contemporary sources, the blacksmith is generally called a *kuznets* but occasionally also a *molotoboets* or "hammerer." The latter term is more strictly limited to an industrial setting and reflects a greater division of labor than the term *kuznets*; however, *kuznets* was also a major occupational designation in large metalworking factories.

[7] Eric Hobsbawm, "Man and Woman in Socialist Iconography," *History Workshop Journal* 6 (autumn 1978): 127–28.

[8] See my essay "The Representation of Women in Early Soviet Political Art," *Russian Review* 50 (July 1991). Two major works present this image: "1-oe Maia vserossiiskii subbotnik" (May 1 All-Russian Voluntary Workday) by D. Moor (May 1920), and "Oruzhiem my dobili vraga" (We Finished Off the Enemy with Weapons) by N. Kogout (October 1920). Moor's poster appears in *The Soviet Political Poster* (Middlesex, England, 1985), p. 28. For Kogout, see RU/SU 1280.

1. "God proletarskoi diktatury" (Year of the proletarian dictatorship), by A. Apsit (1918)

2. "Oruzhiem my dobili vraga / Trudom my dobudem khleb / Vse za raboty tovarishchi" (We finished off the enemy with weapons / Through labor we will procure bread / All to work, comrades!), by N. Kogout (1920)

never served as blacksmith's helpers, the imagery can only be interpreted allegorically. The female worker derived her heroic status from her association with the male worker; her representation as his helper—holding the hot metal on the anvil-altar while he fashions it into a new object-world—reinforces the theme of male leadership, or as we now put it, male domination in the ranks of the proletariat.

In the course of 1919, the image of the male blacksmith began to function as a virtual icon in Bolshevik visual propaganda. The blacksmith appeared in posters and holiday displays, on stamps and official seals, even on pottery and fabric. No other visual symbol—except for the emblems of the red star and the hammer and sickle introduced in the spring of 1918—was as widely disseminated in Bolshevik Russia or as closely associated with the new regime. This image remained central until 1930, and then was abandoned.

The Background

The origin of the blacksmith image in Bolshevik iconography remains uncertain. The first examples I have located date back to the revolution of 1905. An easing of tsarist restrictions on the press led to a proliferation of left-wing journals and newspapers in 1905–7. A number of them contained visual material, mainly satirical. Among the sources I have examined, very few visual representations of the worker can be found during these years. By way of illustration, the left-wing Odessa journal *Svitok* published a picture by D. I. Shatan in its third issue for 1906. Titled "Zakliuchenie soiuza" (The conclusion of a union), it shows a muscular worker shaking hands with a woman in red, presumably Russia, while minuscule blue figures in crowns (the court?) cower at her feet. The worker has a trim beard and a sleeveless shirt. In January 1907, the journal *Volga* featured a grim-looking blacksmith on its cover, his right wrist in a handcuff. Below is the caption "Staryi god" (The old year). This early example incorporated a specific set of attributes or class markers that later became part of the standard image: the mustache, the Russian shirt, the apron, and the hammer.[9]

Between 1907 and 1917 visual propaganda remained the exclusive prerogative of the government and the Church, who were very slow to ex-

---

[9] V. V. Shleev, ed., *Revoliutsiia 1905–1907 godov i izobrazitel'noe iskusstvo*, 3 vols. (Moscow, 1977–1981). The Shatan picture appears at 3:39; the illustration from *Volga*, at 2:102. Other examples of representations of workers from this period can be found at 1: 18, 22, 31, and 3:6. Most of these present images of the blacksmith; one shows the head and torso of a "generic" worker in a cap and Russian shirt. There were also occasional illustrations of the blacksmith's hammer. See, for example, 3:24.

ploit its potential. A few official political posters were issued in 1904–5, at the time of the Russo-Japanese War, but it was only during the First World War that the tsarist regime invested significant effort in visual propaganda as a means of mass mobilization. The image of the blacksmith does not appear in tsarist posters issued between 1914 and 1917, although other types of workers were featured in posters aimed at raising funds for war bonds. One example is the poster by Rikhard Zarin', "Patriotichno i vygodno!" (Patriotic and profitable), featuring a young, serious-looking munitions worker in an apron standing in front of a lathe.[10] Although tsarist political posters did not include images of the blacksmith, the blacksmith's *hammer*, together with the anvil, was quite common in traditional Russian armorial art.[11] Furthermore, monumental sculpture during the final decades of the old regime sometimes included representations of blacksmiths. In Helsinki, Finland, for example, there are several notable statues of blacksmiths in the central area of the city.

The image of the blacksmith made an occasional appearance in the propaganda of social-democratic and other left-wing groups in 1917. In August 1917, a satirical journal, *Spartak*, featured a blacksmith wearing a Russian shirt on its cover. He stands with his legs parted, leaning both hands on a hammer.[12] During the election campaign for the Constituent Assembly, the Committee of the Communist Party of Bolsheviks of the Ukraine distributed a poster featuring a blacksmith holding a proclamation with the heading "Tovarishch!" (Comrade!). Standing against a stark background of factories with smoking chimneys, he wears a red shirt in the Russian style, an apron and boots, and holds a hammer in his left hand (figure 3).[13] Another poster, issued by the All-Russian League for the Equal Rights of Women during elections to the Constituent Assembly, illustrates the broad appeal of the blacksmith image and its appropriation by various groups. This poster depicts a rather haughty-looking woman holding a piece of hot metal on an anvil, while a male worker strikes it with a hammer. The male worker has a muscular bare torso; his face is only partially visible (figure 4).[14]

[10] RU/SU 1226.

[11] Richard Stites, "Adorning the Revolution: The Primary Symbols of Bolshevism, 1917–1918," in *Sbornik: Study Group of the Russian Revolution*, no. 10 (Leeds, 1984), p. 40 and figs. 3 and 4.

[12] The drawing is by E. V. Orlovskii. A reproduction of it appears in *V. I. Lenin*, p. 15.

[13] RU/SU 1262.

[14] RU/SU 18. The League was registered in 1907; it became active at the end of 1909, mainly on behalf of women's suffrage. Before 1917, it attracted about one thousand members, making it the largest feminist organization in Russia. After the February Revolution, it organized one of the first mass demonstrations in Petrograd. On March 20, some 40,000 women marched to demand suffrage for women in elections to the Constituent Assembly. Richard Stites, *The Women's Liberation Movement in Russia: Feminism, Nihilism, and Bolshevism, 1860–1930* (Princeton, N.J., 1978).

3. "Tovarishch!" (Comrade!) (1917)

4. "Golosuite n. 7" (Vote for no. 7) (1919)

Bolshevik imagery of the collective heroes of the revolution began to take form during 1918. In April Bolshevik leaders adopted their first official emblem: a crossed hammer and plow inside a red star, to serve as a breast badge of the Red Army. Soon afterward, a jury of artists and officials gathered to select an official seal for the Soviet state. Out of the many submissions, they chose a design with a hammer and sickle.[15] The adoption of a hammer as the emblem of the working class must have encouraged the use of blacksmith imagery, but as late as November 1918, there was still no consensus over how the worker should be represented. Some artists depicted a generic worker (no specific occupation) with a cap, on horseback, or in a chariot.[16] Boris Kustodiev's famous panels for Ruzheinaia Square in Petrograd in November 1918 included images of artisanal workers: a tailor, a carpenter, a shoemaker, and a baker. In addition, the panels showed a young man in an apron (a blacksmith?) with the title "labor" and images of women who were designated as "reaper" and "abundance."[17] Another artist depicted a miner with a pick ax and called him "Rabochii" (The worker).[18] Artists often represented the worker fully clothed, wearing an apron and a Russian shirt, but some, for example, M. P. Bloch and T. K. Savitskii, depicted him with a naked torso.[19]

The diversity of representations in 1918 indicates that a standard image of the worker had not yet been established, as it would in the course of 1919. More fundamental still, the various visualizations of the worker show that the term initially encompassed a broad range of occupational groups. Aleksandr Apsit's poster, "God proletarskoi diktatury, Oktiabr' 1917–oktiabr' 1918" (Year of the proletarian dictatorship, October 1917–October 1918), produced for the first anniversary of the October Revolution, can be considered the first major statement of the new image in Bolshevik iconography (figure 1).[20] This famous poster depicts a worker and a peasant standing on either side of a window. In the distance, a long winding demonstration of people with red flags is visible, with a factory in the background and the stylized rays of a rising sun. The debris of the old order (imperial shield, crown, double-headed eagle, chains) are strewn across the foreground. The worker, on the left, has a mustache and wears

[15] Stites, *Revolutionary Dreams*, pp. 85–87. The original drawing for the seal also included a sword, but Lenin requested its removal.

[16] V. P. Tol'stoi, ed., *Agitatsionno-massovoe iskusstvo. Oformlenie prazdnestv* (Moscow, 1984), fig. 32; O. Nemiro, *V gorod prishel prazdnik: Iz istorii khudozhestvennogo oformleniia sovetskikh massovykh prazdnestv* (Leningrad, 1973), pp. 17–18.

[17] Mikhail Guerman, ed., *Art of the October Revolution* (New York, 1979), plates 187–93; Tol'stoi, *Agitatsionno-massovoe iskusstvo*, figs. 43–47.

[18] V. I. Kozlinskii, in Tol'stoi, ed., *Agitatsionno-massovoe iskusstvo*, fig. 63.

[19] Ibid., figs. 79, 82; see also figs. 89, 94, 110, and 112.

[20] RU/SU 801.

a leather apron and boots. His right hand rests on the handle of his hammer. Opposite him stands the male peasant, wearing a Russian shirt and bast shoes and holding a scythe in his right hand and a red banner in his left. Each man has a red ribbon on his shirt, and there are two decorative wreaths with red ribbons hanging above them. Apsit (his real name was Aleksandrs Apsitis and he was born in Latvia) was one of the first major poster artists of the Soviet era, and he produced some of the most memorable and widely circulated early works in that genre. His own father had been a blacksmith,[21] and his image of this figure created in the fall of 1918 soon acquired "archetypal" status in Bolshevik visual propaganda.

Two basic variants of the worker-blacksmith emerged during the years that followed. In the first, exemplified by Apsit's 1918 poster and many others, the blacksmith was depicted with a composed and dignified demeanor, a hammer by his side. A second variant portrayed the blacksmith in the act of striking an anvil (figure 2) or in some other physical act, such as slaying a hydra, doing battle with the enemy, or warding off a rapacious eagle.[22] These contrasting images emphasize different aspects of the worker-icon: skill, dignity, and poise are accentuated in some representations, physical power in others. The two aspects of the worker image—contemplation and action—also characterized the imagery of Hercules in the French Revolution.[23] And as in France, the dualism betokened quite different ways of representing and conceptualizing the collective heroes. In one set of action-oriented images, the proletariat emerges as powerful and aggressive, capable of great acts of prowess. It should come as no surprise that these images appeared most frequently during the civil war years. The imagery of the motionless worker conveyed a very different message, emphasizing instead the self-possession and confidence of the victorious proletariat proudly presiding over the new epoch. The latter image predominated in the 1920s. During the civil war, the blacksmith symbolized the collective hero of the Bolshevik Revolution, the working class; the hammer and sickle and the red star symbolized the new Soviet state. What the visual repertoire lacked was a representation of the other central element in Soviet Russia: the Bolshevik Party and its mem-

[21] For a discussion of Apsit's life, see Stephen White, "The Political Poster in Bolshevik Russia," in *Sbornik: Study Group on the Russian Revolution*, no. 8 (Leeds, 1982), p. 26, and his study *The Bolshevik Poster* (New Haven, Conn., 1988).

[22] See, for example, Apsit's posters, "Obmanutym brat'iam" (To the deceived brothers), 1918, RU/SU 1546, "Internatsional," 1918, RU/SU 2282; B. Zvorykin, "Bor'ba krasnogo rytsaria s temnoi siloiu" (The struggle of the red knight with the dark force), 1919, RU/SU 1285; P. Kiselis, "Belogvardeiskii khishchnik" (White predator), 1920, RU/SU 1287. I discuss the Kiselis poster later in this chapter.

[23] Hunt, *Politics, Culture and Class*, pp. 109–10. The image of Marianne also appeared in several different versions. See Hunt, p. 93, and Agulhon, *Marianne*.

bers. One notable exception is the arresting image in Kustodiev's famous 1920 painting, "Bol'shevik" (The Bolshevik). Here was a larger-than-life man striding across the Kremlin. He is dressed in winter clothing, carrying a red flag, and has an intense, almost maniacal expression.[24]

In the course of the 1920s, this gap in the visual vocabulary was rectified. The depiction of the worker-hero—the signifier—remained unchanged. But a subtle change occurred in the signified. The blacksmith image came to symbolize the Bolshevik worker—the party member, the loyal follower of Lenin. Thus, by 1927, the tenth anniversary of the October Revolution, the image of the worker was designated not just as a revolutionary but as a standard-bearer for the Bolshevik Party. The 1927 poster, "Oktiabr' na severnom Kavkaze" (October in the northern Caucasus), exemplifies this development. Here the traditional worker carries a red flag with the inscription: "With the Leninist party for the victory of the worldwide October [Revolution]." Photographs of six leading Bolsheviks (Lenin and Bolshevik heroes of the Caucasus) are in the center of the frame.[25] In this poster and in many others of the late 1920s, the blacksmith acquired a far narrower focus than ever before.[26] The revolutionary worker had become the Bolshevik worker. The shift in visual propaganda coincided with the intensified campaign against Trotsky and other left-wing opposition groups and the consolidation of the monolithic party-state.

The exceptional status of the worker was manifested in the visual syntax, that is, the relationship among images. Images of peasants (male and female) or the woman worker seldom appeared alone but nearly always in pairs or clusters. Their position in the Bolshevik hierarchy of heroes was defined by contiguity, by their close visual association with others. Thus male peasants often appeared with male workers or female peasants; male and female peasants were depicted together or with workers. By contrast, the figure of the male worker did not depend for definition on a relationship of contiguity. The presence of the male worker conferred heroic status on those nearby. The worker himself, however, needed no other figure to establish his position in the hierarchy of heroes. He sometimes appeared alone, sometimes in a larger-than-life format. Only the Red Army soldier, as depicted during the civil war, occupied a syntactic position similar to that of the worker. A. T. Matveev's famous monu-

---

[24] Guerman, ed., *Art of the October Revolution*, fig. 9.

[25] A52120, poster collection, Muzei revoliutsii, Moscow.

[26] Agulhon provides an example from French iconography that illustrates how a symbol can acquire not only complex but even contradictory meanings. Following the establishment of the Third Republic in 1870, the female allegorical figure of Liberty-the-Republic came to symbolize both the state and the movement directed against the state. Maurice Agulhon, "On Political Allegory: A Reply to Eric Hobsbawm," *History Workshop Journal* 8 (autumn 1979): 170.

mental sculpture completed in 1927, "Oktiabr'skaia revoliutsiia" (October Revolution), illustrates the visual language that served to delineate heroic images. The sculpture shows three nearly naked men. The Red Army soldier, identified by his Budenny hat, is kneeling; the worker stands in the center, resting his arm on his hammer; the peasant with a beard sits, with his left hand outstretched. The commanding presence of the worker in this composition leaves no doubt about the hegemonic status of the proletariat.[27] The constellation of figures and their hierarchical arrangement betoken a particular worldview—a view propagated by the Bolshevik Party and enshrined in their official ideology.

Cultural Frameworks for Interpreting the Worker-Icon

During the Civil War, chaotic conditions and poor communications prevented the establishment of a centralized authority in poster production. By the end of 1920, there were some 453 separate organizations producing posters in the country.[28] Despite the dispersion and lack of coordination, there was remarkable consistency and uniformity of the imagery beginning in 1919, especially the representation of the worker-hero. The adoption of the hammer and sickle as the official Soviet emblem in the spring of 1918 must have provided strong support for the blacksmith image. But the appeal of such an image and its widespread adoption by Bolshevik political artists rested, above all, on its extraordinary polyvalence. The figure of the blacksmith meant many different things to different people. It resonated with folk and religious art, the imperial art of the old regime, and the traditions of Western art and socialist iconography. Moreover, the blacksmith was an important figure in urban centers and rural villages, in giant factories and small artisanal enterprises. He crossed many boundaries.

What kinds of associations did contemporaries have with the image of the blacksmith? Given their preexisting cultural frameworks, how did artists, officials and viewers "read" this image? Of course, there was not just one interpretation but a multiplicity of different responses depending on the viewer's social class, education, gender, geographical location, and

---

[27] 50 Let Sovetskogo Iskusstva (1917–1967): Skulptura (Moscow, 1967), fig. 25. Posters produced for the tenth anniversary of the October Revolution also emphasized the leading role of the worker. See, for example, P. Shukhmin, "Pod znamenem VKP (b)" (Under the banner of the VKP[b]), 1927, which shows a worker in the forefront, followed by a Red Army soldier, a woman worker, and a male peasant. The Soviet Political Poster, p. 48.

[28] The largest organization was the Literature and Publishing Department of the Political Administration of the Revolutionary Military Council of the Republic (Litizdat PUR RVSR), established in October 1919 and headed throughout the civil war by Viacheslav Polonskii. See White, Bolshevik Poster, pp. 39–40.

other factors. Our information about the audience for political posters during the civil war years is quite limited, but it appears that most were displayed in locations accessible to urban dwellers and to soldiers.[29] Even if poster displays were for the most part limited to these groups, the viewers included a broad spectrum of the population (most soldiers were recruited from the peasantry), and it is not possible to identify a single interpretation of a particular image. Artists, officials, and spectators conceptualized and interpreted the new worker-icon within diverse cultural frameworks shaped by a variety of traditions as well as practical experience and observation.

Of all the types of workers associated with nonagricultural labor, the blacksmith might arguably be considered the most nearly universal. The term *kuznets* was applied in a wide range of contexts: rural and urban, artisanal and industrial. In the countryside, every village had a blacksmith who produced agricultural implements, tools, wheels, and many other necessities for the local population. His basic equipment—a hammer, an anvil, and a forge—was a familiar sight. At the same time, the kuznets could also be found in all types of manufacturing, from the traditional artisanal-type blacksmith shop in a village or city to a large industrial plant.

The status of the blacksmith in society depended on his location. In the village, he belonged to the elite by virtue of his skills, his relative prosperity, and his critical function in rural life. A city blacksmith, working in a small shop, occupied an intermediary position within the ranks of artisanal craftsmen. The kuznetsy in a large metalworking plant, laboring in the "hot shop" *(goriachii tsekh)*, were looked down on because of their peasant ways and the physical as opposed to mental effort involved in their work.[30] The kuznets had a lower status than his fellow workers in the machine shops, such as metalfitters and lathe operators. But if the blacksmith remained inferior to the metalfitter within the plant's status hierarchy, he nonetheless occupied an important position within the enterprise. Unlike the unskilled laborers in metalworking plants, textile mills, or food-processing plants, the kuznets performed a critical function in industry requiring skill and training and considerable physical prowess.

The exceptional significance and role of the blacksmith were reinforced by Slavic folklore, which contains many references to the blacksmith who was thought to possess "concealed sacred abilities." Wedding songs spoke of the blacksmith as hammering out the wedding crown, the ring, the wedding itself. There were also references to the blacksmith hammering

[29] François-Xavier Coquin, "L'Affiche revolutionnaire sovietique (1918–1921): Mythes et réalité," *Revue des études slaves* 59, no. 4 (1987): 737.
[30] A. Buzinov, *Za Nevskoi zastavoi* (Moscow, 1930), p. 21. The "hot shop" included the smelting, rolling, and blacksmith shops.

out a tongue-language-speech. A blacksmith had god-like features and could perform heroic feats.[31] The supernatural attributes of the blacksmith were readily carried over into Bolshevik propaganda. A popular revolutionary song was titled "My—kuznetsy" (We are blacksmiths). Composed in 1912 by a factory worker, Filip Shkulev,[32] the song was sung in the aftermath of the February Revolution and especially during the civil war. Its effectiveness was due, in large measure, to the skillful combination of popular mythology and political ideology. The first stanza sets forth the miraculous powers of the blacksmith:[33]

> We are blacksmiths, and our spirit is young,
> We hammer out the keys to happiness,
> Rise ever higher, our heavy hammer,
> Beat in the steel breast with greater force, beat,
> Beat, beat!
> We are hammering out a bright road for the people,
> We are hammering out happiness for the motherland [rodina],
> And for the sake of cherished freedom
> We all have been fighting and shall die,
> Die, die!

For some urban and educated groups in Russian society, the blacksmith image was also familiar from Western art. In late nineteenth- and early twentieth-century Europe, representations of the worker became more and more important in monumental, decorative, and political art. And images of the blacksmith, in particular, served as a symbol for all types of workers associated with the new age of manufacturing. The Belgian artist and sculptor, Constantin Meunier, greatly influenced the representation of workers by presenting them (both male and female) in a heroic mode. He sculpted many figures connected with the metalworking industry. Among them is a statue of "Der Schmied" (The blacksmith), shown as a youthful half-naked figure with regal bearing, seated with a hammer between his legs.[34] Though some of Meunier's workers show signs of heavy labor and

---

[31] On these points, see V. V. Ivanov and V. N. Toporov, "Problema funktsii kuznetsa v svete semioticheskoi tipologii kul'tur," in *Materialy vsesoiuznogo simposiuma po vtorichnym modeliruiushchim sistemam I (5)* (Tartu, 1974), pp. 87–90. The sacred attributes of the blacksmith were not only celebrated in Slavic folklore but can be found in many popular traditions in Indo-European culture.

[32] Shkulev was born in 1868, the son of poor peasants. At the age of fourteen, he lost his right hand in a factory accident. He wrote a number of songs; this was his most popular. *Sovetskie pesni* (Moscow, 1977), pp. 14–15; *Russkie revoliutsionnye pesni* (Moscow, 1952), p. 127.

[33] *Antologiia Sovetskoi pesni, 1917–1957* (Moscow, 1957), 1:27.

[34] Brandt, *Schaffende Arbeit und bildende Kunst in Altertum und Mittelalter* (Leipzig, 1927), p. 269, fig. 343. According to Brandt, this was Meunier's greatest work (p. 342).

exhaustion, they also convey pride, dignity, and strength. During the Third Republic in France, blacksmiths provided the subject matter for many public monuments as well as the decorative facades of public and private buildings.[35] The blacksmith image, as we have seen, was remarkably polyvalent and evoked an extremely rich set of associations.

Considering the powerful effect of religious icons, it is not surprising that conventions in Church art affected how both artists and viewers approached political art. The religious icon, as I have already suggested, had a tremendous influence over Bolshevik political art. The first great master of the Bolshevik poster, Apsit, had extensive prior training in icon painting.[36] The blacksmith does not appear, to my knowledge, in icons of the Russian Orthodox Church, but Soviet artists borrowed a number of key features from icons and used them to sacralize the new worker-hero.[37] During the civil war, the worker-hero was sometimes depicted as St. George slaying the dragon of capitalism.[38] A poster produced in the fall of 1920, "Da zdravstvuet pobeda truda" (Long live the victory of labor),[39] incorporated the single most important symbol of religious art: the cross. In this remarkable poster, a blacksmith is seated on top of an altar, surrounded by a globe and the works of Karl Marx. The altar rests on a platform and the entire structure bears resemblance to the shape of a cross.[40] He holds a hammer in his right hand; his left hand is raised, bearing a wreath encircling a hammer and sickle. Scenes depicting the past and present surround the central image, much as marginal scenes *(kleima)* appear in icons, conveying characteristic episodes from the life of a saint.[41]

Color symbolism drew on associations with religious art. The color red served in religious icons to identify the sacred (black was the color of evil).[42] In Apsit's 1918 anniversary poster, the worker and peasant both

---

[35] Agulhon, "On Political Allegory," pp. 170–71. To date, my research has not turned up examples of the blacksmith image in German socialist sources prior to 1918. The blacksmith appeared in other cultural spheres of that era, however. Richard Wagner's *Ring of the Nibelung*, a major cultural landmark, featured a blacksmith as one of its principal characters.

[36] White, "The Political Poster in Bolshevik Russia," p. 26.

[37] In the discussion that follows, I have benefited greatly from Boris Uspensky, *The Semiotics of the Russian Icon*, ed. Stephen Rudy (Lisse, Belgium, 1976).

[38] An example is Apsit "Obmanutym brat'iam" (To the deceived brothers), 1918, RU/SU 1546. See also White, *Bolshevik Poster*, p. 34.

[39] A52250, poster collection, Muzei revoliutsii, A52250.

[40] The alter carries the inscription: "Vsia vlast' sovetam. Rabochii k stanku! Krest'ianin k plugu! Vse za upornyi trud vo imia pobedy kommunizma" [All power to the soviets. Worker, take your place at the work bench. Peasant, take your place at the plow! Let us all work steadfastly for the victory of communism].

[41] Uspensky, *Semiotics of the Russian Icon*, p. 55.

[42] Ulf Abel, "Icons and Soviet Art," in Claes Arvidsson and Lars Erik Blomquist, *Symbols of Power* (Stockholm, 1987), pp. 152–53. Contemporary Soviet artists were highly conscious

wear red ribbons; the peasant holds a red flag and wreaths tied with red ribbons hang above each figure. It was quite common for the blacksmith to wear a red shirt, hold a red flag or be surrounded by the color red. To be sure, the color red also had positive connotations in Western European socialist art. But the great majority of Russian spectators were probably far more familiar with the icon, which graced the *krasnyi ugol* in every hut and urban household, than with European art.

Other devices common to religious icons were applied to Soviet political posters.[43] In religious icons, key images are presented with full or three-quarter face views. Soviet political artists almost invariably presented the blacksmith with a frontal view, and his gaze was seldom turned directly to the spectator (by contrast, some key posters of Red Army soldiers utilized the direct gaze).[44] Perspectival distortions of the background are quite common in religious painting and "semantically important figures are less subject to perspectival deformations."[45] The device of perspectival distortion was occasionally used in early Soviet political art (it becomes very common in the 1930s), though in a different manner from the religious icon. Typically, the worker-hero was the subject of perspectival distortion and appeared as a giant figure towering over pygmies. In one other respect Soviet political iconography reversed the canons of religious art. In religious icons the most important figures are represented at rest, the less important ones are shown in motion.[46] In many Bolshevik posters, the worker-hero is also depicted at rest; but in others he appears in the act of striking the anvil.

How contemporaries "read" the image of the blacksmith was also influenced by the use of allegory drawn from Russian folk and Western classical traditions. From 1918 until the end of the civil war, Bolshevik political artists combined various types of allegory with the worker image. Thus we find examples of the blacksmith on horseback wielding shield

---

of color symbolism. See, for example, comments by Dmitrii Moor on this subject in *Brigada khudozhnikov*, no. 4 (1931): 14.

[43] Posters issued by the Whites in the civil war also drew extensively on religious themes and imagery. In one poster, the Russian people are symbolized by Jesus Christ carrying the cross to Calvary while Trotsky looks on scornfully from the sidelines. RU/SU 898. In another poster, reminiscent of Dante's *Inferno*, the Bolsheviks are falling into a pit of flames and subjected to punishments for various crimes. RU/SU 1042. Still another depicts two scenes, one presided over by the devil (the Bolshevik side), the other with a cross suspended from the clouds. RU/SU 1782.

[44] According to one major Soviet study, the hero turned directly to the spectator in civil war posters, but seldom did so in 1920s posters. In the 1930s, he again directly faced the viewer. G. L. Demosfenova, A. Nurok, and N. Shatyko, *Sovetskii politicheskii plakat* (Moscow, 1962), p. 84.

[45] Uspensky, *Semiotics of the Russian Icon*, p. 60.

[46] Ibid., p. 68.

БОРЬБА КРАСНОГО РЫЦАРЯ С ТЕМНОЙ СИЛОЮ.

5. "Bor'ba krasnogo rytsaria s temnoi siloiu" (Struggle of the red knight with the dark force), by B. Zvorykin (1919)

and hammer as the "Red Knight," or *rytsar'* (figure 5).[47] A 1921 May Day poster from Kiev depicts a blacksmith carried by giant birds, against the background of a red star and a sun.[48] And whereas Hercules served to symbolize the sansculottes in the iconography of the French Revolution, the Russian proletariat sometimes became associated during the civil war years with the titan Prometheus. In visual propaganda, this is exemplified by the 1920 poster by P. Kiselis, "Belogvardeiskii khishchnik terzaet telo rabochikh i krest'ian" (The White Guard beast of prey is tearing the body of workers and peasants to pieces).[49] The sovietization of the Prometheus myth had the proletariat bound to the rock of capitalism and attacked by an eagle, the official emblem of the old regime.[50] In this poster, the beleaguered worker-Prometheus holds a hammer in his right hand to ward off the attacking eagle. In literature, music, drama, and ballet, the myth of Prometheus Unbound attracted special attention during these years.[51]

The New Function of Political Art

In 1930, the traditional image of the blacksmith disappeared from Bolshevik political art; only occasional and schematic representations remained. This development took place with remarkable swiftness and was nearly completed by the time the Central Committee issued its resolution of 11 March 1931, placing all poster production under the auspices of the State Publishing House for Visual Arts (Izogiz) directly subordinate to the Central Committee. The centralization and coordination of visual propaganda reinforced the trend already under way among poster artists to replace most of the old iconography from the civil war period with a new visual language suited to the Stalinist era.

Criticism of the established worker imagery can be dated from 1930.

[47] B. Zvorykin, "Bor'ba krasnogo rytsaria s temnoi siloiu" (The struggle of the red knight with the dark force), 1919, RU/SU 1285. This poster was issued for the second anniversary of the revolution.

[48] A26318, poster collection, Muzei revoliutsii. This poster, "1 Maia—zalog osvobozhdeniia mirovogo truda" (May 1—the guarantee of the liberation of world labor), by A. Marenkov, was produced in Kiev in an edition of five thousand.

[49] RU/SU 1287. A different version showed a snake rather than an eagle attacking the worker. B. S. Butnik-Siverskii, *Sovetskii plakat epokhi grazhdanskoi voiny 1918–1921* (Moscow, 1960), p. 229, entry 869.

[50] James von Geldern, *Bolshevik Festivals 1917–1920* (Berkeley and Los Angeles, 1993), p. 183.

[51] Ibid., pp. 32, 162, 183. For example, in November 1918, the Bolshoi performed Scriabin's symphonic poem "Prometheus." In 1919, the Red Army Studio prepared a drama, "The Russian Prometheus"; in 1920, there was an amateur production, "The Fire of Prometheus," performed by Red Army theater groups and a May Day plan for a mass drama based on the myth of Prometheus.

N. Maslenikov, author of a book on posters, described the standard image as "petty bourgeois *[meshchanskii]* in ideology."[52] When a rare poster appeared in 1932 depicting two muscular men standing at an anvil with hammers in hand, a Moscow critic commented that "the image does not take into account the essence of socialist labor and is based entirely on a bourgeois conception of workers' labor. The artist was entirely wrong in drawing from the archive of poster clichés these stereotypical blacksmiths with heavy sledgehammers."[53] Thus, the blacksmith image, which had occupied a central place in Bolshevik iconography before 1930, was considered unacceptable and "bourgeois"—a grave epithet—by 1932.

The abandonment of the conventional worker-icon coincided with the implementation of the First Five-Year Plan and a reevaluation of the hero in Soviet society.[54] In literature, writers and critics advocated a turn away from the earlier emphasis on individual heroes (they disappeared almost entirely from literary works until 1932) and their replacement by what Katerina Clark has called "the cult of 'little men,' " that is, ordinary workers. Literature was "deheroized," and writers focused, instead, on the emerging future society or on production.[55] This development had its counterpart in political art. Many posters produced in 1930 and 1931 relied heavily on the silhouette, a technique which had been utilized in some civil war posters but had lapsed during the 1920s.[56] The silhouette, with its lack of detail or facial expression and its general vagueness, appealed to political artists groping for new imagery in a period that stressed the ordinary man.

The anonymous 1931 poster, "B'em po lzheudarnikam" (Down with the False Shock Workers) is a typical example (figure 6).[57] It depicts three

---

[52] N. N. Maslenikov, *Plakat* (Moscow, 1930), p. 39.

[53] *Produktsiia izobrazitel'nykh iskusstv*, no. 3–4 (1932): 10.

[54] For an excellent discussion of this topic, see Katerina Clark, *The Soviet Novel: History as Ritual* (Chicago, 1981), and her essay, "Little Heroes and Big Deeds: Literature Responds to the First Five-Year Plan," in Sheila Fitzpatrick, ed., *Cultural Revolution in Russia, 1928–1931* (Bloomington, Ind., 1984).

[55] Clark, "Little Heroes," pp. 200–201.

[56] The silhouette dates from eighteenth-century France and was named after Etienne de Silhouette, a French magistrate, who attempted to restrict the king's spending. His silhouette was placed in windows as part of an effort to ridicule his effort ("Man reduced to a mere outline no longer inspired the same respect"). Robert Philippe, *Political Graphics: Art as a Weapon* (New York, 1982), pp. 12–13. During the civil war, the enormously successful ROSTA posters, as well as some other notable posters, employed the technique of silhouette. For examples of ROSTA posters, see *The Soviet Political Poster*, pp. 34–36, White, *Bolshevik Poster*, chap. 4. Another well-known example from the 1920s is Ye. Kruglikova, "Zhenshchina! Uchis' gramote!" (Woman! Learn to read!), 1923, RU/SU 519.

[57] RU/SU 1748. For other examples of silhouetted workers with hammers, see F. Lain, "My raportuem!!!" (We are reporting), issued on the occasion of the All-Union Shock Worker Day (1 October 1930), RU/SU 1670; "Sol'em udarnye otriady v skvoznye udarnye brigady" (Let us merge the shock teams into shock brigades), 1930, RU/SU 1963; and "Udarnym tempom" (Let us work in a shock tempo), 1930. White, *Bolshevik Poster*, p. 55.

6. "B'em po lzheudarnikam" (Down with the false shock workers) (1931)

silhouetted workers (painted orange) wielding hammers against those who violate work rules. This poster is one of many produced in 1930–1931 in connection with the shock worker campaign, a mass campaign that re-cruited 1.5 million workers in the first four months of 1930s alone.[58] We see here a suggestion of the blacksmith image but now it is presented in an entirely new way. The old class markers of the worker have vanished, except for the hammer. Workers are now presented in groups rather than individually—the visual counterparts of the "little heroes" who populated Soviet novels of these years. Virtually all such posters emphasize motion, one of the distinctive features of the new visual language that emerged during the First Five-Year Plan. As the old class markers began to dis-appear, color symbolism became more important than ever before. The silhouetted figures of workers were usually represented with red or or-ange. Contemporary reviewers did not always approve of posters using silhouettes. A critic of another 1931 poster with images similar to those discussed above criticized the work for its "extreme schematism." Instead of live builders of socialism, there were "mechanized dolls."[59] In the wake

[58] Lewis H. Siegelbaum, *Stakhanovism and the Politics of Productivity, 1935–1941* (Cam-bridge, 1988), p. 45.
[59] *Za proletarskoe iskusstvo*, 31 February 1931, p. 12. It is noteworthy that works of literature produced in the early 1930s style were also being labeled "schematic" by critics in early 1931.

of such criticism (similar comments were made about literary works emphasizing the "little men"[60]), artists soon moved away from the use of the silhouette and by the mid-1930s one seldom encounters posters of this type.

In the course of 1931, the official policy toward heroes began to change once again. The official party newspaper *Pravda* launched a campaign under the title "The country needs to know its heroes," designed to publicize leading shock workers. The same year, Izogiz published a book under that title and another called *Udarniki* (Shockworkers).[61] By the time the First Congress of the Union of Writers assembled in 1934, official policy had shifted dramatically. The glorification of anonymous little heroes had been replaced by emphasis on the individual hero. Speaking at the congress, Andrei Zhdanov proclaimed that the new Soviet literature should emphasize "heroization."[62] In a similar vein, Maksim Gorky spoke at length about the role of heroes, reminding his audience that oral folklore had created the "most profound type of heroes," figures such as Hercules, Prometheus, and Dr. Faustus, as well as others from Russian folktales.[63]

During the 1930s, heroic status was accorded first to shock workers and then, from the fall of 1935, to Stakhanov and his fellow Stakhanovites. Katerina Clark and Lewis Siegelbaum have drawn attention to the important shift that occurred in the middle of the decade when the cult of the individual hero acquired central focus in official propaganda, presided over by Stalin.[64] Elevated to the status of national heroes and exemplars, Stakhanovites were compared to Hercules, the unbound Prometheus, and the warrior knight of Russian folk epics, the bogatyr'. In official rhetoric they were portrayed as representing a new order of humanity.[65] Together with the shock workers and others who performed great feats (for example, reaching the North Pole), they acquired unprecedented recognition in the Soviet pantheon. The worker-hero of the civil war, who had become the Bolshevik worker-hero by 1927, was again transformed in the course of the 1930s into the "new man" *(novyi chelovek).*

The "new man" was, of course, a worker—though not, as we shall see, exclusively so. But what kind of worker? One paradoxical aspect of the

[60] Clark, "Little Heroes," p. 203.
[61] Regine Robin, "Stalinisme et culture populaire," in Marc Ferro et al., *Culture et revolution* (Paris, 1989), p. 158; *Brigada khudozhnikov*, no. 7 (1931): 27. The shift in orientation appears to have taken place following a speech by Stalin in July 1931, in which he emphasized the need for good leaders and managers. Clark, *Soviet Novel*, p. 118.
[62] Clark, "Little Heroes," p. 206.
[63] Ibid., p. 155. On this subject, see also Clark, *Soviet Novel*, pp. 147–48.
[64] See Siegelbaum, *Stakhanovism*, and Clark, *Soviet Novel*.
[65] Clark, *Soviet Novel*, pp. 72, 119, 148.

First Five-Year Plan is that official propaganda became obsessively pre-occupied with the theme of class war. Class designations acquired more significance than ever before, but at the same time, rapid social and demographic change fundamentally altered the class structure of Soviet society so that class distinctions became, in practice, much more muddled. Large numbers of peasants migrated from villages to cities and factory centers. They were now officially designated as "workers" but it was the village, not the factory, that shaped their outlook and conduct.[66] At the same time, tens of thousands of workers were promoted into the ranks of managers and technicians. What it meant to be a "worker"—much less a heroic Bolshevik worker and new Soviet man—became increasingly uncertain. The shock worker and Stakhanovite campaigns were designed, at least in part, to provide a blueprint for becoming an exemplary worker and a new Soviet man.

Visual propaganda provided another major means for transforming inner as well as outer conduct.[67] The Central Committee resolution on political art, issued on 11 March 1931, left no doubt about the aim of visual propaganda. It was to serve as "a powerful tool in the reconstruction of the individual, his ideology, his way of life, his economic activity" and a means of "entering the consciousness and hearts of millions [of people]."[68] The pronouncement accentuated the ambitious task of political art in the Stalin era: to change people's structure of thinking at its deepest level.

The disappearance of the figure of the blacksmith from political art signified not only a change in imagery, but more important, a fundamental shift in the function of this imagery. Political art in the 1930s aimed not merely at exhortation but at the "reconstruction of the individual." Previously, the worker-icon functioned as a symbol—a symbol of the heroic proletariat, which, according to Bolshevik mythology, had made the October Revolution. The image of the blacksmith was meant to capture some elements of what it meant to be a worker (hence the significance of the polyvalence of the blacksmith image). The worker-icon, initially representing the broad category of collective heroes of the revolution and later the more select group of Bolshevik worker-heroes, was rooted in a

---

[66] Moshe Lewin, *The Making of the Soviet System: Essays in the Social History of Interwar Russia* (New York, 1985), pp. 219–22, 241, 248–50. In 1931 alone, 4.1 million peasants joined the factory labor force, creating a "ruralization" of the cities. Lewin, pp. 219–21. See also Hiroaki Kuromiya, *Stalin's Industrial Revolution: Politics and Workers, 1928–1932* (Cambridge, 1988), pp. 92–107.

[67] The urgency and importance of this task can scarcely be underestimated. As Lewin puts it, "a semiliterate if not illiterate, predominantly rural labor force had to be broken into the industrial world and taught, simultaneously, to use machines, to get used to an unfamiliar, complicated organization, to learn to read, to respect authority, to change their perception of time, and to use a spitoon." Lewin, *The Making of the Soviet System*, p. 242.

[68] *Brigada khudozhnikov*, no. 2–3 (1931): 1–3.

symbolic tradition of representation. During the 1930s, the imagery of the worker in political propaganda had a different purpose. Now the image of the worker functioned as a model, an ideal type. Its purpose was to conjure up a vision of the new Soviet man, to provide a visual script for the appearance, demeanor, and conduct of the model Stalinist citizen.

This new function performed by visual propaganda led contemporary commentators to focus intensively on the problem of *tipazh*. In the Soviet lexicon, the term "tipazh" implied a correct rendering of a particular social category. But the essence of tipazh was not typicality but, rather, type casting or typicalization. As Lunacharsky put in an article published in *Brigada khudozhnikov* in 1931, "The artists should not only describe what is, but should go farther, to show those forces which are not yet developed, in other words, from the interpretation of reality it is necessary to proceed to the disclosure of the inner essence of life, which comes out of proletarian goals and principles."[69]

Lunacharsky's prescription, with its respectable metaphysical pedigree and its close resemblance to the definition soon given to the emerging concept of socialist realism, encapsulates the difficulty facing poster artists in the early 1930s. Having abandoned the standard image, which Soviet critics labeled "stereotypical" and "bourgeois," artists were faced with the daunting task of making visually precise social types that corresponded not to contemporary experience but to current party analysis of the "inner essence of life," which would be fully realized only in the hoped-for future. This reformulation of the artist's task marked a fundamental shift from a historically credible representation of the past and present to a new mode of visual representation which depicted the present not as it actually was but as it should become. The trick was to create the illusion of an imaginary future in the visual terms of the present.

The application of tipazh in the first half of the 1930s did not imply a fully elaborated iconographic image comparable to the blacksmith. Correct tipazh required that the image of the worker convey a certain demeanor and expression, a combination of physical strength, energy, fortitude and intelligence. One reviewer complained that tipazh in a 1932 poster was uncharacteristic because "the face is not intellectual, not warmed by creative thought. It does not have the joy of mastering knowledge, curiosity, absorption in study."[70] This emphasis on the intellectual and cultural attributes of workers was part of a more general trend that found expression in the Stakhanovite campaign beginning in September 1935. The model Stakhanovite was not merely capable of great physical feats but also a person who valued learning and partook of high culture.[71]

[69] *Brigada khudozhnikov*, 5–6 (1931): 13.
[70] *Produktsiia izobrazitel'nykh iskusstv*, no. 14–15 (1932): 5.
[71] Siegelbaum, *Stakhanovism*, chap. 6.

The Semiotics of Stalinist Visual Propaganda

Even a cursory survey of the 1930s political posters discloses a dramatic shift in aesthetic sensibility. These posters cannot easily be confused with those of the civil war or the 1920s. In terms of images, syntax, and technique they belonged to a very different world—a world of feverish reconstruction, in which "higher, farther, and faster" became the new incantations.[72] The technique of photomontage was widely applied in the first half of the 1930s by political artists seeking to respond to new political tasks. Unlike the silhouette, which stripped the image of all detail and distinctiveness, photomontage accentuated the particularities of the representation, making it more concrete and less abstract. Photomontage had been used extensively in film and commercial posters during the 1920s, but far less often in political propaganda.[73] Led by Gustav Klutsis, the master of photomontage in Stalinist propaganda, a number of key artists turned their attention to photography as a way to visualize the worker-hero of the First Five-Year Plan.[74] Photomontage marked a sharp departure from the previous style of representing the worker. Photographs, unlike drawings and paintings, projected the aura of objectivity and were based on the principle of realistic as opposed to symbolic representation. The power of the image derived from its seemingly authentic representation of the real world, its verisimilitude.[75]

Photomontage was in some ways the quintessential application of socialist realism in the visual sphere. Using actual photographs of Soviet workers, it created the impression of "is" where before there had only been "ought." Since photographs conveyed, as did no other medium except film, a seemingly "real" picture of the world, photomontage perpetrated an illusion that the future and present were indistinguishable. Relying on actual photographs, political artists developed a new approach to the problem of representing workers in the Stalinist era. Instead of subsuming all workers into a single image of the blacksmith, they began

---

[72] Ibid., p. 225.

[73] The German painter George Grosz claimed that he and John Heartfield invented photomontage in 1916. Heartfield subsequently became a major practitioner of this technique, and his work greatly influenced Soviet artists. M. Contstantine and A. M. Fern, *Work and Image: Posters from the Collection of the Museum of Modern Art* (New York, 1968), p. 58.

[74] The technique of photomontage was not without its critics, and the early 1930s witnessed lively debates over its application in a revolutionary context. See, for example, the discussion by M. Neiman, "Fotomontazh khudozhnika B. Klincha," in *Produktsiia izoiskusstv*, no. 7 (1933): 3–5, and Demosfenova, Nurok, and Shatyko, *Sovetskii politicheskii plakat*, p. 77.

[75] There were three different types of photomontage in the Soviet Union in the 1930s. The first and most widely used approach combined various photographs into a montage. This was the style used by Klutsis. The second combined photographs and drawings. The third used photographs that incorporated visual tricks and distortions. Neiman, "Fotomontazh," p. 3.

to portray workers as miners, construction workers, metalworkers, tex-
tileworkers, and so on. There was no longer a single prototype of the
worker.

A 1931 large-scale poster by Klutsis, "Dadim milliony kvalifitsirovannykh rabochikh kadrov" (We will produce millions of qualified workers'
cadres), exemplifies the application of photomontage (figure 7).[76] The
poster consists of a column of workers (male and female) moving toward
factory buildings in the distance. They belong to different occupational
subgroups. Most are smiling, and some are looking directly at the viewer.
Not all 1930s posters utilized the silhouette or photomontage to depict
the worker. There were many others that relied on conventional techniques of painting and drawing to convey their message; in the second
half of the 1930s, these posters once again predominated. Experimenta-
tion with technique was part of a larger effort, under way throughout the
1930s, to create a new visual language suited to the era of Stalinist industrialization. This language no longer depended on the repetition of
certain fixed iconographic images (though there was a return to this style
in the period of high Stalinism following the Second World War). Instead,
artists brought their imagery in line with official ideology by incorporating
visual elements designed to serve as markers for the new Soviet rather
than the "proletarian" man. A distinct set of attributes (though not all
were present at the same time) became the marker for heroic citizens in
the Stalinist epoch.

These attributes included, first and perhaps most important, youth
and a general appearance of vigor, freshness, and enthusiasm. The emphasis on youthfulness corresponded to actual changes in the labor
force. By the end of the 1930s, the bulk of factory workers were under
twenty-nine.[77] Second, the new Soviet man—the worker-hero of the Stalin era—was a perpetual builder of socialism and he was usually shown
in motion. Whereas formerly the worker had often been depicted in a
static pose, now political artists were expected to represent workers engaged in action.[78] Indeed, the composition of 1930s posters—with their
use of the diagonal—accentuates the idea of motion. Journals devoted
to poster reviews sharply criticized posters that failed to include images
of workers in motion. Thus, the 1931 Klutsis poster discussed above
(figure 7) was received with reservations by a critic who noted that the
figures were motionless and posed.[79] A third attribute of the Stalinist
hero was his stature. Like Gulliver towering over the Lilliputians, he

[76] RU/SU 2281, pts. 1 and 2.
[77] Lewin, *Making of the Soviet System*, p. 250; Kuromiya, *Stalin's Industrial Revolution*,
pp. 90–92.
[78] Demosfenova, Nurok, and Shatyko, *Sovetskii politicheskii plakat*, pp. 86–87.
[79] *Produktsiia izbrazitel'nykh iskusstv*, no. 1 (1932): 8.

7. "Dadim milliony kvalifitsirovannykh rabochikh kadrov" (We will produce millions of qualified workers' cadres), by G. Klutsis (1931)

ДНЕПРОСТРОЙ ПОСТРОЕН

8. "Dneprostroi postroen" (Dnepostroi is constructed), by A. Strakhov (1932)

was depicted as larger than life. Perspectival distortion, as noted earlier, had been used occasionally during the civil war years but disappeared in the 1920s. It was restored during the 1930s as a standard way of graphically depicting the heroic worker and others such as collective farm workers, whose feats transformed them into "supermen" and "superwomen."[80]

Another important element of the emerging visual sign system was the attribution of emotion. The blacksmith, as well as the silhouetted figures of the early 1930s, generally lacked emotional expression. In the course of the 1930s, political artists began to represent workers with feelings. The emotional range was limited to two basic dispositions: intense effort and determination on the one hand, joyfulness on the other. A 1932 poster by the artist Adolf Strakhov exemplifies this trend (figure 8).[81] In this poster, "Dneprostroi postroen" (Dneprostroi is constructed), we see

[80] A 1931 poster by V. Efanov, "Proletarii" (Proletarian), RU/SU 1632, exemplifies this technique. Efanov's poster shows a larger-than-life worker in leather jacket, cap, and leather boots (these are all visual markers for a Bolshevik), carrying a book in one hand and gesturing forward with the other (rather in the pose Lenin often assumed in posters). His mouth is open as though he is calling to someone. The poster urges workers to study in technical schools in order to create "proletarian cadres." For a discussion of the "remarkable people," see Clark, *Soviet Novel*, pp. 119–21. Women were also portrayed in the larger-than-life format during the 1930s, especially collective farm women.

[81] *Soviet Political Poster*, p. 69.

the face of a worker beaming with emotion: his joyous expression and raised arm are a response to the opening of the Dneprostroi dam pictured in the background. Joyfulness and "lofty emotional agitation" *(vzvolno-vannost')* become characteristic emotions ascribed to workers in the second half of the 1930s, facilitated, no doubt, by Stalin's declaration that Soviet life had become merrier.[82]

Finally, posters of the 1930s make use of the direct gaze. With the exception of a few Red Army posters produced during the civil war, heroes seldom looked directly at the spectator. This was consistent with religious iconography, which also avoided the direct gaze. But in the 1930s, political artists sometimes depicted workers looking directly at the viewer. Viktor Govorkov's 1933 poster, "Vasha lampa, tovarishch inzhener!" (Your lamp, comrade engineer!), uses this device (figure 9).[83] The poster shows a youthful larger-than-life figure holding out a lamp in his right hand. He confronts the viewer with a penetrating direct gaze. The frequent use of this device altered the conventional relationship between the viewer and the image. Whereas formerly, the viewer was an observer looking in at the world of the image, now the relationship was reversed. The image confronted the viewer. It might not be far-fetched to compare this phenomenon with the presence of the all-seeing eye *(velikii glaz)* in Orthodox iconography.[84]

The famous monumental sculpture by Vera Mukhina, "Rabochii i kolkhoznitsa" (Worker and Collective Farm Woman), created in 1937, exemplifies the coalescence of these elements composing a new semiotic system (figure 10).[85] In what was no doubt a very deliberate choice, Mukhina revived the image of the male blacksmith. It is precisely the reference to this early image that makes her sculpture so arresting, for Mukhina's blacksmith belongs to a very different world from his earlier counterpart. He is strikingly youthful and handsome, in the clean-cut masculine way that became standard for male workers in the late Stalin era. Rather than a static pose or the conventional hammer striking the anvil, his left arm is thrust forward on the diagonal. He holds up a hammer (she raises a sickle) not in an act of labor but rather in a gesture of triumph. His intense expression and direct gaze, brows slightly furrowed, indicate strong emotion and determination. He is the prototype for the new Soviet man.

[82] On this general point, see Demosfenova, Nurok, and Shatyko, *Sovetskii politicheskii plakat*, pp. 105–9. Demosfenova concludes that the image of the workers is transformed in these years and the "worker becomes a master [khoziain] of his life, fully empowered and proud."

[83] *Soviet Political Poster*, p. 72.

[84] Uspensky, *Semiotics of the Russian Icon*, p. 39.

[85] The statue is located at the site of the Exhibition of Economic Achievements (VDNKh), Moscow.

9. "Vasha lampa, tovarishch inzhener!" (Your lamp, comrade engineer!), by V. Govorkov (1933)

10. "Rabochii i kolkhoznitsa" (Worker and collective farm woman), by V. Mukhina (1937)

Stalin as the Sacred Center

One of the most striking developments in the 1930s is the gradual but unmistakable decline in the importance of the worker in Soviet political art. Prior to the adoption of the First Five-Year Plan, the official ideology focused, above all, on legitimating the October Revolution. These efforts reached their apogee in 1927. A key element in this effort was sacralization of the proletariat, which had performed its world-historical mission and earned its status as the chosen people by bringing the Bolsheviks to power. With the adoption of the First Five-Year Plan, the vast Soviet propaganda machine directed its attention to a different issue: the legitimation of the Stalin Revolution. Workers constituted an important group in this massive transformation, but the Stalin Revolution was to be made not by a single class but by a whole society. It required total national mobilization. Despite the incessant rhetoric of class warfare, the key category in the 1930s was not class but citizenship.[86] Stalin, after all, was the Father of the People, not the Father of the Proletariat.

The changing position of workers in visual propaganda can be judged from poster editions. In 1932, the average press run for posters was about thirty thousand; between 1935 and 1941, many poster editions ran as high as one or two hundred thousand. But just as poster editions expanded astronomically, those devoted to industrial themes—those featuring workers—occupied a diminishing place in the now centralized production of political art. Thus, in 1937, posters on the theme of Aviation Day and the death of Lenin were produced in editions of one hundred thousand. A poster celebrating Soviet aviation to the North Pole appeared in an edition of two hundred thousand.[87] The largest press run of a poster on an industrial theme was thirty thousand, compared to seventy-five thousand for posters dealing with agriculture. Of the sixty-one different posters commissioned that year, only four were devoted to themes featuring workers.[88]

Workers and industrial themes had lost their hegemonic position in the visual syntax. Earlier, the male worker's incomparable status had been expressed relationally: he stood in front of or loomed over peasants, female workers, even Red Army soldiers (as in Matveev's sculpture dis-

[86] This argument is elaborated in Gregory Freidin, "Romans into Italians: Russian National Identity in Transition," in Gregory Freidin, ed., *Russian Culture in Transition: Selected Papers of the Working Group for the Study of Contemporary Russian Culture, 1990–1991* (Stanford, 1993), pp. 241–74.

[87] RU/SU 2288. The artist was Piotr Karachentsov. The poster shows a red flag, airplane, and globe with a route drawn from Moscow to the North Pole; it includes a quotation from Stalin: "There are no fortresses which Bolsheviks cannot conquer."

[88] TsGALI, f. 1988, op. 1, ed. khr. 34, l. 11; Demosfenova, Nurok, and Shatyko, *Sovetskii politicheskii plakat*, p. 105.

cussed above). In the 1930s, however, workers took their place alongside collective farmers, aviators, and athletes—all of them inducted into the Stalinist hall of fame. Workers no longer had a special claim to sacralization; this honor was now bestowed on all those who performed exceptional feats for the Stalinist party-state.

These developments in visual representation correspond to what Moshe Lewin has described as the workers' "fall from grace" in the 1930s. As he puts it, workers enjoyed preferential treatment during the NEP, for theirs was "the right of social origin." By the end of the 1930s, this situation had disappeared, and workers "had become inferior to other groups and, most irritatingly, to the pettiest officials." The party, once the bastion of "conscious workers," had become "a vehicle for officialdom and specialists."[89]

A fundamental shift was taking place in the country's system of stratification, with far-reaching implications for the symbolics of power. As the proletarian worker—once the very essence of Bolshevik mythology—receded in importance in visual propaganda, the image of Stalin came to occupy a central and sacred place in Soviet iconography. Representations of the *vozhd'* (leader) occur very early in political art. Lenin's image was incorporated into posters during the civil war and throughout the 1920s.[90] Stalin's appearance in political posters coincides with the First Five-Year Plan. At first, he is shown in a subordinate relationship to Lenin. But as early as 1932, Stalin's image was given equal status with Lenin's and soon he begins to emerge as the more important figure.[91]

A 1935 poster by A. Reznichenko, issued in connection with the Stakhanovite campaign, brings into sharp relief the complex of images and ideas that characterized the Stalinist visual discourse on power. In this poster, Stakhanov is shown carrying a red flag that bears an image of Stalin's face (figure 11).[92] Behind him is a crowd of workers and beyond them, the Kremlin. The poster uses the visual trope of metonymy to associate by contiguity the heroic worker Stakhanov, Stalin, and the Kremlin (symbolizing continuity of the Stalinist state with the ancient Russian tradition of the state). Although Stakhanov is placed in the center of the

[89] Lewin, *Making of the Soviet System*, pp. 247, 254–55.

[90] François-Xavier Coquin, "L'Image de Lenine dans l'iconographie révolutionnaire et postrévolutionnaire," *Annales ESC*, no. 2 (1989): 223–49.

[91] An early example was the anonymous 1932 poster "Pobeda sotsializma v nashei strane obespechana" (The victory of socialism in our country is guaranteed), which featured a larger-than-life photograph of Stalin's face and a large crowd below, with Lenin's small image on a flag in the background. Lenin Library Poster Collection, p4.vii.6.pobeda. I examine these issues in my forthcoming study *The Iconography of Power: Soviet Political Art, 1917–1953*.

[92] RU/SU 1824.

СТАХАНОВСКОЕ ДВИЖЕНИЕ—
ЭТО ВЫСШАЯ ФОРМА СОЦСОРЕВНО-
ВАНИЯ И УДАРНИЧЕСТВА ЭПОХИ
СОЦИАЛИЗМА, КОТОРАЯ ВПИТАЛА В
СЕБЯ ВСЕ ЧЕРТЫ ПРЕДЫДУЩИХ ФОРМ
СОЦИАЛИСТИЧЕСКОГО СОРЕВНОВАНИЯ
И ОБОГАТИЛА ИХ ОВЛАДЕНИЕМ В
СОВЕРШЕНСТВЕ ТЕХНИКОЙ СВОЕГО
ПРОИЗВОДСТВА.

П. П. ПОСТЫШЕВ.

11. "Stakhanovskoe dvizhenie" (Stakhanovite movement), by A. Reznichenko
(1935)

poster, peripheral elements (Stalin's image on the red flag and the Kremlin tower) dominate the composition and define the worker-hero. The significance of this constellation must have been unmistakable for contemporaries. Stakhanov's stature and greatness were inextricably linked to Stalin and the Kremlin; the worker-hero drew from them his inspiration, direction, and superhuman powers. Only ten thousand copies of the Stakhanov poster were printed, a very small edition for the mid-1930s but consistent with the general pattern noted above. Nevertheless the prototype of this poster was used again and again to celebrate the feats of explorers, aviators, athletes, collective farmers, and construction crews.[93] Now the visual script was complete. Entry into the Soviet pantheon required not only joyful and diligent labor but also a talisman engraved with the image of Stalin. It was Stalin, the Great Helmsman,[94] and not the worker-blacksmith, who generated the sacred powers that would make it possible to hammer out "the bright road for the people . . . happiness for the motherland." The affinity between the two figures did not elude Osip Mandelstam, who immortalized it in his irreverent 1933 epigram on the murderous Hephaestus in the Kremlin:[95]

He hammers ukazes one after another, like horseshoes—
One gets it in the groin, one in the head, one in the brow, one in the eye.
Each execution for him is a treat.
And the broad chest of an Ossete.

[93] See, for example, "Da zdravstvuet Sovetskie fizkulturniki" (Long live Soviet physical culturists), RU/SU 565; V. Deni, N. Dolgorukov and Dubchanov, "Da zdravstvuet sokoly nashei rodiny, stalinskie pitomtsy" (Long live the falcons of our motherland, the Stalinist disciples), 1938, RU/SU 1816; G. Kun, V. Elkin, K. Sobolevskii, "Privet velikomu Stalinu kanal Moskva-Volga otkryt!" (Greetings to the great Stalin. The Moscow-Volga canal is open!), 1937, RU/SU 2151; P. Iastozhembolii, "Vsesoiuznaia sel'sko-khoziaistvennaia vystavka" (The all-union agricultural exhibition), 1939, RU/SU 1832.

[94] Designations for Stalin in the 1930s included *vozhd'*, *vozhd' i uchitel'*, *rukovoditel'*, *boets*, *otets*, and *krepkii khoziain*. Robin, "Stalinisme et culture populaire," p. 152.

[95] Quoted from Gregory Freidin, *A Coat of Many Colors: Osip Mandelstam and His Mythologies of Self-Preservation* (Berkeley and Los Angeles, 1987), p. 242. The epigram dates from November 1933. Mandelstam was arrested soon afterward.

13

Moshe Lewin

Concluding Remarks

Between Personality and "Class"

The "biographical method" proposed by Reginald Zelnik in Chapter 1 is a good starting point for the conclusion. Zelnik hints at the problems that lead to tension between the sociological method that prefers broad impersonal agglomerations and trends and the "biographical" method, which begins with concrete persons and individual lives.

The clash here is between two theories of reality, the deterministic-structural approach and the personalistic approach, which actually posit their mutual exclusion. Thus two exclusive approaches, verging partly on different ideologies, namely methodological collectivism versus methodological individualism, compete with each other. (Interested readers may find a sample of this problematique in Jon Elster's book on Marx.)[1]

According to the latter approach, there is no society except as it works in individual minds; therefore, study must begin and end with the reading of individual minds. Elster saw Marx as partially redeemed from irrelevance because he endorsed the erroneous, that is, the former, approach but applied it inconsistently, since he was also aware of the correct view and hence managed to gain some staying power. But in the supposedly more correct conception, collective bodies have no reality by themselves.

The contradiction between these "opposites," is, to my mind, artificial. The macrodimension is indispensable and the final objective. To deny the reality of collective bodies amounts to denying that the individual is "social." Yet the "sociological" approach, denying or refusing to incorporate the lessons learned from studying human psychology and individuality, is equally faulty. The big theoretical battle should be about how to relate

[1] Jon Elster, *Making Sense of Marx* (Cambridge, 1985).

and merge the two and not about how to counterpose them; such a task, however difficult, is the real one.

Thus, the discovery Zelnik makes of the importance of the individual's biographic memory, such as how Gerasimov's experience of being an orphan (*pitomets*) was a shaping force in his political activism, enriches and complicates the task of the generalizer without denying the existence of a factory system with its class realities. Most of the contributors to this book, as expected, try to grapple with "class," but most seem to doubt the validity of this concept and the related one of "class consciousness." But class consciousness, whether from the standpoint of the role of ethical concepts (Steinberg), or the empirical reconstruction of the actual making of such a consciousness (Hogan), or in connection with dependency relations with immediate supervisors (Smith), must be recognized as historically real on condition that "class" itself has a historical reality; that such a consciousness is time- and context-bound, which means that in time it can form itself and re-form itself into something else; and that in context it depends on the existence, reactions, and self-consciousness of other factors, such as factory owners, other layers in the plants, the state, the social origins of the workers themselves, and the political situation (revolutions, reforms). The list of factors is longer, but there is no class consciousness from within itself without such context.

It is here that Marx's concept of class *an sich* is important. Masses of people, must have a commonality of situation, position, and income for a consciousness of this situation to take root. "Above" does not always imply *direct* exploitation, because there are classes that exploit somebody but not each other. "Domination," which Steve Smith prefers to "exploitation," and which refers to workers in factories or other employment where there are bosses, is, to my mind, a better, more inclusive description. There can be no exploitation without the presence of domination (except for "suckers" in interpersonal relations, which means psychological weaklings—but this also implies domination). Still, there may be different concepts of "exploitation." It is often not acknowledged when expressed in the usual Marxist terms, but it is broadly recognized in all cases when the working conditions are below usual, normally acceptable standards.

So classes exist whether they know it or not. They rarely fail to know it and many students of these matters would reject the idea of a class that was not aware of its own existence. But one only has to think of how revolutionary movements after taking power, the Bolsheviks in their leather coats among them, seem unaware at first that they are a ruling class, not a popular or a working class anymore. Accusations that they have become exploiters and oppressors are met with the most sincere denials, at least at first. This was certainly true of the Bolsheviks. In the early stages of the system, they saw themselves as authentic, red-blooded revolutionaries. But others were already telling them, with good reason, that they were a ruling class, at least *an sich*, if not yet *für sich*. A switch from one state of self-consciousness to another, from *an sich* to *für sich*, can be triggered by different events or circumstances, a classic example of such a trigger being the massacre of a religious procession of workers by the tsar's guard during "Bloody Sunday" in 1905. The *an sich* state of things was suddenly transformed into a *für sich* class consciousness.

There can be moments of solidarity in other groups, but if these groups are quite heterogeneous in character, the ties may disappear once a particular irritant or problem is removed. Thus a group such as " the intelligentsia" could, quite often, share opinions and lines of action, but lacking a real infrastructure, could not maintain a capacity to defend clearly perceived group interests, as trade unions do for the working class.

Consciousness Coming and Going

The consciousness of a class *für sich*—that is, the appearance of a self-awareness with an ideology and accompanying political programs—does not mean, as the Bolsheviks often tried to make us believe, the adoption of some particular program or party. We have to accept a consciousness as it is. Indeed, we must even recognize "a false consciousness" in cases in which a class, or large strata of it, has allowed itself to be led astray by politicians and ideologies that did them a lot of harm. This has happened quite often to different popular classes and layers; upper classes too have paid a heavy price for being similarly misled.

All these phenomena related to political self-awareness change in changing circumstances. Indeed, we can see and often have seen the "consciousness" and the underlying social structure undergo sometimes quite unrelated, or seemingly unrelated, transformations. From our observations we can reconstruct the social history of each class as it undergoes transformations under the impact of social, technological, educational, and political circumstances; as it evolves through transitional stages; as it gives birth to groups that are new and different; and as, at times, it just ceases to exist—sometimes for good, sometimes temporarily. Isn't this exactly what we are studying? So, if we drop any explicit or implicit claims that classes and "structures" are immutable, if we accept that social realities can be, and often are, very fluid, then the concept of class becomes real and useful, but our work becomes more intricate because we have ceased to take class and class consciousness for granted. Now we must rediscover class and class consciousness empirically (and conceptually), without preconceived notions about their appearance or their "consciousness." We will also have to learn how to live with fluidity, that is, in situations that are as often transitional as they are firm and fixed.

It seems relevant to propose a parenthesis at this juncture: the tsarist regime after 1905, whenever it calculated and plotted its electoral policies, operated already, partly at least, with class terms, despite its preference for thinking in terms of *sosloviia* (estate). The establishment of a workers' curia is a clear sign that both "sides" considered classes to be distinct realities, and neither side had to read Lenin for this. Later, when reading the memoirs of General A. I. Denikin and P. N. Miliukov, written after the civil war, we find that both were thinking in clear-cut class terms— workers, bourgeoisie, peasantry (including kulaks as a category separate from other peasants), and *pomeshchiki* (landowners).[2] And they too made errors in using this kind of grammar. This usage of class terms was not necessarily a result of Marxist influence, but of an advancing new stage in economic development in which more clear-cut class formations kept emerging, making obsolete and irrelevant the official categorization by *sosloviia.*

Yet during later stages of development, as observed in countries we are living in now, the rigid and massive configurations of class are replaced by a more complex differentiation. Classes become less prominent and coexist with a variety of social groups and layers that acquire ever more weight and importance in the social system but do not respond to terms that connote broader sociopolitical entities. If we subscribe to the aforementioned conditions, we are, I believe, in business. We find constantly in Russian history—as well as elsewhere—examples of the metamorphoses and transitions just described.

Let us add that the contributors to this book very appropriately address additional dimensions of social reality—gender, family, different forms of contact and coping (clientele, patronage, patriarchalism), a variety of cultural factors, ethnic identities, and different systems of ethics (communal, religious-orthodox, religious-sectarian, and so on). They are all indispensable. These dimensions of social reality—together with internal social differentiations and networking of all kinds—constitute the texture of any social aggregate without which a reality of a social aggregate is just "void."

It is interesting that Steinberg should underline, as he did when speaking about ethical ideals, that his topic was morals, not class. Why, if the evoked phenomena pertain to "culture" or "ethics," should "class" be

---

[2] A. I. Denikin was commander of the Volunteer Army and the Armed Forces of Southern Russia, white armies that fought the Reds during the civil war. P. N. Miliukov was a history professor, leader of the liberal Kadet (Constitutional Democratic) Party from 1906 to 1917, and minister of foreign affairs in the Provisional Government (March–April 1917).

evicted? Demands for justice, stemming from a reality of an oppressive environment and system in the labor process, is easily about class, and it is not important whether this class is fresh from somewhere else, new, or does not ask for anything in class terms. How is "nas za liudei ne schitaiut" [They don't consider us people] *not* an expression of a class reality, though not just of one particular class?

All these aspects of social reality have nothing to do with bursting asunder the broader covering concept, which may land us in an unenviable situation of having the working class or classes "disappear" when they are all over the place—in factories, workshops, construction sites—clearly visible to everyone who wants to see them and different from their bosses, *chinovniki* (officials) and everyone else.

This does not mean, as I said, that classes do not occasionally disappear. Yes, a working class, but also states, parties, institutions, and systems can evaporate, even before this is realized, exactly as they may already be in existence without being noticed. That is inherent in the very character of changing and shifting social realities. Such is the character of this historical field, and such is the power of the illusions and myths that accompany any human reality. Still, history is mostly a nondivine comedy, which means that it does exist whether the curtain is up or down.

Thus, from chapter to chapter, the squads of workers described change their composition, attitudes, politics, and ideology: Zelnik's 1870s versus the 1890s; Hogan's *metallisty* before and during the revolution; Kuromiya's miners, a non-classy thing *par excellence*, and yet a political powder keg ready to fight like no other more "classy" layers did; Koenker's printers, highly articulate and ready for socialism, entering into a battle for sheer survival against the Communists as they probably would against anyone else in certain conditions, and accepting the same Communists in other circumstances. Let us add Gábor Rittersporn's supposition about his working class becoming "an urban laboring mass"—disputable, no doubt, but belonging to the same register.

So here it is, and here it isn't, and this is the name of the game. Sometime in actual reality, sometime just as a stage of the study when at the beginning all seems to be "decomposing." Dan Orlovsky discovers even a whole "hidden class" where there was not supposed to be one—the white-collar employees. Other authors, as soon as they go into details, invariably become aware that the preferred group is layered, even multi-layered, and before long, something initially perceived as class begins to crumble. Peasants are an entity we may take for granted as long as we know little about them, but when we begin to study the local varieties, we have our hands full of social layering again. The peasants suddenly become something tricky and elusive. A version of such a sociological disappearing act comes up also every time we deal with uprooting and re-uprooting, as in the case of the massive influx of people of a different background, even civilization, the highly "traditional" peasants, engulfed by massive industrialization and urbanization, speedy and widespread waves of change. Can a reality "vanish"? It can, but saying that it has is just a stage of research. After the "deconstruction," reconstruction will follow. The only problem is that in the language of some writers it looks as if "somebody," maybe even the writers themselves, are doing the reconstructing. If so, this would be a nice case of megalomania. The real thing, being a multitude of acts by a multitide of individuals, is therefore a *process,* that is, it constructs and reconstructs itself, and that is why, if we work well and come across vanishing or reappearing realities, we can grasp them *because* they are processes. The more shifty and "bubbly" qualities of social reality do not invalidate concepts like class. Nor can it be claimed that these qualities are more real than life, are there before they emerge, or are still there as they transit from stage to stage until finally, like the peasantry in most industrialized countries—and social structures overall—they actually do make their exit from history.

Finally, another caveat is still in order: a reality in flux that dissolves our concepts continues to be a reality, potent and active in shaping historical outcomes. This is why the metaphor of "bubbly" should not deceive anyone.

Hidden Classes, Hiding Classes

When reading about Orlovsky's "hidden class," one could object that officials were hardly hidden during NEP despite the proletarian mantle they were offered in some speeches and statistical tables. Incidentally, it would be good to ascertain when the term "proletariat" was first used for workers and employees and when this usage was discontinued. The reason though for such a "mislabeling," to put it mildly, is clear. It stems from the ideological assumption that the state is proletarian. Therefore, all those it employs, except for the obvious "bourgeois specialists," should be included in the "proletariat." By the same token, such an inclusive view of the proletariat made that underpopulated class look bigger and made it easier to show its growth. Here already is an instance of the tendency to use class terminology to mystify, which led at a later stage to a full-blown "mythological sociology," a key trait of the Stalinist period, a practice that made social theory entirely devoid of any relation to life and destroyed the social sciences altogether. Stalin's "two friendly classes and one layer" (*prosloika*), or the quite unsuccessful effort to drape the poorly schooled mass of Soviet employees of the 1930s in the toga of the supposedly massive "intelligentsia," instead of their previous inclusion in the proletariat, are examples of such a mythical sociology. Another is the category of *byvshie liudi* (former people), those who really became, if not hidden, then at least a hiding class. They, as well as numerous "alien elements" that fled dekulakization, became an object of a frantic chase in the early 1930s and a ruthless rooting out from factories, *sovkhozy* (state-owned farms), offices, and academic institutions, more often than not because of what the person, or the person's father, did or owned before the revolution.

But there is another way the idea of something "hidden" about employees can be revealing. They were or became an important support of the regime. Early on this fact was "hidden" because the employees themselves did not immediately acknowledge it, and the regime was not happy about such unwanted support. It remains a key fact in the social and political history of the Soviet system that this support was finally not only accepted on both sides, but that the bureaucracy, especially its upper layers, supplanted the working class as the mainstay and power holder. This fact actually was made almost official, though not without some ideological manipulations. Ideological makeup still continued to be used but it was fading away as quickly as the "workers' state" itself. An unwanted ruling class, if you will, took over. As long as that class still consisted of old tsarist employees, they were a support *malgré soi*, because they depended on their employer, the state, although many ended up becoming quite loyal to it. But they were, mostly and traditionally, inimical to the working class and there is no reason to assume that this attitude changed very much.

The story is more complicated with employees and cadres of popular extraction, but social origin, although important, did not block the process of the "status revolution"—or counterrevolution, if one prefers—in Soviet state-building in the 1930s. The leaders and the main groups of servants of this state had to emerge, sooner or later, into the open as the power holders that they actually were. In this context, the term "administrators," even "administrative class," as part of a broader category known as bureaucracy, should be mentioned. Whether called in Soviet parlance *vysshii komandnyi sostav, otvet-rabotniki, otvet-politrabotniki,* or even just *rabotniki,* they had to emerge, quite logically, as superior to and ruling over the popular strata, be they workers or low-level employees. These *rabotniki* need also, urgently, their historian. When talking about the Soviet phenomenon of "mythical sociology," we should be reminded that the reality of classes gives rise to a lot of trafficking, posturing and manipulating in every society.

A whole sociopolitical choreography on the themes of class and power can be observed everywhere because deep interests are involved and much is at stake. The realities behind the terms and the identities of those who want to present or misrepresent them must be discovered and rediscovered in every country. What was it that the Soviet system, our topic here, tried to hide at different times, notably by making impossible any serious sociological study or honest class analysis? Quite a lot, no doubt. Yet, it can be summed up very simply: the realities of power and of rule. This is what it is always about. Grappling with class therefore should be a bona fide scholarly endeavor, but it can never be a politically innocent one. Grappling with class can easily become offensive to power relations, and thus deeply enmeshed in ideology, whatever the system.

A Proletariat without Capitalists?

I will not dwell on the precise stages in the formation of the working class. The contributors to this book have done so, and much more is still to be done. But it is worth reiterating that the key trait of most of those years were waves of varying intensity of influx from outside (important outflows too), mostly into cities, and the decomposition and recomposition of social groups on a large scale.

This book is focused on the making of a tsarist working class and on the recreation in the postrevolutionary period of an actual proletariat instead of a hoped-for, liberated working class. This engendered quite a lot of "fiddling" with the class reality, notably by using the already quoted formula of "two nonantagonistic classes plus one *prosloika*" (the latter term being a reference to the intelligentsia) at a time when somebody else up there was actually ruling over the economy, the state, culture and . . . "the two nonantagonistic classes" themselves. These nonantagonistic classes were provided on average with no more than three to four years of elementary schooling and were thus barely literate, literally as well as politically. That the statist system did not have a classical bourgeoisie and ruling class to match the term proletariat is important. Without a capitalist class one cannot speak of capitalism. Here we have a riddle: we have a working class reminiscent of the old capitalist system but a ruling stratum (later, class) reminiscent of what? An even older, precapitalist system? There is no doubt that these forms were indicative of a stage and of a continuity that has to be considered and explained. But a continuity of what?

In the search for answers, it may be useful to turn to, say, 1905 and then to skip directly to the 1930s and later too. It is not surprising and worth noting that so much of what our contributors show us about the prerevolutionary period is also true of the Soviet period. The sexual harassment and exploitation of women was still very widespread. So was the fawning before or rebelling against *mastera* (shop-floor superintendents). But the role of *master* shifted in different periods, and this can be reconstituted only by empirical study. Material cited by Hogan on poor incentive systems, obsolete machinery, and so on, in the Russia of 1905 sounds so similar to what could be observed in 1975 or 1985, the parallelism pointing no doubt to a system in decline in both cases. But this is said only in passing.

The industrial system in its early stages is deeply authoritarian if not despotic everywhere, and its essence is that owners command labor. This statement encourages one to look at the Stalinist system as being the outcome of a "marriage" between a deeply patriarchal social reality of rural Russia, still powerful in the 1920s, with the despotic traits of the smokestack industry of the day. The situation of workers during these years, the type of environment in which they lived, and the social vortex from which they came and which they faced illustrate with greater intensity than before the validity of the aforementioned heuristic formula. It is also possible to expand the discussion of Stalinism to the uneasy symbiosis between a bureaucratic system and the Stalinist despotism that occurred against the broader social framework alluded to by this formula.

And so, even where there are no private owners, we still hear the demand for respect that is due *nashemu bratu* ("to our brother") but is not to be found. Many of the bosses of the Soviet era were from working-class origins, and we do know that many of the most despotic foremen and superintendents in tsarist Russia were too. What does this mean, sociologically and politically?

As I implied, we may be dealing with a version of a state that has, externally, some similarities with an older imperial combination of despotism and bureaucracy, except that in fact our "version" belongs to the twentieth century. It is an industrial or industry-oriented bureaucracy, implanted on a bedrock of a patriarchal peasantry, leading to the phenomenon of the "economization" of the political system, including the monopolistic party, the economy having become its main function and raison d'être.

But it is far from unimportant that "the bedrock" was changing too and with it, the very constitutive parts of a new "intelligentsia," which was novel in its character and scope. At the same time, we cannot overlook the enormous numbers of *chernorabochie* (unskilled laborers), not less officially than 65 percent in 1940, still about 35 percent in 1985. Actually, these figures concern only the *osnovnye* or basic jobs. Among the auxiliary workers, the rate was 95 percent. So, for a time, the social base of the country consisted of the physical labor of the peasants, working mostly with their hands despite the tractors, and the mostly physical industrial labor, also working *rukami, bez mashin* (with their hands, without machines). If there was a certain reintegration of the labor force, as

Ken Straus put it at the conference, it happened inside this sociological base at the bottom of the industrial system in the form of an enormous, still poorly differentiated, unqualified industrial labor force. The transformation of the factory into a provider, actually into a replica of Western company towns, fits this primitive stage of industrial development, as does the existence of a powerful controlling and constraining system which a primitive and poor labor force may have needed, but for which it paid heavily with accrued dependence. The low initial standards of living allowed for these arrangements to produce an improvement, in certain respects, but we are also aware that those standards, low as they were, were under a constant downward pressure. During and for a few years after the civil war, authors spoke of the dangers of malnutrition, if not starvation, workers faced. Housing was also a tough problem, and became a catastrophic one in the thirties. The food situation and standards of living improved during the twenties (not lodging though), but they deteriorated from 1928 onward. Some Soviet calculations, taking 1928 as 100, show a drop to 80 by 1932, a rise to 90 in 1937, and a new deterioration from 1938. Worse, the purchasing power of the average worker or employee did not go above the 1928 level until the mid-1950s. This is why, from the rationing of 1928–29 on, food and some other supplies could be used as a deliberate tool of policy for discipline and reward. Lodging too, when it was more than just a *zemlianka* (dugout) became an instrument of control in the hands of factory administrations when dealing with workers. This was yet another side of Soviet factory-town practice, where not just disciplining but simply retaining the labor force was the aim, a problem that cannot detain us here. The low cost of labor favored keeping labor surpluses, the surpluses hindered raising professional standards, and low standards meant low labor productivity. All these factors together contributed to the appearance of the phenomenon I call *rabsila*—a crude labor force, rather than a working class, that the managers treated as such unless labor shortages forced them to act differently. Workers resisted in many ways, including "voting with their feet," and by other means, but we have no room here to explore this topic further.

The aforementioned developments have to be supplemented by at least some basic data on "culture," and in the first place, on schooling and levels of skill. The existence of the mass of *chernorabochie* is already a testimony to the low professional level of most workers, and it goes with an education that does not exceed, say, three years of elementary schooling in the 1920s, probably less than four in the late 1930s (with only a small proportion of about 8 percent having gone through seven years and more). It is interesting that the 1926 census did not yet ask a worker about his or her *obrazovanie* (education), only about *gramotnost'* (literacy). Could a "ruling class" be so poorly literate or partly illiterate? Yes, if we are speaking about the entourage of Charlemagne in the eighth century A.D. In the twentieth, the requirements were different. Among the population, foul language was used not only and not necessarily at somebody; it was also often a way of speaking, almost a way of life. I have even heard of competitions in swearing in which the swearer was not allowed to repeat himself and the arbiter had a timer in his hands. It was, I think, developed in the tsarist fleet, and continued, to my knowledge, well into the 1930s, if not later.

"Comrade Nachal'nik, Sir"?

One of the general trends, for the 1930s and for some time thereafter, consisted, as said, in the following: the bulk of the industrial working population switched from one type of mainly physical labor in agriculture to another type of mainly physical labor in industry. The difference was significant because the industrial system was a new and different stage of development. But it was not yet enough to make this social base sufficiently powerful to force the top leaders and institutions into changing the pyramid of status and power. The index of the standards of education is crucial here: averages may hide improvements and a layer of better-educated and better-qualified labor, but they also reflect the effects of the influx from rural areas where standards were still very low.

Whatever our opinion of the deskilling process, the fact remains that, at times, the method of adapting to low levels of worker competence by an ever deeper simplification of tasks was tried out, but was found to be excessively complicated to organize and psychologically and culturally damaging to labor. Whatever the methods or solutions actually adopted, the key sociological feature remained: the bulk of the labor force were *chernorabochie*, and nothing is changed even when one calls them "semi-skilled."

The other problem raised, the one of socialization by the system and acceptance of it by the workers, is tricky. We did not yet chart fully periods of worker alienation versus periods of, more or less, acceptance. We know well about the period ending in 1922. Here we have it from Zinoviev telling the Twelfth Party Congress that "we really reconquered this time the working class and its faith in us," making it clear that it was lost for a time. We can also document waves of strikes in 1927–28. Later again, in 1932, we hear central committee secretary and future Ukrainian paty boss P. P. Postyshev saying that the moods of the workers are "ochen' skvernye" (very ugly). The better known campaigns for labor discipline can also be read politically. There certainly was much acceptance of or identification with the regime at different times but still, seen by the party, it was not as good or not as positive on its own terms. Otherwise, why would they have constantly bewailed the "petty bourgeois *stikhiia*" (chaos) that kept swamping workers from inside and outside? Why would they constantly cleanse the factories of "alien elements," or fight those numerous categories of *letuny* (rolling stones), *rvachi* (self-seekers), and so on, all of them varieties of shirkers? The acceptance is political, and even political indifference has a political meaning. But the opposition to norm-raising or to Stakhanovism (which was actually tamed, I suggest, by a united front of management, technicians, and workers themselves), resentment against rude bosses, against the privileges that they reserved for themselves was widespread and recurring and could also, at any time, turn political in a direction unwanted by the regime. Especially when workers, as I myself witnessed during my factory spell in the Urals, tended to develop a clear consciousness of "them" (the *nachal'niki*) and "us" (*nash brat*) as two separate entities that could harden into a dangerous polarization. And if it was there in 1941–42 when I witnessed this phenomenon, there must have been enough of it before or after. We should therefore try to identify stages of the workers' perception of *nachal'stvo*, yes, as a class, and of the system at large. I wrote about the status revolution in the 1930s, but did it, probably, very unconvincingly. Our contributors seem not to be aware of this at all and I do not understand why.

During NEP this might have been partly obfuscated by the division of bosses into "red" directors and "bourgeois specialists." Maybe so, but later it is different. Remember also that in the 1930s supplies were differentiated by status, and top administrators (like higher ranks in the army) never took meals in the same factory cafeterias. They had their own, much better ones. This occurred already on the level of the shop floor, not just of the central management (*zavodoupravlenie*). The joke of those years about the ORS is telling.[3]

The continuation of the "Vy" and "Ty" well into the postwar period is not less revealing about the reality of status. "Ty i Vy" was still a theme for a social psychologist writing in the 1970s. Some ambiguity existed, at first because for a worker to address the director in the "Ty" mode could still be a relic of the revolutionary period and its egalitarianism, at least inside the party. But "Vy" reappeared in official circles and, at the same time, "Ty" became the way a boss talked to a worker or other lower ranks, whereas the boss was addressed respectfully by them as "Vy." These terms are no trifle. They are not just expressions of relative status

---

[3] The initials of Otdel Rabochego Snabzheniia (Department for Workers' Supplies) were read, in a widespread joke, as "Obespech' Ran'she Sebia" and then reread as "Ostal'noe Rabochim i Sluzhashchim" (Take care first of all of yourself, what remains—give to the workers and employees).

and power, but also of an authoritarianism in a civilization that did not depart enough from the culture of crude domination, wielded directly and potently so that there were no misunderstandings.

And the reaction "from below" was equally characteristic: on the one hand, an acceptance of the right and position of the boss, including his crude attitude; on the other, quite often, also a sense of indignation for lack of respect implicit in the way of *tykat'* (jabbing) the workers while they had to remain deferential. There is no need of pompous and cere-monial titles from medieval courts, such as *vashe vysokoblagorodie* (Your Exalted Highness) or even *velichestvo* (Your Majesty), to express social chasms. Simpler words can effect subordination and social distance just as well. Take even the term *tovarishch* as a telling example. When a sub-ordinate is *not allowed* to address a superior directly and personally by given name and patronymic but *must* preface them with *tovarishch*, then "comrade" has become a title denoting a higher status.

So this "Ty" problem is a meaningful indicator of the culture of power relations and of its substance. Formally polite address may still hide, even accentuate, the actual power gap between the interlocutors, but there is a difference of historical system between a Vy to Ty and a Ty versus Vy. You do not see a feudal lord having to be polite, because polite address was reserved by definition only for equals, or at least for "the free." It would be inadmissible to use polite terms towards a serf.

The crude treatment meted out to workers—here it is industry we have in mind—points also to a stage in the history of industrialism. The foul language and the beating and abusing of women are (or should be) fa-miliar to students of American history when the workers were recruited "from the gate," as in Russia, from mostly a poor mass of émigrés, and here too the whole gamut of the sociology of industrial and labor relations comes to play, with many features similar to those our contributors de-scribe. The "crudity" and the despotic foreman begin to disappear at later stages in the United States and more slowly in the Soviet Union as well. But the phenomenon is not an exclusively Russian or Soviet one.

In Russia, the rather humble sounding requests to be treated "like hu-man beings" that our contributors allude to, the ethical self-image behind it leading on occasion to a violent reaction against administrative person-nel, are a continuation of a similar outcry coming from peasants who carried it from the depth of serfdom. I do not know well the peasants in serfdom, to what extent they expressed the same relations to their owners, and especially in what terms. But, clearly, the demand for respectful treat-ment had to become more pronounced when emancipation was not fol-lowed by an improved status. The disappointed expectations certainly had to emphasize this demand expressing the growing self-image of personal value and outrage at the refusal to recognize their human dignity.

The problem specific to the 1930s was that collectivization reinforced or regenerated, for a historical period, the crude forms of coercion in relation to peasants, their heightened dependence, and the arbitrariness of the behavior of state and party officials. The outcry against the fact that "nas za liudei ne schitaiut" and similarly the preference for, at least, paternalistic forms (that would constitute progress) were very much in evidence in the 1930s and much later until these features began to fade away, though not universally, with rising educational standards.

To conclude, Stalin's cult was more than just the apotheosis of a person. It was a version of an apotheosis of the state, and when Stalin's cult declined, the broader version remained and blossomed. But workers (as others), under both versions, had to do as they were told, including assimilate and display a *chuvstvo khoziaina* (sense of proprietorship), although the *khoziain* was somebody else and it was their fault, stemming from the petty-bourgeois residues in them, if they felt that they actually had no say in the business.

But here something baffling can be mentioned, similar to the phenomena we explored when speaking of classes. The superstate, so immensely powerful on the face of it, and accepted as such by the world, was itself losing the *chuvstvo khoziaina* and not just once. Stalin's seemingly immense and undisputed power was displaying clear signs of struggling for the reigns that were constantly eluding him. Some twenty years after his death, the state system at large actually stopped being a real *khoziain*: it presided over a *beskhoziaistvennost'* (proprietorlessness) of monumental proportions until it entered into a stage of full decomposition. It was, or became, an iceberg. Not that icebergs are not heavy or powerful, but an iceberg already may be in the process of melting away, whereas the subjects and observers remain impressed by its enormous weight. So here we have yet another case of the historical game of "hide and seek"—here it is and here it isn't—but when it is, observers and contemporaries often do not know what it is, and when it actually isn't anymore, they tend to think it is still there.

☆

Contributors

VICTORIA E. BONNELL is Professor of Sociology at the University of California at Berkeley.

SHEILA FITZPATRICK is Professor of History at the University of Chicago.

HEATHER HOGAN is Professor of History at Oberlin College.

DIANE P. KOENKER is Professor of History at the University of Illinois, Urbana-Champaign.

STEPHEN KOTKIN is Assistant Professor of History at Princeton University.

HIROAKI KUROMIYA is Associate Professor of History at Indiana University.

MOSHE LEWIN is Professor of History at the University of Pennsylvania.

DANIEL ORLOVSKY is Professor of History at Southern Methodist University.

GÁBOR T. RITTERSPORN is researcher at the Centre National de la Recherche Scientifique in Paris.

LEWIS H. SIEGELBAUM is Professor of History at Michigan State University.

S. A. SMITH is Professor of History at the University of Essex.

MARK D. STEINBERG is Assistant Professor of History at Yale University.

RONALD GRIGOR SUNY is Alex Manoogian Professor of Modern Armenian History at the University of Michigan.

CHRIS WARD is Lecturer in Slavonic Studies at the University of Cambridge.

REGINALD E. ZELNIK is Professor of History at the University of California at Berkeley.

Index

Absenteeism, 185, 259, 307, 322, 337
Accidents. *See* Work safety issues
Aleksandrov, Diomid (worker, b. c. 1851), 40–42, 46
Alekseev, Petr (worker, b. 1849), 32, 46–49
Anti-Semitism, 140–41, 148
Apprenticeship, 51, 53, 56
Apsit, Aleksandr (poster artist), 344, 350
Artel', 40, 45–46, 62, 143
Authority, workshop. *See* Foremen; Labor–management relations; Managers; Workers

Baltic Shipbuilding Works, 87–88, 95, 106; conciliation boards in, 131–32; foremen in, 124; 1905 Revolution in, 118; *zemliachestvo* in, 117
Blacksmith: criticism of poster image of, 360; as iconic representation, 343–52, 365–66, 369, 371; as "lower" type of worker, 30; polyvalence of image of, 353–59, 363
Bloody Sunday (Jan. 9, 1905), effects of, 76, 378
Bolshevik Party: bureaucratization of, 188, 190–91; debates over nature of socialism and labor relations of, 159–61, 164–67; and Donbas miners 140, 147–48, 150–51, 155–58; electoral victories of, 104, 149; iconic representation of, 351–52; language of class and, 193; Menshevik-dominated printers' union and, 170–73, 180–82, 184–85. *See also* Communist Party
Bourgeois specialists. *See* ITR; Specialists
"Breakdown-prone workers," 298, 301–2
Bribery of foremen, 117, 124–25; in cotton mills, 210; in mines, 143
Buntarstvo, 140, 142, 144
Bureaucratization, 188, 190–91, 226–27, 229, 234, 238–39; social pressure for, 246–47

Campaigns, 21, 23, 191, 231, 234, 282–83, 362, 364; class analysis and, 279; culture of, 249; political meaning of, 386–87; political uses of, 262–63, 268, 287

"Carting out" of managers, 80, 89, 129–30, 145
Ceremonies, workshop, 77, 124–27
Chaikovtsy group, 39, 47, 56
Child labor, 35–36, 39, 41–43, 46, 51; and abuse by foremen, 120–22; criticized, 47; replacing skilled adults, 106
Civic participation (*obshchestvennost'*), 230, 233–34, 237, 244, 247; expressions of, 305–6; and white-collar workers, 240–41
Civil war: in Donbas, 139, 147, 151–56; effects of, 14–17, 160
Class, definitions of, 1–2, 12–14, 17–20; and assistant foremen, 128; in socialist state, 179–80, 188, 194–96; by Stalin, 381–83
—language of, 5–6, 17; and Bolshevik Party, 193; and moral judgment, 78–80, 83–84, 379–80; and role of foremen, 136–37; in state socialism, 172
—use of concept of: and "culture," 4–7; in debates about state socialism, 167; in social analysis, 3, 376–77, 380–83; in Soviet historiography, 12–14; by Soviet state, 279–80; by tsarist regime after 1905, 379
Class consciousness, 3, 7–8, 15–16; context of, 377; among Donbas miners, 155–58; foremen's place in, 123, 125–29; among metalworkers, 109–11; moral principle of, 83–84; among peasants, 276; among printers, 75–78, 81; among textile workers, 216; transitoriness of, 378–79; among unemployed, 97–98, 100
"Class exclusiveness," 59–60
Class formation, 4–6; in Imperial Russia, 9–11, 85–86, 103–4, 379, 383; and industrialization, 277; and labor process, 216–17; in October Revolution, 13; and role of state, 249–51; in Soviet industrialization, 23–26, 253–54, 383; in Western Europe, 28–29; and white-collar employees, 225
Class identity. *See* Social identity

393